Governing America

The Politics of a Divided Democracy

Edited by

Robert Singh

OXFORD
UNIVERSITY PRESS

OXFORD

UNIVERSITY PRESS

Great Clarendon Street, Oxford OX2 6DP

Oxford University Press is a department of the University of Oxford.
It furthers the University's objective of excellence in research, scholarship,
and education by publishing worldwide in

Oxford New York

Auckland Bangkok Buenos Aires Cape Town Chennai
Dar es Salaam Delhi Hong Kong Istanbul Karachi Kolkata
Kuala Lumpur Madrid Melbourne Mexico City Mumbai Nairobi
São Paulo Shanghai Taipei Tokyo Toronto

Oxford is a registered trade mark of Oxford University Press
in the UK and in certain other countries

Published in the United States
by Oxford University Press Inc., New York

British Library Cataloguing in Publication Data

Data available

Library of Congress Cataloging in Publication Data

Data available

ISBN 0–19–925049–9

10 9 8 7 6 5 4 3 2 1

Typeset in ITC Stone Serif with ITC Stone Sans
by RefineCatch Limited, Bungay, Suffolk
Printed in Great Britain by
The Bath Press, Bath

Governing America

Editor's preface

Governing America is a new and innovative textbook on American government and politics. Bringing together a range of international scholars of American politics to write on their respective fields of expertise, it seeks to provide a comprehensive, clear, and balanced analysis of contemporary American politics at a time of substantial flux. The volume covers in four main sections the major Historical and Theoretical Context, the key governing Institutions and Intermediary Organizations, Public Policy, and a series of Issues and Controversies. Although the contributors differ in their views on many issues concerning domestic American politics and US foreign policy, together the chapters offer a rounded and dispassionate assessment of government and politics in the United States. Each contributor has sought to highlight how their particular subject both reflects and reinforces the notion of America as a 'divided democracy', paying particular attention to the influence of the US Constitution, the problem of defining key terms, the key academic debates about the topic, and the extent to which the American context differs from or resembles those of other industrialized liberal democracies. As far as possible, we have sought to present the material in an accessible and coherent form, making particular use of useful learning aids, such as:

- **reader's guides** at the beginning of each chapter
- **boxed sections** that present key concepts, important facts, case studies, and key debates
- **key points** organized into bullet point summaries at the end of sections within chapters
- **discussion/essay questions** to assist critical reflection and argument
- **further readings** on the subject covered
- **internet sites** to assist in examining the subject and key political actors further.

A **comprehensive, consolidated bibliography** is included towards the end of the book, along with a copy of the **United States Constitution**.

Acknowledgements

I should like to express my profound thanks to the distinguished contributors to this volume for their participation and support in an innovative project on a tight publication schedule. The idea of an edited textbook was first broached by Angela Griffin of Oxford University Press, and I owe her a particular debt of gratitude for her expertise and extensive work in launching and supervising the early stages of the project. Sue Dempsey took over from Angela midway through, and I was indebted to another wonderful source of advice, support, and encouragement. Along with Ruth Anderson, Katy Plowright, and the other staff, I'm extremely grateful to the professionalism and dedication of the OUP staff who did a wonderful job on a particularly demanding enterprise. I should also thank Andy Coath, who also gave extensive support in the editing of the text and was a generous source of advice and support. Finally, my warmest appreciation goes to my colleagues in the School of Politics and Sociology at Birkbeck College, University of London, for their professionalism, kindness, and good humour.

RS
London, January 2003

Contents

Part One The historical and theoretical context

Part Two Governing institutions

Part Three **Public policy**

Part Four **Issues and controversies**

Detailed Contents

List of figures

List of boxes

List of tables

About the contributors

Elizabeth Bomberg is a Senior Lecturer in Politics at the University of Edinburgh, where she teaches US, environmental, and EU politics. Her main area of research is environmental politics, especially from a comparative perspective. She is author of *Green Parties and Politics in the EU* (1998), co-author of *Decision-Making in the EU* (1999) and co-editor of *The EU: How Does It Work?* (2003). She is currently researching the politics of sustainable development in Europe and the US.

Nigel Bowles is Vice-Principal and Balfour Fellow in Politics, St Anne's College, Oxford. His research interests are the United States presidency and Congress. His main publications include *The White House and Capitol Hill* (1987) and *Government and Politics of the United States* (1993 and 1997).

Steve Bruce is Professor of Sociology and Head of the School of Social Science, University of Aberdeen. He is the author of numerous books on religion and politics, the sociology of religion, and terrorism, including: *Conservative Protestant Politics* (1998), *Choice and Religion: A Critique of Rational Choice Theory* (2000), *Fundamentalism* (2001), *God is Dead: Secularization in the West* (2002), and *Politics and Religion* (2003).

Stephen Burman is Reader in American Studies and Dean of Humanities at Sussex University. He was formerly a research analyst on US foreign policy in the British Foreign and Commonwealth Office. His published works include *America in the Modern World* (1991) and *The Black Progress Question* (1995). He is currently working on a book, *Rethinking American Hegemony: National Interest and Global Responsibility*.

Michael Cox is Professor of International Politics at the London School of Political and Economic Science and editor of *International Relations*. He was formerly Professor of International Politics at the University of Wales, Aberystwyth, and Director of the David Davies Memorial Institute. His most recent work includes *E. H. Carr: A Critical Appraisal* (2000), *American Democracy Promotion* (with G. John Ikenberry and Takashi Inoguchi) (2000), and *Empires, Systems and States* (with Tim Dunne and Ken Booth) (2001). In 2002 he was appointed Senior Fellow at the Norwegian Nobel Institute in Oslo where he completed his book, *Cold War: History Wars–Narratives of the Great Contest*.

John Dumbrell is Professor of American Foreign Relations at Keele University. He is the author of several books on US foreign policy and most recently of *A Special Relationship: Anglo-American Relations in the Cold War and After* (2001). He is currently working on the history of US–Soviet relations during the Presidency of Lyndon Johnson.

Martin Durham is Senior Lecturer in Politics at the University of Wolverhampton. He has written extensively on right-wing politics and sexual morality in both the USA and Britain. Recent publications include *The Christian Right, the Far Right and the Boundaries of American Conservatism* (2000) and 'The Conservative Party, New Labour and the family', *Parliamentary Affairs* (2001).

John Francis is Professor of Political Science at the University of Utah. He has written extensively on comparative regulatory policy in areas such as land use, religion, and education. He has been a contributing editor for two volumes on western American politics. He is the author of *The Comparative Politics of Regulation* (1993) and co-author of *Land Wars: The Politics of Property and Community* (2003).

Francisco E. González is a British Academy Research Fellow at Nuffield College, Oxford. His Oxford University doctoral thesis was on 'The political economy of dual transitions: economic liberalization and political democratisation in Mexico and Chile', and he is currently preparing this for publication as a book. His research interests are democratisation, dual transitions, and comparative politics.

Donald P. Haider-Markel is Assistant Professor of Political Science at the University of Kansas. He has authored and co-authored over twenty refereed articles and book chapters on a variety of social policies. He recently co-authored *Gay and Lesbian Americans and Political Participation* (2002) with Raymond Smith, and has been recipient or co-recipient of grants from the EPA STAR program, the American Psychological Foundation, and the National Science Foundation.

John Hart is Reader in Political Science in the Faculty of Arts at the Australian National University. His primary research is on American government and politics with a particular focus on the American presidency. He is the author of *The Presidential Branch: From Washington to Clinton*.

Vivien Hart is Professor of American Studies at the University of Sussex and currently a Senior Research Fellow at the United States Institute of Peace in Washington, DC. She has written on gender politics and on constitutionalism; her publications include *Writing a National Identity: Political, Economic and Cultural Perspectives on the Written Constitution*, co-edited with Shannon C. Stimson (1993), *Bound by Our Constitution: Women, Workers, and the Minimum Wage* (1994), and the forthcoming *Making Constitutions, Seeking Peace*.

Richard Hodder-Williams is Pro-Vice-Chancellor and Professor of Politics at the University of Bristol. His publications include *Politics in Britain and the United States* (ed.) (1986), *From Churchill to Major: The British Prime Ministership since 1945* (ed.) (1995) and *Judges and Politics in the Contemporary Age* (1996).

Eric Kaufmann is Lecturer in Comparative Politics, University of Southampton. He is the author of *The Rise and Fall of Anglo-America: The Decline of Dominant Ethnicity in the United States* (2003). His main interest is WASP/White dominant ethnicity. He has published on this and related themes in, among others, *Geopolitics* (2002), *Historical Sociology* (2001), *Ethnic and Racial Studies* (2000), *Canadian Review of Studies in Nationalism* (2000), *Journal of American Studies* (1999), and *Comparative Studies in Society and History* (1998).

Desmond S. King holds the Andrew W. Mellon Chair of American Government at Oxford University and is a Fellow of Nuffield College, Oxford. His most recent book is *Making Americans: Immigration, Race and the Origins of the Diverse Democracy* (2000).

Pete Lentini (BA, Rhode Island; PhD, Glasgow) is a Senior Lecturer in Politics in the School of Political and Social Inquiry, and Associate Dean (Research), Arts Faculty, Monash University, Melbourne. He has published work on Russian, American, cultural, and identity politics. His current work concerns the relationship between media culture, identity, and terrorism.

Burdett A. Loomis is a Professor of Political Science at the University of Kansas. He has written or edited more than twenty-five books in various editions. A former American Political Science Association Congressional Fellow, his scholarship focuses on legislatures, interest groups, and policy-making. At present he is at work on a large-scale study of the industry of politics for the Brookings Institution.

Robert Mason is a Lecturer in History at the University of Edinburgh. He is currently completing a book about Richard Nixon as an electoral strategist, *The New Majority: The Nixon White House and the Missing Realignment of American Politics*. His next project is a history of the Republican Party since the 1920s.

Candice J. Nelson is an Associate Professor of Government at American University in Washington, DC, and director of American University's Campaign Management Institute. She is a former American Political Science Association Congressional Fellow. Her research interests include congressional and presidential elections, campaign finance and campaign finance reform, and the US Congress. She is co-author of *The Money Chase: Congressional Campaign Finance Reform* and *The Myth of the Independent Voter*, and is co-editor of *Campaign and Elections American Style*, *Campaign Warriors*, *Crowded Airwaves*, and *Shades of Gray: Perspectives on Campaign Ethics*.

John E. Owens is Professor of United States Government and Politics in the Centre for the Study of Democracy at the University of Westminster. He is co-author (with Michael Foley) of *Congress and the Presidency: Institutional Politics in a Separated System* (1996). Most recently, he co-edited *Political Leadership in Context* with Erwin Hargrove of Vanderbilt University, a special issue of *Politics and Policy*. He is also co-editor of *The Republican Takeover of Congress* (1998) and co-author of *After Full Employment* (1986). His articles on the United States Congress have appeared in the *British Journal of Political Science*, *Political Studies*, *Politics and Policy*, and the *Journal of Legislative Studies*; and he has contributed to a number of edited collections on United States government and politics. He has been chair and vice-chair of the American Politics Group of the Political Studies Association of the UK, a Guest Scholar at the Brookings Institution in Washington, DC, and consultant to the Congressional Research Service at the Library of Congress. He is also a member of the editorial boards of the *Journal of Legislative Studies* and the *Presidential Studies Quarterly*.

Mark Carl Rom is an Associate Professor of Government and Public Policy at Georgetown University in Washington, DC. He received his BA from the University of Arkansas (*magna cum laude*) and his MA and PhD in political science at the University of Wisconsin, Madison, in 1992. He studies American politics and public policy, especially social welfare policy. He has written *Fatal Extraction: The Story Behind the Florida Dentist Accused of Infecting His Patients with HIV and Poisoning Public Health* (1997), *Public Spirit in the Thrift Tragedy* (1996), and, with Paul E. Peterson, *Welfare Magnets: A New Case for a National Welfare Standard* (1990), among other chapters and articles. His dissertation, 'The Thrift Tragedy: Are Politicians and Bureaucrats to Blame?', was co-winner of the 1993 Harold Lasswell Award from the American Political Science Association as the best dissertation in the public policy field.

Fiona Ross lectures in politics at the University of Bristol. She is currently completing a book on the partisan politics of welfare restructuring. She has published a series of journal articles and book chapters on welfare overhaul in comparative perspective.

Robert Singh is Lecturer in Politics at the School of Politics and Sociology, Birkbeck College, University of London, where he is also the Director of the MSc/MRes in American Politics. Among his publications are *The Farrakhan Phenomenon* (1997), *The Congressional Black Caucus* (1998), and (editor) *American Politics and Society Today* (2002).

Introduction

Robert Singh

THE aim of this book is to provide a clear, comprehensive, and balanced guide to contemporary American government and politics. *Governing America* offers a detailed overview of current American government and politics that is sensitive to historical context and the constant and complex interaction of domestic and international politics, but without being overburdened by unduly lengthy historical narratives, excessive description, or too narrow an institutional focus on government. That is, the contributors to this volume have treated 'politics' in its fullest sense, as encompassing far more than simply the institutions of America's federal (national) government—Congress, the executive branch, the federal judiciary, and the bureaucracy. It is hoped that the volume will certainly encourage the reader to think critically and at length about those particular governing institutions (both individually and in terms of their many complex interactions). But the volume also seeks to illuminate the social base of American politics, to examine the critical role of important intermediary organizations such as political parties, the mass media, and interest groups, and to analyse a series of recent issues and controversies in American politics. It is hoped that the reader will thus be able to arrive at an informed and independent assessment of the distinctive—even unique—properties and processes of modern American government, politics, public policies, and society.

Studying American politics

After the terrorist attacks of 11 September 2001, many academics outside America lamented the decline of 'area (or regional) studies' in universities. This had contributed, they claimed, to the failure of public life to generate an informed and broad understanding of the reasons for the attacks on the World Trade Center and the Pentagon. An important area of the world had been neglected, so much so that it remained unfamiliar to millions, rarely visited by foreigners; if foreigners did visit, it was rarely to cities or locales that were representative of the broader region. As such, the public image of the diverse peoples of the region was distorted and partial, a reflection of simple stereotypes and brute prejudices all too easily gleaned from popular culture—not least misleading films and television programmes and partial newspaper coverage. To some, it was ironic that the area that these commentators had in mind was the Middle East, since similar points could equally have been made regarding the United States of America.

Long before 9/11, America excited strong emotions and intense disagreements, both within and outside the United States. The nation's singular global influence after 1945—military, economic, diplomatic, and cultural—placed the United States at the centre of the international system. Indeed, as Michael Cox notes in the final chapter of this volume, what 9/11 revealed was already apparent to several scholars of international relations during the 1990s; the extent to which America had achieved an unparalleled global influence—one whose only relevant historical precedents were the Roman and British empires. Whether such power amounted to an American 'empire' was contestable in many respects, but to many observers the twentieth century had undoubtedly been 'the American century'. The ubiquity of American culture, from popular films and music to clothes and food, ensured that few of us who were born or grew up during the second half of the twentieth century felt unfamiliar with either the nation or its people. The particular policies of the incumbent administration, both domestic and foreign, meant and continues to mean that what the United States does matters profoundly to those outside, as well as within its borders, in a way that cannot be said to be true of any other nation-state.

For the student of American politics, such a context of apparent familiarity represents both a blessing and a curse. On the one hand, the prominent coverage accorded to matters American in the mass media, and the extensive reach and popularity of American films, television, and music, together ensure that the United States is somehow 'closer' to us than most, if not all, other nations. From *The Simpsons* and Hollywood movies through McDonalds and Gap to rap, jazz, blues, country, and rock, few nations outside America are unfamiliar with its many cultural products. Non-Americans have probably learnt as much about the United States vicariously through films, television, and music as through travelling in America, talking to Americans, or reading books on America (whether their information is accurate is another matter, of course). No other nation has produced such a remarkable volume and array of cultural products

that—lest it be forgotten—have achieved such immense popularity outside its own borders.

On the other hand, such familiarity can be problematic for serious students of American government and politics. The depictions of America presented in much popular coverage—from Oliver Stone's *JFK* to *The West Wing*—are often partial, misleading, and inaccurate. Rather than informing, they can often misinform and confirm negative conceptions based less on reason and rounded, reflective judgement than on brute prejudice. It is easy enough, for example, to depict as grievously insular a nation whose baseball 'World Series' has nothing to do with the rest of the world and only one-sixth of whose citizens possess passports. But how insular is a nation that dedicated billions of dollars, personnel, and thousands of lives around the world to the containment and defeat of communism for almost fifty years after the Second World War? Equally, it is straightforward enough to contrast a nation whose Declaration of Independence from Britain promised 'life, liberty and the pursuit of happiness' in 1776 with one that currently executes dozens of death row inmates annually, possesses the world's largest prison population, and remains seared by racial inequality and exclusion. But if such features are so distasteful to so many, why has the United States remained the primary destination for emigrants around the world seeking to flee religious and political persecution and economic disadvantage in order to better themselves and their families? If voluntary mass immigration represents the starkest form of comparative flattery, America is evidently doing something right that other industrialized democracies are not yet able to match.

The problems attending the study of American politics are not, however, merely a function of familiarity with American popular culture. International news coverage of the United States also tends to focus on the more lurid and colourful aspects of American public life—from the dubious delights of celebrity culture and daytime talk shows to the distress caused by seemingly routine gun massacres and urban riots—that cannot but serve to distort the more mundane character of daily life in the United States. Instead of a dispassionate examination of American politics, such images and stories can serve simply to confirm ingrained prejudices and stereotypes about America and Americans. Take, for example, a recent—not entirely untypical—summary of the world's premier democracy:

The United States is, aw shucks, many things to many people. The biggest, most successful, consumer-oriented, gum-chewing—'Hi, howyadointoday? My name is Peggy Sue. I'm your server this evening. I'm here to make certain you have the best evening of your life. How may I be of assistance?'—back-to-front baseball cap-wearing, gun-slinging, Bible-bashing, neurotic, 100-per-cent knuckleball economy in the history of the world. Home to the biggest bunch of self-centred, money-grabbing, hang tough, planet-polluting, golf-obsessed, hamburger-heads of all time, who all hit Prozac for depression . . . think it's sophisticated to use a knife and fork; intellectual to eat burgers, watch TV and drink beer at the same time (and) go to the office wearing a baseball cap, shorts, shoes (no socks) carrying a two-gallon can of Coke or a one-gallon Starbucks . . .   (Biddlecombe, 2002: 1)

Extending the 'only in America' approach, the writer Martin Amis, noting how 'British politics has long ceased to be sexy', has by contrast observed how 'one yearns . . . for the banjos, the majorettes, the misappropriated campaign donations, the sweating vaudevillians of the American scene' (2002: 20). Even an influential, prolific, and dispassionate American observer, Judge Richard Posner, has commented—in assessing Aldous Huxley's landmark novel *Brave New World*—on how the 'society of happy, thoughtless philistines depicted by Huxley seems merely an exaggeration of today's America' (2001: 260).

Such comments may be gross caricatures, but, to millions outside America, they seem more or less accurately to describe a nation, government, and people simultaneously riveting and repellent. On this conception, most notably, American foreign policy is widely regarded as not so much inconsistent or equivocal as essentially hypocritical and unrelentingly self-serving. During the cold war, America supposedly protected the 'free world' against the communist bloc, but in doing so it supported nations, from Pinochet's Chile to apartheid South Africa, that hardly merited the designation 'free'. The United States supported the right of self-determination, yet attempted to intervene either covertly or overtly to deny that right where its exercise threatened to yield a communist regime

(from Italy in 1948 to Vietnam in the 1960s). Similarly, the Bush administration's 'war on terrorism' seemed not expressly to include terrorists in areas such as Colombia and Kashmir. Whatever the flaws and counter-arguments on such matters—and they are many—these notions have helped to 'inform' a view of America outside the United States that is at best ambiguous and frequently downright hostile.

In the context of these popular notions, however, the first step to a balanced understanding of American government and politics requires a willingness to move beyond such easy and familiar preconceptions. This is not to say that such popular notions are wrong, either partially or totally. Many contain at least a grain of accuracy. But three qualifications are generally in order when examining American politics.

First, America, like all nations, is an 'imagined community', for those within as much as those without the United States. The idea that most, much less all, Americans, espouse the same values and views is unsustainable—whether the topic is the Middle East or abortion rights. Indeed, it is precisely from within the United States that some of its most forceful and influential critics—from Gore Vidal and Edward Said to Noam Chomsky—are invariably (and perhaps ironically) to be found. The virtual stalemate results yielded by the 2000 presidential and congressional elections—with a president elected on a minority of the popular vote and a Senate tied at 50:50—themselves rested on, in effect, 'two nations' in America that differed profoundly on matters ranging from environmental protection to health insurance. In examining a polity of whose social base the central feature is a remarkable ethnic, racial, regional, religious, and economic diversity, treating the United States as a homogeneous entity is invariably unwise.

Second, it is worth noting that many of the features of American life that critics frequently find uncongenial are inseparable from other aspects that they typically admire or respect. For example, many political scientists see the type of federal arrangements that have emerged in the United States since 1787 as an important guarantor of the rights of local communities, especially within a notably heterogeneous and diverse nation-state. But these guarantees of local autonomy also mean that, for instance, thirty-eight states can currently sanction the death penalty and forty-two can allow the carrying of firearms concealed by their citizens. It is therefore worth distinguishing certain substantive policy outcomes from the design, historical evolution, and processes of American government. Just as American judges can and do draw a distinction in the cases before them between the questions 'What outcome would I prefer?' and 'What is required by law?', so students of American government and politics can and should be able to draw a distinction between the questions 'What outcomes do I prefer or dislike?' and 'What do these outcomes suggest about the operations and quality of American democracy?'.

Third, popular conceptions of America are invariably worth challenging in terms of their accuracy. America is an avowedly capitalist political economy, for example, but it is also one that sees business more heavily regulated by government than most of its comparable liberal democracies. America does allow widespread legal access to firearms to its private citizens, but most Americans do not own—far less carry—guns, thousands of laws and regulations condition their sale and usage, and the overwhelming majority of gun-owners use them responsibly. America did intervene extensively around the globe to combat the spread of communism during the cold war, but many of these interventions were 'by invitation' of host states in Europe, Latin America, Asia, and Africa, rather than unwanted impositions by an imperial Washington. Equally, while America has acted unilaterally in the international arena on many occasions, objections to such actions are frequently based not on that approach but on the outcomes it has sought. A Bush administration intent on enforcing environmental measures twice as stringent as those in the Kyoto Protocol and dispensing billions of aid to Iraq and Iran—without consulting its European and Middle Eastern allies—would in all probability win plaudits rather than censure for its unilateralism in Brussels, Paris, and Damascus.

In sum, a prerequisite to the study of the United States is a willingness to suspend simple and familiar preconceptions and to challenge these at every turn. This is not to discount the importance of popular culture, since much therein offers valuable instruction into American public and private life, from the comic Rich Hall's 'poor white trash' persona, Otis Lee Crenshaw, to the observations on 9/11 of Bruce Springsteen's *The Rising*. (Even the supposedly subversive cartoons *The Simpsons* and *South Park* arguably represent remarkably strong affirmations of traditional American values (Singh 2002).) But an enlightened scepticism towards conventional wisdoms is invariably useful in this regard, in approaching the study of American politics as a means to examine—not simply to confirm—pre-existing notions about America. As the noted American jurist Judge Learned Hand once observed, 'The spirit of liberty is the spirit that is not too sure it is right.'

America as a divided democracy

The subtitle of this book, *The Politics of a Divided Democracy*, provides an important indicator of the volume's overall approach to its subject. The United States is a 'divided democracy' by constitutional design, historical evolution, and current societal divisions over public morals and values, established public policies, and America's governing institutions. To some extent one can identify most, if not all, industrialized democracies as exhibiting similar types of division. But the particular scale, scope, and character of the three features identified here powerfully distinguish the United States in comparative terms. In particular, three elements underpin the notion of America as a divided democracy.

First, the conflict between democratic values (in its crudest form, representative government or majoritarianism—'majority rule') and liberalism (encompassing the notions of limited government, the protection of individual and minority rights, and constitutionalism) provides a central element in American politics at federal, state, and local levels. Second, the conflict between the constitutional authority and appropriate roles—and effectiveness—of the federal (i.e., the national) government and the fifty individual states has become a prominent feature in analyses of American institutions, policies, and controversies. Third, the conflict between what can broadly be categorized as 'traditionalists' and 'progressives' has emerged since the 1960s as a crucial, broad, and enduring struggle on matters from taxation and welfare policy to trade policy and the environment. Since these three features are indispensable to understanding the nature of American politics, and run through the chapters that follow in this book, it is worth devoting some preliminary remarks to each in turn.

American democracy

There are several reasons why the study of American politics matters. Most obviously, as noted already, the unparalleled international influence of the United States means that American economic, security, environmental, and other public policies can exert profound effects on the rest of the world. If the jury remains out on the extent to which the world is increasingly 'globalized' and interdependent, there can be no doubt that few—if any—nations are insulated from America's particular reach.

But beyond such brute facts is the distinctive character of American government. Whether the American model provides lessons for others that are worth emulating or avoiding is a matter that the reader can assess throughout the book; but at a minimum, analysis of American democracy yields important comparative insights into the nature of democratic governance more broadly. If the conflicts that exist in America are hardly unique and may legitimately be regarded as being universal, the particular manner in which the United States has sought to resolve them certainly is novel—not least, while many aspects of the Bill of Rights have been 'exported' since 1791, no other nations have sought to emulate the particular configuration of national governing institutions and the balance of power between them that the Constitution provided for the United States.

The term 'democracy' appears nowhere in the Constitution of the United States, and for many students of American government the very notion that Americans should continue to operate under a constitutional system designed in and for the eighteenth century is reason enough for bafflement. That so many Americans should not simply accept but actively celebrate the longevity of the Constitution and its distinctive arrangements often adds to the bewilderment. But as the following chapters make clear, the Constitution was a revolutionary statement whose values and design have endured. In designing a democratic form of government in which the ability of those in power to govern rested on the consent of the governed, the principle of majority rule was established as a cornerstone of the American system. But by tempering that with a series of institutional checks and balances and a Bill of Rights that placed powerful impediments to the untrammelled exercise of majority will—policed by federal and state courts—the Constitution also pitted the rights and liberties of the individual (and minorities) against those of the majority. As such, the Constitution entrenched at the heart of the American system an abiding conflict that—ultimately—placed strong hurdles against the type of centralized and unchecked government power common (today as much as in 1787) in erstwhile 'democracies' such as the United Kingdom.

Federalism

One of the most common problems encountered by students of American politics is the extent to which the United States cannot be treated as a unitary or homogeneous entity. Central to the evolution of the nation has been the relative autonomy of the individual states. This is not simply a matter of the sheer scale of the American landmass and the fact that a nation-state such as the UK occupies roughly the same area as a relatively 'small' American state such as New Mexico. With three time zones and immense variations in state size, population density, ethnic, racial, and religious make-up, and even climactic conditions, the physical dimensions of the American landscape are consequential, of course. But other physically large nations—from the former Soviet Union to Russia, Canada, and Australia today—have existed without the type of entrenched protection for their individual sub-units that exists in America.

Federalism is therefore a crucial second dimension to the notion of the United States as a divided democracy. Certain powers are reserved to the states, and the federal government is accorded only specific and limited powers and functions. In practice, that neat and tidy distinction has become inescapably blurred and subject to constant alteration as the federal government has gradually expanded its reach, programmes, and responsibilities—particularly since the Depression of 1929 and American involvement in the Second World War after the Japanese attack on Pearl Harbor of 7 December 1941. Moreover, the federal government has become increasingly creative in devising ways—from incentives to sanctions—by which it can encourage individual states to harmonize and standardize their public policies and programmes.

The fact remains that, for most Americans most of the time, their experience of public and private life is powerfully conditioned by the individual states in which they reside. Even national news is frequently disseminated and interpreted through a local, parochial lens ('What do cuts in federal farm subsidies mean for sugar growers in Louisiana?'). The result is that while we can, for purposes of explanation and analysis, speak of 'American' government, this often obscures more than it reveals. Because what issues are important to American voters may often be very different in Kentucky and Kansas as opposed to Wyoming and Wisconsin; and even where similar issues are in play—from education vouchers to gun control—how these are tackled, and the policy outcomes, vary tremendously from state to state.

Cultural value conflicts

The third pivot on which the divided democracy notion rests concerns the conflicts that have arisen—particularly since the 1960s—over what have been termed 'culture wars': issues and controversies that entail competing public conceptions of right and wrong. America has never lacked political conflicts centred on competing sets of values and beliefs about morality, religion, and individual rights

and freedoms. Political struggles over slavery, Prohibition, and civil and voting rights, most notably, were informed by such contending conceptions of the public good. But since the 1960s, the conflicts between traditionalists and progressives has become broader in scope and more enduring as a force in American politics.

The reasons for this are threefold. First, as noted above, the reach of the federal government grew steadily after the New Deal. This was controversial even when centred on economic concerns such as minimum wage and social security laws rather than moral concerns as such. But from the second half of the twentieth century federal laws increasingly encompassed non-economic concerns, such as the place of religion in American public life (and prayer in school in particular), pornography, capital punishment, abortion, and gay rights. The intervention of the federal government on such matters broadened the ranks of those millions of Americans who felt psychologically, as well as physically, distant from Washington, DC. Whilst clear majorities expressed confidence in the federal government as late as 1964, for example, thirty years later these majorities were reversed.

Second, many of the federal interventions stemmed not from the elected branches of government (the presidency and Congress) but from the unelected and unaccountable United States Supreme Court. Moreover, the constitutional basis for the Court's interventions were often regarded as controversial and unclear. Invoking terms (such as the 'right to privacy') that did not explicitly exist in the text of the Constitution, the Court appeared to be acting as a quasi-legislature, making laws rather than interpreting them. To many Americans, then, not only was the scope of the federal government's interventions excessive but the source of the intervention was also politically illegitimate. With several of the Court's novel interpretations of constitutional law themselves resting on the narrowest majorities in 5–4 decisions of the nine justices, such exercises of 'raw judicial power' appeared all the more flagrant. The failure of elected officials to reverse many of these rulings and their effects—whether through lack of commitment or ineffective strategies and tactics—compounded the egregious character of the federal intervention.

Third, the response to these federal interventions institutionalized conflict over a broad swathe of issues that animated the core values and belief systems of millions of Americans. For many progressives, energized by concerns over civil rights, women's rights, gay rights, and the environment, the idealized picture of 1950s America so beloved of traditionalists was a rebuke to American ideals of equality. To progressives, the interventions of the federal government on matters of racial and sexual equality, the rights of criminal defendants, birth control and abortion—whether by the Democratic administrations of John F. Kennedy and Lyndon B. Johnson or the Supreme Court under Earl Warren (1953–69)—were not only emancipatory but long overdue.

To many other Americans, however, the federal encroachment on ways of life and public policies that had been in place for decades was sufficient cause for a new political mobilization. Among these, the emergence of a politicized Christian community was one of the most influential causes of a steady reaction to the liberalizing measures that occurred in the 1960s (and continued under Presidents Nixon, Ford, and Carter). The mobilization of these two broad coalitions placed a new set of issues on the agendas of America's governing institutions and elected politicians alike. In so doing, they accorded battles over the character of American culture an enduring presence in American politics at national, state, and local levels.

American exceptionalism

If the three elements outlined above together distinguish the United States as a divided democracy, is America still different in nature or degree to other nations? Was it, and is it, even possible to speak of a 'unique' nation or people?

Such questions are not merely tangential to the analysis of American politics. For both proponents and opponents of the 'exceptionalism' thesis have used it to celebrate and censure America, alternately to praise its design of government, its people's values and their beliefs, and to castigate many of its domestic policies and its role in the world. Especially in the aftermath of 11 September, the extent to which 'American' and 'Western' values became synonymous or interchangeable became a highly controversial matter, one in which those seeking both to unite and divide non-American democracies from the United States sought to advance particular political agendas. The presence on bestseller lists of books such as *Why Do People Hate America?* in 2002 and 2003 suggested that, in Europe as much as Asia and the Middle East, something 'different' clearly animated the United States and—implicitly— accounted for the putative animus it generated around the globe.

Many Americans, whether deliberately or unwittingly, also reinforced a conception of a 'chosen people' and a nation that represented a 'city on a hill'. In his second inaugural address on 20 January 1997, for example, President Bill Clinton observed:

What a century it has been. America became the world's mightiest industrial power, saved the world from tyranny in two world wars and a long cold war, and time and time again reached across the globe to millions who longed for the blessings of liberty. Along the way, Americans produced the great middle class and security in old age; built unrivalled centers of learning and opened public schools to all; split the atom and explored the heavens; invented the computer and the microchip; made a revolution in civil rights for minorities; and extended the circle of citizenship, opportunity and dignity to women. Now, for the third time, a new century is upon us, and another time to choose.

For some critics, the notion that America is different or even unique has been used not simply to describe and explain but also to justify and legitimate its actions. In some guises, this has suggested that the nation's interventions abroad have been guided by a 'special providence' (Mead 2001). Isolationists have invoked America's 'standing apart' as a nation and as a people to press for an insular foreign policy, fearful that involvement in the concerns of other nations might somehow sully and taint the special American virtues. Internationalists, equally, have invoked America's 'unique' or 'special' character to justify US interventions abroad, whether defensive (to contain or roll back communism or pre-empt terrorism) or benign (to promote democracy and human rights and to prevent genocide).

Certainly it remains relatively clear that, in several dimensions, American politics and public life is distinctive. For example, the Democrats and Republicans are conventionally regarded as the 'left' and 'right' parties respectively in American politics. Whilst this is an oversimplification of a much more complex reality (and history), it is the case that, for instance, British Conservatives have forged ties with the Republican Party whilst 'New Labour' party officials in Britain benefited from studying 'New Democrat' approaches to both electioneering and governing during the 1990s. Yet, whilst an erstwhile American 'progressive' such as Hillary Rodham Clinton supports measures such as minimum wage increases, abortion rights, and laws against 'hate crimes', she also supports capital punishment and does not favour a prohibition on the legal ownership of handguns. Equally, whilst the conflict between gun rights and gun control groups over firearms regulation is emotive and intense, what is perhaps most striking is the degree to which both occupy common ground compared to non-Americans— remarkably few gun control groups press for a total ban on private ownership of firearms or contest the constitutional 'right to bear arms'. While the nature of partisan conflict is intense and sharp, the boundaries of ideological conflict in America have been—and remain—more confined than has been historically the case in most other industrialized liberal democracies.

Such observations appear to continue to provide credence to the view of the eminent American historian Richard Hofstadter when he stated that the fate of America has been 'not to have ideologies, but to be one'. Moreover, it is clearly the case that, in terms of mass attitudes, Americans display a remarkable antipathy towards government, such that the expansion of the federal government's responsibilities and programmes from 1933 to the 1970s now appears more the aberration in American

history than the norm. This anti-government political culture is not simply a matter of *the* government—the particular occupant of the White House at a given time (the Clinton or the Bush administration)—but to government in its broadest sense. While Americans typically celebrate their system of government—the collective design of federalism, the separation of powers, checks and balances, the Bill of Rights, and constitutional judicial review—they tend to look unfavourably on the institutions of government. Scandals such as Watergate have compounded such attitudes, and the revelation of misdeeds and corruption in high offices (from the FBI's monitoring of figures from Martin Luther King to John Lennon to the 1993 attacks on the Branch Davidian compound in Waco, Texas) have fuelled conspiracy theories, popularized in programmes such as *The X-Files* and movies such as *Murder at 1600* and *Arlington Road*. Even in the aftermath of the 11 September attacks, the rise in confidence in the institutions of the federal government was brief and temporary. In few democracies is government regarded with such suspicion and scepticism.

But any assessment of the nature and extent of American distinctiveness requires qualification. Despite the agendas of those who use exceptionalism to castigate or celebrate America, there is much that the United States shares with the rest of the world. All industrialized states have seen a growth in the scope and scale of government intervention in the regulation of the marketplace, and the introduction of measures regulating social security, minimum wage and hours, and health care assistance. The differences are ones of degree and, to some extent, direction (increased regulation versus deregulation). For all the suspicion that Americans express towards government, American citizens and business alike readily accept its subsidies, tax breaks, social security benefits, and military installations.

Similarly, the classic statement of American exceptionalism ('Why is there no socialism in America?') can now equally well be asked of most, if not all, industrialized liberal democracies. Even nations such as Australia and the UK, where leftist parties retain the label 'socialists' or 'labour', no longer promote a political programme that challenges the free market capitalist model, instead seeking to 'manage' it more competently than their more avowedly pro-free market 'conservative' opponents. In this sense, the European and Australasian left has been 'Americanized'. Where American party politics remains most obviously distinctive, in comparative terms, is less in its lack of an influential socialist movement than in the absence of an influential Green Party. But even here, the strong environmental lobby that exists in America offers opportunities for exerting influence on government in ways arguably at least as significant as those exercised by Green parties in Europe.

In sum, the character and extent of American distinctiveness requires careful analysis. Again, the chapters that follow should assist the reader to reflect on precisely how—and if so, why—the United States stands apart from its democratic peers.

Conclusion

In restoring undivided Republican control of the federal government, the 2002 midterm elections confirmed three current realities of American politics. First, 9/11 has restored issues of national security as priorities for a people that has rarely experienced direct attacks on the American homeland. Second, against the historical precedent of the White House party losing seats in a midterm election, the results confirmed the remarkable political influence of President George W. Bush at home as well as in the international arena—despite the fear and derision with which he is frequently depicted outside the United States. Third, the elections confirmed the existence of a broad domestic political division between a heavily Democratic electorate on the two coasts of America and a strongly Republican heartland in between them. As such, the 2002 results testified to the existence of the divided democracy that this book seeks to analyse.

Dispassionate analysis of American politics is neither easy nor straightforward. Students of the United States often object to aspects of American domestic practice (from the historical legacies of slavery and state-enforced racial segregation to the current use of capital punishment or the importance of religion in public life) and American foreign policy in general—and that of George W. Bush's administration in particular. The more garish elements of American life can easily encourage a distaste for, and even a ridicule of, all things American. Certainly, there exists something rather curious about a nation where the same states that pass laws to prohibit midget-tossing and the sale of 'marital aids' permit the carrying of guns concealed on the person and leave millions without access to adequate health care. But to yield to such stereotypes and prejudices is as misplaced in regard to America as to any other nation. Indeed, it is arguably especially ill-advised in this case. Precisely because 'common-sense' knowledge of America is often all too common and not always sensible, the importance of a balanced and informed approach is all the more imperative.

American politics offers a canvas as rich in its colour as it is complex in its operations, constant in its change, and consequential in its domestic and international effects. Were the Founding Fathers somehow transported to the America of the first decade of the twenty-first century, there is much that they would no doubt be amazed and, perhaps, appalled by (from the invention of the Internet and some of its content to the conduct of certain recent occupants of the White House). Equally, however, they would probably be struck—and possibly shocked—by the remarkable continuity that exists, from a Constitution with only seventeen additional amendments since 1791 to a regular celebration of the ideals of individual liberty, equality before the law, and liberal democracy that informed the revolution against Britain and the establishment of the 'first new nation'. In the chapters that follow, the contributors therefore address a range of questions that typically animate interest in American politics:

- What accounts for the longevity of a Constitution designed in and for the eighteenth century?

- Does American government 'work', and, if so, is this because or in spite of the US Constitution?

- What accounts for the relative success of the United States as an economic and military power?
- Can the president exercise effective political leadership in the face of the powerful obstacles posed by Congress, the courts, the bureaucracy, and other influential political actors?
- What accounts for the apparent weakness of American political parties?
- How influential are organized interest groups and lobbies?
- How can we explain American public policies on matters from the environment and social policy to gay rights and gun control?
- Who controls American foreign policy and to what ends?

The reader will encounter a range of responses to the above questions, and will we hope be able to arrive at an independent assessment in the light of the many arguments and extensive data that we offer. The chapters—individually and taken as a whole—aim not only to provide a solid overview of their subject matter but also to offer much material to stimulate critical and balanced reflection. Whether the views of the United States, the American people, and domestic and foreign policies that the reader brings to this volume will alter, and in what directions, is less significant than their being challenged to justify those views with evidence, examples, and careful reasoning. In that way, whether the view that emerges of American government and politics is positive or negative (or a combination of both), it will it is hoped be informed, reasoned, and dispassionate.

Part One

The historical and theoretical context

In the first part of this book we examine two major themes. First, we seek to provide a historical underpinning to our understanding of American government and politics. In particular, the evolution of the United States from a predominantly agrarian set of thirteen states on the eastern seaboard of America to the world's most influential economic and military nation-state provides a key focus for discussion. Second, we emphasize the existence of competing approaches and interpretations of America's development as a divided democracy. In terms both of America's domestic upheavals and of its relations with the wider world, several factors have been identified by scholars of American development as providing vital influences to the relative 'success' of the United States. The contributors elaborate on how recognizing the multiple influences on American political development is necessary to understanding the historical and contemporary character of politics in the United States.

America and the world

Michael Cox

READER'S GUIDE

This chapter examines America's 'rise to globalism': how an economically weak and militarily insignificant entity, situated on the periphery of a European-dominated international system, emerged by the middle of the twentieth century as both the dominant power in world affairs and the axis around which global politics would revolve thereafter. Earlier generations of nationalist American historians often framed this rise in terms of the construction of an 'exceptional' nation peopled by heroes and brave individuals (invariably white and male) who first fought the British and designed the US Constitution, then went on to carve a new type of frontier society out of the wilderness, continued their grand work by helping preserve the integrity of the republic from those who would sunder it by secession in the Civil War, and eventually forged an economic powerhouse that ushered into being the 'American' twentieth century. In this chapter the multiple explanations for America's ascendancy are analysed, and the linkages between 'internalist' and international factors are examined. In the process, the inaccurate use of American 'isolationism' as the term often used to describe America's 'natural' relationship to the world is explained.

Introduction

On 24 May 1607, 105 English settlers established a small and rather primitive village at Jamestown in what was later to become known as the Commonwealth of Virginia. After having nearly collapsed on more than one occasion, it went on to become the first successful permanent settlement to be established by Britain in America. How it survived has become one of America's many foundational myths;

yet within a century of its creation, a number of states had emerged along the eastern seaboard, none especially powerful in its own right, each one subordinate to London, and all created in the shadow of a larger European struggle for supremacy that was to shape the history of North America throughout the eighteenth century. Final victory in that struggle did not go to the colonists, of course, but to Great Britain, whose control of the whole continent was finally confirmed at the Treaty of Paris in 1763. Yet within only ten years, some of the more irate citizens of Boston were jettisoning that tea into that famous harbour; and two years on, the more material expressions of opposition to English rule had metamorphosed into a war for independence—one that was very nearly lost but, in the end, fought

to successful conclusion in part because of the support extended to the colonists by Britain's principal European enemy, France.

On 4 July 1776, the American Congress approved a Declaration of formal Independence (see Box 1.2 below). The first 'new state' had come into being. Born in the first instance out of economic resistance to metropolitan control rather than any developed theory of nationalism or because of any particular dislike of English political ideas—rebellion in the end was justified in terms of natural rights, not self-determination—the new sovereign power finally emerged in 1783 after having concluded peace terms with the mother country. A year later the first US merchant ship flying an American flag set sail for China, and in 1789 (a date significant in more

---

Box 1.1 The development of the United States: a concise chronology

1776	Declaration of Independence	1941	Attack by the Japanese on Pearl Harbor and entry of the USA into the Second World War
1781–7	Articles of Confederation		
1787	Constitutional Convention, Philadelphia		
1789	Ratification of the United States Constitution	1947	The Truman Doctrine and the beginning of the cold war
1791	Ratification of the Bill of Rights		
1823	Monroe Doctrine declared	1950–3	Korean War
1860	Abraham Lincoln elected president	1954	*Brown* v. *Board of Education* ruling by the US Supreme Court declares segregated schooling unconstitutional
1861–5	The Civil War		
1865–77	Reconstruction and passage of the Thirteenth, Fourteenth, and Fifteenth Amendments		
		1963	John F. Kennedy assassinated
		1964–75	Escalation and eventual end of the Vietnam War
1890s	Mass immigration from southern and eastern Europe		
		1964	Passage of the Civil Rights Act
1896	*Plessy* v. *Ferguson* ruling by the US Supreme Court upholds 'separate but equal' racial facilities	1965	Passage of the Voting Rights Act
		1965–2000	Mass immigration from Central and Latin America and Asia
1898	Spanish–American War	1968	Assassinations of Martin Luther King, Jr. and Bobby Kennedy; election of Richard M. Nixon
1917	The USA enters the First World War		
1919	The US Senate refuses to ratify the Treaty of Versailles		
	Eighteenth Amendment ratified, ushering in the era of Prohibition	1974	Resignation of Richard M. Nixon
		1980	Election of Ronald Reagan
1920	Nineteenth Amendment ratified, guaranteeing the right to vote for (white) American women	1989–91	Revolutions in Eastern Europe and collapse of the Soviet Union end the cold war
		1991	US coalition victory in the Gulf War
		1992	Election of Bill Clinton
1929	Wall Street Crash	2000	Election of George W. Bush
1932	Election of Franklin D. Roosevelt and beginning of the 'New Deal' era	2001	11 September terrorist attacks on the World Trade Center and the Pentagon

ways than one in the history of the world) George Washington was inaugurated as the first president of the United States.

This chapter seeks to explain how this economically weak and militarily insignificant entity, situated on the periphery of a European-dominated international system, emerged by the middle of the twentieth century as both the dominant power in world affairs and the axis around which global politics would revolve thereafter. The story has been told many times before, more often than not by an earlier generation of nationalist American historians much taken with their own particular story about the construction of a very exceptional kind of nation peopled—in their view—with heroes and brave individuals (almost always white and usually male) who first fought the British and wrote a Constitution, then went on to carve a new type of frontier society out of the wilderness, continued their grand work by helping preserve the integrity of the republic from those who would sunder it (this is why Lincoln and the Civil War are so important), and finally built the country into an economic powerhouse which made the 'American' twentieth century possible. It is all very heady stuff.

Fortunately, this kind of morality tale about the birth of a nation with few victims, and even fewer losers, has gone out of fashion since the 1960s, and today historians in the United States are far more critical about the rise of America than they once used to be. Still, many continue to view its emergence as one of the great stories of the last 200 years. And in many ways it is. Indeed, viewed from the perspective of America's critical entry into the First World War in 1917, the even more vital part it played in the defeat of Germany and Japan in the Second World War, and then the central role it performed in underwriting world order during a long and successful forty-year cold war struggle fought against the Soviet Union, one can easily see why people should think in these terms. Many factors made the international history of the modern world. But one would be hard pushed to think of one more significant than the rise of the United States.

Mention of America's global role in the twentieth century also raises a second question about how the United States became a major international player. More often than not those who have written about this have tended, in the main, to focus on specifically American factors: the size of the country, its many geographical advantages, its relative isolation, and the simple fact that it is surrounded by two vast oceans east and west and nothing more dangerous than Canadians to the north and Mexicans to the south! This approach certainly conforms to how most Americans think of their own history. It also contains more than a germ of truth. However, an 'internalist' explanation cannot, in the end, account for how the United States became a serious factor in world affairs in the modern era. Other things had to happen as well before it could reach the position it was to hold: and what happened, quite simply, were two world wars. The first provided America with a massive economic and political boost (Leon Trotsky later observed that whereas on the eve of the First World War the world revolved around Europe, by its end it revolved around the United States). The Second, however, left it in a position of almost unrivalled supremacy. Fighting and winning global wars does not provide the whole explanation as to why the twentieth century was to become the American century, no more than becoming a superpower made victory in the cold war inevitable. But without war and success in war, which in turn presupposed a massively productive economy which could meet the needs of war, the United States could never have risen to the position it held by the beginning of the new millennium. This is why three dates—1918, 1945, and 1989—are not just significant in world historical terms, but central moments in the history of the United States as well.

Any serious assessment of America's 'rise to globalism' thus has to address two fundamental issues: one concerns the domestic conditions which led to its expansion in the nineteenth century and its emergence before the First World War as a 'world power' amongst others; and the other is the impact of international conflict on its position in the world. Naturally, becoming a superpower was not cost-free. Nor was it smooth or inevitable. Indeed, at different points in time some Americans at least (especially in the interwar period) were less than enthusiastic about the US becoming politically and militarily entangled in the affairs of those people whose destiny it could not control—hence the much-discussed phenomenon known as

Box 1.2 The Declaration of Independence (1776)

In Congress, July 4, 1776

The Unanimous Declaration of the thirteen United States of America

When, in the course of human events, it becomes necessary for one people to dissolve the political bonds which have connected them with another, and to assume, among the powers of the earth, the separate and equal station to which the laws of nature and of nature's God entitle them, a decent respect to the opinions of mankind requires that they should declare the causes which impel them to the separation.

We hold these truths to be self-evident: That all men are created equal; that they are endowed by their Creator with certain unalienable rights; that among these are life, liberty, the pursuit of happiness; that, to secure these rights, governments are instituted among men, deriving their just powers from the consent of the governed; that whenever any form of government becomes destructive of these ends, it is the right of the people to alter or abolish it, and to institute new government, laying its foundation on such principles, and organizing its powers in such form, as to them shall seem most likely to effect their safety and happiness. Prudence, indeed, will dictate that governments long established shall not be changed for light and transient causes; and accordingly all experience hath shown that mankind are most disposed to suffer, while evils are sufferable, than to right themselves by abolishing the forms to which they are accustomed. But when a long train of abuses and usurpations, pursuing invariably the same object, evinces a design to reduce them under absolute despotism, it is their right, it is their duty, to throw off such government, and to provide new guards for their future security. Such has been the patient sufferance of these colonies; and such now is the necessity which constrains them to alter their former systems of government. The history of the present King of Great Britain is a history of repeated injuries and usurpations, all having in direct object the establishment of an absolute tyranny over these states. To prove this, let facts be submitted to a candid world.

He has refused his assent to laws, the most wholesome and necessary for the public good.

He has forbidden his governors to pass laws of immediate and pressing importance, unless suspended in their operation till his assent should be obtained; and when so suspended, he has utterly neglected to attend to them.

He has refused to pass other laws for the accommodation of large districts of people, unless those people would relinquish the right of representation in the legislature, a right inestimable to them, and formidable to tyrants only.

He has called together legislature bodies at places unusual, uncomfortable, and distant from the depository of their public records, for the sole purpose of fatiguing them into compliance with his measures.

He has dissolved representative houses repeatedly, for opposing with manly firmness, his invasions on the rights of the people.

He has refused for a long time, after such dissolutions, to cause others to be elected; whereby the legislative powers, incapable of annihilation, have returned to the people at large for their exercise; the state remaining, in the mean time, exposed to all the dangers of invasions from without and convulsions within.

He has endeavored to prevent the population of these states; for that purpose obstructing the laws for naturalization of foreigners; refusing to pass others to encourage their migration hither, and raising the conditions of new appropriations of lands.

He has obstructed the administration of justice, by refusing his assent to laws for establishing judiciary powers.

He has made judges dependent on his will alone, for the tenure of their offices, and the amount and payment of their salaries.

He has erected a multitude of new offices, and sent hither swarms of officers to harass our people and eat out their substance.

He has kept among us, in times of peace, standing armies, without the consent of our legislatures.

He has affected to render the military independent of, and superior to, the civil power.

Box 1.2 **continued**

He has combined with others to subject us to a jurisdiction foreign to our constitution, and unacknowledged by our laws, giving his assent to their acts of pretended legislation.

For quartering large bodies of armed troops among us;

For protecting them, by a mock trial, from punishment for any murders which they should commit on the inhabitants of these states;

For cutting off our trade with all parts of the world;

For imposing taxes on us without our consent;

For depriving us, in many cases, of the benefits of trial by jury;

For transporting us beyond seas, to be tried for pretended offenses;

For abolishing the free system of English laws in a neighboring province, establishing therein an arbitrary government, and enlarging its boundaries, so as to render it at once an example and fit instrument for introducing the same absolute rule into these colonies;

For taking away our charters, abolishing our most valuable laws, and altering fundamentally the forms of our governments;

For suspending our own legislatures, and declaring themselves invested with power to legislate for us in all cases whatsoever;

He has abdicated government here, by declaring us out of his protection and waging war against us.

He has plundered our seas, ravaged our coasts, burned our towns, and destroyed the lives of our people.

He is at this time transporting large armies of foreign mercenaries to complete the works of death, desolation, and tyranny already begun with circumstances of cruelty and perfidy scarcely paralleled in the most barbarous ages, and totally unworthy of the head of a civilized nation.

He has constrained our fellow-citizens, taken captive on the high seas, to bear arms against their country, to become the executioners of their friends and brethren, or to fall themselves by their hands.

He has excited domestic insurrection among us, and has endeavored to bring on the inhabitants of our frontiers the merciless Indian savages, whose known rule of warfare is an undistinguished destruction of all ages, sexes, and conditions.

In every stage of these oppressions we have petitioned for redress in the most humble terms; our repeated petitions have been answered only by repeated injury. A prince, whose character is thus marked by every act which may define a tyrant, is unfit to be the ruler of a free people.

Nor have we been wanting in our attentions to our British brethren. We have warned them, from time to time, of attempts by their legislature to extend an unwarrantable jurisdiction over us. We have reminded them of the circumstances of our emigration and settlement here. We have appealed to their native justice and magnanimity; and we have conjured them, by the ties of our common kindred, to disavow these usurpations, which would inevitably interrupt our connections and correspondence. They, too, have been deaf to the voice of justice and of consanguinity. We must, therefore, acquiesce in the necessity which denounced our separation, and hold them, as we hold the rest of mankind, enemies in war, in peace friends.

We, therefore, the representatives of the United States of America, in General Congress assembled, appealing to the Supreme Judge of the world for the rectitude of our intentions, do, in the name and by the authority of the good people of these colonies, solemnly publish and declare, that these United Colonies are, and of right ought to be, FREE AND INDEPENDENT STATES; that they are absolved from all allegiance to the British crown, and that all political connection between them and the state of Great Britain is, and ought to be, totally dissolved; and that, as free and independent states, they have full power to levy war, conclude peace, contract alliances, establish commerce, and do all other acts and things which independent states may of right do. And for the support of this declaration, with a firm reliance on the protection of Divine Providence, we mutually pledge to each other our lives, our fortunes, and our sacred honor.

Box 1.3 Admission of states to the Union (common abbreviations in parentheses)

1. Delaware (DE)	7 December 1787	26. Michigan (MI)	26 January 1837
2. Pennsylvania (PA)	12 December 1787	27. Florida (FL)	3 March 1845
3. New Jersey (NJ)	18 December 1787	28. Texas (TX)	19 December 1845
4. Georgia (GA)	2 January 1788	29. Iowa (IA)	28 December 1846
5. Connecticut (CT)	9 January 1788	30. Wisconsin (WI)	29 May 1848
6. Massachusetts (MA)	6 February 1788	31. California (CA)	9 September 1850
7. Maryland (MD)	28 April 1788	32. Minnesota (MN)	11 May 1858
8. South Carolina (SC)	23 May 1788	33. Oregon (OR)	14 February 1859
9. New Hampshire (NH)	21 June 1788	34. Kansas (KS)	29 January 1861
10. Virginia (VA)	25 June 1788	35. West Virginia (WV)	20 June 1863
11. New York (NY)	26 July 1788	36. Nevada (NV)	31 October 1864
12. North Carolina (NC)	21 November 1789	37. Nebraska (NE)	1 March 1867
13. Rhode Island (RI)	29 May 1790	38. Colorado (CO)	1 August 1876
14. Vermont (VT)	4 March 1791	39. North Dakota (ND)	2 November 1889
15. Kentucky (KY)	1 June 1792	40. South Dakota (SD)	2 November 1889
16. Tennessee (TN)	1 June 1796	41. Montana (MT)	8 November 1889
17. Ohio (OH)	1 March 1803	42. Washington (WA)	11 November 1889
18. Louisiana (LA)	30 April 1812	43. Idaho (ID)	3 July 1890
19. Indiana (IN)	11 December 1816	44. Wyoming (WY)	10 July 1890
20. Mississippi (MS)	10 December 1817	45. Utah (UT)	4 January 1896
21. Illinois (IL)	3 December 1818	46. Oklahoma (OK)	16 November 1907
22. Alabama (AL)	14 December 1819	47. New Mexico (NM)	6 January 1912
23. Maine (ME)	15 March 1820	48. Arizona (AZ)	14 February 1912
24. Missouri (MO)	10 August 1821	49. Alaska (AK)	3 January 1959
25. Arkansas (AR)	15 June 1836	50. Hawaii (HI)	21 August 1959

---

isolationism. But one should not buy into this particular myth too easily. Isolationist sentiments coupled with a more basic parochialism have always influenced public opinion. Indeed, in 1940, when Europe was ablaze, Franklin D. Roosevelt had to promise the American people that the United States would remain neutral. Even after the Second World War, many Americans still felt more comfortable staying at home rather than supporting an active foreign policy abroad. However, one has to exercise some care here. After all, isolationism did not hold the United States back when it claimed special rights in Latin America under the terms of the Monroe Doctrine, and this was in 1823. Nor did it deter Admiral Perry and his 'black boats' from threatening Japanese prestige in 1853, or prevent it driving the Spanish out of the Caribbean in 1898, or declaring

an Open Door in China a year later. Nor, moreover, did it stop the US intervening militarily several times in Central America before 1914, attempting to subvert the Russian revolution just after 1917, playing a major role at the Paris peace negotiations in 1919, getting involved in the economic affairs of Europe in the 1920s, or becoming a great naval power in the same decade (Britain being the other). Isolationism is often used to describe America's 'natural' relationship to the world. In reality, this idea obscures more than it reveals about the United States in the international arena, even before the second half of the twentieth century. However, before going on to discuss the specific ways in which America influenced international relations and inserted itself into the affairs of the world, it is useful to discuss how it became a major force in the first place.

Manifest Destiny

The history of international relations, it has often been suggested, has primarily been the history of the great powers. As a classical writer from antiquity once put it (and I paraphrase) the strong are important because they can choose what they want to do while the weak simply have very little choice at all. Thus it has always been, and no doubt will continue to be. Which raises the inevitable question: how did the United States become a great power at all? After all, at the beginning of the nineteenth century it was almost an irrelevant player on the international stage, with a small population of around five million persons and an economy that was not only largely rural in character but still very much dependent economically on Great Britain. Nor did it possess much in the way of military firepower. Furthermore, unlike other great powers—aspiring or real—it had few of the trappings of a powerful state. In fact, the American state in 1800 was particularly weak and underdeveloped.

Yet the 'first new nation' had enormous potential. For one thing, it was a long way away from Europe and Europe's wars. It also had few serious enemies worth talking of. Its rivers afforded an adventurous people cheap and relatively easy means of access to the American interior. And its climate and soil made possible the cultivation of a very much greater percentage of its land than, say, Canada or Russia (both of which were geographically more extensive). It had a number of other important assets too. One was a vibrant, rumbustious, decentralized political system which made possible the rapid turnover of elites; another was a powerful set of driving myths about America's special destiny to become a bright shining example to others; and a third was an extraordinarily positive view about the future based on the idea (not entirely unrelated to material reality) that this was a country of genuine opportunity where hard work and effort would be rewarded. Marx also noted something else as well: that the United States was never hampered in any way by old feudal forms. It was from the outset a purely bourgeois society where traditional status counted for very little. This was critically important, in terms not only of

encouraging a far more positive attitude to the making of money—this, after all, is what America was originally set up to do—but of ensuring that there was no resistance by key groups to economic development.

To these more general advantages one should add five fairly specific factors which, when combined, together helped transform America after 1800: continental expansion, a steady supply of labour, the experience of civil war, industrialization before 1914, and the particularly brutal but highly productive form of capitalism which took root in the country. Some indeed would argue that the huge success experienced by the United States after 1865 owed less to natural advantages and more to the very human creation known as the free enterprise system, one which under American conditions was highly exploitative in character, but because of its sheer size and scope was able to generate more wealth more rapidly than any other known in history.

But first, continental expansion—often referred to in the films as 'How the West was Won'.

Continental expansion

If, as some people believe, a special providence has looked after the affairs of the United States through its history, then part of this concern has been geographical. To realize its geographical destiny, however, the continent first had to be conquered. This process took the best part of a hundred years as the frontier of white civilization was pushed forward in one of the more dynamic—and brutal—periods of American history extending until the 1890s. In this relatively short period of time, Americans took over more than one-third of North America, including much of its best land—a broad swathe stretching from sea to sea across almost twenty degrees of latitude. The sheer scale of the enterprise almost beggars belief. But in less than a hundred years, from the surrender of British forces at Yorktown in 1781 to the final settlement of the line of demarcation between the United States and Canada, the US grew by leaps and bounds, acquiring vast amounts of land, initially from the British themselves in the late eighteenth century, then from its original native inhabitants, and last but by no means least, from anybody else who happened to stand in the way.

The continental expansion of the United States in the nineteenth century took place in several great waves. Until the opening of the nineteenth century, all territory east of the Mississippi was deemed to be American. In 1803, however, the French astounded the Americans by offering them a huge area that comprised all the land between the Mississippi and the Rocky Mountains. This immense acquisition, known as the 'Louisiana Purchase', was obtained for the princely sum of $15 m. Then, in 1819, the United States bought Florida from Spain for $5 m. The next great continental expansion occurred between 1845 and 1848 and comprised the entire area (formerly Mexican and Spanish in influence) from the West boundary of the Louisiana Purchase—including Texas—to the Pacific Ocean. More land was then acquired in the south-west as a result of the Gadsden Purchase. Lastly, in 1867, the United States purchased Alaska from Russia.

In this fashion, the broad geographical parameters of what came to be regarded as the United States of America were established. At times it involved diplomacy, at others the threat (and the use) of force, and always a vision of a nation whose purpose could only be realized once the writ of the US ran from the Atlantic to the Pacific, from the borders of a defeated Mexico in the south to the relatively weak 'hostage' state of Canada to the north. The whole exercise involved three wars and the payment of only $48 m. The means employed were rarely less than effective, the ends achieved remarkable. But a price was paid: by Mexico, which lost vast tracts of territory to the militarily more energetic Yankees, and by Native Americans, who lost nearly everything—their land, the right to roam the plains, and, in hundreds of thousands of cases, even the right to live. The West was won, but at a high price. Yet something truly extraordinary emerged: in effect, a nation that was not just very big, but so enormous as to embrace all, and more than all, the geographical variations found in Europe.

Building a country—peopling the nation

This immense continent formed the foundation upon which the United States was subsequently built. However, without a people to till the land, work in the factories, and fight the wars, the nation would have amounted to very little. An expanding country required an expanding population. And perhaps the second most remarkable aspect of American history in the nineteenth century was the extraordinarily rapid rise in its mainly white European population. Much of this resulted from what demographers refer to as natural growth, an increase in numbers occurring in a country in which a relatively prosperous people, with no serious medical or manmade threats to their existence, continue to reproduce over time. Certainly, this natural upward cycle would account for at least a reasonable percentage of the increase in population which took the US from around 5 million in 1800 to 23 million in 1850, 31 million in 1860, 76 million in 1900, and nearly 100 million on the eve of the First World War.

But this was only part of the story—and perhaps not the most important part. Ultimately, this stupendous transformation was made possible by the greatest human migration in history, one that took millions across the Atlantic from Europe to the distant shores of the United States. To this extent, the peopling of the US was not a national but an international achievement. Basically, America in the nineteenth century became the destination, of the bulk of Europe's surplus population. Before 1860 most of these came from England, Ireland, and the Rhine valley; thereafter primarily from Germany and Scandinavia (at least until the early 1880s); and then, finally, from the Mediterranean, East Europe, and Russia—and included within the latter a sizeable Jewish population. In the process a nation was constructed whose patchwork quilt of peoples had to be consciously socialized and integrated into the 'American way'. But even as Americans, they rarely forgot their homeland, and continued to take a keen, often quite romantic and belligerent interest in the affairs of the country from whence they had originally come. Whether any of this often noisy clamour ever decisively changed the course of American foreign policy remains an open question. However, the existence of such ethnic pressure groups did have consequences for the way in which the United States conducted its international affairs when it became more involved in world politics in the twentieth century. Indeed, in one very special case—President Truman's decision in 1948 to recognize Israel—the existence of a powerful Jewish lobby had a major impact on a decision that was to have serious long-term implications for US relations with the Middle East.

The American Civil War

Economists now agree that long before the Civil War, the United States was developing rapidly and fast establishing the framework for a modern capitalistic system. In the twenty-year period before 1860, for example, the annual growth rate was never less than 8 per cent in any one year. Nonetheless, in 1860 the United States remained a land of small-scale, local, handicraft industry, with well over 40 per cent of its people living and working on farms. It was, however, a nation with a potentially fatal fissure running right through its heart: between those states in the South where slavery was the foundation of a material civilization whose economic ideology at least was free trade and open markets, and those in the North, where the twin creeds were those of 'free labour' and high tariffs. Ultimately, the two could not coexist, and in a move designed to maintain a particular way of life, the South seceded from the Union, thus precipitating a long and brutal conflict between the states which left nearly 600,000 people dead and the South in economic tatters.

The impact of the Civil War upon America and America's position in the world was profound. Most obviously, it stimulated an economic boom in the North that laid the material substructure which made possible the rapid industrialization of the country that followed. The Civil War was, in this respect, a forcing ground for American industrial development. Secondly, it revealed to the rest of the world (the European countries in particular) that here was a power to be reckoned with. Significantly, many of the features of modern warfare—the fast repeating rifle, trenches, and the mobilization of millions of civilians—were first deployed in the Civil War. Finally, victory for the North preserved the integrity of the Union, and by so doing forever laid to rest the question of the national unity of the United States. The significance of this for American foreign relations was enormous. Governments in Washington from now on would be able to conduct foreign affairs without fearing their immediate impact on domestic cohesiveness. Foreign powers took note. And it was not insignificant, of course, that even before the outcome of the war was known, none seriously became engaged in its conduct. In reality, so formidable had the United States already become that between 1861 and 1865 neither Britain nor any other major European power dared risk the lasting enmity that intervention would bring. And as the war swung in the direction of the North, leaders abroad became even less enthusiastic about upsetting the winning side, no doubt realizing that having won the war and unified the nation under one government, the new industrial nation that was fast emerging was bound to become a major player in world politics.

Industrial colossus

Power in international politics depends, in the last analysis, on a nation's economic strength, and by 1914 the United States possessed more material capabilities than any other nation. It was this, more than subtle diplomacy, the quality of its intelligence services, or the bravery of its soldiers, that made it into a serious great power long before Europe plunged into a bloody war that would finally pull the United States, albeit reluctantly at first, onto the centre stage of international politics.

The results of rapid economic growth after 1865 were remarkable and impressive. Certainly, by the time the First World War began, the United States was far outstripping all the major powers in national as well as per capita income terms. Britain, its closest economic rival and most obvious competitor, had only one-third the national income and two-thirds the per capita income by the time WWI broke out. All told, the national incomes of all the European powers combined, only just exceeded that of the US in 1914. The structure of US exports also began to change, from being predominantly agricultural before 1860 to becoming mainly manufacturing by 1900. Moreover, the high quality and low prices of these goods played a major role in forcing changes in the economies of Europe and other nations. This in turn was accompanied by a very rapid increase in the American share of world trade, which having remained at around 4 per cent through the 1880s, then rose rapidly almost annually until war broke out. Over the same time period, the US also moved from being a debtor to a creditor nation as its exports surged. US companies began investing abroad too, and although little direct investment went to Europe (its major trading partner) it did begin to increase its presence in Canada, Mexico, Cuba, and South America. The United States also pioneered the techniques of mass production. Great economies of scale were thus achieved by US manufacturers, whose levels of productivity far outstripped the nation's nearest rivals. Significantly, when Europeans began to talk after 1900—as they did with increasing frequency—of a growing American threat, they were not referring to the United States as a security problem (though its navy was causing eyebrows to be raised in many quarters) but to the sheer productivity of the American economic machine.

Capitalism—American style

Finally, any assessment of America's rise to power has to take some account of the particularly effective economic system that was established in the United States. Other forms of capitalism have been productive; but there was something very distinct about the private enterprise system in the US which endowed it with an enormous resilience and an almost limitless ability to innovate. The most obvious measure of this was the sheer capacity of the American economy to out-produce and out-compete nearly everybody else. A more subtle indicator perhaps was the weakness of any serious, organized opposition to the system. The contrast with mainland Europe could not have been more stark. Here socialism in one form or another was to become a mass movement. In the United States however it was a pale, and mainly imported, imitation of its counterpart across

the Atlantic. Indeed, while serious social theorists in Europe could not avoid the existence of mass organized parties opposed to capitalism—and wrote at great length about it—in the US there was no such literature. On the contrary, one of the most frequently asked questions was not when the United States would become like Europe but why the United States was so different.

Capitalism thus managed to sink especially deep roots in the United States, reflecting the fairly self-evident fact that the system happened to work especially well under American conditions. Indeed, it is difficult to conceive of the rise of America except as a capitalist civilization. Even the values associated with capitalism—individualism, the undisputed right to property, the accumulation of wealth—came to be regarded as quintessentially American. Nor did politics stop at the water's edge. Consequently, an ideology born under American conditions necessarily influenced the way in which the US related to the world at large. Certainly, its powerful ideological commitment to free enterprise provided the United States with a general, but not unimportant, road map which it would use as it charted its way through world politics. Thus, while it might support the cause of political freedom (though not always) and even challenge local oligarchs, it could never support any cause that threatened those economic institutions that had guaranteed success in the US. It would simply be 'un-American'. In a nation where few questioned the moral or economic logic of private enterprise, this made very little difference. However, when this world began to change—as it did increasingly after the First World War—this inevitably placed the United States on the side of those favouring the economic status quo. This in part helps explain one of the great ironies of the modern world: why a nation born out of one kind of revolution in one age increasingly came to be regarded as fundamentally opposed to revolutionary change in another.

Key points

- America's 'rise to globalism' was anything but inevitable. At the beginning of the nineteenth century, the United States was almost an irrelevant player in the international system, possessing only a small population of around five million persons and a largely rural economy that still depended heavily on Great Britain.

- American economic and political development benefited substantially from abundant natural resources, distance from European wars, and a

political culture that was strongly receptive to capitalism.

- America was transformed after 1800 by five key developments: continental expansion, a steady supply of labour, the experience of Civil War, industrialization before 1914, and a particularly brutal but highly productive form of capitalism.

The birth of an American empire

Within little more than a century, therefore, the United States had become a very different kind of nation from the one it had been in 1800. And this change in capabilities was very rapidly reflected in the way in which American elites perceived their own role in the world—and by the same token in the way in which foreigners looked at the United States. It was no accident, of course, that whereas most European diplomats regarded a posting to the US before the 1880s as a form of social and political exile, by 1892 all of the major powers (with the sole exception of Austria-Hungary) had upgraded the position of their legations in Washington by raising them to the status of full embassies. More general foreign interest also began to increase in this upwardly mobile, brash power that outwardly possessed few of the graces of a major European state. Indeed, watching its economic development in the 1880s provided Europeans with much food for thought. Often, in dispatches and letters back home, they would wonder and worry what the implications of the rise of American economic power would be for their own prosperity. The conclusions they arrived at were not always happy ones. Thus a German observer in 1881 feared that not only Germany but Europe as a whole could easily 'succumb to the United States in the battle for supremacy in world trade'. Within twenty years, other Europeans were speaking in even more apocalyptic terms of an 'American peril' or even perhaps the 'Americanization' of the world caused by the sheer size and efficiency of the US economy. Certainly, as one century gave way to another, few doubted that the balance of power was

fast changing. As a future French prime minister was heard to remark in 1908, nobody now could question the fact that America had become a major player with the right to sit at that table where all the great powers sat.

The great turning point in all this, however, was to be the critical decade of the 1890s. Obviously, what impressed and scared foreigners most was American economic growth, in turn paralleled by a much more aggressive stance taken by US business abroad. In fact, one of the constant talking points at the time within the United States was the perceived need to find foreign markets which could then absorb the surplus generated by a highly energetic economy that was producing far too much for its own domestic needs. However, the real transition from one era to another was not just an addition of more factories within the US itself, but rather a burst of serious international activity undertaken by the United States in the second half of the decade, especially the period between 1896 and 1900. Whether we argue that America had greatness thrust upon it, or that it chose the route of expansion, still remains a hotly debated issue amongst historians. What is not in doubt is that both Americans and others living in the late 1890s readily understood that they were witnessing a major historical turn.

A number of events contributed to this feeling that a corner was fast being turned. One, interestingly, was the publication of a book that seemed to catch the spirit of the age. Written by a naval officer, Captain Alfred Thayer Mahan, *The Influence of Sea*

Power upon History, 1660–1783 (1890) advanced the not entirely original thesis that empire was the logical consequence of power but that to secure an empire one had to control the sea. The Romans had done it—he argued—and so had the British. And if the United States aimed to become a serious international force, then it too would have to construct a proper navy equal to its requirements and ambitions. Mahan, however, was not entirely indifferent to economics. Indeed, what made his arguments particularly popular amongst some business circles was the additional point he made that American surplus production required overseas markets; but in order to obtain and protect these, the US would require a serious force projection, and this again could only be undertaken with the building of a strong navy. Finally, Mahan advocated and strongly urged the building of what he called an Isthmian canal. This, he argued, would connect the Atlantic and Pacific oceans and thus reduce the distance between the east and west coasts of the United States; but it would do something else as well: make the United States into a truly global actor. Being a good imperialist, though, Mahan was not afraid to draw out the implications of his analysis. As he noted, in order to secure this new vital asset (later called the Panama Canal and completed in 1914) the United States would have to take control of the region through which it ran. This not only made sense in terms of ensuring safe movement through the waterway. It would extend American rule into Central America too.

Mahan's extraordinarily influential ideas about the need for the United States to assert itself was in part recognition that in a more general age of imperialism, where the European powers were extending their reach to the four corners of the earth, the United States could not be left out or behind. It also reflected a growing sense amongst key elites that a country the size of America with its vast assets and resources had to become, and act, more and more like a great power. This was in the nature of things: it would in turn fulfil that glorious destiny for which the republic had been preparing following several decades of expansion across the great plains. Indeed, the notion of America as a constantly expanding entity, whose very survival and prosperity quite literally depended on extending the frontier

of its experience, was another powerful ideological myth that lent weight to the argument that the United States had little choice, in a brutal world where only the fittest survived, but to expand overseas.

It is not coincidental, therefore, that in the same era that witnessed a frenzied burst of foreign policy activity supported by a range of arguments—from 'white man's burden' to Christian 'civilizing mission' through to Social Darwinism—the frontier in the United States was officially declared over. But it was left to a young University of Wisconsin professor (Frederick Jackson Turner) to draw out what he saw as the implications for the future of the republic; and in perhaps the most influential essay ever written by an American about the United States, he argued that the very vitality of the nation had hitherto depended upon an ever-expanding frontier presupposing an abundance of freely available land; however, now that that land had been seized and acquired, the country was bound to face a host of new problems that would challenge it to its core. One answer was to engage in serious reform—a solution favoured at the time by many ordinary Americans. But for those without such ideas, and who opposed any talk of change (and feared it), there was another answer: to look for new frontiers abroad. Indeed, Turner himself drew out the implications of his own thesis. Surveying the American scene with an increasingly jaundiced eye, he argued in 1896 that with the disappearance of one frontier, it was now more important than ever to engage in a vigorous foreign policy that would extend 'America's influence to outlying islands and adjoining countries'. The days of self-sufficiency were over.

Turner and Mahan together were sensitive indicators of a mood change then taking place at the higher levels of American society. Naturally, not all members of the elite favoured expansion. Some, in fact, were strongly anti-imperialist. However, the intellectual tide was turning. The passive period of relative inaction that followed the Civil War (later referred to by some as the 'Dutch disease' and others later as 'imperial understretch') was fast drawing to an end. But it required two things for the transition to finally take place: the building of a more powerful state without which the United States could not assert itself with any degree of effectiveness; and a major international incident. This was to be provided by the Spanish–American war of 1898.

There were several causes of this 'splendid' and relatively cost-free conflict (at least cost-free to the Americans). These should not detain us. But what should are the results. And these were most impressive. Most obviously, Spain was expelled from Cuba and the Philippines. The United States also fought and won a series of relatively minor but internationally significant battles both at sea and on land. Moreover, a public opinion was created which, though divided, was still very much excited about this assertion of American power. The war moreover closed the growing gap that had hitherto existed between America's increasing economic power and its international weight in the world, and it encouraged further self-confident expansion—into Latin America and the Caribbean, as well as across the Pacific. Thus by 1900 the US had acquired a series of interests stretching right across that vast ocean (the Midway Islands had been acquired in 1867, Samoa in 1889, Hawaii, the Philippines, and Guam in 1898, and Wake Island in 1899) which made it into a significant actor in the region. Indeed, it was no coincidence that within a year of acquiring control of the Philippines, Washington was already declaring an interest in China, and that within two or three decades, serious people on both sides of the Pacific were talking seriously about the coming clash for control of Asia between the United States and Japan. Admittedly, this was forced upon the United States by an unprovoked attack much later, in 1941. However, the seeds of the rivalry had been well and truly planted nearly half a century before as the US began to move eastwards across the Pacific Ocean.

Finally, the great turn of 1898 ushered in an important shift in American alliance strategy, and no alliance was to be (or become) as important to the United States as that which it very obviously constructed with Great Britain towards the end of the nineteenth century. Like any normal international state-to-state relationship, this one was not free of rivalry. Britain after all was the former metropolitan master that continued to practise colonialism with great enthusiasm around the world. To many Americans this made the British the number one enemy, as did Britain's enormous financial weight in a global system where the pound still dominated transactions. Yet both sides recognized their mutual interests, supported by a shared sense of Anglo-Saxon superiority, several important transatlantic marriages (Winston Churchill being the product of one), and a strong connection forged by speaking the same language. Britain, moreover, was far-sighted enough to concede the United States its dominant position in Latin America. It also realized that with the growth of German power in Europe it would need American support, to balance the increased weight of its main European rival if war could be avoided, but if not, then to provide the UK with much-needed support. This was a wise move indeed: when war finally did break out in 1914, though the United States remained officially neutral for three years, there was little doubting where its sympathies and money lay.

Key points

- The crucial turning point in America's approach to international relations was the critical decade of the 1890s, when both rapid industrialization at home and the assertion of American power abroad accorded the United States the status of a key global power.

- The Spanish–American war of 1898 closed the growing gap that had hitherto existed between America's increasing economic power and its international weight in the world. It also encouraged the expansion of American power into Latin America, the Caribbean, and the Pacific.

The First World War: Europe's distress—America's advantage

The coming of a great European war posed several difficulties for the United States. The least of these, however, was to determine which side it would support. Though under strong pressure from Irish and German Americans not to favour the perfidious British, Woodrow Wilson—one of the most pro-English US presidents—was in no doubt where America would, and should, stand. A strong admirer of the British Empire, and an even more forceful advocate of a British-style constitution for the United States, Wilson however was not quite the liberal saint painted by his many admirers and several subsequent enemies. A firm supporter of the use of American force in Central America and the Caribbean, and an even stronger believer in the natural inferiority of those unfortunate enough not to have been born white, Wilson since becoming president in 1912 had been active in pushing American influence. There was little chance therefore that he would remain indifferent to what was now happening on the battlefields of Europe. Nor was he unaware of its impact on American prosperity in fact, as the war continued and demand for US goods by the Allies shot up, the US economy began to boom. However, as America boomed the Allies ran out of money, and thus required further loans from the United States to continue the fight. And the loans began to flow in very meaningful amounts from 1915 onwards, leaving both France and the UK in great debt to US banks by the time the war concluded. As a result the United States was to emerge by 1918 as the world's real economic arbiter. In this way (and not for the first time in history) Europe's own devastating conflicts were working to America's advantage.

The shift in the balance of economic power was in turn accompanied by the more serious political involvement of the United States in European affairs. The sinking of the passenger liner *Lusitania* made military intervention inevitable: however, American entry was facilitated by two other, more powerful factors: one was a fear that, with Russia's possible elimination from the struggle in 1917, Germany could end up winning the war and so dominate Europe—an outcome that filled Washington with some dread; and the other was a realization that without becoming more involved directly, the United States would only play a marginal part in shaping the future of the world that would be constructed once the guns fell silent. Wilson, naturally enough, justified America's involvement with grand phrases about extending the liberal principle of self-determination to the oppressed nations of Europe (though not Asia and Africa). He also promised to make the world safe for democracy. And such idealism should not be discounted altogether. If nothing else, it helped mobilize support at home while clothing America's actions in a garb of fine words. However, below the surface there were far more pressing reasons for becoming more actively engaged and trying to get the world to conform to American standards. Furthermore, in a situation where ordinary people were yearning for peace and tired of what had by now become known as the 'old diplomacy', an injection of liberal hope through the United States meant that it would be that nation, and not the European powers, that would be able to control the international agenda when the peace-makers sat down to speak.

Much ink has since been expended by historians on Wilson's failure to build a new world order at Versailles. Even more has been used up explaining how and why he failed to convince the American electorate about the necessity of getting involved in the newly created League of Nations. But in many ways these obituaries on Wilson's lack of achievement (sometimes put down to the fact that he was too liberal and sometimes to the fact that he was not liberal enough) seriously obscure what actually happened during and after the tortuous negotiations in Paris. For in the end, whatever was said or agreed within the corridors of power could not do much to control the elemental forces that had been unleashed by years of war. Nor could they alter the realities outside the splendid rooms where the big powers tried and failed to create a new world order. The United States might have played a key role in 1919, reflecting its newfound influence in the world. In many ways, however, it was not yet quite powerful enough. After the First World War only the United States had the capacity to recast Europe. Unfortunately, the conditions were not yet ripe. As more balanced historians of the period have noted, it is tempting to argue that the United States lost an opportunity to bend Europe to its will. It is equally tempting to say that if only the United States had not retreated into isolationism (of a kind) then all would have been well. But this is simply wishful thinking. Europe was not yet primed for a long peace, no more than America was willing or even able to do what it did at the end of the next major war. In reality, what it was capable of doing some years later, it could have done after the First World War. In 1945 the United States was a superpower and the European nations were much weakened.

But in 1919 it was not yet so much stronger than the other great powers that it could impose a plan on the world. Germany, Japan, France, Italy, and even—and perhaps especially—Great Britain were still serious factors in the international system. And it was only when they no longer remained so (and it took another war to convince them of that) that the US would be able to set the sort of agenda that it was unable to set after the First World War.

Key points

- The First World War was one instance where European conflicts worked to America's advantage in the international system.

- Although the United States' refusal to join the League of Nations ushered in a new era of American isolationism, it is doubtful whether America could have imposed a lasting peace in Europe after 1918.

The Second World War and the rise to globalism

In many ways the interwar period should not be regarded—as it often has been—as but a prelude to the next war. Much happened during these years which needs to be studied in its own right. However, at the end of the day, the various efforts by the status quo powers (including the United States) to either appease or deter aggression by Germany and Japan amounted to nothing. Nor could they prevent the world depression and the collapse of an integrated world economy based on free trade. However, from these dark days at least three important lessons were drawn by US policy-makers that were to guide them through the Second World War and deep into the postwar period of reconstruction. First, that if the United States did not lead then nobody would; second, that the conditions for international order required the creation of a more open, multilaterally organized international economy; and third, that

without sufficient power there would never be peace in the world. Not all the lessons drawn from the past were as brutally realist as this last one. Nonetheless, there were few members of the policy elite on the eve of the Second World War who had not arrived at the conclusion that if the United States was to get involved (and presumably be on the victorious side) in yet another war, this time round it would also have to win the peace as well—and the only way it would be able to do this was from a defined position of strength.

How strong the United States was to become as a result of the Second World War has been the subject of many fine studies; and for the majority of international historians, the most obviously important consequence of a global war which left somewhere close to fifty million dead was not the Holocaust, the decline of European power, or even the spread of

Soviet influence, but the rise of the United States; and the most obvious measure of this was economic. In very simple terms, production for war (carried out by capitalism but directed by the state) broke the back of the American Depression in less than two years, doubled the size of US GNP in four years from just under $100 bn. in 1940 to just over $200 bn. in 1945, and led to one of the most remarkable periods of scientific and technological innovation in the history of the American free enterprise system. The outcome was staggering. Basically, when the war concluded, the United States controlled over half of the world's industrial output and owned 70 per cent of the world's merchant marine, 75 per cent of its planes, and nearly 90 per cent of its petroleum. This was truly remarkable. Nor was there a Chinese wall separating war from peace. Indeed, the basis of America's postwar economic preponderance was laid in these critical years when the great corporations like Boeing, Ford, Goodyear, and General Electric were directed by government to innovate, create, and out-produce the enemy in the great battle for the future of humanity.

The Second World War also transformed the military position of the US. The experience of war fought across two oceans and three continents turned it into a military hegemon of the first order. Britain may have remained influential and Russia retained a sizeable army that had proven its mettle on the eastern front after 1941. But only the United States emerged in such a state of all-round preparedness by 1945. Thus the end of the Second World War, the US was the undisputed master of the seas: it had at last achieved its ambition of becoming (as Mahan had hoped it would) the truly dominant sea power. Its air force was also the world's strongest. And it alone had control of the atomic weapon, a monopoly position it would exploit to the full until the USSR exploded its own first weapon of mass destruction in 1949.

Nor was this all. While America flourished between 1941 and 1945, others suffered grievously. Hence Europe at war's end was in tatters, Britain was virtually bankrupt, Germany destroyed, and Japan on its knees. Never before in the history of the great powers had one of them so towered above all the rest. Moreover, while the USSR had some of the appearances of an equal 'superpower', it had serious weaknesses that would always hamper it in its struggle against the United States, and which some would now claim always meant that it could never equal America—indeed, was always like to remain its inferior. Economically, for example, it was never in the same class. In fact, until it recovered from the terrible damage inflicted upon it by the Second World War (during which time it lost over twenty-five million people) it was almost a backward Third World country by comparison. Nor did it possess the same sort of allies. Thus while the US after the war could count on the willing support of all of the advanced capitalist countries—including defeated Japan and West Germany—the USSR could only count on the mainly unwilling support extended to it by the more backward countries of Eastern Europe. Even in the Third World, where it made much of its anti-colonial past, it did not have the material wherewithal to sustain stable long-term relations with the more significant actors on the periphery.

Of course, the Soviet Union did have certain ideological advantages over its free-world rival after 1945: and one of these, we should recall, was the fact that it presented some economic alternative to the type of capitalism championed by the US. However, in the end, its repressive and brutal political regime was hardly likely to win it many converts. The United States, on the other hand, had many obvious ways of attracting positive support from millions around the world. Significantly, while many ordinary people seemed to be constantly trying to escape from communism, in their many millions they were always attempting to get into the United States. Once again, in this way, the reality of mass immigration (though under very different circumstances) worked to strengthen the international position of the US. So too did the many images that the United States was able to project around the world. Much of this was propaganda which tended to play down some of the less savoury features of American life. But the US did produce the goods and it did generate wealth—as it had done many times before in its past and as it did again during the Second World War. Abundance in turn created the conditions of choice, and choice, it was felt, was the foundation stone upon which true freedom would be built.

Key points

- American decision-makers drew three lessons from the interwar years that lasted well into the second half of the twentieth century: if the United States did not lead then nobody would; the conditions for international order required the creation of a more open, multilaterally organized international economy; and without sufficient power there would never be peace in the world.

- American economic and military power was transformed by victory in the Second World War, leaving the United States as the most influential global player in the international system.

Conclusion

If the Second World War laid the basis for much of what followed in the postwar period—policy-makers having dutifully learned the painful lessons from the interwar period—it also provided the US with the experience necessary to run and organize the world. Much has been made of what US leaders learned from the British—the 'Greeks' to what some regarded as the new American Romans. There is something in this. Britain after all had underwritten the nineteenth century international system (colloquially known as *Pax Britannica*); and the British were conscious too that as the war went on their power would slip while that of the United States would rise. Many resented this bitterly. The overwhelming majority, however, soon came to terms with the fact, and the most influential tried in their own rather patronizing fashion to educate their younger American cousins in the ways of the world. But perhaps the Americans needed far less tutoring than the British suspected. Not only had the war itself provided several valuable lessons; so too did American history. Indeed, one should take care not to overstate influence or to underestimate America's own experience, first in the process of becoming a major power at the end of the nineteenth century, and then as a real force during the First World War. Nor should one ignore its historical role in Latin America and the Pacific. Indeed, even in the interwar period, when it was thought to be entirely disengaged, it was still a critical factor in international relations.

In fact, as we have tried to show, the United States had for several decades been an aspiring power before finally becoming a superpower in 1945. The fact that its 'empire' did not come to resemble that of the British, or that its policy-makers often masked (and legitimized) their own actions by evoking powerful liberal themes drawn from America's own experience as a functioning democracy did not make it any the less effective. Indeed, the fact that it was able after the Second World War to build order out of chaos and go on to defeat the USSR would suggest that it was a most worthy heir to superpower status—with one obvious difference: whereas its former colonial suzerain finally declined as a serious superpower, the United States continues to flourish. And it surely says something about those who built this remarkable edifice that fifty years after it finally announced its presence, it still continues to flourish. This is why many would argue—and with some force—that the United States has proved to be the most exceptional great power in history.

QUESTIONS

1 What best explains America's 'rise to globalism'?

2 'Since the United States has pursued its international interests with vigour for most of its history, the term "isolationism" is an inappropriate description of American foreign policy.' Discuss.

3 To what extent has America's influence in the international system rested more on military than on economic power?

4 Critically assess the causes and consequences of American participation in either the First or the Second World War.

5 'The influence of the United States in the world has relied at least as much on the failures of other states as it has on American virtues.' Discuss.

FURTHER READING

W. Brands (1998), *What America Owes the World: The Struggle for the Soul of Foreign Policy* (Cambridge: Cambridge University Press).

N. Graebner (ed.) (1984), *America as a World Power: A Realist Appraisal from Wilson to Reagan* (Delaware: Scholarly Resources Inc.).

W. LaFeber (1994), *The American Age: US Foreign Policy at Home and Abroad—1750 to the Present* (New York: Norton).

A. McGrew (ed.) (1994), *The United States in the Twentieth Century: Empire* (London: Hodder & Stoughton).

E. R. May (1961), *Imperial Democracy: The Emergence of America as a Great Power* (New York: Harcourt, Brace & World).

D. Slater and P. J. Taylor (eds.) (1999), *The American Century: Consequences and Coercion in the Projection of American Power* (Oxford: Blackwell).

D. W. White (1906), *The American Century: The Rise and Decline of the United States as a World Power* (New Haven, Conn.: Yale University Press).

O. Zunz (1998), *Why the American Century?* (Chicago: Chicago University Press).

WEB LINKS

www.google.com/unclesam Search engine for all aspects of the US

www.foreignaffairs.org/ Foreign Affairs, the journal of the Council on Foreign Relations

www.foreignpolicy.com/ Foreign Policy, a journal on international politics

www.riia.org Royal Institute for International Affairs

www.iiss.org/home.php Institute for International and Strategic Studies

www.csis.org Center for Strategic and International Studies

odur.let.rug.nl/usanew/ A hypertext on American history from the colonial period until modern times, Department of Humanities, University of Groningen, The Netherlands

www.state.gov US State Dept.

www.thomas.loc.gov/ US Congress service

www.lcweb.loc.gov/ Library of Congress

www.census.gov US Census Bureau

www.cia.gov Central Intelligence Agency

www.defenselink.mil The Pentagon

www.fas.org Federation of American Scientists

2 The United States as a divided democracy: competing interpretations

Francisco E. González and Desmond S. King

READER'S GUIDE

This chapter examines the ten most influential theoretical approaches developed by contemporary scholars to make sense about the changing character of American democracy. In the first section we define American politics and government as stemming from a divided democracy. We highlight the fact that the American polity has remained relatively divided, in the sense that political institutions in the United States express a horizontal separation of powers between the branches of government and a vertical separation through the territorial divisions enshrined in federalism. In addition, the United States is also a divided democracy in the sense that progressive versus traditionalist debates and conflicts have shaped—and continue to shape—the complex and multifaceted character of American politics and government. Scholars have used several different theoretical approaches to try to understand this complex and ever-changing political and social reality. In the sub-sections of this chapter we discuss in detail ten influential approaches or 'analytical lenses' through which scholars have tried to make sense of America's divided democracy. We conclude by arguing that no single approach can claim fully to explain the complex reality of American politics. The distinct approaches can and should be combined in order to achieve a rich and solid understanding of American democracy and the way the United States is governed.

Introduction

Alexis de Tocqueville (1805–59), one of the shrewdest observers of American politics and society, was aware that the rise to prominence of the United States on the international stage from the early nineteenth century meant in the long run 'the advent of democracy as a governing power in the world's affairs, universal and irresistible' (Author's Preface to the twelfth edition of *Democracy in America*, 1848). After all, powers that had exercised a strong influence upon the destinies of their worlds thus far,

from the Romans to the British, had been governed by aristocratic institutions (Tocqueville: 236, v. 1, 1990). Since then, the puzzles, dilemmas, strengths, and weaknesses of American democracy have fascinated scholars interested in the study of politics. In this chapter we review ten theoretical approaches developed by contemporary scholars to try to understand and explain how the complex, changing character of American democracy has shaped the way the United States is governed.

American democracy and the character of politics in the United States

If the clue to a good understanding of American politics and government lies in that country's particular democratic character, what type of democracy is the United States in contrast to other countries? Democracy in the United Kingdom, for example, has been embodied in a parliamentary regime under a constitutional monarchy since the Glorious Revolution of 1688, and with it the end of the absolute monarchy. It is also a unitary as opposed to a federal country. Given these basic characteristics, democratic rule in the UK has approached the model of unified democracy. By unified democracy we mean that the governing process has usually been majoritarian and territorially centred in Westminster. With respect to majoritarianism, most of the time a disciplined party with a majority in the House of Commons has been effectively in charge of creating, passing, and implementing its legislation—

which is to say that whichever party has a simple majority in Parliament is very much in charge of the governing process in Britain. With respect to the centralization of the governing process in Westminster, and despite the devolution of powers initiated by New Labour after it swept into power in 1997, the UK has been and remains a unitary state. In a unitary state there is no separation of powers and jurisdictions between the national government and the smaller units of governance in a given country (i.e. provinces, regions, departments, shires).

By contrast, democracy in the United States has been embodied in the political order enshrined in the 1787 Constitution. The constitution established limited government through the separation of powers into legislative, executive, and judicial branches (articles 1, 2, and 3). It also established the territorial separation of powers (article 4) allowing for federal, state, and local governments to coexist within the Union. Democratic rule in the United States has thus approached more the model of divided democracy. By 'divided democracy' we mean that in the United States no single institution or body is in charge of the governing process. In effect, in order to govern America the concurrence of the executive, legislative, and judicial branches of government is required. This can be regarded as a horizontal separation of powers. But there is also a vertical separation. Federalism provides it by establishing federal, state, and municipal levels of government throughout the United States. Thus, in order to govern America the concurrence of the different levels of government is also required.

Moreover, the idea of the United States as a divided democracy not only refers to the separation of powers and federalism. In addition, it refers to the fact that the great social, ethnic, regional, and cultural kaleidoscope that has characterized such a large immigrant society as America has also created more or less permanent social and political conflicts between progressive and traditionalist views of politics and society. In the chapters that follow, the key notion of America as a divided democracy given the three dimensions of separation of powers, federalism, and progressive versus traditionalist conflicts, is used as the fundamental ordering principle of this book. With respect to this chapter, the basic objective is to review the ten most influential theoretical approaches to the study of American democracy, and the way American politics and government has been shaped. Such theoretical approaches have highlighted to a varying degree different aspects of the three dimensions that we have identified above, and which have shaped the character of America's divided democracy. Our objective is thus to make these connections explicit and to discuss how each of these approaches has tried to map and understand the way that changes in America's divided democracy has directly contributed to how America is governed.

American exceptionalism

The first approach that we review is the so-called American exceptionalism. Among political scientists and historians of the United States a prevailing assumption has tended to be how different this political system is from all others. Several features, drawn from a comparison of the United States with other liberal democracies, are believed to differentiate it to such an extent that it must be studied separately because it is 'exceptional'. These factors, it has been claimed, include the absence of class-based politics, the early extension of the franchise for certain groups, the mythology surrounding America's vastness as an inexhaustible frontier, the ideology of American nationhood as one of freedom, and the institutional sophistication of the Founding Fathers' constitutional model. Negative features about the character of American politics have also been noted. Most notably, the United States was a state founded at the expense of an indigenous people, Native Americans, and one in which a significant part of the population consisted of Africans brought by force to the United States, confined to enslavement until the 1860s, and segregated thereafter until the late 1960s.

Adherents to this perspective maintain that political, social, economic, and geographical conditions so differentiated the United States' founding and development from other liberal democracies that its trajectory is most accurately characterized as exceptional. The influence of this approach has been extraordinary: for many political scientists it is the automatic point of departure for analysis of American political development. But analytically the framework is limited by the plurality of factors implied by 'exceptional'.

Historically, scholars who support the 'American exceptionalism' thesis have worked from the question of 'why the US has lacked a socialist or labour political party?' (Sombart 1976). To address this query scholars have pointed to the nation's abundant natural resources and the values brought

---

Box 2.1 American exceptionalism

The conventional narrative about American exceptionalism was portrayed in classic works such as Seymour Martin Lipset's *The First New Nation* (1963). It highlighted the United States as the first country in modern history to shake off colonial rule and to build a liberal democracy. In contrast to this idea, scholars who have focused on specific institutions, rules, and norms of American politics, and their historical development, have highlighted the argument that despite the United States' early start as an independent, modern nation-state, it became a Dahlian 'polyarchy' comparatively much later than most Western European and Commonwealth liberal democracies. By 'polyarchy' we mean a full liberal democracy expressed in empirical rather than in normative terms. Robert A. Dahl developed this view in his classic *Polyarchy: Participation and Opposition* (1971). He defined real democracy through procedural criteria: a political regime characterized by free and open elections, genuine political competition, and wide protection of civil liberties. From this perspective, American democracy took longer and lagged behind the majority of today's advanced post-industrial democracies. The USA was not a 'polyarchy' until relatively recently because free and fair participation and contestation as well as the protection of civil rights were not guaranteed until the passage and implementation of the 1964 Civil Rights Act and the 1965 Voting Rights Acts. Until then the United States remained a 'restricted democracy' (Therborn 1977; Lijphart 1999).

---

by voluntary immigrants to America (McElroy 1999). They have also highlighted its initially vast territory (expanded in the nineteenth century through war such as the Mexican–American war of 1847, which yielded to the United States half of Mexico's territory in what became the states of New Mexico, Arizona, and California) (Lipset 1996). Economic wealth and expanding frontiers facilitated a distinctive ideology of American identity imbued with individualism and self-reliance, while growing income undercut the appeal of socialism.

The ideological views created by the idea of American exceptionalism has endured in recent expressions of America's national identity. In 1985, for instance, speaking at his second Inauguration, President Ronald Reagan evoked the US's founding as a continuing source of American values: 'our new beginning is a continuation of that beginning created two centuries ago when, for the first time in history, government, the people said, was not our master. It is our servant.' Several months earlier, Reagan had employed an allusion to the Founding Fathers to celebrate American exceptionalism: 'the dream conceived by our Founding Fathers [to have] the ultimate in individual freedom ... We don't celebrate Dependence Day on the Fourth of July. We celebrate Independence Day.' For Louis Hartz (1955), America's exceptional conditions gave life to the distinctive brand of American liberalism, what Gunnar Myrdal (1944) earlier characterized as the 'American creed'. For Hartz, America's lack of a feu-

dal past gave its citizens a greater sense of egalitarian individualism; cemented by new generations of voluntary immigrants, this distinct history created the conditions for robust and regularly renewed individualism.

The 'exceptionalism' thesis has helped distinguish American democracy from other countries' types of democracy. It helps to understand, for example, the fact that despite the influence of English settlers and European political traditions, the United States developed into something different and unique, something distinctively 'American'. Some of the basic elements of this new, 'American' political world-view were the ideas of republicanism, federalism, and the rise of a free, liberal individual, a 'new man'. What were aspirations for many British in the metropolis at this time—through the demand of basic civil rights as expressed by John Locke—were realized in the United States under the inspired manifesto of Thomas Paine's *Common Sense* and the American War of Independence.

This approach's strengths have to be qualified, nonetheless, by highlighting its key weaknesses. First, it disregards the temporal dimension of American democratization. Why did the United States not become a full democracy until much later than many other Western European countries? Why did a restricted democracy endure for almost two centuries of independent political life, even after the two world wars made the United States government the most powerful defender of liberal democracy in the world? A second weakness of this approach concentrates more on its logical structure. Did America's divided democracy produce the country's exceptionalism, or did a series of exceptional circumstances produce America's peculiar divided democracy? This circularity problem means that the 'American exceptionalism' thesis veers toward tautology. By this we mean that we cannot tell which was first, the chicken or the egg. In addition, an approach that is able to apply the same cross-national indicators to the United States as well as to other liberal democracies is needed if we are to make sense of American politics and American political evolution in the light of other countries' political records. To do this we now turn to an approach based on contrasting views according to which modern democracies can be either elitist or pluralist. Who governs in America's divided democracy?

Elite *versus* pluralist theories

One of the first academic debates after the Second World War was what kind of society lay behind the formal political and government arrangements of American democracy. Two views dominated the debate. On the one hand, some scholars thought that a powerful small group of people (a minority) ruled America. This so-called elite theory argued that the governing process in America was in the hands of an identifiable and stable minority that shared key characteristics such as vast wealth, privileged education, and political and business connections. The classic author was C. Wright Mills (1956), who argued that in America a powerful few in society managed to define the issues and to constrain the possible outcomes of government decisions to suit their interests. Indeed, according to this view, despite attempts to limit the exercise of power by one person, or few, or any kind of minority in America through the establishment of a divided democracy, in reality wealth dominates politics. The conclusion was that economic and political power was very concentrated in America, and this allowed the powerful few to bypass the democratic system and impose on the rest their policy preferences.

On the other hand, those who opposed elite theory were known as pluralists. Pluralism, as classically articulated by Robert Dahl, argued that it was simplistic to characterize the American governing process as rigidly divided between a majority and a minority. Instead, pluralism sees many minorities vying with one another in different policy areas. Governments have to accommodate these struggles and channel them into specific government decisions. The end result was that, in Dahl's formulation, a single, well-defined, permanent group did not and could not rule America. Who governed? Many different, loosely defined, changing groups organized to further common interests through the policy process (Dahl 1961). In this view the divided character of American democracy actually provided many entry points to the governing process in order that different groups could freely press their claims in competition with one another. Divided democracy thus fostered and encouraged pluralism (Dahl 1967).

Elite theory and pluralism became the standard lenses through which American democracy was seen and evaluated in the 1950s and 1960s. However, by the 1970s several authors were dissatisfied because elite theory and pluralism did not highlight enough the strong ideological content of politics and the governing process in a democracy, including the United States. A solution to this was to focus on the extent and content of class-based politics in America.

Class politics

Analysis of class politics in America has particularly concentrated on the absence of a political party based on the working class. This absence distinguished early twentieth-century America from other advanced industrial societies such as Britain, France, and Germany, where strong labour-based political parties developed to represent the interests of workers (or farmers) in legislatures and in politics, bringing about gradual democratic reforms. For example, in a recent work Lipset and Marks (2000) highlighted that the early 'gift' of the suffrage in the United States weakened the appeals of socialist parties. They claim that suffrage for white males prior to industrialization integrated the working class into mainstream parties along ethnic and religious lines. 'Class' thus diminished as a source of party-political cleavage, and this greatly diminished the socialists' message and political appeal. Added to this was the massive flow of immigrants into the United States, particularly from the 1880s onward. Immigrants' political views were not uniform. They comprised people with radical, conservative, confessional, and secular political views and ideals. In turn, this great cultural-political heterogeneity created deep and long-standing ethnic divisions among the masses of working-class immigrants. And this also helped to weaken the drive for a labour or socialist party representing immigrant workers along class lines.

This argument also connects with the fact that the United States is often portrayed as a classless society in two further senses. First, the egalitarianism of immigrants—the rejection of the idea of social superiors—was reproduced in the culture and society. Second, the vast majority of Americans believe themselves members of the middle class: despite income inequalities, this category is broad enough to be socially integrative.

American understanding of class and attitudes toward labour organizations are unquestionably key evidence for this approach. However, quite how to interpret these factors is less straightforward. For instance, it is certainly the case that American workers' membership of trade unions has been lower—historically and contemporaneously—than

in other industrial countries: it was a mere 15 per cent of workers in the mid-1990s, and throughout the twentieth century never rose above 35 per cent (Goldfield 1997). This figure can be contrasted with countries such as Sweden and Denmark, where density averages over 70 per cent of the labour force, or the UK where close to 50 per cent of workers are unionized, or Australia, where the figure is 40 per cent (Huber and Stephens 2001).

Other authors interested in class analysis have focused on a macro-historical perspective to place America's divided democracy in a comparative perspective. In a classic work, Barrington Moore, Jr. showed how the different socioeconomic structures of the American North and South—free industrial labour versus plantation slavery—led to an increase in political conflicts that culminated in the American Civil War (1861–5). This war constituted, according to Moore, 'the last revolutionary offensive on the part of what one may legitimately call urban or bourgeois capitalist democracy' (1966: 119). From this perspective, American political development is not exceptional. Rather, it is comparable to countries such as England (1688) and France (1789), where 'bourgeois revolutions' took place prior to the American Civil War.

By linking the analysis of class coalitions in such diverse countries as France, the United States, China, and India, this approach put American politics and the way they have evolved into a comparative perspective. It does this by applying the same categories and indicators cross-nationally. However, the class approach based on macro-sociological observations also has important weaknesses. Foremost among them is the fact that any research strategy based on class analysis underestimates the centrality of other sociological cleavages in American politics such as religion: comparatively, Americans have high levels of religious affiliation and church attendance, attributes which translate into politics through a concern with social issues such as abortion rights and family values. The enduring racial and ethnic cleavages in the USA also have to be highlighted (Goldfield 1997; Haney Lopez 1996; Kelley 1994;

Box 2.2 Class politics in America

The conventional view has been that the United States has not experienced class politics. Yet the United States experienced some of the most brutal industrial conflicts of any capitalist country in the closing decades of the nineteenth century and opening ones of the twentieth. These conflicts—often riotous and involving many deaths (for instance, the Homestead Lockout in 1892 included the death of seven steel workers and three Pinkerton agents, and was quelled only by the presence of 8,000 state militiamen deployed by Pennsylvania Governor Robert Pattison in support of the Carnegie-owned steel-making company)—occurred in a context different from these in other countries. White workers purposefully excluded African American workers from shared union membership, thus dividing the working class (Nelson

2000). Thus, within the white working class the tight ethnic ties defining neighbourhood life often proved more alluring than devoting time to organizing politically on a nation-wide basis, and under the banner of a class identity. This preference produced a schism between organized, cross-ethnic conflict at work and ethnic solidarity in the community. Thus, the brutalities of capitalist life certainly existed in the United States—in heightened form in some ways compared with other countries because of the scale of its industrial production. However, its effects upon workers were mediated distinctly by race and ethnicity. Thus, no strong working-class movement developed in the United States, in contrast to countries like Germany, Great Britain, and France.

Jordan 1968; Fields 1990). These cleavages have not given rise to distinct parties, but their presence has saturated the way in which America's two main political parties have formed and evolved (Ware 1996).

Another weakness of some scholars working with this approach has been the assumption that the American state remained divided into sub-national political systems. For example, Rueschemeyer, et al. (1992: 122) used Moore's macrosociological, class analysis to explore the relationship between capitalist development and democracy in, among many countries, the United States. They contend that the North and the West achieved full democracy from the Jacksonian period (1829–36), while the

South remained a restricted democracy from its colonial origins to the late 1960s. From the perspective of the territorial unity of the nation-state this account is unsatisfactory. That is so because it unduly sub-divides the United States by region, even though, for example, racism and segregation were not regional phenomena but national ones (King 1995). Added to this is the fact that simply to declare the US a democracy despite some regional 'blemishes' is, in our view, intellectually and historically unpersuasive, as well as morally wrong. That is why we now have to review an approach that gives precedence to the role of ideas and ideologies in the forging of America's divided democracy.

Multiple traditions

In the first part of this chapter we highlighted the fact that one of the cleavages that has fed the divided character of American democracy was the debates and conflicts between individuals and groups with progressive or traditionalist views about politics and society. The so-called 'multiple traditions' approach has highlighted this cleavage (Smith 1993; 1997). According to this argument the US's political culture is not the pre-eminent example of modern liberal democracy, as claimed by classic authors such as

Alexis de Tocqueville, Gunnar Myrdal, and Louis Hartz. In reality illiberal, inegalitarian ideologies have shaped the participants and the issues of American politics as deeply as liberal democratic ones.

For example, until the 1950s, ineligibility criteria based on 'racial, ethnic, and gender restrictions' were 'blatant, not latent'; and for 'these people, citizenship rules gave no weight to how liberal, republican, or faithful to other American values their political

Box 2.3 **Rogers Smith on multiple traditions**

The political scientist Rogers Smith has aptly defined the 'multiple traditions' approach:

For over 80% of US history, its laws declared most of the world's population to be ineligible for full American citizenship solely because of their race, original nationality, or gender. For at least two-thirds of American history, the majority of the domestic adult population was also ineligible for full citizenship for the same reasons. Contrary to Tocquevillian views of American civic identity, it did not matter how 'liberal', 'democratic', or 'republican' those persons' beliefs were. The Tocquevillian story is thus deceptive because it is too narrow. It is centered on relationships among a minority of Americans (white men, largely of northern European ancestry). (Smith 1993: 549)

Smith based his arguments on a detailed analysis of 2,500 US Supreme Court decisions concerning citizenship, issued between 1798 and 1912. Citizenship laws illustrate the competing pressures—'civic ideologies that blend liberal, democratic, republican, and inegalitarian, ascriptive elements'—constitutive of the multiple traditions framework. They are driven by political pressures that resulted in inequalities and hierarchies rather than in Tocquevillean or Hartzian egalitarianism.

beliefs might be' (Smith 1997: 15; and see Haney Lopez 1996). The civil rights movements of the 1960s did much to redress these illiberal practices. Since Congress's passing of the 1964 Civil Rights Act and the 1965 Voting Rights Act there has been a less unequal playing field for participation in politics throughout the United States. However, since America's divided democracy is multifaceted and ever-changing, the 'multiple traditions' analysis implies that illiberal arguments could recur in the future in debates about American nationhood. Certainly, debates about immigration policy often manifest these dual qualities.

The multiple traditions thesis finds that US politics and history is full of examples of members of the political elites attempting to define American identity as one rooted in inegalitarian, ascriptive themes. This explanation provides the ideational context in which coexisting political ideologies have fought to attain dominance (Stears 2001). As an antidote to conventional claims about the US's progressive march toward an exemplary democracy it is instructive. Putting emphasis on the rich ideational basis of American politics has helped these authors to transcend the overgeneralizing explanations based on American exceptionalism, elites versus pluralism, and class politics. However, the 'multiple traditions' explanation also has some limitations. Foremost among them is the absence of

Box 2.4 **Orlando Patterson on multiple traditions**

The sociologist Orlando Patterson has also used the idea of 'multiple traditions' to make sense of the coexistence of individual freedom and slavery in the nineteenth century and, later on when slavery was abolished, of individual freedom and racial segregation in the United States. He highlights the fact that:

[in] American political history we find the development of three modern versions of democracy. . . . A reinvention of the primal form itself based on the modern system of slavery; an elite capitalist democracy; and an inclusive pluralist democracy. . . . The enormous complexity and apparent contradictions of modern American politics spring from the fact that its history can be read as a record of the shifting alignments between

these three versions of democracy . . . While all three forms advocate three notes of freedom each tends to make one fundamental, playing down the other two. Pluralist democracy emphasizes the idea of freedom as political equality and, under the welfare state, as equality in economic security and social citizenship. Elitist capitalist democracy strongly emphasizes personal liberty as the fundamental freedom, even opposing it to equality and, implicitly, democracy. Modern versions of the primal form of democracy, which tolerated slavery, have made the notion of freedom as power—the powerful people, the powerful state, the powerful leader—and honor, both individual and collective, the central note in the chord. (Patterson 1999: 160) a well-defined agency that helps to promote or thwart these competing ideologies. Ideas on their own do not transform political institutions and decisions. They need human beings—or 'actors', as individuals tend to be called in social science parlance—to effect such changes. The absence of a well-specified agency—that is, political actors making choices and organizing for political action—thus makes it almost impossible to account for basic pol-icy changes, that is, the critical moments when one or another of these competing ideologies in the United States have gained the upper hand, and how their advocates have thus proceeded to implement important political reforms. These omissions lead us to review an approach based on how specific political groups and forces—for example, the civil rights movement—have pushed for changes that have, time and again, recast America's divided democracy.

Social movements and political participation

Since the founding of the United States, but particularly since the conclusion of the Civil War, American politicians have confronted a problem of nationhood. The problem has been how best to integrate the millions of citizens and residents in the United States in a way which both creates a common and shared sense of 'American nationhood' and avoids devaluing citizens' other sources of identity, notably race, ethnicity, or national background. The loyalties and cleavages arising from these latter group ties, and their mobilization for political action, have promoted important changes to the character of American democracy.

The source of social diversity becoming so intertwined with America's divided democracy lies in American history and the federal government's policy toward the groups making up the 'American people'. The United States' engagement with Native Americans throughout the nineteenth century was bloody, brutal, and extinctionist: that is, American policy presumed the expiration of Native Americans (Stannard 1992). When extinction was no longer a certainty the federal government embarked, from the 1880s, upon a strident policy of 'Americanization' of Native Americans, imposing common-law property arrangements upon Native American lands and 'Americanizing' Native American children through schools. 'Americanization' became a

---

Box 2.5 Social diversity and American identity

Two examples illustrate the significance of the problem of social diversity in the United States, and the way this has shaped American democracy. In 1917, as he took the US into the First World War, President Woodrow Wilson chastised some ethnic Americans—and he had in mind especially Irish Americans and German Americans—for lacking a complete sense of American identity, and for retaining their ethnic loyalty with their American nationality (King 2000): 'you cannot become thorough Americans if you think of yourselves in groups. America does not consist of groups. A man who thinks of himself as belonging to a particular national group in America has not yet become an American.' He condemned 'hyphenated Americans' as un-American. The second example comes in the wake of the terrorist bombings in New York and Washington on 11 September 2001. Within days of the attacks President George W. Bush purposefully visited an American mosque and expressed support to Arab and Muslim Americans, and told Congress: 'we respect your faith. It's practised freely by many millions of Americans. The enemy of America is not our many Muslim friends. It is not our many Arab friends. Our enemy is a radical network of terrorists and every government that supports them.' Bush's action and statement was meant to project a more integrative and inclusive version of American nationhood than that articulated by Woodrow Wilson. The transition between these contrasting presidential discourses toward minorities has been complex and on occasions violent.

standard tool of policy toward immigrants from the opening decades of the twentieth century. Fearful that the millions of Eastern and Central European immigrants were incompatible with the dominant American population—a perspective already for-malized in exclusionary policy toward Chinese labourers (in 1882) and Japanese immigrants (in 1908)—policy-makers organized 'Americanization' campaigns for new immigrants in communities and at work. They urged immigrants to learn English and to naturalize. And all these restrictions and contestations about who was an American pre-sumed the segregation of African Americans, whose second class status prompted intellectual W. E. B. Du Bois to fulminate, in 1920, about the hypocrisy of America assuming a global role as a defender of democracy:

it is curious to see America, the United States, looking on herself, first, as a sort of natural peace-maker, then as a moral protagonist . . . No nation is less fitted for this role. For two or more centuries America has marched proudly in the van of human hatred . . . making the insulting of millions more than a matter of dislike . . . rather a great religion, a world war-cry: Up white, down black.

The US Supreme Court, an institution responsible for upholding the package of formal rights guaranteed in the Constitution, mostly concurred in these divisions between Americans on the basis of ethnicity, race, or national background. It was only in the 1950s and more substantially in the 1960s that the barriers to equal citizenship were incon-trovertibly removed. The legacies of this pattern of unequal treatment have made the content of American nationhood problematic. An assimilation-ist melting-pot ideology glosses over real differences of historical experience and fairness.

Without the civil rights movement, led by Martin Luther King Jr., America's divided democracy might still be restrictive and exclusionary (Morris 1984; Chong 1991; McAdam 1999). The civil rights movement proved the crucial agent shaping democratic reforms. Such movements and their leaders have been powerful agency forces behind democratic reformism in numerous countries. As political scientist Sydney Tarrow (1994) argues, opportunities for successful protest open and pro-vide resources for the use of even weak or disorgan-ised groups to engage in collective action.

Box 2.6 **Civic and racial nationalisms**

The historian Gary Gerstle (2001) has captured the com-peting tendencies of assimilation and multiculturalism with his distinction between racial nationalism and civic nationalism. Gerstle argues that what he terms America's 'civic nationalism' (the bundle of beliefs about equality and individual rights) has coexisted with a 'racial nationalism', whose proponents conceive of 'America in ethno-racial terms, as a people held together by com-mon blood and skin colour and by an inherent fitness for self-government'. Both are traceable, ironically, to the founding of the republic that simultaneously endorsed individual rights and the restriction of naturalization to free white persons. The resulting contradictions and racism pervading US political culture rendered the American Dream, in Malcolm X's pithy comment, 'the American nightmare'. For Gerstle, it is only with a juxtaposition of these competing nationalisms that American national identity can be understood.

The tension between Gerstle's civic and racial national-isms is an enduring one. Progressives and reformers looked to civic nationalism as a set of ideological beliefs and values which could be gradually but consistently widened to enlarge the definition of who was an accept-able American; racial nationalists fought this process tooth and nail. Yet even within the civic tradition Gerstle uncovers real barriers to expansion. Interaction between the two nationalisms produced what he terms the 'Rooseveltian nation' (named after Presidents Theodore Roosevelt and Franklin D. Roosevelt) which structured politics between the 1930s and mid-1960s: committed to economic opportunity for those present in the United States, this ideology was accompanied by clear restric-tions (racial, ethnic, and national) upon who was an American. This restricted conception of American nation-hood imploded in the 1960s as the US's tolerance of racists and institutionalized, judicially legitimated dis-crimination ceased. This implosion arose principally from the years of protest fomented by the civil rights move-ment (Morris 1984), coinciding with the social divisions unleashed by America's involvement in Vietnam.

In the US the Department of Justice began to issue *amicus curiae* ('friend of the court') briefs favouring the National Association for the Advancement of Colored People (NAACP) in civil rights litigation in the final years of President Franklin Roosevelt's administration, and continued to do so more rigorously in the 1950s and 1960s. It submitted an *amicus* brief to the Supreme Court when the justices were deciding on the *Brown* v. *Board of Education* case (1954), regarding which they ruled in favour of desegregation, a decision which made it arguably the most significant of the twentieth century. This Justice Department role provided important opportunities that helped to strengthen the civil rights movement. The American civil rights movement was able, through the strategic framing efforts of Martin Luther King and the SCLC, to shape media coverage, win the support of bystander publics, constrain movement opponents, and influence state author-

ities that underpin the agency behind them (McAdam 1999).

An accurate account of the changing character of American democracy has to have as one of its major components the civil rights movement from the 1940s to the 1970s. But a purely domestic-based explanation of relatively recent changes to American democracy is incomplete. Despite the aspirations of isolationists, the United States has never been a self-contained country. Moreover, as Michael Cox noted in the previous chapter, the United States' relationship with the wider world, at least since the Spanish–American war of 1898, needs to figure prominently in a serious account of American democracy. The United States' role as the decisive member of the triumphant Allied countries after both world wars, and its status as the most powerful defender of liberal democracy during the cold war, helped to shape America's divided democracy, particularly during the second half of the twentieth century.

America's international impact

America's role in the world has been fundamental to the character of American democracy in two senses. First, the US has been the most powerful defender of liberal democracy in the world since the end of the Great War (1914–18). In April 1917 President Woodrow Wilson declared in Congress:

the world must be made safe for democracy. It is a fearful thing to lead this great peaceful people into war, into the most terrible and disastrous of all wars, civilization itself seeming to be in the balance. But the right is more precious than the peace, and we shall fight for the things which we have always carried nearest our hearts—for democracy, for the right of those who submit to authority to have a voice in their own governments, for the rights and liberties of small nations, for a universal dominion of rights by such a concert of free peoples as shall bring peace and safety to all nations and make the world itself at last free.

The Wilsonian image of a liberal world order of states failed to materialize, but nonetheless set a standard for subsequent US foreign policy.

Woodrow Wilson's mantle was echoed by President Franklin D. Roosevelt in 1941 and embraced

fully by President Harry Truman in 1947 as he led America into the cold war years. And on 20 September 2001 President George W. Bush told Congress:

the hour is coming when America will act, and you [the armed forces] will make us proud. This is not, however, just America's fight. And what is at stake is not just America's freedom. This is the world's fight. This is civilization's fight. This is the fight of all that believe in progress and pluralism, tolerance and freedom. We ask every nation to join us.

The second factor is America's role in global politics from the 1940s, as the principal exponent and defender of liberal democracy opened up its domestic institutions and practices to foreign scrutiny (Dudziak 2000). Especially during the cold war years (1947–89) the US's enemies were keen to find domestic blemishes, and alighted upon the failure of federal policy toward African Americans, Native Americans, and other minorities to guarantee equality of rights. The country faced what we term the Wilsonian contradiction: on the one hand, the

---

Box 2.7 America and the international arena

International pressures on American democracy became particularly strong after the Second World War and the advent of the cold war. The USA became the superpower behind the support of liberal democracy in the world against the communist Soviet Union and its allies. The contradictions were obvious. The champion of liberal democracy in the world upheld an exclusionary, racially segregated order back home. This inconsistency was a fundamental weakness for the West's fight against communism. The Soviet bloc could attract allies—particularly among the community of recently decolonized states—to

its cause by highlighting alleged American hypocrisy. Potentially more lethally, communists could exploit this internal contradiction in the USA itself by getting American progressive forces to fight the segregationist order and install a complete democracy: by the end of the cold war, the US was the world's unquestioned superpower and leading democracy. But this status does not mean the end of external scrutiny of American democracy as recent criticisms of capital punishment, for instance, illustrate.

---

country's government preached liberal democracy in the international arena (a position first formulated in Woodrow Wilson's Fourteen Points plan for the post-First World War global order). At the same time that government domestically acquiesced in and upheld a segregationist political order (Wilson famously watched over the introduction of segregation in the federal government in Washington) (Rosenberg 1999). This contradiction became unsustainable after 1945. Mass mobilization for both world wars, but particularly in 1941–5 (Kryder 2000), was a catalyst for democratic reform, a pattern observable

in other industrial democracies (Bollen 1979; Therborn 1977).

Thus, international pressure on the US to reform civil rights played an important role in shaping contemporary American democracy. To understand why the US was exposed to such international pressures and domestic tension it is necessary to turn to the next approach, which is based on the analysis of the American state. Indeed, the American state has commonly been characterized as appearing much more highly centralized and effective as an actor in international politics than in domestic policy.

America's weak state

The previously reviewed six approaches give insufficient attention to the distinctness of the American nation-state. The United States' founding political institutions produced important legal and bureaucratic 'stateness' problems that thwarted, for almost two centuries of independent political history, the establishment and development of liberal democracy in that country. Mounting contradictions derived from the ideological dimension of the state—the slowness in upholding rights of citizenship—produced important pressures for democratization at different historical junctures of American political development, expressed, for example, in the Civil War (1861–5), and the civil rights movement (1940s–1970s). Out of such con-

flicts the American state was gradually reshaped, until by the end of the 1960s the United States could be considered a full liberal democracy.

Scholars emphasize the importance of the modern state for the development of liberal democracy. In the United States, the state is a distinctive institution in large part because of features of the US's political institutions and society. The Founding Fathers purposefully created a political system in which power was diffused horizontally and vertically. Horizontally, the separation of powers—between the executive and legislature—and the system of checks and balances—particularly the judiciary— ensured the absence of a powerfully concentrated centre of political authority. The exception to this arrangement is the presidency, whose incumbents can exercise executive power on certain occasions, citing both constitutional authority and a popular mandate. Often such power is exercised more effectively in respect to foreign policy than domestic reforms.

Vertically, the power is disseminated through federalism (about which more below). Each of the fifty states has a constitution and set of laws; each elects politicians. Federal authority and the US Constitution is always superior to state law when they clash, but the federal system is an institutional arrangement which contributes to a weaker national state. Furthermore, America's civil society has been robust: for instance, religious affiliation and voluntary organizations have often enjoyed high levels of participation compared with other countries.

Historically, the federal system has mediated social and political pressures. For instance, political parties (about which more below) must mirror aspects of the federal system to organize successfully, and the wide dispersion of power and interests in the United States makes the two major political parties, the Democrats and Republicans, coalitions of interests rather than organizations structured around tightly formulated ideologies in the way observable in other democracies. The federal system permits—

indeed invites—significant variations in social practices across the fifty states, but it should not permit any variation in the equality of rights experienced by citizens.

Given the separation of powers and federalism, Washington DC, the seat of the US federal government, has commonly been described as small compared with the central state in other industrial democracies. This description refers to the size of the public sector relative to GDP, the number of public employees, and the scope and content of public policy (Nettl 1968). This characterization overlooks the fact that there have been important periods of initiative during which federal activity increased significantly in American society (Sparrow 1996). And these periods have changed America's divided democracy, and the way the country is governed.

This theoretical approach—the state-centric perspective—has helped to make sense of key changes to the American state (through the expansion or shrinking of intervention by the federal government), which have helped to shape the character of American democracy and the way the country is governed. 'Stateness' problems and pressures derived from the state's legal, bureaucratic, and ideological dimensions have to be highlighted to make sense of nineteenth- and in particular twentieth-century

---

Box 2.8 FDR and the New Deal

One of the most famous instances of the expansion of the federal government was the set of programmes collectively known as the New Deal, a phrase captured and publicized from the programmes' architect, President Franklin D. Roosevelt. Elected president in 1932 in the midst of the twentieth century's greatest economic depression Roosevelt promised Americans a 'New Deal' to address the domestic calamity. The initiative consisted in a set of economic policies, inspired by Keynesian economics, to stimulate the American economy (including a public works programme and a variety of work schemes such as those associated with the National Youth Administration, the Civilian Conservation Corps, the Agricultural Adjustment Administration, the Tennessee Valley Authority, the National Relief Administration, and the National Industrial Recovery Act), and a set of social policies designed both to strengthen the position of

workers (such as the Wagner Industrial Relations Act, creating the National Labor Relations Board) and to protect them against future misery (such as the introduction of unemployment insurance and pensions, known as social security). Many of these latter programmes were augmented during the Second World War, the 1950s and particularly in the 1960s as part of President Lyndon Johnson's 'Great Society' reforms. Both the economic and social dimensions of federal activity were small compared with those undertaken in other industrial democracies (and Keynesian policy in the US was limited to macro-economic initiatives), but nonetheless they marked major extensions by the US central state. However, it is important to note that New Deal programmes retained, and in some instances strengthened, the segregated status of African Americans in US society.

Box 2.9 Reaganomics

The period ushered in by Ronald Reagan's election as president in 1980, and known as 'Reaganomics', is another period of high federal state activity, though on this occasion with the aim of reducing the public sector's size and re-empowering the fifty state governments in relation to the federal government. In the twelve years of Reaganomics, comprising the Republican presidencies of Reagan (1981–9) and his successor, George Bush (1989–93), Congress enacted—at White House direction—significant tax cuts, launched a programme of New Federalism, reduced the framework of social and economic regulation, and initiated reform in federal welfare programmes, all designed to restructure the role of the federal government in American society. Externally, the US pursued an aggressive anti-communism manifest, both in support for anti-communist allies in Latin America and in a substantial build-up of military resources to challenge the Soviet Union. The period left a profound mark on American politics and on expectations about the role of the national state. Externally, the policy succeeded spectacularly with the fall of communism in the Soviet Union and its ousting from satellite states—heralded by the physical destruction of the Berlin Wall in November 1989. Domestically, Reaganomics had mixed effects. The build-up of military expenditures combined with tax cuts induced a huge federal deficit, only briefly eliminated in 2001; but the 1990s were years of immense job growth and economic growth. Politically, Reaganomics set an agenda which the Republicans seized with their 'Contract with America' initiative, while Democrats also found themselves committed to maintaining low taxes and reforming government programmes: a powerful example of Democratic commitment is the 1996 Welfare Reform Act signed by President Clinton. Major periods of policy initiative such as the New Deal years or Reaganomics leave a mark on the parameters of state activity, and thus on the character of American democracy for many years.

American politics. But what about some of the more specific institutional and political arrangements which are part of any liberal democratic state—such as a territorial division of power (unitarian versus federal countries) and political parties (two-party versus multi-party systems)? We now turn to them to see how they have also helped to shape America's divided democracy.

Federalism in America

One of the recurrent approaches used by scholars to understand the 'divided' character of American democracy is federalism. Some authors have argued that federalism is a good way of separating political power territorially because this allows the states or local governments to decide on their policy priorities, the way resources are channelled, and the types of law they want. Other authors have contended that federalism also creates problems. If all the government sub-units in a federal country are allowed to apply their subjective standards to their public affairs, then the national government will usually find it very hard to guarantee fairness and equal protection of the laws throughout the territory, in this case, of the United States. Some states are richer than others, and some are more politically powerful than others. How can the ideal of equality, which is central in democracies, be reconciled in this case with respect to America's divided democracy?

Some authors think that American democracy has worked better since the 'devolution revolution'. By devolving powers to the states since the early 1970s, the federal government in Washington has allowed government programmes to work more efficiently. Moreover, such states' decisions should remain closest to those governments that are nearest to the grass roots, where citizens can see immediately the costs and benefits of government's laws, rules, programmes, and resources (Eggers and O'Leary 1995).

Box 2.10 **Confidence in the federal government**

Richard Nixon's election in 1968 began a period of reaction against the expanded powers of the federal government that has continued to this day. For the most part Nixon did not try to roll back the functions of the federal government, but instead deregulated the federal grant system and gave more power over grants to states and localities. The election of Ronald Reagan in 1980 inaugurated a more radical phase of the new federalism (as seen in Box 2.9 above) in which efforts were made to return to the system that existed before the New Deal, when the federal government left many domestic policy functions to the states. Although confidence in all levels of government has fallen since the 1960s, the drop in confidence has been most severe for the federal government. A 1995 CBS/*New York Times* poll found that 48 per cent of respondents felt that the federal government had 'too much power', whereas only 6 per cent felt that the states had too much (Miroff et al., 2001: 53).

Other authors have criticized devolution enthusiasts. They argue that federal decentralization can hamper the chances for Americans coming together to accomplish things they cannot accomplish separately. If each state of the Union acts independently of each other, the things that all Americans share, public goods or the 'commons' (Ostrom 1990), such as air quality, water, and fisheries, can be damaged. These authors think that the gains from decentralization in America have been exaggerated. Investors and big business also choose to settle in some states rather than others. This depends very much on the types of incentive that state laws, norms, and regulations offer business. From this it results that some states received much more investment than others, and that socioeconomic inequality between states has increased in America. Devolution, instead of acting as a 'laboratory for democracy', as those who favour federalism think, can actually result in a 'race to the bottom', as state authorities try to lower their standards and regulations in order to attract business activity (Donahue 1997).

The balance in federal–state relations in the United States ebbs and wanes periodically. It is a complex, dynamic relationship which is being shaped and reshaped constantly. It has contributed to define America's divided democracy and some of the key domestic political challenges that Americans have confronted with respect to economic development, individual and group rights, federal regulation, and the limits of the law. To understand a more partisan element that has also divided Americans throughout their history we now have to review America's political parties.

American political parties

A long-enduring feature of America's divided democracy has been its two-party system. Two parties have dominated national politics in the United States since the early nineteenth century. Up to the 1960s partisan loyalties remained a fundamental source of identity for most Americans: either one was a Republican or else a Democrat. As some authors put it, 'Partisan identities meant having a general orientation to others, to citizenship, to history, and to government' (Miroff et al. 2001: 207). However, as Chapters 5 and 6 below explain, since the 1970s partisan identities have diminished greatly. This process is called dealignment. It means that since the 1970s the majority of the electorate in America does not vote for a party out of loyalty or conviction. Voters have focused more on short-term criteria such as the state of the economy, the 'deals' that the parties offer in their electoral manifestos, or the type of personality that individual candidates manage to project through the media. What have these changes produced in America's democracy and the way the country is governed?

Some authors have welcomed the process of dealignment because they argue that the Republicans and the Democrats have had to adjust to the dynamic, fast-changing, information-driven contemporary world in order to remain effective and representative parties. The parties have found ways to keep on reaching voters and of financing their activities through increasing private contributions. From this perspective, parties are and should be encouraged to be even more professional organizations (Kayden 1989). Their key functions are to articulate and represent policy views to implement them when they are in power. From this perspective the idea of divided democracy in the United States refers much more to the cleavage between those who participate and those who don't in the political and the governing processes in America. Americans' rate of electoral participation is strikingly low in comparison to most other advanced democracies. Electoral turnout in the United States has remained below 45 per cent since the 1980s. This compares negatively with 84 per cent in the Netherlands, 81 per cent in France, 75 per cent in the UK, 73 per cent in Canada, 71 per cent in Japan and 59 per cent in India.

The implication of low turnout is that even if American parties have become very effective and wealthy organizations, they cater for the minority of Americans who are interested in politics, participate, and try to influence the debate inside such parties. The rest of Americans, a majority it seems, remain outside this process (Putnam 2000). Thus, the United States remains a divided democracy between those who participate and those who don't.

There is another way in which American political parties have also helped to shape America's divided democracy. For some authors the Democratic and, particularly, the Republican parties have become stronger at the expense of grassroots democracy. This criticism echoes the perspective of elite theorists that we reviewed under our second approach. The parties express their closeness to the people, but in reality they only manipulate the public around agendas and party manifestos that are very similar to each other. The Democrats and the Republicans do not represent, therefore, real political alternatives. Both parties basically support similar, middle-of-the-road policies, leaving the majority of Americans without the capacity to exercise their political choice meaningfully. In short, both parties are elite institutions which only represent the interests of the rich and powerful (Greider 1992).

Parties and their evolution have had a big impact on the character of America's divided democracy. The first and most evident way in which it has contributed to a stable bipartisan political division of the country has been through the long-standing two-party system itself. Likewise, it has contributed indirectly to shape America's 'dividedness' through the split between the minority of

---

Box 2.11 **American political parties**

Despite the process of de-alignment, the two main American political parties have not become weaker. Some authors think that they have actually become stronger since this happened. For example,

in 1995–1996, the national parties together raised and spent $263 million, a 300% increase over just four years before. By 1998 and 2000, the national parties were raking in even greater amounts of cash and 'soft money.' In the past American parties were primarily local and state organizations. Today parties own their own buildings in Washington DC, gain the support of an ever-growing list of small and large contributors, and direct formidable media and advertising machines. (Miroff et al., 2001: 208)

The early 2002 finance scandal over the largest bankruptcy in American history, that of the giant energy corporation Enron, drew public attention toward the vast amounts of money that big business donates to the parties—in this case to George W. Bush's presidential campaign—in exchange for access and influence in the policy process in Washington. The Enron case also highlighted the fact that a corporation does not necessarily operate politically in a single country. Enron not only financed the Republican Party in America but also made contributions to both the Conservative and Labour parties in the UK. The strong influence of big money in contemporary democracies is thus an increasing phenomenon. The way different governments tackle this problem will clearly shape the way individual democracies will operate in the future.

Americans who vote and the majority who don't. Lastly, the privately funded parties have also divided Americans between those who can make themselves heard in a clearer and louder voice by the parties' candidates—through private donations—and those who cannot. We now turn to an approach that has tried to make sense of some of the key ideas that we have discussed particularly in the last three sub-sections; in the approaches that concentrate on the study of American political institutions (i.e. state-centric, federalism, parties and party system).

American political development

The term 'political development' is an old concept in political science, recently revived. During the 1950s and 1960s American social scientists, with some European colleagues, focused on the position of new states after decolonization in Africa and Asia, and formulated elaborate but highly general theories about the 'stages' of 'political development' facing these new states (Binder et al. 1971). This position came under systematic attack. It was charged with 'functionalism' (the idea that social and political systems have 'needs' that must be satisfied by certain key 'functions' in order to survive, a view associated with the sociologist Talcott Parsons) and 'ethnocentrism' (the practice of studying and making judgements about other societies in terms of one's own cultural assumptions or biases).

The concept was rehabilitated in the 1980s to further the study of American politics in a historical vein without losing the discipline provided by formal methodology. As a result, 'American political development' (APD) has come to represent a major approach to the study of US politics and government. Its exponents have employed historical examples and methodology to study American politics. Famous examples include Stephen Skowronek's account of the early American state, in which he concluded that between the 1870s and 1920 the US was dominated by a system of 'courts and states' rather than a strong central state (1982). Another influential contributor, Theda Skocpol, examined the rise of America's welfare state (1992) and, with Margaret Weir, placed the post-1932 expansion of the US federal government in comparative context (Weir and Skocpol 1985). Since these publications, further APD studies have appeared on numerous topics including party ideology (Gerring 1998), party organizations (Coleman 1996), women's suffrage (Banaszak 1996), segregation (King 1995), the history of Congress (Whittington 1999), agricultural policy (Sheingate 2001), and the party system (James 2000). Other authors such as Orren and Skowronek (1998) applied the 'American political development' framework to analyses of America's federalism as well.

This approach has also had implications for the study of the changing character of American democracy. First, these scholars have underlined the historical development of core US institutions such as the courts, Congress, the presidency, the bureaucracy and federal government, and political parties. In this way they have been able to map and explain how America's divided democracy has evolved. And second, their historical analysis of these phenomena is firmly rooted in a methodology that highlights the opportunities and constraints of the US's political institutions. Such opportunities and constraints include the separation of powers, the pressures generated by significant regional divisions, and the role of party political ideologies. This emphasis converges to some extent with the rational choice approach's interest in how political institutions structure the choices and behaviour of political actors.

The aim of the revival of the idea of American political development has thus been to recast the study of American politics through a methodology that considers the historical context behind the evolution of American democracy.

Conclusion

American politics and government can be understood in a rich and solid way if we think about the United States as a 'divided democracy'. The openness and complexity of American democracy have shaped its politics and the way the country is governed in many different ways. In turn, the character of politics and the government style at particular points in time have also changed and reshaped the type of divided democracy that America is. The sheer immensity and complexity of the task of understanding properly American politics and government can be seen from the fact that scholars have developed and used many theoretical approaches to enhance their understanding about

particular problems and challenges derived from America's divided democracy. We have reviewed ten influential approaches. None of them could be used on its own to explain the great variety and complexity of issues, processes, and ideas that animate American politics and government. Rather, they should be actively combined and deployed to understand particular instances of the American governing process. All the historical examples that we have reviewed should provide a basic model about the way the ten different approaches allow scholars to identify, order, analyse, and interpret particular instances of American politics and government.

QUESTIONS

1   Why is America a 'divided democracy' and what implications has this had in shaping the character of American politics and government?

2   Is America exceptional? To what extent? Has exceptionalism increased or eroded in the last fifty years?

3   Does an elite or a pluralist model apply better to contemporary America? Can these contrasting views co-exist? Is America an elitist society?

4   To what extent have class politics shaped America's divided democracy? Can class politics ebb and wane, or are they a phenomenon of the past?

5   Why have both liberal and illiberal ideologies existed and been preserved in the United States? Do liberal democracies around the world experience 'multiple traditions'? Can liberal views triumph once and for all? Can illiberal views become eradicated?

6   Why have social movements been so important in the changing character of American democracy? Have social movements become a less influential political force in the United States since the 1980s? What is the nature of contemporary social movements such as the anti-capitalist and anti-globalization movements?

7   Why was the American state traditionally weaker and less developed than the state in most other industrial democracies? To what extent can democracy thrive without a national state that possesses a strong capacity to overlook and implement its policies?

FURTHER READING

R. A. Dahl (1961), *Who Governs?* (New Haven, Conn.: Yale University Press). The classic exposition of the pluralist account of American democracy.

D. King (1995), *Separate and Unequal: Black Americans and the US Federal Government* (Oxford: Oxford University Press). Details how the federal government not only failed to challenge but also perpetuated the segregation of African Americans in the first half of the twentieth century.

D. King (2000), *Making Americans: Immigration, Race and the Origins of the Diverse Democracy* (Cambridge, Mass.: Harvard University Press). An influential study that examines the 'racialized' nature of American national identity.

S. M. Lipset (1996), *American Exceptionalism* (New York: Norton). A defence and explanation of the 'exceptionalist' account of America.

S. M. Lipset and G. Marks (2000), *It Didn't Happen Here: Why Socialism Failed in the United States* (New York: Norton). Examines the competing explanations for the failure of a significant socialist movement to develop in America.

R. Putnam (2000), *Bowling Alone: The Collapse and Revival of American Community* (New York: Simon & Schuster). An influential but contested account of the decline of 'community' in America since the 1960s.

WEB LINKS

www.apsanet.org/ American Political Science Association

www.psqonline.org/ Political Science Quarterly, journal of the academy of Political Science

www.cnie.org/nle/ National Library for the Environment, with access to many reports by the Congressional Research Service

For links to a vast range of US material, try one of the following sources:

www.bl.uk/services/information/american.html Eccles Centre for American Studies

www.americansc.org.uk American Studies online

www.keele.ac.uk/depts/as/links/index.htm Keele University links

cwis.livjm.ac.uk/mcc/programmes/american/links/ John Moores University

www.georgetown.edu/crossroads/ Georgetown University

www.norc.uchicago.edu National Opinion Research Center, polling experts

www.gallup.com/index.html Gallup Organization

www.lib.uconn.edu/RoperCenter Roper Center/public opinion surveys

www.ssdc.ucsd.edu/ssdc/pubopin.html Social Science Data Collection

www.liszt.com Directory of e-mail discussion groups from arts to health

www.nara.gov/1 National Archives and Records Administration

www.fedworld.gov FED World

Part Two

Governing institutions

Having introduced the broad historical and theoretical context to the study of American government and politics, we move on to consider the key institutions of government in Part Two, along with the intermediary organizations that provide the key links between those institutions and American citizens. Central to American government is the US Constitution (the text of which is contained in the Appendix to this volume and which you should read thoroughly before proceeding further). This established the particular design of government that includes federalism, the separation of powers, checks and balances, and constitutional judicial review. That design not only influences the distinct roles, powers, and authority of the key institutions of the federal government (Congress, the presidency and the federal judiciary) but also shaped how political parties operate, how elections are fought, and how citizens petition government through interest groups. In addition, the roles of the mass media and the vast federal bureaucracy exert profound effects on how government operates. Although each of these political actors is accorded a distinct chapter, their roles and effectiveness cannot be fully understood other than in the context of their constant interaction. Before moving on in Parts Three and Four to consider the substance of a range of public policies, it is therefore essential to study the full range of important influences in, and on, American government.

Governing Institutions

The US Constitution

Richard Hodder-Williams

READER'S GUIDE

This chapter examines the Constitution of the United States. It explains the context in which the Constitutional Convention was established for the sole and explicit purpose of constitutional revision. It describes what took place in Philadelphia between May and September 1787 and how the Constitution emerged in the form it did. It shows the various ways through which it can, and has been, amended before discussing its role in any evaluation of 'Americanism'. Finally, the chapter introduces a number of debates that took place around the Bicentennial challenging the general view that the Constitution contributes positively to the effectiveness of the American political system.

Introduction

Probably no country takes its Constitution more seriously than the United States of America. Although the original document was drawn up more than 200 years ago, it still provides the basic rules and establishes the basic institutional structures through which politics is practised. There have been only twenty-seven amendments during the life of the Republic, and the most significant ones have emphasised the continual tension between the commitment to democracy, as represented by citizen participation and majoritarian rule, and the commitment to limited government, as represented by institutional checks and balances and the protection of individual rights against elected governments.

Few chapters in this book fail to mention the Constitution, so it is important to have read and become familiar with it. This is essential when the Congress or the President are examined, whose powers are set out quite explicitly in Articles I and II. It is also relevant when reviewing many policy areas, since the Constitution is 'the supreme law of the land' and thus limits what elected politicians can do. Precisely what these constitutional limitations are is contested, by scholars and politicians alike. Public disagreements are regularly couched in constitutional terms and are resolved by the Supreme Court, one of whose responsibilities is to apply the Constitution in disputed cases. No study of the Supreme Court can possibly be undertaken without a familiarity with the Constitution.

This centrality of the Constitution in any study of the country's politics marks the United States off from other countries. It is not only a document to which reference is regularly made and over which much argument ensues during the normal process of politics. It also lies at the heart of what holds together the multi-ethnic, immigrant aggregate of peoples who make up the American nation. So its importance is at once both instrumental and symbolic. It is quite proper, therefore, that the first substantive chapter on the institutions of the United States should be devoted to the Constitution.

Prelude to the Constitution

The Declaration of Independence on 4 July 1776 was a ringing justification of decolonization (see Box 1.2, p. 16). It expressed most vividly the American colonists' rejection of past political arrangements but it said little about how the future might be organized. The Articles of Confederation (1781–7) provided the framework through which the thirteen former colonies organized themselves. It gave limited power exclusively to a legislature, the Continental Congress, composed of representatives from the individual colonies (now states). In 1775 there had been considerable discussion about establishing a single centralized United States of America, as the nationalist fervour that led to the War of Independence encouraged the idea of a strong, centralized state. But victory against the colonial power reduced nationalist feelings, and in the event the thirteen colonies set up their own formal institutions, with their own constitutions and political leaders. The Continental Congress, which had coordinated matters in the colonial war against Britain, continued with only limited powers, with no central executive, and with a system in which each state, whatever its population, cast a single vote. It had little ability to compel states to follow the decisions taken by the Congress; indeed, some states simply refused to acquiesce and most failed to pay their financial dues.

The common view about the Continental Congress is unfavourable. This is somewhat unfair. Its diplomats managed to speak for the new nation in the international arena and, nearer to home, it resolved the divisive issue of western expansionism. Nevertheless, by the early 1780s it was clear to many leading American politicians that serious thought needed to be given to the institutional framework under which the former colonies were governed. A number of factors made this reconsideration urgent. Three in particular may be mentioned here. First was the international situation. Although the War of Independence had driven the British colonial power out, Britain remained a world power, with troops and interests in Canada and the West Indies. Spain, which still considered itself a global force, was active in Florida to the south of the newly independent colonies and also across on the Pacific seaboard. France, an ally in the War of Independence, still had major interests in Canada, the West Indies, and Louisiana. If the French and the British were to go to war again, the United States might well become embroiled in fighting.

Second, an economic downturn, due to many factors such as excessive competition between the individual colonies, an economic depression in Europe, and the small scale of individual state economies, was resulting in genuine hardship both for the primary producers of the southern states and for the traders of the northern states. As a consequence, five of the more important states agreed to hold a meeting in Annapolis in 1786 to discuss possible ways forward.

Third, and as a consequence of economic conditions, small farmers in debt and landless immigrants were desperate enough to challenge existing governments by force. Shays's Rebellion in Massachusetts reflected this desperation, and also symbolized the apparent inability of a state to keep law and order within its own territory.

The Annapolis Convention recommended to the states and to the Continental Congress that a constitutional convention should meet in Philadelphia in the following year 'to take into consideration the situation of the United states [and] to devise such further provisions as shall appear to them necessary to render the constitution of the federal government adequate to the exigencies of the Union'. Some states actually chose delegates before the Continental Congress responded. When it did so, it accepted the recommendation from the Annapolis Convention, but added that 'the sole and express purpose' of the Philadelphia Convention was 'revising the Articles of Confederation'.

The legislatures of each state, apart from Rhode Island, selected delegates for the Philadelphia Convention. For the most part they represented the most experienced, able, and influential public figures within the new country. Many had signed the Declaration of Independence and had had experience of devising constitutions for their own states. A few major figures were not there, either because, like Thomas Jefferson and John Adams, they were abroad on national business or because, like Patrick Henry, they feared that the Convention would establish a strong national government and weaken the sovereignty of the individual states.

Key points

- The Articles of Confederation, which provided the thirteen states of North America with their Constitution after the War of Independence, were proving inadequate. States did not pay their dues, often introduced economic policies that harmed the general economy, and had difficulty in controlling internal insurrection.

- The Great Powers (United Kingdom, Spain, and France) remained major threats to the survival of the new state.

- The Continental Congress was, therefore, persuaded to call a Convention in Philadelphia in the summer of 1787, but for the sole and express purpose of revising the Articles of Confederation.

Making the Constitution

The story

The Constitution of the United States was crafted over four hot, sticky months in the summer of 1787 in Philadelphia. The Continental Congress had set the second Monday in May as the starting date for the Convention. But few delegates had reached Philadelphia by then. Travelling was difficult; businesses and farms had to be organized; funds had to be acquired to pay for accommodation over an extended stay in the city. So the delegations arrived, in dribs and drabs, during the month.

It was not until 25 May that the Constitutional Convention was properly organized and George Washington voted in unanimously as its presiding officer. On 28 May the Convention agreed its processes. They still provide an excellent lesson for today. They emphasized the importance of an orderly procedure and respect for the presiding officer, a limitation on the number of times any individual could speak on a particular matter, and the right of each member to participate before early speakers could return to the fray. More importantly, the Rules Committee laid down two major principles: the Convention could return to an issue, even if a vote had already been taken, and the

Convention's discussions should remain entirely confidential until business was completed. To these was added the important rule that there should be no formal record of how each member voted. The consequences were twofold.

First, debate and argument could, and did, result in people changing their minds without any sense of embarrassment or failure and without the outside world knowing what had, at any stage, been agreed. In this way, a genuine dialogue could take place in which members were free to shift their positions without fear of public criticism. (These are still sound principles for difficult negotiations.) The second consequence was less favourable. By the keeping of silence—and in comparison to the leakiness of contemporary Washington, the confidentiality of the Convention is astonishing—those absent from the discussions could, and did, imagine all kinds of skulduggery going on.

Business started in earnest on 29 May, when Edmund Randolph introduced what came to be called the Virginia Plan. One of the earliest delegations to arrive had been the powerful team from Virginia. Having established themselves in lodgings, they wasted no time in putting together a set of proposals. This was certainly no attempt to *amend* the Articles of Confederation. It was, quite simply, the sketch of a governmental system for a new United States of America. It provided the agenda for all further discussions and the basic principles for the finally agreed Constitution. This, too, represents an important principle of political negotiation. Whoever sets the agenda enjoys an advantage. Randolph's speech outlined fifteen Resolves, or propositions, which together made up the skeleton for a national government, with a national executive, a national judiciary, and two legislative bodies, the first elected by the people themselves, who would then elect the second. The size of each legislature would be related directly to population. This ran counter to the central principle of the Articles of Confederation, where each state, regardless of population, carried the same weight.

It is remarkable how little dissent was expressed at this stage. Virtually every delegate seems to have agreed on, and voted for, the principle of a central government with a chief executive which would act directly upon the people of the United States rather than on the states themselves (as the Continental Congress was obliged to do), would enjoy substantial powers to regulate economic affairs, and whose representatives would be based on the principle of population rather than state equality. The consensus that state sovereignty should give way, in part, to a national sovereignty was revolutionary in the context of the Articles of Confederation. But it hid deep divisions.

The Virginia Plan worried the representatives of the smaller states primarily for two interconnected reasons. It seemed to provide a potentially powerful new central government and this government would be determined by the population principle, which would inevitably benefit the large states. Virginia, Massachusetts, and Pennsylvania between them had 45 per cent of all white people in the United States. William Paterson, representing New Jersey, proffered an alternative model on 15 July that proposed a single legislature with limited powers in which the states, rather than representatives, voted. This scheme was voted down on 19 June by seven states to three (with one divided).

Clearly, the two sets of proposals were in conflict and neither was likely to win the approval of a substantial majority of the states. Either the Convention would collapse in disagreement or else some negotiated middle way needed to be imagined. The weeks following the rejection of the New Jersey Plan were difficult ones. Disagreements now became more common than agreements and a degree of bitterness developed in the Convention. At the heart of the disputes was quite simply the principle upon which power should rest. The smaller states, as had the Articles of Confederation, preferred a system in which the states voted as equal states (as, indeed, was the practice in the Convention itself). The larger states preferred a more popular form of accountability with the legislatures being based upon population. The weather, like the debate, became hotter. The first defections took place when two of the New York delegation left in principled opposition to the whole idea of a national government dependent upon popular vote. It looked to many as though the Convention might well break apart.

The situation was salvaged on 17 July. The Great Compromise emerged which balanced the ambitions of the larger states with the concerns of the smaller states. It was simple in conception but quite novel, and had in fact been suggested by Roger Sherman a few days earlier. There would be two legislatures of approximately equal importance, one based upon the population principle and one upon the principle of equal states. The House of Representatives is still based upon the population principle and the Senate is still based upon the principle of state equality; each state is allocated two senators regardless of the number of its inhabitants or its wealth.

This compromise reduced the potential power of the large states. When the vote was taken, ten state delegations were present and the new scheme was approved by five states to four, with Virginia and Pennsylvania in the minority and Massachusetts equally divided. It can hardly be said that this was an overwhelming endorsement. Yet all but a small handful of the delegates recognized that, without this compromise, the chances of agreeing upon any constitutional framework would be minimal. It was, however, so important to the more populous states that there should be some form of national government as the outcome that they could not reasonably walk away from the Convention at this stage. Thereafter, the delegates from all the states worked together to put detail onto the bones. But it had been a very close-run thing.

On 26 July the Convention appointed the Committee of Detail, a group of five men tasked with reworking the original resolutions in the light of the debate and votes so far taken. Their work became, in effect, the first draft of the Constitution. The authors divided the document into a series of Articles, most with sections, in the form that now survives. This was not, however, just a bureaucratic tidying-up operation, necessary to provide the basis for further discussions leading to a conclusion, although it did perform that function. It expressed the very idea of a Constitution. William Randolph had jotted down some ideas before the group got to work. Only the essential principles, he noted, should be included so that future governments, operating in different times and under different circumstances, would not be circumscribed by too many detailed constraints; the language should be simple and precise and state general propositions; for 'the con-

struction of a constitution of necessity differs from that of law'. The Committee of Detail thus presented the Convention with a document that for the most part contained clear statements of principle. As we shall see, the final document departed slightly from this model, and it was not so precise and clear that disputes did not later arise about its meaning and application.

There followed five further weeks of vigorous debate. The principles were now broadly accepted, although a few delegates continued to challenge them unsuccessfully. Now was the time to grapple with some of the policy issues that had been ignored while the bigger picture was being worked out. Much of the argument related to the exact powers to be given to the new Congress and to the question of a Bill of Rights, which the Convention decided was not needed. But, above all, the question of slavery arose. Here, the Constitution forsook generalization and became prescriptive. Apart from counting slaves as three-fifths of a person for the purpose of counting the population base for representation, the Constitution explicitly denied Congress the power to prohibit the importation of slaves before 1808.

By the end of August, the self-imposed deadline for the completion of the Convention's work was close. Of the fifty-five delegates who had been present at the start, eleven had already left, a handful because they had no wish to be party to the events, most to return to their livelihoods. A few were present who had arrived long after the start; the last member reached Philadelphia on 6 August. Another working group was now set up, the Committee of Style and Arrangement, to revise and polish the draft prepared earlier by the Committee of Detail. By 12 September it had completed its work and only a few small amendments were thereafter accepted. On 17 September, the final version of the proposed Constitution was signed individually by the people still in Philadelphia. Only three of those present did not sign.

It is interesting to note that only three of the Virginian delegation that had provided the initial driving intellectual force actually signed. William Randolph, who had presented the Virginia Plan on which the Constitution was significantly based and who had masterminded the Committee of Detail, did not sign. Only one of the New York delegation signed. These were important states. It was clear, therefore that the near unanimity of those still in Philadelphia might not be translated into widespread support across the whole nation. It was entirely possible that the Constitution would not be ratified.

Ratification

The Philadelphia Convention discussed at length how the new Constitution should be ratified. Ultimately, it settled upon two requirements. Article VII of the Constitution provided, in direct contrast to the Articles of Confederation which required unanimity, that the Constitution would come into existence when nine states ratified. This Article also refers to state conventions and, in a side letter to the Continental Congress, the Convention recommended that each state should elect a 'Convention of Delegates' to whom the proposed constitution should be committed.

Its approval was by no means a foregone conclusion. As we have seen, the New York delegates, apart from Alexander Hamilton, who was unrepresentative of the dominant political forces in the state at the time, had not endorsed the Constitution. Some influential figures from Virginia had refused to sign. Some respected and powerful people, like Patrick Henry, had refused even to go to Philadelphia and were waiting their chance to attack a system that seemed to destroy state sovereignty and provide no protection for individual rights. The silence from Philadelphia throughout the summer had provided plenty of opportunities for people to imagine that a very distinguished elite was establishing a system to suit that elite. Popular doubts and worries were widespread, particularly in the larger states, without whose participation the whole exercise would be useless.

The smaller states, for which the security of the Union was essential, were the quickest and most enthusiastic about ratification. Delaware was the first state to ratify, unanimously, on 6 December. New Jersey followed ten days later, again unanimously. Georgia ratified on 2 January and Connecticut a few days later. The large states, however, were embroiled in fierce debates, carried out initially through an active press and latterly in protracted conventions.[1] The arguments were broadly similar, although each state had some local issues, of policy or personality, that enriched the dialogue. There was no lack of passion, and prognostications for the future were often excessively pessimistic, just as the motives of those participating in the Philadelphia Convention were traduced.

The opponents of ratification in the various states, called the anti-federalists, shared common themes. They foresaw a powerful central government ready to use its taxing and military power to destroy state sovereignty; they saw an urban and intellectual elite determined to use new constitutional powers to disadvantage still further the small, indebted farmers; they believed that the Constitution was more conservative (in its treatment of slavery and acceptance of long terms of office for senators and presidents) than their state equivalents; above all, they worried that there was no Bill of Rights to protect the small individual against what they envisioned as a mighty national government.

In the event it was a close-run thing. Pennsylvania was the first of the larger states to ratify, by 46 to 23, and here the passion carried on in the taverns after the vote. Massachusetts, with 355 delegates, was the next critical state. Only after the governor had been persuaded to suggest that approval should be linked to proposed amendments did a tiny majority, 187–168, finally emerge to bring the number of approving states to six. The losers here accepted their defeat with grace, and agreed that there had been a fair debate and that the majority should prevail. This was deliberative democracy at its best. Maryland voted 63–11 in favour in April, but again with reservations, appending thirteen amendments to its approval. South Carolina voted 149–46 late in May. Only one more state was now technically needed, but a Union without Virginia's participation would be a feeble state.

---

[1] The most famous of the printed arguments is *The Federalist Papers*, a series of brilliant essays in defence of the proposed Constitution, written by James Madison, Alexander Hamilton, and John Jay. While it is now the classic contemporary exposition, at the time its influence, even in New York State where it was published, was not particularly great.

The Virginia debate was probably intellectually the outstanding one. As the arguments flowed first this way, then that, the essence of the issue became clearer and clearer. The sovereignty of the individual states, of which many inhabitants were so proud, had to be weighed against the advantages, economic and military, of a larger Union. (There are powerful echoes of the debates about European unity.) New Hampshire just beat Virginia to the vote and so became the crucial ninth state, on 21 July 1788, to ratify. Virginia finally approved by 89 to 79 (with proposals for twenty amendments), William Randolph now voting in favour. The defeated protagonists, as their equivalents in Massachusetts, accepted defeat with magnanimity and promised to work towards its success. The news reached New York in early July. It was deeply disappointing to the powerful anti-federalist group in the state. Whether it was a resigned pragmatism or the strength of the arguments, New York followed the example of the large states and approved, with a tiny majority

of 30–27. By August 1788 eleven states had signed up to the new Constitution; South Carolina and Rhode Island came along in time.

The Constitution had been ratified. But it had been ratified with implicit strings attached. There was a broad acceptance that it was, in one important respect, incomplete and defective: it needed a Bill of Rights. The first action of the first elected Congress was to prepare a Bill of Rights and on 25 September 1789 Congress transmitted to the state legislatures twelve proposed amendments, two of which, dealing with congressional representation and congressional pay, were not adopted (though the latter was ratified as recently as 1992—the Twenty-Seventh Amendment). The remaining ten were ratified and became effective from 15 December 1791. Although, strictly speaking, these are not part of the Constitution formulated at the Philadelphia Convention, they are effectively part of the initial constitutional project which gave birth to the United States as we now know it.

The ideology of the Constitution

Several principles underlie the Constitution. They are sometimes in conflict. Over the years, arguments have developed not only about the application of these principles but also about their relative importance. Many of the cases decided by the Supreme Court, and most of the literature on the proper role of the Supreme Court, derive from the internal contradictions within the Constitution and the lack of universal agreement over which principle should prevail when there is a conflict.

The first principle was a commitment to limited government. These two words have two distinct implications. Governments need to have appropriate authority and capacity to fulfil their roles. Part of the problem with the Constitutional Congress was its lack of capacity. But balancing this is the belief that governments need to be constrained. The sovereignty of parliament, so much praised in the British system, would have been anathema to the Founding Fathers. Madison's words in *Federalist 51* are eloquent on this point:

If men were angels, no government would be necessary. If angels were to govern men, neither external nor internal controls on government would be necessary. In framing a government which is to be administered by men over men, the great difficulty lies in this: you must first enable the government to control the governed; and in the next place oblige it to control itself. A dependence on the people is, no doubt, the primary control on the government; but experience has taught mankind the necessity of auxiliary precautions.

Notice here several things. Madison is fully aware that governments need the capacity to control the governed, in effect to establish law and order, to raise necessary taxes, to regulate behaviour. But he is also well aware that power can be misused. His first protection is the people, his second auxiliary precautions.

Let us take these in turn. Dependence on the people, echoing the Declaration of Independence, requires governmental accountability to the people. In sharp contrast to practice in Europe at the time, all

---

Box 3.1 **The separation of powers and checks and balances**

Branches of government	Powers of government		
	Legislative	Executive	Judicial
The legislature can:	Make laws	Confirm executive appointments (Senate) Ratify treaties (Senate)	Impeach Create and eliminate courts
The executive can:	Veto laws Recommend laws	Enforce the laws	Grant pardons Nominate judges
The judiciary can:	Review laws	Review executive acts Issue injunctions	Interpret laws

---

those exercising power over their fellow citizens were legitimized by elections. Members of the House of Representatives enjoyed only two-year terms (longer, it may be noted, than some state legislators). They were directly accountable to an electorate whose qualifications were set by the states, and therefore differed across the Union, but enfranchised many more people than in Europe.

However, the democratic commitment was not absolute. Women and slaves were not given the vote and qualifications limited the number of men enfranchised. Furthermore the House of Representatives was to be balanced by a Senate, whose members were to be indirectly elected and serve for six years, and a President, who was also to be chosen indirectly through an electoral college. Unconstrained male democracy was thus tempered, but tempered in such a way that nevertheless required regular elections. The people, Madison presumed, would generally vote out of office those who abused their trust.

While the democratic nature of the American system was very progressive for its time, the most remarkable aspects of the Constitution are the 'auxiliary precautions'. They come in two forms. First are the institutional arrangements: the federal system whose division of powers (or divided sovereignty) left most of the matters of direct relevance to ordinary people in the control of state and local politicians and the governmental system's principle of separation of powers. By providing checks and balances in this way, the Founding Fathers hoped to prevent any individual, or small group, from gaining control of all the organs of the state, stifling liberties, and imposing authoritarian rule on the people (see Box 3.1).

The second form of 'auxiliary precautions' was the Bill of Rights (see Box 3.2). The commitment to 'a government of laws, not of men' can be seen in the supremacy clause of the written Constitution[2] and in the belief that governmental excesses can be constrained through written documents. The passionate debates over a Bill of Rights, and the consequent passing of the first ten amendments emphasize the belief that governments could not be trusted and that, perhaps, even the people could not altogether be relied upon to control them. So there was a need for clear rules, supreme over ordinary legislation, to help individuals protect themselves against the misuses of power.

The principle of accountability, with its democratic implication that politicians may legitimately enact whatever laws the people approve, clashes with the principle of limited government and its constitutional support in a Bill of Rights. In the United States, the power of politicians duly elected by majorities may be constrained by those rights of minorities set out in the Constitution. The tension between majorities, and minorities' rights runs through American political history and was established at the very outset in the Constitution.

[2] 'The Constitution, and the Laws of the United States which shall be made in Pursuance thereof . . . shall be the supreme Law of the Land; and the Judges in every State shall be bound thereby, any Thing in the Constitution or Laws of any State to the Contrary notwithstanding.'

Box 3.2 The Bill of Rights

The First Amendment: prohibits the infringement of freedom of speech, religion, press, assembly or of petitioning the government.

The Second Amendment: prohibits the infringement of the 'right to keep and bear arms'.

The Third Amendment: prohibits the quartering of troops in private property during peacetime.

The Fourth Amendment: prohibits unreasonable searches and seizures of private property.

The Fifth Amendment: prohibits double jeopardy (standing trial twice for the same crime) or self-incrimination, creating rights in criminal cases.

The Sixth Amendment: guarantees rights to a fair trial.

The Seventh Amendment: guarantees rights in civil cases.

The Eighth Amendment: prohibits cruel and unusual punishments.

The Ninth Amendment: states that the *rights* not specified ('enumerated') in the Constitution are retained by the people.

The Tenth Amendment: states that the *powers* not listed in the Constitution are retained by the states and the people.

Explaining the Constitution: rival theories

Telling the story as has just been done implicitly reflects a theory of why the Constitution turned out as it did. Put simply, it assumes that the Founding Fathers were so committed to the conception of one United States of America that, through negotiation and compromise and aware of recent history, they agreed on a system of government that satisfied no single group but reflected some of the wishes of all the groups.

The theory can, and should, be elaborated. It needs to remark on the crucial significance of the Virginian delegation's 'setting the agenda'. It needs to note the significance of Randolph's conception of a Constitution as a broad set of principles. It needs to recognize the skills of the wordsmith in Gouverneur Morris (the principal writer). It needs to remember that the Constitution had still to be ratified by the individual states. In other words, we cannot forget the importance of agency, the distinctive contributions of individuals to the final document.

Even this, however, is far from adequate. For one thing, the stress on compromise should not hide the reality of that consensus that prevailed during the first three weeks and sought an effective national government. We may accept the central importance of pragmatic compromise as part of the explanation.

But other forms of compromise were possible and other principles could have dominated the debates. What is missing is the intellectual context of the time and the ideas familiar to the Founding Fathers. Many of those at the Convention were very widely read. They had studied classical authors such as Aristotle and had themselves researched political systems elsewhere. Many had participated in writing their own state constitutions. Virtually all had been brought up or educated in a system that was essentially British. Hence, the argument during the Convention, often implicit rather than explicit, was coloured by considerations of the British monarchical tradition, the historical experience of colonialism, a bicameral legislature with different legitimations, and a judiciary of high status. The Founding Fathers reacted to their own experiences.

The Declaration of Independence clearly had its origins in the ideas of John Locke. At the heart of any social contract theory is the notion of accountability. It is recognized that only in the very smallest of groups can all members participate equally in the running of the organization. There must be some form of representation. Theories differ over the principles of that representation. Social contract theories, put simply, claim that the people give up their right to participate fully in the day-to-day running of the state to others on condition that those who do exercise power must be held accountable for that use. This idea is strongly embedded in the Constitution.

A second text which was well known and much referred to in the Convention was Montesquieu's *L'Esprit des Lois*. Among the many ideas in this book, the conception of the separation of powers was perhaps the most influential. Often thought of as the most virtuous aspect of the British system and copied in some of the state constitutions, the idea is that the functions of government should be carried out by quite distinct people. All political systems make rules (or laws); all political systems apply those rules; all political systems need to interpret those rules and adjudicate on disputes about their meaning. Hence, separation of powers asserts that the legislature, where the rules are made, the executive, where the rules are applied, and the judiciary, where the rules are interpreted, should be composed of different people and that their responsibilities should be demarcated and separate.

Because the powers of the state are distributed among several institutions, individual liberty, it was held, might be protected. So the Founding Fathers carefully wrote into the Constitution a large number of shared functions to provide checks and balances. For example, laws must originate in the legislature and must be passed by both houses of the legislature, but they do not become law until they are signed by the head of the executive branch—the president. While the justices of the Supreme Court may not be members of either the legislative or the executive branches, they are nominated by the president and confirmed by the Senate, thus involving all three branches.

Nor should one forget Thomas Paine. The experience of colonial government ensured that suspicion of government itself remained a powerful emotion. The federal system and the limited powers granted explicitly to the Congress express this fear. Yet there were still many, especially among the anti-federalists, who wanted still stronger defences against governmental power. One such approach, which grew naturally out of Paine's writings and speeches, was to enshrine the rights of individuals in

the Constitution in such a way that they could not be abridged by governments, even elected governments. The Bill of Rights, which was in part the price that had to be paid for ratification, is the embodiment of this view.

For the first century of the Republic's life, this picture of great figures, intellectual and pragmatic, principled and far-seeing, dominated explanations of the Constitution. At the beginning of the twentieth century, however, progressive ideas were influencing the academic community as they were also generating political movements challenging the dominant forces of unbridled capitalism. It seemed to many that the revered Constitution was really the bulwark of powerful economic interests and, therefore, the enemy of more egalitarian and populist policies. The most influential work setting out this view was Charles Beard's *An Economic Interpretation of the Constitution*, which was published in 1913.

In this book, Beard attempted to show that the Founding Fathers saw the Constitution as a critical opportunity to establish a government strong enough to pay the national debt, regulate commerce, prevent fluctuations in the currency, and, above all through its checks and balances and emphasis on indirect election, control the excesses of popular majorities in their attack on private property and creditor rights. The ratification debates lend general support to this broad overview. Those who gathered in Philadelphia were professionals, urban people, and men in established businesses, whose interests were well reflected in the Constitution's ideals. The anti-federalists tended to be poorer, rurally based, less established, and often debtors.

For four decades Beard's thesis dominated analysis of the Constitution, even though several major historians challenged its empirical base. In the 1950s, with the publication of Robert Brown's *Charles Beard and the Constitution* and Forrest McDonald's *We the People*, Beard's thesis came under an attack which it could not entirely survive. The specific financial interests of the delegates at Philadelphia were not as concerned with government stock as had been claimed; the economic interests of the anti-federalists were less dissimilar; indeed, the real divisions were political and ideological: between those whose visions embraced a single powerful United States of America and those whose parochial loyalties to individual states feared such a project. What was now stressed was the democratic and representative nature of those who were elected to the ratification conventions and hence the degree to which the Constitution reflected a majoritarian view rather than a small elite's preferences.

Key points

- Delegates were chosen from all states, except for Rhode Island, and met in Philadelphia between May and September 1787. These men constituted an impressive body of experience, intellect, and political sophistication.

- The Virginia delegation set the agenda, but its emphasis on the population principle as the basis for allocating representation antagonized the small states. The New Jersey delegation offered an alternative model, quite similar to the Articles of Confederation, but this was not accepted. There appeared to be stalemate until the Great Compromise, which apportioned the House of Representatives according to population and gave each state two members of the Senate.

- The Committee of Detail prepared a draft Constitution, which set out the general rules for the political system, and the Committee of Style and Arrangement refined the text to produce the Constitution as we know it.

- The Constitution starts 'We, the People of the United States . . . ', and the people, through their representatives, were to ratify it. But there was strong opposition to the Constitution (the anti-federalists) and the voting in the large states was extremely close. In some states, approval was given only with the expectation that some changes would be made, especially the incorporation of a Bill of Rights.

- The Constitution embraced several principles: the separation of powers, the division of powers (federalism), and the notion of the Constitution as the Supreme Law. There was a tension between a belief in popular accountability and fear of too strong a central government. Consequently, the Constitution has many checks and balances within it to constrain governments.

- There are rival arguments to explain why the Constitution emerged in its precise form. Pragmatism, intellectual arguments, and economic self-interest have all been offered as the most significant forces.

Amending the Constitution

The formal amending process

Perhaps the most astonishing aspect of the Constitution is the fact that it has been so little amended. If we accept that the first ten amendments were, in effect, part of the original constitutional settlement, there have been only seventeen amendments in over 200 years.

One explanation is that the Founding Fathers deliberately made amendment of the Constitution difficult. Article V sets out the methods by which the Constitution may formally be amended. Here are the important clauses:

The Congress, whenever two thirds of both Houses shall deem it necessary, shall propose Amendments to this Constitution, or, on the Application of the Legislatures of two thirds of the several States, shall call a Convention for proposing Amendments, which, in either case, shall be valid . . . when ratified by the Legislatures of three fourths of the several States, or by Conventions in three-fourths thereof, as the one or the other Mode of Ratification may be proposed by the Congress.

There are thus two ways by which an amendment may be proposed for ratification (see Box 3.3). To date, only the first method (a resolution approved by two-thirds of *both* the House of Representatives and the Senate) has been successful. Such special majorities have been incorporated into the constitutions of other countries, but have not prevented many amendments being proposed. The explanation why this has not occurred in the United States is twofold: on the one hand, there have been few years in which any party has enjoyed such majorities in both Houses of Congress at the same time. On the other hand, it appears as though American leaders feel that amendments should only be successful under very special circumstances. We return to this point later in the chapter.

Just as there has only been one method by which amendments have been proposed, there has also only been one method by which they have been ratified. Congress has always called for ratification to be completed by the legislatures of the states. On some occasions, the proposal approved by the Congress has fixed a time period within which ratification must take place; on other occasions, no such limitation is set. The proposals for an Equal Rights Amendment in 1972 had an initial time limit; this was then extended. When the extension period ended and an insufficient number of states had ratified, the amendment fell. It could be argued that decisions of the Supreme Court, which had increasingly struck down laws that differentiated on grounds of gender, had made an amendment no longer necessary. By contrast, the latest (27th) amendment had no such limit and over two hundred years passed between proposal and ratification. An interesting issue, not resolved by the Constitution, is whether states can withdraw their approval, once granted. This was a matter of considerable concern where the Equal Rights Amendment was concerned.

The second method of amending the Constitution formally is for the states to petition Congress to call a Convention to amend the Constitution. This has never occurred, and nobody knows precisely what should happen if the requisite number of states did indeed call for a Convention. By the end of 1985, it only needed two more states to vote in favour of a Convention to consider an amendment forbidding the national government from operating a deficit

---

> **Box 3.3 Amending the US Constitution**
>
> *Proposal stage*
> Two-thirds vote of members present in both houses of Congress (34 amendments proposed)
> or
> National convention by Congress at request of two-thirds of state legislatures (no amendments proposed)
>
> *Ratification stage*
> Three-quarters of state legislatures (26 amendments ratified)
> or
> Constitutional conventions in three-quarters of the states (one amendment—the Twenty-first—ratified)

---

budget. On other occasions in the past, the votes for a Convention have nearly been reached. Between 1893 and 1911, thirty-one out of the thirty-two states required called for a Convention for the direct election of Senators, while between 1906 and 1916, twenty-seven of the thirty-two called for a Convention to consider the constitutionality of polygamy; between 1957 and 1969, thirty-three out of the required thirty-four states called for a Convention to consider negating the effects of the Supreme Court's decision requiring all state constituencies to be of equal size.

It is difficult to gain the special majorities required by the Constitution unless there is a broad consensus. Where change has come, it has tended to be either the clear expression of majority opinion or an extension of democratic rights which are implicitly part of the American ideal, even if not an explicit part of the Founding Fathers' vision. As Alan Grimes has summarized it:

What the people have done to the Constitution has been to make it a far more democratic document than the one they inherited from their ancestors. The amendments, in fact, constitute a formal record, in the fundamental law, of the growth of democracy in America. Although the amendments were written to meet the needs of specific historical situations, they present in their entirety a remarkably consistent democratic theme.

The successful amendments fall into five comparatively busy periods. The first twelve, ratified between 1791 and 1804, are effectively the completion of the Convention's business.[3] The Thirteenth to Fifteenth Amendments, ratified between 1865 and 1870 may be seen as the northern amendments consolidating victory in the Civil War. The Sixteenth to Nineteenth Amendments, ratified between 1913 and 1920, reflect the populist and progressive power of the western states. The fourth period, from 1933 to 1953, is a tidying-up period. The final period, the so-called urban or metropolitan amendments, ratified between 1961 and 1971, flow from a shift in the centre of political gravity towards the Democratic urban constituency. Out of a 200-year history, action on amending the Constitution occupied only thirty-five years. Each period coincided with a shift in the balance of domestic power; each strengthened, as was intended, the dominant coalition of the day.

The amendments that have been passed fall, for the most part, into clear categories. They increase the democratic participation in the national system; they establish further rights to protect individuals against governments; and they resolve organizational matters that the original Constitution failed to take into consideration. The tension inherent in the original Constitution between majorities and minority rights is replicated throughout the nation's history.

There remains an apparent paradox. Congressmen do not seem backward in *proposing* amendments; but they are backward in *supporting* amendments. In recent years over 150 amendments have been introduced annually. Only a very small number indeed, however, are ever given time by Congress for consideration. There are two reasons for this. In the first place, all but a handful are proposed for purposes purely of publicity, to show constituents that certain Congressmen feel strongly on some matter or another. In the second place, the dominant political view remains that of William Randolph: that a constitution is different from ordinary law and should only embrace the major principles upon which government is to be carried out. American politicians are content that the Constitution does set out appropriate principles for the governance of their country.

Informal means: reinterpretation

The words of the Constitution have barely changed. The *meaning*, and therefore impact, of the Constitution has changed enormously. How can this be? The simple answer is that the justices of the Supreme Court, in the process of dealing with cases brought to them, refine the meanings of particular phrases and words in a way which affects the political structure or the rights of individuals, as the case may be. Three themes can illustrate this briefly.

The first theme is the power of Congress. Article I, section 8, enumerates several policy areas where Congress was expected to act. Much is crystal clear. But some grants of power are imprecise, as Randolph had recommended. What, for example, is encompassed by the power 'to regulate Commerce . . . among the several States' or 'to make all Laws which shall be necessary and proper for carrying into Execution the foregoing Powers', or 'to provide for . . . the general Welfare of the United States'? These questions were answered ultimately by the Supreme Court in its role as the highest court deciding litigation generated by disputes over the meaning of the Constitution.

In *McCulloch* v. *Maryland* (1819), the Court decided that the 'necessary and proper' clause permitted the federal government to establish a national bank, even though this was not actually enumerated in section 8. For the first century, this interpretation had little impact, because national governments were not expected to intervene much in the day-to-day social and economic affairs of the country. Towards the end of the nineteenth century, however, the pressure to legislate to constrain unbridled capitalism was strong, and national laws to regulate the railways and monopolies, for example, were introduced to 'regulate commerce'. The Great Depression of the 1930s resulted in President Franklin Roosevelt's New Deal. Many of the New Deal laws were designed to regulate commerce, broadly defined; limitations on production were established, social welfare programmes set up, rights of workers created, and business freedoms curtailed.

---

[3] It was not until 1939 that Massachusetts and Connecticut actually ratified the first 10 amendments.

This was, in size and scope, quite new. It interfered a great deal with commercial matters and expanded the reach of the 'general welfare' clause into a range of activities that were not enumerated. A slender constitutional majority of the Supreme Court struck down these hastily drafted pieces of legislation, and a Constitution crisis was only averted by a combination of better-drafted laws and a change of personnel in the Court. As the old justices retired and new justices, fully supportive of the New Deal, were appointed, Washington found itself with enhanced authority. The activist governments of the 1960s and 1970s built upon this, supported by popular opinion expressed through the democratic process and the Supreme Court's expansive reading of the Constitution.

As the national government extended the policy areas in which it wished to be involved, it inevitably began to legislate in areas traditionally presumed to be the exclusive responsibility of the individual states. The second theme, therefore, concerns the practice of federalism, deciding precisely where the limits of state sovereignty lie. In the early years of the Union, the division of powers between the central government and the individual states was relatively unambiguous. The new national government was responsible for the defence of the United States and its foreign relations, and it was charged with ensuring a free market of goods between the states. For the vast majority of day-to-day affairs the states remained the primary law-makers. This system, in which the two levels of government had their own specific areas of competence, came to be called 'dual federalism'.

President Franklin Roosevelt's New Deal programme extended the range of activities in which the federal government wanted to get involved dramatically. The basis for a widespread involvement by the government in Washington in areas which had hitherto been thought of as the prerogative of the individual states had actually been laid more than a century earlier. In *Gibbons* v. *Ogden* (1824) the Court asserted that, where a particular activity was being regulated by both the federal government and state governments (in this case, coastal shipping), the federal law, based upon Congress's powers to regulate commerce among the several states, should take precedence. Supreme Court

approval for central government priorities was further extended as a result of the centralization caused by the military requirements of the Second World War. Progressives approved, since the resources available to Washington were substantial and the chance to establish national standards for welfare depended upon that dominant position. Traditionalists complained that the Constitution was being improperly revised. It is but another reminder that the United States Constitution, although written, can be quite as flexible as the unwritten British Constitution.

A third issue relates to the exact definition of an individual's rights. The first amendment starts: 'Congress shall make no law . . .', but the next eight do not start in that way. They are straight assertions of rights. They were generally held to be constraints on the new central government, whose power many had feared. What was not certain in the early part of the nineteenth century was whether these rights could be asserted against state governments as well. *Barron* v. *Baltimore* (1830) decided that they could not.

One aftermath of the Civil War was the passing of the Thirteenth, Fourteenth, and Fifteenth Amendments. It was the Fourteenth which came, in time, to provide the protection of individual rights against *all* governments. Two clauses were responsible, the equal protection clause and the due process clause. Initially, the Supreme Court interpreted them very narrowly and states were permitted considerable latitude in what they did. In 1896, for example, the Court decided in *Plessy* v. *Ferguson* that states were permitted to provide 'separate but equal' transport facilities. This grace was extended from transport to the full range of state activities so that, by the end of the 1940s, the southern states were constitutionally permitted to provide public provision on a segregated basis, from the cradle to the grave literally (from segregated hospital facilities to segregated cemeteries). In 1954, however, a unanimous Supreme Court struck down segregated junior schools as inherently unconstitutional (in *Brown* v. *Board of Education*), and, bit by bit, the Court reinterpreted the equal protection clause to outlaw all racial discrimination and, in time, much differentiation on grounds of gender.

The due process clause has a more complicated

history. Initially, it was held to require states merely to pass their laws and regulations in a proper manner according to the process set out in state constitutions and laws. This was referred to as 'procedural due process'. But, initially in the case of free speech (*Gitlow v. New York*, 1925), the Court then decided that due process in fact embraced some substantive rights that made for a civilized society. In seeking to set out these rights, the Court selected a number of so-called 'natural rights' (the right to chose a marriage partner, to travel between states, to educate children in a school of choice) and then extended the rights protected by this clause to embrace all those set forth in the Bill of Rights (Abraham 1988: 38–117). In the 1950s and 1960s, the decisions of the Supreme Court reversed the initial understanding that these rights were limitations only on the federal government, and extended them against the states.

The consequence of this jurisprudential revolution was profound. States found that their financial support for church schools was unconstitutional; that their unequal constituencies were unconstitutional; that their requirement for prayers to begin the school day was unconstitutional; that their procedures for dealing with suspects and criminals were often unconstitutional; that their methods of obtaining evidence were often unconstitutional, resulting in some evidence and confessions being excluded from trials; that they were obliged by the Constitution to provide counsel for the accused at trials; that their limitations on abortion laws were unconstitutional; that their prison systems and other state-supported institutions were often operating unconstitutionally. The Court's attempt to apply equally across the whole country its interpretation of the meaning of the Bill of Rights seemed to strike at the very heart of the federal idea.

In the last quarter of the twentieth century, there was at first a halting of this development and then a gentle reversal. Once again, the Supreme Court was responsible for the way in which some of the absolutes set out in the 1950s, 1960s, and early 1970s were softened. The powers of Congress were given limitations; the rights of states when in conflict with the federal government sometimes prevailed; the ability of states to constrain the application of the Bill of Rights was reinstated. At this stage, what needs to be noted is that the meaning of the Constitution is never crystal clear and that its contemporary meaning will be decided by the Supreme Court. At first glance, this ability of unelected judges in effect to amend the Constitution appears a major derogation from democratic principles. But, as the conclusion to this chapter and the discussion in Chapter 8 suggest, it is not as straightforward as that.

Key points

- The formal method of amending the Constitution requires substantial majorities in Congress and in the individual states. These are difficult to achieve and there have only been twenty-seven Amendments, the first ten being introduced in the very first Congress.

- With a few exceptions, the amendments have increased the democratic nature of the American political system and extended the protection of individual rights.

- The Constitution has been informally changed through judgments of the Supreme Court which has given specific meanings to some of the general phrases of the Constitution. In this way, the Constitution has been flexible enough to adapt to changing needs and popular expectations.

The Constitution as symbol

As noted in Chapters 1 and 2, the United States is largely composed of immigrants or the descendents of relatively recent immigrants. They have come from virtually all parts of the globe, bringing with them different languages and different customs. Creating a sense of common nationhood has been a task consciously undertaken by American leaders over the years. The Constitution is very much part of that common nationhood.

In the 1940s Max Lerner, in a famous and much quoted article, suggested that the Constitution was 'totem and fetish' and was thought by Americans to possess 'supernatural powers' (Lerner 1945–6). In the middle of the 1950s Jack Pole could write that 'the people of the United States are united above all by their Constitution' (Pole 1957). Similar emotional views were expressed by Senator Sam Ervin (D-SC) in 1967:

The good and wise men who fashioned the Constitution had earth's most magnificent dream. They dreamed they could enshrine the fundamentals of the government they desired to establish and the liberties of the people they wished to secure in the Constitution . . . I know that apart from its faithful observance by Congress, the President and the Supreme Court, neither our country nor any single human being within its borders has any security against anarchy or tyranny . . . The good and wise men who wrote and ratified the Constitution knew the everlasting truth subsequently phrased . . . in this way: 'Whatever government is not a government of laws is a despotism, let it be called what it may.'

And in 1987 President Reagan observed in his address commemorating the Bicentennial of the Constitution that it evoked not merely 'simple admiration, but also a feeling more of reverence'.

This has not stopped vocal groups challenging that Constitution's application to a range of social issues. When *Brown* v. *Board of Education of Topeka* outlawed racial segregation in primary schools, southern politicians fought vigorously to prevent its application. As has been mentioned, the Supreme Court struck down as unconstitutional a range of practices that the states had presumed to be exclusively within their own discretion. All these decisions stimulated powerful, even (where abortion

was concerned) violent, currents of opposition to the Court, and persuaded many to attempt 'reversal' of these decisions.

Because the Constitution *is*, in the last analysis, 'what the judges say it is', it is essential to distinguish between the Constitution itself and the contemporary application, or meaning, of it. Most Americans seem able to make this distinction. But some of the most disadvantaged still see the Constitution through the eyes of a modernized Charles Beard. Intimately aware themselves of poverty, racial discrimination, and political impotence, they blame their plight on the very Constitution the majority venerates. Most Americans, however, argue that it is not the Constitution's fault that schoolchildren are forcibly bussed, God is excluded from the classroom, law enforcement officials are constrained by technicalities favouring the criminal, the right to life is obliterated by the right to an abortion, and blacks and women are given preferential treatment over white males through affirmative action programmes. These are the fault of the justices of the Supreme Court.

The reverence given to the Constitution is one explanation for the very small number of constitutional amendments. The cult of the American Constitution, as Clement Vose has written, is 'akin to the reliance on Biblical text of religious fundamentalism'. For all its imperfections, the Constitution *must* seem to be perfect. Regular revisions, in the eyes of most politicians, would diminish that perfection unacceptably. Explaining this symbolic authority is complex. It lies in part in the reverence for law itself, in the belief in 'a government of laws, not men'. But it also lies somewhere in the unresolved dilemma of deciding what it is to be 'American', an identity much sought after and often disputed. The influx in the latter part of the nineteenth century of immigrants from non-Anglo-Saxon Europe—and Catholics to boot—was enriched by the gradual emancipation of black Americans and the more recent arrival of men and women from Asia and Spanish-speaking Central America. Shared language, shared history, shared religion, shared heroes no longer bound the people of America naturally into a nation, as they had once upon a time. The melting pot needed some glue. So the primary schools had to play a consciously political socializing role, and the oath of allegiance is still recited by the vast majority of young people in the country's schools. Above all, however, the cement binding the disparate ethnic groups which make up American society became a veneration for the Constitution or, perhaps more accurately, a veneration for an idealized conception of the Constitution. Using the word 'veneration' implies

something religious, and there is some sense in thinking of Americans' attachments to their institutions, particularly the Constitution, as part of a civil religion.

Key point

• The Constitution has, over time, become part of a civil religion and has played a major role in defining Americanism and binding a heterogeneous people together.

The Constitution in the twenty-first century

Changing context

The Bicentennial celebrations of the Constitutional Convention in 1987 provided the opportunity for a public reaffirmation of its virtues. At the same time, however, it spawned considerable debate, largely among academics, that questioned its applicability at the end of the twentieth century. The point was commonly made that the Constitution was drawn up in an age when transport and communications were difficult, when the expectations of government were few, when the United States was a new and weak state in the international system, when loyalties were essentially parochial, when there were no national parties. All this had changed.

Now the United States is *the* superpower. Its responsibilities and potential impact globally are enormous. The rest of the world, sometimes in fear, sometimes in hope, looks to the United States to solve international problems and to take a lead in international affairs. It is essential, so it is held, that there should be a strong government, fully accountable to the people of the United States, and readily identifiable. It is no longer acceptable for a president, like Bill Clinton, to approve enhanced funding for international organizations and then find that the Congress will not vote the necessary money. Madison was not alone among the Founding Fathers to realize that effective government requires

effective powers. As the expectations placed upon governments increased through the latter part of the twentieth century, the ideal of limited government came to seem outdated.

In other words, both the empirical realities of the modern age and a shift in normative perspectives have challenged some of the central principles on which the Constitution was based. The constitutional emphasis on the division of powers, the separation of powers, and the rights of individuals against governments seemed to many people to provide altogether too many checks and balances.

The ideology contested

The spark that fuelled the debate was an article published in the journal *Foreign Affairs* and written by President Carter's legal counsel, Lloyd Cutler (Cutler 1980). It was called 'to form a government' and argued that the checks and balances in the Constitution made it virtually impossible to form a government that would be both responsible and representative. Cutler's chief concern related to the separation of powers principle. A little earlier, a powerful attack on the 'imperial judiciary' had been made by Nathan Glazer and had provided the intellectual basis for a continuing critique of the Supreme Court's role in interpreting the

Constitution. And in 1985, Ronald Reagan's Attorney-General, Edwin Meese III, delivered a speech to the American Bar Association in which he lamented what he believed to be the end of federalism, blaming, for the most part, the handiwork of the Supreme Court. Three of the Constitution's central principles—the separation of powers, federalism, the Constitution as Supreme Law—became the subjects of critical debate.

Failures in the 1970s and 1980s to manage the economy, to combat poverty, to provide proper welfare services, and to protect the dollar began to be explained in terms of system failure. As Cutler argued, the system of separation of powers, if it did not actually cause governmental failure, encouraged it. Members of the Congress were obsessed by the need to curry favour with the most articulate and well-resourced members of their districts and were consequently driven by parochial and thus, by definition, minority interests. The president, elected from the national constituency, reflected a different set of popular wishes. In such a situation, it was difficult to 'form a government' capable of carrying through a single coherent and internally consistent set of public policies in the national interest. As the two branches of government consequently pulled in different directions, there were altogether too many checks and balances and not enough effective government.

Here the normative arguments in favour of limited government clash with the normative arguments in favour of effective government. Those who worry about the effectiveness of the system tend to see the president as the central figure in an efficient policy-making system. This is particularly true in the field of foreign relations, where the Constitution, practice, and common sense have granted the president the dominant authority. Such has been the case for a long time, especially through the period of the cold war. Occasionally, the Supreme Court or Congress has briefly restrained presidential power. But the ideal conception of balanced authority as set out in the Constitution, in which Congress plays its constitutionally empowered role and presidents theirs and the courts manage the disagreements, rarely holds for long. The president soon regains the upper hand.

From the perspective of the White House, the separation of powers has always been an unwelcome institutional limitation on effective diplomacy. The relations between the president and the Congress, however, became more strident in the 1980s when the president was a Republican and the majority of the House of Representatives was composed of Democrats. Hence, a natural institutional competition between legislature and executive was made worse by the party competition between Republicans and Democrats.

In thinking about the separation of powers, three points need to be considered. First, the principle of the separation of powers presumes that liberty is best protected where three different sets of people are responsible for rule-making, rule application, and rule adjudication. It is a quite different view from the British model that believes parliamentary accountability will protect liberty. Second, the needs of modern government and the consequences of the United States' status as superpower have shifted responsibility for most proactive measures towards the executive branch. Third, precisely how the competition for power between Congress and the presidency works out depends ultimately upon political factors, on the skills and willingness to compromise of the parties involved, and on the ideological distance between the legislative and executive branches.

In thinking about the division of powers, it is interesting to start with an external view. Harold Laski, the socialist professor of government at the London School of Economics and Political Science, published a study of the United States in the late 1940s and wrote of the 'obsolescence of the federal idea' (Laski 1948: 50). He had in mind both a normative argument (that is, he thought that federalism *ought* to be at the end of its useful life) and an empirical observation (that is, he thought federalism was *actually* collapsing in the United States). His normative argument depended upon a firm belief in central planning, especially of the economy, in the primacy of economic activity over all others, and in the ultimate value of equality which could only be achieved through a single overarching government. Federalism, by preserving the sovereignty of individual states, obstructed rational central planning and protected inequality, especially in the southern states, where racial segregation was the order of the day. But he also thought that the New Deal was, through its regulation of much economic activity and its equalizing policies through welfare programmes, sounding the death-knell for the autonomy of the individual states.

Laski was proved wrong. His ideological position fell upon stony ground. In the United States commitment to private enterprise, to individualism, to the free market meant that arguments in favour of centralized planning made little progress. On the empirical side, however, he came nearer to the truth. From the days of the New Deal for the next half-century, a majority of the American people did look to Washington for answers to many of the economic and social problems of the day. The 1960s probably reflect the high point, when the national government took the lead in trying to end racial segregation, address the problems of poverty, establish a more inclusive political process, and strengthen the national science base in the face of the Soviet Union's space successes.

What frightened people like Edwin Meese was that Laski's empirical analysis might be right. Meese was alarmed at the way that the massive financial strength of Washington, the judgments of the Supreme Court, the dominance of a nationwide media and culture, was effectively destroying the sovereignty of the individual states. In thinking about the division of powers, or federalism, three points need to be considered. First, the division of powers between the central government and the individual states shifts, as a matter of fact, over time in line with political pressures within the country and Supreme Court judgments. Second, divided sovereignty is a heritage bequeathed to the current generation of Americans, nurtured in the individual states for 200 years, and inculcated in Americans as a natural and sensible form of government. It will take much to break such an internalized belief. Third, in the abstract, the division of powers will result in different priorities and policies in different parts of the country (and, therefore, inequalities), but this may be the necessary price to be paid for both good governance and representation in a nation of 240 million people.

Finally, Nathan Glazer's picture of the imperial judiciary suggested that the Constitution as the great unbiased bulwark of American values and protection of liberties was no longer viable. For when the supreme law is vested in a written document, the importance of those who interpret and apply it gives them a very significant role in the political process. That has always been the case. In the 1930s, progressives were incensed by the way traditionalists applied the Constitution. In the more modern period it has been the traditionalists who have been incensed by the way progressives have applied it. Simply, no constitution, not even the hugely long ones, can resolve all the issues that come before the courts for adjudication.

There is always a tension between democracy, in the sense of popular participation, and efficiency, in the sense of speedy decision-making. Defenders of the United States' system would argue that efficient government is not primarily about the procedural effectiveness of devising and passing legislative responses to political problems rapidly and coherently. They would certainly include in the concept the idea that efficient government must reflect the various priorities and preferences of the people whom government is supposed to serve. British observers might stress unfavourably the lack of coherence and the long-drawn-out process of decision-making in the United States; American observers would stress unfavourably the small number of leaders involved in policy-making in the United Kingdom and their distance from popular pressures. Thus, any appreciation of the United States system of government needs to be clear about the meaning and relative weight to be given to such concepts as democracy and efficiency.

Key points

- The conditions at the beginning of the twenty-first century are obviously very different from those at the end of the eighteenth. What people expect from governments, the role of the United States in the world, and technological advancement have all challenged some of the central principles held by the Founding Fathers, most obviously the idea of limited government.

- At the time of the Bicentennial celebrations, many thoughtful Americans questioned whether the constitutional system did not have too many checks and balances. The separation of powers was thought to reduce the effectiveness of government, and the Supreme Court too often found laws and regulations passed by elected governments unconstitutional; perhaps the Constitution was now outdated.

Conclusion

The major principles upon which the American political system is based are set out in the Constitution drawn up in 1787 and subsequently amended a mere twenty-seven times. All constitutions affect the distribution of power within a state and the US Constitution is no exception. So it is essential to be familiar with the Constitution itself in order to understand how political power is formally arranged.

The formal constitutional arrangements begin, but do not end, with the words of the Constitution. The Supreme Court has over the years elaborated on the general phrases in the Constitution to establish detailed rules, especially where such elastic concepts as 'interstate commerce', 'general welfare', 'equal protection', and 'due process' are concerned. Despite the minimal number of amendments, *in effect* the Constitution has been amended throughout the Republic's history, providing an astonishingly flexible instrument to deal with changing problems and changing values.

The Constitution may be flexible, but, as will be seen in Chapter 8, it flexes within limitations. Those limitations are essentially ideological (a respected Constitution should not be repeatedly altered) and political (the process by which new majorities on the Supreme Court emerge reflect major shifts in political forces). However, the process by which the Constitution adjusts to the exigencies of the times depends upon membership of the Supreme Court, men and women who appear to have no democratic legitimacy. It is also important to remember that it failed to manage the crises that resulted in the Civil War.

This is an issue which will be picked up again elsewhere in this book. For now, the point that needs to be made is this: the Constitution may have been democratic for its age but it was clearly based on the two potentially conflicting ideals of popular accountability and limited government. To ensure the latter, the constitutional system is full of checks and balances. The federal principle (the division of sovereign powers), the separation of powers, and the supremacy of law, especially where individual rights are concerned, were designed expressly to prevent governments from acting without very substantial and broad support. In this way, liberty was to be protected against the potential threat of unconstrained governments.

There is one final observation of great significance that needs to be made. The consequence of federalism is fifty-one separate governments; the consequence of the separation of powers, mirrored in the individual states, is three areas of government independent of each other but all playing some part in public policy-making; the consequence of seeking 'a government of laws, not of men' is both to enhance the importance of lawyers and to provide further opportunities for disappointed people to challenge the actions of government and their agents. Put these together and the end product is a political system with multiple points of access. An individual or group can initiate, or obstruct, public policy in many political arenas.

The opportunity to participate in politics in the United States is unparalleled. A highly educated and on average well-resourced population can make use of such opportunities. In many ways this is highly democratic. But, as will be shown, those opportunities are not equally distributed, and some people benefit from the constitutional system at the expense of others. So open a system can also be inefficient and ineffective, because governments lack the power and the legitimacy to drive through unpopular policies in the national interest.

This leaves a final and troubling problem. If somebody flew in from Mars and asked to be taken to the government, it would be hard to know what to do. Fifty-one state governments exercising some sovereignty through institutions bestowing *some* democratic legitimacy to many people operate very actively alongside a national government in which both a president and the members of Congress enjoy the legitimacy derived from popular election. The fascination of studying American politics lies in two fundamental questions. The normative question asks where legitimacy should ultimately lie: in the states, the White House, the Congress, the Supreme Court as guardians of the Constitution as 'the Supreme Law'? The empirical question asks where power actually lies within the political system. The answer to that difficult, and fascinating, problem shifts over time and dominates the rest of the chapters in this book.

But, in answering that empirical question, it is rare indeed that some reference to the Constitution is not made and some constitutional issue does not arise. In that sense, the American political system is surely exceptional.

QUESTIONS

1   What did the Founding Fathers think were the major problems the Constitution had to deal with?

2   How much does the Constitution owe to the Virginian delegation?

3   What historical analogies and theoretical ideas did the Founding Fathers bring to Philadelphia?

4   Why did so many Americans disapprove of the Constitution?

5   Why are there so few formal amendments to the Constitution?

6   Is there an irresolvable conflict between popular accountability and a belief in constitutionally protected individual rights?

7   What part does the Constitution play in the construction of the American ideal?

8   Are there too many checks and balances in the Constitution for the twenty-first century?

9   The American political system is characterized by multiple points of access. How does the Constitution contribute to this?

FURTHER READING

The Constitution of the United States. The essential starting point is to read, and become familiar with, the Constitution itself and its twenty-seven amendments.

C. Drinker Bowen (1986), *Miracle at Philadelphia* (Boston: Little, Brown). A very good popular account of the Constitutional Convention.

M. Farrand (ed.) (1937), *The Records of the Federal Convention of 1787* (New Haven, Conn.: Yale University Press). The best collection of primary material on the Convention.

A. Grimes (1978), *Democracy and the Amendments to the Constitution* (Lexington, Mass.: D. C. Heath). A useful book on amending the Constitution.

R. Hodder-Williams (1996), 'A new Constitution?' in R. Maidment (ed.), *The United States in the 20th Century: Democracy* (London: Hodder & Stoughton for the Open University). Summarizes recent debates about the contemporary appropriateness of the Constitution.

F. McDonald (1958), *We, the People* (Chicago: University of Chicago Press). A more academic study of the Convention.

James Madison, Alexander Hamilton, and John Jay published as *The Federalist Papers* (in many editions). A brilliant contemporary analysis of the arguments in favour of the Constitution.

H. Storing (1985), *The Abridged Anti-Federalist* (Chicago: University of Chicago Press). The arguments of the Anti-federalists are well presented here.

C. Vose (1972), *Constitutional Change: Amendment Politics and Supreme Court Litigation since 1900* (Lexington, Mass.: D. C. Heath). A good guide to amendment politics.

WEB LINKS

www.lcweb2.loc.gov/const/fed/fedpapers.html The Federalist Papers

www.santacruz.k12.ca.us/vft/constitution.html US Constitution, *The Federalist*, historical speeches

www.findlaw.com/11stategov/indexconst.htm A useful source on all federal and state laws

www.iwc.com/entropy/marks/stcon.html State constitutions

www.ncsl.org/statfed/afipolicy.htm National Conference of State Legislators (materials on how federal policies affect the states)

http://press-pubs.uchicago.edn/founders *The Founders' Constitution* (eds. Philip B. Kurland and Ralph Lerner)

www.voxpop.org: 80/jefferson Federalism debated

4 Federalism

John Francis

READER'S GUIDE

Understanding federalism is vitally important to understanding how public policy is made in the divided democracy of the United States. This chapter begins with a survey of federalism and the American constitution and the important role of the US Supreme Court as the most authoritative interpreter of federal practice. The chapter then examines major interpretations of American federalism—dual federalism, cooperative federalism, and devolutionary federalism—that have been used to described how American federalism works. These interpretations are put into the context of American politics, from the New Deal of Franklin Roosevelt during the 1930s to the 'compassionate conservatism' of George W. Bush in the early twenty-first century. The chapter concludes that the long-standing American debate between advocates of a stronger role for the federal government and advocates of locating power at the state level is driven more by the level of government which is expected to be sympathetic to a specific policy position than by formal descriptions of the exercise of appropriate constitutional authority.

Introduction

American federalism is frequently defined as state and federal governments sharing power. Consistent with this definition, but more to the core of American politics, is the description of federalism as a form of government for a people not sure whether they are one or many communities. In general, federalism is understood as the exercise of power by at least two levels of governments within the same country. In a federal system, power is divided or shared between the national government and subsidiary governments. Most federal systems devote a good deal of time to sorting out which level of government is responsible for specific policy areas. It is also common for federal systems—particularly the American one—to address regularly the extent to which a state is bound to accept a national policy it contests. Such debates over the relationship between states and the federal government preceded ratification of the American Constitution and have continued unabated ever since.

In American politics, federalism is not so much a constant as a persistently changing variable in shaping major policy debates. The ever-shifting fortunes of states' rights versus federal power have as much to do with which level of government favours or opposes a particular substantive policy as with the structure of federal institutions. From the storage of nuclear waste to the testing of reading skills in primary schools, policy advocates seek out the level of government most favourable to their cause. Proponents of nuclear waste storage who conclude that no state will be willing to accept the wastes are likely to favour placing the decision at the national level. Critics of nuclear power, on the other hand, are likely to favour granting states veto power over whether nuclear waste can be stored within their borders. American federalism is often pragmatic in practice, in the sense that strong policy preferences shape where a person or group stands on whether decision-making should be located at the state or the federal level.

Conservatives and liberals alike have exhibited both support and antipathy in respect of locating decisions at a particular governmental level. Conservative groups in the 1790s saw in national power a bulwark against popular radicalism which they feared would take hold in some states. The establishment of an initially modest, federally sponsored welfare state in the 1930s would in time shift conservative thought away from the federal government as a brake on the excesses of states. The conservative shift to advocacy of states' rights was built on a new appreciation of the states as reliable supporters of property, limiters of taxation, and, except on the east and west coasts, defenders of traditional values.

Another aspect to this pragmatic understanding of American federalism is apparent in times of national crisis. Major crises result in a reinvigorated role for the national government. American politics in times of crisis is remarkably capable of concentrating decision-making in the federal government. Notable examples include the Civil War, the Depression, and to some extent the cold war. The crisis of 11 September 2001 generated such resurgence of federal power, at least in the short term. When national crisis seems to recede, the practice of American federalism recovers its ambiguity and returns to its normal contentiousness.

Federalism is thus the stage on which major conflicts in American democracy are played out. Conflicts between democratic and liberal values, or between traditionalists and progressives, may move back and forth from federal to state levels. At the end of the nineteenth century, for example, a number of states such as Wisconsin and California had powerful progressive administrations and the federal government did not. A few years later, under Theodore Roosevelt, parts of the progressive agenda became the federal agenda. During the middle of the twentieth century, the progressive tradition became less and less associated with the states. The evocation of states' rights on issues ranging from civil rights to welfare during the middle of the twentieth century became largely a vehicle for the defence of traditionalism. More recently, innovations in environmental policy and welfare policy at the level of state government suggest that the celebration of states' rights can no longer be associated with traditionalism in all areas. The apparent conflict between democratic values—notably majoritarianism—and liberal values—notably the defence of rights for both individuals and groups—has been a major source of tension in American politics. Over the past half-century, issues of individual and group rights have shifted from the federal to the state level. Issues ranging from affirmative action to same-sex unions to the right to die have increasingly been abandoned or avoided at the federal level. Where they have found a home is at the state level, albeit in only a handful of states. Thus it is in the state–federal relationship that the debates over progressivism and traditionalism are expressed in American politics.

Key points

- The ever-shifting fortunes of states' rights versus federal power have as much to do with which level of government favours or opposes a particular substantive policy as with the structure of federal institutions.

- Federalism is the stage on which major conflicts

in American democracy are played out. Conflicts between democratic and liberal values, or between traditionalists and progressives, may move back and forth from federal to state levels.

- Major crises such as war or economic depression reinvigorate the role of the national government in the American federal system.

The shaping of federal institutions

As Richard Hodder-Williams noted in the previous chapter, the US Constitution is not, as constitutions go, very long. It prescribes what government is *not* to do in more detail than it prescribes what it is to do, particularly with respect to the responsibilities of the national government and the states. Nonetheless, the Constitution is a framework for national government and therefore very different from its predecessor, the Articles of Confederation. The Articles, the American colonies' first effort at forming a nation, relied on voluntary cooperation among the confederated states to realize the purposes of the United States. From the perspective of the states, the primary purpose of the Confederation was to preserve the autonomy of each of the member states. Ironically, under the Articles of Confederation, the very local interests that preoccupied the states contributed to the Confederation's failure. State political leaders were unable to respond to local demands to protect public lands, to free families from occupation, and to pay local constituents for past services to the nation. All these local needs required a central government that the new Constitution provided, one capable of taking independent action rather than relying on the voluntary contributions foundational to the Confederation (Dougherty 2001). But the Constitution's presumption in favour of stronger central government was not spelled out in detail, for there was little consensus over how strong the central government was to be.

The terse constitutional outline

The Constitution sets out duties that are exclusively within the sphere of the federal government. The federal government was, from the outset, a government of enumerated powers. Article I, section 8, provides that Congress shall have the power to levy and collect taxes, to pay debts, and to provide for the common defence and general welfare, among other powers. Section 8 concludes by giving Congress the power to make all laws that are 'necessary and proper' to execute these enumerated constitutional powers. Some interpret the necessary and proper clause as an open invitation to expand federal power, while others view it as a constraint on the limits of federal power. The same divided reading is apparent in interpretations of the Article VI provisions that the Constitution and federal law are the supreme law of the land and that when the federal government assumes responsibility for an area under state law, it pre-empts existing state statutes. Federal law controls, but there are limits to federal laws, for Congress is itself constrained to the limits of the enumerated powers of the federal government.

Even in these enumerations of federal power, much is left open. For example, how inclusive is the 'general welfare' and how does it embrace the states? How does this congressional power comport with the police powers of the states? To take an example of national power, it is quite clear that the federal government has exclusive responsibility to conduct foreign policy and to provide for the national defence. Yet many states keep trade offices abroad and presumably seek to capture the interests of foreign powers and their firms, in a modest exercise of foreign policy. Admittedly, the efforts of American states do not hold a candle to the overseas offices of some Canadian provinces, but they are efforts nonetheless. In some areas, the national government and the states exercise concurrent powers; both can levy taxes, for example. The role of federal concurrent power was greatly enhanced when, in 1913, the Sixteenth Amendment to the Constitution was adopted that allowed the federal government to levy an income tax. Today, this power is the foundation of federal fund transfers to the states.

The Supreme Court and Congress

The third branch of the federal government, the Supreme Court, has become the most powerful interpreter of what the Constitution means. This judicial role resonates with that of the Constitutional Courts in other federal systems such as Germany and Canada. The American Supreme Court came to assume the role of arbiter in the first decades of the new federal republic under the leadership of Chief Justice John Marshall. In deciding *McCullogh* v. *Maryland* in 1819, Marshall skilfully established for the Court the power to determine whether an act of Congress violates the Constitution. The Court upheld the power of Congress to establish a national bank, even though the power to establish a bank is not enumerated in the Constitution. The Court ruled that Article I's necessary and proper clause allowed Congress considerable latitude in crafting policy, as long as the end was constitutionally legitimate. The State of Maryland could not tax the bank, for the power to destroy implicit in taxation would place the state above the federal government. In *McCullogh*, Marshall wove the necessary and proper clause together with the supremacy clause. The power to interpret the Constitution has undoubtedly contributed in a number of eras to the expansion of federal power, but at other times, and certainly more recently, it has effectively protected the states from federal intervention.

Clearly the Supreme Court matters, but the agenda for federal action has more often than not been set by Congress. In the last seven decades, congressional action has been a major force in shaping federal-state relations. The congressional role is particularly apparent in how both Congress and the Supreme Court have celebrated the 'Commerce Clause'. Under the Clause, Congress, as described earlier, is given the power to regulate commerce with foreign nations, among the several states, and with Indian tribes. Although brief, the Commerce Clause is large in consequence, for it is the foundation of the national market that shapes the American economy. The power to eliminate all barriers to trade clearly has modern resonance in the European Union's long-term project to create a Europe-wide market. It is a useful contrast to point out that in some areas the American states can regulate in ways now denied EU member states. A striking example is professional licensure. To practise law in a specific state within the United States requires permission of that state. In the European Union, certification to practise in one member nation is certification to practise in all member nations. Regulation of the professions raises a question that regularly goes to the Supreme Court: what may be reasonably included in the ambit of interstate commerce? Obviously, air transport is included. But (as Chapter 19 explains) the Supreme Court has decided that congressional control over commerce does not extend to banning firearms near schools. Congress has never acted to regulate the legal profession, and the Court has not had to rule on whether such regulation would lie within interstate commerce.

Box 4.1 Constitutional influences

I: the Supreme Court and the shifting fortunes of federal power—selected decisions

McCullogh v. Maryland (1819) held that the states could not tax a federal bank created by Congress, because the power to tax was the power to destroy. The decision read the 'necessary and proper' clause as sufficiently elastic to go beyond the enumerated powers found in Article I.

Dred Scott v. Sanford (1857) held that states could confer state citizenship on people living within a specific state, but could not make a resident of the state a citizen of the United States. As a consequence, blacks were excluded from federal citizenship. States which did not recognize slavery were nonetheless bound to return those held as slaves in other states to their owners. This decision helped to precipitate the Civil War.

Brown v. Board of Education of Topeka, Kansas (1954) struck down the educational policy of 'separate but equal' school systems, segregated by race, found in a number of southern states. *Brown* employed the equal protection clause of the Fourteenth Amendment to conclude that separate schools could not be equal.

Garcia v. San Antonio Metropolitan Transit Authority (1985) held that general federal legislation, such as the Fair Labor Standards Act, was applicable to state governments. The decision suggested that the Tenth Amendment has little practical impact on generally applicable federal legislation. *Garcia* has been weakened by later Supreme Court decisions.

United States v. Lopez (1995) ruled that congressional authority under the Commerce Clause did not extend to regulate the possession of firearms in a school zone.

Printz v. US (1997) struck down the background check provisions of the 'Brady Handgun Protection Act', signalling judicial retrenchment of Congress's power to regulate interstate commerce.

Alden v. Maine (1999) held that sovereign immunity protected states from congressional action authorizing suits against state governments in state court. The specific issue was whether the federal Age Discrimination in Employment Act authorized suits by state employees against state governments. *Alden* affirmed a recent, earlier decision that Congress could not abrogate the sovereign immunity of states against suits in federal courts. The Court held that the Eleventh Amendment was designed to reaffirm the original constitutional aim of protecting the sovereign immunity of the states.

In a number of amendments to the Constitution, federalism has been revisited and reconsidered. The Eleventh Amendment protects the states from lawsuits brought against one state by citizens of another state or a foreign state. This amendment has gained increased attention in recent years, with Supreme Court decisions that strengthen the sovereign immunity of states from suits both in state and in federal courts. Most famously, the Tenth Amendment to the Constitution grants states all non-enumerated powers—that is, all powers not granted to the federal government. The Tenth Amendment sought to clarify the allocation of power between the states and the federal government by providing that the powers not assigned to the national government and not forbidden to the states are reserved to the states or to the people. But this provision, too, is subject to interpretive dispute. Are the powers delegated to be interpreted in a narrowly restricted fashion or more broadly? Different states at different times have challenged the authority of federal legislation and federal court decisions. In the early days of the Republic, Jefferson and Madison believed that states could nullify acts of Congress that the state(s) regarded as unconstitutional. A similar position was held by Wisconsin before the Civil War, when it declined to honour a federal requirement to return fugitive slaves. During the civil rights movement of the 1960s, some southern states attempted unsuccessfully to revive the nullification argument to resist equal treatment of black citizens. Nullification has local appeal even today, nearly a century and half after the Civil War, but numerous Supreme Court decisions have eliminated it as a viable political option.

The outcome of the Civil War, 1861–5, settled the issue that a state could not leave the Union. It also extended the protections of the Constitution to citizens residing within the states by adoption of three amendments right after the war's end, the Thirteenth, Fourteenth, and Fifteenth Amendments. The Amendment which has had the greatest impact on federal–state relations is the Fourteenth, which declares that all persons born or naturalized in the United States are citizens of the United States and of the states wherein they reside. The Fourteenth Amendment reversed the 1857 *Dred Scott* decision, which effectively denied citizenship to blacks. Section 2 of the Fourteenth Amendment prohibits state action that deprives persons of 'life, liberty or property' without due process of law. It continues by prohibiting state action that denies persons

Box 4.1 continued

the equal protection of the laws. This celebrated section has been applied to require strict scrutiny of categorizations based on race, and heightened scrutiny of other problematic categorizations such as gender.

In 1913 the Constitution was amended twice. The Sixteenth Amendment allowed the federal government to levy an income tax. The Seventeenth Amendment required the direct election of US senators (formerly they had been selected by their respective state legislatures). The task of sorting out the relationship between the national government and the states has been largely left to action by the president, Congress, state legislative initiatives, and ultimately to the Supreme Court in its frequent interpretations of what federalism under the Constitution means.

Key points

- The Constitution provides a framework for national government. In so doing, it is unlike its predecessor, the Articles of Confederation, which had as its primary purpose the preservation of each member state's autonomy.

- The federal government was from the outset a government of enumerated powers. But there has been long-standing debate over whether clauses in the Constitution such as the 'necessary and proper clause' in Article I, section 8, are an open invitation to expand federal power.

- Amendments to the Constitution have revisited and revised federal–state relations. The fourteenth Amendment has had great impact by prohibiting state actions that deprive persons of life, liberty, or property.

- The third branch of the federal government, the Supreme Court, has become the most powerful interpreter of what the Constitution means. The power of the Supreme Court to interpret the Constitution has undoubtedly contributed to the expansion of federal power in some eras. In other times, and certainly more recently, the Court has effectively protected the states from federal intervention.

The politics of federalism

Over the past two centuries, different groups, different industries, and, of course, different regions have shifted—sometimes dramatically—in the support or powerful antipathy they manifest towards the federal government. It has been fairly common to frame deeply controversial political issues as though they were conflicts over the location of decision-making, which is the hallmark of federal politics. Indeed, this preoccupation with where to make the decision rather than directly with the issue can be observed in contemporary debates over welfare, religious observance in public places, and nuclear waste disposal, to name but three.

Political controversy and federalism

The respective roles of national power and states' rights are deeply contested issues in the American polity. Probably the sector with the most complex position on the question is American business. Business leaders have often welcomed placing decisions such as land use, taxation, and incorporation policies at the state level. The argument for state or even local governmental control in such policy areas is that many large firms are able to negotiate tax relief and zoning variances by playing one state off against another in decisions about plant location or closure. On the other hand, firms or industries competing in national markets may object to significant variations in economic and social regulations that govern how products are made, distributed, and sold. Over the course of the twentieth century, national firms and their respective associations have been consistent supporters of national regulation, both to reduce costs associated with varying regulatory regimes and to promote standards that raise the bar to entry for new firms in sympathetic states.

The understanding of the conflict and fortunes of federalism has most shaped public consciousness at the regional level. For example, a remarkable number of ranchers and other rural residents in the mountain states, like their parents before them, hold the federal government and its environmental and land use regulations responsible for their recurring economic woes. They believe these difficulties threaten the existence of their local communities and the ways of life expressed therein. In contrast, many black communities in the American South welcomed federal civil rights legislation in the 1960s and its enforcement in their home states. Southern blacks had little expectation that states' rights would work in their interests. Federal initiatives helped them to secure the protection and resources needed to exercise their rights of citizenship. Indeed, from the 1960s on, a sea change in southern party politics took place as the Republican Party, the party of Lincoln, was abandoned by southern blacks in the favour of the Democratic Party, then judged the party of federal power. Southern whites in droves entered the Republican Party, now perceived as the party of states' rights.

Environmental groups have exhibited a good deal of strategic shifting in their assessment of the respective merits of federal and state power. As Elizabeth Bomberg details at length in Chapter 16, it is not uncommon for environmental organizations to be both critical and supportive of state and federal power at the same time. Support or opposition to an enhanced federal presence depends on the issue at hand. If the federal government is threatening to allow new drilling for oil in the Alaska wildlife refuge, wilderness advocacy groups in opposition to the drilling are committed to finding ways to block federal power in order to stop the drilling from

taking place. On the other hand, when federal regulations to raise the standard for unacceptable levels of lead in drinking water were announced by the Clinton administration and, after some debate, sustained by the Bush administration, environmental groups greeted the stiffer regulations with enthusiasm, even though they reduced the autonomy of local governments to set their own respective standards.

Given the fundamental and perpetually unresolved nature of the debate over what federalism does and should mean, it would seem reasonable to conclude that federalism is the source of much of the conflict and stalemate in American politics. Institutional ambiguity contributes to political gridlock and frustration. If the United States were to adopt a set of political institutional relations characterized by delineated responsibilities and greater clarity of constitutional expectation, so the argument goes, there would be correspondingly less conflict and frustration in American politics. But this analysis ignores the flexibility American federalism has demonstrated in dealing with a substantial number of contentious issues in American politics. The ambiguity of American federalism that seems so associated with conflict and delay may also promote the useful pragmatic approach that creates the space to deal with some of the most divisive issues that characterize American politics. Controversial issues can be construed as federal debates in locating decision-making, while decisions can be concentrated in the national government during times of crisis. To be sure, the risk of casting major policy debates as debates over where to locate decisions is the risk of delay and obfuscation. Nonetheless, the advantage to framing an issue as one of federalism is that a deeply divisive issue may be recast as a decision-making problem, not as a problem of profound social division.

The enduring debate over where to lodge—or, more to the point, where not to lodge—controversial decisions generates both opportunities and obstructions. States may resist national initiatives to assure civil rights for black Americans, as did a number of southern states during 1960s with the claim that states' rights trumped both Supreme Court decisions and federal legislation. On the other hand, some state initiatives such as Hawaii's state-wide land use planning or Oregon's right to die initiative are most unlikely to have been enacted by Congress for the nation as a whole. Thus, states may serve to promote a diversity of public policy responses to contemporary issues. A number of people and groups throughout the country will praise these state initiatives for their bold new directions, but others of course will denounce some of the state-based polices as wrongheaded. In a country the size of the United States, with its impressively diverse population, there may be a good deal of political sense in promoting a federal system that encourages controversial issues to be addressed in quite different ways by different states.

The decentralization of controversial public policy issues allows a particularly divisive national policy issue to escape being cast as a stark choice, adopted or rejected for the entire nation. If, for example, the debate over whether there should be a right to aid in dying for the terminally ill were cast as a choice available to all Americans or to none, then the debate would become even more intense than it is now in a society that is deeply divided on the moral acceptability of physician-assisted suicide. Would the spectre of national land use planning raise the same divisive concerns? For some in the United States, land use planning is a direct assault on private property. For others, it is a way to save open spaces. If decision-making is shifted to the state level, some states may opt for quite different policy responses to the issue, thus contributing to the national debate but without the high stakes of an all-or-nothing game. But there are limits to the strategy of local variation and the avoidance of a national policy, as the history of civil rights clearly demonstrates. For advocates of policy change, there is the related concern that the road to national adoption of a new policy direction is often tedious and frustratingly slow.

On the other side, the assertion of national authority in times of crisis has been a long-standing feature of American federalism. The normal politics of federalism move slowly to achieve policy consensus, but by no means always. There are significant eras where change is rapid and concentrated at the federal level. American federalism in times of crisis often demonstrates an impressive capacity to concentrate and to exercise authority at the national level. From Lincoln in the Civil War, and Franklin Roosevelt in the Great Depression, to a resurgent federal government under George W. Bush after 11 September, this capacity has been demonstrated. In the aftermath of a crisis, the federal government appears to dismantle or at least retreat from the concentrated authority it had come to exercise. But over the twentieth century, federal responsibilities expanded at every level, particularly in both economic and social regulatory areas, even though the expansion was challenged as overreaching during much of the 1980s and 1990s. There is little doubt that the federal government does a great deal. Even when President Clinton stated that the era of big government was over, the federal government continued to do a great deal. Although in some areas such as social welfare the federal government has played a reduced role with the transfer of resources to the states, in other areas such as land use the federal government has come to play a larger role, with federally owned tracts of land newly designated as national monuments.

Varieties of federalism

The importance of locating a decision where it helps to achieve a policy goal drives much of the practice of American federalism. But another dimension to understanding the shifting fortunes of states' rights and federal power is the connection to unresolved debates over whether the United States is a national community or a community of communities. Some scholars argue that what characterizes federalism in the United States is the ambivalence people have about the ends it should serve. Is the end to be served a federation of separate communities or is it a national community, federally organized? These competing ends have led to two very different understandings of what American federalism should mean.

Over the years, these two understandings have been given many names but they are best known today as dual federalism and cooperative federalism. These understandings of federalism have coexisted, often uneasily, for much of the nation's history. Dual federalism assumes two distinct and separate spheres of authority: one sphere for the states and one sphere for the national government. This duality is often described as 'layer cake' federalism. In contrast, cooperative federalism emphasizes that different levels of government exercise their separate constitutional powers collaboratively to develop and implement public policy for the nation as a whole. Often this model of cooperation is described as 'marble cake' federalism. Such pastry metaphors have long been popular in analyses of federalism.

Both layer cake and marble cake understandings of federalism have raised more questions than they have answered. The layer cake conception of responsibilities raises the obvious and fundamental question of whether two separate spheres really exist. Perhaps the energy and force of American politics and its intrusive policy consequences render sorting out what belongs in the state sphere or the national sphere an absurd exercise. Policy areas from arsenic in drinking water to medical care for the elderly seem to involve all levels of government

---

Box 4.2 Definitions: conceptions of federalism

Confederation. Federalism as a union of states, not of the people residing in the states. The United States was governed by Articles of Confederation from approximately 1781 to 1787.

Dual federalism. Federalism as two distinct and separate layers of power, one for the national government and the other for the states. This 'layer cake' understanding of federalism prevailed in theory but often not in practice from the adoption of the Constitution to the New Deal in the 1930s.

Cooperative federalism. Many programmes and policy areas from the New Deal to the present are shared between the states and the federal government. It becomes difficult, if not in some cases nearly impossible, to distinguish where one level of government leaves off and another begins. A marble cake with its swirling colours is an often-used image of cooperative federalism.

Creative federalism. During the 1960s and to some extent in the succeeding years, federal grants grew greatly and extended to local governments and to non-governmental organizations. Creative federalism embraced organizationally much more than the relationship between the federal and state governments.

New federalism. During the 1960s, 'new federalism' was the term used to describe expanded federal–state cooperation. But by the 1980s and throughout the 1990s, it became the term of choice to describe a retreat by the federal government in a number of domestic policy areas and a corresponding commitment on the part of federal authorities to respect and to enhance the discretionary powers of the states.

Devolutionary federalism. A variation on the new federalism of the past decade. It is the commitment to devolve or transfer to the states programmes that have largely been under federal direction. The argument is that the state level of government is closer to the concerns of citizens and therefore better able to address their needs. In a sense, devolutionary federalism is a return to dual federalism, but without the assumption that it is constitutionally mandated.

Box 4.3 Funding transfers from the federal government to the states

Grant in Aid. A transfer from the federal government to another level of government for a specific spending purpose. 'Grants-in-Aid' describe the range of grants described below.

Categorical grant. A grant-in-aid that specifies in some detail how the funds are to be spent. A classic example is transportation, where federal funds are designated for building highways or airports.

Formula grant. A categorical grant that transfers funds to the state according to a specific funding formula, such as the percentage of the population in poverty or population density.

Block grant. A transfer from the federal government to a state(s) for a generally stated purpose, allowing a good deal of latitude in determining how the funds are to be spent. Examples of block grants included some health services and welfare.

together. Cooperative federalism raises its own immediate challenges as to what is entailed in the cooperation between states and the national government. Perhaps its major quandary is how to engage states that do not want to cooperate with the national government in a particular policy direction. Such engagement is an ever-present problem in policy areas, from end of life decision-making to land use to nuclear waste disposal. These difficult questions challenge both dual federalism and cooperative federalism to confront the ambivalent expectations that Americans have long held about federal state relations. It is also easy to see why federalism is both a flash-point for political conflicts and the forum where political conflict is played out.

Key points

- It is fairly common in American politics to frame deeply controversial political issues as though they were conflicts over the location of decision-making rather than the content of the policies, which is the hallmark of federal politics.

- Over the course of the last century, national business leaders have favoured national regulation over state regulation as a way to reduce costs and to raise the bar to entry for new firms in sympathetic states. On the other hand, the same business leaders have often welcomed local or state control over taxes and land use in order to secure more favourable terms for the location of a branch office or factory, on the assumption that local authorities may prove to be more amenable negotiators.

- A sea change in American politics took place during the 1960s when southern blacks abandoned the Republican Party, the party of Lincoln, in favour of Democrats judged to be more disposed to using federal power to secure the rights of citizenship in the South.

Box 4.4 **Constitutional influences**
II: clauses pertinent to federalism

Article I, section 8 (the 'Commerce Clause'). 'The Congress shall have Power To lay and collect Taxes, Duties, Imposts and Excises, to pay the Debts and provide for the common Defense and general Welfare of the United States; but all Duties, Imposts and Excises shall be uniform throughout the United States;

To regulate Commerce with foreign Nations, and among the several States, and with the Indian Tribes.'

Article I, section 8 (the 'Necessary and Proper' Clause). 'To make all laws which shall be necessary and proper for carrying into Execution the foregoing Powers, and all other Powers vested by the Constitution in the Government of the United States, or in any Department or Officer thereof.'

Tenth Amendment (1791). 'All powers not delegated to the United States by the Constitution, nor prohibited by it to the States, are reserved to the States respectively, or to the people.'

Fourteenth Amendment (1864). 'All persons born or naturalized in the United States, and subject to the jurisdiction thereof, are citizens of the Unites States and the State wherein they reside. No state shall make or enforce any law which shall abridge the privileges or immunities of citizens of the United States; nor shall any state deprive any person of life, liberty, or property, without due process of law; nor deny to any person within its jurisdiction the equal protection of the laws.'

Sixteenth Amendment (1913). 'The Congress shall have power to lay and collect taxes on incomes, from whatever source derived, without apportionment among the several States, and without regard to any census or enumeration.'

Seventeenth Amendment (1913). 'The Senate of the United States shall be composed of two Senators from each State, elected by the people thereof, for six years; and each Senator shall have one vote. The electors in each State shall have the qualifications requisite for electors of the most numerous branch of the state legislatures.'

- The enduring debate over where to lodge—or, more to the point, where not to lodge—controversial decisions can shift a party's commitment to states' rights. The Democratic Clinton administration favoured allowing Oregon to permit medically assisted suicide. The Republican Bush administration has opposed right to die initiatives and sought to stop Oregon from allowing such assistance to continue.

From cooperative to devolving federalism

The twentieth century was characterized by a steady expansion of federal responsibilities, notably in social and economic regulation. Traditional federal responsibilities such as defence, monetary policy, public works, pensions, public land management, and international trade all expanded greatly—so greatly that in many areas they appeared to be transformed as many new programmes came into being. States, particularly in the final third of the century, developed a level of managerial sophistication, and provided a wide range of services that stood in sharp contrast to perceptions of their political performance earlier in the century. The understanding of what federalism meant underwent radical revision between the 1930s and the 1960s. It would change again in the 1980s and 1990s. Now, the twenty-first century may be bringing a new shift in understanding or a recovery of past approaches.

During the Great Depression of the 1930s, the federal government began to assume a much greater role in domestic affairs, ranging from welfare to economic and social regulation to federal financing of research in many areas. The federal government under President Franklin Roosevelt's New Deal expanded into areas that were traditionally the domain of state and local governments, such as care for the indigent. More to the point, perhaps, some of these areas were not undertaken by any level of government. This expansion of governmental activity in the 1930s as a response to the depressed economy intertwined various levels of government through the strategy of federal administrators providing grants-in-aid to the states. But it left to the states and local governments administration of the programmes funded by these grants. This collabor-ation between the states and the national government became known as cooperative federalism and appeared to herald the end of dual federalism.

By the 1950s cooperative federalism was well established, even with a Republican administration in office whose members were deeply sceptical about the direction that the New Deal had taken. The Eisenhower administration did not roll back the New Deal, but extended cooperative federalism by construction of the national highway system. Congress appropriated 90 per cent of the funds and set the standards for the freeway system. Construction of the roads themselves was undertaken by the states. National defence was used by Congress to justify its funding for the highway system, but its use was largely civilian.

During the 1960s, it appeared that metaphors of the layer cake and even the marble cake were melting into a large sheet cake thickly covered by an icing of federal programmes. The Democratic administration's Great Society during the 1960s trebled the number of federal grants to the states, many of which were directed to local governments and other entities. The Great Society shifted from the model of grants-in-aid to categorical grants. Categorical grants required that applicants meet specific standards as to how the funds were to be expended. Federal categorical grants that specified terms were detailed for a growing number of programmes designed to end poverty. During the 1960s it seemed that federal engagement, in seeking to solve or at least to ameliorate the condition of the disadvantaged, was bypassing state governments and going directly to localities and private organizations. Increasingly, federal pre-emption of

Box 4.5 Is America different?

Federalism as an example of American exceptionalism

American federalism clearly goes a long way towards shaping the nation's major public policy debates. It is hard not to conclude that it looks in theory and practice like no other system. Yet if one examines specific institutions of American federalism in comparison with other federal systems, there are obvious and often compelling similarities. Courts as final arbiters matter a great deal in American federalism, but they also clearly matter in Germany and Canada. American states are famously diverse in size, population, and wealth, but such diversity is true of India, Australia, and many other federal systems. Debates between the federal government and the states is rancorous and sometimes bitter in the United States, but similar debates occur in all federal systems.

Nonetheless, the case can be made that federalism in the United States is an apt example of American exceptionalism for the following reasons. The United States is now an 'old' federal system of over two centuries, guided by a Constitution that is remarkably terse in defining the boundaries between federal power and state authority. The brevity of the written word has contributed since the beginning of the republic to the courts, Congress, and the states often competing to define and redefine what federalism means or should mean. The result is a federal system constrained by an ever-expanding number of precedents yet occasionally given to bursts of radical innovation in programmes that as a result redefine state–federal relations in particular areas. Unusual though it may be, it should be noted that there was once a time when very few nations were federal. Today a growing number of countries, notably in Europe, have adopted federal institutions over the past several decades. Indeed, the European Union has some quasi-federal institutions. In the future, there will be greater opportunities for the United States to learn from federal experiments abroad.

---

sub-national programmes became a tactic of choice for federal policy-makers. Pre-emption allows the federal government to take over programmes that are failing to meet defined federal standards. By 1985, the Supreme Court in its *Garcia* decision appeared to eliminate all barriers to federal involvement in public policy. The Court suggested that the Tenth Amendment, which reserved all un-enumerated powers to the states, had little practical impact on general federal legislation. By the 1990s, subsequent decisions had much weakened the scope of *Garcia*.

Debates over fund transfers to the states had been, since the 1930s, emblematic of the controversy over the shifting balance of power between the states and the national government. During the presidency of Richard Nixon, the federal government expanded its social regulatory agenda, notably in the area of environmental policy. Indeed, the ground was laid for a larger federal presence in subsequent administrations. At the same time, the Nixon administration sought to reorganize fund transfers to the states into the form of block grants, thus enabling the states to exercise greater discretion in how to spend the transferred funds.

During the 1970s, the perception of a stagnating economy and growing social tensions seemed to connect to a politically persuasive argument that the federal government was contributing to the problems facing the nation rather to solving these problems. In 1980 Ronald Reagan was elected on the platform that the federal government was the problem at home for being too strong and the problem abroad for not being strong enough. In his inaugural address, President Reagan seemed to revive dual federalism with his statement that the federal government was the result of a compact among the states.

Key points

- An unresolved debate in discussion of American federalism is whether or not the United States is a community of communities or a national community.

- Dual federalism assumes two distinct and separate spheres of authority: one sphere for the states and one sphere for the federal government.
- Cooperative federalism emphasizes that different levels of government exercise their separate constitutional powers collaboratively to develop and to implement public policy for the nation as a whole.

- Both dual federalism and cooperative federalism have often raised more questions than they have answered. On the one hand, there are few areas where there are sharp and distinct differences between the federal sphere and the state sphere. On the other, cooperative federalism does not seem to provide a mechanism for a state to choose not to cooperate with the national government in a particular policy direction.

Reagan to Clinton, 1981–2001: devolving federalism?

In his first inaugural address, Ronald Reagan stated his understanding of what American federalism should be. Federalism, it seemed, should return to the dual federalism of old: 'All of us need to be reminded that the Federal Government did not create the States; the States created the Federal Government.' This view was contested, but it presaged a change in the nature of the relationship between the states and the national government. There was a change in the expectation that the national government would continue to expand, and to do so at the expense of the states. Fourteen years later, the critique of central power had become a mandatory mantra for Republicans and a number of leading Democrats. In January 1996, a Democratic President, Bill Clinton, in his State of the Union Address, declared that 'the era of big government' was 'over'. In the executive branch, Congress and the Supreme Court reached decisions that shifted the balance of power between the states and the national government, in some areas quite significantly. A major example—analysed in detail in Chapter 17—was the shift of welfare from a federal entitlement programme to a block grant programme for the states.

In many ways the Reagan administration evoked the language of states' rights. But its record was one of supporting pre-emption and for the most part imparting new managerial values and directions to the conduct of government rather than shifting decision-making to the states. The Reagan adminis-

tration did cut federal taxes, however, thus reducing or at least challenging the capacity of the federal government to undertake new initiatives.

Two congressional initiatives shifted power to the states from the federal government during the Clinton administration. One of the two, welfare reform, was a fundamental shift. The other initiative, a limit on unfunded mandates, was rather less important but symbolically significant: legislation designed to limit the practice of the federal government acting to impose programmes on the states without the resources to implement them. The understanding of welfare payments shifted in the mid-1990s from a federal entitlement to a limited block grant from the federal government to the states, which were given a good deal of discretion in the use of the funds.

The power to pre-empt state laws when they conflict with federal acts is impressively elastic. The steady growth of federal legislation in many areas allowed the federal government to require—that is, to establish a *mandate*—that states undertake a specific activity, such as job training for welfare beneficiaries or lead reduction in drinking water. The federal government can also undertake the obverse by stopping—that is, imposing a *restraint*—on states from undertaking certain actions. Under the Clean Water Act, for example, states may be prohibited from highway construction that endangers certain wetlands. But it was the growth in mandates that became a major issue in the early 1990s. Congressional action to expand benefits or programmes without providing additional funding had encompassed over 150 such mandates by the early 1990s. The Republicans in the 1994 election made such 'unfunded mandates' an issue. In 1995, Congress passed the Unfunded Mandates Relief Act. Under this Act, when Congress requires the states to implement new legislation that demands significant expenditures without transfers of federal funds, a separate vote must be scheduled to determine if Congress wishes to impose such an unfunded mandate on the states.

Certainly one of the most dramatic changes in federal–state relations during this period was the shift in the federal welfare programme. In 1996, Congress passed the Personal Responsibility and Work Opportunity Act. The heart of the new Act was a new direction in federal funding and in federal purpose. PROWRA was wide-ranging in the changes it brought to welfare, from searching out non-custodial parents to pay child support to the near-elimination of welfare benefits for non-citizens. The heart of PROWRA was the shift in the welfare funding assumption by replacement of Aid to Families with Dependent Children (AFDC) with Temporary Assistance for Needy Families (TANF). The old AFDC programme was funded by open-ended federal matching payments to the states. The more people added to a state's welfare roll, the greater the federal contribution. Open-ended federal funding was criticized for providing an incentive to the states to add clients to their respective welfare rolls, since their share of the costs was often less than half for each client added. Under TANF, the block grant for each state is a fixed amount, with some limited provisions for adjustment. States may not use federal funds for clients who have been on the rolls for more than five years. States which help clients leave the rolls through job training or other methods may retain the federal funds that otherwise would have been spent on welfare benefits. Expectations for the states are clear. States over time are expected to see half of the clients on their rolls working at least thirty hours a week, or to reduce the numbers on their rolls. If neither the rolls are reduced nor more clients work, the state runs the risk of a reduction in the size of its block grant. From the mid-1990s until 2001, nearly all states saw a decline in the numbers of residents on welfare. In some states, the decline was massive. Several explanations have been offered for the fall in the numbers. Perhaps the most persuasive explanation is the sustained growth in the economy during the 1990s, but the changes in the rules governing federal fund transfers to the states should not be discounted. The capping of federal fund transfers meant that states would not gain additional funds by adding additional recipients.

It is clear that states are now participating in a new welfare regime. The new regime does not see welfare as an entitlement, but categorizes welfare payments as short-term funds to help individuals and families during times of economic dislocation. Welfare benefits, under the present model, are designed to bridge periods between jobs. Indeed, states are expected to offer job training programmes in conjunction with welfare benefits. These programmes are designed to help clients to reintegrate or to integrate into the workforce. If states do not offer, or if they greatly reduce, their job training programmes, they run the risk of having their federal funding reduced. It remains to be seen if during a protracted economic downturn the national government will add new funding or re-establish welfare as an entitlement.

It should be recognized that welfare in federal–state relations may be closer in image to President Clinton's observation that the era of big government is over. The consequence of capping funding for welfare recipients is a smaller national welfare state. But it is also apparent that federal funding to the states for welfare benefits does still come with clear federal guidelines. The states may vary a great deal in the level of attention they give to training beneficiaries to return to the workplace, but train they must if they wish to receive federal funding. A shift in values is not the same thing as a shift in power from the federal government to the states.

Key points

- During the 1960s, many federal programmes bypassed state governments by going directly to localities and private organizations. The federal government pre-empted state programmes that did not meet federal standards.

- During the 1970s, the perception of a stagnating economy and growing social tensions contributed to an increasingly popular view among voters that the federal government was contributing to the nation's problems, not resolving them.

- The Unfunded Mandates Relief Act of 1995 prevented Congress from requiring states to implement legislation that required new funds without the transfer of federal funds to pay for the new programmes. The Act was a signal that federal power appeared to be in retreat.

- In 1996, President Clinton stated that the era of big government was over. His support for a major overhaul of the nation's welfare system seemed to support a federal retreat from social programmes.

The Bush era: a resurgent federal government?

George W. Bush came into office as the son of a former president, with very wide-ranging connections to a set of former officials who had served his father eight years earlier. His administration boasts considerable sophistication about how the national government works. Yet President Bush stressed in his campaign his scepticism about Washington and the federal government, and celebrated both private initiatives and the role of the states. He drew attention to his tenure as governor of Texas to portray what could be accomplished on the state level. The centrepiece of his campaign as the Republican candidate for the presidency was a major reduction in taxes, partially justified on the grounds that the federal government should have fewer funds to spend and, correspondingly, the individual citizen should have more.

True to his platform, President Bush was able to gain congressional support for his substantial tax cut. Although this commitment to reduce taxes was certainly the centrepiece of his programme, it was by no means the only commitment for his presidency. Two other areas have also been paramount. Education reform is an important part of President Bush's programme, particularly the establishment of a federal commitment to improve writing and mathematical skills for elementary school students. The new federal initiative in elementary education is a major expansion of federal power and federal standards in an area traditionally thought to be the preserve of local, let alone state,

governments. Second, a more general commitment to the socially conservative wing of the Republican Party was to deploy federal power in defence of moral issues such as opposition to abortion or to physician-assisted suicide. Oregon's right to die initiative, Measure 16, has been a central target of this commitment. The working assumption is that important moral values should be woven into the national legal framework, not subject to the moral predisposition of individual state choice.

The terrorist attacks of 11 September changed the president's agenda. The attacks inaugurated a time of crisis, when federal authority achieved a prominence that has come to characterize federal government activity in other times of crisis. But this time of crisis should not obscure the fact that in other policy areas the Bush administration had clearly advanced an enhanced role for the federal government *before* the events of 11 September. The two policies just mentioned, education and moral commitment, have generated significant controversy. Both illustrate the pragmatic nature of American federalism: even when rhetoric is sceptical of federal decision-making, the practice may be to enhance the federal role.

In 1994 and again in 1997, Oregon voters approved the Death With Dignity Act—a law permitting physician-assisted suicide. The Act permits a terminally ill patient to request a prescription for lethal medication that must be self-administered by the patient, if two doctors clearly conclude that the patient has less than six months to live. Between

Box 4.6 **Core academic debate**
Federalism

The core of the academic debate over federalism is sometimes understood as a division of powers question: which responsibilities rest with the sub-national and which governing tasks are to be assumed by the national government? It is a debate that is never resolved, in large measure because what governments do and how they do it is subject to change, often of fundamental dimensions. The more compelling dimension to the debate over federalism is whether to have a federal system at all—that is, two levels of government formally sharing power. The formal lodging of authority at a sub-national level requires, at least in some policy areas, that the federal government secure the consent of the state(s) or recognize that the state may adopt policies that counter those adopted by the federal government. Federal systems constitutionally recognize that where you live within a nation's borders prevails in the making of public policy. Federal divisions can and often do win out politically over other social and economic divisions, such as religion, race, ethnicity, or economic status.

The appeal of federalism as a way to organize exercise of political power is probably greater today in the United States than it has been for past generations. The Depression, the cold war, and the civil rights movement offered compelling economic, national security, and moral arguments for viewing the federal government as a driving force in American politics, with the state acting more as either an intermediary or as a roadblock to change. But in recent decades scepticism has grown over both the achievement and what should be the future direction of the federal programme. States have typically seemed 'closer' to the people than has the federal government. States seem more likely in recent years to undertake different approaches to a number of public policy questions. Some states demographically are much more diverse than others, suggesting that responses to diversity at state level may provide instructive guidance for a changing nation. The shift to the states is evident in the debate over federalism, but that provides little practical guidance as to what the federal or state governments should do.

1999, when the law went into effect, and 2001, some seventy people had actually taken the overdose. Oregon stands alone in shielding physicians from criminal or civil liability for dispensing controlled substances with the explicit aim of ending a patient's life, under terms of the law. In its 1997 decision in *Washington* v. *Glucksberg*, the Supreme Court concluded unanimously that there is no federally protected constitutional right to aid in dying. At the same time, in a panoply of concurring opinions, the justices left a variety of strategies open to the states for dealing with aid in dying.

Under the power to regulate interstate commerce, the federal government regulates certain drugs through the Controlled Substances Act. The supremacy clause holds that when state laws contradict federal laws, federal laws prevail. Opponents of the Oregon law were unable to persuade Oregon voters to defeat physician aid in dying, nor was the initiative struck down by the federal courts. In 1998 Janet Reno, Attorney-General in the Democratic

Clinton administration, saw no evidence that Congress in the Controlled Substances Act had intended to displace the states as the primary regulators of the medical profession. In November of 2001, however, John Ashcroft, the Republican Attorney-General in the George W. Bush administration, issued an order that the Oregon law violated the Federal Controlled Substance Act (CSA). In April 2002, United States District Judge Robert Jones ruled that Congress had not made explicit in the CSA any intent to regulate the practice of medicine, and that without such explicit indication the statute could not be read to displace such an area of traditional state power. The debate over the Oregon initiative since 1994 has continued unabated but has to some extent now shifted to a debate about federalism: where public policy decisions are to be located. Assisted suicide is now framed as a debate over who gets to make the decision on whether it is to be permitted: the national government or the state of Oregon. Even opponents of the law in Oregon objected to federal intervention in the announced public policy of their state.

Traditionally, primary and secondary education has been the responsibility of local governments, while state universities and colleges have been within the ambit of a state's responsibility. There has been a role for the federal government in education, including setting aside public lands to support public education and establishing land grants for state universities that would provide education for farming communities throughout the nation. During recent decades, American secondary education has come under criticism for what were judged as limited successes in preparing students for future education and ultimately the workforce, notably in the areas of mathematics and verbal skills. The federal role in primary and secondary education has in large measure been one of providing grants and data analysis. The Federal Department of Education's modest portfolio hardly compares to a European ministry of education. Nonetheless, the department has still been the subject of serious political challenge for over two decades, as reflected in the Republican Party platform in 1980 that called for the abolition of the department.

In 2000, the Republican Party presidential candidate, George W. Bush, advocated a stronger role for the federal government in making sure that all the nation's schoolchildren achieve academic proficiency within the coming decade. As president, Bush proposed that states where students were not making adequate yearly progress would risk losing federal education funds. The president's initial proposal requires states to test students in maths and reading every year in grades three to eight. The proposal is entitled 'No Child Left Behind', a title chosen to emphasize that the expectation for improved performance extends to all racial and ethnic minorities as well as to the economically disadvantaged. The president's commitment to establishing a strong federal presence in educational achievement was reinforced in the first nine months of his presidency by frequent trips around the country to muster support for the plan. Indeed, on 11 September, the day of the terrorist attack, the president was reading to students in a Florida elementary school.

Critics of the president's educational standards plan raised challenges within his own party. Republican governors, concerned that diverse students within their respective states raised problems for performance standards, lobbied successfully to loosen the requirement that all students reach proficiency. The challenge for the administration remains the extent to which the states are to be held to federal assessment standards or be given much more latitude to provide their own standards and assessment methods. Other critics who thought the president's proposals do not go far enough have pressed for additional funds to provide tutors to help disadvantaged students meet the proposed standards in mathematics and reading.

The bill passed by Congress in December of 2001 and signed into law by President Bush on 8 January 2002 contains at its core the substance of the president's proposals. The new law requires annual testing in reading and maths during grades three to eight. States are expected to narrow the gaps in test performance between poor and wealthy students. If scores for low-income students do not improve, they may receive tutoring or transportation to another school. Schools districts can use federal teacher quality funds for hiring or training teachers. Some funds are set aside for experimental approaches to improved maths and reading performance. Public report cards are issued for each school, rating the students' test performance.

It is clear that the federal role in education will be substantial, with the acceptance of what are likely to turn out in practice to be quite precise categorical grants rather than block grants. Education is just one example of how policy commitment drives where policy decision-making is to be placed, rather than a general commitment to states' rights. If the policy objective is the improvement in maths and writing skills of the nation's students, then even an administration committed to states' rights will centralize educational standards at the national level rather than keeping educational autonomy at the state and local level. The importance of achieving a particular policy objective, even at the expense of states' rights, is not only found in the Education Act but is also apparent in the Bush administration's attempt to halt the use of federally regulated drugs under Oregon's physician-assisted suicide law. Both issues reflect the importance of values and policies in driving the practice of federalism. The commitment to national power or its alternative of granting greater autonomy to the states has much less to do with overarching commitment to a particular conception of federalism and much more to do with the depth of commitment to a specific policy objective.

Key points

- George W. Bush was critical of federal power during the 2000 presidential election campaign, although he campaigned for and signed into law

in January 2002 a greatly expanded role for the federal government in the American educational system, historically a local and state responsibility.

- The aftermath of the terrorist attacks in New York and Washington, DC, brought forth major new federal initiatives in domestic security and in rebuilding lower Manhattan. New federal initiatives have ranged from subsidies for farming to relief for the unemployed. These programmes confirm that in times of crisis the expectation of federal leadership has not diminished.

Conclusion

Federalism is an enduring feature of American politics. Equally enduring is the fact that American federalism is characterized by conflict and change. The understanding of federal–state relations is different from what it was a generation ago. It is also different from what it was before the terrorist attacks of 11 September 2001. It is not surprising that change and conflict characterize American federalism, for it is continuously shaped by the courts, acts of Congress, the presidency, and of course the states themselves.

Over the past century, as expectations for government have expanded and shifted, the qualifying adjectives for federalism have proliferated, from dual to creative to new and new once again. But these are just a few of the ways in which federalism is described. The proliferation of names reflects the unresolved debate in American politics over what federalism is expected to accomplish. Is American federalism a means for a national government or is it how states cooperate to form a union?

It is in this unending debate that the other core debates of American politics are played out. The search for progressive or traditional policies, the defence of group rights, or the protection of individual rights, shifts from the states to the federal government, and shifts again. These shifts certainly invigorate the debate, although there is a risk that arguments on behalf of the states or federal government can be more rhetorical than substantive. The question of expectations of federalism is not answered in large measure because to answer it might rigidify the nation's federal system to such an extent that its capacity to accommodate divisive policy debates or to respond to major crises could be constrained. American federalism in practice has been pragmatic, particularly during the past seventy years, when time and again its very ambiguity has accommodated a remarkable number of quite distinct policy regimes and exhibited in times of crises a formidable ability to concentrate and project power.

QUESTIONS

1   Critically assess the benefits and costs of federal arrangements for American democracy.

2   Why, and in what ways, has federalism altered since the early years of the twentieth century?

3 To what extent would the Founding Fathers recognize the type of federalism that currently exists in the United States?

4 Is the federal government excessively or insufficiently powerful in regard to state governments?

5 'The reality of American federalism bears little resemblance to the constitutional description of federal and state powers and responsibilities.' Discuss.

FURTHER READING

A. Brinkley, N. Polsby, and K. Sullivan (1997), *New Federalist Papers: Essays in Defense of the Constitution* (New York: Twentieth Century Fund). Nineteen short and provocative essays on American democracy, most providing a robust defence of the federal and separated system and its public policy results.

D. Elazar (1984), *American Federalism: A View from the States*, 3rd edn. (New York: Harper & Row). Provides a comprehensive analysis of the relationship between the federal government and the fifty state governments.

J. Freedland (1999), *Bring Home the Revolution: The Case for a British Republic* (London: Fourth Estate). A British journalist's overview of the differences between America and the UK on a range of policies, arguing strongly in favour of America's decentralized governing arrangements.

J. F. Zimmerman (1992), *Contemporary American Federalism* (New York: Praeger). A lucid and readable account of national–state relations and recent changes in them.

WEB LINKS

www.fedworld.gov FED World

www.bea.doc.gov Bureau of Economic Analysis

www.census.gov Bureau of the Census

www.ssa.gov Social Security Administration

www.hcfa.gov Explanations of Medicare and Medicaid

www.law.vill.edu/Fed-Agency/fedwebloc.html Federal government

www.npr.gov National Performance Review 'reinventing government' programme)

www.law.cornell.edu/uscode US legal code

5 Political parties and the party system

Robert Mason

READER'S GUIDE

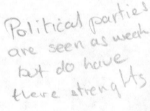

Political parties are seen as weak but do have there strenghts

This chapter outlines the nature of the American party system and the roles of parties in US politics. American political parties are distinctive in a number of significant ways from their counterparts in other democracies. They usually play a smaller role both in campaigning and in governing, and they are relatively weak as organizations. By contrast, individual politicians and their personal organizations are more central to politics in the United States than elsewhere. It is for these reasons that observers generally view American parties as weak, and this weakness has absorbed a great deal of attention from scholars who have studied the party system. Many believe that growing weakness is its key characteristic over the past thirty or forty years. Paradoxically, in other respects the parties also exhibit significant strength. In particular, the Republican and Democratic Parties together succeed in completely dominating American politics to the virtual exclusion of any rival. As well as examining the nature of their weakness, the chapter therefore investigates the reasons for the success and durability of the two-party system in the United States.

Introduction

The roles played by political parties are of critical importance in a democracy. The parties are the principal link between the public at large and office-holding and office-seeking politicians, aggregating the policy preferences of the people. The diversity of the United States and the fractured nature of its system of government makes the role of parties especially important.

There is an urgent need of a cohesive force within its politics.

On the one hand, parties act as a unifying force within the nation's divided democracy, creating connections between politicians in different branches of government, and seeking common ground between voters of vastly different socio-economic, cultural, religious, and racial backgrounds. Institutionally, then, the role of parties is to heal: to promote governmental coherence and to encourage intra-party consensus. On the other hand, parties animate the contentious debates at the heart of politics in the divided democracy. Ideologically, their role is to aggravate: to shape inter-party conflict and to give voice to the signifi-cant differences among Americans on issues of public policy.

But parties are often unsuccessful in performing these roles of seminal significance to American politics. Many see the party system as ineffective. This is because they are often weak by comparison with their counterparts in other Western nations—both as campaigning organizations and as associ-ations of like-minded politicians. But the precise extent of their weakness and its roots are the source of disagreement among observers of American politics. This chapter begins by examining the functions of political parties in the United States, investigating both their strengths and their perceived inadequacies.

The roles of political parties in American politics

Many scholars have employed a tripartite con-ceptualization of the role played by parties in American politics, following the classic work of V. O. Key (1942). This approach involves a consider-ation of the party as a collection of elected officials in government, the party as an organization of like-minded citizens who engage in political activity, and the party as a broad coalition of voters who usually lend it their support at the polls. The view of parties employed here differs from Key's formulation in considering separately the 'party in the electorate', which normally does not undertake active engage-ment in politics beyond voting. The following discussion looks at the functions of political parties both during campaigns and in government, as well as at the continuing organizational existence of parties beyond their direct connection with these aspects of politics.

Parties in campaigns

Electorally, parties play a significant role in pro-viding a label under which most candidates run when seeking major office. Even though the two parties are broad coalitions that encompass poli-ticians of many different views, the party labels nevertheless remain meaningful to most voters in providing general information about a candidate's broad approach to policy-making. At the start of the twenty-first century, it is reasonable to assume that a Republican candidate supports more con-servative policies overall than a Democrat. It was common to observe in 2000 that little of sub-stance separated presidential candidates George W. Bush and Al Gore. Yet the party platforms on which they stood included stark differences; so did their rhetoric. Party matters as a general indicator to voters of a politician's beliefs. In cases where the interests of business and environ-mentalism came into conflict, for example, Bush was more likely than Gore to support business. Similarly, if a choice emerged between a tax cut and an increase in federal spending, Bush was more likely than his opponent to prefer a reduction in taxation.

Yet differences in the detail of policy are decided by individual politicians. Although the party con-vention agrees a platform for the presidency every four years, there is no overall party programme which candidates are required to adopt. Candidates have much freedom to develop their own pro-grammatic identities, thus fostering an ideological looseness within the party overall.

Still, it is in large part because party labels carry meaning that many candidates choose to conduct an a-partisan campaign. They often downplay or even ignore their party affiliation, in order to win over voters who usually prefer their opponent's party, as well as voters who are suspicious of parties altogether. Instead of party attachment, candidates emphasize personal qualifications for office and concern for their constituency's needs. To a surprising extent, therefore, parties may not be visible in a campaign.

Yet another aspect of electoral politics provides an additional example of the parties' weakness. Leaders and key activists frequently do not control the selection of their party's candidate for elected office. Instead, aspirants compete for the nomination in a primary election, in which party supporters are responsible for the choice. The system of primary elections dates from the Progressive era at the turn of the twentieth century, when it was embraced by reformers who explicitly aimed to undermine the influence of party leaders, often fairly seen as having a corrupting effect on politics.

It is, however, possible to exaggerate the extent to which leading figures within the parties are excluded from the process of candidate selection. Many politicians become serious contenders for office because their peers within the party consider them to have promise. It is not improbable to suggest that, entirely in the absence of primary elections, both Gore and Bush would still have won the presidential nomination of their respective party if the choice had been in the hands of party leaders. Nevertheless, the parties enjoy no more than indirect influence over the choice of candidates, and not direct control.

Parties in Congress

As John Owens explains in Chapter 10, the parties are responsible for the organization of Congress, as well as that of many other legislative bodies at lower levels of the federal system. The party with a majority in the Senate or the House of Representatives controls its business, appointing the chairs of congressional committees and setting the legislative agenda—the source of considerable influence over the policy-making process. Its significance was vividly demonstrated when in 2001 Senator Jim Jeffords of Vermont left the Republican Party, throwing control of an almost exactly balanced Senate to the Democrats. The political direction of the body was entirely transformed.

But there are limits to the power of parties in Congress. Whenever it seems appropriate, members of Congress emphasize the needs of their own constituency above party loyalty. To secure such loyalty, Congressional leaders have relatively few rewards to offer or punishments to impose. As a result, party discipline is notably poor. The behaviour of the parties in Congress thus offers weighty support to the thesis that American parties are weak.

Historically, a significant example of the incoherence of parties in Congress was the 'conservative coalition', which emerged in response to the New Deal of the 1930s and which remained visible in important roll-calls until the 1990s. The conservative coalition included conservative Democrats, usually from the South, and Republicans. Although the Democratic Party controlled Congress for much of this period, many of the liberal policies favoured by its non-Southern wing failed to secure enactment because of opposition from the conservative coalition.

The ideological coherence of the parties has increased in recent decades, however. Table 5.1 documents its increase. The change has taken place in large part because conservative Democrats from the South were gradually replaced in Congress by Republicans. The conservative coalition across the parties largely disappeared. A more temporary source of ideological coherence arrived with the 'Republican revolution' of 1994, when Republicans gained control of both houses for the first time in four decades. In the House of Representatives, speaker Newt Gingrich made a determined effort to impose party loyalty in order to secure the measures that made up his 'Contract with America'. Gingrich succeeded for a time in mobilizing House Republicans behind his leadership, achieving unusual levels of party discipline. But the initiatives of the Contract foundered in the Senate; before long, Gingrich's leadership did so, too. Altogether, party coherence was higher in the 1990s than in previous decades; the average annual score of congressional

Table 5.1 Party unity in Congress, 1964–99

The table shows the average level of party unity in Congressional votes—both in the House of Representatives and the Senate—that divided the parties. It should be noted that many votes do not take place along party lines. In 1999, for example, 47 per cent of House votes and 63 per cent of Senate votes divided the parties.

Year	Reps (%)	Dems (%)	Year	Reps (%)	Dems (%)	Year	Reps (%)	Dems (%)
1964	69	67	1976	66	65	1988	73	79
1965	70	69	1977	70	67	1989	73	81
1966	67	61	1978	67	64	1990	74	81
1967	71	66	1979	72	69	1991	78	81
1968	63	57	1980	70	68	1992	79	79
1968	62	62	1981	76	69	1993	84	85
1970	59	57	1982	71	72	1994	83	85
1971	66	62	1983	74	76	1995	91	80
1972	64	57	1984	72	74	1996	87	80
1973	68	68	1985	75	79	1997	88	82
1974	62	63	1986	71	78	1998	86	83
1975	70	69	1987	74	81	1999	86	84

Source: Congressional Quarterly 1999 Almanac (Washington, DC: CQ, 2000), B-18–19.

party unity stood at 83.6 per cent for the Republicans and 82.0 per cent for the Democrats during the decade as a whole (compared with figures of 66.4 and 64.1 per cent during the 1970s). Nevertheless, the heights of unity reached under Gingrich did not last.

Parties as organizations

The parties also exist as groupings of like-minded politicians and activists. As organizations, each national party is a decentralized and loose confederation of state parties and of other affiliated groups. The central body of each party is the national committee, made up of representatives of each state organization; its lack of influence over policy matters is indicated by the paucity of scholarly work on this institution.

American parties do not have a mass membership of dues-paying individuals. Instead, they are relatively small groups of leaders and activists who participate in finding candidates for office and in helping their candidates. In the absence of a dues-paying mass membership, the parties rely on fundraising initiatives for financial support. They are therefore closer to Maurice Duverger's classic model of a 'cadre' party rather than that of a 'mass' party (1954).

There are organizational rivals to the parties. At many levels of politics, candidates set up their own groups of leaders and activities to run campaigns. These leaders and activists do not necessarily wish to undertake similar roles on behalf of other candidates in the same party. As well as volunteers, there are paid employees, part of a body of political professionals which has developed in recent decades. These politicos may specialize in polling, campaign advertising, or campaign management. Available for hire, they are employed by candidates rather than by the party, although most usually work for politicians of similar views. A crucial building block of political organization in the United States is not, therefore, the party, but the personal campaign organizations of individual candidates.

The proliferation of candidate-centred organizations has coincided with the revitalization of the national committees, a development especially pronounced on the Republican side. The coincidence is at first sight paradoxical, but these extra-partisan committees have, in fact, created a new role for the parties. This new role involves the central provision of services and resources useful to these organizations, while the national committee remains ideologically neutral. William Brock, as Republican national chairman, was innovative in carving out a new role for the central organization of his party along these lines during the late 1970s.

Raising money, an item of central importance to

Box 5.1 **Constitutional influences**
The US Constitution and the party system

The Constitution does not mention parties. This was a deliberate omission, because the document's framers thought that parties exerted a negative influence on politics. Instead of promoting effective deliberation of issues and selfless identification with the national interest, they encouraged political decision-making that selfishly favoured particular groups of the population. In his farewell address of 1796, George Washington, the first president, issued a vivid warning of the dangers of party politics, which he claimed 'agitates the Community with ill-founded jealousies and false alarms, kindles the animosity of one party against another, foments occasional riot and insurrection'.

The activities of the first US politicians soon made it clear that politics without parties was an unrealistic goal. No more than a few years after the adoption of the Constitution and even while Washington was still president, political factions emerged in government, reflecting very different visions among politicians for the nation's

future. Even though in many cases these politicians opposed the idea of party, they formed ongoing alliances among themselves, and proposed policies which some groups in society supported and others opposed. In other words, they began to act in a partisan way, and before long their factions would form the foundation of America's two-party system.

Indeed, despite the desire of the Constitution's framers to construct a republic without parties, their design paradoxically emphasized the need for parties. The system of separated powers, creating divisions between branches and levels of government, meant that some form of connection between different politicians was important, and parties provided this connection. At the same time, the federal system contributed to the diffuse weakness of American parties. Federalism, as established by the Constitution, encouraged within parties the persistence of multiple centres of power and the lack of any centralized national leadership.

American campaigns, is a function where the parties enjoy success, even while candidate organizations also seek funds. The legal requirement that 'hard money' is raised in small amounts from each donor has encouraged the development of sophisticated finance operations at party headquarters. Moreover, the provision that allows 'soft money' to be collected with few restrictions helps the parties, too; the distinction between restricted 'hard money' and unrestricted 'soft money' is based on the premise that the latter is devoted to party-building activities, unconnected with the promotion of a particular candidate.

Alternatives to parties

Parties once enjoyed a much more powerful presence in American politics. One reason for their decline over time is the emergence of institutions which are their rivals with respect to key respects of the intermediary process. It is not only candidate-centred

campaign organizations which have reduced the role of parties in American politics.

During much of the nineteenth century, the parties shaped national debate and ran federal, state, and city governments that inspired mass political participation at a scale unknown more recently. This was a party-dominated period, when American anti-party impulses were largely transcended. An early loss of their functions was associated with the emergence of a welfare state and a professionalized bureaucracy. In many cities, political machines once fulfilled such roles, dispensing patronage in return for activism and welfare support in return for votes.

Then, in the second half of the twentieth century, new forms of politics developed that increasingly marginalized the parties. First, the development of the mass media—in particular television—created new means for individual politicians to communicate with voters, free of the party. Television commercials reduced the need for door-to-door, block-by-block mobilization of the vote. A large budget therefore became more important than a large body of party activists.

A second development was the growth of interest groups. Although interest groups have always been a feature of American politics, their significance increased sharply during the twentieth century. They are an alternative force for the aggregation of different interests, and they act as an alternative intermediary between politicians and the people by lobbying in support of their members' position on issues of concern. The key difference between interest groups and parties is that the former are narrow organizations of people who share the same economic, religious, racial, ideological, or social interest, while the latter seek to bring together a broad coalition of interests in search of elected office. Arguably, the former now offer a more promising route by which a group might pursue its political goal.

This survey of the parties' functions indicates the need to be terminologically precise in discussing their strengths and weaknesses. Most local party organizations have seen their strength decline with the rise of candidate-centred organizations. Yet the national committees have gained strength in capably adapting to the demands of modern politics and in developing as fundraising and resource-providing organizations. Nevertheless, the national committees have become no more influential in mapping out strategic or ideological goals for their party. It is probably fair to observe, therefore, that there are both weakening and strengthening tendencies within political parties today. The challenge in studying the party system is to identify the precise nature of both trends, as well as to trace their origins and to understand their implications for American politics.

Key points

- Parties are the basic unit around which American politicians organize themselves both when campaigning and when governing. But they are often overshadowed by the independent activities of the candidates, who are remarkably free to run their own campaign and to advocate their own set of policies.

- Over time, the role for parties within American politics has become smaller. Arguably, however, at the start of the twenty-first century parties are ideologically more cohesive than during most of the twentieth century. They have also responded well organizationally to the development of candidate-centred politics.

Party identification

American parties lack a mass-membership base. But many Americans feel a sense of durable affinity with one of the parties. Known as 'party identification', this connection between voter and party is a source of great interest among scholars. Although a voter's party identification is the most accurate predictor of the candidate whom she or he will support in any election, the concept of party identification is loose enough to allow defections; in any election, a nominal Democrat, for example, may decide to vote for more Republican candidates than Democratic candidates, while retaining identification with the Democratic Party. Indeed, the electoral successes of Ronald Reagan during the 1980s were based in large part on the votes of 'Reagan Democrats', ready to support the conservative president but not to rethink their traditional affiliation with the party he opposed so strenuously.

An influential group of early scholars traced the origins of party identification to a period of political socialization; they argued that voters usually formed a sense of affinity with one of the two parties during their youth, and that they then tended to retain this allegiance throughout their life (Campbell et al. 1960) More recently, Morris Fiorina has rethought the nature of party identification, suggesting that it represents instead a cumulative assessment of the parties' past performance (1981). The latter view

Box 5.2 Is America different?

Parties compared

Politics in the United States is less party-centred than that in most other Western democracies. Parties are weaker, playing a less pivotal role in the organization of legislative politics and in the election of office-holders. It is common for representatives of the same party to vote differently on an issue in Congress; it is also common for a politician to win office through a campaign that does not mention the party to which she or he belongs. Even those scholars who challenge the thesis of weakening parties do not reject this claim that the American party system is weak by international comparison.

The doctrine of separated powers and the system of federalism ensure the distinctiveness of the party system. So does an entrenched and widespread distrust of parties, a set of suspicions which informed the drafting of the Constitution towards the end of the eighteenth century, and which outlived the emergence of the party system in the nineteenth century.

1. The durability of the two-party system is remarkable, as is its dominance of American politics. The party system in no major democracy rivals the purity and longevity of the American.

2. American parties have neither a system of mass membership nor an institution of central leadership. They collect together rather loosely various groupings of politicians and activists. In observing day-to-day politics, personality is usually more visible than party.

3. There is state regulation of political parties to a distinctive degree in the United States. Much of it emerged from an anti-party reform impetus around the turn of the twentieth century. The most notable element of regulation is the primary election, run by the state, which transfers the responsibility for choosing candidates—an important function and a potential source of great influence—from party leaders and activists to a larger electorate.

4. The size and diversity of the United States, together with the institutional disincentives against the creation of multiple parties, encouraged the development of parties as distinctively broad coalitions of different interests, and discouraged the emergence of explicitly class-based parties.

more easily accommodates changes in party identification over time, but, in either case, fundamental to the concept is its extraordinary durability from election to election. In electoral politics, where fortunes of individual politicians so easily rise and fall, party identification is an unusual source of lasting stability.

Based on observations in the 1960s, an apparent decline in the incidence of party identification and a rise of political independence fed a growing belief that the United States was moving towards a non-partisan form of politics. Independence means that a voter has no sense of affinity with either of the major parties, and views politics free of a partisan perspective. Traditionally, political independence was relatively uncommon, and was generally associated with citizens who had little interest in and knowledge of politics. But the 1960s and early 1970s seemed to witness a sharp rise in its incidence and its spread to Americans with a greater level of political

engagement and sophistication. It was widely feared that the change signalled the inability of the parties to represent such broad coalitions of interest with any effectiveness (Broder 1972).

But concerns about the future of the party system proved to be exaggerated. The rise in political independence did not continue, and instead reflected a historically unusual response to political upheavals such as racial conflict, opposition to the Vietnam War, and the fears of governmental abuses generated by the Watergate scandal. After the early 1970s, the onward march of non-partisanship came to a halt; the number of independents levelled off at what nevertheless remained a high point by historical comparison.

Another important feature of weakening ties of partisanship among voters was the increasing incidence of 'ticket-splitting' in elections. Rather than demonstrate a commitment to the nominees of a single party, many voters pick and choose among candidates from both parties, perhaps supporting a Republican for the presidency but Democrats for Congress and still more Republicans for state-level office.

Some scholars view the change as grounded more in rhetoric than substance. They observe that the number of 'pure independents'—who stubbornly refuse to voice any affiliation with a party—has remained roughly stable. What accounts for the increase among independents is the category of 'partisan independents', who first tell pollsters that they are independents but who then speak of a preference for one of the parties (Keith 1992). The voting behaviour of partisan independents is dissimilar from pure independents and instead reveals a continuing tendency to support one party over the other. It is therefore true that many citizens feel a less strong sense of attachment to a party; but almost nine in ten still see the Democratic Party or the Republican Party as representing their political interests to a greater or lesser extent.

Key points

- Figures suggest that the strength of many Americans' affiliation with one of the parties is less potent than it once was. Voters are often unwilling to follow a party line at the polls.

- These developments demonstrate that between thirty and forty years ago there was a marked increase in popular scepticism about the political process and particularly about the party system. But—despite ticket-splitting—party identification remains the best predictor of a voting decision.

Two parties

A key characteristic of the American party system is its dominance by the two major parties. Indeed, they enjoy a position of such political pre-eminence that there are very few office-holders who are not affiliated to the Republicans or the Democrats—although, unusually, the unicameral state legislature of Nebraska is organized on a non-partisan basis. A rare exception in recent years is Jesse Ventura, a former professional wrestler and radio host, who became governor of Minnesota in 1998 as the candidate of the Reform Party—the organization assembled by Ross Perot—but did not stand for re-election in 2002. On Capitol Hill, only Bernie Sanders is outside the two parties. Since 1991, he has served as Vermont's representative in the House as an independent.

Minor-party candidates are a frequent feature of presidential politics, but they rarely perform well. Among their number in 2000 was Harry Browne (Libertarian), who secured 0.36 per cent of the popular vote, and Earl F. Dodge (Prohibition), who won a grand total of 208 votes. Most successful was Ralph Nader (Green); some supporters of Gore claimed that Nader's 2.74 per cent share of the vote deprived their candidate of victory by appealing to a more liberal contingent of voters who otherwise would have chosen the Democrat.

The institutional obstacles to third-party successes are formidable. First, the 'first past the post' system of American elections spells difficulties for any third party which needs to convince voters that a vote against its two major opponents is not wasted. Second, the executive is a singly elected office which cannot be shared by the parties. (It is common for presidents to offer a cabinet position to a politician from an opposing party, but such an appointment is personal and not partisan.)

A third party also faces the challenge of convincing would-be contributors that donations are not a wasted investment. The funding problems of third parties are exacerbated by federal campaign laws that grant financial support much more easily to the two established parties. Moreover—despite some successful legal challenges to such practices— electoral law in many states has frequently offered privileges to the major parties, such as special prominence on ballot papers. In addition to the obstacles, American politics offers insurgent politicians an incentive to remain within a major party; the system of primary elections allows them to

Table 5.2 American society and political parties: party identification, 2000

This table shows the party affiliation of Americans by group. Those who report independence, but then a preference for one of the two parties, are categorized as party supporters rather than as independents (Keith et al. 1992).

% of group	Democrat	Republican	Independent
Males	46	41	12
Females	53	34	12
Whites	44	42	13
Blacks	83	7	10
Grade school, some high school	58	30	11
High school diploma	53	29	16
Some college, no degree	48	40	11
College degree/postgraduate	44	48	8
Income 0–16 percentile	62	22	14
Income 17–33 percentile	52	29	13
Income 34–67 percentile	47	40	13
Income 68–95 percentile	50	40	10
Income 96–100 percentile	36	54	10
Professionals	46	44	10
White-collar	50	37	12
Blue-collar	55	31	13
Unskilled*	50	25	23
Farmers*	51	41	8
Housewives	48	38	12
South	47	37	14
Non-South	51	37	11
Born 1975 or later	51	27	21
Born 1959–74	45	41	12
Born 1943–58	51	37	11
Born 1927–42	50	40	10
Born 1911–26	63	31	5
Born 1895–1910*	59	21	19
Liberals	79	14	7
Moderates	52	34	14
Conservatives	26	67	8

Asterisks indicate that the group contains a small number of respondents.

Source: National Election Studies, 3-point scale of party identification
(www.umich.edu/~nes/nesguide/2ndtable/t2a_2_1.htm,
www.umich.edu/~nes/nesguide/2ndtable/t2a_2_2.htm,
www.umich.edu/~nes/nesguide/2ndtable/t2a_2_3.htm, accessed 4 Feb. 2002)

mount a challenge to the status quo without leaving their party.

In face of these disadvantages, third parties have generally emerged throughout American history to cater for a sizeable minority with interests ignored by both of the major parties. Even if they secure a modest degree of success, the success tends to be transient. Either the concern is passing one, and so the rationale for the third-party movement disappears, or one of the major parties seeks to win over its supporters by emulating the issue stance which

won success for the movement. Table 5.3 discusses some examples of twentieth-century third parties.

By some measures, the most successful third-party movement of American history surrounded the presidential candidacies of H. Ross Perot during the 1990s; he achieved a larger proportion of the vote in successive elections than any previous third-party candidate. Perot mobilized voters who were disenchanted with the political process, particularly because of the way in which politicians had failed—according to Perot—to tackle the nation's economic

Table 5.3 Third parties

This table identifies some of the more successful third parties of the twentieth century, highlighting the reasons both for their emergence and for their disappearance.

1912: Progressive ('Bull Moose') Party. Former Republican president Theodore Roosevelt returned from retirement to challenge his successor, William Howard Taft, for the party's nomination, citing dissatisfaction with the more conservative direction of the Taft administration. When he failed, he launched a third party as the vehicle for his candidacy, splitting the Republican Party between Taft's 'stalwarts' and his 'progressives'. Winning 27.5 per cent of the vote, he took enough support away from Taft to allow Woodrow Wilson, the Democrat, to win. By 1916, Roosevelt had returned to the Republican fold.

1948: States Rights Democratic Party ('Dixiecrats'). A group of Southern conservatives, who broke away from the national Democratic Party in protest at its commitment to civil rights for African Americans. Its presidential candidate, Strom Thurmond (who joined the Republican Party in 1964), carried four states in the South. The Democratic policy on civil rights was more cautious in 1952, preventing a repetition of the walk-out.

1968: American Independent Party. Similarly to Thurmond, George Wallace, a Southern segregationist, launched his candidacy in protest at the racial liberalism of the national Democratic Party. He first sought the Democratic nomination before starting the third-party effort, eventually winning five states. In 1972 he entered Democratic primaries again, but an assassination attempt removed him from active presidential politics.

woes meaningfully. As an independent, he won 18.9 per cent of the popular vote but carried no states in 1992. He also played an important role in persuading politicians in the two major parties to tackle the problems of the deficit. By 1996 he had organized and in large part personally funded the creation of the Reform Party, under which label he ran again. Not only had the novelty of Perot's idiosyncratic approach to politics worn off, but many of his supporters also decided that the major parties were now dealing adequately with the issues which he had raised. Besides, the classic disadvantage of the third-party candidate emerged once again. It was widely accepted that Perot had no realistic chance of winning the White House, so to support him was to waste a vote. In 1996 his

support slipped to 8.4 per cent of the popular vote. By 2000, following his retirement from electoral politics, the Reform party was beset by factional conflict and lost still more support. Its presidential nominee, Patrick J. Buchanan, won just 0.4 per cent of the vote.

Key point

- A significant strength of the two major parties is their success in crowding out serious sources of opposition in most cases. Yet institutional factors explain the problems of third parties as much as the ability of the major parties to mobilize broad coalitions of support.

The impact of the post-1968 reforms

The key development within the party system during modern times is the set of institutional reforms that took place after 1968. According to Byron Shafer (1983), these reforms amounted to a 'quiet revolution' in American politics. The impetus for reform began at the Democratic national convention of 1968, when party delegates selected Hubert Humphrey as their presidential nominee, despite a

lack of enthusiasm for Humphrey among many party activists.

The decisive impact of the reforms was to remove the power of choosing the presidential nominee from party leaders, and to place it in the hands of a wider group of party supporters. Primary elections became the crucial forum for this choice; in order to win, a presidential aspirant now needed to cultivate support among a wide array of ordinary voters. Within the Democratic Party, another reform—later revised—was a requirement that state delegates to the national convention should include more representatives of groups historically marginalized in politics.

Reform, in the eyes of many scholars, produced a great irony. Wider participation in the process of presidential selection was a democratizing measure that did not choose candidates of greater appeal to a majority of voters. The problem seemed particularly acute in the Democratic Party, where a galaxy of groups played a role in choosing the nominee, often with reference to their own concerns rather than the question of national electability. The party frequently found it difficult to win the White House during the two decades between the reforms and the election of Bill Clinton; some saw the procession of apparently unappealing candidates as the product of a nomination process which rewarded those who won over the rank-and-file Democratic supporters, rather than those who might win over voters as a whole. The Republican Party, by contrast, did not suffer the same plight because of its greater degree of internal cohesion (Mayer 1996). Some analysts even argued that party reform tended to produce weaker presidents, because the skills required to win the nomination were vastly different from those needed to govern the nation. It was also observed that reforms bolstered the role of the news media, which communicated information about the contenders to those who would select among them; not infrequently this function allowed journalists collectively to exercise influence over the selection process by deciding which presidential aspirants were worthy of attention.

The extent to which the post-1968 reforms shaped the party system of today is open to question. Some see them as significantly weakening the parties: by firmly placing presidential selection in the hands of a larger electorate, a key structural rationale for the existence of party organizations was undermined. But others question the extent of the impact. In surveying the organizational development of the Democratic Party in a number of states, Alan Ware (1985), for example, found little connection between reform and weakness. Instead, he observed the importance of many other factors, including the declining interest of trade unions in Democratic politics and the emergence of new campaign techniques that allowed candidates to operate independently of party.

Key points

- Reform of the presidential nomination process was the most significant development in the party system during the latter half of the twentieth century. But disagreements emerge in defining its significance.

- To some, it is a principal agent within the trend towards party weakness. To others, it should be considered in conjunction with other factors to explain this trend.

Conclusion

America's party system has periodically attracted a considerable amount of criticism from the scholars who study it. In 1950, an American Political Science Association committee issued a report outlining the need for its revitalization. The report, 'Toward a more responsible party system', argued that the nation's politics suffered because of the weak, decentralized, and ideologically confused nature of its parties. Democratic accountability would be improved, the committee maintained, if voters were able to identify policy initiatives clearly with the politicians who proposed and enacted them; voters could then reward or punish the relevant party appropriately. A model worthy of emulation, it maintained, was the British parliamentary system of party responsibility.

During the 1970s, another group of academic critics coalesced as the Committee of Party Renewal, an organization that is still in existence. The motivating force behind the group was concern over

Table 5.4 The party system over time

The two-party system has shown remarkable durability. Since the early years of the United States, two parties have almost always dominated politics. The balance between the parties has changed from time to time, however. The dominant issues in American politics have also changed. More rarely, changes in the national debate have left one of the parties obsolete, and a new party has taken its place.

1. The first party system (1800–24)
Factional conflict over economic and foreign policy became institutionalized when the parties emerged at the time of the 1800 presidential election.

The Federalists supported an active government committed to building the nation, but became America's shortest-lived major party, disappearing after the war of 1812.

The party of Thomas Jefferson, the Democratic-Republicans, enjoyed success in promoting a localist, agrarian vision against the Federalists' centralized, commercial view.

2. The Jacksonian system (1824–56)
The development of mass politics marked the start of this era; the gradual emergence of tensions between North and South created political conflict which the party system eventually could not resolve.

The Whig Party, formerly a faction of the Democratic-Republicans, emerged in opposition to the leadership of Jackson. It sometimes transcended the obstacle of minority status by winning the White House with a military hero.

The Democratic Party developed in support of Andrew Jackson during the mid-1820s. Jackson and his successors assembled a broad coalition, more representative than the Whigs of the 'common man'.

3. The Civil War system (1856–96)
After the Civil War, party differences on issues were often relatively small, but the ethno-cultural and sectional identities of the parties fuelled political conflict.

The Republican Party emerged during the sectional crisis on the northern side. The Civil War established its strength as the protectors of the Union.

Following the Civil War, the Democratic Party gained strength in the South, and also enjoyed success among many Catholics in the northern cities.

4. The system of 1896 (1896–1932)
Economic upheaval during the 1890s led to the short-lived agrarian protest party, the Populists. In 1896, the Democrats took up Populist positions on economic issues, precipitating change within the party system.

The Republican Party, generally upholding the tenets of laissez-faire economics, dominated politics throughout this period. Progressive reform was another important element of the party's thinking at the start of the twentieth century.

Concentrated still more in the South and among the new immigrants of the North, the Democratic Party rarely won national elections. When its populist cast diminished, many Democrats shared the Progressivism of the pre-First World War era.

5. The New Deal system (1932–68)
Issues linked with the New Deal and its aftermath were especially significant; they concerned the extent of government activism.

The Democrats enjoyed a long period of dominance in American politics as the nation's majority party with a powerfully broad coalition.

Only war hero Dwight Eisenhower won the presidency for the Republican Party, which controlled Congress for just four years (1947–9, 1953–5).

6. The sixth party system (1968–   ): the era of divided government
'Bread-and-butter' issues remained important, while social issues and foreign policy were also often electorally salient.

The Democratic Party dominated Congress until 1994, but experienced less success in winning the presidency.

The Republican Party won control of the White House in most elections, but on Capitol Hill managed to gain the Senate only for six years (1981–7) until the breakthroughs of 1994.

declining figures of party identification as representative of the parties' increasing inability to act effectively as an intermediary between voters and the political process. Stronger parties are essential, they argue, to act as a unifying force to counteract the centrifugal tendencies of the political system. These critics who advocate party renewal differ from their predecessors, who spoke of party responsibility in readily accepting the obstacles that the constitutional doctrines of federalism and separated powers pose to the development of a different kind of party system. They simply wish to see parties more visible at every level of American politics.

This chapter has shown that there is much evidence in support of the critics. There is therefore good reason why those who study parties often

Box 5.3 **Core academic debate**
Realignment

Few debates in American political science have attracted sharper controversy than that surrounding the concept of partisan realignment. The debate is a quest for a systematic explanation of upheavals within the party system over time. It began when V. O. Key, Jr. oriented the attention of political scientists to moments of upheaval within a party system otherwise usually characterized by constant stability. Key introduced the concept of 'critical elections' (an idea later broadened to include 'critical periods') to describe times of special change, when party coalitions altered significantly before settling down to a fixed pattern again (Key 1955; 1959). Table 5.4 presents a widely accepted understanding of the key eras within the history of the American party system. A realignment refers to the process by which one era was replaced by the next, the process by which, for example, the 'system of 1896' was replaced by the 'New Deal system' during the years of the Great Depression.

A realignment of the party system included the long-term transfer of majority status from one party to another, a fundamental shift in the party loyalty exhibited by social groups, and the emerging prominence of new issues in politics. It was a time when political conflict was particularly intense, when inter- and intra-party debates were very contentious, and when voter turnout was high. Although a broad consensus emerged about the essential features of a realignment of the party system, individual scholars placed different emphases on these features as causal factors. James Sundquist, for example, argued that Key stressed excessively the role of social groups in causing a realignment, preferring a focus on the emergence of important new issues for the nation to tackle (1983).

Empirical investigations of realignments created more controversy. One example concerns the realignment of the party system during the 1930s. Kristi Andersen argued influentially that changes during this period were generated by the mobilization of new Democratic-supporting voters, who had not previously participated in elections (1979). But other scholars claimed that the crucial agent of party upheaval consisted instead of former Republican voters, who abandoned their existing political loyalty to support Franklin Roosevelt and the New Deal (Erikson and Tedin 1981).

Realignment theory inspired much work both within politics, the scholars of which sought to refine the concepts, and within history, the practitioners of which examined a variety of critical periods within American politics (e.g. Kleppner et al. 1981). An unusual feature of realignment theories as a focus for academic debate was their success in gaining attention outside the scholarly arena and among an informed wider public. For more than thirty years, a presidential campaign has rarely passed without political journalists writing about the possibility of a realignment; such talk was especially prominent in 1968, 1980, and 1984.

The utility of realignment theories in political science was questioned primarily for two reasons. First, some scholars argued that the application of the paradigm to many different cases sapped the concept of its meaning; it was necessary, they suggested, to revise the theory too much to accommodate each instance of change within the party system. Moreover, an emphasis on realignment often tended to obscure quieter, but still important, transformations of the coalitional bases of party politics. Second, many within political science claimed that the concept of realignment was particularly unhelpful in understanding the transformation of the party system since the 1960s. It was clear that the Democrats lost their majority position, but equally clear that the Republicans were not their replacement in this dominant role within the party system. Instead, it was 'the era of divided government'. Ironically, the very period in which scholars actively investigated realignments apparently revealed the shortcomings of the model (Shafer 1991).

The most recent contribution to the literature represents a culmination of this revisionism. David Mayhew subjects the work of realignment scholars to critical scrutiny and argues that each of their claims lacks analytical robustness (2002). It remains to be seen whether realignment theorists succeed in rebutting Mayhew's arguments and therefore in reigniting this scholarly debate.

Box 5.4 Definitions

Democratic Party. The oldest party in continuous existence anywhere in the world. The Democratic Party traces its origins back to the presidency of Thomas Jefferson in the early years of the nineteenth century, but it reformed in support of Andrew Jackson during the 1820s. In recent times, the party has usually adopted positions more liberal than the Republicans, and its coalition often includes Americans less socially, economically, and educationally privileged than the supporters of the Republican Party. As a group, African Americans are strongly Democratic, and for the past few decades more women than men have supported the party.

Republican Party. Founded in 1854 during the sectional conflict preceding the Civil War by groups who opposed the extension of slavery to new territories in the West. More conservative on most issues than its Democratic opposition, the Republican Party today has a coalition of wealthier and better-educated Americans, as Table 5.2 shows. The party is often known as the GOP ('Grand Old Party'). a term that emerged during the 1880s.

Primary election. A state-regulated election to choose a party's candidate for elected office. The mode of primary election varies from state to state, and the key source of variety is between a closed primary and an open primary. In a closed primary, only voters who are self-declared Republicans or Democrats may participate in the relevant election. In an open primary, all voters may decide to choose among either the Republican candidates or among the Democratic candidates; there is no requirement that they announce a preference for either party.

Party caucus. A meeting of party activists at which a candidate for office is selected. Some states—notably Iowa—still employ a caucus system for presidential selection.

National convention. The meeting at which a party's nominees for the presidency and vice-presidency are officially selected. Historically, the conventions were often the location of intense intra-party debate and disagreement. In recent decades, however, the process of primary elections has ensured that the identity of the presidential nominee is decided before the start of the convention. The parties use national conventions today as an opportunity to set out their agenda to the public and to promote their presidential ticket, rather than to discuss matters of policy.

Political machine. A strong form of party organization at the local level, for many years now virtually extinct. Political machines sought to achieve a political stranglehold over a local government through material means, awarding jobs and contracts to activists and donors.

National committee. The central party organization, a loose confederation of state parties. The national committees have become more important in recent decades as central fundraising and resource-distribution bodies. The significance of the national chairperson varies, according to the influence and prominence of the incumbent individual, but the office rarely enjoys dominance within the party.

---

suspect that a strong system is in the interest of democratic accountability and governmental efficiency. There is also good reason why the American party system has followed a distinctive line of development, beginning with a constitutional design hostile to party. In the face of the institutional and cultural constraints on partisan activity, it is up to each observer of American politics to judge the functional effectiveness of the party system and its normative implications.

QUESTIONS

1 To what extent is realignment useful as a tool to understand electoral change in the United States?

2 In what ways is the current party system different from the New Deal party system?

3 Analyse the impact of the post-1968 reforms on the party system and on American political parties more generally.

4 To what extent does the United States have anti-party politics?

5 In what ways have the news media reduced the importance of American political parties?

6 To what extent is the scholarly debate about party weakness helpful in understanding the nature of the American party system?

7 Explain the increasing incidence of party independence and of ticket-splitting since the 1960s.

8 In what ways have American political parties become stronger since the late 1980s?

9 Who has the power of leadership within an American political party?

FURTHER READING

J. H. Aldrich (1995), *Why Parties: The Origins and Transformation of Party Politics in America* (Chicago: University of Chicago Press).

J. F. Bibby (2000), *Politics, Parties, and Elections in America*, 4th edn. (Belmont, Ca.: Wadsworth).

L. D. Epstein (1986), *Political Parties in the American Mold* (Madison: University of Wisconsin Press).

J. G. Geer (ed.) (1998), *Politicians and Party Politics* (Baltimore: Johns Hopkins University Press).

D. McSweeney and J. Zvesper (1991), *American Political Parties: The Formation, Decline and Reform of the American Party System* (London: Routledge).

L. S. Maisel, (ed.) (2002), *The Parties Respond: Changes in American Parties and Campaigns*, 4th edn. (Boulder, Colo.: Westview).

D. R. Mayhew (1986), *Placing Parties in American Politics: Organization, Electoral Settings, and Government Activity in the Twentieth Century* (Princeton, NJ: Princeton University Press).

M. P. Wattenberg (1998), *The Decline of American Political Parties, 1952–1996* (Cambridge, Mass.: Harvard University Press).

WEB LINKS

www.democrats.org A gateway to websites associated with the Democratic Party

www.greenparty.org The website of the Green party

www.lp.org The website of the Libertarian party

www.reformparty.org The website of the Reform party

www.rnc.org The Republican National Committee offers links to other Republican websites

www.umich.edu/~nes The National Election Studies site, offering data on party identification, among others, from 1948 until the present

6 Elections

Candice J. Nelson

READER'S GUIDE

This chapter examines elections in the United States and the key factors that affect the outcome of elections. The chapter begins by looking at public opinion and partisanship, and the importance of each to American elections. It then turns to a discussion of political participation in American politics, with particular emphasis on turnout in American elections. Finally, it discusses presidential and congressional elections, with a brief overview of state and local elections.

Introduction

Elections in the United States engage the fundamental question of representation in electoral politics. The American electoral system is a single member district system, not a proportional system, as in some other Western democracies. As a result, the candidate that gets the majority (or, in a multiple candidate race, a plurality) of the vote is elected to office. Once in office, the office-holder must decide to whom he or she owes allegiance—the majority of voters who elected him or her to office, or all the citizens of the district or state he or she represents.

Most elected officials believe they represent the entire citizenry of the district or state, but the electoral system does not guarantee that the views of the minority are heard.

Because the United States is largely a two-party country, citizens who identify with third or minority parties, such as the Green or Libertarian parties, have a difficult time making their voices heard. Even in debates before the presidential general elections, minority party candidates have routinely been refused the opportunity to participate. The only exception was in 1992, when Ross Perot was given permission to participate in the presidential debates that year.

The restrictions of the single member district system are ameliorated, however, in part by the distinct federal and state electoral systems. With close to half a million elections in the United States every two years, for offices ranging from United States Senator to local school board member, there are many opportunities for different points of view to be expressed. The sheer number of elections in the United States, and the number of candidates that seek office, means a wide variety of issues and concerns will be aired. Citizens often feel that they have too many opportunities to participate in politics, not too few.

The American electoral system has changed greatly since the drafting of the Constitution. Suffrage, the right to vote, has been expanded to women, African Americans, and people between the ages of 18 and 20. Candidates for office are no longer selected by political party machines, but by very public primaries and caucuses in which voters have an opportunity to hear and vote for candidates. Yet there are still debates between traditionalists and progressives as to reforming the electoral process even further. Some argue that internet voting is only a matter of time, while others worry that internet voting would create opportunities for fraud and corruption in elections. Some would like to see a uniform election process throughout the United States. Their opponents argue that the right to administer elections should be retained by individual states.

This chapter examines both electoral procedures in the United States and the factors that affect the outcomes of elections. The chapter explores the information and activity Americans bring to the electoral arena, and the consequences for presidential, congressional, and state and local elections.

Public opinion

Following the tragic events of 11 September 2001, Donald Rumsfeld, the US secretary of defense, was a daily fixture on television news programmes in the United States. However, in late February, six months after the American public's constant exposure to Rumsfeld, only 34 per cent of the public could correctly answer the question: 'Can you tell me the name of the current secretary of defense?'

Examples like this are often cited to illustrate how ill-informed the American public is on issues of public affairs. The views that individuals have on issues of public concern is called **public opinion**. The traditional view of the American public is that Americans are not very well informed on issues of public affairs. *The American Voter*, one of the earliest studies of public opinion in the United States, found that Americans lacked knowledge of political actors and events. However, more recent studies have argued that while Americans may not be able to identify the secretary of defense, Americans learn about politics through their daily life experiences. In *The Reasoning Voter* (1994) Samuel Popkin presents what he calls the by-product theory of political information. Popkin argues that while individuals may not understand the details of the various energy proposals before the United States Congress, they have a general sense of energy policy simply by following the price of gas at the gas station.

There are five characteristics of public opinion: direction, intensity, stability, specificity, and salience. Direction is simply whether an individual is for or against a particular policy, supports or opposes a candidate or issue, or approves or disapproves of a policy or behaviour. A common survey question that measures direction is: 'Do you approve or disapprove of the job [insert name of public official] is doing as [insert name of position]?' Intensity measures how strongly the individual holds his opinion, and is gauged by asking a question such as: 'Do you strongly approve, somewhat approve, somewhat disapprove, or strongly disapprove of [insert issue being measured]?' Stability refers to how likely the opinion an individual has at one point in time will be held over time. Specificity refers to how well-informed an individual is about an issue or how much information an individual has about a candidate or public official. On many policy issues, Americans do not have much specific information. Finally, saliency refers to how important an issue is to an individual.

The five characteristics of public opinion are related. Opinions which are strongly held (intensity) also tend to be stable over time (stability), better informed (specificity), and important to an individual (saliency). Opinions that have all five of these characteristics are called directional opinions, meaning individuals have strong, stable, informed opinions, and want public officials to move in a particular direction on the policy on which the opinion is held. Examples of directional opinion would be opinions on gun control, abortion, and school prayer. Most Americans have a pretty good idea what their opinions are on these three issues. For most public policy issues, however, the only public opinion characteristic Americans hold is direction. Individuals may have some idea if they support or oppose an issue, but that opinion lacks intensity, is not very stable or well informed, and the issue may or may not be particularly important. Opinions on issues such as these are called permissive: public officials are free to act in what they think are the best interests of the citizens.

Elections in the United States begin with most Americans knowing little about the candidates running for office. If one candidate is an incumbent, he or she has been in office for at least one term, so potential voters may know something about the incumbent's record in office. However, even with long-time office-holders, most potential voters

know little about the candidate, and it is the object of the campaign to educate the voters about each candidate.

Public opinion is typically measured by survey research. Survey research is scientific polls in which everyone in the population being surveyed has an equal chance of being selected to answer questions. Because the polls are scientific, generalizations about issues of public policy can be made from the answers of a relatively small number of people surveyed, called respondents. Polls to measure public opinion are conducted by news organizations, such as newspapers and television networks, by independent survey research firms, such as Gallup and Harris, and by universities. During election campaigns, candidates also conduct surveys to identify the opinions of potential voters.

Key points

- Americans are not always well informed on the details of public policy issues, but they learn a great deal about politics through their everyday activities.

- There are a few public policy issues, such as abortion, gun control, and school prayer, about which Americans have strong opinions.

- On issues on which Americans are not well informed they generally trust elected officials to enact policies in the best interests of citizens.

- Public opinion is measured by survey research, most notably through scientific public opinion polls.

Partisanship

One of the most important factors which affects the outcome of elections in the United States is the **partisanship** of the electorate. Partisanship is a core orientation towards politics. It is a long-term force in elections that doesn't change from year to year or election to election. Most Americans identify with one of the two major political parties. Partisanship is

important for voters because it gives them a way to evaluate candidates and issues when little else is known about the candidate or the issue. For example, if a voter knows nothing about a candidate other than that the candidate is a Democrat or Republican, knowing the candidate's partisanship helps the voter evaluate where the candidate stands on particular issues. Partisanship is not a foolproof way to evaluate candidates: for example, there are Republican candidates and office-holders who are pro-choice on abortion, even though the Republican Party's official position on abortion is pro-life. However, absent other information about a candidate, partisanship is a way for voters to make some informed voting choices.

Partisanship is also important for candidates in an election, because it is a way of predicting behaviour and allocating resources. Because partisanship is a long-term force, people who have voted for Democratic candidates in the past are likely to vote for Democratic candidates in the future. A candidate can look at the percentage of Democratic and Republican votes a candidate got in a state or district in a past election, and be reasonably certain that a particular candidate will get a similar percentage of the vote in a future election. While how an individual votes in an election is secret, statistics are kept on the percentage of votes each party gets in a particular area, and candidates can use that information to allocate campaign resources. For example, a Republican candidate may not spend a great deal of time in an area with solid Republican voters, because those voters are likely to vote Republican no matter who the candidate is. The Republican candidate might better spend his or her time in areas of the district or state that are not solidly Republican, in order to persuade voters who don't always vote Republican.

The partisanship of the American electorate can be measured in one of three ways. First, partisanship can be measured by looking at membership in party organizations, that is, people who join a party organization by becoming party members, paying dues, and attending party meetings. However, this is not a very good measure of party affiliation, because only 3 per cent of Americans actually belong to a party organization.

A second way to assess party affiliation in the United States is to look at party registration: people who, when they register to vote, register as a member of a party. However, this too is not a good measure of party affiliation, because in slightly less than half of the states—twenty-two—party registration is not required.

Consequently, the way party affiliation is most commonly measured in the United States is through self-identification. The typical survey research question that is used to measure party affiliation is: 'Generally speaking, do you think of yourself as a Republican, a Democrat, an Independent, or what?' If the respondent answers 'Republican' or 'Democrat', the follow-up question that is asked is 'Would you consider yourself a strong Republican/Democrat or a not very strong Republican/Democrat?' For respondents who answer the initial question 'Independent', the follow-up question is: 'Do you think of yourself as closer to the Republican Party or to the Democratic Party?'

This series of questions leads to a seven-point measure of party identification. The partisan composition of the United States in 2000 is shown in Table 6.1.

There are several points to be made about these figures. First, as noted by Robert Mason in the previous chapter, the United States is very much a two-party country. The vast majority of Americans identify with the Democratic or Republican Party. Less than 1 per cent think of themselves as affiliated with a minor party. Among those major party identifiers, there are more Democrats than Republicans, and this has consistently been the case since the New Deal in 1932. While control of government shifts between the Republican and Democratic parties, more Americans think of themselves as Democrats than Republicans.

A second consideration in looking at these data is how to think of those respondents who initially identify as Independents. In the mid-1960s the number of Americans who initially identified themselves as Independents jumped from 25 per cent of the electorate to one third. This increase in Independents led to the conclusion that there was a decline in the importance of party identification, and that there was a substantial group of voters, the Independents, who were up for grabs by third-party candidates.

While in 2000 40 per cent of Americans initially identified themselves as Independents, it is a mistake to treat Independent Democrats, Pure Independents, and Independent Republicans as one group. Research has shown that Independent Democrats and Independent Republicans, while thinking of themselves as Independents, vote just like those survey respondents who initially identify

Table 6.1 Partisanship in the United States, 2000

	%		%
Strong Democrat	19	Democrats (Strong, Weak, Independent)	49
Weak Democrat	15		
Independent Democrat	15		
Pure Independent	12	Independents (Democrat, Pure, Republican)	37
Independent Republican	13		
Weak Republican	12		
Strong Republican	13	Republicans (Strong, Weak, Independent)	38
Other/Minor Party	0.5		

Source: National Election Studies, University of Michigan.

themselves as Democrats or Republicans (Keith et al. 1990). Independent Democrats and Independent Republicans are just as likely to vote Democrat or Republican as outright party identifiers. Moreover, people who consistently identify themselves as Pure Independents are those least likely to vote and to pay attention to politics. Thus, while over the last thirty years there has been consistently one third or more of the American electorate who report weakened party ties, the voting behaviour of the majority of these Independents shows no lessening of party loyalty. As a result, despite an increase in the percentages of Americans who describe themselves as Independents, third party and minor party candidates, with a few exceptions, have not been able to draw support from these Independents.

Despite the findings of Keith and his colleagues, there has been an ongoing debate in the United States as to the continued relevance of partisanship in American elections. Following the increase in the number of Independents in the 1960s and 1970s, a substantial body of scholarship argued that there had been a **dealignment** in American politics, and that party identification was no longer of primary importance in voting decisions (Wattenberg 1998; Nie et al. 1979). In the 1992 presidential election Reform party candidate Ross Perot received 19 per cent of the popular vote, further fuelling the dealignment argument. Also, in light of the success of the Republican Party at the presidential level between 1968 and 1988—the Democrats captured the White House only once in that twenty-year

period, in 1976—there was even some speculation that there had been a **realignment** in American politics, and the Republican Party was the majority party. However, while a majority of Americans voted for a Republican candidate for president in 1968, 1972, 1980, 1984, and 1988, those votes were not a reflection of changes in party identification. The Democrats were and, as seen in Table 6.1, continue to be the majority party in the United States.

Key points

- The vast majority of Americans identify with either the Democratic or Republican Party. Very few Americans think of themselves as members of a third or minority party.

- More Americans think of themselves as Democrats than as Republicans, even though Republicans controlled the White House and the House of Representatives in 2001–4.

- A third of Americans identify themselves as Independents, but the majority of those Independents vote for Republican or Democratic Party candidates. While the decline in party identification suggests there may have been a dealignment in American politics, voting behaviour suggest there has not.

- There is no strong evidence that a realignment in partisanship has occurred in American politics.

Box 6.1 **Core academic debate**
Dealignment or realignment?

When asked which political party they identify with, roughly one third of Americans initially answer that they think of themselves as independent of a political party. In 1992 Ross Perot, running not as a Democrat or Republican but as the candidate of the Reform party, received 19 per cent of the popular vote in the presidential election. In 1998 Jesse Ventura, a former professional wrestler, was elected governor of Minnesota on the Reform party ticket, beating the two better known and more politically experienced Democratic and Republican candidates.

These examples, coupled with a 'candidate-centred' electoral system in which the political parties have little say in which candidates run for office, are often cited as examples of the dealignment of American politics. Proponents of dealignment argue that political parties are no longer as relevant to American politics as they were when candidates were chosen by party bosses in back rooms, and political party machines controlled the outcome of elections. Dealignment proponents suggest that with the widespread access to the media, candidates are able to take their campaigns directly to the voters, and that voters in turn evaluate candidates without the filter of the political parties.

Other students of American politics argue that not a dealignment but a realignment has occurred. In 1980 Ronald Reagan was overwhelmingly elected president, ousting incumbent President Jimmy Carter, who got only forty-nine electoral votes. The Republicans also gained control of the Senate that year for the first time since 1954, and picked up thirty-three seats in the House of Representatives, their largest seat gain since 1966. The Republicans also picked up four new governorships and 189 state legislative seats, giving the party five new state legislatures with Republican majorities. The Republicans controlled the White House for the next two elections. In 1994 the Republicans regained the control of the Senate, which they had lost in 1986, and gained a majority in the House of Representatives for the first time in forty years. In the 1994 election the Democrats lost fifty-two House seats, the largest mid-term loss of seats since 1946, and all of the thirty-one House incumbents that were defeated were Democrats, including the Speaker of the House and two important committee chairmen. Of the twelve open gubernatorial seats ten were won by Republicans, and the four incumbent governors who were defeated that year were all Democrats. Following the 2000 election the Republicans briefly controlled the White House and both branches of Congress, until Senator Jim Jeffords switched his party allegiance from Republican to Independent, giving the Democrats a one-vote majority in the Senate. All of these Republican successes are cited as evidence that a realignment has occurred in American politics, and that the Republican Party, not the Democratic Party, is in fact the majority party in the United States.

As suggested in the body of this chapter, the empirical voting evidence does not support either the dealignment or realignment theories. However, a third argument is that the Republican Party more successfully represents the American public's views on a majority of issues in the United States, but that public opinion has not led to a commensurate shift in partisanship. One example might be the issue of education. An important part of George W. Bush's campaign platform was education; his message was 'Leave no child behind'. Education had historically been considered a Democratic issue, yet in the 2000 election, among those voters who thought education was the most important issue, almost half, 44 per cent, voted for Bush.

Political participation

Despite increases in educational opportunities and liberalization of registration and voting requirements over the last few decades, turnout in the United States still lags far behind turnout in other industrialized nations. In the 2000 presidential election, one of the closest elections in the nation's history, just under 50 per cent of those eligible to vote actually voted. In congressional elections, only one third of those eligible to vote actually do so, and in down ballot elections—elections for state and local offices—turnout is lower still.

A number of explanations are offered for low voter turnout. First, in the United States voting is a two-step process: individuals must first register to vote, and then vote. In most states individuals must register to vote thirty days before an election, a time when many people are not yet paying attention to the elections. Also, individuals who move from one location to another must re-register at their new location, even if their new home is not far from their former residence.

In 1993 President Clinton signed a law to make it easier for Americans to register to vote. The bill, nicknamed the 'Motor-Voter Bill', allows citizens to register to vote when they apply for or renew a driver's licence, register a car, or receive services at a social service agency. The idea behind the legislation was to make it easier for people to register to vote as they were carrying out other daily activities. While the legislation has made it easier to register to vote, it has not increased turnout in elections to the level that the bill's supporters had hoped.

Other efforts in the United States to make it easier to vote include liberalized absentee voting laws, all-mail voting, and early voting. In some states individuals may vote an absentee ballot for almost any reason—a change from the days when the only excuse for voting absentee was being out of the state on business, and knowing well enough before the election that this would be the case to secure an absentee ballot. In Oregon citizens vote only by mail; there are no longer voting booths in the state. In other states citizens may vote early, typically up to three weeks before the election. All of these reforms have been instituted to try to increase turnout, but thus far with only limited success.

There have been other proposed reforms to increase turnout. Proposals have been made to move election day to a Saturday, instead of the current Tuesday, or to make election day a holiday, so people would not have to take time off from work, or vote before or after work, as is currently the case. Legislation has periodically been introduced in the Congress to allow election day registration; rather than having to register prior to an election, individuals could register at their polling places on election day. The argument behind election day registration is that more people would vote, because the barrier of having to remember to register prior to election day would be removed. Three states in the United States currently allow election day registration, and turnout is somewhat higher in those states than the national average. However, local election officials often argue that election day registration would be too difficult to administer, and would open the possibilities of election fraud. A third reform that some predict will eventually occur is internet voting, but again, until concerns of potential voter fraud are allayed, internet voting on a massive level is still years away.

While fewer than half of all Americans typically vote in elections, other forms of political participation engage even less of the American public. Table 6.2 describes Americans' participation in politics, apart from voting. While four out of five Americans report discussing politics at some point, only one third try to influence how others might vote, and 10 per cent or less report engaging in other forms of campaign activity.

There is disagreement in the United States about the meaning of low turnout and even lower participation in other election-related activities. Some argue that Americans don't vote because they are satisfied with the government's performance. Others suggest that the time and effort involved in becoming informed about candidates outweigh the chance that any one vote will decide the outcome of an election. Still others suggest it is best if uninformed citizens don't participate in the process. Lastly, some argue that low turnout means voters do not see meaningful differences between candidates,

Table 6.2 Participation in American politics

	% responding 'Yes'
Ever discuss politics	81
Try to influence vote of others	35
Display button/sticker/sign	10
Go to meetings/rallies, etc.	6
Do any other campaign work	3
Contribute to candidate	7
Give money to political party	6

Source: 2000 National Election Studies, University of Michigan.

and thus do not think elections present the voters with real choices.

Key points

- Only half of all Americans eligible to vote do so in presidential elections, and turnout is even lower

in congressional and state and local elections. Legislation to make it easier to register and to vote has not increased turnout.

- Americans engage in other forms of political participation in even fewer numbers than they vote.

- There is no one explanation for the low level of turnout in American elections.

Presidential elections

American presidential elections occur every four years. There are three general phases in the election process: the nomination process, the nominating conventions, and the general election. The nomination process is by far the longest, often starting years before the actual election year.

The nominating process

To gain the nomination of the Democratic or Republican Party, a candidate must receive a majority of the delegates to the party's national nominating convention. The Democratic and Republican parties have slightly different rules for becoming the party's presidential nominee, but the general process is relatively similar. Each candidate running for president seeks to gain delegates through primaries and caucuses held in each of the fifty states, plus the District of Columbia.

Primaries are elections that occur on different dates in different states throughout the late winter and early spring. Citizens cast their votes for candidates on the ballot. In the Democratic Party, each candidate receives a number of delegates to the national nominating conventions proportional to the percentage of total votes he or she receives in the primary. In the Republican Party, the allocation of delegates varies by state. In some states the allocation of delegates is proportional, the same system as in the Democratic Party, but in other states the candidate who gets the majority of the votes receives all of that state's delegates to the convention.

Candidates who are well known and well funded tend to be most successful in primaries, because voters know the candidates' names. **Caucuses**, on the other hand, favour candidates who are well organized. At a caucus, voters gather in homes, schools, and offices in precincts across a state, usually on the evening of the date of the caucus, and spend several hours discussing the candidates before selecting delegates for each candidate. Because caucuses require a commitment of time longer than just a trip to the voting booth, candidates need to organize their supporters to come to a caucus and remain at the caucus for several hours before the vote for delegates actually occurs.

The first caucus is held each election year in the state of Iowa, and the first primary is held in the state of New Hampshire. Though both states are small and send few delegates to the party nominating conventions, the importance of these two early nomination contests is disproportionate to the size of the states or the number of delegates elected in each state. Because these are the first election contests, candidates and the press alike pay particular attention to these states. Potential candidates begin visits to New Hampshire one, and sometimes two, years before the primary. A win in Iowa and/or New Hampshire sends a signal to both the press and the public that the candidate is a serious competitor for the nomination.

Primaries begin with New Hampshire in early February and continue through April. Under Democratic Party rules, the New Hampshire primary can occur no more than a week before the start of the other primaries, and the Iowa caucus no more than fifteen days before the start of the primary period, excluding New Hampshire. Over the past few elections, the time frame in which primaries are held has shrunk. Ten years ago primaries were held over a four-month period—from mid-February to early June. In 2000 a number of states, including California, moved their primaries from later in the spring to earlier in the election period. California, for example, which in earlier years had a primary in June, moved its primary to early March. In 2004 the time frame in which the election of delegates to the conventions occurs will be even more telescoped than it was in 2000. In 2000, over half the delegates to the conventions were elected by mid-March; that will also be true in 2004.

Because the majority of primaries and caucuses occur within a six-week period, candidates who are well known and well funded tend to fare better than lesser-known and less well-funded candidates. As a result, potential presidential candidates spend the year before the election raising money and seeking endorsements. In June 1999, the then presidential candidate George W. Bush announced that he had raised $37 million for his election campaign, an amount far greater than any of his competitors. Over the ensuing summer months several of those competitors withdrew from the race, knowing that they could not compete with Bush in the 'money primary', as the effort to raise money prior to the election year is often called.

Nominating conventions

In July and August the Democratic and Republican parties hold their nominating conventions. By tradition, the party that does not control the White House holds its convention first. The purpose of the nominating convention is officially to nominate the party's candidates for president and vice-president. Until the mid-twentieth century, the party's nominees were actually chosen at the conventions. In 1924 it took the Democratic Party 103 ballots to decide its nominee for president. However, since 1960 the outcome of the conventions has been known prior to the conventions themselves. At the conclusion of the primaries and caucuses, each party's nominee has had enough delegates to secure the nomination. In 2000, both George W. Bush and Al Gore were challenged for their party nominations by John McCain and Bill Bradley, respectively, but by mid-March Bush and Gore had secured enough delegates to be assured the nominations.

While the party conventions are no longer contests for the nomination, they still officially nominate the party's presidential and vice-presidential nominees. In addition, the conventions serve other important purposes. It is at the conventions that the party's rules for the coming four years are established, and the party's platform, the statement of what the party stands for, is debated and approved.

While conventions are important for their formal role in the nomination process, they are just as important for the informal roles they play in presidential elections. If there has been a divisive primary, the convention provides an opportunity for the contesting candidates to reconcile their differences. This often, but not always, is done by offering to include some of the proposals of the losing candidate or candidates in the party's platform.

In the most recent presidential elections, when the two parties' nominees were known months in advance of the conventions, competing candidates had time prior to the convention to work out their disagreements. In these years, the conventions were less the culmination of the nomination process and more a kick-off to the general election. The conventions provide an opportunity to rally the party faithful on behalf of the presidential and vice-presidential candidates, and get the party faithful excited about working for the ticket in the autumn election. The conventions also provide the first opportunity to introduce the candidates to the electorate at large.

Throughout the nomination phase of the election the candidates primarily aim their messages at their own party's identifiers. While there is opportunity for party identifiers of the other party to hear candidates, most voters pay little attention to the candidates apart from the primary or caucus in their state. Once the nomination is secure, however, the nominees focus on the general election, and the conventions provide the first opportunity to do so.

When television first became a widespread broadcast medium in the United States, presidential nominating conventions were covered gavel to gavel. However, as the number of news outlets expanded with the development of cable television, and as the nominees of the parties' conventions became a foregone conclusion months before the actual conventions, network coverage of the conventions was scaled back. By the 2000 conventions, the major networks devoted only an hour of prime time coverage to the Democratic and Republican conventions. As a result, each party scripted the hour to appeal to various groups within the electorate. In both the 1996 and 2000 presidential elections, the nominating conventions were a kick-off for the general election for both the Democratic and Republican parties.

General election

The strategy for winning the presidential election in the United States is unique, because it does not matter who gets a majority—or, in cases when there are more than two candidates, a plurality—of the popular vote. The candidate who is elected president every four years is the candidate who gets a majority of the electoral college vote. Each state gets a number of electoral votes equal to the number of Senators and Members of Congress from the state, and the District of Columbia gets three electoral votes. There are a total of 538 electoral college votes, so to be elected president a candidate must get 270 or more electoral college votes. The electoral college votes are winner-take-all in each state, meaning that the candidate who wins a plurality of the vote in the state gets all of the state's electoral college votes.

Because the nationwide popular vote is not important in deciding the winner of the election, but the total number of electoral college votes is, presidential candidates devise a strategy to win 270 electoral votes. Typically this means identifying states that the candidate thinks he can win, and campaigning almost exclusively in those states. States with few electoral votes and states that are predominantly Democratic or Republican receive little, if any, attention from presidential candidates.

During the 1992 presidential election the Clinton campaign divided all fifty states, plus the District of Columbia, into four categories: 'top end', 'play hard', 'big challenge', and 'watch only'. There were thirteen 'top end' states, plus the District of Columbia, with a total of 182 electoral votes. These were the states that the campaign was confident it would win, and included California, New York, and Illinois. The eighteen 'play hard' states had a total of 194 electoral votes; these were the states where the campaign expected the election to be decided, and where the campaign focused its resources. Among the 'play hard' states were the perennial background states in most presidential elections: Pennsylvania, Ohio, Michigan, North Carolina, and Georgia. Together, the 'top end' and 'play hard' states had a total of 376 electoral votes, more than enough to ensure victory. There were ten 'big challenge' states, with a total of 63 electoral votes; these were states Clinton didn't think he could win, so few resources were allocated to those states. Finally, the 'watch only' states had a total of 99 electoral votes; these were states where the campaign planned to spend no time or resources. Interestingly, one of the 'watch only' states for the Clinton campaign in 1992 was Florida, the state that became key to Al Gore's loss in 2000. On election day Clinton won all the 'top end' states, lost only one 'play hard' state, North Carolina, and won one 'big challenge' state, Nevada, for a total of 370 electoral votes.

In almost all presidential elections in the United States little attention is paid to the electoral college by voters. In all but three elections in the history of the country the winner of the popular vote has also won a majority of the electoral college votes. The 2000 election was the first time since 1888 that the winner of the popular vote did not also win a majority of the electoral college votes. In the closest election in American history, the then Vice-President Al Gore won the popular vote by half a million votes, but George W. Bush won 271 electoral votes, and was elected President of the United States. Controversy surrounding the counting of votes in one state, Florida, left the outcome of the election in doubt for a month, but in the end Florida's 25 electoral votes went to George W. Bush.

After every close presidential election in the United States there is discussion of abolishing the electoral college, and replacing it by either a popular

Box 6.2 **Constitutional influences**
I: the 2000 presidential election—federalism in action

The major television networks in the United States use exit polls, conducted by a survey research organization called Voter News Service, to predict the outcome of the presidential election in each state. On election night in 2000 the major television networks first predicted that Al Gore would win the state of Florida, and consequently the state's twenty-five electoral votes. Later in the evening the networks retracted their prediction, because the outcome in the state seemed too close to call. Shortly after 2 a.m. on election night the networks predicted that George W. Bush would win in Florida, and become the forty-third president of the United States. Vice-President Gore called then Governor Bush to concede the election, and to congratulate him on his victory. However, as the actual counting of votes in Florida continued in the early morning hours, the difference between the two candidates narrowed. An hour after his first call to Bush Al Gore made a second call, retracting his concession. By Wednesday morning, twenty-four hours after voting had begun in the presidential election, the outcome in Florida was still in doubt, and the people of the United States did not know who the next president would be. The outcome of the election depended on which candidate won Florida's twenty-five electoral votes.

Bush led Gore in Florida by less than 2,000 votes. Florida state law required an automatic machine recount of the ballots, because Bush's lead was less than one half of 1 per cent of the total votes cast. However, the Gore campaign

wanted a hand count, not just a machine count, of ballots in four Florida counties, because the campaign argued that the older, less accurate voting machines used in Florida missed some votes. Over the next month hand counting of ballots in Florida started, stopped, started, and stopped again, based on administrative decisions by Florida's election officials and legal decisions by Florida's courts and, ultimately, the United States Supreme Court.

Because of the division of political power between the national government and the state government in the United States, described in Chapter 4 of this volume, state and local governments have the responsibility for the administration of elections. Even though the office in question was a federal office, the presidency, how votes were cast and counted in that election was determined by state and local officials in Florida. Between 10 November and 12 December Florida election officials, responding to decisions by the Florida courts and the US Supreme Court, conducted an on-again, off-again hand counting of ballots in four Florida counties. Bush never trailed in the recount, but at one point Gore was only behind by 300 votes. The varying and ongoing scenarios in the Florida recount case were the strangest in American presidential elections, but the interplay between the state election officials, the Florida court system, and ultimately the US Supreme Court was an illustration of the sharing of powers between the state and federal governments designed so long ago by the Founding Fathers.

vote for president or some modified form of electoral college vote. Because most states are winner-take-all, the electoral college tends to exaggerate the vote for the president; the electoral college vote is often a larger percentage of the vote than is the popular vote, enabling the newly elected president to claim more of a mandate for his policies than might actually be the case. The electoral college also enhances the importance of the most populous states, because they have the most number of electoral college votes. A third consequence of the electoral college is that it reinforces the two-party system in the United States. Because the electoral college is winner-take-all in most states, a third-party candidate has virtually no chance of winning even one state, much less a

majority of the electoral college vote. In the 1992 election Ross Perot, the Reform party candidate, received 19 per cent of the popular vote, but not one electoral college vote.

Interpreting election results

Issues play an important role in the outcomes of presidential elections in the United States, and one of the ongoing debates is whether Americans vote retrospectively or prospectively. **Retrospective voting** means that voters look at what an incumbent—or, if there is no incumbent, what the incumbent's political party—has done over the past term of office. If voters like what the incumbent or his or her party has done, they vote for the incumbent or the party; if they do not like what has been done, they vote for the opponent. For example, during the 1980 election presidential candidate Ronald Reagan asked the question: 'Are you better off now than you were four years ago?' For many Americans, the answer to that question was no, and incumbent President Jimmy Carter was voted out of office. Four years later, President Ronald Reagan asked the same question, but by then the economy had turned around, and the answer was yes, leading to Reagan's re-election. In 1992, one of the mantras of the Clinton campaign was: 'It's the economy, stupid.' Many Americans felt that President George Bush, the father of the current president, had led the country into a recession (even though economic indicators suggested the country was coming out of the recession by the autumn of 1992). Those Americans who were unhappy with the economic policies of the Bush administration voted for Clinton, and he was elected president.

Table 6.3 presents some examples of possible retrospective voting in the 2000 presidential election. Voters who thought the country was on the right track voted almost two to one for Gore; of those voters who thought the country was on the wrong track, three-quarters voted for Bush. Similarly, those who thought the military had grown stronger during the Clinton administration voted for Gore, while those who thought military strength had declined voted for Bush. In a variant of the Reagan question in the 1980 and 1984 elections, those voters who

thought their families' financial situation had improved during the Clinton years voted for Gore, while those who thought their families financial situation had declined supported Bush.

In deciding who to vote for, Americans not only look back on an incumbent or his party's record but also look forward to what the two candidates promise to do if elected. **Prospective voting** is an examination of the campaign promises of the candidates for office, and voting for the candidate whose issue positions are closest to the voter. Table 6.3 also gives some examples of prospective voting in the 2000 election. Voters who thought the next president's policies should be the same as President Clinton's supported Gore; those who thought policies should be more conservative voted for Bush. Voters who thought the United States needed a fresh start supported Bush; those who wanted the new president to stay the course supported Gore. Finally, those voters who wanted more government action voted for Gore; those who wanted the government less involved voted for Bush.

As Table 6.3 suggests, both retrospective and prospective voting can occur in an election. Retrospective and prospective voting are most likely in presidential elections, when voters know a great deal about the policy positions of the candidates. For congressional and state and local candidates, voters often know less about the policy positions of challengers and candidates for open seats, so the election is more often a referendum on the incumbent, that is, retrospective voting.

Table 6.3 Retrospective and prospective voting in the 2000 presidential election

	Retrospective voting (%)			Prospective voting (%)	
	Gore	Bush		Gore	Bush
Country is on:			Next president's policies:		
Right track	61	36	Same as Clinton	87	11
Wrong track	20	74	More conservative	13	88
Military under Clinton:			US needs:		
Stronger	68	36	Fresh start	24	71
Weaker	25	72	To stay on course	68	29
Families' financial situation:			Government should do:		
Better	61	36	More	74	23
Worse	33	63	Less	25	71

Source: Voter News Service 2000 Exit Poll.

Financing presidential elections

In 1972, following the scandals of President Nixon's re-election campaign, a new campaign finance system was put in place for presidential elections. The Federal Election Campaign Act of 1972 (FECA) provided for full public funding of the general election and partial public funding of the pre-nomination phase of the election. In order to qualify for public funds in the primaries and caucuses, candidates have to raise $5,000 in amounts of $250 or less in each of twenty states. Once a candidate qualifies for public funding, each individual contribution of $250 or less to the campaign is matched by an equal amount of money from the US treasury. In accepting partial public funding, candidates must agree to an overall pre-nomination spending limit, as well as state-by-state spending limits. In the 2000 election the overall pre-nomination spending limit was $40 million; the total amount of public funding a candidate could receive was $16.5 million. The amount of money available to the major party candidates in the general election in 2000 was $67 million. In accepting public money in the general election, candidates must agree to accept no private contributions.

Between 1976, when the FECA took effect, and 1992, only one presidential candidate declined federal funds in the primary, and no candidates declined federal funds in the general election. In 1992 Ross Perot, running as a third-party candidate in the Reform party, declined public funding in both the primary and general elections, and in 1996 Steven Forbes, running in the Republican primary, declined partial public funding in the primary. Both Perot and Forbes are millionaires, and could afford to finance their own campaigns. Because Forbes did not accept public funding, he was not bound by the state spending limits or the overall limit. Bob Dole, the eventual Republican Party presidential nominee in 1996, spent the overall limit early in the primaries to try to match Forbes's spending. Consequently, Dole found himself without campaign money to spend between April and the Republican convention in the summer, and could not compete with President Clinton's spending in support of his re-election in the spring and summer.[1]

Having watched the constraints on the Dole campaign in 1996, the then Governor George W. Bush decided to decline partial public funding in the primaries and caucuses in the 2000 election. As a result, Bush was able to out-raise all of his opponents in the primaries and caucuses, and, despite a brief challenge by Senator John McCain, win his party's nomination with relative ease. Both Bush and Gore accepted public financing in the general election.

Public funding of the general election was designed to remove the influence of wealthy individuals in presidential elections. Amendments to the FECA in 1974 limited the amount of money individuals could contribute to candidates for federal office: individuals may contribute $1,000 in the primary and $1,000 in the general election. The combination of these two laws went a long way towards removing excessive political contributions in federal elections. However, in 1979 an amendment to the FECA was passed that allowed unlimited contributions to political parties—not candidates—for so-called 'party-building' activities. These unlimited contributions are called **soft money**, and became a way for large contributions to find their way back into federal elections.

Party-building activities were initially understood to be activities such as voter registration and get-out-the-vote drives, but by 1996 they had become something quite different. When Bob Dole used all the allotted pre-nomination funds in his battle to win the Republican nomination, the Republican Party stepped in and began running 'issue ads' presenting the virtues of the Republican Party and its nominee. The ads were very similar to actual Dole campaign ads, but because they did not use words such as 'vote' or 'support', expenditures for the ads were not counted against Dole's pre-nomination spending

---

[1] The Democratic Party may face a similar problem in 2004. President George W. Bush is not expected to be challenged for his party's nomination, and he is expected, as he did in 2000, to forgo partial public funding in the pre-nomination period. There will likely be a number of Democrats vying for their party's nomination, and all are expected to accept partial public funding during the primaries. A contentious nomination battle could leave the eventual nominee with no money to spend between the end of the primaries in March or April and the convention, while President Bush will have no limit on the amount of money he can spend before the convention. Moreover, if the soft money ban for the national parties included in the Bipartisan Campaign Reform Bill of 2002 is upheld by the Supreme Court, the Democratic National Committee will not be able to run ads on behalf of the party's nominee, as the Republican National Committee did for Dole in 1996.

limit. By the 2000 election both the Democratic and Republican parties raised and spent large amounts of soft money, each party raising close to a quarter of a million dollars.

Because there are no limits on the amount of soft money an individual can contribute to political parties, the growth in soft money allowed wealthy individuals, removed from the political process by the FECA in 1974, back into the process of financing campaigns, through contributions to the parties. After years of calls for a ban on soft money in federal elections, in 2002 Congress passed and President Bush signed legislation, The Bipartisan Campaign Reform Act of 2002, which prohibits the national Democratic and Republican parties, and candidates for federal office, from raising and spending soft money. The Act will take effect following the 2002 elections.

Key points

- Delegates are selected to the political party nominating conventions through a series of primaries and caucuses held in the winter and early spring of the election year. The Iowa caucus and New Hampshire primary are traditionally the first caucus and primary, and as a result get a lot of attention from the media and the candidates.

- Presidential candidates are officially nominated at the political parties' nominating conventions in the summer of the election year. These conventions serve as the unofficial start of the general election campaign.

- The electoral college, not the popular vote, determines who will be the president. A successful presidential candidate must receive at least 270 electoral college votes. Because the popular vote does not decide the election, candidates devise an election strategy to get at least 270 electoral college votes, and then campaign in the states they need to win.

- Issues play an important role in voters' decisions. Voters may look back on an incumbent's performance in office, and cast a retrospective vote, or may compare what the candidates promise to do if elected to office, and vote prospectively.

Box 6.3 Constitutional influences
II: freedom of speech

One characteristic of American elections is their length. Members of Congress no sooner close their campaign offices than they begin raising money for their next election. This is particularly true of members of the House of Representatives, who run for office every two years. Candidates running for president start visits to Iowa and New Hampshire years before the election. The consequences of the 'permanent campaign' are the length and cost of campaigns.

Occasionally there are suggestions that the length of campaigns be restricted, and candidates allowed to campaign only within a prescribed time frame, as is the case in the UK. However, there is general agreement that such restrictions would very likely be held unconstitutional, as a violation of the first amendment guarantee of freedom of speech.

A second, more difficult issue is the role of money in elections. As the costs of running for office continue to escalate, there are ongoing proposals to limit the amount of money spent in elections. In *Buckley* v. *Valeo*, the 1976 US Supreme Court case that upheld contribution, but not spending, limits in federal elections, the Court ruled that money was a form of speech, and thus could not be limited in federal elections. The only exception was if a candidate voluntarily accepted public financing, then limits could be placed on the amount of money the candidate spent.

The Bipartisan Campaign Reform Act of 2002 limits the amount of money that groups and organizations can spend on issue ads. The Act is being challenged in the courts as a violation of the First Amendment right to freedom of speech. The court case is the first major challenge to *Buckley* v. *Valeo*, and it remains to be seen if the Supreme Court will continue to hold that spending is a form of speech, and thus cannot be restricted under the First Amendment.

- Candidates may choose to qualify for partial public funding in the pre-nomination period and full public funding in the general election. Candidates who accept public funding in the general election may not accept any private contributions.

- In recent elections soft money has become a way for wealthy individuals to contribute large amounts of money to the political parties. The Bipartisan Campaign Reform Act of 2002 prohibits political parties from accepting soft money after 5 November 2002.

Congressional elections

Congressional elections are held every two years, in even-numbered years. All 435 members of the House of Representatives run for re-election every two years. US senators serve staggered six year terms, so every two years one third of the Senate stands for election. There is no electoral college for congressional elections; the candidate that gets the plurality of the vote is elected.

Like presidential candidates, candidates for the US Congress compete in two elections: a primary election to determine each party's nominee, and a general election in the autumn. The US Constitution prescribes that the general election for candidates for federal office will be held the first Tuesday after the first Monday in November. Primary election dates are set by each state; the earliest primaries are in March and the latest in September.

Congressional candidates fall into one of three categories: incumbents seeking re-election to the House or Senate, challengers who are seeking to defeat those incumbents, and open seat candidates. Open seats are created when an incumbent decides not to seek re-election. The resources and strategies each type of candidate brings to the election are quite different.

Incumbent candidates are at an advantage in almost every election, and as a result, voting in most congressional elections is more retrospective than prospective. Because they have the resources of their congressional offices during the preceding two years (for House members) or six years (for senators), incumbent candidates have high name recognition. Because incumbents presumably have worked hard while in office to meet the demands of their constituents, they also generally have high job approval

ratings from the citizens in their district or state. Incumbents also may have more political experience than their opponents, and, because they have run and won their campaign at least once, they have more campaign experience. Incumbents, because they are office-holders, also find it easier to get coverage in the media. Finally, for all of the above reasons, incumbents generally find it easier to raise money, and are able to raise more money, than their opponents. In the 2000 election House incumbents raised, on average, slightly less than a million dollars each, while House challengers, on average, raised just $175,000. Senate incumbents out-raised their opponents four to one. As a result, over 90 per cent of all House incumbents who seek re-election are re-elected; the re-election rate for Senators varies more depending on the election year, but is still upwards of 70 per cent.

Challengers, conversely, face an uphill fight in their efforts to unseat an incumbent. Challengers first need to develop name identification, build a base of support, and give voters reasons to support them and to 'fire' the incumbent. Given the limited financial resources with which challengers start elections, all of the above is difficult. Also, because they are less well-known than the incumbents they face, challengers have a hard time raising money and getting media coverage of their campaigns.

Open seat races are the most competitive, because there is no incumbent running for re-election. However, the number of open seat races that are competitive is relatively small, because many districts, by party registration or party identification, lean heavily towards the Republican or Democratic Party. In any given election cycle there are probably only twenty or thirty House seats that are competitive, and ten to fifteen Senate seats.

The US Constitution requires that there be a census conducted every ten years to determine the number of people living in the United States. Every ten years, following the census, congressional districts in each state are redrawn by each state's legislature to make sure that each congressional district has approximately the same number of people in the district. In states where the legislature is fairly evenly divided between Democrats and Republicans, district lines generally are drawn to protect incumbents of both parties. Democrats are given districts with large numbers of Democratic voters, and Republicans are given districts with large numbers of Republicans. Drawing districts this way leads to the relatively few competitive open seats mentioned above, even when there is no incumbent in the race. In states where the legislature is dominated by one party or the other, the strategy in redrawing congressional districts is to maximize the number of seats in the hands of the majority party. One way to do that is to draw the district in such a way that two incumbent members of the minority party are in the same district, and must run against each other. Every ten years, following re-districting, there are a handful of elections in which that occurs.

Money in congressional elections

Unlike the presidential elections, there is no partial or full public funding of congressional elections in the United States. Candidates have four sources of funding: themselves, individual contributors, political action committees (PACs), and the political parties. While the FECA of 1974 put limits on the amount of money individuals, PACs, and political parties could contribute to congressional candidates, there is no limit on the amount of money a candidate can contribute to his or her own campaign. For example, in the 2000 election, wealthy Democratic businessman Jon Corzine contributed $60 million of his own money to his successful New Jersey Senate campaign.

Individuals may contribute $1,000 to a congres-sional candidate in the primary election, and another $1,000 in the general election. These figures were doubled in the Bipartisan Campaign Reform Act of 2002. Beginning with the 2004 election, individuals will be able to contribute $2,000 to federal candidates in the primary election and another $2,000 in the general election.

Political action committees (PACs) are committees formed by interest groups, labour unions, trade associations, and corporations to solicit money from their members for political candidates. Federal law prohibits corporations and labour unions from contributing treasury funds to candidates for federal office, so political action committees were created as a way to allow these groups to participate financially in elections in the United States. A PAC may contribute $5,000 to a candidate in the primary election and another $5,000 in the general election.

Political parties can contribute money to federal candidates in one of three ways. The parties may make a contribution directly to the candidate. The national (Republican National Committee or Democratic National Committee), Senate (the National Republican Senatorial Committee or the Democratic Senatorial Campaign Committee), and the congressional (the Congressional Republican Campaign Committee or the Democratic Congressional Campaign Committee) committees may each contribute $10,000 directly to candidates for the House of Representatives. The national and Senate committees combined can contribute $17,500 to Senate candidates, and the House committees can contribute another $10,000 to Senate candidates.

A second way the party committees can help finance congressional elections is through coordinated expenditures on behalf of congressional candidates. The Senate and House committees may pay for a poll, or a campaign advertisement for a candidate, but the money does not go directly to the candidate, so the party committee has some say over how the money is spent. The amount of money available each election cycle is indexed to inflation; in the 2000 election it was $33,780 for House candidates, and ranged from $135,120 to $3.2 million for Senate candidates, depending on the population of the state.

A third way political parties can financially participate in congressional elections is through soft money expenditures. In congressional elections, just as in presidential elections, soft money has, in recent elections, most commonly been spent on issue advocacy. As with presidential elections, as long as the ad does not advocate the election or defeat of the candidate but simply provides information about him or her, there is no limit on the amount of soft money political parties can spend to elect or defeat congressional candidates in this manner. However, if the campaign finance bill passed by the Congress in 2002 is upheld by the courts, 2002 will be the last congressional election in which soft money can be used by the political parties.

Key points

- Elections for the House of Representatives are held every two years. Senators serve six-year terms.
- The majority of incumbents who run for re-election win, because they are better known, better liked, and better financed.
- Every ten years, following the census, House districts are redrawn to ensure that each district has approximately the same number of citizens.
- congressional candidates raise money in four ways: self-financing, contributions from individuals, contributions from political parties, and contributions from political action committees (PACs).

State and local elections

While presidential and congressional elections often receive the most attention from the media, and are typically the most expensive, they are only the tip of the iceberg in terms of the number of elections in America. There are approximately 450,000 state and local elections held in America every two years (Beaudry and Schaeffer 1986). These elections include high-profile elections, such as those for state governors and large city mayors, but most of these state and local elections are for offices that are less high-profile. State legislative offices, city councils, school boards, and other offices have elections as well. Turnout in these elections is generally lower than in presidential and congressional elections, particularly when there are no federal elections on the ballot. Turnout could be as low as 5 or 10 per cent of those eligible to vote in these very local elections (Francia and Herrnson 2002).

It is in these elections that party identification is usually the most important determinant of the vote. Voters typically know little, if anything, about these candidates other than the candidate's party affiliation, which is on the ballot. Knowing nothing else about the candidate, voters cast their vote for their party's candidate. Often these elections involve first-time candidates, who have little or no political experience. While these elections are typically less expensive than races for federal or state-wide offices, even state and local elections are becoming more expensive. Estimates are that spending increased 70 per cent in state legislative races in the United States between the mid-1980s and the mid-1990s.

Key points

- There are hundreds of thousands of elections to state and local offices held every two years in the United States.
- Most candidates for state and local offices are not well known by the voters, and do not have the resources to run high-profile campaigns.
- Turnout in state and local offices is generally lower than in congressional elections.
- Party identification is often the primary determinant of the vote in state and local elections.

Box 6.4 **Is America different?**
Elections compared

America is different from other Western democracies in a number of ways. First, the date of the general elections for federal office—the presidency and the Congress—are prescribed by the US Constitution, but the dates and times of primary elections for federal offices, as well as the dates and times of state and local elections, are determined by state governments. This division of power between the federal and state governments means that there is a plethora of elections in the United States. At almost all times in the country, someone is running for some office somewhere.

Second, because the First Amendment has been interpreted to mean there can be no limit on the time spent campaigning, campaigns for some offices take many months, or even years. Candidates start running for president not six weeks, or six months, before the election, but often two or three years. No sooner had the Supreme Court finally decided the outcome of the 2000 presidential election than speculation began about Al Gore and Joe Lieberman's relative prospects in 2004.

Third, despite few restrictions on voting in the United States, turnout in elections is much lower than in many other industrialized states. While voters in emerging democracies stand in line for hours to exercise their right to vote, half of all Americans are too complacent or too disillusioned to vote for even the nation's highest office, the presidency.

Finally, political parties play a very small role in who runs for office. While the parties provide financial and campaign assistance to candidates in elections, the nomination of the party for any particular office is decided by the voters, not the parties. The candidate-centred nature of American politics means that sometimes the party's nominee is not the strongest representative of the party, or even acceptable to the party. For example, in 1991 former Ku Klux Klansman David Duke ran for governor of Louisiana as a Republican, much to the chagrin of the Republican Party.

Conclusion

Elections proliferate in America, and the amount of money spent to elect candidates to office increases every year. There is always an election in progress in the United States. Yet even with the number of elections, there is still concern that incumbent office-holders have a decided advantage in elections, and it is difficult for a challenger to run a competitive race.

The costs of elections is also an ongoing concern. Some argue that the costs of running for office, even increasingly at the state legislative level, mean that candidates without independent wealth or access to financial resources will not be able to participate in the political process. Others argue that not enough money is spent on elections, and there should be no restrictions on the amount of money individuals, political parties, or interest groups can contribute to candidates.

The presidential election of 2000 illustrated some of the flaws in the American electoral process. With no uniform voting standards in the country, different states have different practices and procedures. Some states have state-of-the-art electronic voting machines, while others, such as Florida, still rely on paper ballots and machines prone to counting errors. Efforts to create national standards face resistance from states which want to retain control of elections.

Election reform has been an ongoing discussion since the United States was founded, and will continue into the twenty-first century. The role of the electoral college, internet voting, voter registration reform, poll closing times, and media coverage of election returns will all continue to be debated, as the nation tries to balance the goals of a fair electoral system for all while retaining differences in individual participation in the electoral process.

Box 6.5 Definitions

By-product theory of political information. People learn about politics through events that happen in their everyday lives.

Caucuses. A gathering of people affiliated with a political party to choose delegates to the party's nominating convention.

Challengers. Candidates who run for an elected office in which the current office-holder is running for re-election.

Dealignment. A lessening of the importance of partisanship in American elections, resulting in fewer Americans identifying themselves as Democrats or Republicans.

Electoral college. The process by which candidates are elected president of the United States. Each state is assigned a number of electoral votes equal to the number of senators and representatives elected to Congress by that state. A presidential candidate must receive at least 270 electoral votes to be elected president.

Incumbent. A candidate who is running for re-election to the office he or she already holds.

Open-seat candidates. Candidates running for an elected office in which there is no incumbent seeking re-election.

Partisanship. A long-term identification with a political party that constitutes a basic orientation towards politics.

Political action committee. An organization formed to solicit voluntary contributions to be given to candidates for political office. PACs are often but not always affiliated with an interest group.

Primaries. Elections involving candidates of the same political party to determine the party's nominee in the general election.

Prospective voting. Voting on the basis of a comparison of candidates' promises on policy issues if they are elected to the office they seek.

Public opinion. Opinions about public policies and public officials by a collective number of people.

Realignment. A fundamental, permanent shift in political affiliations such that the minority party becomes the majority party in the country.

Retrospective voting. Voting on the basis of an incumbent's—or, if there is no incumbent, the incumbent's party's—performance in office.

Soft money. Unlimited contributions which may be given to political parties for 'party-building' activities.

Survey research. The scientific study of public opinion, by polling randomly selected individuals.

QUESTIONS

1   How important is it to have an electorate informed on policy issues and familiar with candidates running for office?

2   Does it matter that only half of those eligible to vote in the United States vote in presidential elections, and even fewer vote in sub-presidential elections? Does the level of turnout affect the legitimacy of government? Should elected officials represent the views of those who vote, or all the citizens?

3   Some people think that election laws should be liberalized to make it easier for citizens to vote, while others think the electoral system works well as it is. What would be the advantages and disadvantages of moving towards a more universal suffrage system?

4   What are the consequences of the high rate of re-election of incumbents for governmental responsiveness to the opinions of citizens? Are incumbent office-holders likely to be more or less responsive, knowing their positions are by and large secure?

5 Does money have too great a role in American elections? Does the expense of running for office keep some talented candidates from seeking office?

6 Should the electoral college, created by the Founding Fathers for a country very different from the United States today, be continued, or should presidential candidates be elected by popular vote, as are all other office-holders in the United States? What would be the consequences of having presidents elected by popular vote?

FURTHER READING

A. Corrado et al. (1997), *Campaign Finance Reform: A Sourcebook* (Washington, DC: Brookings Institution). A detailed reference book explaining the history of campaign finance and campaign finance reform in the United States.

W. Flanigan and N. Zingale (2002), *Political Behavior of the American Electorate*, 10th edn. (Washington, DC: CQ Press). A comprehensive study of public opinion and partisanship in the United States during the second half of the twentieth century.

K. Jamieson and M. Waldman (2001), *Electing the President 2000: The Insider's View* (Philadelphia: University of Pennsylvania Press). An excellent discussion of the strategies of presidential candidates George W. Bush and Al Gore in the 2000 election by key Bush and Gore staff.

D. Magleby (ed.) (2002), *Financing the 2000 Election* (Washington, DC: Brookings Institution). A comprehensive account of campaign finance in the 2000 presidential, congressional, and state and local elections.

M. Matalin and J. Carville (1994), *All's Fair: Love, War and Running for President* (New York: Random House). An entertaining and informative discussion of the 1992 presidential campaign from the perspectives of the authors, one a key strategist for George Bush and the other a key strategist for Bill Clinton.

S. Rosenstone and J. M. Hansen (1993), *Mobilization, Participation, and Democracy in America* (New York: Macmillan). An excellent examination of the reasons for low turnout in American elections.

D. Von Drehle (2001), *Deadlock: The Inside Story of America's Closest Election* (New York: Affairs). A comprehensive account of election night 2000, and the 36-day recount in Florida by reporters of the *Washington Post*.

WEB LINKS

National political party campaign committees

www.rnc.org The Republican National Committee

www.democrats.org The Democratic National Committee

www.nrsc.org The Republican Senatorial Campaign Committee

www.dscc.org The Democratic Senatorial Campaign Committee

www.nrcc.org The Republican Congressional Campaign Committee

www.dccc.org The Democratic Congressional Campaign Committee

Campaign finance

www.fec.gov The Federal Election Commission

www.cfinst.org The Campaign Finance Institute

www.opensecrets.org The Center for Responsive Politics

Media sources

www.cnn.com/ALLPOLITICS Cable News Network (CNN)

www.washingtonpost.com/wp-dyn/politics *The Washington Post*

www.campaignline.com *Campaigns and Elections Magazine*

Other sources of information

www.vote-smart.org Project Vote Smart: information on candidates' voting records

www.pollingreport.com The Polling Report: trends in American public opinion

www.american.edu/spa/ccps Center for Congressional and Presidential Studies at American University

7 The mass media

Pete Lentini

READER'S GUIDE

The purpose of this chapter is to provide an overview of the mass media's role in contemporary US politics. Upon completing this chapter, the reader should have gained a more thorough knowledge of this topic within five main areas: the general characteristics and functions of the US media; the politics of the news media; the relationship between the media and the political process; the politics of 'new' and non-traditional media; and media politics in the age of globalization. Overall, this chapter is concerned with presenting the media as a site of perpetual contest within American society. Americans view a free media as an important component of their form of divided democracy. Additionally, the chapter highlights the tensions between American values of freedom of expression and how they can often conflict with the practices of the free market. This chapter also interrogates the extent to which the media broaden notions of American identity and whether they can serve as mechanisms to reduce America's declining voter turnouts and stimulate other forms of political participation.

Introduction

The first part of this chapter outlines such issues as the range of media Americans use and the relationship between media ownership, content, and political power. Additionally, the chapter is concerned with the role of the media in the American democratic process. Hence, it investigates how the media constitute battlegrounds for free speech, debates, and access. Additionally, it asks how the media can serve to assist in the political socialization process and to help generate a sense of national identity over a broad land mass. The next section examines the relationship between news and institutional politics, in particular, addressing issues like what constitutes news. It goes further, to discuss how editors' and producers' decisions on who and what to cover and the manner in which they are presented are political issues. Amongst one of the most important questions this chapter seeks to address is how politicians, their staffs, and the media interact within the context of agenda setting. The next section focuses on the media and its relations to political participation. In particular, it looks at the ways in which the media's market-driven orientation affects election campaigning and offers the potential for political engagement through social movements.

Politicians' use of media to convey their messages to the population is an important component of US politics; however, it is by no means the only manner in which there is contact between the governors and the governed. Citizens also use various forms of media to conduct politics. However, because of the nature of American media's operating procedures, not all citizens' viewpoints are accommodated through the mainstream mass media. The fourth section of this chapter, therefore, questions why American citizens turn to sources of political information and communication that are not within the mainstream. In particular, it queries the political significance of new and non-traditional media like

talk shows and talk radio, the increasingly important role of the internet as a means of political discussion and organization, and other personalized media such as zines. It also addresses whether these media are indeed open to all, and if they enhance the process of democratic participation.

Finally, most people's initial contact with the US comes from either news or entertainment media generated by American-owned or American-based media conglomerates, centring on American politicians, starring American actors, or focusing on American themes. These forms of media content are increasingly becoming more internationalized through the process of globalization. Politicians, civic groups, and citizens living outside the US have become increasingly concerned that the availability of American products or American themes that are broadcast overseas is challenging established notions of national identity. Therefore, the final section of this chapter is concerned with the politics of American media and its contribution to the globalization process. In particular, it is concerned with whether American media's contribution to the globalization process challenges other countries' identities, and the measures that those living outside the US have taken to counter or to embrace these media artefacts.

General overview

Struggles over the media

The politics of the mass media is inherently linked to culture, and culture is political. According to Raymond Williams, Glenn Jordan, and Chris Weedon (1995: 9–13) culture can be defined as 'a general process of intellectual, spiritual and aesthetic development'; 'a particular way of life, whether of a people, a period or a group'; 'a way of life that is informed by a common spirit'; 'the works and practices of intellectual and especially artistic activity'; and 'the signifying system through which necessarily (though among other means) a social

order is communicated'. Alan Finlayson's (1999: 134) arguments concerning the political consequences of culture correspond quite logically with de Jouvenal's, Easton's, and Lasswell's definitions of politics (see Box 7.1):

Culture only becomes an issue, something that is explicitly thought about, because certainties about our way of life have been called into question. . . . The wide dissemination of culture raises important issues. It is not adequate to answer the question 'what is culture'? by defining it as 'the best'. This simply raises further queries. Who decides what 'the best' is? Who has access to 'the best'? To put it another way, who is to count as cultured? This is a question of power and democracy.

Box 7.1 Definitions

For most students—and even professional analysts of politics—the term 'politics' is associated with (or perhaps more precisely ghettoized as) 'the science and art of government, the science dealing with the form, organization and administration or a part of one, and with the regulation of its relations with other states' (*Shorter Oxford Dictionary* cited in Tansey 1995: 5). In reality there are many more aspects and definitions of politics. Stephen Tansey (1995: 6–8) employs four additional definitions which broaden political study's scope: 'a way of ruling divided societies by a process of free discussion and without undue violence' (Bernard Crick); 'who gets what, when, how' (Harold Laswell); 'man moving man' (Bertrand de Jouvenal); 'the authoritative allocation of value' (David Easton). Aside from the obvious sexist bias in de Jouvanal's definition, these approaches greatly expand the borders of politics to areas outside the official corridors of power of 'grey buildings' where 'grey men and women in grey suits' promote 'grey policies'.

Jordan and Weedon (1995: 13) argue that those who control culture—or aspects of culture—possess a range of powers, including the power to name, the power to represent common sense, the power to create official versions, and the power to represent the legitimate social world. Therefore, they argue: 'In each case, what is at issue is the power to define what things mean. How meanings are defined largely determines who has access to wealth and the social resources that are necessary for a decent life.'

It is with these points in mind that it is necessary to pursue the politics of American mass media. The struggles portrayed in the media and the conflicts over what is presented within them are linked to questions of culture and power. They are often concerned with some of the most basic values that Americans consider essential to their concepts of democratic governance and the quality of governance. Important, therefore, are issues such as: What is presented in the media? Who is presented in the media, and in what manner? Who has access to the media? What constitutes a significant political issue? What forms of media permit the greatest level of interaction between the governors and governed? What forms of media best permit citizens to engage in dialogue with each other?

The politics addressed in the American media occurs within three often overlapping spheres: personal, public, and policy. Much of Americans' (and others') media consumption occurs within a personal realm: watching television news within their own homes, hearing about politics on the radio and reading newspapers and books, and, for those who have web access, surfing politically oriented internet sites. Nevertheless, even within these confines, there are interactions between the personal and public realm and the policy sphere. Bennett and Entman (2001: 2–3) define the public sphere as 'comprised of any and all locations, physical and virtual, where ideas and feelings relevant to politics are transmitted or exchanged openly'. However, while acknowledging that politics can occur within a broad range of instances, from people's normal everyday interactions to the highest levels of government, they make a further distinction by introducing a policy sphere which they define as 'the subset of the public sphere where ideas and feelings explicitly connect with—are communicated to, from, or about—government, and officials, parties or candidates for office who may decide the outcomes of issues and conflicts facing society' (p. 4). Peter Dahlgren (2001: 38) contends that 'the public sphere often deals with private matters, such as the personal lives of politicians and celebrities on general topics having to do with "lifestyle" questions or moral issues about how we live (e.g., abortion)'. The mass media and the public figures and citizens who use them engage and articulate politics on all these levels to attempt to influence and interpret politics, to receive political information, and to organize politically.

The media in everyday life

Americans use media abundantly. There is also a wealth of American media, their freedom to report constitutionally protected by the the First Amendment (see Box 7.2). Philip John Davies (1998: 337) argues that this is politically important because Americans possess

an average of 5.6 radios ... and 2.2 televisions per household, [so] all the family can listen and watch. The 80 per cent of households with VCRs spend $6.6 billion on film rental, and cinemas receive a further $6.5 billion in receipts. Total newspaper distribution is around 60 million.

Douglas Kellner (1995: 1) argues that most advanced democracies—America included—can be considered part of a media culture which encompasses various audio, visual, and digital recordings, and their means of distribution, packaging, reception, and marketing. Hence, media culture encompasses film, the internet, music, the press, the book industry, radio, and, particularly television, which he argues is situated 'at the centre of media culture' (Kellner 1995: 1). Jamieson and Campbell (1997: 9) note that, 'Americans spend more time watching television than doing anything else except sleeping and eating!' The media, including television, help to set and legitimize political agendas. According to Michael Parenti (1986: ix),

For many people an issue does not exist until it appears in the media. ... Even when we don't believe what the media say, we are still hearing or reading their viewpoints rather than some other. They are still setting the agenda, defining what it is we must believe or disbelieve, accept or reject.

Amongst all their various forms of media, Gary C. Woodward reports from Roper poll data, Americans consider television the most credible source of information:

when asked 'if you got conflicting or different reports of the same story from radio, television, the magazines, and the newspapers,' over half of all respondents (55 per cent) said they were most inclined 'to believe television', with newspapers coming in a distant second (21 per cent). Radio and magazines were the first choices of less than 8 per cent of respondents. (Woodward 1997: 58)

The United States has three major television networks: NBC, which is owned by General Electric, ABC, owned by Disney, and CBS, owned by Westinghouse. During the late 1980s another channel emerged, Rupert Murdoch's Fox Channel. The three main networks all have local affiliates in major cities. In addition to the free-to-air terrestrial stations, cable television—which offers its subscribers a range of specialized programming including movies, sports, and news—like CNN and the congressional channels C-SPAN I and C-SPAN II and other channels, began to emerge throughout the country from the 1970s. However, while free-to-air television is certainly widely available, cable television's distribution is somewhat more limited. Davies notes: 'in 1991–92, over 70 per cent of adults with household income over $50,000 were watching cable, as opposed to fewer than 50 per cent of adults with household incomes lower than $30,000' (1998: 343). Thus it is important to note that Americans with lower incomes do not have access to some of the most important sources of political information—CNN, for instance, especially for overseas news, and the C-SPAN channels for national issues.

Americans also consume a wide range of magazines and newspapers. Unlike many other advanced democracies, however, America does not possess a national newspaper. A wide range of newspapers circulate on a national level, like the influential *Wall Street Journal*, *New York Times*, *Los Angeles Times*, and *Washington Post* and the popular tabloid *USA Today*. Weekly magazines such as *Time* and *Newsweek* are also sources of Americans' information.

Box 7.2 **Constitutional influences**
The First Amendment

Congress shall make no law respecting an establishment of religion, or prohibiting the free exercise thereof; or abridging the freedom of speech, or of the press; or the right of the people peaceably to assemble, and to petition the government for a redress of grievances.

Media ownership and political power

What is also important to note about the American mass media is that they are private corporations:

the primary function of the mass media is to attract and hold large audiences for advertisers. They also inform and entertain, of course; but informing and entertaining are only means to the end of providing a mass audience for advertisers. (Jamieson and Campbell 1997: 4; original emphasis)

Woodward argues:

Consumers tend to view the media as providers of specific forms of content: programs we want to see or items we want to read. But the media themselves, along with those who evaluate them as potential investments and advertisers generally consider the media as audience delivery systems. (Woodward 1997: 41–2)

Another significant feature of the American media is that since the 1980s they have become increasingly concentrated in the hands of fewer and fewer individuals and business groups. Hence, these features raise questions that are essential to the core themes of this volume: Does the corporate nature of American media serve to provide American citizens with the diverse range of sources of information and opinion that are necessary to construct a pluralist order? What degrees of access do Americans have to the mass media? Do the American media help to strengthen feelings of national identity? Do they enhance divisiveness? These very questions prompt a discussion of the fundamental roles that the media play in democratic states.

Over the past two decades, mass media in the US have gone through several changes, and have had significant impact on the manner in which the media portray politics, who owns the media and what is disseminated, and who has access to the mainstream media. These issues reflect the core questions associated with the politics of culture, and affect how the mass media can perform as an intermediary institution in US politics. Blum and Gurevitch note that economic factors such as the rapid growth from national to transnational corporations, corporate takeovers which have led to increased media concentration, the proliferation of media outlets through satellite and cable systems, and the abundance of 'personal and in-home' communications and reception equipment such as VCRs, CD burners and, increasingly, the internet, have led to 'intense competition for audiences [which] favours populist cultural forms and appeals' and reduces leeway for policy goals other than the building and earning of long-term competitive positioning (Blum and Gurevitch 1996: 124–5).

From the 1930s, the Federal Communications Commission (FCC) has been the body responsible for regulating the public airwaves in the United States and performing such duties as issuing and revoking licences for broadcast media outlets such as radio and television (Stevens 1982: 60, 135, 141). Throughout most of the twentieth century, the FCC and the US government more broadly attempted to keep media outlets and ownership fairly diverse. Christopher H. Sterling notes that the 1934 Communications Act, which brought the FCC into existence, initially mandated that no single media owner could possess more than one radio (and, subsequently, television) station at any one time. However, he also notes that some two decades later, the FCC altered this pattern to what is referred to as the '7–7–7 Rule', which enabled owners 'to control up to seven AM, seven FM, and seven television stations, nationwide, not more than five of the latter to be VHF outlets' (Sterling 2000: 57). He goes on to note that compared to contemporary standards, concentrated media ownership was at that stage still quite small: 'By 1980, even the largest group owners controlled no more than twenty-one stations, though three-quarters of the country's stations were owned by such groups' (Sterling 2000: 57). However, after the Republicans won control of the US Congress in 1994, Congress passed the 1996 Telecommunications Act which enabled media owners to control greater numbers of media outlets. Sterling contends that their philosophy was that media, like other US businesses, needed to become larger in order to be competitive in a global environment. Additionally, he notes that many credible studies suggested that media concentration could potentially enhance diversity in programming and content and that the increased competition that this would stimulate would benefit consumers (Sterling 2000: 66–7).

Sterling reports that there were many tele-communications company mergers as a result of the 1996 legislation. For instance,

Where companies had been restricted to owning no more than twenty AM and twenty FM stations [before 1996], 'within a month of the law's passage, the two largest national group owners had 52 . . . and 46 stations respectively. . . . By mid-year merger activity led to the first group owner with more than 100 stations.'

Additionally, two years later some radio station group owners possessed nearly 400 stations (Sterling 2000: 62, 64). There were also significant mergers within the television industry in which 'the largest 35 group owners who held 25 per cent of the market in 1996 owned 36 per cent in 1998', and to illustrate the degree of ownership of some of these groups Sterling points to Paxson Communications, which by 1999 'owned fifty television stations serving more than 30 per cent of the nation's TV homes'. More-over, the largest cable television owners' holdings increased from 45 per cent of the market in 1994 to 74 per cent in 1998 (Sterling 2000: 64).

In addition to concentrating ownership, the new legislation and the subsequent merger frenzy threatened media diversity in another important way. From the 1970s, the federal government had been attempting to increase the number of media outlets owned by ethnic minorities. The govern-ment used incentives like tax concessions to help provide these communities with avenues to present programming which they controlled and which reflected their cultures and interests. However, Sterling suggests that these struggling media owners would have faced serious disadvantages when the legislation came into effect. The increased com-petition would have raised the prices of the media outlets. Additionally, the federal government with-drew the tax concessions. Nevertheless, Sterling also notes that the minority communities may have had some opportunity to remain in the game through the provision of a Telecommunication Development Fund. Small businesses like the minority-owned stations could utilize these monies to purchase stations (Sterling 2000: 61). Despite this provision, Sterling contends that overall, the legislation bene-fited the companies because, in the end, consumer prices rose and 'the law that many Congressmen

expected to expand competition seemed instead to promote growing merger activity' (p. 67).

Mass media in a democracy

The new media environment has altered signifi-cantly the role that the mass media are supposed to perform in a liberal democracy. James Curran argues that the media are supposed to carry out three main functions in a democratic environment: public watchdog, public representative, and a source of public information. He contends that the literature which relates to the media and the public sphere underlines the proposition that market conditions will best enable the media to perform these func-tions. For instance, private rather than state owner-ship will provide the media with the proper environment in which to monitor the government for corruption and malfeasance. Similarly, the mar-ket can permit the media to serve as a public repre-sentative because it is better suited for delivering programming led by consumer demands. Finally, the market can serve the media better in its public information role because it is already geared towards diversity (Curran 1996: 83–97).

However, Curran also notes that the new market-oriented media conditions have not necessarily served to enhance democratic practices within advanced democracies, including the US. For one, the public watchdog function need not be restricted to government and its officials. The media can also serve to monitor the private sector. However, he notes that 'one of the consequences of the changing patterns of ownership is that the media enterprises have sometimes refrained from criticising the activities of the giant conglomerates to which they belong' (Curran 1996: 86). He suggests further that these theories of media and the market are inadequate because in the new conditions the media often cannot serve adequately as public representa-tives because 'the new oligopolies have reduced media diversity, audience choice and public con-trol', and 'the rising capitalisation of media has restricted entry into the market' of those who do not possess adequate financial means. Furthermore, these theories also ignore matters such as the fact that media owners are not politically neutral and often insert their own agendas into their media. Finally, the media do not adequately perform their informational role because the media are not the only sources of political information in contemporary society. These include peer groups, political parties, and non-mainstream sources of information. Additionally, while the media, particularly print media, could adequately perform the task of bringing information to the citizens of liberal democracies during the eighteenth to early twentieth centuries, they have more difficulties today because there are more information outlets and audiences are more fragmented as a result of mobility, and the abundance of broadcast and reception technologies (Curran 1996: 90–102; Blumer and Gurevitch 1996).

Mass media and national integration

This latter point draws attention to the role that the media play in helping to foster national integration. Benedict Anderson (1983/1999) argues that the nation is an 'imagined community'. By this, Anderson means that the size of any given nation-state and the population groups that constitute the nation are so vast that all the people within them can never meet each other personally. As a result, the nation, which can best be defined as a group of people sharing a common history, common culture, and in some cases common territory and who consider themselves as a group distinct from others (Gellner 1983; Smith 1991), needs to imagine itself in order to maintain its coherence. Anderson argues that mass media, beginning with the process of print capitalism, helped to bring nations together in the absence of face-to-face interaction. He contends that the mass media help to spread the narratives of history and everyday life which bind people together as a nation. The media also help to generate the common myths and struggles in which the individuals and groups define their sense of identity, a term that Jordan and Weedon (1995: 15) claim 'implies a conscious sense of self'. Kellner (1995), Blumer and Gurevitch (1996: 123), and Herman and Chomsky (1988/1994: 1) all agree that the mass media help to spread values which provide the building blocks

from which people can formulate their senses of self and of difference from others. Kellner also suggests (1995) that the nature of contemporary media under conditions of globalization (which is discussed at greater length below) is to establish what could be considered to be elements of a common global culture.

It needs to be highlighted, however, that it is not only 'serious' media—quality newspapers and periodicals, mainstream radio and television news, and internet news sites—which contribute to the construction of national identity. The mass media's persistent images and references to particular ethnic and social groups begins to naturalize and to define these groups' relationships to the broader national corpus. Those groups which appear most frequently and in the most positive light are often seen to embody the national community. Using the war-film genre as a case study, historian Robert Burgoyne demonstrates that until the 1980s most war films focused overwhelmingly on white males' roles in military service. Hence the film industry (and viewers) validated this conception by producing and consuming motion pictures which followed this line. While it is well known that other groups of men and women played significant roles in American history, their absence (or negative portrayals) excluded them from being written into what Burgoyne considers 'the official narrative' of American identity through film. During the 1980s, however, this process began to change when filmmakers, many from non-European backgrounds, began to make movies depicting members of their ethnic groups as positive contributors to American history. Burgoyne contends that a film such as *Glory*, which depicts African American soldiers' combat roles (albeit led by white officers) in the Civil War, helped to expand the cinematic portrayals of those who contributed to American history. Hence, these films and other media helped to expand the celluloid representations of those who contributed to the nation's history. In these respects, the media helped to broaden the conceptions of inclusiveness, citizenship, and identity (Burgoyne 1997).

This analysis need not be confined to film. For instance, Sue K. Jewell (1993) demonstrates how other mainstream media have stigmatized African

American women with negative images and how these women have challenged them. Similarly, Tricia Rose (1994) contends that young African Americans use hip hop to create social spaces where they can affirm and celebrate their cultural experiences, reflect on socially relevant issues, and contest negative stereotyping on their own terms. Television has certainly begun to show women as far more empowered citizens than they were in the 1950s. However, it is important to note that while popular productions like *Buffy the Vampire Slayer* may cast a positive light on young women's roles in America, and depict representatives of sexual minorities in progressive and affirming circumstances, they still have a long way to go in providing more inclusive definitions of what it means to be young and female other than white, suburban, and middle-class (hooks 1981; 1994; Edwards 2002). Hence, the mainstream media do not offer comprehensive conceptions of national identity.

These examples demonstrate one of the problems that contemporary media face in attempting to create a sense of national identity and integration. The US is a diverse country with many ethnic groups, and with peoples of varying religious and sexual identities. These factors, plus the points to which Blumer and Gurevitch and Curran draw attention—increased media outlets, many forms of personal communications, and other developments like the internet—make it increasingly difficult for the mass media to generate a sense of common identity, as they did during the eighteenth to early twentieth centuries. Observers have noted that often the new media arrangements stimulate people to receive their information from sources which are more closely aligned to their views and interests (Cook 2001: 185; Dahlgren 2001: 42–4; Blumer and Gurevitch 1996: 126–7). Moreover, Bennett and Manheim (2001) suggest that some of the strategies and policies of the owners neither enhance the quality of information nor aim to attract broad audiences. Drawing on Robert Dahl's work on polyarchy, they argue that 'the quality and communication of political information is central to the evolution of democracy', and that if polyarchy is to evolve beyond a state of capture by policy elites, the key lies in 'maximizing the free flow of information in the policy process', and they contend that this is best

served by 'creating independent communication channels for transmitting reliable knowledge to citizens, and facilitating broadly inclusive deliberation on policy related decisions' (Bennett and Manheim 2001: 279, 280). They suggest that 'the use of information and communication by various organised interests in the United States indicates movement in just the opposite direction of that advocated by Dahl'. They contend that these groups target

the smallest audiences likely to be helpful to their political aims, and to deliver information that is designed not to promote informed deliberate engagement on the part of those selected citizens. Rather, information is typically publicized to mobilize and demobilize segments of the public to serve narrow strategic interests, often masking the identity or intent of the communicator in the process.   (Bennett and Manheim 2001: 280)

Despite these factors, the mass media are still mechanisms which reinforce American values such as diversity of opinion and which help promote pluralism. Additionally, they remain the primary source of information on major national and international affairs. In these ways, they still serve as an important intermediary mechanism for maintaining national identity, and for monitoring nationally significant issues and issues in international politics that concern the US. Indeed, Diana C. Muntz and Paul S. Martin posit: 'Exposure to conflicting views is deemed a central element—if not the sine qua non—of the kind of political dialogue needed to maintain a democratic citizenry. . . . In contrast, political talk that centres on reinforcing a shared viewpoint does little to encourage deliberation on multiple perspectives or promote a public space' (Muntz and Martin 2001: 97). They contend that people generally seek direct relationships with people who share their most common viewpoints. Conversely, they tend to avoid those with whom they will have the most differences. Hence, in these circumstances, they tend to receive little differentiation in political views. However, Muntz and Martin argue that, by using the mass media, viewers and consumers are exposed to far greater varieties of opinion than they get in their everyday interactions. This is largely due to the fact that most mainstream news outlets—newspapers, radio, television news—are structured to present a broad range of issues and perspectives:

It is easier to avoid exposure to the views of personal acquaintances than the views expressed in the national news. With daily newspapers and most national television news, the ability to exercise choice on the basis of partisanship is severely limited. Few communities have more than one daily newspaper from which to choose; moreover, few newspapers have readily recognized political complexions that facilitate selective exposure to like-minded political views. Likewise, the political tone of national television news is very similar across channels. Of course, the same cannot be said about news magazines, talk shows and political web sites. In more specialized media, people may well be able to select a news source that shares their political bent.   (Muntz and Martin 2001: 99)

These features mean that the mass media still have a much more important role in exposing citizens to divergent viewpoints than do interpersonal networks and the specialized media. They therefore continue to serve as perhaps the most important form of media outlets that have the ability to strengthen national cohesion and to promote pluralism (Muntz and Martin 2001: 109–10).

Commentators have correctly acknowledged that new technologies such as the internet are challenging the American mainstream media's abilities to reach national audiences with important information. However, Doug Underwood (2001: 112) underlines the fact that 'mainstream commercial media organizations still provide much of the information—or at least most of the credible information—upon which society's communication pyramid is erected', and W. Russell Neuman's research (2001: 311) suggests: 'Web users do not use news sources on the web to replace regular media exposure but rather to supplement it'.

The politics of news

Selecting and defining news

The previous section suggested that market-driven media and new media have challenged the manner in which the mass media promote national identity. However, it is also important to question how these factors affect the mass media's abilities to serve their roles as public watchdogs and sources of information in liberal democracies. Indeed, the main questions posed here are whether the media are giving the people what they want; whether the drive for consumers has come at a cost to the democratic process; and whether these measures have increased the range of ideas necessary to stimulate a pluralist system.

Commentators have noted that these market demands have come at a cost to newspeople, the quality of the news they generate, and the items that they address. First, there is some consensus that market-driven journalism has transformed the notion that what is important to audience members is to be responsible citizens into what is 'relevant' to audience members as individuals and consumers (Underwood 2001: 101; Delli Carpini and Williams 2001). As such, news outlets have greatly reduced the analytical space given to political events, replacing them with tabloid-style graphics, increasing stories devoted to lifestyle issues, and centring on sex scandals rather than policy issues. There also appears to be a paradox within the media in their coverage of local affairs. While the media have increased their attention to items of local significance such as lifestyle issues, they have done so at the expense of local-level politicians. Indeed these authors contend that the political figures who tend to maintain media presences are the president, some cabinet members, and select congressional leaders (Underwood 2001: 102; Delli Carpini and Williams 2001: 167).

Woodward contends that these economic factors have contributed to 'black hole areas in the news', where issues (and countries) which the media once covered and to which outlets allocated staff, are no longer deemed financially viable (Woodward 1997: 155). Underwood argues, for instance, that market-driven journalism has substantially reduced foreign news coverage: it remains largely reported by CNN, and media outlets occasionally draw on satellite feeds from foreign broadcasters (Underwood 2001).

Box 7.3 Core academic debate
What counts as 'news'?

Culture is a site of political contest, and those who are in positions to influence or control media wield considerable power. Defining what constitutes news is one such power. The nature of global communications technologies facilitates fairly rapid changes of stories within the news media. Stories reported in the various news outlets alter and progress on a daily basis. In some circumstances, when news stories break they disrupt normal news presentation patterns. Generally, however, news appears to be an everyday occurrence; it is regarded as a fairly normal part of our daily lives. Nevertheless, while news is routine, routine is not news. Only select events, people, and issues are significant enough to be considered focal points for mainstream news. Moreover, American media realities and political values may clash in the process: the need to generate revenue does not always necessarily coincide with the duty to inform. This news selection process is not only political in the sense of conferring power, which, as Easton contends is 'the authoritative allocation of values'. What is defined as news also has the potential 'to move people' (de Jouvenal) and can have the opportunity to influence 'who gets what' (Laswell).

Jamieson and Campbell (1997) provide very useful information on how news emerges and how it is created. They contend that news transcends '"the facts"', that it is 'selected, even created by news people' (1997: 39). Moreover, they contend:

News is gathered, written, edited, produced, and disseminated by human beings who are part of organizations and who have beliefs and values. Organisations, such as networks, have functions and goals as well as relationships to government, to regulatory agencies, to advertisers, to their parent companies, and to the vast audiences they seek to attract. These beliefs, values, functions and interests are bound to influence the messages these networks publish and broadcast (1997: 39).

They maintain that 'no neat, satisfactory answer to [what is news] has been found. . . . The best answer seems to be that news is what reporters, editors and producers decide is news' (1997: 39). The nature of American media predisposes its managers to select items which portray various themes. As these topics suggest, most news stories reflect conflict (1997: 51):

1. *Appearance versus reality*. This reflects an emphasis on conflict and the 'objective' role of sceptical newsgatherers who uncover hypocrisy.

2. *Little guys versus big guys*. This theme reflects an emphasis on the personal and individual by taking a particular interest in the underdog or outsider or exposing corrupt and self-interested actions by the powerful against the powerless.

3. *Good against evil* . . . [T]his theme is related to crime as a news model and to investigative journalism as a norm for reporting.

4. *Efficiency versus inefficiency*. This is usually an attempt to uncover waste and mismanagement, illustrating the emphasis on politics and government in the news.

5. *The unique versus the routine*. Reflecting a stress on normality, this is illustrated by the human interest stories appearing at the end of most newscasts or in syndicated newspaper columns.

Finally, Jamieson and Campbell (p. 55) note that there are particular factors which influence how news is gathered and presented. These include 'access, costs, and limitations of time and space. News stories must attract and hold on to audiences and avoid offending advertisers, audiences and media owners. These factors influence what choices newspeople make and ultimately determine which stories will be printed and aired.'

Lang and Lang (2000: 300) present data which illustrate how reportage of international events has declined over two and a half decades:

the time that the networks devoted to news from abroad had fallen from 45 per cent of program time in 1970 to an emphatically tiny 13.5 per cent in 1995 (Moisy 1996). The space in newspapers given to foreign news had similarly declined over roughly the same period. In 1971, it filled 10.2 per cent of the newshole, in 1982 this was down to 6 per cent (NAB cited in Hoge 1997). Seven years later, another content analysis found only 2.6 per cent of the non-advertising space in ten leading newspapers carrying news from abroad (Emery 1989). News magazines have exhibited the same downward trend. Between 1985 and 1995, the space devoted to international news declined from 24 to 14 per cent in *Time*, from 22 to 12 per cent in *Newsweek*, and from 20 to 14 per cent in *US News & World Report* (magazine editorial reports, cited in Hage 1997).

These factors seriously diminish many Americans' knowledge of international and national affairs, and may affect Americans on the lower side of the income scale. Indeed as Davies has indicated, many of those with lower incomes will not have access to the international news presented on cable television channels like CNN.

Left-wing critics such as Herman and Chomsky (1988/1994) and Michael Parenti (1998) maintain that it is not just the demands of the news-making system that inhibit the media from providing more diverse news and news that runs counter to elites' viewpoints. They argue that media owners often share the perspectives of the ruling elites, so that they are ideologically predisposed not to present certain information, or to present dissenting information in a negative light.

Nevertheless, this should not suggest that Americans are solely subjected to one-sided or trivial media. Michael Kahan (1999) rightly indicates that criticisms of the media often underestimate the fact that individuals receive, perceive, and interpret information largely on the basis of their personal experiences, and that Americans have access to a very wide range of (often very credible) sources of information outside the mainstream media.

Access to news and manipulating the news

Following from the previous section, it is important to note that news selection is not just the province of editors, journalists, producers, and news managers. Political actors—elected politicians and candidates for elected office, political activists, terrorists—understand that they are required to generate news-worthy events in order to publicize their causes and to build support for their political objectives. Moreover, these political actors have also learned to use specific tactics to help them in the process of agenda setting, or highlighting specific issues and

downplaying others, in order to generate positive publicity and to maintain control over news content and tone. Woodward (1997: 1) argues:

The relationship that exists between the political world and the mass media often seems like an unusual form of courtship. Each needs the other, but the bonds of attraction are based more on suspicion than affection. Participants representing each side have clearly learned all the right moves, and the names for them. They plan their steps carefully, using a familiar language that signifies their caution in pursuing the relationship.

Additionally, Street maintains (2001: 2), 'Politicians are adapting to the medium upon which they have come to rely. They design their campaigns and their approach to fit the media. Their schedules are timed to coincide with journalists' deadlines; their public performances are intended to look good on screen.'

Woodward, for instance, provides useful illustrations of how the president relates to the press, and how both president and media each attempt to set the political agenda. He notes that during his time in office, the president will 'maintain a perpetual campaign', orienting his actions as if he were still attempting to win elected office. As such, the president consistently relies on public relations advisers so that he can best manage the media and be able to define and select the most important political issues. Additionally, Woodward notes that the president will coopt his former campaign advisers to his personal staff (Woodward 1997: 128–35). Most importantly, these factors help to contribute to a news management model of the presidency in which

the administration largely sets the agenda of events and ideas to be covered. The press is generally placed in a reactive role responding to those carefully prepared events with a combination of summaries and scepticism. The news management model of presidential power presumes that the White House holds most of the cards in the poker game of seeing favourable coverage.   (Woodward 1997: 139)

Ronald Reagan's Saturday speeches are among the best examples of a president managing the news.

One of the reasons the Reagan White House began the modern tradition of fifteen-minute Saturday messages is because it presents a chance to control the political news agenda. Saturday is a light news day in Washington, since Congress and the Federal agencies are usually closed. The

President's message exists through Sunday as something that others in the loop of national politics may need to deal with. The Sunday morning talk shows with their small but politically active audiences, for example, often include interviewers who use the President's remarks as a basis for their own questions to Congressional and political leaders. (Woodward 1997: 134).

Key points

- The politics addressed in the American media occur within three often overlapping spheres:

personal, public, and policy. Americans spend more time watching television than on any activity other than sleeping and eating.

- The freedom of the press is constitutionally protected in the First Amendment to the US Constitution.

- Journalists exercise a 'gatekeeping' function in American politics: what counts as 'news' or 'newsworthy'—from election results to politicians' sex lives—is inextricably tied to journalists' judgements.

The mass media and political participation

Various social movements also strive to present their causes and gain political support for their objectives (see below). The mainstream media also provide avenues through which non-institutional actors can become politically significant. Indeed, the media's market-driven orientation, the conflictual qualities of some events which make newsmakers select them as newsworthy stories, and the politics and activities of some mass social movements (e.g. the environmental movement, organized labour, the feminist movement, and various gay, lesbian, and queer movements and ethnic movements)—strikes, demonstrations, sit-ins, occupations—generate what could be considered a symbiotic relationship (Pakulski 1991: 3–51). William A. Gamson (2001) notes that often the media can assist various social movements merely by focusing attention on them, even if this is negative attention: that by using these 'cracks' provided by the media the members of such movements can gain media attention. However, what is more important is that these examples have been demonstrated to enhance citizens' perceptions that they are not powerless and that they can change their political situation, a process to which he refers as collective agency. The media, he claims (pp. 61–2), help to further these movements' causes when they:

- present social movements and their causes as 'taken seriously' by officials even when presented negatively;
- present citizens as potential agents that can change the conditions they consider negative;
- convey information which can be used to stimulate collective action and to publicize their goals.

Gamson suggests further that there are certain restrictions on their effectiveness. For instance, he claims that this exposure would very often be 'issue-specific'; those issues concerned with class struggle, such as labour disputes, have received far less exposure, and positive commentaries, than, for instance affirmative action and abortion issues. Nevertheless, he concedes that these conditions are also affected by the administration and its policies towards these issues. His research indicates that the mainstream mass media occasionally serve those interests that can run counter to the elites' perspectives by 'frequently and inadvertently keeping alive and helping transmit images of group protest, treating citizens as potential agents and challenging exclusion by opening the ruling governing policy discourse' (Gamson 2001: 72).

New media and political participation

Gamson's research provides credible evidence that the mass media, particularly television, have the potential to complement, and on occasion assist in, formal political participation. Kahan notes that before the rise of, for instance, the mediated presidency of Franklin Delano Roosevelt in the early 1930s, political parties were often the main sources of political information and political socialization. Thereafter, however, the mass media took over this role (Kahan 1999). Nevertheless, there are some critics who have argued that the mass media have not adequately fulfilled this function and that they—television in particular—have actually contributed to Americans' disengagement from politics (see examples in Bennett 1998: 742–4). Others have argued that the increased reliance on the media in politics and everyday life has not bred apathy, but rather has generated further evidence of a swing towards conservatism. Radio talk shows, which have been popularized by such notable figures as the 'shock jocks' Rush Limbaugh (his conservative viewpoints contributed to his being named an honorary member of the Congress, elected in 1994) and the libertarian Howard Stern, and by former disgraced political figures brought back from the dead such as the Watergate burglar G. Gordon Liddy and Lt. Col. Oliver North of Iran-Contra fame, offer media formats which reduce the potential for progressive or, at times, informed political discourse. This supposed 'anti-politics' is actually another manifestation of conservatism: the station owners tend to be Republicans, they appeal to a commuting audience which is overwhelmingly male (Gitlin 1996: 79–80), and like Clint Eastwood-type films, they allow for immediate audience actions (responses) without having to go through bureaucratic procedures like civilized discourse. Susan Herbst (1995) contends that people listen to, and communicate with the presenters, and sometimes other listeners, during these programmes because they often feel that the political mainstream does not give them adequate outlets for formal political participation. For instance, they consider the mainstream news media to be ' "too high-brow" ' for

them. She also notes that these shows are empowering because they permit the average citizen to 'police the public sphere' in areas where they feel that the media and certain politicians are too liberal in their points of view.

Although their politics differ radically, talk show listeners, and some left-wing activists who use the internet to disseminate their views share a common trend in political participation: they have turned their energies towards additional and sometimes alternative sites of politics, outside the formal institutional outlets and frameworks. In this sense, the new media have become both a site and an intermediary institution of politics. Scholars have noted that the decline in party identification and voter turnout in the US have been accompanied by participation in other civic groups and in some of the social movements that have been acknowledged earlier (Bennett 1998; Dahlgren 2001). As Bennett and Entman (2001) point out, these political activities certainly stimulate politics on both a personal and public basis. However, they often tend to weaken these individuals' and groups' stakes in the policy sphere. Indeed, even liberal scholars who applaud the diversity that identity, lifestyle, and difference politics can contribute to the public sphere concede that they often end up fragmenting the progressive and liberal forces and can strengthen conservative politics (Grossberg 1992).

It is with these points in mind that it is necessary to approach the politics of the internet. The internet promotes a contradictory politics and has been accused of both strengthening and weakening the public and policy spheres (Neuman 2001: 299). Originally conceived as a means for maintaining computer communications in case of a Soviet military attack, the internet spread from military to academic to civilian use (Everard 2000: 6). The National Telecommunications and Information Administration (NTIA) of the US Department of Commerce notes (2002: 1) that as of 'September 2001, 143 million Americans (about 54 per cent of the population) were using the internet—an increase of 26 million in 13 months. In September 2001, 174 million people (or 66 per cent of the population) in the United States used computers'. These statistics demonstrate that most Americans are both computer-literate and have used the internet at some time. Therefore, these data suggest that the internet has the potential to become a significant political tool for many Americans. Nevertheless, what these statistics do not reveal is that there is a digital divide within America. For instance, those people who have not used the internet or who do not have internet access are the most disadvantaged politically, economically, and socially. The NTIA notes that the 'off-line population' includes (2002: 75):

- people in households with low family incomes—75.0 per cent of people who live in households where income is less than $15,000 and 66.6 per cent of those in households with incomes between $15,000 and $35,000;

- adults with low levels of overall education—60.2 per cent of adults (age 25 +) with only a high school diploma [sic] and 87.2 per cent of adults with less than a high school education;

- Hispanics—68.4 per cent of all Hispanics and 85.9 per cent of Hispanic households where Spanish is the only language spoken;

- blacks—60.2 per cent of blacks.

These data suggest that this digital divide could reproduce, and possibly enhance, socioeconomic and, subsequently, political inequality amongst those with internet access and those who lack it. Dahlgren notes that the internet possesses several features which give it the potential to be a significant politically empowering tool for those who have access. These include the fact that it is an 'extension of mass media', meaning that it reproduces 'on-line versions of television, radio stations, news services, and daily newspapers, often with enhanced interactive components'; the internet also enables a combination of 'one-to-many communication as well as many-to-many communication' (Dahlgren 2001: 46–7). Additionally, Underwood (2001: 108) and Delli Carpini and Williams (2001: 175–6) draw attention to the fact that the internet has influenced how the mainstream news media present their broadcasts by identifying how sources like Matt Drudge's *Drudge Report* often set the mainstream media's agendas during the Clinton–Lewinsky sex scandal in 1998. Moreover, political groups with

varying political agendas have used the internet to engage in political activities such as organizing civic demonstrations, challenging the negative consequences of globalization such as exploitation within sweatshops, generating racist politics, and organizing terrorist activities (Shaw 1999; Gabriel 1998; Southern Poverty Law Center 2001; Arquilla and Ronfeldt 2001). The internet has also been a site of contest for censorship, free speech, and freedom of expression similar to the wars over popular music in the 1980s and 1990s (Grossberg 1992, chs. 5–8). Conservative opponents objected to the availability of pornography and other sex sites as well as horror, occult, and violent images, arguing that these images corrupted both children's and the country's moral values. Many (but not all) feminists criticized these types of sites because they demeaned and objectified women, arguing further that these sites could be considered as violence against them. Liberals and cyber-libertarians, by contrast, sought to uphold democratic freedoms to permit these sites to exist, claiming that censoring or eliminating these sites from the internet would cause greater damage to the political system by weakening the country's constitutional commitments to freedoms of expression (Rushkoff 1994; Slater 2001).

Nevertheless, Dahlgren acknowledges that, of all the activities on the internet, those related to politics are certainly not amongst the most popular. In this regard, the internet is an under-utilized political tool. Citing the 1998 research of Hill and Hughes, he reports that 'the word "politics" occurred in only 6.6 per cent of approximately 3000 Usenet groups'; 'by comparison, "computers" appeared in 38.2 per cent of news groups, "sex" in 23.3 per cent, "movies" in 10.7 per cent, "TV" in 9 per cent, "religion" in 6.3 per cent and "recipes" in 3.4 per cent' (Dahlgren 2001: 47–8). He notes an additional paradox within the politics of the internet: whereas most American internet users tended to be liberals, those who engaged in political activities were more often conservatives. He also draws attention to the fact that, 'Of the sites that had to do with politics ... about 20 per cent fell outside the political mainstream reflected by the mainstream media' (Dahlgren 2001: 48).

Key points

- The media offer both opportunities and obstacles to participation in American political life.

- Although most Americans use the internet, its use is not primarily geared towards politics, and a 'digital divide' ensures that those with least access tend to be the more disadvantaged and poorer sections of American society.

Globalization

The process of globalization has certainly been amongst the most significant developments of the past few decades. Ray Kiley (1998: 3) considers globalization as 'a world in which societies, cultures, politics and economies have, in some sense, come closer together'. It involves activities within all these spheres. Despite the best wishes of supporters of neo-liberal economic globalization, there are still huge gaps between the haves and have-nots. This is reflected, for instance, in the distribution of communications media. According to Kiley (1998: 4–5):

Much has been made of the potential of the internet, as a basis for reconstructing and democratising social relations throughout the globe. Although it would be unwise to totally discount the ways that it can be used to rapidly disseminate progressive ideas across the globe, there is still the reality of the massively unequal distribution of communications. At least 80 per cent of the world's population still lacks access to the most basic communications technologies, and nearly 50 countries have fewer than one telephone line per 100 people. There are more telephone lines in Manhattan than there are in the whole of sub-Saharan Africa. While the United States has 35 computers per 100 people, even rapidly developing South Korea has only 9, while for Ghana the figure is as low as 0.11. Although the number of internet users has expanded dramatically in recent years, its use is still largely confined to Western Europe and the United States. Moreover, the overwhelming proportion of internet activity takes place at work. Even if computer prices fall to levels where they become easily affordable, there are other expenses for potential users. These include specialised cabling, advanced modems and online charges. . . . Clearly then, the information superhighway has passed by most of the world's population and is likely to do so for the foreseeable future. This point applies not only to the poorest parts of the so-called Third World, but also to many people living in global cities such as Los Angeles, where new telecommunications networks have produced 'electronic ghettoes', in which access is restricted to television screens. Clearly, then, time-space compression is experienced differently across the globe. For the people excluded, this is not even life in the slow lane. It is life on the hard shoulder.

In addition to acknowledging the power differentiation in access to media technologies, Ziauddin Sardar (1998: 19–20) contend that the cultures of the oppressed have often been commodified and demeaned in the process of globalization, such as the use of some tribal rhythms in various techno songs. These instances, he argues, constitute further cultural disempowerment, to the benefit of the wealthier nations of the northern hemisphere.

Key points

- There exists among many commentators a concern that the globalization of American media and its artefacts will equate with the erosion of national cultures outside the United States.

- Simultaneously, to the extent that globalization offers opportunities for hybrid forms of media communication to develop, the spread of specifically 'American' forms of communication can be resisted.

Box 7.4 **Is America different?**
A culture of globalization or cultural hybridity?

There is often a concern that globalization of American media and its artefacts will equate with the erosion of national cultures, and that this will occur not only in the developing world but also in the industrialized democracies. For instance, Shuker (1994: 62–71) notes that developed countries like Canada and New Zealand have either established quotas or discussed similar ceilings for foreign-originated, particularly American, music in order to promote and protect their own artists' works and their national musical identities. In certain circumstances, American media artefacts are broadcast because it is cheaper than producing domestically made programming. Ellis Cashmore (1994: 195) notes that 'a Copenhagen programmer can lease an hour-long episode of *Dallas* for under $5,000; that is less than the cost of producing a single minute of Danish drama.' Additionally, not all media artefacts are consumed blindly. Mike Featherstone (1995) argues:

the process of globalisation suggests two images of culture. The first image entails the extension outwards of a particular culture to its limit, the globe. Heterogeneous cultures become incorporated and integrated into a dominant culture which eventually covers the whole world. The second image points to the compression of cultures. ... The world becomes a singular domesticated space, a place where everyone becomes assimilated into a common culture. ... [A] global culture [can be considered] the culture of the nation-state writ large.

However, much of the global media culture, such as music, that originates in the US tends to get hybridized once it travels overseas. For instance, while hip hop may have started out within the urban cultures of young African Americans, it has been adopted in other cultural settings, and this broad form of cultural expression incorporates experiences of young people in the UK, Italy, French people of North African origins, New Zealand Maoris, and Turks in Germany, to name but a few (Bennett 2000; Mitchell 1996; 2001; Wright 2001). Australian punk bands incorporate issues relevant to daily life in the Antipodes into their musical repertoires, challenging the notion that punk is an American (or Anglo-) form of culture (Lentini 2002). Electronic music, which often does not rely on lyrics, can and does serve as a broad forum for incorporating the cultures of many countries and often incorporates the politics of protest (St John 2002). Additionally, it should be known that there are many foreign financiers, artists, and sports personalities who contribute to the global culture originating in the US. By hybridizing the broad cultural forms, or by contributing to America's popular culture, people living outside the US both create new senses of their existing identities and enhance the 'citizenship' of global media culture.

Conclusion

American media serve as an important if flawed intermediary institution within the contemporary American political system. There is an abundance of media outlets from which Americans can receive their information, and they have various means at their disposal to influence the media. The media performs the role of monitoring politicians, and can also assist in the promotion of political participation. Nevertheless, some of the greatest conflicts within the American media system concern the tensions between the free market and democratic freedoms. Increased media concentration has reduced diversity in news formats, and has greatly diminished the information on foreign affairs and some aspects of national affairs. While new media such as the internet have the opportunity to expand the potential access to information, and to serve as mechanisms for political participation, there still exist huge discrepancies between those groups who have access to the internet and those who do not. Those without are largely located on the lower socioeconomic rungs and are, consequenty the most disempowered. There have been debates over internet content and use. Similarly, there is the potential threat that America's global projections through its media culture have disturbed notions of identity in other countries. The mass media are therefore both the conveyors and the sites of hotly contested political struggles.

QUESTIONS

1 To what extent and why is the mass media important in American politics?

2 'The influence of the mass media in American politics is much less than commonly supposed.' Discuss.

3 How has the rise of 'new media' affected the role and operation of the mass media in America?

4 'The benefits of an adversarial media far outweigh the costs.' Discuss.

5 Critically assess the contribution made by either press or television to the quality of American democracy.

FURTHER READING

R. Burgoyne (1997), *Film Nation: Hollywood Looks at US History* (Minneapolis: University of Minnesota Press).

K. H. Jamieson and K. K. Campbell (1997), *The Interplay of Influence: News, Advertising, Politics and the Mass Media*, 4th edn. (New York: Wadsworth).

D. Kellner (1995), *Media Culture: Cultural Studies, Identity and Politics Between the Modern and the Postmodern* (London: Routledge).

J. D. Stevens (1982), *Shaping the First Amendment: The Development of Free Expression* (London: Sage).

J. Street (2001), *Mass Media, Politics and Democracy* (New York: Palgrave).

WEB LINKS

www.abc.com ABC

www.cbs.com CBS

www.nbc.com NBC

www.cnn.com CNN

www.c-span.org C-SPAN (focus on Congress)

www.npr.org National Public Radio

www.pbs.org Public Broadcast Service

www.newslink.org/menu.html Links to newspapers and magazines

http://pomo.nbn.com/people/hemmerle National Political Index, guide to political information on the web

8 The federal judiciary

Richard Hodder-Williams

READER'S GUIDE

This chapter examines the third branch of government, the federal judiciary, concentrating upon the Supreme Court. It explains why the courts must play a political role in the United States system and how this affects the Court, first by delimiting the matters upon which it is asked to adjudicate, second by influencing who actually sits on the courts. It describes the process by which an initial dispute reaches a decision and the forces that affect this process. It then examines different empirical theories about why justices decide as they do and different normative theories about the principles upon which judges ought to decide. There follows an examination of the Supreme Court's actual power in the United States political system, and the chapter concludes by discussing how an unelected body like the Supreme Court can retain its legitimacy within an avowedly democratic system such as that of the United States.

Introduction: the Supreme Court as a political institution

To start a chapter by stating boldly that the Supreme Court of the United States is a political institution may seem odd. Courts are surely legal, not political, arrangements. The difficulty about understanding how the Supreme Court works is that it is *both* political and legal. In the 1920s and 1930s, many people claimed that courts in America were strictly legal institutions that 'found the law' by simply applying the Constitution and federal laws to the disputes before them and announcing an inevitable, objective, logically required, result. We may think of this as 'slot machine jurisprudence': line up the facts beside the appropriate laws and the consequences will follow automatically. Such a view finds expression in part of a famous judgment written by Justice Owen Roberts in 1936:

The judicial branch of Government has only one duty—to lay the article of the Constitution which is invoked beside the statute which is challenged and to decide whether the latter squares with the former. (*United States* v. *Butler*, 257 US 1, at 62–3 (1936))

By the 1950s and 1960s, quite the opposite perspective became dominant. Many people began to argue that the Supreme Court was no more than another political branch, deciding cases according to its own subjective policy preferences. Justice John Marshall Harlan the younger expressed this view in 1964:

These decisions give support to a current mistaken view of the Constitution and the constitutional function of the Court. This view, in a nutshell, is that every major social ill in this country can find its cure in some constitutional 'principle', and that the Court should 'take the lead' in promoting reforms when other branches of government fail to act. The Constitution is not a panacea for every blot upon the public welfare, nor should this Court, ordained as a judicial body, be thought of as a general haven for reform movements. (*Reynolds* v. *Sims*, 377 US 533, at 624–5 (1964))

Most of this chapter is designed to compare these views and provide the theoretical framework and empirical evidence to decide which of them is more accurate. Before we get involved in the details and in the arguments, we need to examine the whole idea of what it is to be 'political'. There are in fact at least six different aspects to the Supreme Court's political role and these need to be clarified at the outset (Hodder-Williams 1992). Much of the disagreement between protagonists arise because they are using the word in different ways. We shall look at each of these meanings at appropriate points in this chapter.

Box 8.1 Six notions of 'political'

The Supreme Court is often thought of as a political as well as a legal institution. But what is meant by 'political' is not always clear. Six senses can be identified in which the court can be seen as exhibiting expressly political features.

Definitional. As an appellate court of last resort, and more broadly in adjudicating between competing legal claims, the Court allocates values and powers authoritatively.

Empirical. Since the power of constitutional judicial review gives it potentially awesome influence, many other American political actors—from elected and unelected public officials to interest groups—attempt to persuade the Court by filing *amicus curiae* ('friends of the court') briefs with the court to try to influence the justices to share their view of the litigation before the Court.

Influence-seeking. Each Supreme Court justice wishes to prevail in arguments within the Court, but each needs to convince a majority of their fellow justices to endorse their particular view of what the Constitution and law requires in a given case. As in Congress, forging a majority frequently requires justices to bargain—not least by making concessions and compromises—much as elected law-makers do.

Prudential. The Court frequently considers the likely consequences of its decisions before coming to a ruling, recognizing that it does not operate in a political vacuum, sealed off from American society. In the case of landmark and controversial decisions, the justices strive to achieve a unanimous or near-unanimous ruling to confer particular authority to the decision.

Policy-oriented. Supreme Court justices are often viewed as strategic politicians, using the Constitution and the law as embellishments for achieving their particular favoured policy results. On this view, progressives vote for liberal outcomes, conservatives for conservative ones. Both groups can normally find some kind of constitutional rationale for their favoured policies because the document is so vague and ambiguous.

Systemic. Supreme Court rulings often have knock-on effects for other branches of government and politicians more generally. In deciding issues such as criminal defendants' or abortion rights, the Court introduces new questions to American public life, ones that elected officials, bureaucrats, and candidates in campaigns are forced to take positions on. Equally, by declining to consider cases (such as segregation from 1896 to 1954) the Court preserves the status quo against change.

To start with, we need to understand why the courts will necessarily be political. This arises from the very definition of politics. The purpose of a political system is to manage the various demands made upon the state by its inhabitants and to produce laws and regulations under which the inhabitants live. Two simple points need to be stressed. First, if everybody agreed about everything, there would be no need of politics. Political decisions are the consequence of one set of values (priorities or ideology, for example) prevailing over another. Second, the decisions emanating from the institutions of the state are authoritative, in the sense that its inhabitants must obey them. As David Easton once put it, politics is a process through which the authoritative allocation of values takes place (Easton 1956–7). The critical words are 'values' and 'authoritative'.

Disputes reaching the Supreme Court by definition divide people. Whichever way the Court rules, it will be expressing some value (a particular way of interpreting the Constitution or a particular way of applying a statute) and, because it is the supreme court in a system where the Constitution is the supreme law, its decisions will be authoritative. The Supreme Court necessarily, therefore, authoritatively allocates values.

We need to pause briefly at this point. The Constitution does not explicitly state that the Supreme Court will be the final arbiter of the meaning of the Constitution. It is now taken for granted that it is; but this has not always been the case. The Court's claim to be able to exercise judicial review (that is, to review the acts of the other branches of government and the states and declare them null and void as in conflict with the Constitution) originated in the case of *Marbury* v. *Madison* in 1803. Here Chief Justice John Marshall wrote that it 'is emphatically the province and duty of the judicial department to say what the law is'. Such a claim is consonant with much of the writing (such as Alexander Hamilton's *Federalist* No. 78) and practice of the time, but it was by no means unanimously the view then, nor was it for decades thereafter, that the courts should have the *final* say on the meaning of the Constitution. Judicial review thus allows the Court, in certain areas, to be superior to the executive and legislative branches, since it can strike down their actions as unconstitutional. As we shall see in a later section, this can give rise to a criticism that the judiciary is 'imperial'. At this stage we need only note that the federal courts, through judicial review and their normal power to interpret statutes, will inevitably have a political impact.

Key points

- When looking at the federal judiciary, and the Supreme Court in particular, we need always to be aware that it is both a legal and a political institution.

- When we say that the Supreme Court is a political institution, we may be making six quite different types of observation.

- Political in the sense of seeking to achieve predetermined public policy outcomes—the essence of a politician's role—is only one sense in which the Supreme Court may be political, but it is the sense that takes it furthest from its ideal.

The federal courts in the US political system

The formal position

Article III of the Constitution sets out the basic framework for the judicial branch. Section 1 makes it clear that the judicial power of the United States should be exercised by a single Supreme Court and such other inferior courts as the Congress shall establish. This became important in the 1970s, when an increase in the workload of the Supreme Court persuaded many influential people to consider dividing its work (and so creating more than one Supreme Court). Although no agreement emerged to alter the status quo, this episode serves to remind us that the Supreme Court really is the 'court of last resort'. Once it has reached its decision and opinion, that *is* the law of the land.

Section 1 also states that there can be inferior courts and section 8 confirms this, with authority being granted to Congress 'to constitute Tribunals inferior to the supreme Court'. So far as structure is concerned, therefore, Congress may legislate, provided that there is a single supreme court. This power has been regularly used as Congress has extended the federal judiciary system in line with society's needs. The history of the growth of the federal judiciary mirrors the history of the United States. As the frontier moved towards the Pacific Ocean in the nineteenth century and population drifted towards the south and west in the twentieth, so the court system grew in response.

At the beginning of the twenty-first century there was, in essence, a single system. At the bottom of the pyramid were the district courts, or courts of first instance. Each state has at least one; the more populous states have several. Here litigation begins. A plaintiff (the person who brings the complaint) enters a plea against somebody, or some institution (the respondent). Each case will have a name (e.g. *United States* v. *Nixon*), with the plaintiff first and the respondent second.

Above the district courts are the Circuit Courts of Appeal, so called because in the early days the country was divided up into circuits in which a particular Justice of the Supreme Court rode to act as an ordinary judge. Each justice is still responsible for one, or more, circuits. These courts hear appeals from the district courts. In turn, their judgments may be appealed, this time to the highest court in the land: the Supreme Court of the United States.

We need to be clear what cases it considers and what cases it does not. Americans often say that they will appeal right the way to the Supreme Court, but in most cases they cannot. Once again, the Constitution itself is a good place to start. Section 2 of Article III states that the judicial power 'shall extend to all Cases . . . arising under this Constitution, the Laws of the United States, and Treaties'. This is very important. Most legal disputes, whether between neighbours over land matters or between a government official and a citizen over parking offences, are subject to state, not national, laws. The vast majority of all litigation

in the United States begins and ends in the states' courts.

The federal courts deal primarily with what are called statutory cases: that is to say, a conflict arising out of a statute, or law, passed by the Congress in Washington. The civil rights laws, the social security laws, the tax laws, and so on provide the day-to-day business of the courts. These can raise far-reaching issues and have profound consequences, but in the last analysis the court's interpretation of the statute can, if the legislators believe it flawed, be reversed simply by amending the statute to meet the particular point of disagreement. This is not true of cases involving the Constitution.

Constitutional claims can arise in both federal courts and in state courts. If they start in a state court (as many of the great civil and social rights cases of the 1960s did), they usually wind their way through the state judicial system until there are no higher courts to which an appeal could be made. At this stage, the plaintiff can take his or her appeal direct to the Supreme Court for final adjudication. When the Court decides what the Constitution means in a particular case, that becomes the supreme law of the land and can only be changed through a constitutional amendment or through a future Supreme Court deciding differently.

We are here talking about what is termed jurisdiction. The Constitution, statutes, conventions, and Supreme Court judgments lay down quite precisely what cases are eligible for Supreme Court consideration. There must be a real case or controversy, the issue must still be alive (if there is no continuing dispute, the case is called 'moot'), the problem must be justiciable (that is to say, amenable to judicial resolution), and the appropriate stages of litigation completed. The Constitution is quite clear. Except for a limited number of clearly specified instances when the Supreme Court is the court of first instance, it has appellate jurisdiction only.

A structure must now have people to operate it. The Constitution is relatively clear about this, too. We have to move to Article II, section 2 (the presidential article), which states that the president 'shall, and with the Advice and Consent of the senate, shall appoint . . . Judges to the supreme Court, and all other Officers of the United States . . . which shall be established by law'. So the Congress established the court system, through Judiciary Acts, including establishing by law how many judges there shall be, and the president, in cooperation only with the Senate, fills those positions.

The number of justices composing the Supreme Court has changed over the years. Consecutive Judiciary Acts have increased the number (to ensure representation from the Western states as the frontier moved inexorably on) and, once, reduced the number, but the convention—and it is only a convention—is that there shall be nine members. In 1937 President Franklin Roosevelt, stung by a series of decisions striking down aspects of his New Deal, proposed to Congress that it should increase the number of justices from nine to fifteen, so that people sympathetic to his policies could be placed on the Court. Despite his popularity, Roosevelt failed to 'pack the court' in this way, and it would now be unexpected if the number of justices were to change. But it is entirely permissible.

Using the courts to advance policy interests

The Constitution is clear that the federal courts can only deal with 'cases' and 'controversies'. This means that other people must initiate a dispute and the dispute must be a real, not a hypothetical, one. A court, as Justice Jackson once put it, is by nature 'a substantially passive instrument, to be moved only by the initiative of the litigants' (Jackson 1955: 12). It becomes important, therefore, to discover who the litigants are and how they behave.

A simple model describes how an individual, believing that his or her rights have been personally infringed by a particular action of some state official, sues that official in federal court. This is, indeed, still the formal process. Several of the most important cases in the last half-century have been due to determined individuals taking their claims right to the Supreme Court. Clarence Earl Gideon did that in the early 1960s to establish the constitutional right to a lawyer (*Gideon* v. *Wainwright*) and Allan Bakke took his case against rejection by the Davis Medical School to establish the principle that crude affirmative action was unconstitutional

(*Regents of the University of California* v. *Bakke*). But these are exceptions. The cost of carrying a case through the district court and the Court of Appeals finally to the Supreme Court itself is enormous. Governments have the resources; large corporations have the resources; the very poor, whose basic legal costs can be covered (as were Gideon's), have the resources. Most people and small firms need assistance.

The cases that reach the Supreme Court for final adjudication almost without exception raise issues of concern for many people. Individual citizens or corporations might have brought cases to eliminate segregated schooling, or to establish a right to an abortion, or to limit the requirement to make maternity payments to staff, or to prevent anti-monopoly laws breaking up a corporation. Hundreds of others would be affected and, in some cases, many millions of dollars might hang on the outcome. These others can, and do, get involved in litigation.

One method is by filing a brief *amicus curiae* (literally 'friend of the court'). Originally, such a brief was provided to help the Court in an area where evidence was hard to acquire or the knowledge of the justices inadequate for the particular dispute. In time, however, it changed its function, and now individuals or groups who can show that they have either a substantive interest in the outcome of a case or specialist knowledge that would help the justices may, with the Court's permission, submit a brief. Normally, such briefs are clearly supportive of one position and are self-generated. There were fifty-seven *amicus* briefs in the Bakke case and over seventy in the *Thornburgh* abortion case. Occasionally, the Court itself may ask for an *amicus* brief from recognized experts and so still use this procedure in its original purpose.

Another method is by providing resources, lawyers and experts, to support a case. *Brown* v. *Board of Education* was ostensibly concerned about the young Linda Brown and her primary schooling in Topeka, Kansas. But it was, in fact, one part of a long strategy funded and orchestrated by the National Association for the Advancement of Colored People. Having failed to prevail in the state legislatures or in Washington, the NAACP calculated that, to end segregation generally, it needed to establish a constitutional decision outlawing segregated schooling. It advanced its public policy goal—the classic purpose of politics—through the judicial system. Interest groups of nearly every kind now litigate in the United States as a normal tactic in their overall political strategies. This emphasizes again the multiple points of access available to the politically interested in the United States. To exemplify this further, when the Supreme Court became less receptive to individual claims against governments towards the end of the twentieth century, progressive groups then litigated in *state* courts, many of which were more sympathetic to their cases.

Interest group litigation is not entirely new. The railroad interests, the anti-Saloon League, and many progressive causes, for example, were involved in litigation at the end of the nineteenth century. But the practice has become much more common. Test cases are sought; public interest law firms seek out litigation they can sponsor and support; the Washington offices of interest groups watch out for cases in which *amicus curiae* briefs may be submitted. In short, many cases that now reach the Supreme Court are less like classic idealized lawsuits between two individual parties than the interest group pluralism associated with the American legislative process. Administrations, too, consciously use litigation to advance their policy goals. President Reagan's was particularly active in this way. In short, the courts in the United States (and that means ultimately the Supreme Court) are drawn into the political business of allocating values by the American people themselves whether they like it or not.

Nominating judges and justices

The decisions of the courts are important, and not only to those immediately involved in the case. It is, therefore, a matter of public interest who becomes judges of the lower courts and justices of the Supreme Court. The Constitution requires federal judges to be nominated by the president and also appointed by the president 'by and with the Advice and Consent of the Senate'. Nomination is the first stage. In the United States, unlike in the United Kingdom, the pool from which nominations may be made is wide. There is no natural progression in a judge's career. It is not expected that a district

judge, because of the respect engendered, would be promoted to a Circuit Court of Appeals and then, on merit, to the Supreme Court. The majority of nominations do not follow this pattern. Rather, aspiring federal judges, at any level, need some active political networks, perhaps as a local legislator or official, or an active party member, and a patron, perhaps a Senator or a member of the current administration. When nominating judges, again at any level, the president will calculate how much such appointments would advance his policy agenda, either through their judgments or through the satisfaction provided to their sponsors or, perhaps, through the general publicity generating electoral support.

On average, a president will nominate a justice to the Supreme Court about every two years. So there is normally a steady turnover of membership. Each new member in effect introduces a new court. At the beginning of 2003, the United States had the longest-serving natural court in its history. The most junior justice, Stephen Breyer, had taken his seat in 1994.

Presidents now devolve much of the work related to nominations to a group, usually within the Department of Justice. This group will be well aware of the kind of person the president would wish to nominate and perhaps champion through the process of confirmation. Sometimes the guiding principle is a particular way of looking at the Constitution, as President Reagan tried to do by favouring individuals whose jurisprudence would produce different results from the courts he had inherited; sometimes it is a desire to change the outward appearance of the judiciary, as President Clinton tried to do by increasing the number of women and minorities. While presidents have the absolute right to nominate, it cannot be guaranteed that the Senate will consent.

Constitutionally, the Senate should advise the president and then confirm nominations. In recent years, the advice has been somewhat reduced. Fifty or more years ago, Senators would expect *their* nominees, often political associates, to be appointed to district judgeships and they so advised presidents. Their expectations were usually fulfilled, since presidents either owed the Senator a favour following the presidential election or wished to build up support across the spectrum of the Senate. Influence on appointments to the Circuit Courts of Appeal were less effective, because several Senators would have an interest in such an appointment. Affecting the nomination of justices to the Supreme Court was even more difficult, but, whenever there was a vacancy, politicians, interest groups, political friends, and the media were very quick to give advice.

The freedom that a president enjoys in nominating to the Supreme Court is constrained by the Senate's obligation to confirm any nominee. Senates usually accept the president's prerogative, especially when the candidate is clearly a person of distinction and probity. But the Senate refuses to confirm often enough for presidents to be well aware that they must anticipate its reactions when bringing a name forward. In recent years, the most notorious such occasion was when President Reagan nominated Judge Robert Bork in 1987. Interest groups were activated, politicians calculated the feelings of their constituents, opinion polls measured the popular pulse. But the administration was unable to hold a sufficiently large coalition of Senators together to win the vote. It was a special occasion, when special factors came together. The Republican president was losing popularity and the Senate was controlled by the Democrats. That sometimes makes confirmation difficult, but rarely is divided control decisive. The administration had made it clear that it wished to see some of the Supreme Court judgments reversed, especially those related to abortion rights and affirmative action. The civil rights lobby had long been extremely concerned about possible Reagan nominations and was ready to act politically as soon as a name came forward. Robert Bork was, as it were, a lightning rod. He had enjoyed publicly challenging the liberal consensus and was on record strongly opposing many of the decisions which the civil rights groups held dear. He therefore brought together a broad band of opposition groups, who orchestrated a sustained attack on his nomination, carefully focusing upon pivotal Senators whose votes would be vital. Throughout the summer, Bork's opponents took the initiative and the administration, troubled by a foreign policy scandal and with a president unable to devote himself fully to the task of championing his candidate, failed to make an impact. The Senate Judiciary Committee

held long hearings and recommended, by nine to five, that the nomination be rejected. The full Senate endorsed that recommendation by fifty-eight to forty-two.

The failure of Bork's nomination is a reminder that the Senate can exercise real power in the matter of appointments. But it does so only when several factors appear concurrently: a president with strong opposition in the Senate, divided control between the executive branch and the Senate, a period where the Supreme Court's judgments are particularly salient, a candidate whose views seem extreme, and an administration in some disarray. Following Bork's rejection, Reagan played safe and nominated Anthony Kennedy, a well-respected judge of the Ninth Circuit Court of Appeals who had played some part in Republican politics in California. When George Bush senior became president, he was concerned not to re-ignite the civil rights groups and nominated David Souter, a little-known and moderate judge of the Second Circuit of Appeals, who had personal links with senior Republican political supporters of Bush's candidacy. His second nomination was very different. When the first African American justice, Thurgood Marshall, retired, he swiftly nominated an extremely conservative African American, Clarence Thomas, to replace him. Thomas's positions on the judicial agenda were well known and his intellectual claims were weak. Bush did not enjoy a majority in the Senate and his initial popularity ratings were falling. But, after bitter hearings involving claims of sexual harassment, Thomas was narrowly confirmed. The difference was that the civil rights lobby failed to hold together and was less organized.

Nominations, therefore, are intensely political. Collecting potential candidates is a major task of the Justice Department; the president will make many political calculations before selecting a name to send to the Senate; the Senate Judiciary Committee's hearings will be couched in jurisprudential language but will be fuelled by policy preferences, as will the final vote on the floor of the Senate; the way in which the process is reported in the media and the way the public, through interest groups particularly, bring pressure to bear upon Senators will be coloured by policy preferences.

Key points

- The federal judiciary is the third branch of the federal government, but the precise way that it is organized is decided by the other branches.

- The courts respond to cases instigated by individuals, groups, or corporations. They are used as another point of access by the politically active to advance their own political agendas.

- Because the courts are important, politicians work hard to try and get their favoured candidates nominated to fill vacant positions. The method of appointment to the federal courts is highly political.

Inside the Supreme Court

The formal process

The Supreme Court is housed in a magnificent classical building on Capitol Hill, at the very heart of American government. Within it are located a suite of offices for each justice (and space is found for retired justices), the conference room, the hall where oral argument takes place, a library, restaurants—for the public and employees—and offices for those who manage the whole process from the post room that receives applications for review to the printing office that arranges the final opinion. It is very self-contained.

Let us follow the history of one imaginary case. It will arrive at the clerk's office to be recorded and given a number. Each term begins on the first Monday of September and the cases are numbered from then, starting at 1–03 for the first case filed in the 2003–4 Term. During a whole year about 8,000 cases will come to the Court. Fewer than 100 will end up with a judgment and an opinion setting out its reasons.

Since the Judiciary Act of 1992, the Supreme Court is obliged to hear virtually no appeals.[1] So the first hurdle to jump is to persuade the Court to hear the case. To do this, our case will need to be granted a writ of *certiorari* (a legal term requiring the lower court to send up the documents of the case) and our

---

[1] Cases arising under its original jurisdiction, of course, are unaffected by this new power.

Box 8.2 The calendar of the US Supreme Court

Activity	Time
Start of term	First Monday in October
Oral argument cycle	October–April on Mondays, Tuesdays, and Wednesdays in seven two-week sessions
Recess cycle	October–April, two or more consecutive weeks after two weeks of oral arguments and at Christmas and Easter holidays
Conferences	Wednesday afternoon following Monday oral arguments (discussion of four Monday cases)
	Friday following Tuesday and Wednesday oral arguments (discussion of Tuesday–Wednesday cases; *certiorari* petitions)
	Friday before two-week oral argument period
Majority opinion assignment	Following oral arguments/conference
Opinion announcement	Throughout term, with bulk coming in spring/summer
Summer recess	Late June/early July until first Monday in October
Initial conference	Late September (resolve old business, consider *certiorari* petitions from the summer)

Source. Adapted from L. Epstein and T. G. Walker, *Constitutional Law for a Changing America: Rights, Liberties, and Justice* (Washington, DC: CQ Press, 1992), 662–4.

application for review will set out, as clearly and precisely as possible, the reasons for taking the case.

Our application for a writ of *certiorari* is copied to the chambers of each of the nine justices. Once, when the number of cases was much smaller, each chamber would review every application independently. Now, however, in most chambers the initial review is more of a team effort. The justices hire each year three of the brightest law graduates to aid them in their work. They are called law clerks. A pool of these are on duty fortnightly and summarize the applications for review, setting out the basic facts, the law, or constitutional provision that is in dispute, and the current precedents to which it relates. Each justice, often in discussion with the law clerks, then makes a preliminary and personal decision about whether it is worthwhile to grant *certiorari*. The chief justice then distributes a list—the discuss list—in which he indicates the cases he feels warrant review. Justices may add any further cases to this list.

At regular intervals throughout the term, but frequently and at some length in the initial weeks, the justices meet in the conference room to transact their collective business. The only people present are the justices themselves. The chief justice presides, but each member of the Court carries equal weight when voting occurs. The agenda normally beginning with a consideration of the discuss list. There is, therefore, no discussion on the vast majority of applications for a writ of *certiorari* since no justice finds any merit in them. In order for a case to be granted the writ of *certiorari*, it requires four justices (just a minority, it should be noted) to vote to hear the case. Those that are rejected have had their last chance, and the judgment of the court from which they were appealed stands. Clearly, this process can give justices enormous power to decide what should go on the public agenda and be reviewed. The considerations that sway justices are varied, and change over time, but they can be categorized as principled and instrumental.

Principled considerations relate to a justice's view of the Court's duties. Cases which raise issues that have been decided differently in the lower courts are usually given a very careful look. Cases which involve the president or the Congress are similarly privileged. Cases which raise questions of statutory interpretation of laws with wide application are scrutinized closely. Cases which raise issues of individual rights with potentially wide ramifications might be given considerable attention. The principle here is one set down back in 1925 when the first major Judiciary Act giving the Supreme Court control over some of its docket was passed. It is simply that the function of the Court is not to consider, and perhaps right, each possible legal claim (there have been occasions enough to do that) but to bring to bear the full attention of the highest court on those issues that might have wide, and significant, consequences.

This introduces the instrumental aspect. Justices may feel that a particular issue (say, the constitutionality of the death penalty for rape) needs consideration, because many petitioners have claimed in the courts that such a punishment is prohibited by the Constitution. Then they will select a particular case which clarifies the issue and is not encumbered with characteristics that might overlay the central question with unhelpful additional factors. *Coker* v. *Georgia* (1977), the case that did deal with this issue, was carefully chosen to ensure that extraneous matters such as the race of the perpetrator or the age of the victim were not important. The problem from the justices' point of view is that cases only reach them at a pace, and in an order, dictated by the litigants and the courts below.

Once a writ of *certiorari* has been granted, the two sides in the dispute prepare briefs setting out their positions. At this stage, a number of outside groups and individuals may submit briefs *amicus curiae*. These are usually accepted, but the justices have the authority to deny people who are not party to the dispute the right to submit. A large amount of printed material is thus generated and finds its way efficiently to the nine justices' chambers. Here each justice operates as he or she prefers. Some work quite solitarily; others involve their law clerks a great deal; all use their law clerks to research, draw up drafts or aide-memoires, and generally provide them with the information they need before oral argument.

In alternate fortnights, the Court sits twice each week to hear oral argument on the cases it has agreed to review. These are often fascinating occasions to witness. Except for a limited number of special cases, each lawyer has just thirty minutes to plead and the time limit is rigidly adhered to. The justices will have read the original *certiorari* brief and the much longer briefs of the parties concerned, and in most cases the *amicus* briefs as well. They come with clear views of what the problems are and where clarification about the constitutional, or statutory, issues is required. The lawyer will be interrupted throughout the presentation as the justices want to test out the strength of a particular line of reasoning, or challenge the appropriateness of the actual precedents cited, or discuss what kind of redress would be possible. Sometimes, the justices argue amongst themselves through the lawyer, using oral argument as a way to pressure a colleague whose position appears contrary to their own. Those who argue before the Court do not provide a class of elite barristers, as in the United Kingdom, and some will only argue a single case in their entire career. A few lawyers are well known and will be used by corporations. The government's position is argued by the solicitor-general, or one of his deputies, whose expertise becomes considerable. But, generally, there is a mismatch between the importance of the case and the quality of the argument.

When the justices meet in their twice-weekly conference, they will discuss the cases where oral argument has taken place. The chief justice will summarize the facts and legal issues and indicate how he would vote (to affirm the lower court's judgment, reverse it, or refer it back for further consideration) and the rationale for his view. In order of seniority, the other justices express their positions. In the past, the justices would then vote in reverse order, from the newest member to the longest-serving and the chief justice. Chief Justice Rehnquist, however, marks the votes as the discussion proceeds and summarizes the voting and the discussion when the junior justice has had his say. Only about one third of cases are unanimous. This contrasts sharply with, say, the Judicial Committee of the House of Lords, where unanimity is the norm. Each year there will be several cases, often the high-profile ones, decided by five to four votes.

The chief justice then circulates a list of these cases, indicating who will be the opinion writer. If he is in the minority, as does happen, the senior justice in the majority nominates the opinion writer.

This power is perhaps the main weapon that a chief justice has to exercise authority over the court. But he is constrained by conventions that require all justices to write about the same number of opinions in any term. Within that constraint, however, the chief justice will tend to allocate the major cases to himself or to a justice who is jurisprudentially close to him. The less important cases can be assigned to others, particular those who often find themselves differing from the chief justice. The opinion sets forth not only the decision of the Supreme Court, whether to affirm or reverse, but the statutory or constitutional basis for that decision. This justification is critical. It can be written in broad terms which will have wide repercussions, as it provides a precedent for other litigation. Or it can be written very narrowly, focusing upon the specific facts of an individual case, and will have little further impact. The supreme law is thus regularly refined and developed through the medium of the Court's opinions. As Chapter 18 details, the balance between the right of a woman to have an abortion and the right of the states to regulate abortions has been crafted through a succession of individual cases, each of which has altered the law and each of which has affected the reality of the availability of abortions to pregnant women.

The justice assigned to write the Court's opinion will bear in mind the views expressed by those justices who agreed with the disposition, but will have substantial freedom to write the opinion to highlight the particular principles or facts he or she wants emphasizing. An opinion may go through many drafts, as the author attempts to take on board comments from colleagues. It may be a personal statement and the basis of a justice's reputation, but it is, after all, the opinion of the *Court*. There will often be a dissenting opinion. Increasingly, there are concurring opinions, in which a justice will concur in the disposition of the case but will be unhappy with the reasoning. Occasionally, no majority can be forged for a single opinion of the Court.

Finally, when the opinion writer is content, the decision will be handed down. The case has been decided and justified. That is now the law of the land and binding upon all the country's inhabitants. But, as we shall see later, this is not quite the end of the story. When the justices finish the term, almost always just before the 4 July holiday, they have done their work. The nation must now respond. Usually, the decisions are accepted and there is little reaction. In several cases, however, political action follows in an attempt to reverse the decision or water down its impact.

Influencing the outcome

Compare the judgments of the Judicial Committee of the House of Lords and you will find unanimity far more often than not. The Supreme Court is much more divided. With the expectation of a divided Court, its members are naturally keen to build up majorities to support their point of view. Some justices have worked extremely hard, and successfully, at this. Others accept diversity and their own independence and merely see how the votes and argument fall. There are few justices, however, who do not try and influence the proceedings.

Practice changes over time. When Earl Warren was attempting to ensure that the opinion in *Brown* v. *Board of Education* was unanimous, he lunched with some of the pivotal justices and encouraged them to share his perspectives. Such personal lobbying is much less common now. Justices have frequently sent messages, some personal and encouraging, some communally and critical, to put pressure on the opinion writer. The threat to write a concurrence or, in the extreme, to dissent are sometimes used to persuade the writer to add a point or tone down an argument or alter a paragraph. Most cases get little such collective input. But the cases which are going to make public impact (and the justices know these well enough) are usually subject to considerable intra-Court discussion, even negotiation, as the opinion's author tries to build a solid majority.

Because the author of an opinion is known, justices have a personal interest in, and commitment to, their writings. The new decision, although handed down in the name of the Supreme Court as a whole, is attributed to the writer. Consequently, justices seek to ensure that their own view of a case prevails and they will act politically, by trying to persuade their colleagues or bargaining with them, to influence their votes.

Models of decision-making

The description of the process by which disputes reach the Court, are granted a writ of *certiorari*, are decided in conference, and emerge as opinions of the Court might suggest two things. First, there are procedures and conventions in place to ensure a level playing field for the litigants; the justices consider the facts and arguments, aided by law clerks, and make intellectually sustainable judgments of a principled nature. This is how the law operates. Able and experienced lawyers review the facts and arguments and then, following the appropriate processes, make their judgments.

But it would also note that, despite this procedural and philosophical regularity, justices conclude differently. Clearly, therefore, the slot machine conception of the legal function is not operating, or perhaps cannot operate. What, then, is happening instead? If there were just a few aberrations from unanimity, there would be little to be concerned about. But so many cases, and so many of the significant cases, depend quite clearly upon the votes of one or two critical justices. We should always remember that many of the most significant cases are decided on five to four or six to three votes. And some justices are absolutely pivotal to what happens. In the 1990s the first woman Justice, Sandra Day O'Connor, for example, was the critical fifth vote in more five to four decisions than anybody else. To some extent, therefore, she was the powerful individual on the Supreme Court.

There is something rather odd about a judicial process depending upon the counting of votes. The justices appear to view the same set of facts, the same set of conflicting arguments, differently. Actually, we should not be surprised by that. Laws are sometimes unclear and rarely manage to take into account the extraordinarily varied behaviour of people, and the Constitution is in many places so general that there is room for disagreement about the outer edges of a particular clause's reach. Judicial systems are established precisely because there are disagreements, and lawyers are trained to make plausible cases for conflicting positions. The Supreme Court for the most part hears the most problematic cases, or addresses issues which have been resolved in quite different ways by judges elsewhere in the system. Surprise should not be our reaction. But we should certainly, as political scientists, want to have some kind of theory or framework to explain the particularities of the disagreements.

The Supreme Court, remember, is *both* a political *and* a legal institution. Its legal nature gives rise to one set of theories and frameworks for explanation. These we discuss in the next section. Its political nature gives rise to a very different set of theories and frameworks. The dominant model here is the 'attitudinal model' associated with Spaeth and Segal.

These political scientists examined the voting records of Supreme Court justices and predicted the votes, first by establishing an ideological profile of each justice and then by applying that profile to his or her performance. They found that, once the initial ideology had been identified, there was a very high correlation between expected voting patterns and actual voting patterns. It seemed that justices had clear notions of what outcomes they sought, voted accordingly, and then justified that position through traditional legal language. In other words, they were highly political, acting in the same way as politicians who first identify their policy goals and then work towards them.

Such a view of the justices was, for many people, difficult to accept. On the normative side, it did seem to destroy the essential belief that judges are *not* policy-oriented politicians but objective judges, applying the law, not making it. On the empirical side, there was concern that the profile was developed by looking at what the justices had actually done and therefore would almost inevitably

predict what they would then do. Furthermore, it failed to take into account the possibility that policy positions might be the logical consequences of different jurisprudences and that the *real* driving force was the particular jurisprudence espoused by the justice. We turn to this in the next section.

Key points

- The justices of the Supreme Court exercise considerable power through their prerogative to issue writs of *certiorari*. This enables them to control the cases that they actually concentrate upon. But only four of the nine justices need to vote in favour for the application for review to be granted.

- The nine justices carry equal weight when voting on a case. The chief justice presides at the conference and allocates opinion writing, but he has no casting vote and no power to instruct colleagues.

- The justices operate basically as nine independent law firms, but they often try to influence the outcome, or the detail of the opinion, through a range of actions, from writing memoranda to talking to the justice writing an opinion.

- Explaining why justices vote as they do (and only one third of cases are decided unanimously) is extremely problematic. Because the Supreme Court is both a political and a legal institution, both political and legal explanations are needed. The attitudinal model asserts that justices' personal ideologies drive their behaviour, rather than jurisprudential theories guiding them to a conclusion.

Arguments over jurisprudence

The need for jurisprudence

The cases that reach the Supreme Court are rarely straightforward. If they were, they would have been resolved in the lower courts and *certiorari* would not

have been granted. A straightforward case would deal with an issue already well discussed, with precedents uniformly pointing to one result, and with parts of the Constitution or federal laws on whose meaning there is no disagreement. Cases that generate new issues (is there a right of privacy?), or could be informed by different and contrasting precedents, or generate problems about application, are difficult cases. The problem facing a justice is *how* to treat such cases.

The first need is to be clear about the facts of the case and the claims being made by the litigants, and so decide what the question of principle before the Court really is. In many cases this is not obvious, because they raise more than one issue. Justices may properly disagree about which issue is critical, just as they may disagree about the significance of the facts before them. Already, we can see why they may diverge in their approach, and hence their conclusion, to a case.

A justice could merely decide what he or she felt was the best public policy and announce that as the judgment of the Court. Adherents to the attitudinal model would assume this, and the implications of Glazer's (1988) argument about the imperial judiciary point in the same direction. An extreme version of Glazer's position has argued that justices use the Constitution 'as a kind of letter of marque authorising them to set sail at will among laws, striking down any they find displeasing' (Berns 1979: 15). The private papers of the justices and the feedback from law clerks indicate that this is not the case. Often there is 'fluidity of judicial choice' as justices change their positions between granting *certiorari* and final disposition.

While in some cases justices may instinctively start out with a conclusion in mind, they need to explain their result in legal terms according to legal conventions. More commonly, they start with some principle of adjudication and apply that to the case in hand. There are, however, several principles that can legitimately be applied and they do not always lead in the same direction. The jurisprudence chosen by a justice will, more often than not, dictate the outcome.

Philip Bobbitt (1991) has usefully identified six modalities, or methods, that a justice can use. The first is *historical*. Here the judge relies on the intentions of those who framed and ratified the provision. Usually referred to as 'original intent', this method seems entirely sensible, but it has serious problems. It is often, perhaps usually, impossible to discover what that original intent was so far as

the specific clause is concerned. It is also difficult to discover whether the relevant creators themselves believed that their intention should be the defining force.

The second is *textual*. Here a judge reads the text literally and applies it to the case in hand. Again, this seems eminently sensible. The problem arises when the text cannot be read literally (e.g. the general welfare or cruel and unusual punishment clauses) because some values are needed to operationalize them. The judge then has to decide whether he uses the historical modality (and intuits what the framers intended) or applies contemporary standards to the phrase.

The third is *structural*. Here the judge infers from the Constitution, read as a whole, how the framers intended the relationships between the institutions of the American government to operate. Such a modality has its place in cases where conflicts between the central government and the individual states are concerned or where the national legislature and executive are in dispute. The judge then develops a philosophy of separation (and division) of powers and applies it. The problem here, apart from the simple fact that it can only apply to a certain number of cases, is that—once again—it is not clear what the Founding Fathers intended.

The fourth is *doctrinal*. Here the judge uses past precedents and, by analogy, applies them to the current set of facts. This traditional method of judging, the norm in most common-law countries, also has its obvious attractions. It should make for stability in the law, and it should limit the freedom of judges to advance their own policy preferences. The problems lie in the difficulty of deciding how the precedents might be applied (the *Roe* decision depended upon a precedent which had found statutory control of contraceptives an unconstitutional limitation on an individual's privacy) and prevents the law developing should earlier precedents appear, as they often do, to have been wrongly decided. The Supreme Court can, and does, reverse itself, thus implicitly acknowledging that this modality, although a good starting principle, cannot always be the binding principle.

The fifth is *ethical*. Here the judge deduces from the general framework of the Constitution and the dominant mores of the country how a particular clause should be applied. This is most obviously seen in the history of the due process clause, which developed from an injunction in favour of all laws that had been passed by the proper processes into a substantive protection of certain practices 'inherent in an ordered society', as Justice Felix Frankfurter once put it. Since there is also a 'natural law' tradition in the United States (that is to say, certain rights are above even the Constitution as absolute rights), this modality has a genuine legitimacy. The right to procreate or send children to a school of the parents' choice have fallen into this category.

The sixth is *prudential*. Here the judge weighs the benefits and costs of deciding one way or another, where there seems to be possible right on either side. At the height of the Depression, for example, Minnesota enacted a law that permitted farm owners with mortgages to postpone paying their mortgages (rather than having to give their farms to the mortgagors). This was sound policy and to the general welfare of the state and country, but it seemed to contradict a textual reading of the contracts clause of Article I. The Court acted prudentially in choosing to support the statute rather than the loan company.

All these modalities have their place in judging. But which one is chosen will depend upon the particular facts of the case and the philosophy of the judge. Over a period of time, justices develop their preferred modalities, and, although few do not use all at some time or another, their selection will inevitably favour one kind of claim, or claimant, over another. Thus, once you have identified the basic jurisprudence of the justice (as well as his or her conception of the role of a judge in the American constitutional system), it is relatively easy to predict how the vote will be cast in any specific case.

Characterizing judges

Most judges and judgments are place into categories, especially by the politically active. These categories—liberal, conservative, activist, self-restrained—normally carry with them pejorative or supportive overtones. They have some use as shorthand for describing the fundamental philosophy of a judge,

but they normally also tell us a good deal about what the user thinks a judge's role should be.

'Liberal' and 'conservative' tend to be used in relation to outcomes. If the consequences of a judge's jurisprudence is to endorse liberal policies, that judge will be categorized as liberal. While the terms 'liberal' and 'conservative' may be contested in political science discourse, there is a broad consensus that associates equality, individual rights against states, particular concern for the less powerful, belief in freedom of expression and behaviour with liberal, and the opposite—differentiation, state authority, support for the powerful, controlled expression and behaviour—with conservative. While those adjectives are frequently used to categorize justices (John Paul Stevens is liberal while Clarence Thomas is conservative), they may tell us something interesting about the consequences of their jurisprudence, but not much about their actual jurisprudence.

'Activist' and 'self-restrained' are more helpful. An activist judge will be prepared to use his or her judicial power quite regularly to strike down laws and regulations passed by duly elected political bodies and to refine the meaning of particular clauses of the Constitution as current needs and views appear to demand. A self-restrained judge, by contrast, will largely defer to elected politicians except in the most egregious instances, and will be reluctant to develop the meaning of clauses of the Constitution. Interestingly, both kinds of judge can be either conservative or liberal. In the 1930s, the activists struck down liberal laws and so protected conservative policies; in the 1950s and 1960s, the activists struck down conservative laws and so protected liberal policies. It is necessary, therefore, to be quite clear about the distinction between substantive and procedural aspects of judging. Justice Hugo Black took a very literal view of the Constitution and, having accepted that the due process clause of the Fourteenth Amendment applied the Bill of Rights to the states, simply applied all the rights contained there to the states. He was procedurally quite self-restrained (if the claimed right was enumerated in the Bill of Rights, he applied it; if it was not, he did not), but he was substantively very active (the consequences of his decisions were to reverberate through the states for two decades).

No senior judge in the United States believes that, in a system of separation of powers with a Constitution as supreme law, the judicial branch should defer entirely to the elected politicians. In some systems, for example the Soviet Union or the People's Republic of China, the role of the judge is to support and sustain the ruling party and its members in positions of authority. In the United States, the debate over the role of the judge really concerns the principles setting out when a judge should not defer to political authority. The various modes of judging described in the previous section provide different answers.

Interpretivism and non-interpretivism

The current debate over the jurisprudence of the Court revolves around the notions of 'interpretivism' and 'non-interpretivism'. Interpretivists concentrate entirely upon the Constitution itself and how to interpret its words. In the strictest sense, they argue that not only the literal text but also the original intention behind that text must govern every judicial decision. This presents considerable difficulties. There is abundant argument over the original intention of those who wrote, and those who ratified, the disputed sections of the Constitution and so no easy answers are available. It is also unclear whether the original intention should cover merely the particular ideas of the generation who write and ratified the provision or the logical extension of those ideas. Thus Robert Bork, who would see himself very much as an interpretivist, reads the Fourth Amendment's prohibition against unreasonable searches and seizures as a prohibition on electronic eavesdropping, even though the first Congress could not have imagined such a thing.

Non-interpretivists, by contrast, see the Constitution as the start of all judging, but not the end. They see the Constitution as in need of constant updating and bringing into line with current mores. Thus, the meaning of 'cruel and unusual' must change over time as the dominant view of what counts as cruel and what proves to be empirically unusual changes. Chief Justice John Marshall once observed that the Constitution was intended to endure for generations and therefore needed to be adapted to different conditions and different expectations. Randolph's guidance to the Committee of Detail was similar. This is well expressed in *Trop* v. *Dulles*, where the opinion says that the Eighth Amendment 'must draw its meaning from the evolving standards of decency that mark the progress of a maturing society' (356 US 86 (1958) at 101).

But there are major, and more obvious, problems with non-interpretivism. It can appear as though judges do no more than write their own ideas of good policy into such clauses as 'due process' or 'cruel and unusual' and seem to act exactly like politicians. The accusation that justices 'legislate' has some credibility.

In truth, most justices can be located between the extremes of these two concepts. Interpretivism retains the ideal of judging, in that the justices' skill is in ascertaining accurately original intention and in applying the specific words of the Constitution to the case. But it is not as simple as that. Different modalities seem appropriate to different kinds of cases. Even interpretivists find themselves on the other side from time to time. In 2002, as Chapter 20 elaborates, a majority of the Court decided that, in applying the Eighth Amendment to capital punishment cases, contemporary standards had changed from the 1970s and so the reading of the Constitution ought to change as well.

The impact of the Supreme Court

Politics as usual

When an opinion is announced and published, those most concerned with the case will, of course, quickly read it and consider how to respond. The press is very selective in the space and attention it gives to opinions and only a few make the front pages even of the *New York Times* or *Chicago Tribune* or are featured in the television news programmes, so the extent to which the general public is aware of Supreme Court decisions is limited. Inevitably, the complexity of the actual opinion is simplified for public consumption and the careful writing of the justices is frequently ignored. The *Roe* decision is extremely long and, although there are plenty of places where an alternative line of argument might be made, most of the criticisms subsequently made are in fact addressed. Justice Harry Blackmun's prose was probably too prolix to make an impact, and the cry that the Supreme Court had created an untrammelled right to an abortion made better headlines. Essentially, decisions affect the public policy process vicariously through intermediaries such as interest groups, particular politicians, or the parties involved.

Justice Robert Jackson once observed that the justices of the Supreme Court 'are not final because we are infallible, but infallible because we are final' (*Brown* v. *Allen*, 344 US 443 (1953), at 540). Like most loved aphorisms, it contains a substantial truth, but also disguises the full truth. To start with, we need to distinguish again between constitutional

---

Box 8.3 **The Supreme Court and abortion**

As Martin Durham explains in Chapter 18, the Supreme Court's intervention nationalized and politicized conflict over abortion rights in America, making abortion a divisive political issue whose salience persists today. The selected decisions below illustrate the variety of cases, and decisions, that come before the Court on just one controversial issue.

Roe v. *Wade* (1973). Ruled (7 to 2) that the US Constitution, through its unenumerated 'right to privacy', protected a woman's right to choose to terminate a pregnancy by abortion. But this right was relative, not absolute. The justices noted that the states maintained legitimate interests in abortion decisions, in particular concerns about preserving maternal health and protecting potential life. The Court therefore sought to balance the competing interests of the mother's right to an abortion against the states' interests within a threefold, or 'trimester', framework that legalized access to abortions during the first two trimesters (or six months) of pregnancy but allowed states greater autonomy to limit access in the final three months.

Doe v. *Bolton* (1973). 7–2. Ruled that states may not make abortions unreasonably difficult to obtain, striking down state requirements that abortions be performed in licensed hospitals, that a hospital committee give prior approval to abortions, and that at least two physicians concur in the approval.

Harris v. *McRae* (1980). 5–4. Upheld the Hyde Amendment, passed by Congress in 1976, that prohibited Medicaid funding of non-therapeutic and therapeutic abortions (except where necessary to save the mother's life).

Akron v. *Akron Center for Reproductive Health* (1983). 6–3. Ruled unconstitutional an Akron, Ohio ordinance that imposed conditions on a woman's right to choose a termination (such as an 'informed consent' provision and a 24-hour delay between signing the consent form and undergoing the termination).

Webster v. *Reproductive Health Services* (1989). 5–4. Upheld state laws restricting abortion rights providing that the laws did not impose an 'undue burden' on women's access to terminations.

Hodgson v. *Minnesota* (1990). 5–4. Upheld a state law requiring parental notification before an abortion could be performed on a woman under 18 years of age.

Rust v. *Sullivan* (1991). 5–3. Upheld Department of Health and Human Services regulations that banned use of Title X federal family planning funds for abortion counselling or activities that advocated abortion as a method of family planning.

Planned Parenthood v. *Casey* (1992). 3–2–4 (no majority opinion). Upheld the restrictive provisions of a Pennsylvania state law similar to those previously declared unconstitutional in *Akron*, effectively ending the trimester system of *Roe*. But simultaneously five justices declare that the basic constitutional right to choose an abortion remained intact.

Stenberg v. *Cahart* (2000). 5–4. Ruled unconstitutional a Nebraska state law banning 'partial-birth' abortions, as too broadly constructed and as imposing an 'undue burden' on a woman seeking an abortion. Also, the law did not contain an exception to protect the woman's health.

cases and statutory cases. The latter can be, and often are, 'reversed' by legislation passed in Congress. In the late 1980s the Supreme Court handed down a number of decisions that cut back on some rights which had, until then, been thought of as encompassed within the existing civil rights statutes. In 1991, the Democrat-controlled Congress passed a further Civil Rights Act which restored the position and effectively reversed the Supreme Court.

But this cannot be done with constitutional cases. The Constitution *is* what the judges say it is, and their decisions can only be overturned through the process of constitutional amendment. As Chapter 3 explained, this is a difficult thing to do. In only four instances have judgments of the Court been expressly challenged and overturned by constitutional amendment (though *Dred Scott* was reversed by two amendments—see Box 8.4). That is not to say that, from time to time, Congressmen do not still attempt to go down this route. When the Court decided that the First Amendment forbade state schools to require the saying of the Lord's prayer in morning assembly, the equal protection clause required the constituencies in every state to be as equal as was possible, and the due process clause gave women limited, but substantial, right to an abortion, Congressmen introduced constitutional amendments to reverse these. None of them succeeded in getting the requisite majorities to send them to the states for ratification. To that extent Jackson was right.

What he left out, however, was the normal way that politics operates in the United States. A Supreme Court decision is an event that, in most cases, immediately generates a political response. It is not the end of the road. What takes place is, in Louis Fisher's words, 'a constitutional dialogue' (Fisher 1988). Opinions, like stones cast into a pond, produce ripples in the political world; sometimes they are seismic in their consequences.

This was true for *Roe*. It galvanized the pro-life lobby into a variety of actions designed to reverse, or decisively cut back, that decision. It organized marches and demonstrations; it kept vigils; it challenged those attempting to have abortions and those who administered them; it attacked clinics; it made it clear to candidates that their position on abortion could determine their chances of electoral success; it hounded Blackmun himself and, to a lesser extent, the other justices in the *Roe* majority. The conservative administrations supported lawsuits that sought to limit the impact of *Roe*, and President Reagan's solicitors-general argued on their side. One consequence of *Roe* was a massive increase in *legal* abortions. But the pro-life lobby was relatively successful in establishing limits on abortion, partly by persuading legislatures not to fund abortions and partly by hedging the right about with further regulatory constraints.

We have noted the reactive nature of the Court, as its agenda is constructed by Americans' propensity to litigate some questions. But the Court is also in some sense proactive, a political actor that energizes the political system itself. Its decisions are legally definitive but rarely final politically, rather the starting gun for further political competition. The more its cases take on the character of interest-group conflict, the more its decisions become yet another part of an ongoing saga. We should not speak of a seamless web, for the Court's actions are clearly discernible moments when the struggle is decisively moved in a definite direction. Just as the Constitution is used as a political resource by political actors (and individuals) and thus impels the Supreme

Box 8.4 Amendments reversing Supreme Court decisions

Amendment	Date ratified	Supreme Court decision overturned
Eleventh	7 February 1795	*Chisholm* v. *Georgia* (1793)
Thirteenth	6 December 1865	*Scott* v. *Sandford* (1857)
Fourteenth	9 July 1868	*Scott* v. *Sandford* (1857)
Sixteenth	3 February 1913	*Pollock* v. *Farmer's Loan and Trust Co.* (1895)
Twenty-sixth	1 July 1971	*Oregon* v. *Mitchell* (1970)

Court into the political arena, so also the judgments of the Court, relating as they so often do to issues on which there are disparate and vocal views, redefine the political debate and thus elicit responses from affected parties.

The power of the Supreme Court

The import of Nathan Glazer's famous article on the 'imperial judiciary' mentioned in Chapter 3 can be neatly juxtaposed with Alexander Bickel's famous book *The Least Dangerous Branch* (Glazer 1986; Bickel 1958). For Glazer, and people of his persuasion, the Supreme Court not only exercised substantial power, even a superior power to the other branches, but did so with no justification. While Bickel accepted that the Court did, and should, exercise some power under certain specified conditions, he saw it as substantially less dangerous to the welfare of the individual than the legislative and executive branches. It is important to make a judgement between these contradictory positions.

Let us start with some incontrovertible observations. Schools *have* been desegregated; children *are* bussed to school; affirmative action plans *have* been approved; Bible-reading at the start of the school day *has* been stopped; limitations on abortions *have* been set aside; electoral districts *have* been equalized. It is plain for all to see. But it would be misleading to imagine that these fundamental changes were achieved by the Supreme Court and the lower federal courts alone.

In one important sense, the Court does not possess the requisite coercive power to *make* people obey its judgments. Its police have no remit outside the confines of the marble palace. So it is entirely possible for its judgments to be disobeyed. Indeed, the 1955 instruction in the second *Brown* judgment to desegregate the public schools with 'all deliberate speed' remains the classic example of non-compliance. By 1971, only 1 per cent of African American children in the schools of the eleven southern states went to integrated schools. Judgments designed to prevent public authorities denying blacks the vote did not enfranchise African Americans; judgments outlawing the saying of prayers or the reading of the Bible at the beginning

of the school day did not immediately put an end to these practices; *Roe* did not enable all the women who wished to terminate their pregnancies earlier to have an abortion. Other people must implement the decisions of the Court.

Rosenberg made this point in great detail in his much-discussed book *The Hollow Hope* (1991), arguing that the Court's impact has been much less than its critics have assumed. In the areas of social policy that he examined, he observed that the expectations of the groups who had prevailed in the Court were disappointed in the actual consequences that followed. Whereas in the 1950s and 1960s, the other branches of government had supported the Court, in the 1970s and 1980s this was not the case. The contrast is a reminder that the Supreme Court needs the voluntary assistance of others if its judgments are to be fully effective. Elected legislators and executive officers need to act, as Eisenhower did to enforce desegregation in Little Rock in 1957 by sending in the marines or as the Congress acted legislatively in the 1960s. It was the Civil Rights Act of 1964 and the Voting Rights Act of 1965 that provided the bases for the integration of schools and the enfranchisement of black Americans; it was the action of the Departments of Health, Education, and Welfare and of Justice that brought federal law and federal prosecutors to bear on these problems. In the 1970s state legislatures, Congress, and the executive used their powers to constrain the impact of *Roe* and to cut back on affirmative action programmes.

Within a federal system of government, there is now a national Bill of Rights. The effective incorporation of virtually all the rights set out in the first eight amendments of the Constitution into the Fourteenth Amendment (hence applicable to the individual states) has created a major source of tension in which the contemporary Court is now forced to participate. It is little wonder that localized hostility to the Court's actions is aroused. Although the United States has experienced cultural homogenizing and centralizing developments in the modern period, major differences in priorities, values, and ambitions continue to exist in the states. The majority view on social matters just *is* different in Oklahoma from Massachusetts. Inevitably, therefore, a national institution espousing national values will tread on parochial toes; attempts to permit local variation (in, for example, what counts as pornography) have been tried but have been dropped as unworkable. Where emotions are intense (as with desegregation or abortion or gay rights) either the willingness to obey by *some* people is withdrawn or the Court's legitimacy is openly challenged.

It is interesting to note, however, that the Court has, both historically and recently, managed to ride these storms of opposition. It does this essentially as a result of the political process that produces the justices for the Court. As public views change nationally, the Washington majority also changes in line with electoral results. Fresh presidents, with new bases of electoral support, mindful of refreshed Senates with changing ideological centres of gravity, make nominations that, over time, brings the Court into line with that majority. At the same time, the justices themselves, acutely aware of the political ambience in which they work and plugged into networks that provide them with good intelligence about the public mood, see where things are going. The Court's decisions on many of the highly salient and divisive issues have tended to be in line with public opinion of the day or the direction of public opinion. Of the major salient social issues, only in matters of church and state and bussing was there a large discrepancy between its landmark decisions and national trends. In other words, the Court has tended either to reflect or to anticipate public opinion.

You will note that the issues focused on by those who favour the analogy of an imperial judiciary are almost entirely social issues, related to the Bill of Rights or the Fourteenth Amendment. This is actually a very small part of public policy taken as a whole. The Great Society, the Vietnam War, the barrage of legislation, and executive orders issuing forth each year from either end of Pennsylvania Avenue, these are the dominant Washington forces affecting life—and death—for American people. It is only when the perspective is state-centred and rights-centred that the Court looms really large.

In many ways, the concept of political power used above is a very crude one. It seems to assume that power is only exercised in direct, observable situations where command and response can both be documented and measured. But there is also a 'second face of power' (Lukes 1961), where the range of choices *realistically* open to citizens is circumscribed by means other than the command–response model. The power to set, or limit, the public agenda is very real, and in a contemporary democracy can be of decisive importance.

It may be here that the primary significance of the Supreme Court is found. It does help to set an agenda; and it does highlight values. Although the desegregation called for in *Brown* would not have taken place when it did without congressional action, congressional action would not have been so high on the political agenda if the *Brown* decision

---

Box 8.5 The Court's decisions and public opinion: criminal rights

Respondents believing courts are too lenient

Year	Percentage	Year	Percentage
1972	66.1	1983	85.2
1973	72.6	1984	80.9
1974	77.0	1985	83.7
1975	78.8	1986	85.2
1976	80.7	1987	77.9
1977	82.9	1988	81.3
1978	84.7	1989	83.6
1980	83.0	1990	82.4
1982	82.3	1991	79.2

Note: Question: 'In general, do you think the courts in this area deal too harshly or not harshly enough with criminals?'

Source: Lee Epstein et al., *The Supreme Court Compendium* (Washington, DC: CQ Press, 1994), 592.

had not lent legitimacy to black civil rights and placed the issue of racial discrimination unequivocally, if embarrassingly, on the political agenda. Similarly, the simple (perhaps over-simple) moral underpinning to *Miranda* or *Reynolds* made the subsequent actions of public officials both necessary and broadly acceptable. Because the Court has such a high standing in the abstract and because its legitimacy does normally result in its judgments being honoured, its major decisions translate what in reality is often a squalid set of facts into a principle of national significance. That is a very real power.

Key points

- At the moment when a decision is handed down, it is the law of the land. In many instances, there is little or no reaction. But in most cases, especially the highly salient ones, the decision is only the starting point for further political action.

So the decisions of the Court are an input into the political system that initiate further political action.

- The power of the Supreme Court can be viewed from two angles. One looks at the immediate impact of its decisions and notes that in most areas of public policy it plays virtually no part but that in some, especially those related to individual rights alleged to have been infringed by state governments, it is much more active. Nevertheless, its decisions are only realized if people accept their legitimacy and freely obey them or, as happened with civil rights particularly, the legislative and executive branches become actively involved.

- The second angle notes that, although the Court needs others to ensure that its decisions are implemented, those decisions themselves affect the national agenda and provide moral support for change.

Conclusion: the Supreme Court and American democracy

The Supreme Court exercises power within the United States political system. Its members are not elected nor are they directly accountable thereafter. How, then, can this non-elected body fit comfortably into American democracy?

First, the dominant principle of American democracy is not unconstrained majoritarianism. The written Constitution was designed to limit what elected politicians could do. The purpose of a Bill of Rights is to protect individuals from the actions of majorities. The Constitution itself denies simple majoritarianism in many places, from the election of the president, through the representation of states equally in the Senate, via the supremacy clause, to the process of amendment. Nevertheless, the present culture is weighted in favour of a system where policy-making is legitimized through the electoral process.

Second, the Supreme Court is indeed the least dangerous branch of government. It cannot initiate policy proposals, although it can expand constitutional meaning or ensure compliance through judgments which certainly create fresh policies in some areas. It needs the elected branches to protect its decisions and to operationalize the principles that it enunciates. Without them, little actually happens as a consequence of its opinions, which are merely pieces of paper.

Third, the means by which nominations are made to the Supreme Court involve the two other elected branches of government. An elected president nominates and an elected Senate confirms. Indirectly, therefore, the justices have as much democratic legitimacy on their appointment as does, for example, the secretary of state or the Attorney-General. Over time, the Court as a whole reflects the changing majority in Washington and thus the changing national majority. Some justices, however, remain in post for many years after the majority they reflected has disappeared. This derogation from representation is balanced against the need for independence from the passing passions that can excite legislators.

Fourth, the Supreme Court is a national court, filled by justices reflecting the balance of power in Washington, not in Baton Rouge or Sacramento. Inevitably, therefore, it is likely to be out of step with the preferences, perhaps prejudices, of some states. It reflects the enduring tension of any federation. By dividing sovereignty between one central government and fifty state governments, the American political system expects, and indeed glories in, diversity across the nation. The Supreme Court, applying the Constitution (especially the Bill of Rights and the Fourteenth Amendment) across the nation, will surely challenge the decisions of some states that do not reflect the current majority view in Washington.

At the heart of the debate is the very nature of America's divided democracy. As prior and subsequent chapters emphasize, this differs from European democracy in many ways. Perhaps the most striking aspect of this difference is the emphasis given to a written, limiting Constitution, to a 'government of laws, not men', to a supreme law. In such a system, democracy is conceived of as a system of government where 'We, the people' are predominant but are limited in our powers. In this conception, a Supreme Court watching over the limits of those powers is at the very heart of its democratic structure.

QUESTIONS

1 In what sense, if any, can the Supreme Court be viewed as an inherently political as well as legal institution?

2 Is the Supreme Court too powerful an institution or not powerful enough?

3 To what extent and why can the role of an unelected judiciary in America's divided democracy be justified?

4 'Charges that the Supreme Court is "imperial" ignore the profound limits to its influence in American politics.' Discuss.

5 Is a search for the 'original meaning' of the Constitution of any legitimacy as a guide to constitutional interpretation in the twenty-first century?

6 'Since judges in America exercise such marked political influence, the people should elect them.' Should they?

FURTHER READING

C. Clayton and H. Gillman (1999), *Supreme Court Decision-Making: New Institutionalist Approaches* (Chicago: University of Chicago Press).

K. Hall (ed.) (1992), *The Oxford Companion to the Supreme Court of the United States* (Oxford: Oxford University Press).

R. Hodder-Williams (1992), 'Six definitions of political and the US Supreme Court' (*British Journal of Political Science*, 22(1)).

R. McKeever (1995), *Raw Judicial Power? The Supreme Court and American Society*, 2nd edn. (Manchester: Manchester University Press).

D. O'Brien (1990), *Storm Center*, 2nd edn. (New York: Norton).

M. Perry (1994), *The Constitution in the Courts* (New York: Oxford University Press).

J. Segal and H. Spaeth (1993), *The Supreme Court and the Attitude Model* (Cambridge: Cambridge University Press).

C. Sunstein (1999), *One Case at a Time: Judicial Minimalism and the Supreme Court* (Cambridge, Mass.: Harvard University Press).

T. Yarbrough (2000), *The Rehnquist Court and the Constitution* (Oxford: Oxford University Press).

WEB LINKS

www.supremecourtus.gov Site of the US Supreme Court

oyez.at.nwu.edu/cases/70–18 Oral arguments of the Supreme Court

www.findlaw.com Comprehensive guide to the US Constitution, cases, and the legal system

www.abanet.org American Bar Association

supct.law.cornell.edu/supct Supreme Court information and cases

www.law.cornell.edu/uscode US legal code

9 The presidency

John Hart

READER'S GUIDE

This chapter examines the power of the president of the United States within a fragmented and separated system of government. It considers the increased responsibilities of the presidency matched against the constitutional powers established for the office over 200 years ago. It describes the principal institutional developments that help presidents cope with the burdens of their job, and it identifies the clientele with whom the president must deal. Finally, the chapter argues that the nature of presidential leadership may depend more on the quality of the electoral choice and the electoral process than on anything inherent in the office of the presidency itself.

Introduction

American presidents stand out as the most important and powerful political individuals in the United States, but they operate within a framework of government that fragments power and subjects the president to a host of political forces with independent sources of power and the ability to obstruct and oppose the president if they choose to do so. Presidents are expected to lead. Many Americans quite naturally see their president as

the focal point of the system of government. Public expectations are high. Presidents are expected to solve the nation's problems and are held accountable when they do not. American voters have rejected the incumbent president or his party in five of the last nine presidential elections. But few Americans fully absorb the impact of the fragmented and pluralistic structure of American government on presidential leadership. It is not easy for presidents to change the way things are. The American Constitution imposes the doctrines of separation of powers, checks and balances, and federalism on its political institutions, which makes the American president subject to constraints and limitations that do not operate on executive government in most other western democracies. The president is constrained by Congress quite frequently, sometimes by the decisions of the Supreme Court, and limited by the difficulties of managing the executive branch of government of which the president is nominally head. Presidents also face potential opposition from political institutions that are not mentioned in the Constitution, such as the media and interest groups. It would be no exaggeration to say that the American public overestimates the real power that resides in the office of president, and imposes on presidents unrealistic expectations.

The responsibilities of the president of the United States have increased exponentially since the middle of the twentieth century. President Franklin Roosevelt's years in the White House marked a watershed in the development of the presidency. Roosevelt's New Deal was nothing less than a national government takeover of public policy in a time of desperation brought on by the economic Depression of the late 1920s and early 1930s, and it is no coincidence that the growth of the modern presidency coincides with the decline of the role of state and local government in America. Since then, the federal government has continued to take responsibility for the nation's most critical problems at home and abroad, but the formal, constitutional powers of the president have not changed to match the responsibilities and public expectations of a presidency that the Founding Fathers could never have imagined. In fact, the American presidency is an inherently weak office. American presidents need to find other sources of power beyond the formal powers granted to them in the Constitution in order

to do what the American public expects of them. They have to operate within the American system of government, not above it—although in times of crises, like the national crisis generated by the terrorist attacks on New York and Washington in September 2001, the president can acquire extraordinary authority to lead the nation and command support from other branches of government. In normal times, however, other branches of government and other parts of the political system impinge on the operation of the presidency, and understanding the nature of the presidency requires an understanding of the nature of Congress, the power of the Supreme Court, and the role of non-governmental political players in Washington.

Those who aspire to the presidency need to possess extraordinary leadership skills in order to make the American government respond to their policies and vision of the future. We can study the American presidency as an institution, but institutional structures and constitutional powers will not tell the whole story. The strength of the presidency depends just as much on the individual who occupies the White House at the time. Presidential power is very personal and, as such, its nature is intangible, elusive, and mysterious. Few presidents these days are considered to be outstanding successes. Indeed, the usual measures of presidential success—legislative success in Congress, achievements as a world leader, maintaining economic growth and prosperity, ability to persuade and generate public support, getting re-elected and ensuring party victories in mid-term congressional elections—may well be beyond the capacity of any politician. The nature of the job and the constraints on power are considerable, and most presidents inevitably fail at some point in their presidency. The presidency, by its very nature, is perhaps the least predictable part of the American system of government.

The creation of the presidency

The Founding Fathers and the dilemma of the presidency

The creation of the presidency was the linchpin of the work of the Founding Fathers at the Constitutional Convention of 1787. The Constitution would not have achieved its major purpose—strengthening the authority of central government within a federal system—had not the Founding Fathers been able to write into the new structure a reasonably strong executive arm of government. The principal weakness of government under the Articles of Confederation had been the absence of sound and stable administration—indeed, the absence of any executive—and the newly created presidency was the mechanism intended to correct that deficiency.

But, while the Founding Fathers pinned so much importance on the presidency, one needs to remember that this innovation was born just eleven years after the former colonies in North America had declared their independence from Britain and renounced a system of government that had demonstrated all the evils of strong executive power. In 1776 the rebel colonists had rejected the tyranny of monarchy as manifested in those detested agents of the king, the colonial governors. Their hatred of monarchy and the association of monarchy with tyranny became entrenched as part of America's revolutionary culture. It was thus hardly surprising that, when the draft Constitution was made public, its critics argued that the Founding Fathers had simply changed the names and substituted president for king: that one brand of executive tyranny had been replaced by another.

The Founding Fathers had done their best to head off this criticism. The presidency, as it appeared in Article II of the draft Constitution of 1787, was shrouded in ambiguity and uncertainty. The powers of the president were far from clear. In the ratification debates that preceded the formal adoption of the Constitution, anti-federalists were able to attack the presidency as the 'foetus of monarchy' and a threat to their liberties, while the Federalists could equally claim that the presidency wasn't powerful enough (see McDonald 1994: 184). As Edward S. Corwin, in his classic study of the presidency, put it, 'Article II is the most loosely drawn chapter of the Constitution' (Corwin 1957: 3).

In many respects, the American presidency was a patched-up compromise that emerged only at the very end of the Constitutional Convention. That was not just because the Founding Fathers were wary about the fate of their handiwork during the ratification process, but also because they were quite divided amongst themselves over a whole range of issues relating to the presidency. They were divided over how to elect the president, over the length of term of office, over whether or not the president should be eligible for re-election, over whether to give the president a cabinet, and how to remove the president from office should the necessity arise. There was even discussion about whether there should be just one president or several presidents—a plural executive. And even when the draft Constitution was agreed, there was hardly any consensus about the relationship of the president to Congress.

The Founding Fathers had to compromise in creating the presidency, but theirs was no standard compromise. They achieved agreement not by finding the lowest common denominator, but rather by leaving the language of the Constitution deliberately vague and ambiguous. Had they been more specific about the powers of the presidency, the Constitution might never have been ratified.

The durability of the presidency

But compromise was shrewd politics in the longer term as well as the short term. The immediate goal of the Founding Fathers was to improve the condition of American government at the end of the 1780s, but one presumes that they also wanted the presidency to be durable and survive in different times and circumstances. As things turned out, the ambiguity they had written into the Constitution in 1787 gave the office of president flexibility, adaptability, and room to grow. Whether or not that was by deliberate design, presidents have been able to find enough scope in the Constitution to broaden executive power when the need has arisen, and to respond to exigencies and conditions that the Founding Fathers could never have foreseen.

One other consequence of the Founding Fathers' ambiguity about the presidency is that they did not have the last word about the scope of presidential power. Arguments about the power of the presidency have continued, and ever since 1787, people who write about the presidency have been trying to redefine the office and its prerogatives to match the circumstances of the time. The arguments have still not been resolved and the debate goes on.

Key points

- The Founding Fathers were constrained in the powers they could allocate to the president because of the revolutionary suspicion of executive power and executive tyranny.

- The presidency in the Constitution represents a compromise achieved by ambiguity in the wording of Article II.

- The ambiguity written into the Constitution in 1787 gave the office of president flexibility, adaptability, and room to grow. It also left open the debate about the appropriate nature of presidential power in the United States.

The president: powers and power

The nature of executive power

Perhaps the best example of the constitutional ambiguity over the scope of presidential power occurs in the very first line of Article II: 'The Executive power shall be vested in a President of the United States'. It leaves no doubt about who has the executive power, but nowhere in the Constitution is the term 'executive power' defined. Compare this with the opening line of Article I which delineates the power of Congress: 'All legislative powers herein granted shall be vested in a Congress of the United States'. The Constitution gives to Congress, not *all* legislative power (as it gives *all* executive power to the president), but only those specific legislative powers that are 'herein granted'. The powers of Congress are specifically enumerated in Article I, section 8.

The president, too, is given some enumerated powers, but it is doubtful whether the Founding Fathers intended these to be the sum total of the executive power. In all, the president is given eleven powers (see Box 9.1), most of them ill-defined—which can often be very useful for a president—and most subject to checks and balances by other branches of government. Article II also gives the president two duties—'to take care that the laws be

faithfully executed' and 'to preserve, protect and defend the Constitution'. Both are, in essence, broad grants of power, particularly in times of national crisis, and would give the president constitutional authority to go far beyond the minimal executive powers enumerated in Article II.

The inadequacy of presidential constitutional powers

Few presidents have thought that their constitutionally enumerated powers adequately matched the responsibilities of their office, and the expansion of presidential power has been an abiding characteristic of the presidency. Thomas Jefferson, for example, had no specific constitutional power to make the Louisiana Purchase in 1803, nor did Abraham Lincoln have the power to suspend habeas corpus or emancipate the slaves, as he did in 1863. The same could be said of Theodore Roosevelt's decision to build the Panama Canal, Richard Nixon's decision to impose wage and price controls, or Jimmy Carter's instigation of a boycott of the 1980 Olympic Games.

Presidents have either stretched the meaning of their constitutional powers or relied upon extra-constitutional authority to achieve their goals.

Box 9.1 Constitutional influences

The constitutional powers and duties of the president

Powers

1. Chief executive—'The Executive Power shall be vested in a President of the United States'—but executive power is not defined.

2. Commander-in-chief of the armed forces.

3. Power to require the opinion of the principal officers of the executive departments.

4. Power to make treaties (with the advice and consent of the Senate).

5. Power to nominate ambassadors, judges, and public ministers and appoint (with advice and consent of the Senate).

6. Power to recommend measures to Congress.

7. Power to grant reprieves and pardons for offences against the US (except in cases of impeachment).

8. Power to receive ambasssadors (i.e. recognize foreign countries).

9. Power to fill vacancies in the administration when the Senate is in recess (by granting temporary commissions).

10. Power to veto legislation passed by Congress (but veto can be overridden by Congress).

11. Power to convene Congress (on extraordinary occasions) and adjourn Congress if both houses disagree on time of adjournment.

Duties

1. To take care that the laws be faithfully executed.

2. To preserve, protect, and defend the Constitution.

They have been able to do so primarily because the ambiguity of Article II gave them enough flexibility and room for manoeuvre. One can only guess whether or not the Founding Fathers deliberately intended future presidents to strengthen the scope of presidential power once the immediate arguments over the Constitution had been forgotten; nevertheless, the narrow range of executive powers enumerated in the Constitution serves as an inadequate guide to what contemporary presidents do in office and how they are able to do it.

The sources of presidential power

The Constitution

Presidential power derives from a number of sources. The Constitution itself is still an important basis of presidential power, not so much for what it says literally, but rather for what presidents have done with the vague grants of power written into Article II. The 'commander-in-chief' clause, for example, has been routinely used by modern presidents to justify their dominance in the making of national security

policy and, particularly, their usurpation of the congressional power to declare war. Only Congress has the power to declare war, but that hasn't stopped a number of presidents from using their power as commander-in-chief to commit American troops to fight in what are obviously wars, irrespective of constitutional niceties. The Korean War was never 'declared' by Congress, nor was the Vietnam War. Did the Founding Fathers intend the commander-in-chief clause to be so expansive? Probably not, but presidents have not been constrained by the intent of those who drafted the Constitution over 200 years ago.

Presidential interpretation

The way in which presidents themselves have interpreted presidential power explains much about the development of the presidency. The classic example of the 'expansive' or 'activist' interpretation occurs in the autobiography of President Theodore Roosevelt (see Box 9.2), in which he expressed his belief that the growth of the president's responsibilities—'anything that the needs of the nation demanded'—justified his expansion of presidential power, except where the Constitution or statute law expressly prohibited any presidential initiative. It was a conception of presidential prerogative shared by many other activist twentieth-century presidents, such as Woodrow Wilson, Franklin Roosevelt, John F. Kennedy, and Lyndon Johnson.

But it was not a view shared by all American presidents. In fact, Theodore Roosevelt's successor, William Howard Taft, directly challenged Roosevelt's activist conception of presidential power (see Box 9.2). Taft had a narrower, more passive view of the powers and duties of the president, a view also held by some of his successors like Warren Harding, Calvin Coolidge, and Herbert Hoover. The debate between the activist and passive (or progressive and traditionalist) interpretations of the presidency is now less potent than it once was. The Taftian conception of presidential power seems to have lost out to the Rooseveltian view: with the possible exception of Dwight Eisenhower, there has not been a Taftian president in the White House since the days of Herbert Hoover. Today, even politically conservative presidents need to be institutionally activist in order to pursue their policy goals.

America as a superpower

A third reason why presidential power has expanded beyond the enumerated powers in the Constitution is the nature of American foreign policy in the latter half of the twentieth century, when the US renounced its isolationist stance and began a new global, interventionist approach to foreign affairs as a world superpower.

The confrontation between the US and the Soviet Union in the latter half of the twentieth century significantly enhanced the president's constitutional power as commander-in-chief. Foreign policy and national security policy became synonymous, and Congress was content to stand back and let presidents take the lead in managing the nuclear risk and cold-war threats. Congressional acquiescence over the direction of national security policy gave rise to what historian Arthur Schlesinger Jr. labelled 'the imperial presidency'—a presidency that was beginning 'to overwhelm the traditional separation of powers' (1973: 208).

On occasions, Congress has attempted to claim back its prerogatives and powers in foreign affairs and national security. In 1973, it passed the War

---

Box 9.2 **Core academic debate**
Presidents define presidential power

The most important factor in getting the right spirit in my Administration was my insistence upon the theory that the executive power was limited only by specific restrictions and prohibitions appearing in the Constitution or imposed by the Congress under its Constitutional powers. My view was that every executive officer in high position was a steward of the people bound actively and affirmatively to do all he could for the people. I declined to adopt the view that what was imperatively necessary for the nation could not be done by the President unless he could find some specific authorization to do it. My belief was that it was not only his right, but his duty to do anything that the needs of the nation demanded unless such action was forbidden by the Constitution or by the laws. Under this interpretation of executive power I did and caused to be done many things not previously done by the President and the heads of departments. I did not usurp power, but I did greatly broaden the use

of executive power. (Theodore Roosevelt, *An Autobiography* (1920))

The true view of the Executive function is as I conceive it that a President can exercise no power which cannot be fairly and reasonably traced to some specific grant of power or justly implied, and included within such express grant as proper and necessary to its exercise. Such specific grant must be either in the Federal Constitution or in an act of Congress passed in pursuance thereof. There is no undefined residuum of power which he can exercise because it seems to him to be in the public interest. The grants of Executive power are necessarily in general terms in order not to embarrass the Executive within the field of action plainly marked out for him, but his jurisdiction must be justified and vindicated by affirmative constitutional or statutory provision, or it does not exist. (William Howard Taft, *Our Chief Magistrate and His Powers* (1925))

Powers Resolution over President Nixon's veto, which was meant to curb the president's power to commit US troops to hostilities without the consent of Congress. No president, however, has accepted the legitimacy of the War Powers Resolution, on the grounds that it infringes their powers as commander-in-chief, and the War Powers Resolution seems not to have constrained the ability of successive presidents to commit American troops to theatres of war. The cold war with the Soviet Union has now given way to the war on terrorism, but the president remains the dominant force in the making of national security policy, and presidential power in this respect remains substantially greater than the powers given to the office by the Founding Fathers.

Public opinion has also played its part in enhancing presidential power and placing the president centre stage in national security matters. When the United States is under threat, public opinion rallies around the flag and presidential popularity suddenly soars, as it did for President Kennedy after the Bay of Pigs fiasco in 1961, for President Carter when American hostages were taken in Tehran in 1979, for President Bush senior when he initiated the Gulf War in 1991, and for his son after the events of 11 September 2001. The combination of a crisis and a presidential popularity rating at 80 or 90 percent is the worst time for Congress to try to challenge the power of the presidency. Issues about constitutionality and process get lost in the enormity of the threat and the overwhelming public support for the one national leader that the Constitution gives to the people of the United States.

The growth of government

The expansion of government activity has also enhanced the power of the president. During the course of the twentieth century, the federal government decided to take on responsibility for social security, unemployment, health care, education, urban development, racial desegregation, environmental protection, and a host of other issues. In most instances that meant increased responsibility for the president, and with the increased responsibility went increased power. In some cases, Congress seemed all too willing to hand over to the president responsibility for complex problems of domestic policy for which it had no answer and it is hardly

surprising that the presidency became the focal point for those groups and interests expecting some government response.

The growth of the mass media

Another explanation for the expansion of presidential power beyond the confines of the Constitution has been the growth of the mass media. The invention of radio and then television provided presidents with an immediate link to their national constituency. It gave them the means to reach out to the country at large and mobilize public opinion in support of their goals, something that could not be done very easily before the development of the electronic media. Television in particular has given presidents a new kind of power base and a tool that can be used to overcome some of the institutional barriers that stand in the way of presidential leadership.

Institutional support

Finally, the American presidency has acquired more power than the mere powers granted in the Constitution because successive presidents have been given the institutional capacity, in the form of an Executive Office of the President, to enable them to do what they could not possibly do on their own. The size and nature of the staff support that presidents have available to them has been a major resource over the last fifty years or so. Indeed, it is so significant in the development of the presidency that it requires a fuller discussion further on.

The reality of presidential power

The US Constitution neither depicts the full extent of the power of the presidency in the twenty-first century nor ensures that presidents will necessarily have the ability to exercise the powers they are given. Most of the meagre powers allocated to the president in Article II are subject to checks and balances, and depend on congressional support and approval. Even broad grants of power to the president—the executive power clause, for example—do not guarantee that presidents will necessarily be able to overcome the obstructions and opposition that they will inevitably encounter from within their own federal bureaucracy. The 'iron triangle' formed by permanent career bureaucrats working with the equally permanent membership of relevant congressional committees and the professional lobbyists who staff the interest groups in Washington can be a formidable network when in opposition to the president's policies. 'Powers are no guarantee of power', wrote Professor Richard Neustadt (1960: 10) in what became one of the most important books ever written on the American presidency.

Neustadt's book grapples with the power problem of the president. It is built around a remark once made by President Harry Truman: 'I sit here all day trying to persuade people to do the things they ought to have sense enough to do without my persuading them. That's all the powers of the president amount to.' Neustadt gives Truman's statement some analytical backbone. He does not dismiss the formal powers given to the president in the Constitution, neither does he think they are insignificant, but he does argue that the formal powers of the president are rarely enough. They do little more than enable him to be a clerk. Neustadt argues that a president's power ultimately depends on his personal capacity to influence the conduct of those who make up the government, and that a president's personal influence becomes the mark of his leadership. The key point that Neustadt makes is that it is not easy for a president to exercise effective power in Washington just because he is the president. Presidential power is limited, and it requires people with extraordinary leadership ability to wield presidential power effectively. Presidential power is the power to persuade, argues Neustadt, and the ability to persuade rests on the president's public prestige and professional reputation among governing elites. Powers and power are two different things when one talks about the American presidency.

Neustadt emphasizes the weakness of the presidency partly to make clear what is necessary for a strong president who is the centre of leadership in the American political system. But, more recently, other political scientists have begun to stress that the American system of government is not a presidency-centred system. It is, as Charles Jones stresses, 'a separated system', and an exclusive focus on the presidency, he warns, 'can lead to a seriously distorted picture of how the national government does its work' (Jones 1994: 2).

Key points

- The Constitutional powers of the president are minimal, and the Constitution is a poor guide to the real nature of presidential power.

- Presidents have stretched the meaning of their constitutional powers or relied upon extra-constitutional authority to achieve their goals, and have been able to do so because the ambiguity of Article II gave them enough flexibility and room for manoeuvre.

- The expansion of presidential power has been aided by the willingness of some presidents to interpret their role liberally and expansively, by the changing nature of American foreign policy, by public support in times of crises, by the growth of government, by the rise of the mass media, and by the creation of institutional staff support for the president.

The presidential branch

One of the most significant developments in the history of the American presidency has been the growth of the presidential staff. American presidents now have a formidable resource at their disposal to assist them in managing the executive branch of government and their relationship with Congress, the media, interest groups, state governors, the national party organization, and other important clients of the contemporary presidency. Presidential staff are also instrumental in developing the president's policy proposals, promoting his public image, and, for the first term at least, providing the president with an unofficial re-election campaign team.

During the nineteenth and early twentieth century Congress had been slow and somewhat reluctant to provide the president with sufficient staff assistance. Nineteenth-century presidential memoirs and diaries are full of complaints about how they and their office were overburdened by routine but voluminous administrative chores (see Hart 1995: 13–26). Even when Franklin Roosevelt moved into the White House in 1933, the staff system he inherited was small, rudimentary, and hopelessly inadequate for the kind of presidency that Roosevelt was about to launch.

But Roosevelt was prepared to make an issue of the need for more appropriate staff support for the president, which he did by establishing a prestigious, hand-picked, three-person committee to investigate the state of the institutional presidency and make necessary recommendations. The report of the President's Committee on Administrative Management (popularly known as the Brownlow Report after the committee's chairman, Louis Brownlow) was to become a landmark document of the modern presidency. The Committee reported in 1937 and recommended the creation of a substantially enhanced staff for the president in the form of an Executive Office of the President (EOP). This was to house the principal management, planning, and budgeting agencies of the government under the direct control of the president, and it also provided an enlarged personal staff for the president in a separate division of the EOP to be known as the White House Office. Brownlow gave Roosevelt exactly what he needed to drag an antiquated presidency belatedly into the twentieth century. Congress eventually approved the staffing proposals when it passed the Reorganization Act of 1939.

The Executive Office of the President has expanded considerably in both size and power since its inception in 1939, and has established itself at the centre of decision-making within the executive branch of government. It provides a very flexible structure of staff assistance to the president because its divisions can be disbanded when they

have outlived their usefulness and new staff units, serving different purposes, can be added when needed. A variety of offices, more than forty in all, have been housed in the EOP since 1939 and only a few have survived the administration that created them. Thus, the structure that Brownlow proposed has the capacity to meet the staffing needs of a succession of different presidents, operating in different circumstances, with different ideas about managing the government of the United States.

The EOP is currently made up of eleven divisions (see Box 9.3). It has an annual budget in excess of three hundred million dollars and a staff of over 1,600. The scope of the EOP is now more far-reaching than originally envisaged by the Brownlow Committee, which saw it primarily as a tool to help the president manage the executive branch of government. The contemporary EOP is broadly engaged in the whole range of policy advice, policy-making, policy implementation, and political strategy, and as a consequence its work necessarily overlaps, second guesses, and sometimes conflicts with the work done in the executive branch departments and agencies. So, although the EOP has given the president a very significant and powerful staff resource, it has also created some tension and division within the executive branch, such that the EOP can often be in competition with the departments and agencies in a struggle to control and determine the direction of public policy. Indeed, the increasing power of the EOP has been at the expense of the department and agencies, such that Nelson W. Polsby coined the term 'the presidential branch' to describe a presidential staff resource that has become a de facto separate branch of government operating in Washington (Polsby 1983: 20).

While the establishment of the EOP has given presidents the capacity to do things they would not be able to do on their own, it has also been a controversial development that has got the presidency into trouble on more than one occasion. The presidential staff, particularly the senior staffers in the White House office, have become powerful political players in Washington, and sometimes their ambition, enthusiasm, and drive has made them less sensitive than they ought to be to other political players in Washington. They speak on behalf of

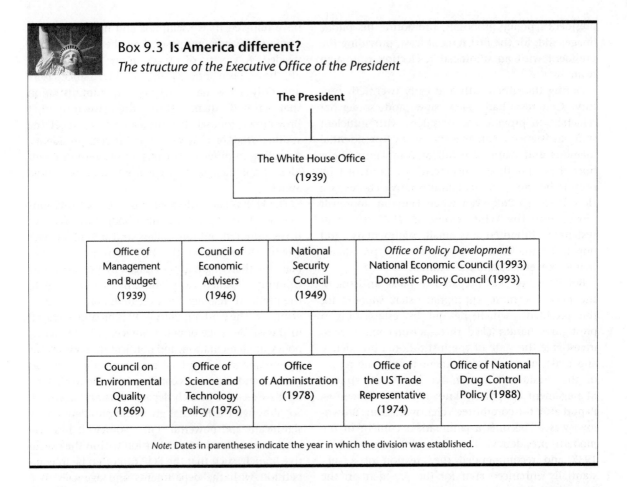

Box 9.3 **Is America different?**

The structure of the Executive Office of the President

The President

The White House Office
(1939)

Office of Management and Budget (1939)	Council of Economic Advisers (1946)	National Security Council (1949)	*Office of Policy Development* National Economic Council (1993) Domestic Policy Council (1993)

Council on Environmental Quality (1969)	Office of Science and Technology Policy (1976)	Office of Administration (1978)	Office of the US Trade Representative (1974)	Office of National Drug Control Policy (1988)

Note: Dates in parentheses indicate the year in which the division was established.

the president, they interpose themselves between the president and cabinet members, they make decisions, they issue orders, and the heady atmosphere of working in the White House leads some of them to forget that they should be exercising power on behalf of the president rather than themselves. There have been occasions when cabinet members have resigned because they came off second best in clashes with senior White House staffers, and there have been incidents like Watergate and the Iran-Contra affair where the presidential staff have abused their power and position to the point of breaking the law.

Some commentators argued, particularly after Watergate, that the presidential staff had become too large, too powerful, too unaccountable, and beyond the control of the president. They blamed the senior presidential staffers for isolating the president, and they were critical of the growing number of presidential staff who were recruited from the president's election campaign organization, with little experience of government. A number of critics argued that the power and size of the presidential staff ought to be reduced and that policy-making responsibility, now centralized in the White House, should be handed back to the departments and agencies, and the Cabinet, not the presidential staff, should be the focus of decision-making in Washington.

Successive presidents have, however, resisted all attempts to rein in their staff and reduce their powers. Notwithstanding, the dysfunctional consequences of a powerful presidential branch of government in Washington, its expansion in size and power has occurred because presidents themselves have wanted it that way. Presidents prefer to operate through close aides whose loyalty is unquestioned and who see things from the president's perspective more clearly than anyone else in Washington. No president since Watergate has tried to reverse the development of the presidential staff system. As far as they have been concerned, reliance on staff has served their purposes better than a system that relies on the cabinet or the executive branch departments.

Key points

- American presidents now have a formidable resource at their disposal in the form of an Executive Office of the President to assist them in managing the executive branch of government and their relationship with Congress, the media, interest groups, state governors, the national party organization, and other important clients of the contemporary presidency.

- The EOP has expanded considerably in both size and power since its inception in 1939, and has established itself at the centre of decision-making within the executive branch of government.

- The development of the EOP since 1939 has been controversial and has got the presidency into trouble on more than one occasion. Some critics have argued that the presidential staff has become too large, too powerful, too unaccountable, and beyond the control of the president. They suggest that its size and power be reduced.

- Presidents have not responded to these suggestions. On the contrary, the EOP has developed into a quasi-separate presidential branch of government.

The presidency and its clientele

In order to give direction to government, presidents always have to confront other parts of the political system that have their own sources of political power, sometimes different perspectives and positions on matters of public policy, and the potential to oppose the interests of the White House. While the American presidency stands out as the archetype of one-person leadership in modern democracies, it is not the case that American government is presidency-centred. Presidents compete for power in a pluralistic and fragmented political system structured by the constitutional doctrines of separation of powers and checks and balances. They must, as Neustadt says, bargain and persuade in order to mobilize support behind their policies. Presidents, save in times of national crises, have little ability to command other governing elites to follow their lead. They can encounter outright opposition or just lack positive support. Either way, the weak foundations of presidential power provide a strong incentive for presidents to think about their relationships with other key institutions in a stra-tegic and systematic way. The presidential staff, housed in the Executive Office of the President, helps them to do this to some extent, but, important as such institutional developments are, the EOP alone does not guarantee that presidents will be able to overcome opposition that they will inevitably face during their term of office. This section examines the inherent problems that presidents encounter in their dealings with four key political forces that can so easily frustrate the aspirations of any occupant of the White House.

The executive branch of government

A new president is chief executive in name only. The vague grant of executive power in the Constitution does not, in itself, provide the means by which presidents can ensure that those who staff the executive branch of government will necessarily follow presidential directions and leadership. There are significant structural barriers to presidential leadership of the bureaucracy, and it is relatively easy for bureaucrats to exploit those barriers to thwart the will of the president.

The size of the federal government alone is a major impediment for the president. No CEO of any private corporation anywhere in the world has as many people working for them as has the president of the United States. In November 2001 there were 2,633,985 civilians employed in the executive branch—almost 3 per cent of the total US workforce.

Moreover, many of those employees stay in their jobs for a considerably longer period of time than the president. Many senior career bureaucrats know that they will outlast the president, and they also know that they have the expertise, experience, continuity of service, and institutional memory that neither the president nor the presidential staff are likely to possess.

And because of their 'permanence' in Washington, career bureaucrats inevitably build strong working relationships with other 'permanent' political actors in Washington, particularly the congressional committee members and staff that deal with their policy area and the key interest groups who demand to be heard in the making of public policy. This relationship is frequently referred to as 'an iron triangle'—a network of influence among permanent operatives in Washington that forms an independently powerful policy-making sub-system which presidents must break down if their views are to prevail.

This is not to suggest that all career bureaucrats are hostile to presidents and cannot cooperate with presidential administrations. In fact, as Mark Carl Rom notes in Chapter 11, the evidence tends to show that the permanent bureaucracy is responsive and does behave in a professional bipartisan way even when incoming administrations have been overtly suspicious about its political leanings and loyalties (see the case studies in Rector and Sanera 1987). But it is inevitable that organizations as large as government departments, working in cooperation with Congress and organized interests over a long period of time, will develop their own perspectives and positions on issues that can be at odds with the policies and programs of newly arrived presidents, often from outside the Washington establishment.

New presidents do tend to be suspicious about the career bureaucracy, particularly when party control of the presidency has changed hands. When the Republican Richard Nixon entered the White House in 1969 after eight years of Democratic presidents, he expressed grave misgivings about the partisan leanings of the bureaucracy. When two political scientists subsequently put Nixon's suspicion to the test by examining the attitudes of 126 career civil servants handling welfare policy, they found, in this case, that Nixon's suspicions were justified, and concluded that even paranoids can have real enemies (Aberbach and Rockman 1976).

There are also significant structural impediments to presidential control of the executive branch of government. The departmental organization of the executive branch is not well matched to the nature of policy problems in contemporary America. Much public policy today transcends the clientele-oriented jurisdiction of individual departments and agencies. Overlapping jurisdiction between government departments on major policy issues is now the norm, and that tends to blur lines of responsibility, encourage turf fights between departments, and generate the need for new coordination and control mechanisms.

What tools do presidents have at their disposal to overcome these problems of managing the executive branch? In short, the answer is not many. There are two features of the system of presidential government in the United States that could help, but neither works very effectively. The cabinet is one mechanism that, in theory, could be seen as a counter to the centrifugal forces of the federal bureaucracy, but operates very differently from the Westminster-type cabinet system and is falling into disuse. While the president's cabinet is made up of the heads of the executive departments, they are rarely power brokers within the president's political party—indeed, presidents sometimes select one or more cabinet members from the opposing political party—and, because of the separation of powers, there is no place for cabinet members in the legislature. The theory of the Westminster-type cabinet does not apply to the United States. Presidents are not politically dependent on the support of the members of the cabinet, nor do they need cabinet approval for anything they do. The cabinet in the United States serves as little more than a symbol of the unity of the executive branch, but is functionally unable to enforce that unity in any politically practical sense.

The members of the cabinet, as individuals, are the president's political appointees and agents in the departments, along with deputy secretaries, under-secretaries, and assistant secretaries (see Chapter 11). They are there to ensure the responsiveness of the career bureaucracy to the president's program, but, in order to be effective political executives in the departments and agencies, they have to divide their allegiance between the president and their depart-ments. This weakens the potential for presidents to rely on their political appointees as agents of presidential control of the bureaucracy.

Presidents have been inventive in their attempts to control the executive branch. Some have tried structural reorganization—abolishing departments or merging several into a super-department—in the hope of breaking down the iron triangles of influ-ence and structuring the executive branch depart-ments in a more rational way. But departmental reorganization requires congressional approval, and Congress has its own interests in the organization of the executive branch. Moreover, because the con-gressional committee structure generally mirrors that of the executive branch, the abolition of a department could well make the relevant congres-sional committee redundant. Congress is more will-ing to create new departments and very reluctant to abolish existing ones, thus limiting the scope of presidential reorganization schemes.

Presidents have been more successful with their efforts to politicize the civil service and make career bureaucrats more responsive to political leadership. The passage of the Civil Service Reform Act in 1978 created a Senior Executive Service and incentives (in the form of financial bonuses) for civil servants accepting less job security and greater political direction. That legislation also allows presidents to make a greater number of political appointments to the bureaucracy.

One or two presidents have resorted to micro-managing the career bureaucracy through the use of personnel policy—punitive assignments and reassignments, performance appraisals, closure of regional offices, staff reductions, etc.—in the hope that these threats will make independent civil servants feel a little less independent.

None of these techniques has worked very satis-factorily, and given the frustrations many presidents feel over the lack of bureaucratic responsiveness, it is perhaps not surprising that they have resorted to what Aaron Wildavsky (1969) once called 'salvation by staff', where presidents have basically given up trying to make the bureaucracy responsive to their leadership and instead have centralized power and decision-making in the White House and turned the Executive Office of the President into a counter-bureaucracy which does what presidents think the bureaucracy ought to be doing but isn't—hence the concept of a separate presidential branch of government.

President and Congress

Presidential influence over Congress is variable. Some presidents have been much more successful than others in getting Congress to enact their legisla-tive proposals and some have operated in much more favourable circumstances than others. Some have worked with a Congress in which their own party has had control of both the House and the Senate (unified government), some have had to deal with one chamber under the control of the opposing party, and some went through the whole of their presidency with both the House and the Senate in the hands of the opposition (divided government). Sometimes, the political leadership of Congress changes during the course of a presidency. President Clinton, for example, began his presidency with the Democrats in control of the House and the Senate, only to lose it at the mid-term election two years later, leaving him to try to work with what turned out to be an aggressively hostile Republican majority in Congress. President George W. Bush had the benefits of unified government for just five months until Senator Jeffords of Vermont renounced his membership of the Republican majority and became an Independent who was willing to support the Democrats. It was enough to give control of the Sen-ate to the Democrats, and that had an immediate and adverse effect on the president's legislative agenda.

There is no single formula for successful presidential relations with Congress, nor is there a totally satisfactory way of measuring presidential legislative success. The traditional methods that presidents have used to win support in Congress range from persuasion on the merits of an issue (and sometimes arguments on the merits can prevail), to more political persuasion through various inducements like patronage, pork-barrelling, and other government largesse (although there is never enough largesse to meet the congressional demand), to an appeal over the heads of members of Congress directly to the public to create the kind of popular pressure that members of Congress cannot resist.

None of the above can ensure success in Congress for any presidential initiative, and specific efforts to win individual votes have been supplemented by the development and expansion of an increasingly sophisticated congressional liaison staff within the White House Office whose job is to monitor routinely and systematically the members of Congress, respond to their needs wherever possible, act as the president's lobbyists on Capitol Hill, and foster a relationship that creates a generally favourable disposition towards presidential legislative initiatives (see Collier 1997).

The individual leadership skill of the president is also a factor in persuading Congress and securing its support, although there is a considerable difference of opinion amongst political scientists about how much difference presidential leadership skill makes to congressional voting behaviour (see Bond et al. 1996: 127–9). What is agreed, however, is that the kind of legislative success that Franklin Roosevelt had with Congress—too often the benchmark against which his successors are unfairly measured—was the product of an unusual combination of circumstances (an economic depression and then a world war, a realigning election in 1932, an extremely popular president, a clear mandate, a coat-tails Congress, and huge presidential party majorities in the House and Senate) that are unlikely to be replicated.

Legislating in the United States is a cooperative endeavour. As John Owens argues in the next chapter, Congress is a 'co-equal partner'. Presidents cannot be assured of support even when their own party forms the majority in both houses of Congress, as President Clinton discovered when he failed miserably to get Congress to pass his number one legislative priority, health care reform, in 1993 notwithstanding the fact that his own party had a majority of eighty-two seats in the House and fourteen in the Senate. The politics of Congress has changed considerably since the abnormal circumstances of Franklin Roosevelt's presidency. Party discipline, although improving, is still weak, incumbency-protection behaviour among members of Congress is strong, and interest group influence on Congress, courtesy of campaign financing practices, has become a formidable obstacle to presidential initiative. Moreover, divided government is now the norm. In only six of the thirty years spanning 1972 to 2002 have the presidency and both houses of Congress been controlled by the same party.

Contemporary presidents may still wish to lead Congress and set its legislative agenda, but they have to recognize that, in normal times absent a crisis, Congress demonstrates a remarkable resistance to presidential direction and presents formidable obstacles to presidential legislative success. Presidents have to cajole and bargain and persuade, but they may also have to accept compromise to avoid politically humiliating defeats. On occasions, they accept programs and laws that they would rather not have. President Clinton, for example, was strategically compelled to sign the Republicans' welfare reform legislation in 1996 even though much of it was unpalatable to him and his party (Mulé 2001: 158–80). George W. Bush was in a similar situation when he signed what was essentially a Democratic education reform bill in 2001 (Ornstein and Fortier 2002: 47–8).

It would appear that presidential success with Congress is getting harder to achieve as time goes on. If one ranks the last nine presidents (see Box 9.4), excluding the present incumbent, George W. Bush, in order of their average yearly success rates then three of the last four are the most recent presidents (Reagan, Bush, and Clinton) and three of the top four are the earliest of the cohort (Eisenhower, Kennedy, and Johnson). It is also interesting to note that the top three performers were the only three presidents in the last fifty years who enjoyed the

Box 9.4 Presidential success in Congress, 1953–98

Ranking	President	Average annual success rate (%)*
1st	Kennedy	84.6
2nd	Johnson	82.2
3rd	Carter	76.6
4th	Eisenhower	69.9
5th	Nixon	64.3
6th	Reagan	62.2
7th	Clinton	59.9
8th	Ford	58.3
9th	Bush	51.8

*Percentages calculated by dividing the number of votes in Congress supporting the position of the president by the total number of votes on which the president had taken a position.

Source: Harold W. Stanley & Richard G. Niemi, *Vital Statistics on American Politics 1999–2000* (Washington, DC: CQ Press, 2000), pp. 252–3.

benefits of unified government for the duration of their presidency.

The president and the media

The American mass media are the vehicle through which the image, the words, and the deeds of the president are transmitted to governing elites and the public at large. The media feed off the president as the most newsworthy individual in American politics, and the president depends on the media to convey favourable impressions that will help to determine his public prestige. The relationship between the media and the president has, for most of American history, been an adversarial one. In terms of the dissemination of news, the interests of the media and the president are very different and often incompatible. They became more so following the Vietnam War and Watergate, when the media identified 'the credibility gap'—the difference between what President Johnson was saying about the conduct of the Vietnam War and what was actually happening in Vietnam—and discovered that President Nixon was lying to them about the Watergate affair.

Post-Watergate media coverage of the president has been aggressively critical, except in times of national crises such as the 11 September terrorist attacks on New York and Washington, and more intensive. The White House is now covered around the clock by specialist White House correspondents who feed off White House gossip, rumour, intrigue, conflict, and personality. They need to make their news interesting. The details of presidential policy are often regarded as less newsworthy than the behind-the-scenes politics related to that policy. What often emerges in the media is not what presidents wanted to be reported. The consequence is that presidents now expend more time and effort in trying to manage the media to get their message across to the public with a minimum of media intermediation from reporters, analysts, or public figures who are likely to oppose them.

Again, the presidential staff has become one of the president's most effective resources in media management. Both the press secretary and, more recently, the White House Office of Communications have expanded in size to manage the White House press corps and control the news that the media report. It would not be an exaggeration to say that the presidential staff who devise media strategy and handle the press want their news to be the news that is reported, whereas professional White House correspondents are inherently suspicious of the 'spin control' that is part of the function of the presidential staff.

Post-Watergate presidents have been inventive in devising strategies and tactics to manage the media to try to get their message across without the media interpreting it to the public in an adverse way. Some of the more interesting innovations are designed to bypass the traditional, mainstream political journalists and exploit media opportunities that are more suitable for presidential purposes. Bill Clinton, for example, did this very effectively during the 1992 presidential election campaign when he tended to avoid the 'hard news' programmes like NBC's *Meet the Press* or CBS's *Face the Nation* and opted instead to appear on the softer chat shows, audience participation programmes, or breakfast television, where the questioning is less confrontational and the atmosphere less adversarial. Clinton also made use of selected media appearances where he could reach a specific target audience such as his MTV appearances which gave him a direct channel to young people.

Clinton used the same techniques for dealing with the media as president. His aim was to go over the heads of the Washington press corps directly to the people. He developed the 'electronic town meeting' where he would respond to questions from a studio audience at a local television station. He exploited new technologies like e-mail to increase direct communication with the public from the White House. He gave interviews to local television stations when travelling outside Washington, where his reception would be rather more reverential than that given to him by the media in Washington. And the traditional method of presidential communication with the media—the formal presidential press conference in the White House—was used less and less. President Clinton gave just forty-one press conferences in his first six years in office compared to the sixty-four given by his predecessor in just one four-year term (Stanley and Niemi 2000:170).

President Clinton's relationship with the media was particularly torrid. The Washington press corps were resentful of the way in which they were being bypassed by what one of them labelled Clinton's 'talk show presidency' (Kurtz 1993), and they responded with unusually critical treatment of the president during the honeymoon period at the beginning of his presidency. In return, Clinton and his media staff made no secret of their hostility to the Washington press corps, and within a few months the war between Clinton and the media had become a major media story itself.

Presidents have a strong incentive to try to manage the news and reduce the ability of the media to intermediate between them and their publics. Their public prestige depends in large part on what people read about and see of the president in their newspapers and on television. Presidents want to speak directly to the people, while the media want to filter those messages through analysis and interpretation. The more the media try to mediate presidential messages, the more likely it is that presidents will find additional ways of getting around that hurdle. And the more presidents succeed in avoiding accountability by the media by managing, controlling, and spinning, so the more critical the media will become. It is an inherently adversarial relationship.

The president and the public

Richard Neustadt's *Presidential Power* emphasized the significance of public prestige to a president's power prospects. 'The prevalent impression of a president's public standing tends to set a tone and define the limits of what Washingtonians do for him or do to him,' Neustadt wrote (1960: 87), and so managing public opinion is as important an activity for presidents as is managing their other clientele. But Neustadt also stressed that public opinion about the president was 'actually a jumble of imprecise impressions held by relatively inattentive people', so managing public opinion is no easy task for the modern president. The increasing number of public opinion polls and the prominence that the media give to poll findings does mean that presidents are never unaware of how they stand with the public, even if that standing is formed by a jumble of imprecise impressions.

Presidents put much effort into enhancing their public standing. The hope is that strong public support will translate into pressure on those in Washington to support their policies and initiatives, and presidents engage in activities designed to achieve just such an effect. Samuel Kernell (1986) has labelled this approach to presidential leadership 'going public', a response to the importance of public opinion in the conduct of the presidency.

Public appearances by the president are strategically arranged and carefully planned by the presidential staff. The words that presidents speak on these occasions are scripted by a team of speechwriters in the White House, aided by the president's communications staff. The timing of these appearances and their geographical setting are also strategically important. The message is visual as well as oral, often symbolic as well as substantial.

The strategy of going public had its origins in the presidency of Franklin Roosevelt. His famous 'fireside chats', where he addressed the American public from the White House via radio, was a particularly effective tool and allowed him to speak on topics of his choice without any third party getting in between him and the audience. All presidents have followed in Roosevelt's footsteps, but have also developed the public appeal to such an extent that it has become a strategy of presidential leadership rather than merely a form of communication.

There are drawbacks to the 'going public' style of leadership. It may not always work. Presidents run the risk of overusing the direct appeal, such that the novelty wears off and interests wanes. It is now less easy for presidents to command prime time television to address the nation. The American electronic media is no longer dominated by the big three free-to-air networks (NBC, CBS, and ABC). Cable television and the internet provide alternatives for viewers and competition for the networks, so the networks have to think very carefully about giving up prime time television just because a president wants to address the nation. When President Clinton decided in June of 1993 to hold his first televised prime time press conference, two of the three major networks refused to broadcast it and the third cut off coverage after thirty minutes.

It is also possible that the American media and the public may be getting a little tired of the over-scripted, stage-managed public appearances of the president. So much staff effort goes into preparing every last detail of a presidential statement, speech, or public event that they are in danger of being interpreted as nothing more than artificial public relations stunts designed to boost sagging presidential popularity. Presidents need to conserve their use of the public appeal in order to preserve its impact for the occasions that matter.

The major drawback with presidential leadership built around 'going public' strategies is that it comes to be seen as an alternative to bargaining and persuading political elites in Washington. No president can go public on every contentious political issue. The art of negotiating, bargaining, and compromise is still paramount in making Washington work. No matter how articulate and charismatic presidents can be on television addressing the nation, the reality of political life in Washington is still very traditional and requires coalition-building skills of a high order.

Presidential efforts to manage and manipulate public opinion are essential in order to maintain or increase presidential popularity, but they have met with mixed success. In general, presidential popularity declines over the course of a presidency: every post-war president has left the White House with his public approval ratings lower than when he entered it. Ironically, the only exception is President Clinton, who, notwithstanding the Whitewater scandal, his escapades with Monica Lewinsky, and his impeachment by Congress, left the presidency in 2001 with higher approval ratings than he had in January 1993. But then, no president had begun his presidency with less public support than President Clinton.

Key points

- To give direction to government, presidents have to confront other parts of the political system that have their own sources of political power, sometimes different perspectives and positions on matters of public policy, and the potential to oppose the interests of the White House. But the US system of government is not presidency-centered, and presidents can easily be frustrated in the exercise of leadership.

- Managing the bureaucracy is difficult for presidents because of its size, the independent power of career bureaucrats through networks of influence in Washington known as 'iron triangles', and the clientele-oriented structure of the departments and agencies. Presidents try to counter this through reorganization, politicization, and personnel policies, but rely ultimately on centralization of power and decision-making in the White House.

- Presidential influence on Congress is variable and there is no single formula for successful presidential relations with Congress. Legislating is a cooperative endeavour, and presidents must be prepared to compromise as well as cajole.

- The relationship between the media and the president has, for most of American history, been an adversarial one. Presidents need the media to communicate with the public, and have been inventive in devising techniques and strategies to reduce the impact of the media intermediating between president and public.

- Presidents put a lot of effort into enhancing their public standing in the hope that strong public support will translate into pressure on those in Washington. This strategy has been labelled 'going public'. It can work well for presidents but can also be overused. Its danger is that it comes to be seen as an alternative to bargaining and persuading political elites in Washington, but no president can go public on every contentious political issue. The art of negotiating, bargaining, and compromise is still paramount in making Washington work.

The presidency and electoral choice

Given the constraints facing the president in a separated system of government, it matters a great deal who is chosen to be president every four years. Neustadt emphasized that presidential power is essentially personal and that only those with extraordinary skill, ability, and temperament can be successful presidential leaders. His message is that, if the United States is to have good leadership in the White House, it will have to choose its president carefully from amongst a very small class of able, experienced politicians who understand the elusive nature of presidential power.

If that is so, then how do American voters know whether they are making the right choice when they vote for their president? Neustadt doesn't answer that question, but James David Barber tries to do so. Barber's book, *The Presidential Character* (1972), ranks along with Neustadt's as one of the most influential and important works published on the American presidency in the last half-century. It is a psychological study in which Barber identifies four personality types that shape the nature of any presidency. One of those types—the active-positive character—is highly desirable and another—the active-negative—

Box 9.5 Definitions: four meanings of 'the presidency'

The term 'presidency' is applied to several distinct perspectives on the office of the President of the United States.

1. Most commonly, and in its narrowest sense, it is employed as a label to refer to the incumbency of one particular president, as in the presidency of Abraham Lincoln or the presidency of Franklin Roosevelt.

2. More broadly, the term applies to the historical development and legacy of a succession of presidencies since the office was established in 1789.

3. In a more precise constitutional sense, the presidency is that branch of government established by Article II of the Constitution of the United States encompassing a set of constitutional and statutory powers and duties of the president together with additional 'implied' or 'inherent' powers and responsibilities not specifically enumerated in the Constitution or statute law.

4. Finally, the term 'presidency' is used to denote the institutional structure of the office of president embracing the Executive Office of the President—a collection of staff units, originating from proposals contained in the Brownlow Report of 1937, that provide the president with the capacity to manage the work of the executive branch of government and to liaise with the principal constituents of the president, namely the Congress, the media, and interest groups.

Source: J. Hart, 'Presidency: United States', *International Encyclopaedia of the Social and Behavioural Sciences* (Oxford: Elsevier, 2001), p. 11998.

is rigid, inflexible, and dangerous and to be avoided at all costs. Even more alarming is Barber's assertion that presidential character is fixed long before the individual contests a presidential election, and there is not much that can be done to change a personality type once that personality is occupying the White House. Barber intended his book to be a tool for voters to help them anticipate a potential active-negative President. It is a controversial work and his psychological typology is not accepted by all presidency scholars but nevertheless, his argument that not much can be done about bad presidents once they have been elected is always a timely one, and emphasizes how much responsibility voters carry when they exercise electoral choice. Once installed in the White House, presidents can only be removed from office by the impeachment process—a form of accountability of last resort and one that works imperfectly, as the attempted impeachments of Andrew Johnson and Bill Clinton demonstrated.

In other words, electoral choice lies at the heart of presidential leadership. While the success of any individual president will depend on the ability of

that individual and the circumstances of the time, ultimately it is electoral choice that makes the difference between good and bad presidents in the United States; and so the nature of the presidency may ultimately turn on the quality of the electoral process rather than anything to do with the nature of the presidential office itself.

Key points

- Presidential leadership is personal and elusive, and requires extraordinary temperament and ability from those elected to the office.

- Presidential character is fixed by the time a president reaches the White House, and nothing much can be done to alter presidential personality once a president has been elected.

- The quality of presidential leadership ultimately rests on electoral choice, and that in turn depends on the quality of the American electoral process.

Conclusion

The presidency is the single most significant political office in the United States. No other figure possesses the legitimacy conferred by a national election and a national constituency. Only the president can speak both to and for America, and only the president possesses the resources (formal and informal) to galvanize a notoriously fragmented and conflictual system. In short, only the president can lead. But as George

W. Bush has found, even in the most demanding of crisis situations the president must recognize that he operates in a separated system of government, not a presidential democracy. Accordingly, whilst most presidents since FDR have rightly seen their office as an especially powerful one, few have held it to be sufficiently so.

QUESTIONS

1 'Sustained presidential leadership is now impossible in America.' Discuss.

2 Can the power of the presidency be reconciled with its inherent weakness?

3 What are the most formidable obstacles to effective presidential leadership?

4 What best explains presidential 'success'?

5 'The president typically possesses authority but not necessarily power.' Discuss.

FURTHER READING

J. D. Barber (1972) *The Presidential Character: Predicting Performance in the White House* (Englewood Cliffs, NJ: Prentice Hall).

J. Hart (1995), *The Presidential Branch: From Washington to Clinton* (Chatham, NJ: Chatham House).

C. O. Jones (1994), *The Presidency in a Separated System* (Washington, DC: Brookings Institution).

S. Kernell (1986), *Going Public: New Strategies of Presidential Leadership* (Washington, DC: CQ Press).

R. E. Neustadt (1960), *Presidential Power: The Politics of Leadership* (New York: Wiley).

A. M. Schlesinger, Jr. (1973), *The Imperial Presidency* (Boston: Houghton Mifflin).

WEB LINKS

www.whitehouse.gov White House

www.whitehouse.gov/WH/EOP/omb Office of Management and Budget

www.bog.frb.fed.us Federal Reserve Board

www.usdoj.gov Department of Justice

stats.bls.gov Department of Labor Bureau of Labor Statistics

dosfan.lib.uic.edu Department of State

www.ustreas.gov Department of the Treasury

www.is.gov CIA

10 Congress: the co-equal partner

John E. Owens

READER'S GUIDE

Within America's separated system of government, Congress is a co-equal partner invested with formidable powers by the framers of the Constitution—although outside Congress the institution is held in popular contempt. To understand how the House of Representatives and Senate operate and organize themselves as representative and legislative chambers we need to understand the nature of contemporary candidate-organized and permanent election campaigns that existing House members and senators run to win re-election. As we have seen in earlier chapters, the policy preferences of House members' and senators' constituents have become more polarized along party lines. In this context, the parties in Congress became much more ideologically homogeneous and polarized, and rank-and-file party members became much more willing to empower their party leaders. Leaders were increasingly expected after the mid-1980s to develop partisan policies and political strategies that would enhance their party's national reputation and improve individual party members' prospects of re-election. Particularly when Congress handles major legislation that is salient among the public and important to the majority party an American form of party government prevails. As parties became the most significant organizations on Capitol Hill, the once autonomous and powerful House and Senate committees were increasingly marginalized, sometimes bypassed. Party government American style is much more potent in the House because of the chamber's majoritarian rules. In the non-majoritarian Senate, contemporary majority leaders find it much more difficult to win approval for party legisla-tion. Despite the strengthening of party in Congress, however, there remain numerous opportunities for individual members and congressional committees to influence legisla-tion and represent their constituents thereby maintaining the enduring tension between Congress' representative and governing roles.

Introduction

In America's separated system (Jones 1994: 28), the president shares power with the Congress, which is the most powerful legislature in the world (Box 10.1). Congress' essentially coordinate role has often been underestimated and undervalued, particularly in the twentieth century–and notwithstanding the assumption made by the framers of the American Constitution that Congress would be 'the govern-ment', and the impressive powers they gave the legislature. As John Hart explained in the previous chapter, throughout most of the period since the election of President Franklin Roosevelt in 1932, the presidency was presumed to be the driving force within the system–as observers, many inside Congress itself, became enchanted by what James Sundquist has called the 'cult of the strong presi-dency' (1977: 223). During this presidentialist phase of congressional-presidential relations, Con-gress' willingness even to claim a position of national political leadership, co-equal with the president, was doubted, as House members and senators frequently permitted, even encouraged, the president and the rest of the executive to insist on exercising leadership on the major issues of the day. For several decades now (Box 10.2), Congress has increasingly insisted on its constitutional pre-rogatives and, particularly since the mid-1980s, come to operate almost as a complete government either alongside or, more commonly, in competi-tion with him, offering policy alternatives and par-ticipating at all stages in the national governing process.

> ## Box 10.1 A separated, not a presidential or parliamentary, system
>
> Even in times of crisis—such as the aftermath of the attacks on New York and Washington on 11 Sep-tember 2001—this defining feature of American government cannot be ignored. For it is Congress that must appropriate monies—for example, to pro-vide financial assistance to New York City and the airline industry; it is Congress that must pass new laws (albeit often at the request of the president)—to combat terrorism, strengthen airline security, and for other purposes; and it is Congress that oversees and scrutinizes the actions of the executive. Unlike in parliamentary systems, the Congress not only has the formal power to say 'no' to the president, but often does so.

Congress in the Constitution

As we saw in Chapter 3, those who thought about republican government in the America of the 1770s and 1780s emphasized political representation. The main complaint of the American colonists against the British government in 1776 was that the Westminster Parliament had violated the 1689 Bill of Rights, which required, they argued, that no taxation should be imposed on those who were not

Box 10.2 **Key events and developments in the recent reassertion of congressional power**

Late 1960s and early 1970s	The 'presidential' war in Vietnam
Early 1970s	Watergate
After 1968	Re-emergence of **split party government** (where Congress and the presidency are controlled by different parties)
Mid-1970s and 1980s	Strengthening of Congress' institutional capacity (increasing staff, growth of subcommittees, greater use of congressional agencies)
After the mid-1980s	Strengthening of party in Congress (especially in the House of Representatives), stronger party unity, and the emergence of sharper policy differences between Democrats and Republicans in most important areas of public policy

represented. Since the colonists were not permitted to elect any members to Westminster and had not authorized anyone to consent to taxation on their behalf, Parliament's actions were illegitimate. Under America's first system of government established by the Articles of Confederation of 1777, similar importance was attached to the election of political representatives who saw themselves primarily as agents of the local people. '[A representative assembly] should think, feel, reason, and act like them,' declared John Adams. The new system had no executive or judiciary—only a representative assembly, the Continental Congress, which would be 'the government'. When the framers of the 1787 Constitution came to write their document, they also emphasized political representation and the importance of the legislature. 'In republican government,' James Madison insisted in *Federalist Paper* No. 51, 'the legislative authority

necessarily predominates.' The very first sentence of the new Constitution declared: 'All legislative Powers herein granted shall be vested in a Congress of the United States.' Section 8 of Article I then provides Congress with virtually all governmental powers conceivable to late eighteenth-century life: to tax, spend, and 'provide for the common defense and general welfare of the United States'. The same section also gave Congress substantial powers in the areas of foreign policy (to declare war, and make treaties with other countries), appointments to other branches of government (to advise on and consent to presidents' nominations, and to impeach), foreign and interstate commerce, national security (to raise and maintain armed forces), selecting the president (in case of stalemate in the electoral college, presidential disability, or resignation), and in proposing constitutional amendments. Finally, clause 18 of the section—the so-called 'elastic clause'—vested in Congress the broad power 'to make all laws which shall be necessary and proper for carrying into execution the foregoing powers'.

Yet, although political representation constitutes an important theme in the 1787 Constitution, as well as in contemporary politics, the wise heads who framed the document were even more concerned that the actions of a Congress invested with such potent powers would not rely exclusively on representatives directly elected by local people. Experience of the states' legislatures following the Declaration of Independence in 1776 had demonstrated in brutal fashion that legislative government produced neither political stability nor responsible government in America's fledgling republic. Influenced by the examples of the British parliamentary system and most of the American states, and by pressing demands from outside the Constitutional Convention, the framers opted for a bicameral legislature that embodied co-equal chambers and reflected competing concepts of representation. The popular, directly elected House of Representatives would represent the views and interests of local people. However, in order to check what Madison and others anticipated would be the 'fickleness and passion' of the directly elected House, and the likely 'rapid succession of new members', there would also be a small Senate to represent the states. Senators would be chosen by the state legislatures, not directly elected by the people, and (hopefully) would be men (*sic*) with more stable temperaments who would promote and defend the broader visions and interests of American society beyond the immediate demands of the people. By providing for two chambers, then—chosen from different electoral bases and in institutional competition with one another (Box 10.3)—it was assumed that 'the aggregate interests of the community' would be represented and that the awesome responsibility for lawmaking and running the federal government would be shared between two competing institutions.

Box 10.3 **The House and Senate in the Constitution**

According to the 'great compromise' reached at the 1787 Philadelphia Convention:

The House of Representatives would be elected every two years from congressional districts apportioned to the states after each decennial census and based on their populations.

The Senate would accord equal representation for each state with seats delineated into three classes, each representing a third of seats up for re-election every two years—with senators serving staggered six-year terms.

Key points

- Republican government in the United States has always emphasized political representation and the importance of legislatures.

- The 1787 Constitution was premised on the need to balance the immediate and parochial interests of the people with those of the collectivity of 'the American people'.

- Bicameralism was built into the Constitution as an essential element for limiting the effects of immediate popular pressures and as a means of diffusing Congress' awesome lawmaking and governing responsibilities.

In the next section, I discuss the contemporary electoral connection between Congress and the voters: how members are recruited, how they are elected, and how they interact with their constituents once they arrive in Washington. This section lays the groundwork for the analysis of congressional organization in the contemporary era characterized by party government: how are congressional parties organized? How influential are they and their leaders in structuring debate and decision-making in the contemporary House and Senate? And how do other congressional structures—notably, Members' personal offices and the committee systems—limit contemporary party government? The chapter concludes by exploring the inherent tensions in congressional politics between satisfying House members' and senators' electoral needs and the efforts of central party leaders to coordinate congressional activity.

Congress' electoral connection

The parochial character of congressional representation

Madison's insistence, in *Federalist Paper* No. 52, that 'the [Congress] should have an immediate dependence on, and an intimate sympathy with, the people' is as important today as it was in the late 1780s. It is manifested, negatively, in popular contempt for Congress that far exceeds that for all other governmental institutions and for nearly all other societal institutions (Hibbing and Theiss-Morse 1995; Kimball and Patterson 1997) and, positively, in the huge efforts that congressional candidates and incumbent politicians undertake to remain in touch with the voters.

None of the 440 House districts[1] or fifty states is identical. Seeking nomination or election from at-large Alaska (586,000 square miles)—whose eastern and western borders are the same geographical distance apart as the distance from Chicago to Washington and thousands of miles from the capital—or Montana (147,046 square miles) is very different from seeking a seat covering 10 or 11 square miles in downtown Brooklyn or Los Angeles. Besides obvious geographical differences such as these, there are considerable variations in wealth, median family income, and other economic and social conditions. Cultural and ethnic compositions of districts and states also vary widely, as do age distributions; and there are wide variations in political conditions, including political ideology and partisan strength, and the number and distribution of different newspaper, television, and radio markets. Individually, very few districts and no states are socially or culturally monolithic. When they seek election or re-election, congressional candidates must accommodate to one of these diverse geographic constituencies (see Box 10.4).

Once elected, local voters *expect* their member of Congress—regardless of whether he/she is a junior member or a senior party leader or committee chair—to provide good constituency service, to be accessible, to communicate with them frequently, and to promote their causes and interests even at the expense of broader general interests, the member's ties to the president, his/her party's presidential candidate, or his/her congressional party leaders. So, when House members and senators decide how they will apportion their time in Washington, what issues they will take up, what committee or subcommittee assignments they will seek, and how they will vote, their first question will be: 'how will my decision affect my district or state?' What David Mayhew calls Congress's 'electoral connection' (1974a) is vital to understanding how members relate to their constituents—at least those who are likely to vote (see Box 10.5)—once they arrive in Washington; and how individual members relate to their constituents and *vice versa* has important consequences for how individual House members and senators relate to their congressional party, but also for how Congress as a collective institution fulfils its constitutional responsibility to share in the task of governing the country.

Box 10.4 The 2000 elections: accommodating to a specific geographical constituency

When Rhode Island Republican Lincoln Chafee sought election in 2000 to a Senate seat to which he had been appointed after his father died, his campaign ran a television advertisement touting his support for proposals to enhance patients' rights and regulate prescription drug prices (incidentally, paid for by funds provided by the National Republican Senatorial Committee) that are supported by Democrats and opposed by most congressional Republicans. Rhode Island is a strongly Democratic state that gave Al Gore 61 per cent of the presidential vote in 2000.

One of Hillary Rodham Clinton's most important tasks in her campaign for one of New York's Senate seats in 2000 was to convince the state's voters why they should vote for a candidate who. was born in Chicago, became a lawyer in Arkansas, and spent the previous eight years in Washington, DC as First Lady to President Bill Clinton, a former Governor of Arkansas.

Congressional recruitment

Candidates seeking election to the House or Senate must meet few formal constitutional requirements apart from age, citizenship, and residency. Congressional Republicans introduced a constitutional amendment in 1995 that would have limited the number of terms that members of Congress could serve but this and other measures were not enacted into law. Similar attempts by twenty-two states failed

---

[1] Currently, the House has four non-voting delegates—from American Samoa (1981), District of Columbia (1971), Guam (1972), and the Virgin Islands (1976)—and one resident commissioner for Puerto Rico (1976), bringing the total to 440. Proposals were made in 1994 to grant delegate status also to the resident representative of the Northern Marianas Islands. Puerto Rico's delegate or resident commissioner is elected for four years, the others for two years. Although not technically members of the House, in the 103rd Congress (1993–4) delegates were allowed by majority Democrats to vote in certain circumstances. Delegates may also speak on the floor, serve and vote on committees, and even hold committee chairs. Republicans ended delegate voting in 1995.

Box 10.5 Low voter turnout in congressional elections

Voting in congressional elections is much lower than levels of other liberal democracies, particularly in western Europe. Despite their frequency and the attention paid to elections in American political culture and by individual members of Congress, most congressional campaigns are sporadic and amateurish, especially for the House, and attract little media attention. Most Americans of voting age do not vote in congressional elections: less than half vote when there is a presidential election (just 48.3 per cent in 2000) and usually only one third when the presidency is not being contested. Survey evidence collected by the American National Election Study (NES) also shows that voters' knowledge of and regard for congressional elections is low. In the 1998 elections, for example, 38 per cent of respondents could not even identify correctly which party controlled Congress; and 48 per cent did not care which party won a round of elections (Center for Political Studies 1995–2000).

when the Supreme Court ruled an Arkansas law unconstitutional in *US Term Limits* versus *Thornton* (1995), and political support for the change dissipated as economic conditions improved and voter anger with politicians waned. In keeping with the system's essentially decentralized character, there is no national congressional election process. Rather, the individual states run a calendar of numerous uncoordinated events that occur on different days over an eight-month period and are governed by myriad state laws and regulations and heavily coloured by highly varied local party-political conditions.

In contrast to parliamentary systems in which strong party organizations act as gatekeepers controlling which candidate(s) bear the party's label in an election, strong party control over House candidate recruitment is now extremely rare, and totally absent in Senate elections, as partisan-led campaigns have been replaced by those that are candidate-centred. Although local, state, and national party organizations and leaders (including the president) often play important roles in recruiting House and Senate candidates and funnelling electorally useful

services—fundraising, media consultancy, issue research, and opinion polling—to them, particularly in that small subset of House districts and selected Senate races that constitute the 'battleground races', and although the vast majority of candidates run as either Democrats or Republicans, in most districts and states parties do not control congressional recruitment in any meaningful sense. Exceptions in the 2000 elections included Democrats in the Illinois-3 and Pennsylvania-1 districts, and Republicans in the New York-3 district. In many ways, more typical were the successful campaigns of two well-known House incumbents—self-described socialist Bernie Sanders, in the Vermont at-large district and former Democrat, Virgil Goode in Virginia-5—who won election as independents.

Whether a congressional candidate decides to run and whether or not he/she wins election depends crucially on his or her individual efforts and strategic calculations, and the quantity and quality of the financial and other resources that he/she personally can muster to run a viable campaign. Of course, contextual factors—including the partisan composition of the particular district or state,[2] the strategic environment (whether the seat is held by an incumbent or open; the likely quality of opponents, local and national economic and political conditions) (Rohde 1979; Jacobson and Kernell 1983; Jacobson 1989; Fowler 1993; Campbell 1993; Jacobson 2001a), and the country's collective policy mood (Stimson 2001)—are also important. However, as one former senator put it: 'you are either a self-starter or a no-starter'. Those most likely to be successful are the so-called quality candidates—politically ambitious men and women who have already invested heavily in a political career; they probably hold office already, and are now seeking to move up the promotion ladder, possibly from the state legislature or local government to the House, or from the House to the Senate. Other quality candidates may include well-known political amateurs (Canon 1989) who are sufficiently well known and appealing to voters: an athlete, like former University of Oklahoma quarterback and Baptist preacher, former Congressman

---

[2] Most districts are safe for one party. In the 2000 elections, for example, 349 (80%) House districts and 24 (73%) of the Senate contests were won by the same party whose presidential candidates won the state (excluding Florida).

and Republican Conference chair, J. C. Watts (R.OK), or the widow of a well-known local politician, like Senator Jean Carnahan (D.MO); or a multimillionaire, like Senator John Corzine (D.NJ), who spent $60 million of his own money to win a Senate seat in the 2000 elections. But best of all are incumbent House members and senators. The single most important fact about contemporary House and Senate elections is that most incumbents seek and win re-election (Box 10.6). Voluntary retirement, not electoral defeat, is the main cause of congressional turnover. There are usually a few more opportunities after a redistricting cycle but towards the end of a decade pickings are very slim indeed.

Elected members and their constituents

Why incumbent House members and senators seek and win re-election tells us something important about the electoral connection between them and their constituents. While Congress as an institution is held in popular contempt,[3] voters love *their* member of Congress (Fenno 1975), as Box 10.7 shows. A reflection of this phenomenon is that incumbents in their first term tend to increase their share of the vote when they seek re-election—the so-called 'sophomore surge'. So, for example, in his first election in 2000, Democrat Mike Ross won Arkansas' 4th district with 51 per cent of the vote but in 2002 he won with 61 per cent. Incumbents also find it easier

than challengers to raise money—largely from wealthy political action committees (PACs) and their parties who seek to invest in success and relative certainty. In the 2000 elections, for example, average contributions to incumbents were twice that of challengers in Senate elections and 247 per cent of those of House challengers—and the gap between incumbents' and challengers' spending has widened sharply over recent years. Even when they lose their seats, House incumbents often spend significantly more than their winning challengers because they try to scare off quality challengers (sometimes unsuccessfully).[4]

One reason why incumbents tend to win is that they allocate time and resources to waging a permanent re-election campaign designed to cultivate close relations with re-election constituencies back home and help them win re-election in two or six years' time. It used to be the case that senators' longer terms allowed them to concentrate their first three to four years attending to matters of state in Washington, leaving the final two or three years for re-election activities. No longer. Now, senators too are occupied from their first year raising money (often to pay off debts from the previous campaign) and visiting their states regularly, and all the time making sure that their voting behaviour complies with the wishes of their constituents. Incumbent House members and senators devise a home style or representational strategy that suits them and their districts or states (Fenno 1978; 1996; 2000). These representational strategies define how much and what kinds of attention they will pay to their constituencies, particularly their re-election constituencies—those voters whom the House member or senator thinks will vote for him/her next time ('traditional Democratic voters', 'core Republican voters', and so forth).

Box 10.6 **The importance of incumbency in congressional elections**

In the 2000 elections, just three House and no Senate incumbents lost their primaries. Six House members and six senators lost the general election: 93 per cent of all House members (403) and 85 per cent of senators whose terms expired sought re-election; 98 per cent (394) of House members and 79 per cent of senators won, including sixty House incumbents and one Senate incumbent all of whom had no major party opponent.

---

[3] Polls taken throughout the 1990s show repeatedly that barely 50% of Americans approve of the job Congress is doing as a collective institution. Since Gallup began measuring congressional approval in 1974, positive ratings have generally remained at less than 50% and in March 1992 reached an all-time low point of just 18% approval. The rise in Congress' approval ratings to 84% in October 2001, following the attacks on Washington and New York, was unprecedented and must be regarded as aberrant.

[4] In the 2000 elections, for example, just 17% of House Republican incumbents and 20% of Democratic incumbents faced challengers that had ever held public office (Jacobson 2001b).

Box 10.7 Voters love their member of Congress (but not Congress)

The American public hold Congress as a collective institution in contempt. Not so their individual member of Congress.

- Survey evidence from five House elections (1992–2000) shows that an average 61.2 per cent of respondents approved of the job done by their incumbent House representative.

- Election after election, almost all voters recognize the names of incumbent House members and senators but only about half recognize the names of House incumbents' challengers. (The differential is less between incumbent senators and their challengers.)

- Voters also feel more positively towards incumbents than their challengers, especially House incumbents.

- Voters evaluate incumbents primarily according to their constituency attentiveness, personal qualities, and experience, rather than by their party connections, ideology, or policy preferences on salient issues.*

* Even so, consistent with growing partisan and ideological polarization among the electorate, the percentage of respondents citing that they liked their House incumbents' ideology or stances on policy issues doubled from 12% to 24% between 1978 and 1998, as did the percentage citing dislike of their House incumbents' ideology or stances on policy issues (from 22% to 43%).

Source: American National Election Survey.

These strategies determine how incumbents present themselves and their activities to their constituents and others; what positions they adopt that are favoured by their voters; how they vote in Congress; how they explain in ordinary language their activities in Washington to constituents, especially on issues of local interest; how and to what extent they claim personal responsibility for 'bringing home the bacon'/'pork barrel'—flood projects, military contracts, research grants, housing and urban aid, and so forth—to their states and districts; and how they allocate their own and their staff's time, energy, and other resources to address salient constituency interests and concerns. Incumbents' representational

strategies and personal styles vary considerably (Box 10.8) but, regardless of specific content, their shared purpose is to emphasize the member's fit with his/her re-election constituency, to promote an aura of trust among prospective supporters back home, to indicate that the incumbent is qualified to hold the office (including whether he/she is honest), to demonstrate that he/she can identify with the attitudes, beliefs, and perceptions of constituents, to empathize with constituents' problems and perceptions, and to demonstrate accessibility to voters.

Helped by generous travel allowances and congressional scheduling that allows for 'non-legislative' work periods during congressional sessions, incumbents make frequent visits to their constituencies, keep in regular contact with constituents either through personal appearances or contacts through the mass media, and avidly publicize their activities. Surveys conducted from 1978 to 1994 by the American National Election Study show that between 10 and 15 per cent of American adults contacted their member of Congress or senator (equivalent to between 55,000 and 85,000 constituents in the average congressional district) at some time, including 6 per cent who wanted to give their opinion on a particular issue. Senators receive even more contacts, especially those representing the largest states. In order to cope with these volumes of enquiries, members have voted themselves generous allowances (Box 10.9). The strategic rationale for paying so much attention to constituency service is obvious: it is a relatively cost-free non-controversial way for incumbents to bolster their re-election credentials and, in certain cases, compensate for

Box 10.8 Contrasting representational styles in Congress

While Senator Robert Byrd (D.WV) and Congressman Robert Brady (D.PA) emphasize close personal contact with their constituents, and winning contracts and projects for their districts and states, Senators Edward Kennedy (D.MA), Phil Gramm (R.TX), and Paul Wellstone (D.MN) tended to emphasize particular policy positions. Many members emphasize a combination of these strategies.

policy preferences or partisanship out of tune with their districts or states.

The so-called incumbency advantage is not, however, automatic in congressional elections: although most incumbents win, some do not; and sometimes incumbents who provide excellent constituency service are swept away by national political tides (as in 1994). Re-election has to be earned—by exploiting the resources of their offices to give their constituents constant attention, by reading accurately the interests of districts and states, by taking care of constituents' concerns, and by scaring off potential quality challengers.

Key points

- Candidates who seek election to Congress must demonstrate their appeal and responsiveness to the parochial values and interests of voters in their individual districts and states.

Box 10.9 **Serving constituents**

In 2002, each House member received personal staff and communications allowances worth up to $2.7 million over a two-year term. Senators received as much as $19 million over a six-year Senate term (even more for committee chairs and party leaders)— in addition to their salaries of $150,000. About 40 per cent of House and 30 per cent of senators' personal staff are assigned to district and state offices.

- Congressional candidates essentially recruit themselves. In the vast majority of districts and states, political parties do not control party nominations. Campaigns are candidate-centred and candidate-organized.

- Most incumbents seek and win re-election by waging permanent re-election campaigns designed to cultivate an aura of trust and effectiveness among constituents.

Congressional organization

Congress is a lawmaking institution as well as a representative assembly. In the American separated system, members of the House and Senate are expected to share in the making of national government policy, as well as pay attention to and represent their constituents. Just as incumbents and other congressional candidates seek election by designing their own election strategies, logically, once these ambitious entrepreneurial politicians arrive in Washington, they want to play meaningful roles in national policymaking, participate fully in Congress' processes, and structure congressional organization so that it serves their political needs and objectives. Indeed, it is because the Congress continues to recruit ambitious entrepreneurial politicians who are overwhelmingly sympathetic to the principles of diffused responsibility, mixed representation, and institutional competition that the institution is able to fulfil its constitutional responsibilities (albeit imperfectly), maintain its institutional autonomy and scope of action, and

largely resist encroaching presidentialism, executive expertise, and coordinated power.

The determination of contemporary members of Congress to fulfil both their representative and lawmaking responsibilities and resist pressures to devote their entire Washington careers to getting themselves re-elected is manifest in the institution's size, organization, and breadth of activities. Congress is a large, bureaucratic, and expensive legislature (see Box 10.10).

While the Constitution enunciates formidable powers for Congress and stipulates rules for electing its members and how often it should meet, the document says next to nothing about how the House of Representatives and Senate should organize themselves. It merely specifies how the House's presiding officer (the Speaker) should be elected and that the Vice-President (or, in his absence, the president *pro tempore*) should preside over the Senate. No mention is made of political parties, congressional committees, or other aspects of legislative

Box 10.10 **Congress' cost and workload**

- Congress occupies eight large office buildings spread over 1.8 square miles on Capitol Hill and costs about $3 billion a year to run (2002)—$5.5 million for every member.

- Although less active than it was in the mid-1990s, America's national legislature remains a highly active, bustling institution. In 2001–2, the House of Representatives was in session for 265 days—about six hours a day; the Senate, for 322 days—seven hours a day.

- In the 107th Congress (2001–2), House members introduced over 15,700 bills (about 13 per member), senators almost 3,900 (32 per senator). Of these, 331 passed into law.

- Over the same period, House members recorded over 615 votes (two a day) and attended over 5,000 committee meetings; senators recorded 633 votes (under two a day) and attended over 2,000 meetings.

organization that are essential to how the contemporary Congress operates. Hence, although the Constitution created a bicameral legislature and requires both chambers to consider and approve all legislation, the members of those chambers have almost complete freedom to evolve their own organ-izational frameworks, internal rules, and behavioural norms.

Not surprisingly, important institutional differences between the House and the Senate have developed (see Box 10.11).

Key points

- Congress is a lawmaking as well as a representative institution. Its members are expected to participate fully in the national policymaking process as well as pay attention to and represent their constituents.

- Just as congressional candidates structure their own election and re-election campaigns, it is logical that members of Congress should want to play a meaningful role in national policy-making, and should structure congressional organization so that it serves their political objectives.

- The determination of contemporary members of Congress to fulfil representative and lawmaking roles serves to uphold Congress' institutional strength and autonomy.

- The Constitution does not prescribe how Congress should be organized internally. Hence, members of Congress enjoy considerable freedom to organize their chambers in ways that best reflect their own collective personal goals.

- There are important institutional differences between the House and the Senate.

Party government American style

In the British House of Commons and all other European legislatures, it is the parties—particularly the majority party, that control the legislature—because most MPs win election as a result of bearing a particular party label and once elected are expected to toe the party line, in the belief that their loyalty to the party will benefit all party MPs and in many cases lead to promotion to the party hierarchy. Members of Congress are individually *purposive*. They must decide their own representational calculus and organize their individual congressional careers with far less instruction or guidance from their party leaders and colleagues. Each member pursues different personal political goals (Fenno 1973: 1) with different degrees of priority and intensity (see Box 10.12). Their own peculiar combination of priorities and intensities guides their congressional activities and determines how

Box 10.11 Important institutional differences between the House and Senate

The House	*The Senate*
Lower prestige.	Higher prestige
Larger (435 members + 5 delegates).	Smaller (100 senators)
Geographical constituencies usually smaller (usually about 500, 000 people) allowing closer contact with constituents.	Geographic constituencies usually larger; more difficult to retain close contact with constituents than do House members. Also huge variations in constituency populations; e.g. the two senators from Wyoming represent just over 495,000 people while their colleagues from California represent 34 million people—69 times as many or 12 per cent of total US population. In consequence, the chamber grossly over-represents small states* and under-represents racial and ethnic minorities (Lee 1997).
More bureaucratic.	More individualistic, much more personal.
More partisan.	Less partisan.
Hierarchically organized.	Fairly flat organizational structure.
Procedural rules much more comprehensive (1,322 pages in the 107th Congress), more formalized, and less flexible.	Procedural rules fewer (just 90 pages in the 107th Congress), highly flexible, and the most permissive of any legislative chamber in the world.
Majoritarian rules designed to ensure that a party majority can effectively control the policy agenda and floor proceedings.	Nonmajoritarian rules that are designed to uphold minority power and protect the legislative prerogatives of individual senators.
Floor debate more tightly controlled by party leaders.	Floor debate not controlled by party leaders; much more protracted.
Attention given by mass media sporadic but less than senators.	Attention given by mass media considerable.
Being larger, the House has a more formal division of labour, so committees tend to be more important and House members are able to consider legislation in greater detail through their committee system.	Being smaller, the Senate has a much less formal division of labour, so committees play a less important role.
Members have fewer committee assignments and their Washington activities are more clearly defined by their committee activities.	Members have more committee assignments and their Washington activities are less defined by their committee activities.
Members are usually able to develop greater policy expertise.	Members usually find it more difficult to develop policy expertise and need to rely more on the expertise of their staff.

* In 2002, just 18 senators represented just over half the population of the United States while 70 senators represented just one-third. These biases are brought into sharp relief when, as in the 107th Senate (2001–2), the majority party's plurality rests on very small majorities in several states.

they employ their time and energy and what policy positions they adopt.

At the aggregate institutional level, the combinations of members' personal goals also determine the kind of congressional chamber they want: depending on whether they are members of the House or Senate, how their chamber is organized internally to serve the collective and individual goals of its members. Given the diversity of House members' and senators' needs and goals, it is not

---

Box 10.12 Fenno's typology of Congress members' personal goals

Some members emphasize constituency service and/or winning re-election. Others concentrate on acquiring prestige and influence within their chamber; and others are most interested in making good public policy. All members probably seek all three goals, but the emphasis they place on each varies and sometimes changes over time.

---

surprising that each chamber of Congress has developed multiple and competing internal power structures the relations among which have changed over time, especially in the House, as the collectivity of members' individual combinations of goals have changed in response to the changing patterns of politics inside and outside Congress. For most of the twentieth century, congressional organization was characterized by committee government—following Woodrow Wilson's well-known description: 'Congress in its committee rooms is Congress at work' (1885: 69). Beginning, however, in the 1960s, the power exercised by congressional committees and the largely conservative barons who chaired them came under increasing challenge from newly elected liberal Democratic majorities who viewed Congress's internal organization as a barrier to achieving their goals of social reform. As a consequence of an institutional reform process that began in the 1960s and resulted in major changes in the 1970s and 1980s, transformations were set in train that led to the reinstatement of an American form of party government.

Political parties have always figured prominently in Congress since the earliest days of the American Republic. So, today, each of the semicircle chambers separates majority and minority members depending on which party has the larger number of seats; members of the majority party sit to the right of the presiding officer, minority party members to the left. Moreover, when a party loses its majority—as in May 2001, when Senator James Jeffords (R.VT) defected from the majority Republicans—party control of a chamber changes, even in mid-term. Yet congressional parties have rarely exerted what

Charles O. Jones calls 'substance-oriented policy leadership' (1982: 175), and certainly not to the extent found in British and other European party systems. However, parties are now the most significant organizational structures on Capitol Hill, and the power and authority exercised by central party leaders—especially in the House—is greater than at any time since the beginning of the twentieth century. Today, parties organize the House and the Senate in more or less all respects (see Box 10.13).

Why parties have become the most significant organizational structures in the House and the Senate is inextricably connected with broader developments in the party system and the electorate. As the discussions in Chapters 5 and 6 explained, after the 1970s the ideological and policy preferences of activists within each of the two main parties

---

Box 10.13 The role of contemporary congressional parties

The majority party in each chamber:

- decides who will be the House Speaker and the Senate Majority Leader;

- decides who will occupy other leadership positions, including committee chairs;

- devises and revises each chamber's rules, including what powers leaders enjoy and which committees shall be created;

- exerts control over committees, assigns members to committees, and fixes party ratios on committees to its advantage;

- refers and schedules all major legislation (although this power is weaker in the Senate: see Box 10.18);

- controls much of each chamber's vast administrative resources.

Most importantly, under conditions of party government, the majority party is now much more likely than the minority to enact its legislative priorities and preferences. Although its non-majoritarian rules and procedures significantly limit this capacity, having a party majority in the Senate—albeit a very slim one—is now much more of an advantage than it was thirty or forty years ago.

became much more homogeneous and divergent from those in the other party. Democratic activists were much more likely to be liberal (typically more liberal than most Democratic identifiers), while Republican activists were much more likely to be conservative (typically more conservative than most Republican identifiers). Increasing ideological and preference divergence among party activists worked with increased electoral partisanship in the 1980s and 1990s to produce much more ideologically homogeneous and polarized bases for each of the parties than was the case previously. Moreover, as budgetary issues increasingly dominated Congress' agenda, and in the context of control of Congress and the presidency split between the two parties, American-style party government re-emerged, particularly in the House (see Box 10.14).

Central to party organization in the House are the House Republican Conference and the Democratic Caucus. Each of these organizations is appropriated about $2.1 million (2002) for their activities each year, in addition to separate funding made available to the majority and minority party leaderships. The Conference and Caucus, respectively, nominate their party's candidates for Speaker, elect a leader, whip, caucus/conference chair and vice-chair, and chair of the election campaign committee (the Democratic Congressional Campaign Committee and National Republican Campaign Committee), ratify the nominations of committee members and chairs made by the parties' respective steering committees (the Republican Steering Committee and Democratic Steering and Policy Committee), establish the parties' legislative priorities, and schedule items for House and party consideration (Foley and Owens 1996: 138–9). The Caucus/Conferences also approve the party's rules (for example, how long a member may chair a committee or subcommittee and what the conditions are for membership), and through the Conference/Caucus chairs and in coordination with the Speaker or Minority Leader assume responsibilities for publicizing the party's legislative efforts and the respective parties' 'spin' on the day's events (a particularly important activity for the party that does not control the White House). More generally, the party Caucus/Conference provides a forum for party colleagues to question committee and party leaders candidly and privately on

---

Box 10.14 **American-style party government**

Under conditions of party government, rank-and-file members of the majority party continued to insist on retaining sufficient latitude to pursue their individual policy interests and particularistic benefits for their districts and states, in order to win re-election; but simultaneously they now insist on and depend upon central party leaders coordinating party efforts and teasing out from an increasingly complex and conflictual policy agenda collectively agreed party legislation that they perceive will help their party win or retain its majority at the next elections. Specifically, when their party forms the majority, rank-and-file House members and senators expect their party leaders to use powers and resources granted them to seek and deliver partisan outcomes that reflect the collective positions and priorities of the majority party and which diverge significantly from the chamber median (Aldrich and Rohde 1997; 2000).

(For a counter-argument that views congressional parties as less important, denies the power of the majority party, and views congressional decisions as reflecting the chamber, rather than the party, median, see Krehbiel (1998).)

---

legislative tactics and policy. Both parties also have mechanisms for expelling members (by a two-thirds vote) but only the Democrats stipulate conditions for expulsion and discipline and sometimes these are not invoked.[5]

Party organization in the Senate follows similar lines. Each party conference and policy committee receives over $2.5 million a year to finance their activities in addition to leadership budgets. However, as we would anticipate from the Senate's individualistic and non-majoritarian character, party organizations and rules are much less formal and less elaborate. Over recent years, hardline conservative Republicans have made various attempts to enforce a kind of party discipline, partly to bring moderate

---

[5] In January 2001, for example, Congressman James Traficant (D.OH) was expelled from the Democratic Caucus after voting for the Republican candidate for speaker. When, however, 11 Democratic subcommittee chairs voted against a leadership recommendation to approve President Clinton's budget reconciliation package in May 1993, no disciplinary action was taken.

colleagues into line, but all these efforts have been unsuccessful. In March 1995, for example, hardliners tried unsuccessfully to strip Republican Senator Mark Hatfield (R.OR) of his chair of the Appropriations Committee following his vote against the party's proposal for a balanced budget constitutional amendment; and when in May 2001 Republican Senator Jeffords defected from his party, fellow

Republican Senator John McCain (R.AZ) denounced his colleagues as 'self-appointed enforcers of party loyalty'. McCain pleaded that they 'learn to respect honourable differences among us, learn to disagree without resorting to personal threats, and recognise that we are a party large enough to accommodate something short of strict unanimity on the issues of the day'.

Majority party leadership and lawmaking in the House

As the congressional parties have become more ideologically homogeneous and polarized, rank-and-file co-partisans have insisted upon more active and stronger party leadership. In the contemporary period, central party leaders of both chambers—but especially of the House—are now expected to develop an agreed party agenda, promote that agenda within their chamber and outside, and structure policy choices and debate on the chamber floor and in committee (if necessary, by obstructing the opposing party)—all as part of a wider effort to deliver collective and individual policy benefits to chamber co-partisans. When they appear on television or other mass media, they are expected to demonstrate skill and appeal in articulating and promoting party priorities and policies to wider publics—as part of their party's efforts to influence the terms of national political debate and enhance the party's public reputation with a view to the next elections. When party control of Congress and the presidency is split between the parties, majority leaders in Congress become effectively leaders of the opposition and organize 'rapid response' teams to counter the president's policy pronouncements and media appearances. Indeed, following the Republicans taking over control of the House in 1995, Speaker Newt Gingrich (R.GA) was even able to insist that his daily news conferences were televised nationwide on C-SPAN. Similarly, when the Democrats took over control of the Senate in June 2001, the new Senate Majority Leader Tom Daschle

(D.SD) was promptly anointed the *de facto* leader of the opposition. The important points are that contemporary congressional leaders now experience considerable public exposure on behalf of their parties, are able to command airtime in the manner of the president, and are unmistakably in competition with him/her; and how they perform in public has some influence over the national reputations of the congressional parties.

Contemporary House majority leadership is characterized by activism, strength, coordinated party organization and policymaking, and accountability to the party's conference or caucus. The majority and minority leaderships comprise large teams at the head of extensive networks of House party committees. This core group, including the Majority Floor Leader, the Majority Whip, and the Caucus or Conference Chair and Vice-Chair—all of whom are elected by the party caucus or conference—who coordinate activities through frequent informal contacts with one another and caucus/conference members, regular meetings of the whips and the steering committee, and consultation with Senate leaders and (when the majority party also controls the White House) with the president. These activities are undertaken with the assistance of a large leadership staff and other resources funded by annual appropriations of almost $5.7 million for the majority leadership and $3.4 million for the minority leadership (2002).

The most powerful office is that of the Speaker,

who is leader of the majority party, the chamber's presiding and chief administrative officer, and the party's chief spokesperson. Because he/she is leader of the majority party in a legislative chamber that is fundamentally majoritarian, the powers of a contemporary speaker are formidable (see Box 10.15).

Whereas twenty years ago House leaders became involved only in a minority of measures (usually only when those issues were brought to the House floor), their contemporary successors are involved in all stages when major legislation is under consideration by their chamber. Leadership involvement under Speakers Jim Wright (D.TX, 1986–9) and Newt Gingrich (R.GA, 1995–8) was particularly

---

Box 10.15 **The power of a contemporary House Speaker**

The Speaker:

- controls the House's legislative schedule;

- greatly influences committee and conference committee assignments;

- appoints and removes majority members of the Rules Committee (which controls which measures are brought to the floor and under what conditions);

- appoints members of ad hoc oversight committees (subject to House approval).

As presiding officer, the Speaker:

- opens each daily session;

- rules on procedural issues;

- decides which members will be recognized to speak and offer amendments;

- judges the results of voice and standing or division votes;

- refers bills to committees;

- appoints the chair of the Committee of the Whole (the parliamentary mechanism through which the House considers most major legislation).

As the House's chief administrative office, he/she also commands substantial administrative and communications resources.

---

intensive and effective. But all contemporary Speakers are obliged to intervene with varying degrees of success. When they are first elected at the beginning of a Congress, all contemporary Speakers announce the majority party's agenda and usually supplement that with additional items they present in reply to the president's statements or speeches, including the State of the Union address and major presidential news conferences. Once those issues that are important to a substantial part of the majority party are identified, the Speaker and other members of the majority leadership team take responsibility for gaining floor passage of these issues—as well as other major legislation in which the majority party has a political stake, including the budget and other major economic legislation. Although most decisions to refer bills to particular committees are routine, the formal power lies with the Speaker, so that when new policy issues emerge or an issue is important to the majority party and a committee is obstructing the majority party's will, the Speaker is able to intervene in the interests of the majority party. In 1993, for example, Speaker Tom Foley (D.WA) sought to improve the chances of winning House approval of President Clinton's huge health care bill by referring it to the strongly led and centrist Energy and Commerce and Ways and Means committees rather than to the fractious and liberal Education and Labor Committee.

Once major legislation is under consideration by one or more committees, central leaders monitor its progress, liaise with committee chairs and rank-and-file members, and begin making strategic calculations as to when and how the legislation will be handled on the floor so as to maximize passage. Leaders may even impose timetables on committees for completion of their work and instruct them to make little or no revisions to the original bills, as Republican leaders insisted when they pushed through their Contract with America legislation in 1995. Strong leadership intervention of this kind is possible because in today's party-oriented environment majority party members of House committees—particularly committee chairs—recognize the legitimacy of their party's wishes and want to respond positively by writing legislation that will command majority party support on the floor. Committee chairs and other majority party members of committees also want to avoid incurring the wrath of the caucus or conference, which has the power to revoke committee chairs and assignments. If committees report legislation that reflects majority party preferences as interpreted by central leaders, they receive the leadership's assistance in winning passage on the floor, where majority leaders exercise almost monopolistic control. If, however, a committee measure fails to satisfy majority leaders, and the legislation is important to the majority party, leaders often intervene to require revisions (Box 10.16).

In most instances, the majority leadership broadly supports measures reported by the committees and then works with the majority members of the Rules Committee to design a special rule that will help win floor passage of a version of the measure that enjoys the support of most members of the majority party— if necessary, by allowing floor amendments supported by the majority party and/or by prohibiting amendments hostile to majority party preferences. If a committee reports a bill that the majority leader-

ship opposes, central leaders may even persuade the Rules Committee (on which the majority party enjoys a 2 to 1 majority) to deny a rule altogether. Since the Speaker selects the majority members of the Rules Committee and usually makes his/her views known, the committee will almost invariably comply with his/her wishes. Indeed, as policy partisanship and partisan polarization has increased in the House, central leaders have resorted increasingly to designing restrictive special rules that limit the offering of floor amendments. In the 105th House, for example, 46 per cent of rules fell into this category. Rules are now an important part of the heavily partisan environment in the House, and reinforce the institution's majoritarian nature (Box 10.17).

Once at least a provisional decision has been made on the type of rule that will be requested, the majority party's whip system (named after the equivalent system in the British House of Commons) comes into operation. As in the House of Commons, a large whip system is now an essential part of

---

Box 10.16 Strong leadership intervention to ensure the majority party's will on major issues

- In 1995, House Speaker Gingrich insisted that the chair of the Commerce Committee sponsor a new sixty-six-page floor manager's amendment that reversed the overall thrust of a telecommunication bill which the committee had reported out by a 38–5 margin. Committee chair Thomas Bliley (R.VA) conceded: 'The leadership has forced me to change the bill in order to win consideration on the floor'. The bill passed the floor in its amended form by a large margin.

- In 1999, House leaders refused to allow the chair of the Education and Workforce Committee to report out a managed health care bill because they feared that advocates of the popular Norwood–Dingell bill, which the leadership opposed, would offer their bill as a floor amendment and win House approval—thereby handing a significant political victory to the Clinton administration, which supported the bipartisan measure.

Box 10.17 Leaders use the Rules Committee to ensure the majority party's will on major issues

- In July 2001, the Rules Committee refused to allow Republican Mark Foley (R.FL) to offer a floor amendment to President Bush's faith-based initiative legislation because the majority leadership perceived that Foley's amendment would attract Democratic support and weaken the legislation.

- In November 2001, the leadership instructed the Rules Committee to report out a structured rule for consideration of the airline security bill on the House floor. The rule permitted only two floor amendments to a version of the bill approved by leaders. Eight other floor amendments were denied consideration. The clear purpose of the rule was to prevent the House from approving a bill that had received unanimous approval in the Democratic-controlled Senate.

majority party management of the House. Between 1995 and 2002, the majority Republican whip organization (2002) included a (non-elected) chief deputy whip, fifteen deputy whips, and forty-four assistant deputy whips, and was headed by Congressman Tom 'The Hammer' Delay (R.TX), a man with a fearsome reputation for successfully rounding up votes for the leadership. Before a bill is brought up on the floor, the whips must build support and gather information on likely parliamentary and political problems, usually working through a special whip task force established for the specific legislation. When legislation reaches the floor, majority whips station themselves at strategic points so that they may discuss the legislation with rank-and-file members before they cast their votes. Majority party members who frequently dissent from the party's positions on major legislation are often excluded from party task forces, overseas visits, and desirable committee assignments.

Finally, if the House and Senate versions of legislation require a conference to reconcile differences, House rules give the Speaker the power to select conferees. In practice, conferees are usually appointed from members of the reporting committee(s). However, the Speaker has discretion both to select additional conferees (which he/she will exercise depending on his relationship with the chair and the nature of legislation under consideration) and to veto conferees he/she does not want. In the 106th House (1999–2000), for example, Speaker Dennis Hastert (R.IL) stacked the House–Senate conference on the bipartisan Norwood–Dingell managed health care bill with Republican opponents and excluded Charlie Norwood (R.GA), the measure's sponsor, as well as other majority party supporters of the legislation. The Speaker also has discretion over which House conferees will handle particular parts of a conference bill, and is often closely involved in the conference itself, arbitrating among several committee delegations and seeking to protect the House majority party's position *vis-à-vis* the Senate.

Through a variety of mechanisms, then, the House majority leadership is in a very strong position to ensure passage of measures supported by the majority party—and to deny consideration and approval to measures supported by the minority party. The extent to which they are able to exercise strong, activist leadership rests ultimately on their ability to retain the support of their party colleagues. When this support disappears, it becomes politically impossible for leaders to continue in office—as Speaker Gingrich discovered after the 1998 elections.

Majority party leadership and lawmaking in the Senate

While House majority leadership is activist and strong, majority leadership in the Senate is activist and weak. Senate leaders produce an annual legislative agenda agreed by their party, meet regularly with party colleagues to consider current legislative strategies and policy issues informally, encourage party colleagues to join the party's team efforts, promote agreed party policy positions, try to monitor and shape floor action, manage their co-partisans and opponents, and provide their fellow partisans with timely and in-depth information on pending issues, schedules, and leaders' statements and views. Both the parties also run whip operations, but their primary role is to monitor floor developments and maintain communications with the party membership rather than twist arms. On the rare occasions that a floor vote count is required, the task falls to the bill's managers, who are usually the relevant committee's leaders or the bill's sponsor, with some assistance from the whips.

The Senate Majority Leader is the single most important senator, but he does not preside over the chamber; that role is assigned by the Constitution to the Vice-President of the United States or to the Senate's President *pro tempore* (a position which is usually awarded automatically to the most senior member of the majority party), although in practice many different senators take turns presiding over the chamber. Lacking the prerogatives and powers of a presiding officer, and required to operate within a chamber that is highly unpredictable, fundamentally non-majoritarian, and strongly upholds the prerogatives of individual senators, the majority leader is not in a position to enforce either his own or his party's policy priorities or preferences. Debate on almost all legislative measures is governed by unanimous consent agreements, which require the assent of every single senator. Even if a bill is reported to the Senate floor unanimously, there is nothing to stop an individual senator from preventing it from being given floor consideration by placing a hold on it.[6] As former Senator J. Bennett Johnston (D.LA) once observed: 'The Senate is run for the convenience of one senator to the inconvenience of 99'. Once a measure reaches the Senate floor, it may then be subject to a filibuster (Rule XXII) whereby one or more senators may speak for an unlimited time on any bill, amendment, or motion so as to obstruct further business. With the advent of greater policy partisanship and partisan polarization, split party government, evenly balanced party competition, and increased constituency, group, and media pressures, there has been a marked increase in the number of floor amendments now offered on the Senate floor, and greater resort to extending debate and obstructing legislation.

The only significant formal weapon available to Senate majority leaders to counter these activities is the right to be recognized first on the floor. So, in order to expedite the majority party's business, the majority leader will use this right—often aggressively—to forestall obstruction (particularly when bills or nominations to the executive and judicial branches are controversial, and involve large stakes for the majority party) by offering complex unanimous consent agreements (rather like special rules in the House) that stipulate exactly which floor amendments will be permitted, who will offer them, who will control debate time, the total time permitted for debate on each amendment (including a specific time at which the amendment will be voted on), and sometimes prohibitions against non-germane amendments. Majority leaders also more readily—even routinely—seek cloture on

an increasing number of measures. (Cloture is the process—other than by unanimous consent—by which extended debate may be ended on an affirmative vote of at least sixty senators.) However, to reiterate: in all these circumstances, a Senate Majority Leader's capacity to lead the chamber rests on his/her ability to win the consent and co-operation of other senators—usually including members of the minority party. Since this is frequently not forthcoming, the inevitable consequence is that contemporary leaders find it difficult to predict floor action, maintain their legislative schedules, and guide legislation important to the majority party through the chamber (Box 10.18).

So, while contemporary Senate majority leaders are expected to advance their party's interests, and co-partisans are much more willing then previously to act together as a majority party team, ultimately there is little leaders can do when consent and cooperation are not forthcoming, except threaten to keep the Senate in session. As Senator Jay Rockefeller (D.WV) observed during a Senate debate on health care reform in 1994: 'The Majority Leader can only offer the rest of us the opportunity to act; he has no powers further than that. Then, it's up to us.'

Key points

- Parties are now the most significant organizational structures on Capitol Hill.

- Since the mid-1980s, an American style of party government has characterized congressional organization, particularly in the House, where party organization is stronger and more formalized.

- Contemporary House majority leadership is activist, strong, and highly interventionist at all stages of the legislative process.

- Strong majority party leadership is precluded by the Senate's non-majoritarian nature.

---

[6] For example, for the first five months of the new Bush administration in 2001, Senator Jesse Helms (R.NC) retained a 'hold' on two appointments to the Treasury Department pending assurances from the administration that protections would be afforded to the North Carolina textile industry.

Box 10.18 The perils of trying to lead the Senate

- In December 2001, Democratic Senate Majority Leader Tom Daschle (D.SD) was forced to abandon enactment of an economic stimulus bill. Majority Democrats refused to support Republican efforts to bring a bill approved by House Republicans onto the Senate floor, while Republicans refused to allow passage of parts of the bill that Democrats wanted.

- Two days earlier, Daschle was forced to concede

defeat on a farm bill that was subjected to seventy-two floor amendments. Three times the majority leader failed to persuade his colleagues to invoke cloture.

- In March 2001 Republican Leader Trent Lott (R.MS) faced similar problems, when a bipartisan coalition of sixty senators forced him to concede a floor debate on campaign finance reform legislation that he and most of his party opposed.

Countering party government: personal entrepreneurship and committees

While parties and leaders seek to coordinate and centralize decision-making when political issues are important to the House and Senate majority parties, as we would expect in a divided democracy that celebrates individualism, pluralism, decentralization, and resistance to majoritarianism, strong and enduring forces in congressional politics—parochialism, the permanent election campaign, and Congress members' personal political goals—serve to reinforce structures and organizations within the House and Senate that compete with and sometimes counter the centralizing forces of party government.

The important point was made earlier that because Congress is composed of highly motivated politicians who have won election to the House or Senate with little help from party organizations, we should expect them to behave in individualistic ways once they arrive in Washington. Hence, within each chamber hundreds of congressional organizations serve House members' and senators' political needs—in addition to the different party and leadership organizations. These include the personal offices of the 540 members, thirty-five standing committees, four select and one special committee, four joint committees, 160 subcommittees, 160 informal caucuses and task forces, and uncountable ad hoc organizations.

Most immediate to House members and senators are the resources of their own personal offices. Varying in complexity, structure, and function, these enterprises are not the shoestring affairs found in the British House of Commons. Rather, they are fairly elaborate, well-resourced, organizations that are customized to the personal goals and political needs of individual members (Box 10.19).

Every House member and senator is able to draw on a wealth of resources not only to serve their constituencies but equally, depending on the members' personal goals and representational strategy, to engage in policy entrepreneurship and other meaningful forms of legislative participation—in whichever subject areas they choose, independent of party leaders, committees, and the executive (Box 10.20). The consequences for congressional organization and decision-making of members having both the opportunities and the resources to develop legislative solutions that differ from those of their colleagues, including those developed by party and committee leaders, are obvious.

It is, however, Congress' impressive committee systems that have traditionally represented the strongest countervailing forces to party rule and centralization of power, especially in the House. At the beginning of every Congress, each chamber

---

Box 10.19 **Congress members' personal office resources**

- Every House member occupies a suite of two to three offices and uses the generous allowances described in Box 10.9 to employ up to eighteen permanent and four part-time members of personal staff.

- Senators occupy more luxurious suites of five to eight rooms and employ an average of forty personal staffers, with those from the largest states employing over seventy.

- Apart from resources generated from their own office budgets, members also enjoy access to House and Senate committees and party organizations of which they are members, as well as the congressional Research Service (CRS) and the congressional Budget Office (CBO).

Box 10.20 **Policy entrepreneurship and legislative participation in Congress**

- In her first year of office in 2001, Congresswoman Jo Ann Davis (R.VA) sponsored and then successfully negotiated the Federal Long-Term Care Insurance Amendment Act through the House Government Reform Committee and the House.

- Her colleague, Mark Kirk (R.IL), a former officer at the World Bank and Counsel to the House International Relations Committee, achieved a similar feat with the Coral Reef and Coastal Marine Conservation Act of 2001.

- Following her successful election campaign in 2000 on a platform of lowering the cost of prescription drugs, Senator Debbie Stabenow (D.MI) led her party's efforts in a Senate floor debate in July 2002 to provide Medicare drug benefits and cut pharmaceutical costs.

- Over recent decades, about half the amendments that are offered to measures reported by committees to the House floor are offered by members who are not members of the reporting committee(s), using the resources of their personal offices and elsewhere. In the Senate, the comparable figure is about 90 per cent.

---

creates permanent standing committees that are empowered to receive, write, and report legislation and conduct investigations. Unlike the temporary, government-dominated standing committees in the British House of Commons—whose role is limited to performing the legislative function on a specific bill—congressional standing committees perform both legislative and investigative functions, conducting countless hearings and investigations on diverse aspects of public policy. All major legislation covering myriad subjects—civil rights, consumer protection, environmental regulation, social security, budget reform, war powers, transport and highway programmes, money laundering and anti-terrorist legislation, farm subsidy programmes, product liability, telecommunication regulation, and many others—has originated in the detailed investigative and legislative work undertaken by congressional committees (Box 10.21). When the Congress is in session, as many as 100 meetings of full committees and subcommittees take place each week, with meetings by the House's nineteen standing committees and one select committee (Intelligence) outnumbering those by the Senate's sixteen standing committees, two select committees (Ethics and Intelligence), and one special committee (Aging) by about two to one.

All committees are different because they deal with different kinds of policy and because different kinds of member choose assignments to different committees that reflect their unique combinations of personal political goals. Thus, for example, at the beginning of the 107th Congress, newly elected Democrat Adam Schiff (D.CA) wanted to use his experience as a former criminal prosecutor and his concerns to seek reform of the juvenile justice system; he sought and won a seat on the House Judiciary Committee. New York Democrat Hillary Rodham Clinton had experience working on education and children's initiatives during her husband's administration: she sought and won a seat on the Senate Health, Education, Labor and Pensions Committee. Congresswoman Jo Ann Davis (R.VA) won an assignment to the Armed Services Commit-

---

Box 10.21 Congressional committees

Roles:

- identify, investigate and study public problems;

- consider proposals introduced by individual members, the party leadership and the president;

- convene hearings (often televised) at which interested parties testify;

- sift through testimony;

- publish reports of their findings;

- decide what needs to be done;

- draft legislative language;

- decide whether to report out legislation.

Landmark committee hearings

- on the conduct of the Vietnam war, by Senator

J. William Fulbright as chair of the Senate Foreign Relations Committee;

- on the events surrounding the Watergate scandal, by a special Senate Committee chaired by Senator Sam Ervin (D.SC);

- Iran-Contra, a joint House-Senate committee chaired by Congressman Lee Hamilton (D.IN) and Senator Daniel Inouye (D.HI);

- on the addictive qualities of tobacco, by the House Health and Environment Subcommittee chaired by Congressman Henry Waxman (D.CA);

- the Lewinsky scandal/Clinton impeachment, by the House Judiciary Committee;

- the failure of the energy trading firm Enron, by the House Commerce Committee chaired by Congressman Billy Tauzin (R.LA).

---

tee, reflecting her district's interests in shipbuilding and other military industries, and the fact that her predecessor was a member of the same committee. Fenno (1973) developed a typology of congressional committees premised on this self-selective assignment process to explain why different committees behaved and interacted with other elements of the political system in different ways and to elicit new insights into congressional behaviour (Box 10.22). Notwithstanding the different motivations of members, prestige and certain policy committees (especially Commerce) are most attractive to most members and their actions subjected to more intensive monitoring by party leaders.

A second consequence of the self-selection assignment process—and one that has a close bearing on contemporary relations between the majority party and committees—is that many committees are unrepresentative of their parent chambers: members from urban and financial centres tend to be attracted to the banking committees; westerners to the House Resources and Senate Energy and Natural Resources Committee; representatives from farming areas to the agriculture committees; those from constituencies with substantial military interests (like Congresswoman Davis) to the Armed Services

committees; those representing ports to the Transportation and Infrastructure Committee, and so on. Interest and policy over-representation is typically reinforced by client interest groups, who tend to concentrate their lobbying efforts and campaign contributions on the members of the committees and subcommittees that handle legislation that most interests them (Box 10.23).

Over-representation mattered in the days of committee government, much more than it does now. For, as the earlier discussion emphasized, House and Senate majority parties and their leaders are now much less willing to see their party's major legislative goals and priorities thwarted by committee decisions that do not reflect their partisan preferences and priorities, especially when voters' concerns and preferences warrant swift and effective remedial changes in public policy.

As a consequence of the strengthening of party government, fewer and fewer legislative measures are subjected to this committee-based process; almost none when legislation is politically salient and important to the majority party or the president. Increasingly, majority party leaders intervene at the referral, committee consideration, and post-committee stages. As a result, contemporary

Box 10.22 Fenno's typology of congressional committees

Prestige committees (Appropriations, Budget, Rules, and Ways and Means) are those that attract members most interested in exercising influence in their chamber. These committees are heavily concerned with budgetary and other issues that are almost always important to the majority party leadership.

Policy committees (Education and Workforce, Energy and Commerce, Financial Services, Government Reform, International Relations, and Judiciary) comprise members who are driven primarily by their pursuit of 'good public policy' and often deal with issues that concern party leaders.

Constituency committees (Armed Services, Resources, Science, Small Business, Transportation and Infrastructure, and Veterans' Affairs) attract members motivated primarily by serving their constituencies and deal with issues that typically do not much concern party leaders.

Finally, members who would rather be on another committee are assigned to *unrequested committees* (House Administration, Standards of Official Conflict, and Select Intelligence).

The typology works better for House committees because senators are much less likely to cite the influence goal, and are generally less sure of and less intense about their preferences. Hence, Smith and Deering's elaboration of Fenno's scheme (1997: 80) often places Senate committees into the mixed constituency–policy category.

Box 10.23 Committees as targets for lobby groups

In the 1999–2000 election cycle, members of the House Agriculture Committee received an average 10 per cent of their campaign contributions from individuals and PACs connected with agricultural interests. House Agriculture Committee Chair Larry Combest (R.TX) and ranking Democrat Charles Stenholm (D.TX) received approximately one third of their contributions from these interests. Similarly, all eleven of the top House recipients of money from military-related industries served on either the House Armed Services Committee or the Defense Appropriations Subcommittee, and six of the top seven Senate recipients were members of the Senate Armed Services Committee.

Source: Calculated from data at www.opensecrets.org/

Key points

- While parties coordinate and centralize decision-making, especially when political issues are important to the majority party, strong and enduring individualistic and centrifugal forces reinforce structures and organizations that compete with and sometimes counter the centralizing forces of party.

- Hundreds of congressional organizations serve House members' and senators' political needs in addition to the different party and leadership organizations.

- The resources made available to members of Congress within their personal offices enable them to develop legislative solutions that may differ from those of their party and committee leaders.

- Congressional committees retain formidable investigative and legislative powers, but when legislation is salient and important to the majority party their actions are likely to be heavily circumscribed or even negated by majority party leaders.

lawmaking in Congress is much more complex, more heavily influenced by the actions of party leaders, and less likely to reflect decisions reached exclusively by committees (Box 10.24). The most important effects of these procedures are to undermine and circumscribe the power of committees and strengthen the hands of party conferences and their leaders so that committees—or, failing that, members of the House—reach decisions that reflect majority party preferences.

Box 10.24 The new 'unorthodox' legislative process in Congress

A major bill—like the Bush Administration's USA Patriot Act, proposed in the wake of the attacks on Washington and New York on 11 September 2001—is likely to be referred to several committees within each chamber (multiple referral), with time limits for consideration and reporting out. Once the bill is reported out by a committee, each chamber's final decisions are then likely to be subjected to uniquely designed procedures and informal processes orchestrated by majority party leaders in both chambers (and the White House) that often overturn committee decisions.

Sometimes, committees in the House and Senate are completely bypassed by a decision of the majority party leadership (although not always without the relevant committee's consent). In the case of the anti-terrorism legislation, for example, House majority party leaders wished to avoid likely public reaction to the appearance of congressional contention on the issue, and proceeded to replace the Judiciary Committee's bill with a substitute bill drafted in secret by the White House and Senate Judiciary Committee leaders that was not even marked up by any committee. No formal House–Senate conference committee was convened on the measure. Instead, key House members met with Bush administration officials to resolve differences. A clean bill was then offered under suspension of House rules (a procedure normally reserved for non-controversial legislation controlled by the House Speaker that does not allow for floor amendments) and approved by both Houses with little debate.

While the circumstances that gave rise to this particular piece of legislation were exceptional, the legislative processes and procedures followed by majority party leaders in both Houses to enact this and other omnibus legislation were not (Sinclair 2000b).

Conclusion

The intention of the framers of the Constitution was for the Congress to share power as a co-equal partner in America's separated system of government. Since 1787, the balance of power between the Congress and the presidency has fluctuated frequently and considerably. In the most recent period, since the early 1970s, Congress has become more assertive and now functions almost like a complete government alongside and often in competition with the presidency. Such a strong and autonomous legislature is unique in world political systems and is especially significant given America's global power since the mid-twentieth century. The roots of congressional power and autonomy lie in the separated system based on diffused responsibility, mixed representation, and institutional competition created by the 1787 Constitution. But congressional power and autonomy continues by constant reinforcement exercised by successive waves of new members—representing diverse constituencies and backgrounds and contributing an assortment of experiences, opinions, and preferences—who insist on exercising

the constitutional prerogatives of their resident institution. The emergence over recent decades of an era of candidate-centred elections and campaigns further reinforces and strengthens this pattern by sending to Congress members who insist on playing significant and autonomous governing and representative roles. Once elected to Congress, these men and women act purposively to create and maintain congressional structures that allow them to fulfil their representative and lawmaking responsibilities and defend the institution's autonomy and scope of action against swelling presidentialism, executive expertise, and coordinated power—even when the United States faces national crises such as that following the attacks on Washington and New York in September 2001.

Yet, as this chapter has shown, in a political system increasingly characterized by policy polarization and partisanship, members of Congress do assert their representative and lawmaking roles and at the same time are increasingly held to account for what their *party* achieves collectively—congressional

Republicans perhaps more so now than previous Democratic majorities. congressional parties are now the most significant organizational structures on Capitol Hill, especially in the House, particularly when policy issues are highly salient and important to the majority party, congressional parties play crucial roles in coordinating action within an essentially decentralized and specialized legislature to the extent of modifying and even overruling and bypassing committees. The increased influence of congressional parties has, however, not eroded an enduring tension in congressional politics between representing and governing. Individual House members and senators have to satisfy the needs and demands of their re-election constituencies *and* the needs and demands of their leaders, whom they increasingly expect to deliver collective legislative products that will enhance their party's reputation for governing and help them win at the next election. In the contemporary era of divided government the costs of ignoring *either* the electoral needs of individual House members and senators *or* the collective needs of the congressional parties are much greater than they were. Even so, the stronger imperative is the representative one. For individual House members and senators to win re-election, they need to satisfy the voters back home sometimes at the expense of acceding to the pleas of their leaders to stick with the party.

QUESTIONS

1 What role does Congress play in the American political system?

2 How is Congress' role in the American separated system different from that of legislatures in parliamentary systems?

3 Why has conflict between the Congress and the president increased over recent decades?

4 How important is bicameralism in national policymaking?

5 Why do Americans love their member of Congress but not Congress as an institution?

6 How does the way Congress is elected influence how the House and the Senate are organized internally?

7 Why are congressional parties more important than they were forty years ago?

8 How powerful are the respective leaderships of the House and the Senate?

9 What roles do congressional committees play in contemporary congressional politics?

10 To what extent are members of Congress better at representing their constituents than governing the country?

FURTHER READING

Introductory surveys

R. H. Davidson and W. J. Oleszek (2001), *Congress and Its Members*, 8th edn. (Washington, DC: CQ Press). Excellent comprehensive introduction that evaluates and synthesises current research on most aspects of the contemporary Congress.

M. Foley and J. E. Owens (1996), *Congress and the Presidency: Institutional Politics in a Separated System* (Manchester and New York: Manchester University/St Martin's Press), chs. 1–5.

Provides a detailed introduction to Congress within the context of relations between the president and Congress.

B. A. Loomis (2000), *The Contemporary Congress* (Boston and New York: Bedford/St Martin's Press). A brief but comprehensive overview of the Congress.

Advanced surveys

L. C. Dodd and B. I. Oppenheimer (2001), *Congress Reconsidered*, 7th edn. (Washington, DC: CQ Press). This edition and its predecessors include top-quality articles on current developments in congressional politics written by leading congressional scholars.

Major theoretical contributions

G. W. Cox and M. D. McCubbins (1993), *Legislative Leviathan: Party Government in the House* (Berkeley, Calif.: California University Press). An influential book setting out a theory of limited party government.

R. F. Fenno (1973), *Congressmen in Committees* (Boston: Little, Brown). The classic work on Congress members' purposive behaviour in the context of House and Senate committees.

R. F. Fenno (1978), *Home Style: House Members in Their Districts* (Boston: Little, Brown). Influential work conceptualizing the relations between House members and their constituents.

G. C. Jacobson and S. Kernell (1983), *Strategy and Choice in Congressional Elections*, 2nd edn. (New Haven, Conn: Yale University Press). Essential reading for understanding in a fundamental way the dynamics of congressional recruitment and elections.

D. R. Mayhew (1974a), *Congress: The Electoral Connection* (New Haven, Conn.: Yale University Press). Another highly influential book that offers a purposive theory of members of Congress being solely motivated by their desire for re-election.

D. W. Rohde (1991), *Parties and Leaders in the Postreform House* (Chicago: University of Chicago Press). Influential book that outlines the origins and practice of 'conditional party government' in the contemporary House.

B. Sinclair (1995), *Legislators, Leaders, and Lawmaking: The US House of Representatives in the Postreform Era* (Baltimore: Johns Hopkins University Press). A major book that offers a principal-agent theory of contemporary congressional leadership.

B. Sinclair (2000), *Unorthodox Lawmaking: New Legislative Processes in the US Congress*, 2nd edn. (Washington, DC: CQ Press). The definitive analysis of the new process, heavily influenced by party leaders, by which most major legislation is enacted in the House and the Senate.

On particular themes

J. R. Hibbing and E. Theiss-Morse (1995), *Congress as Public Enemy* (Cambridge: Cambridge University Press). An important and original analysis of Americans' negative feelings towards Congress and other American political institutions.

G. C. Jacobson (2001a), *The Politics of Congressional Elections*, 5th edn. (New York: Addison Wesley Longman). The most important series on congressional elections within a strong theoretical context.

W. J. Oleszek (2000), *Congressional Procedures and the Policy Process*, 5th edn. (Washington, DC: CQ Press). The most comprehensive and readable text on congressional processes and procedures.

WEB LINKS

www.cq.com The site of the authoritative weekly magazine on congressional activities

www.c-span.org The cable networks' site that includes considerable information on contemporary Congress

www.opensecrets.org/ The site of the Center for Responsive Politics, which provides data on campaign finance

www.thomas.loc.gov Congress' own website, which includes links to numerous other related sites, including those of congressional parties and committees

11 The federal bureaucracy *

Mark Carl Rom

READER'S GUIDE

The federal bureaucracy comprises the administrative organizations of the national government that execute the laws, write regulations, and adjudicate regulatory disputes. This chapter examines how the bureaucracy fits into the American divided democracy; outlines the bureaucracy's function, structure, and personnel; surveys the bureaucracy's historical development; and offers some concluding comments on the role and importance of the federal bureaucracy in the government of the United States.

Introduction

Americans do not trust their government, but they expect it to do great things. The federal bureaucracy is one source of their fears and aspirations. Americans want to have a secure defence, safe and efficient highways and airways, cheap and high-quality food, clean water and air, and a thriving economy. Americans expect the federal government to help provide and protect these goods, among many others. At the same time, Americans often distain the federal agencies that work to support these goals. Americans worry at times that the bureaucracy is too powerful, too remote, and too uncontrolled by elected officials.

How does the federal bureaucracy fit into the United States' political system? What are its functions, and how does it fulfil them? How is it organized and staffed? How has it evolved to meet the changing needs of a growing country? These questions serve as the basis for this chapter's investigation. By the final page, the reader should have a good understanding of the answers.

* A version of this was published in Singh, R. *American Government and Politics: A Concise Introduction* (Sage Publications, 2003).

Democracy and the federal bureaucracy

In the United States, the public believes that the bureaucracy should work for it, not that the people should serve the bureaucracy. States, too, have rights, and state governments are not simply subjects of the federal government, but partners with or competitors to it. Fundamental aspects of the American political culture, especially the belief in popular sovereignty, liberty, and political equality, guide the way Americans conceive of their government and its administrative apparatus, and influence the ways the bureaucracy is organized and staffed as well as the way it functions.

The Constitution

The American government is based on the Constitution. The Constitution never mentions the bureaucracy, however, and scarcely has much to say about it (see Box 11.1). The Constitution nevertheless organizes American government, and American politics, in ways that profoundly influence bureaucratic structure and performance. Because the constitutional founders were intensely worried about government becoming tyrannical, the writers of the Constitution divided powers within the national government and between federal and state governments. (In the American vernacular, 'federal' and 'national' are synonyms.)

Divided control

As Chapter 3 explained, the Constitution established a set of checks and balances so that neither legislative, executive, nor judicial branches would reign supreme, and so that power would be shared among them. Each branch thus exercises substantial control over the bureaucracy. For example, Congress has the power to establish agencies, to give them legislative instructions, to appropriate them funds, and to oversee them; the Senate also confirms (or, at times, rejects) presidential appointments to lead them. The president is the chief executive officer and hence provides the agencies with direction; he also appoints their leaders. The courts have the authority to rule on the legality (i.e. constitutionality) of agency actions and to adjudicate disputes against them.

As you might expect, because the bureaucracy has no undisputed master it can and does at times play legislative, executive, and judicial branches against each other. How does it do this? Subtly. It can turn to Congress to seek what it wants if the president has other priorities, and vice versa. If the courts rule against an agency, the agency can seek additional authority from Congress.

Federalism

The Constitution establishes a federal system, with the national government having authority over certain issues, the states over others, and power over still other issues shared between federal and state governments. But the Constitution is silent about many of the issues with which modern governments concern themselves: it says nothing about which governments are responsible for education, health, transportation, and the environment, for instance. As a result, national and state bureaucracies are both involved in these issues and many others. The national government has a department of education, and so does every state. National and state governments all have departments of transportation, environmental protection agencies, and agencies involved in health care. At times federal and state governments have similar priorities, and so both levels of government work cooperatively; often, however, state and national bureaucracies disagree with each other and so must work to resolve the conflicts.

Popular sovereignty

An essential feature of American politics is that 'we, the people' ultimately reign supreme. The core assumption is that the public need not defer to the bureaucracy, but that the bureaucracy must be subject to popular control. This assumption plays out in at least three main ways. First, bureaucratic decisions are seen as legitimate only to the extent that they are the product of the democratic process. The

Box 11.1 **Constitutional influences**
The US Constitution and the bureaucracy

The Constitution does not specifically mention 'bureaucracy', thought it devotes Article I to the legislative branch, Article II to the executive branch, and Article III to the judiciary. Several clauses are especially pertinent for bureaucratic operations, however:

Congress has the authority to create agencies, provide them funds, and to give them responsibilities:

Article I, Section 8: The Congress shall have the power to . . . provide for the common Defence and general Welfare of the United States. . . . To make all Laws which shall be necessary and proper for carrying into Execution the foregoing powers, and all other Powers vested by this Constitution in the Government of the United States, or in any Department or Officer thereof.

The President has the authority to direct agencies and select their leaders (Congress can impeach and convict these leaders):

Article II, section 1: The executive Power shall be vested in a President of the United States.

Section 2: [The President] shall nominate, and by and with the Advice and Consent of the Senate shall appoint . . . other public Ministers and Consuls . . . and all other Officers of the United States, whose Appointments are not herein otherwise provided for, and which shall be established by Law: but the Congress may by Law vest the Appointment of such inferior Officers, as they think proper, in the President alone . . . or in the Heads of Departments.

Section 4: [A]ll civil Officers of the United States, shall be removed from Office on Impeachment for, and Conviction of, Treason, Bribery, or other high Crimes and Misdemeanors.

The judiciary has the authority to adjudicate claims against agencies:

Article III, section 2: The judicial power shall extend to all cases, in Law and Equity, arising under this Constitution, the Laws of the United States . . . or which shall be made under their Authority;—to all Cases affecting . . . other public Ministers;—to Controversies to which the United States shall be a Party . . . In all Cases affecting . . . other Ministers . . . the Supreme Court shall have original Jurisdiction.

bureaucracy has authority only when it is given it through laws enacted by a majority of a duly elected Congress. If a bureaucracy attempts to over-reach its legitimate authority, it will face a hostile public and, probably, an unsympathetic judiciary. Second, the public expects to be able to have a direct say in bureaucratic decision-making, both by participating in these decisions and by having access to bureaucratic records about how such decisions were made and implemented. These expectations are embodied in laws such as the Administrative Procedures Act (APA) and the Freedom of Information Act (FOIA). Third, individuals believe that they should not be subject to arbitrary or capricious bureaucratic decisions, and they maintain the right to sue federal agencies if they believe their rights have been infringed.

Popular control over the bureaucracy is neither easy nor complete. Elected leaders are not always willing or able to specify precisely what the bureaucracy should do, and so give them substantial administrative discretion. The public is often inattentive to agency decision-making, and so public involvement is minimal (though organized interest groups do pay close attention, and are heavily involved in rule-making and implementation). Individuals are indeed at times mistreated by the bureaucracy, but lack either skills or resources to protest the mistreatment effectively.

Liberty

Americans are passionate about their liberty. The archetypal American is the cowboy on horseback, free to do what he chooses, when he chooses, how he chooses. Many Americans consequently view the bureaucracy as a threat to their freedoms, and indeed it is. Today the bureaucracy touches almost every aspect of life from birth to death through its involvement in health care, education, the environment, and the economy. To be sure, the

Box 11.2 Is America different?

Bureaucracies compared

All nations use bureaucracies to perform the essential tasks of government: collecting taxes, implementing laws, providing for safety and security. Still, the American bureaucracy differs substantially from those in many other affluent democracies in several ways, and for several reasons.

Political culture

'Political culture' refers to widely shared beliefs about who should govern and by what means for what ends. The American political culture espouses liberty, equality, individualism, democracy, and capitalism. It is profoundly anti-bureaucratic and suspicious of government. The Revolutionary War for independence from Great Britain was fought, after all, because the colonialists opposed both what the British bureaucracy was doing (collecting taxes and imposing restrictions) and how it was doing these things (giving orders and making demands). The Declaration of Independence was a long list of complaints against the British Crown.

American political culture has several implications for its bureaucracy. First, Americans are wary of governmental agencies telling them what to do, how to do it, or in any other way restricting their freedom. (Nobody is said to believe the line 'Hello, I'm from the government and I'm here to help you'.) Second, Americans expect that the bureaucracy will treat each citizen equally, and profoundly reject the idea that bureaucrats should give preferential treatment to anyone. Third, Americans believe that the bureaucracy should account for individual differences, both in those affected by the bureaucracy and in those who work for it. Fourth, the belief in democratic control over the government leads Americans to resist deferring to bureaucratic authority or expertise. Americans are inclined to think, 'We don't do what the bureaucracy says; the bureaucracy should do what we, the people, say.' In fact, the American bureaucracy is exceptionally open and accessible to private citizens (and, undoubtedly, to private interest groups). Finally, the American faith in capitalism typically leads to the presumption that private businesses are better than public

bureaucracies, and that free markets work better than governmental regulations. (The astute reader will note that not all parts of the American political culture lead to consistent expectations about the bureaucracy. For example, Americans insist that the bureaucracy promote equality by not giving special favours to others, but allow individualism by making special exceptions for their particular needs. Americans believe that bureaucracies should be made more efficient (i.e. run like a business), but they also expect the bureaucracy to make its decisions through democratic processes that involve public participation).

Institutional structure

The American constitutional system divides power within the federal government, through a system of checks and balances, and across governments, through a federalist system. The US bureaucracy thus differs from those in countries with parliamentary, unitary governments. In the United States, both Congress and the president assert control over the bureaucracy; in parliamentary systems, executive and legislative functions are concentrated in a single branch (with the chief executive selected by the legislature), so the bureaucracy has a single boss. In unitary systems, local bureaucracies receive instructions and budgets from the national headquarters. In the American federal system, national, state, and local governments may all have bureaucracies involved in specific issues (such as education, transportation, or health). State and local bureaucracies have their own budgets, and do not simply take instructions from their federal counterparts. Instead, local, state, and national bureaucracies engage in conflict, competition, and at times cooperation.

Precisely because political control over the federal bureaucracy is divided, the American bureaucracy is in some ways more independent of both legislature and executive than in other countries. As the federal bureaucracy has no single master, it is able to muster resources to seek goals different from what Congress wants, or the president expects.

bureaucracy can enhance liberty in the sense that it helps free Americans from tainted food, dangerous drugs, criminal activity, and many other threats to health, safety, and prosperity. When the bureaucracy does limit freedom, moreover, it legally does so only on the basis of legislation enacted by a duly elected Congress.

Still, Americans might justifiably be concerned about bureaucratic intrusions into personal freedoms, both legal and illegal. When the bureaucracy acts lawfully—say, when the Environmental Protection Agency forbids landowners from draining their property in its effort to protect wetlands—it may face a storm of public protest and ultimately be forced to change its regulations. More ominously, the bureaucracy at times acts illegally, such as when the Federal Bureau of Investigation (FBI) tapped the phones of those suspected of being political dissidents, or the Internal Revenue Service (IRS) harassed citizens for political purposes. More recently, the 'war against terrorism' has again raised the spectre that the bureaucracy will conduct surveillance of large numbers of ordinary Americans in order to identify any terrorists lurking within the nation's borders. While Americans may be willing to tolerate restrictions on liberty for broader public purposes, we can expect them to rise in opposition when these restrictions become too onerous.

Political equality

Americans willingly accept great economic inequality, viewing it as the natural outcome of a capitalist system. They are less disposed to accept political inequality, and vehemently oppose the idea that the government (and hence the bureaucracy) should treat citizens unequally. The concepts of 'equal treatment' and 'equality before the law' are deeply embedded in the American psyche. These ideas have two main implications for the bureaucracy. First, the bureaucracy is expected to treat its employees equally: no race, religion, gender, or political views should be advantaged in the bureaucracy's decisions to hire or promote. The bureaucracy is indeed more egalitarian in its treatment of its employees than any other sector of American life. Second, the bureaucracy is expected to treat citizens equally: the rich and powerful are subject to the same rules as the poor and weak. There are exceptions to these two principles, of course. The most important exception is that organized interest groups are substantially more powerful in influencing bureaucratic decision-making and enforcement than are ordinary, isolated individuals (a subject explained further in the next chapter by Burdett Loomis).

Key points

- The federal bureaucracy is not mentioned in the Constitution, but the Constitution—through its fragmenting control of government and allocation of distinct powers to different branches of government—has profoundly affected the shape of the federal bureaucracy.

- America's distinctive political culture has created suspicion of bureaucracy as part of government whilst simultaneously demanding equality of treatment by government bureaucrats.

The federal bureaucracy

Functions

The federal bureaucracy serves three essential functions for the government. First, the bureaucracy must implement the laws enacted by the Congress. Because these laws typically (and perhaps necessarily) are somewhat vague, the bureaucracy must also write the specific rules that guide how the laws will be executed. That is, the bureaucracy engages in rule-making. Finally, disputes inevitably arise regarding how its rules have been developed or applied. To resolve these disputes, the bureaucracy conducts adjudication. In short, the bureaucracy performs executive (implementation), legislative (rule-making), and judicial (adjudication) functions.

Executing laws

The Constitution (Article II, section 2) specifies that the executive branch will 'take care that the laws be faithfully executed'. The bureaucracy does this whenever it implements the activities spelled out in congressional legislation. When the Post Office delivers the mail, when the Internal Revenue Service (IRS) collects taxes, or when the newly created Transportation Safety Administration inspects baggage at the airports, the bureaucracy is performing its executive functions.

Making rules

As the economy and society have become more complex, and the problems addressed by the government more complicated, it has become more difficult for Congress to specify precisely what the bureaucracy is to do. (Congress may be reluctant to be precise because it lacks the expertise to know exactly what to do, or because it lacks the political consensus necessary to be precise.) Agencies—such as the Environmental Protection Agency, established by Congress in 1970—must therefore follow the steps outlined by Congress in the Administrative Procedures Act (APA). Before adopting any rule that assists the implementation of laws passed by Congress and the president, the APA requires that agencies 'give notice' in the Federal Register that they are planning to develop regulations, that the agency obtain comments from the affected parties through either (or both) written comments or public hearings, and that the agency take these comments into account in promulgating the rule.

Adjudication

The federal bureaucracy is engaged in many complex, controversial issues. Inevitably, disputes will arise between parties subject to the regulations. The APA requires that agencies 'act like courts' when settling these disputes. Bureaucratic adjudication takes the form of a civil trial, with a judicial officer who is structurally and functionally separated from the other activities of the agency making the decisions. The National Labor Relations Board (NRLB), for example, resolves disputes concerning federal labour laws when management and labour present differing interpretations of the law.

What influences the ways that the bureaucracy implements laws, writes rules, and adjudicates disputes? Does the bureaucracy have a partisan bias, favouring one party or another, or preferring liberal or conservative solutions? Does the bureaucracy tend to favour 'traditional' values or 'progressive' ones? Does the bureaucracy typically seek to impose national 'solutions' on the reluctant states? There are no simple answers to these questions, as the federal bureaucracy is large and diverse, with literally hundreds of departments, agencies, bureaus, offices, and corporations directly employing nearly two million people and working with many million more who serve as contractors, grantees, or who fulfil mandates.

It is not at all clear that the bureaucracy as a whole has a partisan bias (that is, that it acts to promote one party over another). There are several reasons for this.

First, bureaucrats' political opinions typically mirror those of the public at large, and the public is divided fairly evenly between Republicans and Democrats. Second, bureaucrats in general appear to take democracy seriously. If their elected leaders are Republicans, they will pursue the goals that the Republicans establish; if their elected superiors are Democrats, they act accordingly. (This is complicated, of course, when one party controls the White House and the other party maintains a majority in Congress.) Third—and importantly—an increasing number of public servants are 'white-collar' (i.e. well-educated specialists in technical and managerial positions) professionals who take their professional responsibilities seriously. That is, they act as they believe that engineers, lawyers, economists, technicians, or analysts should act, rather than acting as a political partisan should. Whether the president is Democrat Clinton or Republican Bush, most bureaucrats apparently take guidance from these elected officials and act in ways consistent with their professional training. If their political superiors promote traditional values, the bureaucracy as a whole complies; if their elected leaders have a progressive bent, bureaucrats tend also to promote these objectives.

As John Francis explained in Chapter 4, the relationship between federal agencies and their state counterparts has changed over time. For much of the nation's history, federal and state bureaucracies essentially operated in 'their' domain and left the other level alone. Between the 1950s and 1980s, however, the federal bureaucracy increasingly saw itself as superior to state bureaucracies and was willing to give them instructions. As state governments became more competent during the 1980s and 1990s, and as the political environment became more favorable to the states, the federal government became more interested in working cooperatively with the states. At the turn of the century, federal–state relationships appear to be based more on mutual collaboration than federal coercion.

Structure

The federal bureaucracy was not logically designed by some master planner to address the nation's needs. It has been created piecemeal over 200 years as the nation's needs, and political priorities, have evolved. As the structure of the federal government is determined by political decision-making—all components of the federal bureaucracy, with the exception of those in the Executive Office of the President, are created through legislation—the structure reflects the goals and needs of the president and Congress.

The federal bureaucracy is massive and complex. There are well over 1,000 civilian agencies that form departments, independent agencies and regulatory commissions, and government-sponsored corporations.

Departments

In 2002 there were fourteen cabinet departments, employing about 60 per cent of the federal workforce, and accounting for the vast bulk of federal spending. Each department but one is led by a secretary, appointed by the president, and confirmed by the Senate. (The exception is the Department of Justice, which is directed by the attorney-general.) The secretary is responsible for establishing the department's policies and administering its

operations, consistent with congressional directives and the president's objectives.

The departments vary widely in their size and budgets. The largest department in terms of employees is the Department of Defense (DoD), which employs about 800,000 civilians (about one half of the total federal civilian workforce) and an additional 1.4 million uniformed military personnel. (The DoD is unique among cabinet departments in that it comprises three other departments, the Departments of the Army, Navy, and Air Force.) The Department of Health and Human Services (HHS) is the biggest player in terms of budget, accounting for about 40 per cent of all federal spending (mainly through the Social Security and Medicare programmes, which respectively provide pensions and medical services to the elderly). In contrast, the Department of Education employs about 5,000 civil servants and has a budget of about $42 billion.

Each department is a multifaceted organization with many components variously called administrations, bureaus, divisions, sections, services, and offices, among other titles. (As there is no consistent labelling scheme, it is not possible to tell by an organization's title exactly where it fits into the departmental hierarchy.) Departments might be sub-divided along functional lines or according to clientele needs.

Independent regulatory commissions

The Congress has created many independent agencies and commissions. Each of these has responsibility for regulating particular sectors of the American economy (such as the Securities and Exchange Commission and securities markets, or the Food and Drug Administration and pharmaceuticals) or regulating certain policy arenas (e.g. the Federal Reserve Board and monetary policy).

The independent regulatory commissions are granted authority by Congress to make, enforce, and adjudicate rules. They are typically headed by a board of directors (or 'commission') rather than a single director, though the commission's chairman generally is the pre-eminent member. (The chairman of the Federal Reserve Board, for instance, is often thought of as one of the most powerful persons in the country.) To insulate the commissions from partisan politics, the commissioners serve fixed terms of office and cannot be removed by the president (although he appoints them and they are confirmed by the Senate, just like the cabinet secretaries). Some commissions, such as the Federal Trade Commission (FTC), are free-standing organizations; others, such as the FDA, are located within a department (in this case, the Department of Health and Human Services, or HHS).

Why would elected politicians be willing to give up control over these bureaucracies by making them independent? One possible reason is that the tasks of the agencies are seen as technical (e.g. approving new medications, determining workplace safety standards) rather than political. A second, complementary reason is that by making the agencies independent, politicians can insulate themselves from the tough choices the agencies often must make. Politicians nonetheless reserve the right to chastise these agencies if they believe they act inappropriately.

Independent executive agencies

The independent agencies look much like cabinet departments, though they typically have somewhat narrower programmatic responsibilities. Like departments, these agencies are led by a single director, appointed by the president and confirmed by the Senate, who serves at the pleasure of the president. The heads of these agencies report directly to the president, rather than to a departmental secretary.

The structural or functional differences between cabinet departments and independent agencies are not at all clear or obvious. They are separated from departments (or may be merged with them) for political reasons, often having to do with symbolism. The Department of Defense has strong interests in missile and satellite technology, and so it might have seemed practical to place the space programmes within that department. Still, President Kennedy created the National Aeronautics and Space Administration (NASA) as an independent agency both to symbolize the peaceful uses of space exploration and to show his commitment to such exploration (NASA was created in response to the Soviet Union's first successful launch of a spaceship).

On the other hand, at times presidents have sought to elevate the prestige of an agency by having it converted to cabinet status. The Veterans

Affairs Administration was an independent agency until 1989, when President George Bush transformed it to departmental status without changing its basic mission or functions. President Clinton sought to convert the EPA from an agency to a department for similar reasons, but was thwarted by Congress.

Government-sponsored corporations

Beginning in the 1930s, Congress has established corporations to perform functions that might otherwise have been carried out by private firms (but which, in the eyes of Congress, were not being done appropriately or at all). Examples of such corporations include the Federal Deposit Insurance Corporation (which insures savings deposits in commercial banks) and Amtrak (which operates most of the nation's passenger trains). The largest government corporation is the US Postal Service; prior to its formation, the postal service had been a governmental agency. It was converted to a corporation to give it greater flexibility to act like a private business, while at the same time maintaining its obligations to serve the entire public at rates less than a private business might charge.

Government corporations remain somewhat controversial. Some argue that the government should not be in the business of business, and that the functions should be turned completely over to the private sector. Others maintain that, because the government is involved in these activities, they should be handled by regular governmental agencies.

Personnel

As Box 11.3 explains, the federal government is the largest single employer in the nation, with a civilian workforce of about 1.8 million individuals (another 850,000 or so work for the US Postal Service, a government-sponsored corporation). How should these individuals be selected? The two main answers are that they should be selected by politicians or hired on the basis of their skills, not political connections. Both answers have been selected for the American bureaucracy, at different times in the nation's evolution.

Box 11.3 The true size of government

Every modern president, it seems, likes to brag about how he has 'reduced the size of government'. To be sure, since the 1970s the relative size of the bureaucracy (federal bureaucrats as a proportion of the total workforce) has been shrinking, and the absolute number of full-time civilian federal bureaucrats has been declining. When President Clinton left office in 2001, he left behind a bureaucracy that had fewer employees (approximately 1.8 million) than most post-war presidents had presided over. (The trend to a smaller federal workforce was interrupted by the nationalization of airport security in 2002, which gave the government the responsibility of hiring approximately 40,000 new baggage screeners.)

But does the number of federal bureaucrats reflect the true size of government? Hardly. To calculate the real scope of the federal workforce, we would want to include the employees who are paid by federal tax dollars or who perform functions mandated by the federal government. In the former category are those who perform contract services for the government or receive grants to do federal work; the latter category involves those who fulfil federal requirements. Federal employees no longer clean many governmental buildings, for instance; privately owned janitorial companies do. Federal employees do not design, build, and maintain NASA's space shuttles; private companies do. These janitors and aeronautical engineers may be privately employed, but they receive their pay through federal contracts. Much health research is funded by grants from the National Institute of Health (NIH), and much basic scientific research is sponsored by the National Science Foundation (NSF). The recipients of these grants are not federal employees, but the federal government nonetheless pays their salaries. When state and local bureaucrats, or private employees, perform tasks required by the federal government—for example, when they collect data regarding compliance with federal laws—they are in effect working for the federal government. If one counts all those who are paid by federal funds, or who spend time complying with mandates, then perhaps an additional 15 million persons might be considered governmental workers.

Why does the federal government not simply put all those who actually work for it on the payroll? The primary reason is political: while Congress and the president want the government to accomplish many diverse tasks, they want also to claim that they are restraining the size of government. At the same time that the bureaucracy is shrinking in size, it is expanding its mission.

Until 1893, almost all federal workers were hired under the 'spoils system', in which the party controlling the White House was able to hire workers as it chose, and usually chose to employ its supporters, as patronage appointments. If the other party won the presidency, it was able to replace those workers with its own. During this period, the vast majority of federal bureaucrats worked for the Post Office.

After the Civil War, reformers grew increasingly critical of the spoils system. In the 1870s, President Rutherford B. Hayes had called for the creation of a merit system by which federal workers would be hired on the basis of their performance on open, competitive exams, but Congress rejected his requests. The window of opportunity for reform opened wide in 1881 when President James A. Garfield was assassinated by a disgruntled job-seeker. The spoils system was also a burden to the presidency because, as others had noted, every time the president selected a person for the bureaucracy he delighted one and disappointed nine others.

The spoils system began fading away in 1883 with the enactment of the Civil Service Reform Act (more commonly called the Pendleton Act after its congressional sponsor, George H. Pendleton). At first the merit system covered only a small share of the federal workforce but, in combination with additional laws and executive orders, it gradually came to apply to over 90 per cent of federal employees. Today the vast majority of federal bureaucrats are career civil servants, supplemented by over 3,000 political appointees. The spoils system is not dead, but it is greatly diminished.

Political appointees

They may be few in number, but they are large in importance. Political appointees—the 1,200 or so who require Senate confirmation, and the 2,000 who do not—hold the top positions in virtually every federal agency. The primary justification for having political appointees in leadership roles is that the bureaucracy should be directed by those with direct connections to the democratically elected president, and that the president ought to have the bureaucratic leaders personally responsible to him. (Given the nation's heritage, it remains exceedingly difficult for the bureaucracy to defend its policies unless they can be directly attributed to democratically elected leaders.)

Are these political appointees loyal to the president and do they doggedly pursue his goals? These are open questions, but consider the following. The president knows few of the appointees directly and well. The appointees have their own goals and preferences. The president does not have clear goals on most issues, if he has much of an opinion at all. The appointees mainly work in the agencies, with career civil servants, not in the White House, with the president and his immediate staff. It is little wonder, then, when these appointees become sympathetic with agency goals (this is called 'going native') or pursue their own policy objectives. Still, it appears that political appointees on the whole act in ways they believe are consistent with presidential wishes.

Who are these political appointees? Do they represent the public as a whole? The answer to the first question does not necessarily lead to the answer to the second. Political appointees, as a group, tend to be much better educated and more affluent than the rest of the public; they also tend more often to be white and male, though less so today than in previous decades. They do tend to represent the dominant views of the current president, and so at least have political views that are sympathetic with those who voted for the president.

For better or worse (and most political scientists take the latter view), political appointees do not normally stick around long. The average tenure is less than two years: appointees come, and then they go. If they support the president, then why do they leave him so soon? Most could earn much more in the private sector, and the temptations to do so are large, especially given the pressures (e.g. a hostile and intrusive media) and difficulties

(the political barriers to enacting the president's vision) of the job. It is quite prestigious to become a presidential appointee and to do the president's work, but this prestige and knowledge can be transformed into more comfortable, and lucrative, private careers.

Civil servants

The federal hierarchy is topped by the thinnest layer of political appointees, but the vast majority of federal bureaucrats are career civil servants selected on the basis of competitive examinations or specialized skills. It is easy to stereotype these employees as mindless paper-pushers, but more than 15,000 job skills (from nuclear physicist to computer programmer to clerk typist) are included in the federal workforce. In fact, the American civil service has some of the best-trained, most skilled employees in the world. It is also highly experienced: the typical bureaucrat is about 45 years old with nearly seventeen years' federal experience.

While federal employment is quite secure—civil servants can only be fired for 'cause' (i.e. poor performance) and not for their political opinions—provides good benefits (health and pensions), and offers substantial opportunities to promote the public interest, it is not nearly as prestigious to work for the government as it is in other countries. Few Americans say, 'I want to become a bureaucrat when I grow up'. Because American political culture is relatively hostile to the government, and quite sympathetic to capitalism, civil servants do not generally receive the high status accorded to those in the private sector. The federal government often finds it difficult to recruit and retain the most talented individuals.

The federal workforce is also as diverse as the public as a whole in terms of ethnicity and gender, though it is better educated. Federal employees are not especially liberal politically, as one might expect of those working in the public sector, but hold roughly the same public opinions as those of the society at large, though bureaucrats are somewhat more tolerant of political dissent. Like the private sector, however, women and minorities tend to be more concentrated in the lower positions, and less common at the top ranks of their organizations.

Key points

- The federal bureaucracy performs three key functions that can be categorized as executive (implementation), legislative (rule-making), and judicial (adjudication).

- The federal bureaucracy contains a vast array of permanent civil servants and a smaller number of temporary political appointees, organized into fourteen departments and a multitude of independent regulatory commissions, independent executive agencies, and government-sponsored corporations.

- Although evidence of systematic political bias—especially partisan bias—is limited, and civil servants are broadly representative of the public at large, politicians typically fear that agencies can be 'captured' by their client interests and that political appointees are likely to 'go native'.

The evolution of the federal bureaucracy

At its inception, the federal bureaucracy was minuscule in size and insignificant in scope. Today, more people work for the federal government than for any other single organization, and the bureaucracy touches every aspect of American life. We might usefully divide this bureaucratic evolution into four phases: the founding years (from the Constitution's ratification in 1789 until the Civil War began in 1861), expanding roles (from the Civil War until the Great Depression of the 1930s), the New Deal era (from the Depression until the 1960s), and the recent episodes.

The founding years

After the Constitution was ratified, Congress quickly established the departments essential to national creation: the Department of Defense (at the time called, perhaps more appropriately, the Department of War), the State Department (handling foreign policy), and the Treasury Department (responsible for the government's finances). The first Congress also established the principle, after extensive debate, that only the president could remove cabinet officials for cause; Congress recognized that for the presidency to be effective those officials must serve at his discretion, not Congress's. President Andrew Jackson removed the Post Office from the Treasury in 1829, so that the postmaster general would have greater control over that essential service. Until the Civil War, almost all federal employees worked for the Post Office. Most federal employees had the job of delivering the mail.

Expanding roles

The Civil War forever changed the nation, and it also changed the size and responsibilities of the federal government. Simply fighting the war caused a huge increase in the federal bureaucracy (the soldiers were, after all, governmental employees). To help ensure a steady supply of food (and to mollify farmer demands), President Abraham Lincoln and Congress created the Department of Agriculture in 1862. In a precursor to the modern Social Security system, the Pension Office was established in 1866 to pay benefits to those who had served in the northern armies. In 1870, the Department of Justice was created to lift the attorney-general and his staff to the same status as the other departments.

The growing national economy, the rise of large (and ruthless) corporations, interest group demands for governmental support, and reformers intent on addressing public problems led Congress to establish several new departments at the end of the nineteenth and beginning of the twentieth centuries. The Interstate Commerce Commission (ICC) was created in 1887 to establish 'just and reasonable' rates for railroad shipping. (The ICC was finally dismantled in 1995 as rates were deregulated.) In 1903 President

Theodore Roosevelt was successful in establishing (through congressional legislation, as always) the Department of Labor and Commerce. President Woodrow Wilson split it into separate departments in 1913, and the next year Congress created the Federal Trade Commission, to protect small businesses from unfair competition, and the Federal Reserve System, with powers to regulate banks and the money supply.

The New Deal and after

The federal government again surged in size and complexity during the Great Depression of the 1930s and again in the Second World War of the 1940s. President Franklin Roosevelt, desperate to restore a failing economy, created a slew of 'alphabet agencies' (as they were all known by their initials) to create jobs and provide economic support; perhaps the most important of these agencies today are the Federal Deposit Insurance Corporation (FDIC), which protects small savers and preserves the stability of the banking system, and the Securities and Exchange Commission (SEC), which regulates the stock market. During this period the Supreme Court, which had been hostile to federal intervention into the economy, reversed its decisions and let these new agencies come into being.

Recent trends

As the 1960s arrive, changing problems, and public demands for new protections, led to a whole series of bureaucratic innovations. The Department of Health, Education, and Welfare (handling functions historically left to state and local governments) was established in 1953, and later split into a separate Department of Health and Human Services and Department of Education in 1979. In quick succession the Department of Housing and Urban Development (1965) and Department of Transportation (1966) were established, as were the

Occupational Safety and Health Administration (1970), the Environmental Protection Agency (1970), the Consumer Product Safety Commission (1972), the Commodity Futures Trading Commission (1974), and the Nuclear Regulatory Commission (1974), among others. The Department of Energy was created in 1977, as was the Federal Energy Regulatory Commission. Most recently, the Department of Veterans Affairs was established in 1989.

The American bureaucracy continues to evolve. The most important recent phenomenon—likely to persist into the future—is the demand for better (i.e. more effective, more efficient) bureaucratic performance. The debate has focused not so much on what government should do (liberals and conservatives alike generally agree that the federal government will continue to play a prominent role in health, education, environmental protection, transportation, welfare, and virtually every other important policy arena) as on how it should conduct itself in these arenas. The clearest examples of political pressure to improve the functioning of the bureaucracy are President Clinton's 'National Performance Review' (better known as its 'reinventing government' initiative) and the Government Performance and Results Act of 1993. Whether or not these efforts pay lasting dividends remains to be seen.

Key points

- The federal bureaucracy has grown substantially in size, responsibilities, and personnel since the Republic's founding, reflecting the expansion of government programmes and the increased intervention of the government on matters from social security to regulating trade disputes.

- Despite American political rhetoric about cutting the size of government, neither liberals nor conservatives dispute the extensive and important role that bureaucratic agencies perform in most policy arenas.

Conclusion

The American bureaucracy fits somewhat awkwardly into its democratic system of government. The Constitution is virtually silent about administration, but its separation of powers and federalism has shaped the political environment in which the bureaucracy operates. The bureaucracy promotes political equality and, to a limited extent, constrains economic inequality. The bureaucracy is a threat to liberty when it becomes overbearing, but in other ways serves to protect freedom by damping the physical threats to it. The bureaucracy is legitimate only when it is subject to popular sovereignty, and public disputes over the bureaucracy have reflected the tension between those who seek a more activist role for the government and those who seek to minimize its size and power.

The bureaucracy has three main functions in the United States. Most obviously, it implements the laws enacted by Congress. Because legislation is often vague, the bureaucracy must also write the detailed rules which make the laws enforceable. As disputes over regulatory meaning inevitably arise, the bureaucracy also adjudicates disagreements over interpretations. It does these things with the powers and procedures given to it through statutes, and with personnel who are primarily career civil servants directed by a small number of political appointees.

The bureaucracy has evolved in ways that the Founding Fathers could scarcely imagine. Today the bureaucracy is much larger, more varied, and more complex than at the nation's inception. Its structure and responsibilities have changed to meet the growing demands of the public and the needs of the politicians elected to serve them. In the future, the bureaucracy will continue to evolve to meet new demands and needs.

QUESTIONS

1 How well does the American bureaucracy fit within its democratic political system?

2 What are the merits of having career civil servants, as compared with political appointees, having leadership positions in the bureaucracy?

3 Should the president or Congress have greater authority over the bureaucracy?

4 What are the advantages and disadvantages of having Congress delegate administrative discretion to the bureaucracy?

FURTHER READING

C. T. Goodsell (1994), *The Case for Bureaucracy: A Public Administration Polemic*, 2nd edn. (Chatham, NJ: Chatham House). Examines the qualities of bureaucrats and their motivations to serve the public, and offers optimistic conclusions.

W. T. Gormley, Jr. (1989), *Taming the Bureaucracy: Muscles, Prayers and Other Strategies* (Princeton, NJ: Princeton University Press). A sophisticated account of how to improve bureaucratic performance, which concludes that no single strategy is optimal.

C. M. Kerwin (1999), *Rulemaking: How Government Agencies Write Law and Make Policy*, 2nd edn. (Washington, DC: CQ Press). Kerwin provides an in-depth look at how federal agencies make the rules that govern US society. He presents basic rule-making procedures, the role of judicial consideration, and historical, practical, and theoretical perspectives.

P. Light (1995), *Thickening Government: Federal Hierarchy and the Diffusion of Accountability* (Washington, DC: Brookings Institution). Explains why the federal bureaucracy has become more complex and how this complicates democratic control.

H. Seidman (1998), *Politics, Position, and Power: The Dynamics of Federal Organization*, 5th edn. (New York: Oxford University Press). Shows how political forces influence how the bureaucracy is organized and how it performs.

J. Q. Wilson (1989), *Bureaucracy: What Government Agencies Do and Why They Do It* (New York: Basic Books). The best single book on the federal bureaucracy. Wilson looks both at bureaucracies' internal characteristics and their external environment.

WEB LINKS

www.firstgov.gov First Gov: offers information about federal agencies, programs, and benefits; also linked to all fifty state government websites. Aspires to provide users the information they seek within 'three clicks of your mouse'.

www.fedworld.gov Fedworld: the homepage connects you to virtually every federal department, bureau, commission, and foundation, as well as to governmental statistics and reports.

www.voxpop.org Jefferson Project: links the viewer to Fedworld as well as scholarly and popular articles and analyses of the federal government.

12 Interest groups

Burdett A. Loomis

READER'S GUIDE

This chapter explores how interest groups affect both the operation and the outcomes of American government and politics. Organized interests stand at the heart of American political life, as all major political figures from James Madison on have understood. The chapter will focus on four core themes: the tension between particular interests and the general interest within America's divided democracy; the logic of organizing interests; various competing perspectives on the influence of interest groups; and the nature of group representation in American politics.

Introduction

All nations are made up of a variety—usually a wide variety—of interests, ranging from farmers to corporations to religious groups. This has been historically true in the United States from the time of the American Revolution to the twenty-first century. Indeed, America has provided extra-ordinarily fertile ground for the growth of interest groups or organized interests. In part this derives from the relatively weak American political parties that Robert Mason discussed in Chapter 5, which can

themselves be usefully characterized as groupings of organized interests. Moreover, the very size and diversity of America has encouraged the representation of a multitude of interests by organized groups.

The Constitution plays a major role in protecting the rights of organized interests, as the First Amendment guarantees the rights of speech, petition, and association. Indeed, as Richard Hodder-Williams noted in Chapter 3, the framers consciously sought

Box 12.1 Definitions

Interest groups have gone by various labels in American politics. They are sometimes called 'pressure groups' or 'special interest groups'. Some contemporary scholars label them 'advocacy groups'. The first two terms are value-laden, and relate to a reformist perspective that viewed groups in a negative light. The 'advocacy group' terminology has some advantages, but it implicitly limits groups to a single activity. The preference here is to use the terms 'interest group' and 'organized interest' interchangeably and broadly. A corporation qualifies as an interest group, as does a university, at least when it engages in lobbying, as frequently occurs in America. Most interest groups have memberships made up of individuals or other organizations (a labour federation, for example), but some organized interests are simply a single entity, be it a corporation or an organization supported by contributions, such as the American Enterprise Institute, a Washington think tank. In short, 'interest group' and 'organized interest' are terms that cover a great many forms of organization in American politics. To a greater or lesser extent, they represent a particular point of view within the political process, broadly defined.

to protect minority rights when they wrote the Constitution in 1787. Over the course of the American experience, citizens have tended to organize to press their case before state and national policy-makers. Still, until the onset of the Depression and the election of Franklin D. Roosevelt, most organized interests had relatively little reason to seek benefits from a government that neither raised nor spent much money.

In the wake of the New Deal and the Second World War, however, a much larger, more active government emerged—one whose policies, ranging from agricultural subsidies to educational loans to defence contracts, both encouraged an expanded federal bureaucratic apparatus (discussed in the previous chapter) and heightened levels of lobbying in Washington. If business dominated the immediate post-war era, groups representing consumers, racial minorities, and environmental interests came to the fore in the 1960s and early 1970s. By 1970, political scientist Ted Lowi (1969) could legitimately argue

that the president and Congress could no longer govern effectively, because so many groups were so well represented that policy-making had simply become a process of continual negotiation.

At the very least, there was a great expansion in the number and variety of organized groups between the 1950s and the 1980s, and a similar growth among lobbyists in Washington. These trends have continued in the new millennium, as the amount and sophistication of lobbying from all quarters of society—as well as the growing importance of interest-group funding of political campaigns—have reached new levels.

Not only has the number of interest groups changed dramatically since the 1950s, so too have the roles of groups in American political life. In the 1950s prominent political scientists such as David Truman and Robert Dahl built broad theories of government (in America, at least) on a 'pluralist' model that posited a rough balance among organized interests within the political process. But the political movements that moved civil rights, the environment, and women's issues into the mix of American politics demonstrated the severe limitations to the pluralist theory of the 1950s. Moreover, as economist Mancur Olson (1965) demonstrated, the formation of interest groups—which Truman saw as a natural occurrence—is anything but natural. Indeed, organized groups with even modest numbers of members must overcome the natural tendency of individuals *not* to join a group, so long as they receive the general benefits (like clean air or national defence) that they could have enjoyed without joining. Groups can and do surmount this problem, but Olson's work demonstrated that interest groups do not form in some automatic way, as some pluralist theories had asserted.

Although journalists and political scientists have written extensively about organized interests since the late 1970s, few contemporary attempts to explain the nation's politics *begin* their analyses with an emphasis on the power and behaviour of interest groups. Rather, most scholars see organized interests as important, but scarcely central, political actors. Still, the tension between the interests of particular groups and some broad, if hard to define, societal interest remains. As scandals in the American business and accounting industries demonstrated, organized interests have often sought, in the most single-minded manner, to enhance their own well-being at the expense of society's welfare. For example, in the 1990s accounting firms lobbied energetically and successfully to kill legislation that would have imposed more stringent accounting standards—standards that would have almost certainly reduced the huge societal costs of a series of corporate failures (such as Enron and Worldcom) in 2001–2.

All in all, organized groups represent a wide array of interests in American politics, and few, if any, significant interests go unrepresented. At the same time, more representation does not equal sustained influence. Whether through providing campaign contributions, gaining access, or presenting information, some organizations—often, though not always, those with the most resources—can obtain systematic advantages within the interplay of interest groups and governing institutions.

The core issues

As New York fought over ratifying the Constitution in 1788, James Madison argued in *Federalist Paper* 10:

The causes of faction . . . are sown into the nature of man. [And] by a faction I understand a number of citizens, whether amounting to a majority or minority of the whole, who are united and actuated by some common impulse of passion, or of interest, *adverse to the rights of other citizens, or to the permanent and aggregate interests of the community.* (Emphasis added.)

From the outset of the American experiment, Madison and his fellow framers held few illusions about the nature of interests, or factions, in any nation's politics. Whether representing a majority or a minority, interests were to be restrained, and they certainly could not be expected to represent the broad interest of the community at large.

The most dangerous factions in a democracy were those that represented majority interests, and the framers took great care to constrain the power of majorities. A large, diverse country could control minority interests, the framers reasoned. In fact, smaller and less popular interests stood in need of protection. During the ratification struggle, Madison and the federalists agreed to add a Bill of Rights to the Constitution, making explicit the rights that they considered implicitly guaranteed by the document. Through the entire American experience, the addition of the Bill of Rights—and especially the First Amendment, which guarantees the freedoms of speech, assembly, and petition—has provided

consistent protections for groups as they organized and sought to influence governmental policies.

At the same time, American citizens—who often belong to multiple groups—have expressed profound distrust of so-called 'special interests'. One survey, conducted for the Council for Excellence in Government (2002), reported that more respondents (38 per cent) considered interest groups the most responsible for 'what is wrong with government today', as opposed to the media (29 per cent), elected officials, or political parties (24 per cent each). Political candidates have long relied on private donations to run increasingly expensive campaigns, and citizens commonly regard members of Congress and other officeholders as beholden to those interests that fund them. Such a conclusion flies in the face of most social science findings, but these have had little impact on public views.

Key points

- Factions (or particular interests) are part of human nature.

- The framers considered organizing a factional interest to be both a valued right and a potentially dangerous activity.

- Citizens are generally wary of so-called 'special interest groups', even though they often belong to one or more such groups.

Pluralism and its critiques

For the most part, political scientists and practising politicians have viewed interest groups in a more benign light than have members of the public. In 1950, political scientist David Truman articulated a theory of American politics that placed interest groups at the centre of a world in competition, however imperfect, that encouraged them to influence public policy in various ways. The complex, layered structure of American government included any number of 'points of access [whose] diversity assures various ways for interest groups to participate in the formation of policy, and this diversity is a flexible, stabilizing element' (Truman 1971: 519). Pluralist theory, derived in part from Madison's notions of faction, posits that there will be many countervailing centres of power, both within government institutions and among outside groups.

Even though a great range of interest groups do exist, whether the idea of countervailing power accurately captures the reality of group competition remains an open question, and any number of scholars, politicians, and journalists have found fault with the pluralist perspective. Two broad, if somewhat contradictory, critiques are especially powerful. The first argues that some interests generally lose in the policy process, while others usually win. Without endorsing elite theory contentions that a small number of interests and individuals conspire to dominate policy decisions, one can make a strong case that those interests with more resources (such as money, access, and information) will do better at achieving their goals than will those with fewer assets. The numerically small, cohesive, and wealthy defence industry, for example, does well year in and year out in the policy-making process; marginal farmers and the urban poor are much less successful. Based on such continuing unequal results, critics of pluralism argue that losing interests are represented unevenly and often ineffectively.

A second important line of criticism generally agrees that inequality of results remains an important aspect of group politics. But this perspective, most forcefully set out by Lowi (1979), sees interests as generally succeeding in their goals of influencing government—to the point that the government itself, in one form or another, provides a measure of protection to almost all societal interests. Everyone thus retains some vested interest in the existing structure of government and array of public policies. This does not mean that all interests obtain just what they desire from governmental policies; rather, all interests get at least some rewards. From this point of view the tobacco industry surely wishes to see its crop subsidies maintained, but the small farmer and the urban poor also have pet programmes (such as guaranteed loans and food stamps) which they seek to protect.

Lowi has labelled the proliferation of groups and their growing access to government 'interest-group liberalism' (see Box 12.2), and argues: 'Interest-group liberal solutions to the problem of power [who will exercise it] provide the system with stability by spreading a *sense* of representation at the expense of genuine flexibility, at the expense of democratic forms, and ultimately at the expense of legitimacy' (Lowi 1979: 62). Interest group liberalism is thus pluralism, but it is *sponsored pluralism*, and the government is the chief sponsor. On the surface, it appears that the unequal results and interest-group liberalism critiques of pluralism are at odds, but they

---

Box 12.2 Interest-group liberalism

Lowi (1979: 52) argues that 'interest group liberalism ... defines the public interest as a result of the amalgamation of various claims' from a wide range of groups. He goes on to contend that decision-makers, whether in Congress, the executive branch, or the bureaucracy, are guided by *'whatever organized interests they have taken as the most legitimate'* and that this perceived legitimacy is the *'only necessary guideline for the framing of the laws'*. In short, there are no clear standards of the public interest, only those frameworks put forth by various individual interests, who compete to shape the policy debate.

can be easily reconciled. Lowi does not suggest that all interests are effectively represented. Rather, there is often only the appearance of representation. As political scientist Murray Edelman (1971) has pointed out, a single set of policies can provide two related types of reward: tangible benefits for the few and symbolic reassurances for the many. Such a combination encourages groups to form, become active, and claim success, whatever their actual track record.

Key points

- At mid-century, the dominant pluralist interpretation of American politics emphasized the representation of most important interests by organized groups.

- Critics of pluralism, as well as events such as the civil rights movement, demonstrated that a benign pluralist interpretation of politics was incomplete at best.

- Lowi's 'interest-group liberalism' concluded that representation of many interests could lead to ineffective governing.

The formation of organized interests

In 1965, the economist Mancur Olson offered a striking intellectual challenge to the pluralists and to all students of interest groups. In his path-breaking study, *The Logic of Collective Action*, Olson argued explicitly that it was neither natural nor rational for individuals (or individual firms) to join large membership groups. Ironically, Olson's work was published on the cusp of a new wave of interest-group organization, beginning in the 1960s and continuing to the end of the century. The theory of interest-group formation appeared to be at odds with the establishment of large numbers of new organizations. As it turns out, Olson was right, but he did not anticipate how effective group entrepreneurs could be in enticing members to join their organizations.

Membership groups and the collective action problem

Olson posited that even individuals who have common interests are not inclined to join organizations that attempt to address their concerns. The major barrier to group participation is the 'free-rider' problem: 'rational' individuals choose not to bear such costs as time commitments or membership fees because they can enjoy the group benefits (e.g. favourable legislation) whether or not they

join. This is especially true for groups that pursue 'collective' benefits that accrue to all members of a class or segment of society regardless of membership status.

Clean air would reflect one such benefit. Likewise, it would be irrational for an individual automobile owner to become part of organized attempts to improve highways since all citizens, members of pro-road groups or not, would reap the benefits of better highways. The free-rider problem is especially serious for large groups because the larger the group the less likely it is that an individual will perceive his or her contribution as having any impact on group success.

Olson argued that the key to group survival lies in providing certain 'selective' benefits to individuals. These material rewards, such as travel discounts, informative publications, or cheap insurance, go only to members. Organizations in the best positions to offer such benefits are those initially formed for some non-political purpose and that ordinarily provide material benefits to their clientele. In the case of labour unions, for example, membership may be a condition of employment. For farmers, the American Farm Bureau Federation (AFBF) has long offered inexpensive insurance, which induces individuals to join even if they disagree with AFBF goals. In professional circles, membership in legal or medical societies may be a prerequisite for occupational advancement.

Overcoming the free-rider problem

While profound and theoretically powerful, the free-rider problem has scarcely proved insurmountable. Olson, an economist, emphasized *material* benefits, but political scientist Robert Salisbury (1969) noted the import of two other kinds of rewards. *Solidary* incentives—the socially derived, intangible rewards created by the act of association, such as fun, camaraderie, status, or prestige—can lead to participation. Likewise, *expressive* (also known as *purposive*) rewards, which come from advancing a particular cause or ideology, help explain why many members join such groups as the National Rifle Association or Planned Parenthood.

Non-material incentives, such as fellowship and self-satisfaction, may encourage the proliferation of highly politicized groups and, according to Terry Moe (1980: 144), 'have the potential for producing a more dynamic group context in which politics, political preferences, and group goals are more centrally determining factors than in material

associations, linking political considerations more directly to associational size, structure, and internal processes'. Indeed, pure political benefits may attract potential members as well, and even collective benefits can prove decisive in inducing individuals to join large groups. Like elected officials, groups may find it possible to take credit for widely approved government actions, such as higher farm prices, stronger environmental regulations, or the protection of Social Security (Hansen 1985).

Key points

- Economist Mancur Olson persuasively demonstrated in the 1960s that groups do not initially form or sustain themselves in some 'natural' way.
- Individuals receive various kinds of benefits—material, solidary, and expressive—as they join groups.
- Even though the free-rider problem is real, the growth of organized interests in the 1960–2000 period demonstrated that it can be overcome in various ways.

The proliferation of interest groups and the growth of government

Not only have the number of groups increased substantially since the 1950s, but organized interests have also increasingly directed their attention toward the centre of power in Washington, DC, as the scope of federal policy-making has grown and groups seeking influence have determined to 'hunt where the ducks are'. As a result, the 1960s and 1970s marked a veritable explosion in the number of groups lobbying in Washington.

Moreover, the composition of the interest-group universe has changed substantially. As Chapters 5 and 6 explained, political parties grew weaker and many citizens sought alternative means of becoming

active in politics. In fact, a participation revolution occurred in the country as many citizens joined an increasing number of protest groups, citizens' organizations, and public interest groups, whose members often seek collective material benefits, such as clean water or air. Olson's free-rider problem has proved not to be an insurmountable barrier to group formation, and many of these organizations do not use selective material benefits to gain support. Since the late 1970s, the number of these groups has remained relatively stable, and they have become well established in representing the positions of consumers, environmentalists, and other public interest organizations (Berry 1999).

In addition, government itself has had a profound effect on the growth and activity of interest groups. Although the government prompted the establishment of agricultural interest groups in the nineteenth century, to say nothing of subsidizing railroad interests, since the 1930s the federal government has become an increasingly active and important spur to group formation. One major New Deal goal was to use government as an agent in balancing the relationship between contending forces in society, particularly industry and labour. One goal was to create greater equality of opportunity, including the 'guarantee of identical liberties to all individuals, especially with regard to their pursuit of economic success' (Beer 1978: 12). For example, the Wagner Act (1935), which established collective bargaining rights, attempted to equalize workers' rights with those of their employers. Some New Deal programmes did have real redistributive qualities, but most, even Social Security, sought only to ensure minimum standards of citizen welfare. Workers were clearly better off, but 'the kind of redistribution that took priority in the public philosophy of the New Deal was not of wealth, but a redistribution of power' (Beer 1978: 10).

The expansion of federal programmes accelerated between 1960 and 1980; since then, costs have continued to increase, despite resistance to new programmes. In what Hugh Heclo (1978: 89) termed an 'Age of Improvement', the federal budget has grown rapidly (from nearly $100 billion in 1961 to $2.1 trillion in 2001) and has widened the sweep of federal regulations. Lyndon Johnson's Great Society—a multitude of federal initiatives in education, welfare, health care, civil rights, housing, and urban affairs—created a new array of federal responsibilities and programme beneficiaries. The growth of many of these programmes has continued, although slowed markedly by the Reagan and Bush administrations, as well as by the Republican capture of Congress in 1994. In the 1970s the federal government further expanded its activities in the areas of consumer affairs, environmental protection, and energy regulation. It also redefined some policies, such as affirmative action, to seek greater equality of results.

Many of the government policies adopted early in the Age of Improvement did not result from interest group activity by potential beneficiaries. Several targeted groups, such as the poor, were not effectively organized. Rather, initiatives typically came from elected officials responding to a variety of private and public sources, such as task forces composed of academics and policy professionals.

The proliferation of government activities led to a mushrooming of groups involved in the affected policy areas. Newly enacted programmes provided benefit packages that encouraged interest-group formation. Consider group activity in the field of policy toward the ageing, for example. The radical Townsend Movement, based on age grievances, received much attention during the 1930s, but organized political activity focused on age-based concerns had virtually no influence in national politics. Social Security legislation won approval without the involvement of age-based interest groups. Four decades later, by 1978, roughly $112 billion (approximately 24 per cent of total federal expenditures) went to the elderly population. By the early 1990s the elderly population already received one third of federal outlays, long-term projections had been revised upward, and the existence of such massive benefits had spawned a variety of new groups as well as encouraging other organizations (e.g. hospitals), often formed for non-political reasons, to redirect their attention to the politics of the ageing.

Across policy areas two types of group develop in response to governmental policy initiatives: *recipients* and *service deliverers*. In the sector devoted to policies affecting elderly individuals, recipient groups are mass-based organizations concerned with protecting—and if possible expanding—old age benefits. The largest of these groups—indeed, the largest voluntary association represented in Washington—is AARP, the group formerly called the American Association of Retired Persons. This change to AARP as the group's official name illustrates its marketing aspirations, in that it wants to appeal to *future* retirees and elderly among the baby boomers and younger generations.

AARP is well over twice the size of the AFL-CIO and, after the Roman Catholic Church, is America's largest organization. In 2001 it comprised thirty-five million members, an increase of twenty-five million in twenty years.[1] Approximately half of all Americans aged 50 or older, or a fifth of all voters, belong to the group, in part because membership is cheap ($8 per year). Much of the organization's revenue is derived from advertising in its bi-monthly magazine, *MM* (formerly *Modern Maturity*). The organization's headquarters in Washington has: its own zip (post) code, a legislative/policy staff of 165; twenty-eight registered, in-house lobbyists; and more than 1,200 staff members in the field. Charles Peters, the editor of *Washington Monthly*, claimed that the 'AARP is becoming the most dangerous lobby in America' given its vigorous defence of the elderly population's interests (Tierney 1988). At the same time, because the AARP represents such a wide array of elderly individuals, it is often cautious and slow in its actions.

Federal programme growth also has generated substantial growth among service delivery groups. In the health care sector, for example, these range from professional associations of doctors and nurses through hospital groups and the insurance industry to suppliers of drugs and medical equipment. Not only is there enhanced group activity, but also hundreds of individual corporations have strengthened their lobbying capacities by opening Washington offices or hiring professional representatives from the capital's many lobbying firms.

Programmatic concerns are not the only motivating forces behind group reactions to governmental actions. In recent years, changes in the campaign finance laws have led to an explosion in the number of political action committees (PACs), especially among business, industry, and issue-oriented groups. Laws facilitating group formation have certainly contributed to group proliferation, but government policy in a broader sense has been equally responsible. Indeed, as the government spends more, taxes in increasingly complex ways, and regulates more aggressively, the need for enhanced representation by a wide range of groups has become apparent.

Thus, not only has the number of membership groups grown in recent decades, but a similar expansion has occurred in the political activity of many other interests such as individual corporations, universities, churches, governmental units,

foundations, and think tanks (Berry 1999). Traditionally, most of these interests have been satisfied with representation by broad trade or professional associations. The chief beneficiaries of this trend are Washington-based lawyers, lobbyists, and public relations firms. The number of attorneys in the nation's capital, taken as a rough indicator of lobbyist strength, tripled between 1973 and 1983, and the growth of public relations firms was dramatic. The current lobbying community is difficult to pin down, but it is large, increasingly diverse, and part of the expansion of policy domain participation, whether in agriculture, the environment, or industrial development. Overall, political scientist James Thurber has calculated that, as of the early 1990s, 91,000 lobbyists and people associated with lobbying were employed in the Washington, DC, area (cited in Phillips 1995). As of 2001, the *Encyclopedia of Associations* (2002) listed approximately 22,200 organizations, up more than 50 per cent since 1980 and almost 400 per cent since 1955. And this number does not include hundreds of corporations and other institutions (e.g. universities) that are represented in Washington.

In addition, as the growth of new governmental spending slows, often eaten up by continuing increases in entitlement programmes such as Medicare (see Chapter 17), legislators and regulators find new ways to affect legions of interests throughout the society. For example, the American tax system has grown more and more complex, as specific groups and coalitions have lobbied effectively for provisions that will benefit their particular organized interest. In the mid-1990s corporations and accountants lobbied to loosen the reporting standards for business transactions (with predictably disastrous results a few years later). And in 1996 the Congress produced its first rewrite of telecommunications law since the 1930s era of the vacuum tube. After extraordinarily contentious lobbying among various industry groups, the bill was passed, and the groups' attention immediately turned to the Federal Communications Commission (FCC), which was charged with implementing the law. Groups continued to have immense stakes in governmental

---

[1] The AARP offers free memberships to spouses, which artificially enlarges its ranks, but it remains—by any count—a huge group.

decisions; only the venue for those decisions— executive, legislature, bureaucracy, or courts—had changed.

Not only do public policies contribute to group proliferation, but government often directly intervenes in group creation. In the early twentieth century, relevant government officials in the agriculture and commerce departments encouraged the formation of the American Farm Bureau Federation and the US Chamber of Commerce, respectively. Since the 1960s the federal government has been especially active in providing start-up funds and in sponsoring groups. One study reported that government agencies have concentrated on sponsoring organizations of public service professions: 'Groups like the American Public Transit Association or the American Council on Education . . . serve as centres of professional development and informal channels for administrative coordination in an otherwise unwieldy governmental system' (Walker 1983: 401).

Government sponsorship also helps explain the recent rise of citizens' groups. Much federal domestic legislation has included provisions *requiring* some citizen participation, which has spurred the development of various citizen action groups, including grassroots neighbourhood associations, environmental action councils, legal defence coalitions, health care organizations, and senior citizens' groups.

The proliferation of American interest groups has proceeded apace into the twenty-first century. With weak political parties, organized groups have always offered an alternative mechanism for the representation of corporate and individual interests. Most

noteworthy in the growth of groups from the 1950s through the present is, first, that the theoretical 'irrationality' of joining groups did not prove a serious hindrance to their proliferation. And second, the government itself—at both the national and state levels—provided many incentives for groups to organize and to interject themselves into the policy-making process. It is no wonder that contemporary interest-group politics has focused, more and more, on exercising influence in Washington, DC, and the fifty state capitals.

Key points

- As the federal government has become more activist over the past forty years, the increasing number of programmes has led to the formation of more and more groups to represent affected interests. Causality here runs in the opposite direction from traditional expectations; groups do not seek new governmental action but rather react to past governmental actions.

- Both programme recipients and service deliverers tend to organize in response to new programmes.

- The government often purposely creates organized groups to represent particular interests—a practice that dates back at least to the early years of the twentieth century.

- The proliferation of groups has led to an explosion in lobbyists who earn their living in Washington; many state capitals have experienced similar booms.

Interest groups and influence in American politics

Although many groups, such as labour unions or corporations, seek to influence governmental policies only as a by-product of their overall organizational goals, many others, like Handgun Control or the Business Roundtable, have come together explicitly to affect policy outcomes. And regardless of the

reason for organizing, interest groups have become increasingly sophisticated in their attempts to exert influence.

It is a mistake to think that organized interests continually approach Congress, the president, and various regulatory bodies with long sets of issues that they hope to see enacted. To be sure, most groups have their favourite proposals, which they would love to see become law, but much of their attention is focused more on resisting changes that they oppose. Likewise, it is unwise to conclude that organized interests 'buy' legislative victories through either campaign contributions or favours heaped upon law-makers. The latter are now illegal, and the former, while significant for congressional campaigns, are of modest import at best. Still, many organized interests do spend a lot on elections or lobbying or both, and they often evaluate what kind of return they are receiving on their 'investment'.

Organized interests attempt to influence policy outcomes either directly, through the process of lobbying, or indirectly, by supporting their favoured candidates for election. Although money is important in both lobbying and campaigning, many other assets come into play, such as large number of members (labour, AARP, NRA), visibility (celebrity involvement), and strong constituency bases across the country (the National Federation of Independent Business).

There is no magic bullet of influence in American politics. With so many groups, so many resources, and relatively weak political parties, organized interests often engage in multiple tactics, despite not knowing exactly what works. In particular, they focus on obtaining *access* to decision-makers, providing *information* to them, and *supporting candidates* in their election campaigns. In obtaining access, providing information, and supporting candidates, wealthier interests have distinct, if not insurmountable, advantages over other groups, largely because money can support almost any set of tactics that a group wants to employ to achieve its strategic goals. During the 1990s, for example, corporations that worked against the election of Bill Clinton could subsequently gain access to the president by hiring lobbying firms with close ties to his administration. Groups with fewer financial resources could not match this capacity to move from the electoral stream of potential influence to a lobbying stream that depended heavily on access.

Most organized interests rely on combining access, information, and electoral support, although some groups do not become involved in political campaigns. Still, there is a lot of overlap, as elections can lead to access, which can allow for the effective presentation of information. Whether or not all these broad techniques ultimately lead to influence remains an open question, at least on a case-by-case basis.

Access to governmental officials

When lobbyists describe how the American political system works, few will publicly admit that its results are frequently skewed to serve the wealthiest, most powerful segments of society. Rather, lobbyists will argue that all they seek is 'access' to decision-makers, so their messages can get through. In truth, there is a lot of merit to this argument. Members of Congress are extremely busy individuals; even their top staff members are overloaded. Getting a chance to make a pitch is a valuable asset for any lobbyist, especially those who must attract clients to their Washington firms.

Access comes in many forms. It can be purchased, up to a point. Campaign contributions do not guarantee access, but even the most strait-laced legislator will admit to returning the call of a large contributor before turning to handle those from other constituents. In the past, well-heeled groups gave legislators large speaking fees for modest amounts of work, often at expensive vacation spots, where they could enjoy several hours of unrestricted socializing on the golf course. Honoraria for speaking have been outlawed and entertaining has been curtailed, but social contacts remain important. For example, more than 125 former members of Congress lobby their past colleagues, and many of these individuals command hefty fees for their service.

In his thoughtful analysis of how members of Congress grant access and how organized interests gain it, John Mark Hansen (1991) focuses on the reduction of uncertainty by both legislators and groups. Interest groups and law-makers can help each other by working together so that each partner in the arrangement reduces the tremendous uncertainties of the legislative process. For legislators, uncertainty arises over winning re-election and rising to higher office. For interests, it relates to the impact of future policies and programmes, especially those seen as potentially injurious.

Box 12.3 The sugar lobby: from iron triangle to policy community

The most important patterns of access are those that occur on a regular basis, over a long period of time. The basic, if oversimplified, pattern here reflects a continuing set of relationships between organized interests, congressional committees, and bureaucratic agencies. Sometimes referred to as an iron triangle, the ties that bind groups, committees, and agencies can become tight over the years, especially when outside groups do not challenge the relationships. Thus, for many years there were strong ties between the congressional agriculture committees, the US Department of Agriculture (USDA), and a small number of US sugar producers, who sought to maintain artificially high sugar prices. In this triangular relationship, personnel often moved from one job within the triangle to another: committee staffers would take administrative positions or lucrative lobbying jobs with sugar producers. As long as no outside interests, such as producers of corn sweeteners or environmentalists, intervened, the triangular relationship could dominate policy-making in this limited area.

The sugar lobby faced stiff competition in the 1970s, when the intervention of new interests with strong political bases created a more open policy community to address sugar issues. In a policy community, the lines of communication are not nearly so tight as in an iron triangle. Rather, legislators, bureaucrats, and interest group representatives of all stripes exist within a loose network of common policy concerns.

The sugar industry regrouped and learned how to play a new game, in which they had to compete with a broader array of interests. The fact that the American sugar industry remains highly protected demonstrates its ability to adapt—as it forged alliances with other crop groups and aggressively pursued its policy goals with effective lobbying and increased campaign contributions.

In sum, access is a two-way street, with each side hoping to obtain higher levels of certainty at the lowest level of cost. In real-world settings, therefore, a long-time legislative supporter of the NRA may find it impossible to swallow that organization's opposition to waiting periods on gun purchases; voting against such a provision might produce too much potential electoral backlash from constituents. Conversely, the NRA might react by cutting off its support for the legislator (see Chapter 19).

Information as the currency of influence

The exchange of information between organized interests and legislators makes up the core of the bonds between them. In particular, scarce and reliable information is most valuable, especially in the uncertain environment of much legislating (Wright 1996). Although policy-based information is important, other intelligence can be equally, if not more, useful. Interactions between interest groups and Congress, as well as other decision-makers, foster needs for three kinds of information:

policy, political (re-election), and procedural (internal to the legislative process). Lobbyists and legislators continually attempt to reduce uncertainties by soliciting and exchanging various kinds of information, often within the context of extended, trusting relationships. This makes sense, in that both major interests, like the auto industry, and key legislative figures, like veteran Michigan Democratic Representative John Dingell, have long-term goals to benefit the various constituencies that rely on a healthy auto manufacturing sector.

The distribution of power in legislatures determines where groups will seek to build strong bonds. In the mid-1950s, for example, the key figures were the top committee leaders, who dominated the legislative process. By the mid-1970s, on the other hand, as both committee and party leaders struggled to provide policy-making direction, organized interests needed to establish ties to dozens and dozens, if not hundreds, of members of Congress, many of whom operated as independent entrepreneurs in a highly decentralized body—and who had become key figures in various policy communities.

One oft-repeated rule of congressional lobbying is that lobbyists must never misrepresent their sponsoring groups. According to the conventional wisdom, being caught in a lie means that the bonds of trust between law-makers and lobbyists will be irreparably frayed. If the untruth is a true whopper, such a judgement may be accurate. On the other hand, the stock in trade for most lobbyists is to present information that is 'interested' rather than disinterested. Sometimes this means shading the truth by ignoring data that fail to support a lobbyist's contentions. More frequently, however, both lobbyists and law-makers will colour the truth through their reliance on policy narratives in the course of developing legislative alternatives (West and Loomis 1998). Regardless of the legislative body, lobbyists and law-makers forge careers of crafting explanations for policies past, present, and future. One way to look at lobbying is to think of it as offering up various policy explanations to legislators, who can then select and adapt the one(s) they want to convey back to their constituents.

In the past, trafficking in narratives has been a relatively private undertaking, with lobbyists making their arguments in personal conversations. All contemporary surveys of interest-group activity note the continuing importance of such communications. At the same time, framing explanations in public—through expensive scientific studies or large-scale public relations/advertising campaigns—has become more commonplace. So-called 'message politics' has grown in importance, as law-makers have come to understand that major policy decisions are often largely determined by how they are framed on the governmental agenda.

Elections and majorities

Whatever the era, the day-to-day lobbying context in Washington relates back to the previous election and forward to the next one. And given the

---

Box 12.4 Public advocacy

Although the idea of lobbying often conjures up dark hallways and whispered conversations, organized interests have increasingly turned to much more public forms of advocacy. On occasion, groups may seek to change public opinion with extensive advertising or public relations campaigns, but such efforts are extraordinarily expensive, running into the tens of millions of dollars. And even then, they cannot compare with the advertising of an auto company or a Colgate-Palmolive, which spends several billion dollars in advertising each year.

Rather, groups tend to target their messages, often focusing on a handful of key legislators in their districts or in the policy-oriented Washington community. Although corporations and other interests have employed such tactics since the early days of the twentieth century, the 1990s witnessed a surge of public advocacy, in part because of the apparent success of the legendary 'Harry and Louise' television ads, which the Health Insurance Association of America (HIAA) used to oppose President Clinton's health care initiative in 1993. Although the total expenditures amounted to only $14 million, and public opinion was not directly affected by the ads, the campaign was a rousing success, in that the news media reported heavily on the witty commercials. With

the defeat of the Clinton plan, many groups rushed to use advertising. For the most part, televised ads are usually highly targeted toward Washington policy-makers, and the groups hope that the news media will extend the reach of their messages.

Organized interests often focus their attention on the small world of Capitol Hill, as they purchase advertising space in *Roll Call* or *The Hill*, the two newspapers that offer extensive congressional coverage. In the 15 July 2002 issue of *Roll Call*, the following groups ran full-page ads, at a cost of about $10,000: Lockheed-Marietta (defence); Better World Campaign (pro-United Nations); Robert Wood Johnson Foundation (children's health); Alliance for Energy and Economic Growth (energy industry); Blue Cross/Blue Shield (health); Southern Company (energy); America's Student Loan Providers; Business for Affordable Medicine (drug consumers); American Forest & Paper Association; Miller Brewing.

Although organized interests do seek to change public opinion, they understand how difficult and costly that can be. More and more, they focus on the views of decision-makers who will determine the fate of their favoured policy positions.

two-year congressional electoral cycle, the next one is always right around the corner. For individual legislators, interest groups are almost always important elements of winning re-election, but the broader electoral relationships between interests and legislators vary according to chamber, partisan margin, the balance of power between parties and committees, the safety of incumbents, and the costs of campaigning.

Thus, in the 1920s, an era of few effective campaign regulations and a dominant Republican Party in Congress, well-heeled interests could 'invest' in a national party and its incumbents, confident in the knowledge that these partisans would control the legislative process for at least the next two years. In the 1980s, Representative Tony Coelho (D.CA), head of the Democratic Congressional Campaign Committee, made it clear to business interests that they would have to deal with a Democratic Congress for some time to come, and corporate contributions shifted sharply away from Republicans over the next few years.

More generally, both congressional and presiden-tial campaigns have grown increasingly expensive since the 1970s, although information on funding before 1974 is spotty at best.[2] The first wave of funding growth came through political action committees (PACs), whose numbers increased from 608 in 1974 until they levelled off a decade later at about 4000. Although PACs have received their share of criticism, in the end they have allowed contributors to pool their support to their favoured candidates.

Where there is a rough partisan balance, organized interests operate within an environment that is both tempting and dangerous. They can make strategic decisions to back one party or the other, in the hope that their favoured partisans will win control of the legislature (Ferguson 1995). But if their party loses, they face the possibility of being shut out of the

[2] The 1974 amendments to federal election legislation mandated the first systematic reporting of campaign contributions. It also pro-vided for public funding of presidential elections, although the pol-itical parties and candidates do not rely just on this source—to the point that George W. Bush rejected all public funding in his 2000 primary election campaign.

Box 12.5 Political action committees (PACs)

Political action committees have a long history in American politics. In the 1950s, numerous labour unions and a few business groups created these organizations, most notably labour's Committee on Political Education (COPE) and the Business–Industry Political Action Com-mittee (BIPAC). Although PACs have frequently been viewed as instruments of special-interest politics, an excellent case can be made that they are important democratic institutions, in that they operate by com-bining the resources of many labour union members, business executives, environmentalists, gun enthusiasts, or beer wholesalers (SIXPAC) in order to present a unified voice within the political process.

After the passage of 1974 campaign reform legislation that allowed for their expansion, PACs became increas-ingly important forces in American politics. These groups could give an individual congressional campaign up to $10,000, and many critics viewed the explosion of PACs as increasing the possibility of corruption on Capitol Hill. By the mid-1990s, however, interests groups and corporations often supplemented their PAC efforts with large contributions (e.g. $250,000) to political parties (so-called 'soft money') or substantial direct expenditures on campaign ads. Given such infusion of big money into campaigns, the $10,000 limit imposed upon PACs appeared positively quaint.

Since 1974 PACs have become integral parts of American electioneering. Overall, they allow large numbers of small contributors to have some small voice in how campaigns are funded. In addition, increasing numbers of elected poli-ticians have formed their own committees. For example the former House Minority Leader Dick Gephardt (D.Mo) has the Effective Government Committee, which raised and spent approximately $900,000 in the 1999–2000 electoral cycle. Although Democrats did not win control of the House in 2000, Gephardt was an attractive target for funds, given his leadership position. As of 2000, more than half of all House members (240 of 435) had organized their own PACs, usually so as to enhance their own power on Capitol Hill. The PAC organizational form has proved popu-lar and malleable, and PACs will be a part of the American political landscape for the foreseeable future.

policy process—at least in terms of the majority party leadership. In this situation, interest group 'investments'—even very large ones—may have modest payoffs, in that narrow margins ordinarily increase the level of uncertainty over legislative outcomes.

In the end, organized interests contribute to the legislative process by competing among themselves, by subsidizing legislators through their provision of information, and by serving as checks on the claims of opposing groups. The linkages between groups and legislators are not always benign, but if they are reasonably well regulated and made as transparent as possible through various reporting requirements, the overall effect on representative democracy is beneficial, even when group motivations are narrow and self-serving.

Key points

- To the extent that organized interests obtain influence in American politics, they win access to decision-makers, they provide information to them, and they offer support, often financial, to candidates for office.

- Although the public often sees campaign contributions as crucial for influence, the effective delivery of information is probably more important.

- In the past, organized interests often gained influence through the cultivation and preservation of 'iron triangles', which tie groups to congressional committees and administrative departments.

Lobbying in American politics

One secret of American lawmaking is that legislators and legislatures *need* lobbyists. Even in Congress and a few highly professionalized state legislatures, where legislators enjoy great staff resources, interest-group representatives provide a continuously flowing river of useful, even critical, information. If legislators want to know something about agriculture, they can call the Farm Bureau and a dozen other, smaller groups such as beekeepers or organic farmers or farm implement dealers. If they want to know what raising the minimum wage will mean, they can talk to the National Federation of Independent Business, the Chamber of Commerce, and the AFL-CIO, as well as representatives from various think tanks. Law-makers will get a range of responses, but they and their staffers will almost always come out better informed. Moreover, legislators know that by seeking information from several sources, especially when they are genuinely undecided, they will increase their chances of taking an appropriate position on a given issue. In addition, over time law-makers come to know whose information they consider most useful and reliable.

One cynical version of the legislative process depicts lobbyists and the interests they represent as showering favours and campaign contributions on law-makers in return for their backing on key issues. Although recent campaign finance reforms may modify these relationships, there is precious little evidence that votes are bought either with contributions or with meals, favours, and trips. What legislators want most—and what lobbyists can provide—is solid, timely information. For lobbyists, this requires access, which allows them to deliver a message at the right time. One lobbyist, a former state senator, noted that if he wanted to talk to a key law-maker, he would get to the Capitol by 7 a.m. and catch the legislator before he got too far into the hurly-burly of the day: 'I can get my business done in two or three minutes, once I can talk to him. Otherwise, it's hard to find an opportunity to have his undivided attention.'

Lobbyists and their interest groups seek to influence legislative outcomes in numerous ways. First, they can try to *persuade* legislators that their positions should be adopted, in terms both of substance (a worthy programme) and politics (a smart vote). Second, lobbyists can try to *mobilize* their grass-roots supporters to pressure their representatives to support a given policy. Third, they can seek to *redefine issues*, so that a given programme, like prescription drug benefits, becomes something else, like a tax increase. Fourth, they can *direct campaign funds* to benefit legislators who agree with them. And fifth, they can seek to *oust legislators* who oppose them. It is worth noting that the first three of these techniques are the most direct, and they rely on information more than money to further the goals of their respective interest groups.

This is not to say that money is not important, either at the state or national level. Top-flight lobbyists command high salaries and large fees. Equally important in contemporary politics are grass-roots campaigns that seek to pressure legislators by mobilizing their constituents. In the past, such grass-roots techniques were used largely by large membership groups, like labour unions or environmentalists, which could prompt their loyalists to call or write to their legislators. In recent years, however, some lobbying firms, such as Jack Bonner's in Washington, DC, have created a specialty in pumping up grass-roots support for legislative action. Often labelled 'astroturf lobbying', such efforts can be expensive, and legislators often sniff out such tactics as artificial. Indeed, one perennial problem for law-makers

is to separate useful information from noise. Again, if lobbyists and their groups can gain a legislator's confidence, they have a much better chance of getting her or him to listen—and this exchange usually works to benefit both lobbyist and law-maker.

Key points

- Despite negative reactions to lobbyists by the public, decision-makers, and especially legislators, often rely on the information provided to them by group representatives.

- Lobbyists seek to persuade legislators that their position is correct, but they also mobilize political support behind their views, as well as working to redefine issues in ways that favour their own interests.

- Lobbying success does not depend solely on the amount of money that is spent, but adequate funding does mean that a group can employ various methods in seeking to influence decision-makers.

Conclusion: organized interests and American democracy

The public generally envisions lobbyists as acting on behalf of the most powerful societal interests. There is no denying that major economic interests are often well represented, but this is a superficial observation in at least two ways. First, even among powerful interests there are great differences of opinion over preferred policies. For example, textile manufacturers have consistently fought to restrict the importation of cheap foreign goods, which reflect the low wages paid in Asia or Latin America. Conversely, Nike lobbies for reduced trade restrictions, as it both manufactures its shoes abroad and sells many of its products around the globe. Labour unions often desire protection for their members' jobs, while, as consumers, these same

union members buy a wide range of imported products from chains like Wal-Mart, which lobbies for policies that will reduce tariffs and barriers to trade.

Second, many of the most powerful interest groups represent large numbers of citizens who do not share a single set beliefs. For example, the conservative-leaning National Federation of Small Business (NFIB) represents hundreds of thousands of small firms, which have some similarities, but many differences as well. The US Chamber of Commerce finds it even more difficult to represent its broad mix of business interests. In addition, many organizations with large numbers of highly committed members represent non-economic interests, as

Table 12.1 The power twenty-five: most influential interests

In the states		In Washington, DC
Schoolteachers' organizations (NEA)	1	American Association of Retired Persons
General business organizations (chambers of commerce, etc.)	2	National Rifle Association of America
Utility companies and associations (electric, gas, water, etc.)	3	National Federation of Independent Business
Lawyers (state bar associations and trial lawyers)	4	American Israel Public Affairs Committee
Traditional labour groups (AFL-CIO)	5	AFL-CIO
Physicians and state medical associations	6	Association of Trial Lawyers of America
Insurance: general and medical	7	Chamber of Commerce
Manufacturers (companies and associations)	8	National Right to Life Committee
Health care organizations (hospital associations)	9	National Education Association
Bankers' associations	10	National Restaurant Association
Local government organizations (municipal and county leagues)	11	National Bankers' Association
State and local government employees (other than teachers)	12	National Governors' Association
Farm organizations (state farm bureaus)	13	American Medical Association
Individual banks and financial institutions	14	National Association of Manufacturers
Environmentalists	15	National Association of Realtors
Universities and colleges	16	National Association of Home Builders
Realtors' associations	17	Motion Picture Association of America
Individual cities and towns	18	Credit Union National Association
Gaming interests (casinos, race tracks, and lotteries)	19	National Beer Wholesalers Association
Contractors, builders, and developers	20	National Association of Broadcasters
Liquor, wine, and beer interests AND K-12 education interests (other than teachers)	21	American Farm Bureau Federation
Retailers (companies and trade associations)	22	American Federation of State, County, and Municipal Employees
Senior citizens	23	International Brotherhood of Teamsters
Mining companies and associations	24	United Auto Workers Union
Truckers and private transport interests (excluding railroads)	25	Health Insurance Association of America

Sources: Fortune Magazine (Dec. 1999); R. Hrebenar, *Interest Group Politics*, 1997

with the Sierra Club or the Christian Coalition. Again, economic interests, such as auto manufacturers, certainly get their message across, but clean-air advocates are also heard. Table 12.1 lists the twenty-five most powerful groups within the states and in Washington, DC. Such rankings should be taken with a grain of salt, but they indicate both the breadth and concentration of influence.

At the national level, many of the usual suspects do appear, including the AARP, the NRA, and the US Chamber of Commerce. Still, there is no evidence for an established 'power elite' of top interests that dominate American politics. For example, the Chamber of Commerce (7) and the Trial Lawyers (6) have long been bitter enemies over the incidence and impact of high-cost liability litigation. Some groups, like the American Israel Public Affairs Committee (AIPAC) or the National Right to Life Committee, attempt to exercise a great deal of influence over a limited slice of policy.

Although environmental groups are notably absent from the national top twenty-five (the Sierra Club ranked forty-third), they are scarcely without power. More importantly, perhaps, the overall balance of interests is remarkable—with the elderly, gun enthusiasts, small-business owners, supporters of Israel, and big labour constituting the top five groups. Furthermore, the variety of interests continues as one moves down the list, encountering beer wholesalers, credit unions, and the governors' association.

Turning to the states, a similar range of interests appears. It is no surprise that education associations lead the list, given their large memberships and wide geographical base. A host of business interests are well established, as we might assume, but many of the most influential groups are frequently at odds with each other (e.g. trial lawyers and physicians, labour and the Chamber of Commerce).

In addition, the most influential groups in

Washington often do not have similar clout in the states, and vice versa. The AARP is far more respected or feared on Capitol Hill than in most state legislatures; likewise, and understandably, AIPAC has little influence in the states, given its focus on foreign policy and military affairs. The National Education Association, while strong in DC, does not come close to exercising the clout there that it does in the states, where education funding easily consumes half of a state's budget and attracts the unwavering attention of teachers' organizations. More generally, the large membership groups such as the AARP and the NRA appear less influential in the states than in Washington. Again, the framers of the Constitution got it right: a federal republic, with its dispersion of authority, has tended to work against the concentration of power among a few interests.

Driving this point home all the more firmly is the growth in the number of interests, both in the states and in Washington, DC, where the number of groups has increased from about 2,000 in 1970 to almost 16,000 thirty years later. Moreover, as Jeffrey Berry (1999) has demonstrated, citizens' groups (Common Cause, campaign finance organizations, environmentalists, etc.) have expanded even more rapidly than interests groups as a whole. Indeed, the number of Washington-based citizens groups has risen from fewer than 100 in the 1970s to more than 2,400 in the late 1990s.

Although the framers of the Constitution could not have imagined how professional lobbying would become, they understood that interests would—and should—seek to influence law-makers. Taken together, the rights of petition and free speech represent an invitation for groups to make their case before the legislature. In the end, this protects us all. Nearly eight in ten Americans belong to an organized group with a policy agenda—from the Christian Coalition to People for the Ethical Treatment of Animals. About 40 per cent of adults are members of two or more groups. Even without formally joining an organization, many individuals identify with that group (e.g. spouses of union members or African Americans who do not belong to the NAACP). In sum, the so-called 'special interests' are not some corrupt elite: they represent citizens in thousands of different combinations.

Given that, interest groups are pervasive in the US, but they are not quite central to the American policy-making process. Too many other elements come into play—ranging from legislators' constituencies to the court system to federalism—to allow for an interpretation of American politics that relies heavily on organized interests. Rather, they are continually part of the process, often accentuating the demands or the positions of certain elements within the society. But, much as Madison and his fellow framers envisioned, modern factions remain held in check both by the overall political system and the very fact that so many interests are effectively represented within that system.

QUESTIONS

1 The large and growing number of interest groups within the US all pursue their own goals. To what extent does the sum of decisions based on the pursuit of individual interests produce an effective approximation of the general societal interest? Who protects the more general interests of society?

2 American political parties have traditionally been viewed as weak. To the extent that this is so, how are organized interests affected? Do they necessarily have more opportunities to influence policy-making? Or must they simply operate in a political setting in which it is difficult to get things done at all?

3 To what extent does money—operating through organized interests—dominate American politics? What other resources come into play that may offset the potential power of well-heeled interests?

4 Organized interests have proliferated in American politics over the past forty years. What are the implications of this increase for how politics and policy-making are conducted in the US?

FURTHER READING

F. R. Baumgartner and B. Leech (1998), *Basic Interests: The Importance of Groups of Groups in Politics and in Political Science* (Princeton, NJ: Princeton University Press).

J. M. Berry (1997), *The Interest Group Society*, 3rd edn. (New York: Longman).

A. J. Cigler and B. Loomis (eds.) (2002), *Interest Group Politics*, 6th edn. (Washington, DC: CQ Press).

T. Lowi (1979), *The End of Liberalism: The Second Republic of the United States* (New York: Norton).

M. Olson (1965), *The Logic of Collective Action: Public Goods and the Theory of Groups* (Cambridge, Mass.: Harvard University Press).

D. Truman (1951), *The Governmental Process* (New York: Knopf).

WEB LINKS

Many interest groups have their own websites, which are often highly sophisticated. You might want to check out: **www.nra.org/** for the National Rifle Association, or Handgun Control Inc. at **www.bradycampaign.org/index.asp**. Some of the most useful websites allow anyone to follow the raising and spending of money in American politics; perhaps the best one is **www.opensecrets.org/** (Center for Responsive Politics). A group of political scientists placed a considerable amount of data on lobbying on the web at **www.lobbying.la.psu.edu**. One commercial site merits attention: **www.influence.biz** serves as a trade publication for the lobbying industry.

Part Three

Public policy

Parts One and Two of *Governing America* should have provided a detailed explanation of the institutions of American government, the key intermediary organizations, and their on-going and complex interaction. In Part Three we move on to consider public policy. In essence, public policy comprises the total sum of government activities as they have an influence on individual citizens' lives. More particularly, we can identify three levels of policy: *choices*, where authoritative decision-makers select between available options; *outputs*, meaning those choices put into action (resulting in the government spending money, hiring personnel, or issuing regulations); and *impacts*, the material effects of policies on individuals, groups, and localities. In this part of the book, we focus on five key policies (economic, foreign, foreign economic, environmental, and social policy). These illustrate how the fragmentation of governing institutions and the competitive efforts of parties, interest groups, and bureaucratic agencies interact to produce particular policy choices, outputs, and effects. The contributors illustrate clearly how America's divided democracy is not only reflected in, but also reinforced by, the public policies that emerge from the processes of decision-making in government.

Part Three

Public policy

Economic policy

Nigel Bowles

READER'S GUIDE

This chapter examines two questions. First, what is distinctive about the formation and content of domestic economic policy in the US? Secondly, why is knowledge of that distinctiveness important for understanding government and politics in the US? The chapter examines how governments in the US make decisions about domestic economic policy and why they make them as they do. It shows what is distinctive about the politics of domestic economic policy, and why knowledge of that distinctiveness matters for fuller understanding of government and politics in the United States. In considering distinctiveness itself, the chapter highlights where it applies and where it does not, and shows how such distinctiveness illuminates the broader themes of this book. These themes are supported with data about key economic indicators, and then illustrated by analysis of fiscal and monetary policy.

Introduction

America's economy is the largest and most efficient in the world: the average American worker produces more than her or his counterparts in other countries. Table 13.1 gives a snapshot comparison of output per capita in the United States with that of some other major market democracies in the year 2000.

For politicians as for their constituents, economic and financial questions are ubiquitous: even non-economic decisions about resource allocation have clear economic consequences. Like politicians in other market democracies, American politicians make political judgements about these questions with special care because their careers depend upon getting such judgements right. The political fate of elected executives—of the president, of state governors, and of city mayors—usually depends upon their achieving (or at least presiding over) steady output growth, low inflation, and high employment.

Table 13.1 GDP per capita, 2000 (current $US)

Country	At current exchange rates	Purchasing power parities
United States	35,619	35,619
United Kingdom	23,887	24,398
Canada	22,783	28,015
Germany	22,712	25,893
France	21,417	24,215
Australia	20,278	26,495
Korea	9,671	15,055
Mexico	5,903	9,152

Where an incumbent's economic policy record is mixed, opponents' prospects are enhanced. Politicians accordingly attempt to influence output growth, inflation, and unemployment because political futures and fortunes hang upon them.

Unfortunately for politicians, however, neither they nor the civil servants and staff who advise and assist them are able to determine these outcomes, because most of the economy lies not in public but in private control. In order to allocate resources most efficiently, companies' managers, not politicians, take the major decisions about their companies' investment, products, employment, and location in a context of demands upon those companies being made freely by other companies and individual consumers. In short, goods and services in market economies are rationed through the operation of market prices rather than through authoritative allocation by politicians and bureaucrats.

However, America's market economy is complex and not easily categorized. It is not a libertarian's dream in which entrepreneurs, buyers, and sellers interact in relationships of supply and demand free of supervision by public authorities. In fact, federal, state, and local governments constantly intrude upon the economy in various guises: as buyers, employers, arbitrators, regulators, and judges. Federal, state, and local governments, in their own right and through the bureaucracies and courts which they establish, are major players in America's market democracy. Governments provide frameworks of contract, commercial, property, land, labour, and constitutional law which shape the rights and obligations of the owners of businesses, and those of the managers and workers within them. The federal government is most obviously

and daily apparent in its role as monopoly supplier and regulator of the single national currency, the dollar.

The federal government, and the governments of every state and of many cities, are themselves major purchasers ('procurers') of goods and services from the private sector. All governments, large and small, employ people directly whether in civilian or military service, and all are responsible indirectly for the employment of many more in the private sector through the demands which they create for goods and services from the private sector. All governments spend public money raised from private citizens

---

Box 13.1 Definitions

Fiscal policy. Those policies directly concerned with public expenditure and taxation.

Fiscal deficit or surplus. The difference between total federal revenues and expenditures in any one fiscal year.

Federal debt. The accumulated sum of federal fiscal deficits less the accumulated sum of federal fiscal surpluses.

Monetary policy. Those policies determining short-term rates of interest set by the Federal Reserve Board's Open Market Committee.

Authorization legislation. Congressional legislation that authorizes the existence and purpose of public policy programmes.

Appropriation legislation. Congressional legislation that appropriates public funds to authorized public policy programmes.

and corporations in taxes. The federal government is a major borrower from US and foreign citizens, and from US and foreign banks and investors through the agency of the US Treasury. The US government's resulting (highly liquid) debt constitutes the world's largest securities market, with some $5.7 trillion worth in circulation globally.

American governments' decisions about the money supply, taxation, expenditure, procurement and borrowing have powerful economic, financial, political, and electoral consequences. Economic decision-making is a thoroughly political process, not a neutral or merely technical one. Every economic policy question is inescapably political because it confers benefits upon some groups and losses upon others. Since politicians need citizens' votes to gain or retain power, public preferences carry weight with those same politicians. That claim could be made of every democracy, but it has special force in the United States, where government is comparatively transparent, where the political system contains multiple, competing, and interactive institutions of government, and where those institutions are highly sensitive to public and group opinion.

A distinctive system?

Let us now turn to the question of distinctiveness, beginning with what is *not* distinctive about economic policy in the United States. The range of available policy instruments is similar to that in other political systems. Monetary policy (to control the money supply through banking regulations and by alterations in interest rates); fiscal policy (encompassing government expenditure, taxation, and borrowing); trade policy (including policy on tariffs, quotas, and protection of certain sectors of the economy from foreign competition); and labour market policy (including policy towards education and training of the labour force, and laws governing unionization and contracts between employers and employees) are all common policy instruments in other economies.

Nevertheless, American politicians and policy-makers have made different use of these policy instruments from their counterparts in most other market democracies. There are three respects in which this distinctiveness has been apparent.

First, the economic doctrine of Keynesianism, which rested on the proposition that aggregate demand could be manipulated by governments through altering the levels of public expenditure and taxation, took root late and incompletely in the United States. Not until Lyndon Johnson's tax cut of 1964 did Keynesianism find full expression in legislation. Just sixteen years later, by the second half of Jimmy Carter's presidency, Keynesianism had lost stable majority support within both Congress and the executive branch. In Congress especially, most conservatives fought Keynesianism from the 1930s onwards because they feared that its adoption would increase federal expenditure on domestic programmes (which, in any case, they opposed) faster than the economy could sustain it, and would thereby result in fiscal deficits with damaging inflationary consequences. Other conservatives opposed Keynesianism because of the doctrine's supposed privileging of reductions in unemployment over reductions in inflation. The new dominant doctrine from the mid-1970s was that of monetarism propagated by Milton Friedman (among others), one whose focus was upon the reduction of inflation expectations by tightly controlling the quantity of money in circulation.

Secondly, total government expenditure in the United States measured as a percentage of Gross Domestic Product (GDP) has been lower than such expenditure in most other market democracies throughout the post-war period. Its composition is also different: the United States spends proportionately rather more than do other major countries such as France, Britain, Italy, Germany, Australia, Brazil, and Canada upon defence and much less upon welfare.

Thirdly, although the federal and state governments do own public corporations (the US Post Office is one example, and the Port Authority of

New York and New Jersey is another), the US has never embraced direct public ownership of industrial or commercial enterprises on the scale that was once common in (for example) Western Europe and Japan. Consequently, there has been less scope for privatization initiatives in America than there has been in Europe, Asia, Australasia, Africa, and Latin America. Rather than owning enterprises directly, federal, state, and local governments have chosen to shape their activities by regulating them. Congress has established many such federal regulatory agencies (often in response to presidential requests), and has devolved responsibility to them for protecting their interests—for example, the Food and Drug Administration is charged with protecting the health and safety of the consumer. State legislatures have acted similarly in response to requests from state governors.

The American political system is also distinctive in two structural respects, each of which has consequences for the formation (and, arguably, for the content) of economic policy. First, formal powers of government are separated horizontally within the federal government between the executive, a bicameral legislature, and a formally independent federal judiciary with powers of judicial review. Secondly, the United States is separated vertically into federal, state, and local governments, comprising three autonomous but interactive and fiscally interdependent levels. Whilst policy instruments in the US are not distinctive, the structure of government certainly is. A consequence is that coordi-nating the system's disparate elements is politically demanding and administratively complex. The federal government is not densely concentrated but open-textured, with dispersed and often competing and overlapping centres of authority whose component bureaucratic agencies have multiple loyal-ties. The loyalties of departments and agencies with jurisdictions over parts of economic policies are not just or even primarily to the president but to Congress and private sector groups, as the examples of the Treasury, Commerce, and Labor all show. Much of the discussion in the following sections deals with some of the problems to which this scattering of power across and within America's political institutions gives rise.

Key points

- The US economy is the largest, most productive, and most innovative in the world.

- Economic decision-making is not merely a technical process, but a highly political one.

- The US economy is distinctive in that public expenditure accounts for a smaller proportion of total national output than is the case in most other market democracies.

- The distinctive structural characteristics of federalism and separation of powers fragments much economic decision-making in America.

Box 13.2 **Constitutional influences**
Is American politics structurally distinctive?

The US's constitutional *structure* is distinctive in that:

- it is federal;

- the federal government is separated into an executive, a bicameral legislature, and a judiciary;

- membership of the three branches of the federal government is completely separate;

- federal executive departments and agencies are Congress's creation;

- federal departments' and agencies' programmes are designed and funded by Congress in the form of law;

- Acts of Congress, actions of the executive, and actions of state and local governments are in principle subject to judicial review by federal courts.

The importance of the distinctiveness of economic policy formation

The questions with which the chapter began illuminate the theme of the 'divided democracy' that informs this book, and from which three propositions can be derived about economic policy's distinctiveness; they also illuminate another division—one of the most problematic relationships in any democracy—between public authority (government) and private capital (markets).

Government and markets

The formation and content of economic policy at federal, state, and local levels in the United States raise questions about where the boundaries between institutions and agencies of governments on the one hand and markets on the other actually lie. These questions are linked to the American economy's distinctiveness, especially with respect to the persistence with which spending by governments at all levels throughout America's industrial history has accounted for a smaller proportion of GDP than is the case in most other market democracies. They are also linked to the supposed absence in America of an industrial policy by which government promotes certain technologies and industries, sponsors industrial change through state corporations and agencies, and takes a directive role in training programmes which the private sector needs but fails to supply.

In fact, America's comparative success in fostering and exploiting intellectual assets, in American companies' technical and organizational innovation, and their resultant success in raising the productivity of labour, do not result solely from private sector activity but instead depend heavily upon the public and charitable sectors for their success and profitability. Such dependence of private companies upon the public and charitable sectors is true of major growth technologies at the beginning of the twenty-first century such as software, pharmacology, and genetics. But in no industry has it been more durably

and dramatically demonstrated than in aerospace, where government and industry are sutured in an intimate relationship which amounts to an industrial policy (albeit one whose terms and character politicians prefer not to acknowledge). Aircraft and aero-engine manufacturers have all benefited greatly and recurrently from government spending on defence research and development, whose benefits manufacturers have transferred to civilian applications made profitable by the federal government's assumption of most research and development costs. In the wake of the terrorist attacks of 11 September 2001, Congress actually wrote into law a provision for large subsidies to Boeing. It did much the same, although less lavishly and with closer public attention, for US domestic airlines. Few parts of the aerospace or civilian airline industry bear much relation to free market theory.

American companies are typically more productive than their competitors in other countries because of their high rates of investment in new physical capital, and their typically superior organization, marketing, training, research, and development. It is indeed true that the private sector in America does assume a significant proportion of the risk in commissioning research and development. Congressional Budget Office (CBO) data show that the business sector's share of such expenditure rose sharply in the 1990s to 67 per cent by the decade's end. However, American companies and the American public also benefit greatly from research and development conducted directly by federal agencies (such as the National Institute for Health) or indirectly by them in support of research by universities and charities (such as support from the National Academy of Sciences). Research universities, many of them private but including several distinguished examples such as the Universities of California, Michigan, Texas, and Wisconsin under the aegis of state governments, also contribute greatly to every sector of America's research base; so, too, do scientific charities—especially those in medical research. The combined total of private, public, charitable, and university research is much larger relative to the economy's size than that in any of America's competitors. Unsurprisingly, therefore, by three measures of research quality—Nobel prizes, patent applications, and citations in scholarly journals—the United States contains the largest single slice of the world's intellectual capital, and the world's twenty or so greatest research universities.

There can be little doubt that rates of product innovation, and the scale and speed of industrial transformation, are exceptionally high in the United States. But the brief preceding examples suggest that they are so not solely because of the superior quality of American companies or of the markets in which they operate but because of extensive relationships between companies, governments, research charities, and universities which themselves suggest that the boundaries between governments and markets are not easily identified but are both fluid and complex.

Policy fragmentation

Conflict over the content of economic policy occurs in all market democracies. If politics comprises, as Harold Lasswell once defined it, the determination of 'who gets what, when, and how', the questions of taxation, expenditure, growth, employment, and inflation which comprise economic policy are those which express that question of resource allocation in its starkest form.[1] Little wonder, then, that every citizen and group should care (often intensely) about who wins and who loses in political struggles, where one group's gain from the inclusion or exclusion of a particular clause in a tax bill is usually another group's loss.

Federal, state, and local government decisions about fiscal and labour market policy shape the condition of the national and of regional and local economies. Despite the US being a market economy, the federal government is the single largest influence upon the country's output, employment, and investment, because its budget is greater than those of all state and local governments combined: its activities account for more than 20 per cent of GDP. More-

over, unlike the constitutions of many states, the US Constitution does not prohibit the federal government from running a fiscal deficit.

Many of the struggles within American government over resource allocation take place in public. Most state legislatures do most of their formal business of writing tax and spending laws in public; so does the US Congress. Interest groups which donate money to politicians to finance their campaigns are, under the laws of the federal (and most state) governments, obliged to disclose the amounts given. There is little room for financiers or politicians to hide. Moreover, in much of America there exists a deep suspicion of government and a pervasive wariness of the exercise of power by elected politicians and unelected officials. Only in monetary policy does the US federal government (in the form of the central bank, the Federal Reserve Board) have a monopoly over short-term policy formation. The Federal Reserve ('the Fed') has full formal authority to set short-term interest rates, although, as we shall see later in this chapter, that does not innoculate the Fed against Congress, the president, and businesses pressing it to adjust monetary policy to their (often conflicting) preferences.

Fragmentation of government fragments policy processes. Transparency of policy-making and distrust of government obtains in a system of government that is better understood as separated rather than presidential. The presidency and Congress are coordinate institutions: each requires the other's active cooperation in order for economic policy initiatives to become law. Unlike in most West European democracies, the US executive has little authority and few sanctions over members of the legislature; nor does either legislative chamber have authority or power over the other. These constitutional rules fragment the making of fiscal, monetary, and labour market policy within Washington as surely as parallel constitutional rules fragment it between Washington on the one hand and state and local governments on the other. This fragmentation has consequences that are powerful, pervasive, and durable both for the style and for the content of economic policy in

---

[1] Lasswell, Harold D., *Politics*, New York, P. Smith, 1950.

the USA. Authority over the making of economic policy is distributed between structurally separate branches of government which the formation of public policy makes both interactive and interdependent.

Not only are there divisions of interest between and among participants in government, but also between and among groups, corporations, unions, and citizens. For governments, citizens, and groups, the stakes are high. Politicians fight elections in order to retain or gain power; workers fight to retain or gain jobs or new terms and conditions; corporations fight to win or hold contracts and sales in order to maximize profits or market share. This is a system of competitive politics which operates at high pressure.

Democratic and liberal values

Economic policy is where government and markets meet. Democratic rules (such as equality before the law, symbolized and expressed in the equal worth of votes) resonate strongly in the rhetoric and sometimes in the practice of politics. By contrast, they resonate only faintly in markets whose dominant ethos is cupidity and within which corporations have huge power over investment and employment. As a result, the meeting of these two worlds is fraught. Everyone's welfare turns on the outcome of economic policy formation, but not everyone's voice counts equally in its determination. For example, city and state governments need the businesses within their borders to remain and develop as major employers and investors; they also need to attract new businesses from elsewhere. City and state governments are therefore bound to listen carefully to businesses' demands and wishes in matters of taxation, public spending, and employment law. Businesses do not *dictate* policies on such matters (not least because different businesses have different, and sometimes clashing, interests). But businesses' voices attract private audiences of government decision-makers especially when constituents' jobs are at stake; that in turn gives businesses leverage over government, especially in respect of taxation and incentives to invest.

Within the federal government, Congress is the key actor. Congress enjoys complete formal authority (the right to act) over tax and spending (appropriations) laws, subject only to the threat or fact of a president's veto and within a political context which the president has the opportunity to shape through his setting of the national agenda in his budget and taxation programmes. However, both power (the capacity and will to act) and authority over tax and spending law within Congress is unequally distributed because of the disproportionate influence of a small number of experienced and resourceful politicians and because of specialist committees' exclusive jurisdictions in aspects of fiscal policy. Appropriations Committees in the House and the Senate have jurisdiction over expenditure. The Ways and Means Committee in the House, and the Finance Committee in the Senate, have jurisdiction over taxation. Committee decisions can be modified or defeated on the floor of either chamber, but rarely are. Representatives and senators who are not members of these four key committees, or of the Budget Committees, influence economic policy only rarely and usually with difficulty.

Values of democracy and liberalism expressed in the forms of representative government and equality are both threatened by politicians' inescapable dependence upon bureaucratic expertise. Those federal, state, and city civil servants whom representative politicians charge with regulating (for example) markets' fairness or workers' and consumers' rights and safety, are typically both experienced and expert. It is in the public interest that they be both experienced and expert: the alternative is unacceptable. But the expertise of bureaucrats makes it harder for (mostly) inexpert politicians to hold them to account. As we shall see in the section below on monetary policy, the Federal Reserve Board's highly concentrated knowledge and intellectual grasp of all aspects of the American economy relevant to its work makes it a major asset for realizing the public interest. But by the same token, none of its officials are elected. Congressmen, senators, or presidents must therefore hold it to account on behalf of the public in congressional hearings, in public comment, and private representations.

Progressive and traditionalist doctrines

Since the nineteenth century, the formation and content of fiscal and monetary policy have highlighted both the tension between progressive and traditionalist doctrines of economics and politics and some of the means by which politicians have exploited notions of 'progressive' and 'traditionalist' in economic policy for their own political purposes.

Differences of interest between lenders and borrowers conditioned the politics of the early Republic during Washington's and Jefferson's presidencies. Conflicts between creditors and debtors shaped American electoral and party politics during the populist revolts of the 1890s, splitting the Democratic vote and confirming the Republicans as the majority party. Sharp differences of economic interest shaped Franklin Roosevelt's New Deal coalition in 1932 and 1936, when American party politics came closer to being aligned to social class than at any other point in US history. Even in 1944, with America still at war, Roosevelt exploited class resentment to energize his core constituency of unionized workers in manufacturing industries. Workers' freedom to organize in unions provoked protracted, bitter, and often violent conflict between corporations on the one side and workers seeking organization rights on the other. There has rarely been widespread public sympathy in America for unions' rights to organize or for their activities: the corruption of some unions, and the involvement of others in organized crime, have contributed to undermining unions' popular legitimacy and support. Not until 1935 did Congress pass the National Labor Relations Act, which enhanced labour unions' rights to organize and bargain collectively, established a National Labor Relations Board, and banned those practices of employers deemed unfair. The measure was initiated by Senator Robert Wagner and at first opposed by the president, only to win his support after the full extent of congressional backing became apparent. In 1938, the Fair Labor Standards Act set a minimum wage of twenty-five cents per hour, and a maximum working week for some workers of forty-four hours. Legislative measures subsequently to increase the minimum

wage have always since provoked resistance from affected employers, drawn support from affected employees, and divided opinion in Congress along ideological lines.

Policy about distribution of the tax burden at federal, state, and local level divides America. It does so in a context in which, as the CBO reported in 2000, inequality of income has grown markedly: the real income of families in the middle of the US income distribution rose from $41,400 in 1979 to $45,100 in 1997, a 9 per cent increase. Meanwhile the income of families in the top 1 per cent rose from $420,200 to $1.016 million, a 140 per cent increase. Alternatively expressed, the income of families in the top 1 per cent was ten times that of typical families in 1979, and twenty-three times and rising in 1997.[2] President Reagan's Economic Recovery Tax Act of 1981 had the intention and the effect of increasing post-tax income inequality. President George W. Bush had a similar distributional purpose in his economic stimulus package of 2001–2. Divisions within Congress about the fairness of such redistribution now coincide closely with partisan affiliation: Republican Congressmen (and, to a lesser extent, senators) have supported reductions of the tax burden on the richest quintile of American taxpayers, while Democrats have usually opposed them. The CBO calculates that between 1979 and 1997 *effective* individual income tax rates fell for the 80 per cent of households with the lowest income and rose for the 20 per cent with the highest income, a result of the extraordinarily large growth of income of those at the top of the distribution increasing that quintile's federal tax liabilities.

State governments rely heavily for their revenue on sales taxes, and local governments (particularly local school districts) upon property taxes. Most states also impose an income tax of their own, attracted by the buoyancy which makes it easier for politicians to avoid raising income tax *rates*. The precise mix of income, property, and sales taxes which states and local governments choose has powerful implications for the distribution of the tax burden. Broadly speaking, the more conservative the state's political representation in the legislature,

---

[2] Krugman, Paul, 'America the Polarized', *New York Times*, 4 January 2002.

Box 13.3 **Is America different?**
The policy process(es)

The US's policy processes are distinctive in that:

- the Presidency has little constitutional authority and only contingent power over economic policy;

- the economic policy forming institutions of government are heavily penetrated by interest groups;

- many legislators who write tax and expenditure laws and who oversee the operation of regulatory laws depend upon interest groups' cash for campaign finance;

- structural separation often makes identification of the core of 'the state' in federal economic policy-making difficult;

- the central bank (the Federal Reserve Board) is an amalgam of public and private interests with effectively complete operational autonomy from elected politicians.

Federal and state governments have relied for more than a century upon large numbers of regulatory agencies to correct for market failure rather than upon direct ownership of industrial enterprises.

---

the more regressive its tax burden. But the distribution is almost always a matter of political controversy, even in a conservative state such as Texas, where low income tax rates might appear to be an article of political faith.

Key points

- Fragmentation of government implies fragmentation of policy processes. There is no single centre of decision-making authority about (for example) taxation either in the United States or even within the federal government.

- American companies' comparatively high rates of product innovation result in part from America's broad and deep investment in research and development. But that research and development from which the private sector benefits owes much to federal, state, local, and charitable support for research institutes and universities.

- The tensions between the values of liberalism and those of democracy come to the fore in the politics of domestic economic policy. The principle of equality before the law collides with the practical concentration of public authority over taxation and spending in legislatures and bureaucracies.

- Distribution of the tax burden is politically controversial and a matter upon which the two parties have contrasting views. Marginal rates of taxation have fallen sharply since 1981.

Fiscal policy

This section describes what 'fiscal policy' means and encompasses, and the politicians and officials who participate in making fiscal policy; and it explains how the four propositions are expressed in it.

The meaning and scope of fiscal policy

Fiscal policy refers to governments' *taxation* of its companies and citizens, and to governments' *expenditure* upon all programmes of public policy and interest payments on the national debt. The key fiscal data for the federal and state governments are receipts, outlays, deficits in any one year, and total debt outstanding. The difference between the flows of taxation and expenditure is the fiscal surplus or deficit. A fiscal surplus in any one year enables a government to reduce its debt by the amount of the surplus; a fiscal deficit in any one year forces a government to increase its debt by the amount of the deficit incurred or to increase its tax revenue to cover all or part of the additional deficit. As Box 13.4 notes,

the federal government usually runs deficits; the constitutions and/or laws of most state and local governments prohibit sub-federal governments from doing so.

Participants in the making of fiscal policy

Federal, state, and local governments participate (and often share) in the making of fiscal policy. Most of the 86,000 governments in America raise public funds (revenue) for their programmes through taxation, and all spend funds which they raise or which are transferred to them by other governments on those programmes or in support of other governments' programmes.

In the US federal government and in each of the fifty states, legislatures write both taxation and expenditure (the latter often termed 'appropriations') laws. In the US federal government and in each state, it is the president and governor respectively who formally propose detailed packages for taxation and expenditure (the budget), following detailed preparatory and drafting work by budget office officials. Neither legislatures in the states nor

---

Box 13.4 **Core academic debate**
Why does the US federal government usually incur a fiscal deficit?

- The President proposes budgets, but Congress writes them into law.

- Congress' main institutional difficulty in budget-making is in aggregating interests rather than merely summing them.

- Congress' capacity to aggregate interests has weakened since the 1960s because of the weakening of hierarchy (especially in the House), and the cultural and attitudinal changes of members of the Appropriations Committees and the House Ways and Means Committee, and because of House and Senate rules changes which have reduced those committees' autonomy.

- There are fewer institutional constraints upon individual congressional politicians' single-minded pursuit and retention of electoral office. That pursuit and retention often involve them in aggressively supporting their districts and states' fiscal interests at the expense of the national interest.

- Such behaviour leads to the systematic meeting of particularistic demands at the price of generalized log-rolling—Congressmen's and senators' support of each other's policy preferences with weak regard to the consequences for the fiscal balance.

the US Congress at federal level are obliged to accept the chief executive's proposals, but they usually modify them rather than reorder them. For all politicians, whether mayors, governors, the president of the United States, or members of city councils, state assemblies, or the US Congress, taxing and spending policies are the products of some of their most consequential decisions. Few areas of public policy have higher salience; few have a greater capacity to make politicians' careers, as Ronald Reagan always understood, or to break them, as his successor, George Bush, belatedly discovered.

As the earlier discussion showed, the politics of taxation and spending are highly contentious; that is so both at federal level and in the states and cities. Voters are, accordingly, vocal participants in fiscal politics. Elected politicians who lose touch with public opinion on taxation and spending risk being defeated by opponents skilled at exploiting popular discontent. It has become common in federal and in state and local politics since the late 1970s for politicians to affirm their support for tax cuts whilst supporting increases in spending upon programmes which they calculate that the median voter will support. That circle has become harder to square as the presumption has gained ground since the late 1970s that the federal budget ought (according to some fiscal conservatives) always to be balanced or in surplus, or (according to those more willing to use the budget as a counter-cyclical tool) to balance over the course of a business cycle.

Groups, in the form of interest groups pressing for higher expenditure upon various public programmes, are prominent actors and lobbyists in fiscal politics. Teachers' unions favouring increased spending by city governments upon teachers' salaries are one example; defence contractors favouring increased spending by the federal government upon their companies' weapons systems are a second. Such groups help finance politicians' election campaigns, organize to support or oppose their election or re-election, fight for public support through television, and lobby city councils, state assemblies, and the US Congress.

The fragmentation of fiscal policy-making

The fragmentation characteristic of so much policy-making in the United States is revealed in a nearly pure form in fiscal policy. As the preceding section showed, the number of governments involved in its formation in this deeply federal country is large: in consequence, tax policy and rates vary by state, city, county, and local school district. Fragmentation of government results in variation of policy outcome.

Even within the federal government, the number of participants within the executive and Congress is large; so is the extent of fragmentation. Participants' perspectives upon fiscal policy differ, as do their interests in the identity of those who benefit from tax and appropriations legislation and those who do not. The simple fact of bicameralism approximately doubles the number of congressional committees involved; bicameralism also requires that the two chambers agree with each other on every clause in every bill that each passes before legislation may be sent to the president for his signature (or, if he chooses) for his veto.

The House of Representatives devolves formal authority over the writing of tax policy to the Ways and Means Committee, subject only to the House's right to alter the Committee's legislative drafts in floor debate. The Senate similarly devolves authority to its Finance Committee. In practice, however, this clarity and concentration of formal authority in two specialist committees throws but a thin cloak over the complexities of process and fragmentation of informal power. Once protected by House rules from amendment on the House floor, the Ways and Means Committee's drafts are now exposed to them. Accordingly, the committee must attempt to anticipate where its legislative drafts might prove vulnerable to amendment on the House floor or, later, in a conference committee of the House and Senate charged with the task of reconciling the two chambers' drafts. On the floor and in conference committees, the number of participants engaged in legislative drafting is greater than in committee; the number and type of influences which Congressmen exercise upon the legislation on behalf of their constituents' special interests rises commensurately. That complicates the task of building majorities, and reduces the prospects of fending off amendments designed not to address national questions of public concern but to privilege sectional interests. Throughout the drafting of legislation, a wide array of lobbying groups press their cases for special treatment upon Congressmen and senators.

The House and Senate also each fragments its procedures for writing appropriations legislation. Sectional interests capitalize upon fragmentation of spending as they do upon fragmentation of taxation, inducing Congressmen and Senators to attach amendments to appropriations bills which make federal grants to favoured commercial enterprises, charities, universities, groups, and local governments. Why, for example, is there a federal programme to support the growing of sugar cane in Louisiana and sugar beet in the Midwest at prices higher than the free market world price? The answer is that minority interests manage to exploit the fragmentation of congressional committees to secure minority benefits because the costs of their favoured treatment are widely distributed among American taxpayers. Moreover, every Congressman and senator has an interest in preserving the fragmented arrangement because each has special interests of his or her own to protect. 'Log-rolling', an implicit bargain between politicians to respect each other's right to defend politically important special interests within a congressional district or a state, is the outcome. Accordingly, a Congressman from Louisiana might acquire or retain a federal subsidy to support the farming of sugar in his district, whilst another member might succeed in defending a federal subsidy for highway construction in her own district. These pervasive characteristics of the fragmented system of fiscal policy-making in the United States apply to conservatives and liberals alike. Many Congressmen and senators serve their districts' and states' interests by directing federal funds and subsidies to them, only to denounce the aggregate outcome of federal spending for being higher than it need be.

Tension between values of democracy and liberalism

The preceding example suggests that citizens' influences on fiscal policy are unequally distributed. Some, especially those who represent sophisticated organizations of important corporations and interest groups, are well situated to influence elected politicians. Most are also well resourced to exercise influence, experienced in doing so, and skilled in lobbying discreetly in private rather than noisily in public. Others either lack the resources to join an existing organization or fail to overcome the collective action problems involved in forming a new one to defend their interests. The poor fit into both categories, as do those forty million Americans without health care. Inequality of resources between citizens is an empirical fact. So, too, is the inequality of influence over fiscal policy which often flows from it. Yet whilst their influence may be disproportionately great, it does not follow that resource-rich individuals and corporations *determine* fiscal policy. If they did, neither the wealthy nor corporations would be taxed, corporations would not willingly permit federal, state, and city governments to impose costly regulations upon them, and the poor might receive even fewer benefits than they do.

We might hypothesize that organized opinion and interests invariably defeat unorganized opinion and interests in struggles for influence over politicians who write tax and spending laws. The hypothesis is especially likely to be confirmed where the organization in question represents an intense opinion or interest and the unorganized opinion is less intense or indifferent. A good example of the latter is the oil-depletion allowance, a tax break provided for many years to US domestic oil producers, most of whom operated in Texas and Oklahoma and for whom the allowance turned marginal wells into profitable ones and profitable wells into bountiful ones. Whilst producers benefited from the allowance, the US Treasury and consumers of oil paid for it in the form of lost federal tax revenue and the distortion of the energy market. Why did the depletion allowance survive for so long in a system of representative government? Like the sugar programme, the number of direct beneficiaries was tiny and the number of losers large. Yet the programme survived repeated attempts to defeat it: in 1951, when the president and Congress were raising taxes to finance the Korean War and urgently seeking new sources of revenue, liberal US senators pressed for the adoption of an amendment to a tax bill reducing depletion allowances on gas and oil wells. Since Texas and Oklahoma had just four votes, sixty-seven votes came from states where consumer interests in respect of oil taxation would appear to have been dominant. Even in those two states, owners of oil and gas wells were a tiny minority. Yet the amendment lost by seventy-one votes to nine. It did so, first because of the implications of the fact that the four senators from Texas and Oklahoma had no political option but to support the oil industry's position. They had no such option partly because of the self-interest and power of oil well owners, potential contributors to Senate campaigns. But it was also the case that hundreds of thousands of leaseholders in Texas and Oklahoma, workers in the oil industry, pipeline constructors, bank owners, employees, and others depended indirectly upon the oil industry's turnover and profitability.[3]

As with federal sugar, dairy, and catfish subsidies, every Congressman and senator represents at least one concentrated local interest and knows that each of his or her colleagues represents at least one of his or her own. A free, unconstrained, private vote of persons whose only object was to create a fiscal policy wholly in the public interest, as opposed to the political interests of 535 congressional politicians, would eliminate tax breaks for favoured industries. It would also end wasteful expenditures upon local public projects which serve only the electoral needs of the politicians proposing them. But representative government is not government by angels; it is government by politicians who calculate where their electoral interests lie, where their parties' interests lie, and where the public interest lies. Politicians usually put electoral interests first; where they do not, they risk defeat. Since every Congressman and senator behaves similarly, small and spatially concentrated interests win political support from other Congressmen and senators with interests of their own to defend.

Tension between progressive and traditionalist doctrines of economics and politics

Fiscal policy goes to the heart of debates and disputes about distribution. How are the burdens of taxes and benefits of expenditure to be distributed between corporations and individuals? Among individuals, how are taxes to be distributed between types of tax—on sales, property, income, wealth, and on death? At what rates are such taxes to be levied? Above what threshold should a citizen be obliged to pay taxes on income? Should exemptions from taxation (such as the oil depletion allowance) be permitted and, if so, under what conditions and for what reasons? What is to be spent on what programmes and for what reason? How much spending is to be permitted and under what economic circumstances? To what extent should the spending and taxing policies of governments in America counteract the business cycle?

Answers to these questions involve the incidence of taxation and, therefore, its distribution. The answers themselves, and the means by which city councils, state legislatures and governors, the US Congress and president reach them are, accordingly, political. In the United States, as elsewhere, politicians think about these questions by calculating the consequences of their decisions for their electoral safety and their prospective political power. But few politicians are merely calculating machines: most make the decisions that they do in part because of the values which underpin their politics. In fiscal policy, we can place most legislators and most presidents and governors on a continuum dividing progressive and traditionalist doctrines of economics and politics. The division appears in every argument between politicians about every tax or spending bill, but the example of President Bush's so-called economic stimulus bill in 2001–2 illustrates it. Most Republican Congressmen and senators sought to draft a bill which would grant significant benefits to business especially by cutting minimum corporation taxes; most Democratic Congressmen and senators sought to draft a bill which would give direct cash benefits to the working poor, and extend health care and unemployment benefits to the unemployed. Complete victory for either side was not possible, given that Republicans formed the House majority, Democrats formed the Senate majority, and a Republican held the White House, and where the division between progressives and traditionalists corresponded closely to the partisan divide. Since passage of a bill into law required the assent of all three institutions, compromise was essential. However, reaching that compromise was complicated by the difficulty which all sides had in reconciling strongly held values with the need to arrive at an agreement from which they calculated that they

[3] Dallek, R., *Lone Star Rising*, New York, Oxford University Press, 1991.

might benefit in the 2002 mid-term congressional elections.

Calculating prospective political benefits and losses through trade-offs of this kind about taxing and spending is everyday politics in Washington—just as it is in state legislatures and city councils. But such everyday politics are made harder for participants, and more interestingly complicated for observers, precisely because politicians do not just calculate but also act within the framework of values that inform their understanding of politics and which their median supporter typically shares. Reconciling interest and principle is not always as straightforward for politicians as some political scientists suppose.

Key points

- The decisions that politicians make about taxation and spending are typically preceded by and cause intense interest and, often, controversy among affected voters and groups. Such decisions are always freighted with electoral significance.

- Fiscal politics illustrate the fragmentation of politics and policy in the United States especially clearly. The federal, state, and many local governments have the authority to tax and spend. Within each level of government, the politics of fiscal decision-making is further fragmented between bicameral legislatures, parties, committees, and subcommittees.

- Neither citizens' nor legislators' voices are equal in the politics of spending and taxation. Within fragmented institutions, authority and power over both are usually concentrated in specialized committees.

- Whilst policy outcomes affecting, for example, a large and well-resourced industry are often close to that industry's interests, it does not follow that the industry's owners or managers determine the outcome. That is partly because those who benefit from the outcome are more numerous than the ranks of the industry's owners and managers, but also because interests within an industry are often competitive rather than homogeneous.

- The progressive–traditionalist fault-line in taxation policy runs along the division between those who favour using the tax system to redistribute income and those who oppose it. That fault-line has since the 1960s increasingly corresponded with the partisan division between Democrats and Republicans, a division more plainly apparent in the US Congress than in some state legislatures. Clashes between progressives and traditionalists in taxation policy are complicated by each side's need to identify and win the allegiance of the median voter.

Monetary policy

The United States is a single capital market, has a single currency, and one central bank—the Federal Reserve Board ('the Fed'). The dollar is the largest traded international currency, is accepted for payment by corporations worldwide, and held by governments and companies in their reserves. All of the world's trade in oil takes place in US dollars, a measure of the currency's dominance and universal acceptability.

Accordingly, the Fed's decisions are important both for the United States and for the rest of the world. Like the European Central Bank, it has sole authority to set short-term interest rates and to employ other policy instruments with the object of controlling the quantity of money in circulation and, indirectly and with much uncertainty, the rates of inflation, unemployment, and the rate of change of the economy's output of goods and services. Congress stipulated in the 1913 Federal Reserve Act, and the Banking Acts of 1933 and 1935, that the president should appoint the board's members 'with the advice and consent of the Senate' to fourteen-year terms. In writing that provision into the legislation, the president and Congress intended that the Fed's members need not worry about having to yield to pressure from politicians. Instead, they were to have decision-making autonomy from the president, Congress, and from business and other groups' lobbying. And that is how it has worked out.

The non-fragmentation of monetary policy-making

The contrast between the making of fiscal and monetary policy could scarcely be greater. In fiscal policy, the Constitution and statute laws divide authority between the federal, state, and local governments and within each of those layers. Fiscal policy is policy fragmentation exemplified; monetary policy is not. Neither the states, nor local governments, nor the president, nor the secretary of the Treasury, nor Congress has any authority over monetary policy under current law. Instead, those laws give the Fed a monopoly of formal authority. The Fed is in a position of monopoly control: its organization into thirteen Reserve Banks around the country is an expression of the influence of federalist values and procedures, but does not significantly qualify the immense operational authority and power which lie at its centre in Washington.

However, since the Fed inhabits a democratic and competitive world, and since Congress and the president could, if they so wished, weaken its authority by amending the laws that govern its existence, form, and operation, it has in practice to make decisions about monetary policy more sensitively than its monopoly of formal authority might imply. The Fed is operationally autonomous of congressional, presidential, public, or market opinion, but independent of none of them.

Tension between values of democracy and liberalism

Monetary policy is made within a democratic context, but it is not democratically made. Decisions about interest rates are made by members of the Federal Open Market Committee, who are unelected officials supported and informed by expert staff economists and others who subject the large quantities of data at their disposal to high-quality technical analysis and give technical advice accordingly. The legitimacy of Fed staff, as of bureaucrats in general, derives from their being recruited on the basis of their intellectual ability and expertise; at any one time, a high proportion of Open Market Committee members are themselves technically accomplished. By contrast, the legitimacy of Congressmen, senators, and the president lies solely in their election.

These two contrasting sources of legitimacy have sometimes caused tension between unelected Fed officials and elected politicians. Some Congressmen and senators, especially those from rural areas in the Midwest and South, have objected to the Fed's operational autonomy because they think that unelected officials (especially those based in remote Washington, DC) should not enjoy monopoly control over such an important area of public policy. However, most elected politicians recognize that if operational decisions about interest rates were their own rather than the Fed's, they would accede to constituents' pressures to privilege job creation over the control of inflation, and accordingly set lower interest rates than autonomous officials would do—an attractive short-term expedient with high long-term costs. A weaker form of the objection, which finds some support in Congress, is that Congress exercises insufficient legislative oversight (scrutiny) of the Fed. Such stronger oversight would not *entail* looser monetary policy, but markets might *infer* that it would. In consequence, market-makers would probably push long-term interest rates upwards because they feared a rise in the inflation rate and, hence, a reduction in the real value of fixed-interest government securities. The trade-off, therefore, is between enforcing mechanisms of democratic accountability and giving unelected officials the freedom to act as they judge appropriate to achieve low rates of inflation.

Tension between progressive and traditionalist doctrines of economics and politics

Congressmen and senators have objected to the Fed's extensive autonomy and authority on other grounds. Some have argued that in practice Congress has inadequate political resources to constrain the Fed's freedom of action, whilst others have objected to what they argue is the Fed's privileging of the interests and preferences of bankers in general and of New York investment bankers in particular over the interests and preferences of their (frequently indebted) constituents. Both objections have implications for the politics of the tension between progressive and traditionalist doctrines.

The first of these two objections is probably correct. Although Congress is an exceptionally well-resourced legislature, most of the expertise within Washington on the subject of monetary policy lies in the Federal Reserve itself. Few members or staff of the key committees whose responsibility it is to oversee the Fed are experts in monetary economics and finance. Consequently, Fed officials who testify before meetings of Senate and House committees invariably have decisive intellectual advantages over their questioners in terms both of expertise and of experience in monetary policy. In practice, asymmetries of this kind are ineradicable. However, only an unwise Fed official would behave as if she or he presumed that the Fed's asymmetrical advantages of expertise gave it complete freedom of action. In a democracy, that would be a self-defeating stance for bureaucrats to adopt because politicians would resist the presumption.

The second objection has to do with the identity of Fed governors and their staff, and what is taken to be the Fed's characteristic perspective upon economic policy. Most governors have, indeed, been male, white, and either academics or bankers close to powerful financial interests in New York. Much Midwestern and Southern opinion is receptive to the notion that Eastern creditors will sacrifice the broader public interest—and particularly the interests of Midwestern and Southern farmers—to their own narrow financial advantage. That view found its most intense expression following a collapse in agricultural prices in 1893, when small Southern and Western farmers and debtors (often one and the same group) bitterly resented the power of Eastern bankers. William Jennings Bryan exploited their discontent by attempting, but failing, to win the presidency on behalf of marginalized voices of rural debtors.

Bryan's cry against bankers has echoed less strongly through the twentieth century. Nevertheless, suspicions of banks and bankers remains a feature of politics in Western and Southern states, and politicians have often divided on the question of whether the defeat of inflation or of unemployment should take priority. Although Congress has not set an inflation target, nor specified its role as being solely to maintain a low or zero inflation rate, the Fed has in practice often appeared to regard its objective as being the maintenance of low inflation rather than the achievement of other, arguably more progressive, goals. This suggests why the Fed has often been a target for progressives, populists, and liberals who have criticized its accommodation of conservative banking interests, and its allegedly limited concern for the interests of borrowers. In 2001 and 2002, with interest rates low and falling, such critics fell silent. But when real interest rates are once again high or rising, the plight of those who have difficulty in meeting payments on their mortgage, agricultural, or credit card debt might again stir the old populist cries of rage against bankers and their alleged protectors in the Federal Reserve Board.

Key points

- In contrast not only to fiscal policy but also to other areas of public policy, monetary policy is made by a single institution (the Fed) where, in the short term, operational authority is highly concentrated. In the medium term, however, the Fed has to take account of other opinions and pressures both from within government and from group and public opinion.

- If an elected body such as Congress were to control interest rates, markets would anticipate a rise in the rate of inflation. That suggests that a body autonomous of elected politicians (of which the Fed is an example) is required to determine short-term interest rates. But autonomy comes at the price of Fed officials not being directly accountable to the electorate.

- Some critics contend that, for much of its history, the Fed has by its decisions privileged the interests of creditors over debtors. However, given the Fed's statutory obligation to limit inflation, it is an outcome that it probably cannot avoid.

Conclusion

The content and formation of economic policy illuminate the themes in this book, the underlying structures and values of American politics, and the differing roles accorded to public authority and private capital in America. We have noted that the fragmentation of domestic economic policy formation shows itself in sharp relief in fiscal policy, where the two elected branches of Federal government, and all three levels of government within the federal system, are politically significant players. Yet we have seen that the familiar account of fragmentation does not hold in the case of monetary policy. In fiscal policy, there are tens of thousands of players in many governments; in monetary policy, there is one player with operational command—the Federal Reserve Board. And so it is that the two aspects of domestic economic policy—fiscal and monetary—present two contrasting windows onto American politics. In the one case, the politics of taxing and spending, we find resounding confirmation of American politics as disaggregated, of authority being dispersed throughout the federal system, and of authority and power over public policy in Washington being divided between the executive branch and a bicameral legislature. Yet we find no such confirmation in the case of monetary policy. Here is a case where Congress and the president, expressing their will in a series of Acts of Congress, have determined that authority over monetary policy shall be aggregated, concentrated, and undivided. In the long term, of course, Congress could write new legislation which changed the rules. But because of the special sensitivity of markets to direct political interference with the conduct of monetary policy, that is unlikely.

We have also noted that the tension between democratic values of representative government and the executive's accountability to the legislature, on the one hand, and the liberal value of equality, on the other, repeatedly show themselves in fiscal policy, the politics of taxing and spending. The equality of every citizen's vote clashes with the inequality of access to politicians and officials in policy-making roles in legislatures, executive agencies (such as the US Treasury), and the Federal Reserve. Special interests often succeed in winning special taxing or spending favours from Congress and from state legislatures. But because such interests are numerous and spatially concentrated, Congressmen, senators, and state legislators acquiesce in symbiotic and parasitical exchanges of mutual support for subsidies.

Finally, this chapter has emphasized the tension between progressive and traditionalist doctrines of economics and politics in a policy area where the results matter to every citizen and politician. No politician can afford to be, or appear to be, indifferent to the levels and incidence of taxation, or to the consequences of (for example) the Federal Reserve running a tight money policy. Voters' jobs, incomes, and general welfare depend upon the choices which politicians and officials make between options for economic policy. Little wonder, then, that a system which makes elections so common a method of recruitment to public authorities and which makes election cycles often so short (every 730 days in the case of the US House of Representatives) should make politicians so sensitive to the political consequences of their choices.

QUESTIONS

1 Who determines economic policy in America?

2 Whose interests does US federal fiscal policy serve?

3 Whose interests does US federal monetary policy serve?

4 Why does the institutional fragmentation of the processes of US economic policy-making not lead to incoherence of policy content?

FURTHER READING

L. Berman (1979), *The Office of Management and Budget and the Presidency, 1921–1979* (Princeton, NJ: Princeton University Press). Assesses one of the key executive branch actors in the formulation of budgetary and economic policy.

S. Collender, *Guide to the Federal Budget* (annual publication, Washington, DC: Urban Institute Press). Clarifies the contentious and complex process of writing budgets into law.

L. Fisher (1975), *Presidential Spending Power* (Princeton, NJ: Princeton University Press). Examines the constitutional powers of the president.

W. Greider (1987), *Secrets of the Temple* (New York: Simon & Schuster). A more sensationalist and entertaining account of the Fed than Woolley (below).

H. Stein (1988), *Presidential Economics* (Washington, DC: American Enterprise Institute). The chairman of the Council of Economic Advisers under President Nixon gives a fascinating account of the often difficult relationship between the two ends of Pennsylvania Avenue.

J. Woolley (1984), *Monetary Politics* (Cambridge: Cambridge University Press). The best simple guide to the history and operation of the Fed.

WEB LINKS

www.ft.com and www.wsj.com, the internet sites of the *Financial Times* and the *Wall Street Journal*, are useful sources of current and historical information upon and commentary upon economic and financial policy.

Official federal government data on economic and financial issues are available at www.fedstats.gov. The Brookings Institution at www.brook.edu and the American Enterprise Institute at www.aei.org provide analysis of economic policies, and links to websites of governments, interest groups, and foundations which publish analyses on economic and financial matters.

14 Foreign policy

John Dumbrell

READER'S GUIDE

This chapter considers both the process and content of contemporary US foreign policy. It focuses on debates in the post-cold war era about the purposes of US foreign policy, and the best means (multilateral or unilateral) to achieve them. The chapter discusses the role of the US president in managing contemporary foreign policy, as well as various challenges to the president's dominance. The chapter concludes with some recapitulation and remarks about the nature of US foreign policy in an era of international terrorism.

Introduction

Non-Americans are generally neither slow nor reluctant to criticize American foreign policy. In so doing, foreign critics of the US tend to bear out the adage that familiarity breeds contempt. In a way that is true of no other country, leading figures in the American foreign policy process appear regularly on television screens across the globe. News coverage of international issues—from the Middle East to the Pacific, Somalia to Serbia, Afghanistan to Northern Ireland—regularly invokes the central importance of US foreign policy.

Foreign perceptions of America's international posture are often contradictory, and also frequently betray a degree of ignorance about how American foreign policy is made. The US is, for example, often accused of being both imperialist (seeking to dominate the world) and isolationist (seeking to withdraw from the world). An informed understanding of US foreign policy could do worse than to begin with two key realizations. First, in international terms, America is different. Secondly, if America is different, then so is its foreign policy.

America's foreign policy traditions embody wide-ranging, and deep-seated, national debates about the true purpose of American international power. Such debates are traditionally structured around an axis of internationalism versus isolationism. These debates constitute part of the division between liberalism and conservatism, a core concern of this book. Some contemporary implications of this debate are drawn out in the following section of this chapter. The US is also different in terms of the nature and extent of its global power. It is the post-cold war superpower—in some formulations, the first ever 'hyperpower'. It enjoys an unmatched 'hard' power, evidenced by its unrivalled military superiority (see Box 14.1). America also exhibits a mighty 'soft' or cultural power, wielded by various international culture warriors—not least in Hollywood and in the new technology empire stretching out from Seattle. In recent times, of course, the US has appeared extremely vulnerable to international threats, whether in the form of oil price rises in the 1970s or devastating 'asymmetrical' terrorist attacks in 2001. Many of America's foreign critics, in fact, do not fully appreciate the limits to American power. Nevertheless, in terms of its international power potential and its actual global power projection, there is no doubt that America is different.

Foreign policy is also different. The US has its own way of making foreign policy. The apparent inconsistency, even hypocrisy, in elements of US foreign policy can often be traced to constitutional doctrines of separation of powers and power-sharing between executive and legislative branches of government. As in so many other areas, majoritarianism and limited government conflict. Foreign policy is also different, however, in a slightly different sense. In the other main areas of American public policy (economic, environmental, social, even foreign economic), policy outcomes are the result of highly decentralized and pluralistic policy-making processes. The US Congress, the state governments, interest groups, and various other actors enjoy considerable influence. The foreign policy process is at once less open and more centralized than in other areas. State governments do not vie with the federal government here. The need for secrecy and dispatch, allied to particular constitutional arrangements, makes foreign policy pre-eminently the province of the executive branch and its presidential head.

Key points

- The US has its own unique foreign policy traditions and processes.
- The US is the post-cold war superpower.
- The making of foreign policy is far more centralized than the making of domestic policy.

Box 14.1 **Is America different?**
American military power

Annual defence spending (US rates as proposed in President Bush's defence budget, February 2002) (billion pounds):

US	246
Russia	30
Japan	27
Britain	23.5
France	16.8
Germany	14
China	4.3

Source: *The Times*, 12 Feb. 2002.

The US defence budget in 2001–2 was greater than that of the next nine countries in the world combined. It spent around three times more on research and development than the next six countries combined.

[handwritten margin note: limited american power]

The search for doctrine

The fundamental purpose of American foreign policy is, to risk stating the obvious, to further the interests of the United States in the wider world. The definition of these interests, of course, poses the problem. For purposes of analysis and explication, we may see US foreign policy as having, throughout its history, two major purposive strands: material interests and export of American democratic ideals. Material interests, which are emphasized by commentators working in the realist tradition of international relations scholarship, are dominated by security considerations. Security for America itself and for American assets abroad constitutes the essence of foreign policy doctrine. Democracy promotion, emphasized by commentators more inclined to the idealist tradition of international relations scholarship, connects directly to the notion of American exceptionalism. US foreign policy leaders, in this view, accept and act on the belief that America is different. The US has a particular historical destiny: to export American-style liberal democracy, set in its capitalist, free-market economic context.

These two purposive strands—material interests and promotion of democratic values—are not mutually exclusive. Most US foreign policy leaders would argue, invoking arguments that derive from Thomas Jefferson, that they are mutually reinforcing. US security can only be strengthened if the world turns to liberal, capitalist democracy. Surely the spread of democratic capitalism can only benefit American prosperity? Unfortunately, the world is usually not so simple. Perceived security and economic interests have often caused the US to support dictatorial regimes in the developing world, and to turn a blind eye to abuses of human rights in other countries. Liberal capitalist democracies can be competitors to the US, not just reliable trading partners. Nevertheless, the rational goal of US foreign policy can usefully be seen as the purposive unification of material interests with the promotion of democratic values.

Doctrines in US foreign policy

During the cold war, most American foreign policy leaders saw their main purpose as the containment of Soviet communism. The central idea here was to defeat Soviet communism by resisting its global expansion. Thus could US interests (extinction of the 'Soviet threat') and values (promotion and protection of democracy) be unified. If prevented from spreading, the communist system would expire from a combination of internal economic inefficiency and unpopularity.

Particular expressions of intent within the history of American foreign relations are often labelled 'doctrines'. Many foreign policy 'doctrines' were, in fact, unilateral warnings to enemies, often designed to mobilize domestic opinion as much as to deter foreign foes. Several doctrines served notice that the US would not hesitate to act to protect key material interests, such as Western hemispheric domination and access to Middle Eastern oil.

Though properly used to refer to the various statements and injunctions summarized in Box 14.2, the term 'foreign policy doctrine' is also used more broadly to convey the sense of a 'grand strategy' or integrating purpose. In cold war conditions, the grand strategy was containment of communism, as devised by George Kennan in the later 1940s. Following the cold war's end, the US had no comparable integrating strategy, beyond a generalized commitment to security, prosperity, and promotion of democratic values. In the early 1990s, State Department policy planners consciously embarked upon a coordinated effort—dubbed the 'Kennan sweepstakes' (Brinkley 1997)—to discover a successor to containment. These doctrinal sweepstakes lasted, in effect, for over ten years after the fall of the Berlin Wall in 1989. Contending views about the merits of democracy promotion, humanitarian intervention, unilateralism, and multilateralism in foreign affairs preoccupied US foreign policy elites into the new century. The framework for these debates, however, was provided by that same dialectical opposition so familiar to students of the history of American

Box 14.2 Some American presidential foreign policy doctrines

- **The Monroe Doctrine** (1823): warning by President James Monroe against European intervention in the Western hemisphere

- **The Truman Doctrine** (1947): warning to the Soviet Union, made in the context of US aid to Greece and Turkey ('containment' of Soviet power in Europe)

- **The Eisenhower Doctrine** (1957): warning to the Soviet Union not to intervene in the Middle East

- **The Nixon Doctrine** (1969): commitment, made during the Vietnam War, to render primarily non-military and indirect military assistance to fight communism in the developing world

- **The Carter Doctrine** (1980): warning to the Soviet Union in the Persian Gulf

- **The Reagan Doctrine** (1985): undertaking to assist anti-communism in the developing world.

(On debates about a possible Clinton Doctrine, see Dumbrell (2002). In June 2002 President G. W. Bush issued a defence of American pre-emptive, 'preventive' military action against possible threats to international security. Some commentators labelled this the Bush Doctrine.)

foreign policy—the paired doctrines of isolationism and internationalism.

The dialogue between isolationists and internationalists relates, albeit in a complex way, to wider conflicts, between traditionalism and progressivism. The issue is complicated by the reluctance of almost everyone—Eric Nordlinger (1995) was an exception—to accept the label 'isolationist'. The word 'isolationism' survives primarily as a term of abuse, evoking images of provincialist bigotry and insularity. In the sense of denoting an absence of international interconnectedness, 'isolationism' may also be deemed a characteristic which has never applied to American foreign policy. However, 'isolationism' and 'internationalism' are terms which summon up, as can no others, identifiable positions within historical and contemporary debates about US foreign policy and its purposes. Whatever the historical complexities, advocates of the two positions also have clear perceptions about themselves: 'isolationists' as upholders of traditional, 'America First' values, 'internationalists' as liberals and progressives.

The isolationist/internationalist dialectical opposition is often expressed in terms of American exceptionalism. Isolationists, drawing upon Puritan doctrines of the 'city on a hill', seek to provide a model for the world by achieving perfection at home. International entanglements, treaties, commitments, protocols, alliances, and obligations are all obstacles to the achievement of that goal. Isolationists see themselves as offering the world the vision of freedom in action.

Internationalists, on the other hand, have dominated US foreign policy-making since the Second World War. They seek to intervene in foreign conflicts, to make treaties and alliances, and to advance the global, preponderant power and reach of the US—all as a way of promoting its values as well as its security. The two traditions draw on differing interpretations of the American 'national interest'.

Democracy promotion

In his second inaugural address, in 1997, President Bill Clinton declared that, for the first time in history, more people on earth were living under democracy than under dictatorship. Clinton presented this as a triumph for the policy of democratic 'enlargement'. An early entry in the Kennan sweepstakes, democratic enlargement was an attempt to place global democracy promotion at the heart of post-cold war foreign policy. It was linked to the idea of 'liberal peace', deriving ultimately from the international relations philosophy of Immanuel Kant (1724–1804). Its central concept was that democracies, especially when linked by trade, do not go to war with one another. Democracy promotion, therefore, promotes enhanced security as well as ideals.

The case for prioritizing democracy promotion may be stated briefly. Enhancing global democracy has economic as well as security benefits. Linked into notions of market opportunity and US-led economic globalization, democracy promotion provides the rationale for a new American internationalism. Moreover, as Clinton apologists always maintained, it does not have to collapse into starry-eyed unrealism. A programme of global democracy promotion could be keyed into US economic and security interests, as well as into a coherent view of which areas of the world were most important to the interests of the United States. Undiscriminating, limitless, 'feel-good' democracy promotion is difficult to defend. It soon collapses into arrogance, over-extension, and resentful retreat. A more balanced version of the doctrine, which somehow manages to balance a sensitivity to interests with an avoidance of blatant hypocrisy, may indeed be a viable basis for a sustainable American internationalism.

In contemporary American foreign policy debates, arguments about democracy promotion usually develop into arguments about military intervention for humanitarian purposes. Towards the end of its second term, the Clinton administration edged clearly towards the view that the US military should be used more frequently, and less hesitantly, for humanitarian ends. Such a policy would have signalled the end of the caution about the application of military power which was part of the legacy of the Vietnam War. Though never entirely abandoning its instincts for pragmatic restraint, the Clinton administration committed troops to Bosnia in 1999 and at least presented the case for a substantive doctrine of humanitarian intervention.

The case against democracy promotion and the kind of 'liberal hawkism' advanced in the later Clinton years is quite straightforward. It is the view that interests always trump ideals. Interests may be dressed up as ideals, but should not be confused with them. One interpretation of the history of the Clinton administration, indeed, would argue that, in practice, democracy promotion is always abandoned for narrower, interests-based realism as events run their course. As well as advocating humanitarian intervention, the later Clinton administration also moved somewhat away from cooperation with allies and international organizations (examples here include the Kosovo bombing without UN

sanction and the 1998 Sudan and Afghanistan air strikes).

Further objections to democracy promotion and humanitarian intervention are not difficult to formulate. Discussions of globalizing democracy, of the kind in which Clinton indulged himself in his second inaugural address, encounter severe problems of definition. Here we encounter the dilemmas, frequently cited in European accounts of these issues, over US cultural imperialism and over variant forms of democracy. American democracy promoters are often held to define 'democracy' in relatively narrow and procedural terms (free elections, competing political parties, and so on) rather than in terms of human rights, including women's and minority rights. Excessive optimism has allowed the US to claim democratic success when various countries have simply opened up to world trade and made cosmetic improvements to electoral procedure.

Critiques of American democracy promotion also often raise the question of leverage. Can democracy be imposed or just encouraged? The US has a range of instruments at its disposal: from education programmes in the developing world, practical help with organizing elections and diplomatic pressure, to sanctions and military force. At least since the era of the Vietnam War, it has tended to balk at democracy imposition and nation-building. Nonetheless, most recent US military interventions (see Box 14.3) have had democracy promotion, indeed nation-building, dimensions.

Unilateralism and multilateralism

In contemporary foreign policy debates, the anti-democracy promotion cause tends to be dominated by arguments for American unilateralism. Unilateralists stand as opponents of liberal internationalism and the commitment to nation-building. Both the George Bush (1989–93) and Clinton administrations tended to support multilateralism, certainly at the level of public rhetoric. Multilateralism—the securing of American power within formal and ad hoc alliance structures—was at the centre both of Bush's New World Order and of Clinton's notion of democratic enlargement. Multilateralism

Box 14.3 Major US military interventions since the end of the cold war

1989–90	Invasion of Panama (President G. H. W. Bush)
1990–1	Gulf crisis and war against Iraq (Desert Shield and Desert Storm: President G. H. W. Bush)
1992–4	Intervention in Somalian civil conflict (Operation Restore Hope: Presidents G. H. W. Bush and Clinton)
1993–5	Air strikes in Bosnia and enforcement of no-fly zone (President Clinton)
1993–9	US participation in United Nations peacekeeping force in Macedonia (President Clinton)
1993–2001	Various air strikes against Iraq (Presidents Clinton and G. W. Bush)
1994	Military intervention in Haiti (President Clinton).
1995–	US participation in NATO peacekeeping and stabilization forces in Bosnia (Presidents Clinton and G. W. Bush)
1998	Air strikes on Sudan (President Clinton)
1998	Air strikes on Afghanistan (President Clinton)
1999	NATO war against Serbia (President Clinton)
2001–2	Onset of war on terrorism, initially involving war against Taleban regime in Afghanistan (President G. W. Bush)

involved a sharing of risk and expense, a widening of the burdens of world leadership, and a way of excluding and exposing 'rogue states'. Above all, it was a way of neutralizing opposition framed in terms of resistance to 'American imperialism'. Secretary of State Madeleine Albright warned in 1998 of 'a widespread backlash, tinged with anti-Americanism, against free markets' (Albright 1998: 55). Chalmers Johnson (2000) coined the term 'blowback' to describe a growing international political and cultural resistance to America's massive post-cold war power. Working *with* allies, *with* international organizations, is seen by multilateralists as a precautionary counter to 'blowback' (see Box 14.4).

From the 'exemplarist' perspective of unilateralism, procedural multilateralism simply limits America's freedom of action. As the global superpower, the US has no need to compromise with allies. Many international decision-making and cooperative forums are actually dominated, so the argument goes, by anti-American sentiment. Contemporary American unilateralism is not necessarily isolationist. Indeed, it can be argued that it is precisely America's special role as the ultimate guarantor of global order which makes America unique, and which makes constraining cooperation inappropriate. Far from entirely rejecting democracy promotion, some conservative unilateralists also argue that the fundamental purpose of US foreign policy is the projection of democratic values (Muravchik 1996). In practice, however, realist arguments for unilateralism predominate over internationalist, idealist ones. Republican (and some Democrat) conservatives exhibit contempt for 'foreign policy as social work'. International co-operation—let us take the example of international arms control agreements—is likely to be dismissed as utopian and inimical to US interests. Arms control agreements, inherently unverifiable and unenforceable as they are, merely inhibit the gains to American security made possible by advances in military technology. They also perpetuate the myth that American power is in any way equivalent to that enjoyed by other countries.

A defensible position in the unilateralism versus multilateralism debate is that ends matter more than means, and that the US should employ such procedures (unilateralist or multilateralist) as are appropriate. After all, unilateralism and multilateralism are modes of power projection, rather than goals in themselves. The putatively 'multilateralist' George H. W. Bush acted unilaterally when he ordered the invasion of Panama in 1989. Few 'unilateralists' actually wish entirely to see the US withdraw from regimes of international law or from the United Nations or NATO. Rather, the debate should be seen in terms of a presumption in favour of either multilateralism or unilateralism. Defined in this manner, we see the contemporary Congress (certainly in the era 1995–2001) as 'unilateralist'. The G. H. W. Bush and Clinton administrations were 'multilateralist', and the

Box 14.4 Core academic debate
Multilateralism versus unilateralism

Arguments for multilateralism

- recognizes global complexity and interconnectedness

- lends greater legitimacy to American international actions

- promotes international security by strengthening international organizations like the United Nations

- minimizes international resentment at the extent of American global power

- promotes efficiency by pooling resources.

Secretary of State Colin Powell: 'You can't be unilateralist. The world is too complicated'. (*Time*, 10 Sept. 2001)

Phillip S. Meilinger: 'Working with allies is a fundamental principle of American foreign policy'. (*Foreign Policy*, Jan.–Feb. 2002, p. 77)

Arguments for unilateralism

- recognizes the reality of American international primacy (America is different)

- recognizes that the US has a particular responsibility to guarantee international order

- recognizes the difficulty of cooperating militarily with less technologically sophisticated allies

- promotes America's freedom of action

- allows the US to focus on its own national interests.

Stephen G. Brooks and William C. Wohlforth, 2002: 'The world finds it unfair, undemocratic, annoying, and sometimes downright frightening to have so much power concentrated in the hands of one state, especially when the United States aggressively goes its own way. But given the weight and prominence of U.S. power on the world stage, some unease among other countries is inevitable no matter what Washington does.' (*Foreign Affairs*, vol. 81, no. 4, pp. 28–9)

George W. Bush administration (at least in 2001–2) 'unilateralist'. The Republican Party has tended strongly to espouse unilateralism in recent years, notably in military and regional policy issue areas. The antagonism between multilateralism and unilateralism, however, is not entirely reducible to a framework of liberalism versus conservatism. On international trade issues, labour and environmental groups—generally associated with the Democratic Party—tend to favour 'unilateralist' options. In a sense, economic globalization (discussed at length in the following chapter) represents the ultimate in contemporary multilateralism.

Key points

- The end of the cold war stimulated a conscious quest for new doctrine.

- Older traditions of internationalism and isolationism have been revived and adapted to post-cold war conditions.

- Democracy promotion and humanitarian intervention have occupied centre stage in recent debates about the purpose of US foreign policy.

- The most conspicuous current debate is between advocates of multilateralism and of unilateralism.

Presidential leadership of foreign policy

As every textbook on the subject points out, the US president has particular constitutional strengths in the area of foreign policy. He is given constitutional authority to negotiate treaties and is commander-in-chief of American armed forces. Presidential domination of foreign policy, however, rests more on practical arguments about the need for strong leadership in a dangerous world than on the Constitution of 1787 (constitutional foreign policy responsibilities are outlined in Box 14.5).

Presidents can, and generally do, dominate foreign policy. Invocation of the need for secrecy, rapid decisions, and sure direction—especially in the eras of nuclear (and other) weapons of mass destruction and international terrorism—bolster presidential authority. Key decisions in foreign policy, however, are rarely made by presidents on their own. Over time—and this certainly was the intention behind the Constitution—the president has to share power. Most obviously, he has to share power with the US Congress. Only Congress can declare war and only Congress has the constitutional authority to raise money for war and diplomacy. The following historical survey of cold war and post-cold war presidential foreign policy leadership will concentrate on the tension between president and Congress. But, as will be drawn out later in this chapter, the president's partners (and sometime rivals) in power also include his own bureaucracy, various organized interests, and US public opinion.

Cold war presidents

Presidential leadership did not go entirely unchallenged, even in the early days of the cold war. President Harry Truman's handling of the Korean conflict (1950–3) was consistently criticized in Congress. The Vietnam conflict, of course, brought major challenges in the form of congressional action, especially in the early 1970s, and organized societal protest. The 1973 War Powers Resolution required presidents to consult Congress before committing troops; once forces were engaged, they

---

Box 14.5 Constitutional influences
Foreign policy responsibilities under the US Constitution

Congress (Article I)

- right to declare war and 'provide for the common defense'

- power 'to regulate foreign commerce'

- Senate confirms major presidential appointments (including secretaries of state and defense)

- Senate ratifies treaties, by a two-thirds majority

- Other relevant powers:
  oversight and investigation of the executive branch
  the legislative 'power of the purse'
  powers to make all laws which shall be 'necessary and proper for carrying into execution' the explicit powers given to Congress in the Constitution.

President (Article II)

- 'The President shall be the commander in chief of the army and navy of the United States . . .'

- nominates major appointees

- negotiates treaties

- other relevant powers:
  'he shall receive ambassadors and other public ministers'
  'he shall take care that the laws be faithfully executed'
  power of veto over legislation.

should be deployed for no more than sixty days unless Congress granted an extension to ninety.

Despite all this, under cold war conditions it was generally relatively easy for presidents to dominate the policy process. In times of crisis (real, imagined, or constructed), Congress, the public, and organized interests ultimately deferred to the leader. A glance at the experience of the final two cold war presidents will help to illuminate this assertion.

The presidential leadership of Ronald Reagan (1981–9) was idiosyncratic in the extreme. Notoriously ill-informed over policy detail and often content to abdicate control, Reagan nonetheless maintained presidential dominance. He had his share of policy reversals, mainly at the hands of Democrats in Congress. These included measures designed to block aid to the rightist, Contra rebels in Nicaragua. The ensuing Iran–Contra scandal, involving the illegal funnelling of money to the Contras from the sale of arms to Iran, called into question Reagan's whole approach to foreign policy leadership. However, the evidence of the 1980s does not justify the view that presidential domination of foreign policy was seriously threatened. Under Reagan, the 1983 invasion of Grenada and covert operations in Central America both proceeded without significant interference from congressional war powers. Above all, Congress stood on the sidelines as Reagan's highly personal dialogue with Soviet leader Mikhail Gorbachev developed, and the cold war entered into its final phase.

President G. H. W. Bush (1989–93) was frequently and publicly contemptuous of the foreign policy prerogative of Congress. Panama was invaded in 1989 with no apparent concern for war powers legislation. Bush did seek legislative authorization before commencing military action against Iraq in January 1991. However, the clear preference within the Bush administration was always for conducting foreign policy by means of presidentially declared National Security Directives. Looking to the post-cold war era, Bush's foreign policy team were concerned to develop ground rules for a new world order in which presidential domination would continue. Bush took his share of criticism, for example, over his perceived failure of leadership as Yugoslavia disintegrated. Senate disapproval of John Tower, nominated by Bush as defense secretary, was an important early

defeat in 1989. Nevertheless, in these years of transition to a completely altered policy-making environment, there was no question where dominant power resided. It resided in the White House.

Post-cold war presidents

By 1992 the old enemy, the Soviet Union, no longer existed. At this juncture, many observers saw the future as one of decentralization and disaggregation of the foreign policy-making process. Congress would, it was widely felt, become more assertive as trade policy, a key priority for legislators, moved up the agenda. Geo-economics seemed poised to displace security and geopolitics. Without the integrating force of the Soviet threat, foreign policy would threaten to spin out of the president's control. Interest groups, even state governments, might come to challenge executive authority. Some years after the cold war's end, James M. Scott (1998: 406) actually proclaimed the arrival of 'the era of interbranch policy making'.

Reviewing the experience of America's first post-cold war president, Bill Clinton (1993–2001), we can attempt to test these prophecies and judgements. Even before the Republican congressional election victories of 1994, the legislature certainly was prepared to challenge White House direction of foreign policy. For the first time since the Vietnam War, Congress flexed its war-funding muscles. Threats were made to cut off funds to US troops engaged in missions to Africa. The early Clinton period, however, also saw significant and successful assertions of presidential authority. The North American Free Trade Agreement was passed by Congress in 1993; Haiti was invaded in 1994 as part of a forceful assertion of executive authority. The trajectory of Clinton's development as a foreign policy leader was profoundly affected by the Republican take-over of Congress at the start of 1995. From that point onwards, Clinton was concerned, by a mixture of compromise, confrontation, and policy pre-emption, to prevent Republican usurpation of key decisions. Challenges over policy towards Bosnia signalled a major shift in direction for the White House. Policy towards Cuba was virtually abdicated to Congress and relevant interest groups.

Nor could public humiliation be entirely avoided, as in the Senate rejection, in October 1999, of the Comprehensive Test Ban Treaty.

All this, however, did not amount to an end of the president's ability to set priorities and to retain control of the broad management of most high-profile policy areas. Clinton was able to claim important victories in regard to the North Atlantic Treaty Organization enlargement of 1998, and to his pragmatic policy of trading with China in 2000. The 1999 Kosovo conflict again illustrated the difficulty of challenging presidents once the decision to take military action has been made. Similar lessons, not least for the War Powers Resolution, were taught by the post-1995 deployment of US troops in Bosnia.

Clinton bequeathed to his successor, Republican President George W. Bush, a foreign policy environment in which presidents (especially in non-economic areas) were able to set agendas. The preferences of the new administration were less multilateralist, more inclined to stout defence of fairly narrowly defined American interests, than its predecessor. Bush found that the new emphasis on unilateralism—notably his withdrawal from the Kyoto Protocol on climate change in May 2001—upset foreign allies far more than it stimulated opposition to presidential leadership at home.

Leading congressional Democrats, especially following the achievement of a narrow Democratic majority in the Senate (June 2001) did criticize Bush's unilateralism. The development of National Missile Defense was seen by many Democrats as threatening to destabilize the international arms control order established by the 1972 Anti-Ballistic Missile Treaty. (In early 2002, the Bush administration announced its rejection of the ABM Treaty.) Congressional criticism of the administration in

2001, however, did not amount to a sustained and significant challenge to presidential direction of foreign policy.

Following the September 2001 terrorist attacks, presidential leadership was reaffirmed. The resolution allowing Bush to wage war in Afghanistan—not a declaration of war, rather a congressional agreement to support the president's discretion—involved a linguistic compromise over the issue of war powers. Unsurprisingly, the overwhelming response to the 2001 terrorist attacks was to look for strong presidential direction. Bob Dole, former Kansas senator and 1996 Republican presidential candidate, described the proper role for president and Congress in wartime as 'to keep their arms around each other'. Yet Bush still was not given a completely blank cheque of authority. In October 2001, for example, Congress denied him blanket authority to impose sanctions on any state suspected of harbouring terrorists. However, during late 2001 and into 2002, the 'war on terrorism' proceeded under strong presidential direction.

Key points

- The cold war was an era of presidential dominance of foreign policy. Its end seemed to point to greater foreign policy decentralization, and to challenges to presidential dominance.

- President Clinton's dominance of foreign policy was frequently challenged, but he managed to retain control of America's foreign policy agenda.

- The 2001 'war on terrorism' appeared to reaffirm presidential dominance.

The foreign policy presidency

The foregoing discussion, principally concerned with presidential leadership of foreign policy in competition with the US Congress, concentrated on the person of the president. The 'foreign policy

presidency', however, consists of more than one person. In this section, we review the roles played by the main foreign policy actors and institutions within the executive branch of the federal government.

Secretary of state and national security adviser

After the president, the principal bureaucratic leader of US foreign policy is the secretary of state. The secretary heads the State Department, an institution which currently employs about 30,000 people, many of them posted in embassies overseas. The State Department is actually something of a bureaucratic minnow. Under threat from budget cuts in the late 1990s, State Department employees took to displaying badges reading, 'JUST ONE PER CENT', as an indication of the proportion of federal tax dollars devoted to the Department's activities. Some recent secretaries of state have been highly effective foreign policy operators. Several of the most effective—such as James Baker under George H. W. Bush—have tended to act as rather freewheeling policy advisers and policy implementers, rather than as managers and leaders of the State Department itself. Colin Powell, George W. Bush's Secretary of State, saw it as an important part of his job to restore strong morale and sense of purpose at the State Department. At least in the early (pre-war on terrorism) phase of the Bush presidency, this preoccupation was seen as weakening Powell's substantive impact on policy.

In seeking foreign policy assistance, presidents tend to prefer advisers with relatively light bureaucratic baggage. They are especially attracted to the national security adviser, who operates from the White House and partakes more of the role of presidential 'courtier' than does the secretary of state. The NSA clearly and unequivocally serves the president, rather than being in any degree of thrall to bureaucratic or legislative interests. Some NSAs have become major public figures. Henry Kissinger, NSA to President Nixon between 1969 and 1974, is the paradigmatic recent example of a powerful, freewheeling foreign policy 'Lone Ranger'. (Kissinger's assumption of the formal role of secretary of state in 1973 did not alter his approach.) Some presidents have tried to ameliorate the potential for conflict between the NSA and the secretary of state by designating the former as 'thinker' and the latter as 'doer'. The job of the NSA and his staff thus becomes one primarily of policy initiation and conceptualiza-tion, while the State Department concerns itself with implementation. In practice, this distinction has always broken down. All recent presidents—George H. W. Bush with Brent Scowcroft, Clinton with Tony Lake, G. W. Bush with Condoleezza Rice—have been tempted to use their NSAs to 'do' as well as to 'think' (see Box 14.6).

The almost ontological scope for bureaucratic warfare between the White House and the State Department can only be successfully managed by firm presidential adjudication. Differences of opinion within an administration can be healthy. As Alexander George (1980) argues, presidents should be exposed to multiple advocacy: the clear articulation of contrasting policy positions. A consistent reluctance by presidents to adjudicate, however, leads to confusion and public harm to the administration. (Most accounts of the presidency of Jimmy Carter, especially in the period 1977–9, see Carter as failing to adjudicate successfully between Secretary of State Cyrus Vance and National Security Adviser Zbigniew Brzezinski.)

The Pentagon and Central Intelligence Agency

During the early part of the presidency of George W. Bush, the central rivalry between foreign policy principals was not so much between national security adviser and secretary of state as between Secretary of State Colin Powell and Defense Secretary Donald Rumsfeld. Again, the president was widely accused of failing adequately to reconcile or adjudicate the opposing positions. Powell tended towards caution and multilateralism, Rumsfeld towards confrontation and unilateralism. (Bush's preferred method of adjudication involved his siding on various issues with two key, or 'swing', figures in his foreign policy hierarchy: NSA Rice and Vice-President Richard Cheney.)

Rivalry between the State Department and the Defense Department (housed in the Pentagon, the world's largest office building, just over the Virginia perimeter of Washington, DC) is not uncommon. State, after all, represents the viewpoint of America's diplomats, the Pentagon that of

---

Box 14.6 Presidents, secretaries of state, and national security advisers since 1989

President George H. W. Bush (1989–93)

secretaries of state: James Baker (1989–92); Lawrence Eagleburger (1992–3)
national security adviser: Brent Scowcroft

President Bill Clinton (1993–2001)

secretaries of state: Warren Christopher (1993–7); Madeleine Albright (1997–2001)
national security advisers: Anthony Lake (1993–7); Sandy Berger (1997–2001)

President George W. Bush (2001–)

secretary of state: Colin Powell (2001–)
national security adviser: Condoleezza Rice (2001–)

America's military. With its massive spending entitlements, the Pentagon is, of course, a massive bureaucratic player. In 2001, even following a period of post-cold war cutbacks, the Pentagon enjoyed a daily spending budget of approximately one billion dollars. It would be quite wrong, however, to regard the Pentagon as an automatic advocate of military aggression. Since the era of the Vietnam War, the US military has been extremely cautious about committing military force in situations where overwhelming American superiority and clear exit points to the conflict are not evident. The US military has also in recent years been engaged in more or less constant redefinitions of mission and internal changes. Rumsfeld himself came into office in 2001 as an advocate of the so-called Revolution in Military Affairs: the injunction to abandon cold war military postures. The 2001 war on terrorism highlighted the problems of asymmetrical warfare, where the US faces apparently weak—yet highly flexible and in some ways technologically sophisticated—foes.

The job of the secretary of defense is to achieve a balance between military modernization and military readiness. Most recent defense secretaries have acted primarily as managers of military affairs, rather than as independent foreign policy principals. In conditions of war, however, the division between defence and foreign policy tends to break down. Secretaries of Defense Robert McNamara, Richard Cheney, and Donald Rumsfeld became major foreign policy actors during, respectively, the Vietnam, Gulf, and war on terrorism conflicts. The defense secretary, always a civilian, also has the responsibility of ordering military spending ambitions and restraining inter-service rivalries. James Forrestal, the first head of the unified Department of Defense (created in 1947), described the military's peacetime purpose as to 'destroy the Secretary of Defense' (Stubbing 1986: 384).

One remaining agency of executive branch foreign policy capability, the Central Intelligence Agency, deserves attention. During the cold war the CIA became a major symbol, often hated and feared in the developing world especially, of American international power. By about 1990 it employed just under 20,000 personnel and had an estimated annual budget of around one and a half billion dollars. Founded in 1947 as an intelligence-gathering and spying agency, the CIA subsequently became notorious for mounting its own covert military operations. Presidential direction of the CIA in the cold war conditions was sometimes lax, but the CIA in its more controversial actions often followed the logic of 'plausible deniability'. Though rarely actually beyond presidential control, the CIA in its more controversial incarnations could be disowned by presidents when the need arose.

Following the collapse of Soviet communism, the *raison d'etre* of the cold war spying and covert operations agency came into dispute. The CIA was accused of having exaggerated the strength of the USSR in order to serve its own bureaucratic interests. After 1989 the CIA began to refashion its role, notably in response to the threat of international terrorism. Under President Clinton, Director of Central Intelligence George Tenet became closely involved in Middle Eastern peace negotiations. The onset in 2001 of the war on terrorism seemed to open the way for an expanded CIA responsibility, despite the agency's failure to intercept the terrorist planning of the September attacks.

Key points

- Policy-making in the executive branch is often dominated by a rivalry between the secretary of state and the president's national security adviser. Conflict between the Department of Defense and the State Department is also common.

- In all cases of conflict, despite the benefits of 'multiple advocacy', clear presidential adjudication is essential.

- In the post-cold war era, the CIA has been searching for new roles.

Challenges to presidential leadership

At one level, presidential dominance is refined and challenged by the foreign policy presidency itself. Even within the executive branch—maybe especially within the executive branch of government—presidents have to share power. Presidential advisers and operatives virtually never, however, offer a real and sustained challenge to their boss. The US foreign policy process is generally hierarchical, and is imbued with the assumption of overriding presidential discretion. When we look beyond the executive branch, we also find a series of potential challengers to presidential dominance who may influence, but who can rarely negate or overturn, presidential preferences.

Congress

Supporters of a strong legislative role in foreign policy argue that unfettered presidential discretion leads to the abuse of power. However, as indicated above, presidents, even post-cold war presidents, have generally been able to resist legislative incursions into their foreign policy-making territory. A fundamental explanation for this relates to the extent to which foreign policy, even in post-cold war conditions, has remained oriented towards presidentially defined crises. *In extremis*, Congress may assert its war and money-raising powers. In practice, and especially when presidents invoke national danger, it rarely does so. Members of Congress do not wish to be seen to be challenging the head of state when he says he is acting in furtherance of pressing national interest.

Congress also conspicuously lacks the kind of detailed foreign policy information, expertise (and, indeed, confidence) which is normally available to the executive branch. Assertions of legislative power tend to occur in the context of rather formalized, set-piece foreign policy confrontations. Important opportunities for challenging, even changing, policy do occur when the Senate moves to confirm appointments and to ratify treaties. Indeed, the most celebrated legislative rebuff of presidential foreign policy authority in US history—the 1919 Senate rejection of the Treaty of Versailles—involved the legislative power of treaty ratification. Congress also is better placed to exert influence when it operates its annual authorizations and appropriations procedures, particularly in relation to foreign aid and defence spending. Set-piece votes may also occur on very high-profile, crisis-oriented policy. The Gulf War authorization of January 1991 and the war on terrorism votes of September 2001 spring to mind. In general, however, the greater (and the more presidentially defined) the crisis, the more discretion is pushed towards the executive branch.

Congress does have several committees which are geared to foreign policy oversight (see Box 14.7). Senators such as Republican Jesse Helms (chair of the Senate Foreign Relations Committee, 1995–2001) and Democratic Joe Biden (who took over Helms's chair in 2001) do base a large part of their national reputation on foreign policy activism. However, most law-makers' priorities are more parochial. Few congressional elections are won or lost on foreign policy *per se*, although foreign economic and immigration issues may have important local impacts. Congress may also, when a partisan majority clearly opposes the discretion of presidential foreign policy, use its various powers to influence that general direction. This was unquestionably the case with the Clinton administration and its move to more unilateralist policies, following the Republican congressional takeover of 1995.

Interest groups

Many of the general points about congressional foreign policy authority apply also to the power of interest groups. When presidents make crisis decisions, they do not consult interest groups. It is manifestly in non-crisis areas (especially in foreign economic policy, where business interests are conspicuously salient) where interest group influence manifests itself. 'Advocacy' groups and non-governmental organizations have proliferated since the end of the cold war, and many have developed effective lobbying techniques on issues such as human rights and world economic development. Various foreign policy 'think tanks', many

funded by business, can also help shape the climate of foreign policy opinion.

The most publicized and researched area of foreign policy interest group activity is that relating to ethnic group politics. The Irish, Jewish, and Cuban American lobbies are probably the most widely known outside the US. The latter, in the guise of the Cuban American National Foundation, has certainly had great success in opposing normalization of US relations with Cuba. The ethnic groups tend to be primarily geared to influencing Congress, often through donations to election campaigns, rather than the presidency. Ethnic groups are also often internally divided; some (as in the case of Indian and Pakistani Americans) face powerful countervailing lobbies. They thrive in areas of policy in which presidents choose, usually for reasons of expediency, to allow Congress to take the lead.

Public opinion and the states

Many foreign policy commentators, especially those working in the realist tradition, tend to see public opinion as an unsuitable guide for foreign policymakers to follow. According to Walter Lippman (1955), for example, public opinion is far too unstable, irrational, and poorly informed to be allowed to shape foreign policy.

Few would argue that US public opinion on foreign affairs is especially well informed. In the post-cold war era, the public has tended vastly to overestimate the extent of America's contribution to international aid and peacekeeping. Only following the September 2001 terrorist attacks did a (very narrow) majority of the American public respond to pollsters that foreign policy was 'extremely important'. Nevertheless, empirical research on poll data tends to find a public which is reasonably consistent in its long-term outlook, if not well briefed on contemporary events. Shapiro and Page (1992) coined the phrase 'the rational public' to describe this phenomenon. In the post-cold war era, the US public has, in some respects, exhibited a preference for insularity and 'America First' attitudes. However, the post-cold war public certainly does not see itself as isolationist, and wishes to see continued

---

Box 14.7 **Congressional foreign policy committees (2002)**

Senate

- Armed Services Committee (chair: Senator Carl Levin, Democrat, Michigan)

- Foreign Relations Committee (chair: Senator Joseph R. Biden, Democrat, Delaware)

- Select Committee on Intelligence (chair: Senator Bob Graham, Democrat, Florida)

House of Representatives

- Armed Services Committee (chair: Representative Bob Stump, Republican, Arizona)

- Select Committee on Intelligence (chair: Representative Porter J. Goss, Republican, Florida)

- International Relations Committee (chair: Representative Henry Hyde, Republican, Illinois)

US engagement in organizations such as the North Atlantic Treaty Organization.

Only in exceptional circumstances does foreign policy assume a high degree of saliency for the American public. Presidents are generally able to lead and shape public opinion, at least in the short to medium term. The degree of attention paid by presidents to public opinion will vary according to the perceived intensity of views held by the public on different issues, as well as the degree to which particular presidents regard themselves as servants or as leaders of the public (Foyle 1999). Public opinion is communicated to presidents via various 'linkage paths' (notably friends and associates of policy-makers, interest groups, the news media, the Congress and local elected bodies, and polls) (Powlick 1995). Several of these linkage paths, of course, themselves serve to shape as much as to communicate public opinion.

As noted at the beginning of this chapter, one of this book's key themes—the tension between government at federal and at state level—scarcely applies to foreign policy. The US constitutional tradition points more or less unequivocally to centralization of authority in Washington. Nevertheless, especially since the cold war's end and notably in the area of foreign trade promotion, some state and local governments have strayed into the area of foreign policy. They have attempted to advance the view that sub-national regions are better placed than nation-states to exploit opportunities opened up by economic globalization.

Key points

- Congress has formidable foreign policy powers, but—for structural, procedural, and political reasons—often finds it difficult to challenge the president.

- Various interests, notably ethnic groups, are able to build themselves into the foreign policy-making process.

- Presidents must attend to public opinion. However, public opinion as such is too unstructured, poorly informed, and insular to be an effective leader of foreign policy.

- State governments defer to the federal government.

Conclusion

The terrorist attacks of 11 September 2001 ushered in a new phase in the history of American foreign relations. A distinct era, the 'post-cold war era', came to a close. This era actually represented a substantial chunk of recent international history, stretching back to the fall of the Berlin Wall in 1989. It was, as we have seen, a period of complex debate, flux, and perceived transition. It witnessed major debates about the nature and purpose of American international power, as well as concerning the procedures for making US foreign policy.

At least by the later stages of the post-cold war era, few commentators were in any doubt about the extraordinary strength of America's global power. Writing in mid-2001, Henry Kissinger concluded: 'At the dawn of the new millennium, the United States is enjoying a pre-eminence unrivalled by even the greatest empires of the past'. The unparalleled American ascendancy ranged from 'weaponry to entrepreneurship, from science to technology, from higher education to popular culture' (Kissinger 2001: 9). The problem of American power at the turn of the millennium centred on the difficulty of finding (and selling to the rest of the world) a consensually acceptable definition of America's international purpose. Should America's post-cold war international purpose be the promotion of global democracy, the narrow protection of American economic and security interests, or the championing of a global regime of free trade? Could it—and should it—be all three? How was the US to deal with the growth of anti-American global resentment? How

Box 14.8 Definitions

American exceptionalism: in foreign policy, the view that the US has a special, historic mission to spread democracy

Anti-Ballistic Missile Treaty (1972): cold war treaty, outlawing defence systems designed to intercept incoming nuclear weapons

asymmetrical warfare: war against state-sponsored or non-state terrorist groups

Central Intelligence Agency (CIA): powerful cold war agency, responsible for intelligence gathering and promoting American covert military operations

Comprehensive Test Ban Treaty: treaty, rejected by the US Senate in 1999, which would have banned all nuclear weapons test explosions (the US originally signed the treaty in 1996)

containment: the major cold war doctrine of the US, involving commitment to prevent the expansion of Soviet power

cultural imperialism: phrase used by opponents of American global cultural penetration

enlargement: doctrine developed in the first Clinton administration (1993–7), involving a commitment to the expansion of global democracy and free markets

idealism: an international relations tradition, emphasizing a normative commitment to international cooperation

internationalism: a commitment to international involvement, usually at least partly for democracy promotion

isolationism: a commitment to the avoidance of international entanglements, usually combined with 'America First' attitudes

Kyoto Protocol: international agreement, rejected by the Bush administration in 2001, to limit greenhouse gas emissions

liberal peace: international peace, rooted in the supposed reluctance of democracies to go to war with one another

multilateralism: a commitment to working with allies and through alliance structures

multiple advocacy: the provision to presidents of a variety of arguments for differing foreign policy positions

nation-building: support by the US for building democratic institutions in war-torn or developing countries, usually involving a sustained military commitment

(National) Missile Defense: programme to develop a comprehensive defence against incoming missiles

national security adviser: the president's chief White House foreign policy adviser

New World Order: President George H. W. Bush's plan for a post-cold war cooperativist, democratic capitalist order, led by the US

North American Free Trade Agreement (NAFTA): the agreement, ratified by the US Senate in 1993, for a free trade zone, comprising the US, Canada, and Mexico

North Atlantic Treaty Organization (NATO): major North American–West European defence organization, originally set up in 1949

Pentagon: headquarters of the US Defense Department; shorthand term for US military leaders

realism: an international relations tradition, emphasizing the prevalence of conflict and power struggles in international politics

rogue states: countries deemed to constitute threats to US and international security

State Department: America's foreign ministry, sited in the Foggy Bottom area of Washington, DC

superpower: exceptionally strong international power, usually with strength in a number of dimensions (notably military, economic, and diplomatic)

unilateralism: a preference for acting and operating without allies

war powers: the congressional right to declare war and to be included (especially under the 1973 War Powers Resolution) in decisions to commit troops

---

were generally internationalist American foreign policy elites to deal with pressures for a narrower, 'America First', and unilateralist foreign policy? The 2000 presidential election was, at some level, a national referendum on these various debates. Disputed, unsatisfactory, and extraordinary as it was, the 2000 election nonetheless clearly nudged

the US in the direction of a unilateralist and 'America First' foreign policy.

The post-cold war era also generated expectations about the making of foreign policy. As we have seen, the anticipated diminution of presidential control in post-cold war international conditions largely failed to occur. Several important features of foreign policy in this era actually were continuations of trends inherited from the cold war. Presidential domination of foreign policy-making was a case in point. The central importance of policy in the Middle East, linked to the need to keep oil flowing, was another. The period also saw a preoccupation, transposed from the cold war, with Russian power, and a concern to manage threats from China. Various cold war institutions, notably NATO, struggled to adapt to post-Soviet conditions. The US also retained a profound reluctance, associated with memories of the conflict in Vietnam, to expose its military forces to the possibility of sustaining high casualty levels.

The era which began on 11 September 2001 certainly did not see a jettisoning of all the features of the post-cold war era. Memories of Vietnam, even some thirty or so years after the exit of American troops from that country, were not suddenly extinguished. Yet the war on terrorism involved a pivotal re-mobilization of American military and foreign policy. In January 2002, President George W. Bush announced a massive increase in military spending: 48 billion dollars more by 2003–4. As Michael Cox elaborates in Chapter 25, the war on terrorism military budget, along with the unchallenged technological sophistication of the American military, again emphasized the gap between the US and all other countries. Some key features of the post-cold war era seemed to be receding. US–Russian and US–Chinese relationships were reconfigured in the light of the new anti-terrorist priorities. The darkening economic outlook, at least in comparison with the years of the 'Clinton boom', cast some doubts over the American ability to sustain its massive military preeminence. Although the Middle East remained at the centre of US priorities, efforts were clearly under way to find new sources of oil, notably in central Asia. The terrorist attacks at first appeared to have halted America's drift towards unilateralism, as Washington sought the cooperation of allies in the war on terrorism. As the new era progressed, however, it became clear that Washington policy-makers were determined

to conduct the conflict on America's terms. The Bush administration retained its preference for unilateralism, despite the apparent multilateralist preferences of Secretary of State Colin Powell. The unprecedented levels of public support for Bush's handling of foreign policy also virtually removed internal checks on the administration's leadership in this area.

It seems appropriate to conclude this chapter with a brief revisiting of the main themes of *Governing America*. In regard to the tension between democratic, majoritarian, and liberal values, again it must be emphasized that foreign policy is different. Presidents—even a president with George Bush's high level of public and congressional backing after the September 2001 attacks—have to share power. Their power is limited by the Constitution and by the exigencies of a relatively open political process. In general terms, America's executive branch of government is more constrained in its domination of foreign policy than are the executive leaderships of most other advanced, industrialized countries— especially those (like Britain) with no written constitution and little sense of the formal independence of the legislature. However, in all recent eras—cold war, post-cold war, and the era of the war on terrorism— presidents have dominated, setting agendas and handling (often self-defined) crises. Checks from the state governments on federal power, despite some of the expectations generated in the post-cold war era, do not apply to foreign policy to any substantial extent. Finally, the debate between traditionalists and progressives has a peculiar and distinct application to foreign policy. The conflict here is between the axis of isolationism and unilateralism on the one hand and internationalism (allied to multilateralism) on the other. The trajectory of US foreign policy in the early years of the twenty-first century was towards a kind of unilateralist, 'America First' internationalism. It is certain that, as the new post-11 September 2001 era in US foreign policy continues, significant challenges to this trajectory will emerge, and will be articulated within American democratic institutions.

QUESTIONS

1 What arguments have traditionally been advanced to explain the underlying purposes of American foreign policy?

2 Is the proper purpose of American foreign policy, especially in the post-cold war international context, the promotion of democracy?

3 Why has unilateralism become so powerful a force in contemporary US foreign policy?

4 What are the main limitations on presidential control of foreign policy?

5 Is it inevitable that presidents should dominate the making of US foreign policy?

6 To what extent is the conflict between national security adviser and secretary of state a major obstacle to the effective conduct of US foreign policy?

7 What impact have the 11 September 2001 terrorist attacks had on the making of US foreign policy?

FURTHER READING

Debates about US foreign policy purposes

M. Cox, G. J. Ikenberry, and T. Inoguchi (eds.) (2000), *American Democracy Promotion: Impulses, Strategies and Impacts* (Oxford: Oxford University Press). Excellent essays on problems and debates surrounding American post-cold war promotion of global democracy.

C. V. Crabb, L. E. Sarieddine, and G. J. Antizzo (2001), *Charting a New Diplomatic Course: Alternative Approaches to America's Post-Cold War Foreign Policy* (Baton Rouge: Louisiana State University Press). A guide to the post-cold war debates.

E. A. Nordlinger (1995) *Isolationism Reconfigured: American Foreign Policy for a New Century* (Princeton, NJ: Princeton University Press). A stout and original defence of isolationism.

J. S. Nye (2002), *The Paradox of American Power: Why the World's Only Superpower Cannot Go It Alone* (Oxford: Oxford University Press). Eloquent defence of multilateralism by a leading academic commentator and former Clinton administration official.

On the American foreign policy-making process

J. W. Dumbrell (1995), *The Making of US Foreign Policy* (Manchester: Manchester University Press). Argues against presidential domination of the process.

B. W. Jentlesen (2000), *American Foreign Policy: The Dynamics of Choice in the 21st Century* (New York: Norton). A reliable guide.

P. E. Peterson (ed.) (1994), *The President, the Congress and the Making of Foreign Policy* (Norman: Oklahoma University Press). Argues for presidential domination of the process.

T. Smith (2000), *Foreign Attachments: The Power of Ethnic Groups in the Making of American Foreign Policy* (Cambridge, Mass.: Harvard University Press). A thoughtful examination of the power of ethnic lobbies.

WEB LINKS

The following sites offer a range of views:

www.fpa.org

www.afpc.org

www.foreignpolicy.com.

Two executive branch sites (**www.whitehouse.gov**; **www.state.gov**) and two congressional sites (**www.senate.gov/foreign relations**; **www.house/gov/international relations**) offer competing perspectives.

Foreign economic policy

Stephen Burman

READER'S GUIDE

This chapter examines the consequences of the end of the cold war for American international economic policy. The collapse of communism has led to an era of globalization in which the American national interest has been redefined and economic policy has become more important in foreign policy. America has responded dynamically to the challenges of the new era, and on the basis of a revitalized domestic economy the US has pursued an aggressive foreign economic policy that has shaped the global economy. It has continued to play a hegemonic role, reconciling the pursuit of national interest with responsibility for the maintenance of a stable and growing world economy. However, there have been harsh consequences of the American approach for much of the world and there is a growing opposition to its domination, most graphically manifest in the terrorist attacks of 11 September. Unless American foreign economic policy is oriented toward equality and justice as well as prosperity in the future, America's position at the apex of the world economy may arguably be placed in jeopardy.

Introduction: after the cold war

It is always tempting to discuss US foreign policy in terms of discrete periods. These may be based on chronology, where individual decades are the most readily employed; or on administrations, as with the Reagan era; or on major episodes, such as the Vietnam War. While the identification of watersheds has an arbitrary quality, some divisions are more plausible and useful than others. In recent years the most significant watershed has been the end of the cold war and the collapse of the Soviet Union. The momentous character of these events has left little unchanged in international affairs, including the role of America in the modern world. During the cold war, security issues were given the highest priority but in the 1990s international economic issues have joined security at the heart of the foreign policy agenda. The change in public attitudes is clear; where in the 1980s there were mass demonstrations about cruise missile deployment and anti-nuclear demonstrations, today the biggest demonstrations affecting foreign policy issues surround the meetings of the World Trade Organization (WTO), an organization that did not exist at the start of the decade and whose business most people would have thought of interest only to specialists.

The first major issue of the post-cold war era, the Gulf War, was justified by the obligation to preserve the territorial integrity of the state of Kuwait and to restore stability to a dangerous region.[1] However, the need to protect the economic interests of the US was a major factor in the decision to intervene. The consequences for American oil supplies had Iraq not been turned back were immense. The intervention, although led by the US, also served to protect collective Western interests. Japan, for example, was even more vulnerable to the threat of disruption to oil supplies than Europe or the US. Hence Japan's financial contribution to the cost of the war.[2] American-led intervention in the Gulf demonstrates that economic and security interests can rarely be divorced from each other, because political and social stability is a pre-condition for a successful capitalist system; investment will not be made where there are threats to the free movement of capital and other factors of production.

The Gulf War was, however, a transitory episode. President George Bush was forced to act in a new environment before its implications were understood. His response centred on the idea of the New World Order. This was a relatively optimistic concept, which was premised on a collective approach to management of world security, drawing on the American experience of leading a successful broad coalition in the Gulf. It did not, however, allay the anxieties in the minds of the American public. These centred on both the nature of American national interest after the cold war and on America's own domestic unfitness to meet the challenges of the new order. Bush's inability to address the concerns of the American public proved costly, and led to his defeat in the 1992 presidential election. Part of the reason for Bill Clinton's victory was his determination to focus on domestic issues. However, Clinton did not simply ignore foreign policy; rather, he recast its role by challenging the distinction between foreign and domestic issues. He grasped that foreign policy would no longer be dominated by the politics of strategic issues but would instead be driven by the need to foster American jobs and prosperity.

In this chapter we will consider how America's response to the challenges of the era of globalization have evolved in international economic policy. We will see that from tentative beginnings America has adopted an increasingly assertive approach to shaping the world economic system. The distinction between foreign and domestic economic policy has become less distinct and the relation of economic policy to broader foreign policy has become more integrated. While the policy framework has become more seamless, the divisions within the American political system, whose importance have been demonstrated in other chapters, will be seen to have affected the conduct of policy in this sphere.

---

[1] It is probable that the situation in the Gulf only resulted in armed conflict because the cold war had ended. US involvement was not going to result in a superpower confrontation, which would have raised the stakes so high that both sides would have avoided it.

[2] The cost of the war has been estimated at $80 bn., of which America's allies paid 80%.

Box 15.1 Definitions

The cold war between the USA and Soviet Union began shortly after the Second World War, which ended in 1945, when America adopted the doctrine of the containment of communism, and of the Soviet Union in particular, as the cornerstone of American foreign policy. It governed policy until the collapse of the Soviet Union in 1991.

Globalization refers to the integration of world markets through trade and investment flows to the point where it is possible to refer to a single global market. Debates rage both about the extent of integration and the political implications of a single market in a world of nation states.

Hegemony is used to describe American predominance in world affairs. It conveys a softer impression than imperialism. Hegemonic leadership concerns cultural and ideological pre-eminence as well as military and economic power, and implies a degree of consensus between the leading power and others.

National interest is the concept by which the vital interests of a nation are articulated so as to provide a guide to foreign policy, the purpose of which is to protect these interests. They centre on security and the protection of the territory of the state, but can be widened to include economic, political, and ideological interests.

New World Order is the term coined by the first President Bush in 1991 to describe the kind of world he wanted to see after the collapse of communism. It stressed American commitment to democracy and human rights and a just distribution of global wealth.

The American national interest

Only a little sense of history is needed to see that the question of what the American national interest is has become central to American foreign policy since the end of the cold war. During that era the US national interest appeared self-evident because the perception was virtually universal that the survival of the US was at stake in the struggle with communism and the Soviet Union. This gave a sense of order to the formulation of policy; since all individual policies, including economic policy, were to be subordinated to the aim of containing communism, questions of coherence and compatibility were easily resolved. Although ostensibly defensive in character, the policy of containment also rationalized American attempts to shape world events in its own interest.[3] By contrast, the defining characteristic of foreign policy in the post-cold war era is that it lacks the overarching principle against which action may be formulated, implemented, and judged.

This uncertainty has led to a major re-evaluation of US national interest both by government and by commentators (Trubowitz 1998; Nye 1999). The consensus has been a broader concept of national security that places the defence of economic interests on a par with traditional security concerns. Under the Clinton administration the goals of foreign policy were also expanded to encompass the idea of democratic enlargement and the promotion of human rights across the globe. The interconnection between economics and security was maintained because the market can only operate on the basis of free movement of factors of production and the sanctity of private property. It is not therefore compatible with any form of political authority that curbs freedom. Because the market enshrines freedom in social organization and produces the greatest wealth in the process, it is a system that requires democracy. And, as has been widely noted and debated, countries in which democracy is embedded do not go to war with each other (Friedman 2000). The global free market has therefore become in the eyes of US policy-makers the key

---

[3] Other doctrines that have guided US policy over long periods include the Monroe Doctrine and Manifest Destiny (the notion that an exceptional America has a special, even unique, role in world affairs).

not only to prosperity but also to security and democracy.

America as an ordinary country

This approach to the national interest was hampered by a duality in American understanding of its role in the post-cold war world. On the one hand, the assumption underlying international economic policy was that, lacking its privileged position on security, the US would have to defend its economic interests on the same terms as other countries. In the last years of the cold war, it became fashionable to argue that the costs of maintaining the empire were such a drain on US economic resources that it was leading to an imbalance between American military might and economic weakness (Kennedy 1988). Fear of economic weakness led to the argument that America should think of itself, in a phrase coined much earlier, as an 'ordinary country' (Rosecrance 1976) that looked after 'number one' by pursuing aggressively an economically led approach to foreign policy. Those who were most influenced by these concerns argued that American responsibility for the success and stability of the international system, which had been so willingly embraced in the cold war, should be jettisoned in favour of a narrower conception of national interest.

On the other hand, many have seen the post-cold war situation as offering an opportunity to turn weakness into strength. The rapid development of an integrated global market has been widely thought of as unmanageable because it transcended the power of all nation-states, even that of the US (Scholte 2000). Optimists proposed that, to the contrary, these forces could and should be harnessed to the vision of a powerful America leading a prosperous and democratic world. They argued that, although promotion of the free market encourages competition between states as well as between firms, it also presupposes that conflict takes place within a consensual framework because conflict is about the division of spoils rather than the method of their production. However, for most countries the environment in which they pursue their national security strategy is a given in the sense that they have little capacity to alter the system of international affairs and must instead marshal their resources to manoeuvre for the best possible position. The difference between ordinary states, whose aspiration is confined to 'punching above their weight',[4] and a superpower is that the latter can shape the world system and indeed has a responsibility to do so if anarchy is not to ensue. On this perspective, globalization gave the United States, as the sole superpower, a unique opportunity to rewrite the rules of international affairs and craft a stable, democratic, and prosperous world order based on its own free market system.

Key points

- The collapse of communism has forced America to redefine its national interest. The concept is less clear than it was during the cold war.

- The new conception of national interest gave greater emphasis to economic interests. Protecting these became the key not only to prosperity but also to promoting security and democracy in the world.

- Policy has also been hampered by a belief that America had overstretched itself in protecting the world from communism. In the new era it would have to concern itself less with its global responsibilities and more with looking after its own interests.

- Globalization also gave America great opportunities, as it is the only country that has the potential to shape the powerful forces that are creating a global market. The goal of international economic policy came to be to take advantage of this opportunity to create a global market system on American principles.

[4] The phrase was coined by British Foreign Secretary Douglas Hurd, who sought to inject some realism into an inflated view of Britain's post-imperial status while retaining a sense that Britain was not just another middle-ranking power.

Domestic prosperity and globalization

There is, however, a significant gap between formulating policy and implementing it. The elimination of the communist threat has allowed greater scope for the multifarious character of American society to exert influence on foreign policy. One consequence has been a reassertion of influence over foreign policy by Congress. This has been a problem because in the modern world the US is by far the leading force in the world economy, and effective discharge of leadership requires clear and decisive international economic policy. If there are too many agendas influencing policy-making this clarity of purpose is lost. The balance between creativity and implementation lying with the executive branch of government and modification of policy reposing in Congress can be constructive, but it depends on a consensus on the goals of policy or, in other words, a common conception of the national interest. Without this, each branch will seek to exert its substantive policy visions through pushing its prerogatives up to and beyond their constitutional limits, and the result is confusion and indecisiveness. These problems are made worse by the power of special interests, notably multinational corporations, which can exert an undue degree of influence not only on Congress but on the administration as well. The close relationship between the Bush administration and the oil industry is a case in point.

The pressures of globalization have led to a new global division of labour. The US has embraced the rapid technological developments that have created virtually a new economy, and has not only become very dynamic by historical standards but has kept ahead of the rest of the world, to which it farms out mass production of artefacts and lower-level service activities. However, this increases its dependency on the world economy, as success at the advanced end of the spectrum depends on the servicing from the lower levels. It follows that the US cannot absolve itself of responsibility for the relationship with the rest of the global economic structure. Sitting atop the global economic pyramid is precarious because the extent of American integration into the world economy has undergone a qualitative shift under globalization. Whereas before the US connection to the rest of the world economy was primarily strategic and its economy was relatively self-sufficient, in the post-cold war world the

Box 15.2 Constitutional influences

An 'invitation to struggle'

There is little in the Constitution dealing explicitly with foreign affairs. Congress has the sole constitutional authority to declare war (Article I, section 8), while presidential authority derives from his constitutional position as commander-in-chief of the armed forces (Article II, section 2). Of more direct relevance to economic policy is the power of the purse, which gives Congress the exclusive power to appropriate funds for all foreign programmes, including foreign aid. This power can be used to limit presidential freedom, but it is a longer-term instrument for shaping policy rather than a means of curbing executive action in the short term or in a crisis. Trade policy is an area in which there has to be a measure of consensus between the administration and Congress. While the administration has the power through the Office of the United States Trade Representative to negotiate trade agreements, Congress must approve any binding agreements that the US enters into. This can be done on a clause-by-clause basis, a process so cumbersome that it would effectively scupper any agreement. Congress can waive this right in part by giving the administration what is known as 'fast track authority', whereby Congress votes only to approve or reject the whole agreement as negotiated by the executive. Congress withdrew this authority from the Clinton administration and this contributed in large part to the stalling of that administration's trade initiatives.

standard of living of average Americans is heavily dependent on the relationship with the world economy. American political leaders, then, for sound domestic political reasons, have to manage the economic relationship between the US and the rest of the world.

In the event, the 1990s saw one of the most sustained periods of domestic economic growth in US history, and this made the balancing of national interest and global responsibility easier. The collapse of Soviet-style command economies gave the American market model a clear ideological run, and domestic economic success gave credence to the idea that the US model was generalizable to the world economy. This success is not unalloyed, however. Integration into the world economy has seen the creation of an hour-glass economic structure in the US, with a dynamic, technologically-driven sector at the top driving the new economy; middle-range skills associated with old industries are exported abroad; while at the bottom there is a pool of cheap labour providing services for the advanced sector. The focus on the high-technology end of the economic spectrum has required great flexibility of the American economy, and the dynamism of its response has been startlingly successful. It has also been dependent on an enlarged, immigrant-based

pool of cheap labour that has driven down wages and curbed inflation in a time of rapid growth. Their contribution to reducing the cost base of the economy has been vital in maintaining profitability and facilitating economic restructuring. Economic inequality has not been eliminated by growth, and as the boom of the 1990s has petered out the problems associated with this new economic structure have become more acute.

Another indicator of the integration of the foreign and the domestic in economic policy is the balance of payments deficit that has been a persistent feature of the US economy. The importance of this is difficult to overestimate, since without the outlet for exports from other countries that the deficit provides, globalization would have had a much rockier path. It has been possible to run this deficit because it is relatively easy to finance and has not led to a decline in the value of the dollar. America is seen as a safe haven for capital in an uncertain world, and international capital is always available to buy the bonds needed to finance the deficit, and to do so without punitive rates of interest. There is a clear virtuous circle here for America: by engaging with the world economy it helps maintain world economic growth, but it also facilitates the restructuring of its own economy, promotes economic

---

Box 15.3 **Core academic debate**
Imperial overstretch

The primary debate concerns the question of whether America is in economic decline. This debate goes well beyond economic policy but that is an essential part of it. The debate began in the last years of the cold war, when Paul Kennedy (1988) coined the term 'imperial overstretch' to describe a situation in which America, like other great powers before it, had taken on so many burdens in fighting the cold war that the cost of maintaining its hegemonic status had drained resources needed for domestic economic renewal. Low productivity, investment, and innovation were the result. The contrast with the alternative and more successful model of corporatist capitalism developed in particular in Germany and Japan was given a great deal of attention. Much of the gloom was dispelled by the victory in the

cold war and in the Gulf, and Henry Nau (1990) published a book attacking the myth of American decline, which received wide approval. The long boom of the American economy, starting in the early 1990s and lasting through the decade, appeared to put fears of decline to rest, especially when combined with growing evidence that it was based on a remarkable reorientation of the American economy away from old industries to high-tech knowledge-based ones. Doubts continued, however, with critics pointing to the unsustainably large balance of payments deficit, excessive consumption built on credit, a stock market bubble, and a virtually negative savings ratio. As the inevitable recession has hit the American economy in the new century, these fears have been revived.

growth at home, confirms the American leadership role in managing capitalism, and so increases its attraction as a home for mobile capital. In other words, by recognizing that different rules apply to the American economy, since no other country could continue to run a deficit, it creates a self-fulfilling prophecy. By acting like a hegemon it confirms its status as precisely that.

Key points

- It has not been easy for US administrations to conduct policy, as Congress has reasserted its rights in this area. There is a danger of stalemate between the executive and legislative branches and of excessive influence by special interests, and this threatens the clarity and decisiveness of foreign economic policy.

- The American economy has become much more integrated into the world economy. Americans' standard of living now depends on the health of the global economy, and this gives foreign economic policy a solid grounding in domestic politics.

- The American economy responded with remarkable dynamism to the challenge of globalization, creating a new economic structure that has prompted a lengthy period of rapid economic growth. Inequality has continued to grow, and as the boom comes to an end the problems associated with this will become more acute.

- American domestic growth combined with a persistent balance of payments deficit has provided an engine for world economic growth through much of the last decade. America's ability to attract the capital needed to finance this deficit confirms its hegemonic status as the safest home for mobile international capital.

Trade policy

Bilateral trade relations

The American approach to bilateral trade relations has focused on the so-called Big Emerging Markets (BEM). Ten countries[5] were targeted as having the most potential for growth, and the resources of the federal government were marshalled in support of American business in building up market share in these countries. This brought the use of America's political influence down from the rarefied atmosphere of grand strategic thinking to the grittier slopes of naked economic interest, and involved a geographical and a philosophical reorientation of American state power. In the cold war era many of the BEMs targeted by the US were virtually ignored or treated as pawns in the grand strategic game, whereas in the 1990s they became the focus of international economic policy that was itself much higher in the priorities of foreign and domestic

policy. The underlying question that this strategy posed was whether the US would reconcile the more aggressive pursuit of its own national interests that the BEM approach implied with its hegemonic responsibilities in managing the free market global economic system. The BEM policy was a reaction to a sense of threat to American dominance, but it was ambitious in conception: trade policy was a vehicle for reasserting American power in the world, not for adapting to decline. Rather than allowing globalization to take its own course, possibly at the expense of American interests, the intention was to manage it in such a way as to make the world safe for continued American domination. A strategy that would merge these two goals is unique to the US, and demonstrates that, even at a time of weakness and uncertainty, American foreign economic policy

[5] The BEMs are Mexico, Brazil, Argentina, South Africa, Poland, Turkey, India, Indonesia, China, and South Korea.

Box 15.4 Is America different?
Superpower hegemony

The fact that the term 'superpower' is used about the USA but about no other country suggests that in this field America really is different. There are other major powers in the world—the EU, Russia, China, Japan—but none has the range of resources to act as a rival to the USA in the contemporary era. In part the difference is quantitative–America has the biggest single economy in the world and trades and invests abroad more than any other country. However, it is also qualitative, since its size and resources gives the USA an unparalleled influence on the development of the world economy. We see this in the fact that it can run a balance of payments deficit of some 2.5 per cent of its economy, that is to say it can import more

than it exports, on a more or less permanent basis without ill effect, while for every other country this would lead to a devaluation of its currency. We see it also in the rules that govern international institutions, which turn these ostensibly independent institutions into extensions of American will. This is to suggest not that the USA can operate alone in international economic affairs but that it has similar interests to other capitalist societies and takes the lead in managing the affairs of international capitalism on their behalf as well as its own. In that sense it rules but does so with the consent, at least of the governments of others countries, if not of all their people. This is why we refer to American power as hegemonic.

was formulated on the basis of different rules to the rest of the world.

Trade in the hemisphere

Bilateral relations are only one aspect of trade policy; cultural and geographical ties generate a regional level of association as a locus for trade relations, and American policy-makers have paid close attention to the creation of regional ties. After several years of negotiation, the North American Free Trade Agreement (NAFTA), covering Canada, the US, and Mexico, was established in 1993. The advantages of a free trade pact with Canada were clear: it increased the mobility of US-based capital and opened up a substantial new consumer market. However, this was not the case with Mexico. Here, NAFTA represented a quantum jump in that it proposed the integration of a highly advanced economy with a developing one. It would be naïve to suppose that the US had not had great influence over Mexico historically, well before NAFTA gave it an institutional framework; but NAFTA made the US commitment far greater. While this carried opportunities for profit and cheaper goods for American corporations and consumers, it also tied the US to the fate of the Mexican economy to an extent never before contemplated.

Not all Americans felt sanguine about this. Many US workers felt that competition from cheap Mexican labour would be at their expense as capital moved existing plants away from traditional sites in the US. This fear created a substantial political constituency that was firmly opposed to the idea of NAFTA, a constituency that became more powerful when joined by environmentalists who feared that capital would relocate to Mexico to escape US environmental safeguards. As a result of opposition in his own Democratic Party, Clinton relied heavily on cooperation from Republicans in Congress to get the legislation that created NAFTA passed. Once NAFTA was established it quickly became evident that the logic of that agreement was not confined to Mexico. Accordingly, at the Summit of the Americas in Miami in December 1994 the Clinton administration proposed a Free Trade Area of the Americas (FTAA), to be achieved by 2005. The purpose, from the American perspective, was to lock Latin America into an agenda of modernization that would entrench not only economic liberalization and market economies but also the progress towards democracy that had been made after the barbarism, instability, and military autocracy of recent decades. The coalition that failed to stop NAFTA renewed the fight against the FTAA, and with more success. Its strongest representation comes from the House of Representatives, where members are subject to pressure from workers/voters who fear their jobs may be threatened by the free trade agenda. The fact is, however, that American economic goals in the hemisphere are being achieved without the need for institutional expression as the US economic relationship with Latin America has prospered. While the FTAA remains US official policy it is not clear that the Bush administration, like that of Clinton before it, will want to expend the political capital necessary to bring the Miami commitment to fruition.

Asia–Pacific

The Asia Pacific Economic Cooperation (APEC) forum is the second side of a triangle of major regional economic associations in American international economic policy. There was much talk in the late 1980s of the centre of gravity of the world economy shifting from the US to Asia. At the time Japan was seen as the potential regional hegemon that would organize the Asian economy to reflect its own economic principles. In the 1990s, while Japan faltered China emerged, and its economic potential is clearly so great that the sense of challenge to America is not diminished. The Asian economic region remains vital as a source of cheap manufactured products, and as a consumer market it dwarfs all others in its potential. The combination of economic dynamism, from which America can profit, and potential political instability, from which it would undoubtedly suffer, is a compelling argument for US engagement in the economic affairs of the region. APEC has not moved regional integration forward as much as had been anticipated, however. US involvement in the Asian economic crisis of the late 1990s was driven by the threat the crisis posed to global economic stability rather than by regional considerations. Further, US policy has focused on security, notably on North Korea's nuclear capabilities and the perennial issue of China/Taiwan. The possible consequences of the growing potential of China focused minds in the US–Japan relationship and persuaded both parties to cool down the trade spats that had come to dominate relations.

The transatlantic economic relationship

What then of the third side of this triangle, the world's biggest economic relationship, that between the US and the EU? America has long supported the development of the EU, partly on the grounds that it consolidates democracy and stability in Europe but also because it creates a strong partner with a similar outlook on world affairs. However, the dividing line between a partner and a rival is not always easy to draw. The US attitude is driven by fear that the line may be crossed and policy is driven by a desire to promote the EU contribution to global economic management while restricting its autonomy. Trade disputes,[6] while easily dismissed as squabbles between friends, may also signal that economic relations lack the discipline characteristic of the security arena. Concern to prevent economic rivalry getting out of hand have led periodically to proposals for a Transatlantic Free Trade Area (TAFTA). This benign view was not necessarily shared by those outside the magic north Atlantic circle, for whom a TAFTA could look very easily like a rich man's club designed to perpetuate privilege and inequality. Rather like the case with Latin America however, little imperative for a TAFTA existed. Tariffs are generally low in trade between the US and the EU, with an average level of 3.5 per cent.[7] It was not worth expending a great deal of political capital on both sides of the Atlantic to remove all tariffs.

The failure of TAFTA to materialize confirms a general pattern in the regional dimension of US international economic policy. Regional agreements are intended to tie the US into all significant areas of economic activity and, equally, to tie other countries to the US, so placing it at the centre of a system of overlapping circles and warding off the development of blocs that might threaten its dominant role in world trade and investment flows. This idea, based on a clear-headed recognition of the new-found dependence of the US on the world economy, built up quite a head of steam but this has

---

[6] There have been a series of disputes on items as various as bananas, beef hormones, and steel.

[7] This does not of course include the intractable area of agriculture, but a TAFTA would not have solved that problem.

fizzled out. In part this has been due to domestic opposition to the free trade agenda, but in addition the health of the US economy has made the need for new institutional frameworks for trade less pressing.

Key points

- The emphasis in bilateral trade relations has shifted to emerging markets, where the resources of the government have been marshalled in support of American business. This has been part of an aggressive trade policy that seeks to shape the global market in such a way as to ensure continued American pre-eminence.
- NAFTA tied the American and Mexican economies together but met with opposition from labour unions and environmentalists. The US proposed a hemispheric free trade area but progress has been slow. This has not prevented the US from reinforcing its pre-eminent position in the hemisphere.
- A combination of political instability and economic dynamism in Asia has given the US good reason to remain heavily involved in the Asia-Pacific region. China has replaced Japan as a rival, but its potential as a market and a supplier of cheap consumer goods gives America a strong incentive to draw it into the world economy.
- The transatlantic economic relationship remains the world's biggest. A series of disputes between the US and the EU have not undermined the growth of trade and mutual investment, and this has made a formal trade agreement redundant.

International economic institutions

The World Trade Organization

The global dimension of US trade policy in the 1990s revolved around the World Trade Organization (WTO). The road to the creation of the WTO was a rocky one but US influence was critical, and now the US has taken the lead in using the WTO as a platform for a new, millennium round of trade liberalization talks. The goal is to ameliorate the potential for conflict escalating from trade disputes, and to get all countries to adopt and accept free market principles in an irreversible way. One illustration is the way in which China's accession to the WTO, brokered by the US, has required it to adopt a series of commitments on free trade that might have taken decades to achieve on a bilateral basis. The virtue of this development is that, to a significant extent, the US has been able to write the rules upon which regulation is based. Given the underlying

competitiveness of its economy, this places the US in a good position even when the WTO as an independent body interprets these rules.

It should be stressed that the object of US foreign economic policy, of which the WTO and a rule-based environment are crucial elements, is the creation of a new management system for international capitalism. The US operates at the centre of an increasingly elaborate network of countries and institutions that have taken responsibility for the management of globalization. Perhaps even more important in promoting an American-inspired view of globalization are financial institutions such as the IMF and the World Bank, which are supplemented by a network of less formal organizations, such as the Trilateral Commission and the World Economic Forum. Although these are multilateral institutions, there is little doubt that US perspectives play a large part in their policies and that in this way they are an effective means of extending the reach of US policy beyond what the American government can achieve directly.

Bail-out

One of the ways in which the increasing confidence of America in its own influence has been manifest is the bail-out of troubled economies. The US on more than one occasion has arranged for funds to be channelled to support Mexico, Brazil, and other Latin American countries via the IMF so as to give their governments the breathing space to put their financial house in order. This pattern of orchestrating financial support to re-establish market confidence was even more strikingly evident in the American response to the Asian economic crisis of 1997. The question was not whether help would be proffered, since the benefits were compelling, but whether it could be on a scale that would be commensurate with the problems. Despite the extent of the challenge, the United States did put together a package of support that created breathing space for adjustment and so restored confidence. This showed that when quick and decisive action was necessary only the US had the capacity to act on behalf of the international capitalist system.

The upheavals associated directly with the end of the cold war provided the greatest challenge in this area. The elimination of communism presented questions about the economic model that should be followed in reconstructing Russia and other former Soviet states. American influence was thrown behind a radical model of economic reconstruction, which pushed for a rapid transition to a full market economy. Much was left to European powers, especially Germany, while the US exercised its influence via the International Monetary Fund, whose strict conditions required movement towards a market system before aid were disbursed. The contrast between American involvement in this sphere, which has been largely indirect, and on security issues, where it adopted a much more direct form of engagement, is striking (Talbott 2002).[8] This conforms to a more general pattern in which economic management is a collaborative exercise where security is essentially a national one. One reason for this lies in the fact that international economic activity, trade, and investment, cannot be carried on in isolation. Although there can be conflicts over trade issues, ultimately working agreements have to be contrived or the activity ceases. In security matters, on the other hand, if consensus cannot be achieved then policy can be implemented by unilateral action, if necessary through force. In neither realm can long-term success be achieved by imposition, but this should not mask the fact that US dependency on the global economy requires it to cooperate with other powers as it tries to orchestrate global economic development.

The pattern that emerges is one of extensive American involvement, indeed leadership, when economic crises break out. The integration of the world economy enhances the domino effect of these crises. American/IMF intervention was intended to send a signal of confidence to international capital markets and so encourage capital to return to the countries affected. The fact that it often does so on terms that have a harsh impact on the poorer sections of the receiving countries does not alter the fact that new finance meets the central concern of US policy, which is to maintain global economic stability. Intervention has not been entirely successful, as is the case with Russia, but the potential for instability in the first post-cold war decade should not be underestimated, and the testament to the American track record has been that of the dog which has not barked.

Although international financial agencies play an important role, nation-states are not willing to pool their sovereignty to allow the agencies to take the lead in making policy decisions. The alternative path to coherent international economic management lies in the form of a hegemonic state which other states recognize is fulfilling a systemic function and is acting in the interest of all. In that sense the hegemon will have to moderate its own policies so that they can be seen to reconcile its national interests with systemic ones. This will never be an easy or a complete process: suspicions will always exist that the system is being run solely for the benefit of the powerful. The point is that this is precisely the role the US has played in the post-cold war world. This

---

[8] See e.g. America's involvement in the de-nuclearization of former Soviet states such as Ukraine.

owes much to America's success in managing the initial stages of globalization. As both the American and the world economy have prospered over the decade, Americans have come to feel that their model and leadership has been largely responsible for this. Success has bred increased confidence that they have the qualities and ideas necessary to lead and that they are, in a phrase often employed under Clinton, 'the indispensable nation' in world affairs. They have thus become bolder than before in taking initiatives and have paid less heed to the demands of other nations. The result has been a growing impression of unilateralism in US foreign economic policy. This began in the later Clinton years and has been reinforced by the philosophy and actions of the administration of George W. Bush. It is important here, however, to insist on the distinction between unilateralism and isolationism; American confidence has not led it to withdraw from world events but to try to manage them more aggressively.

Key points

- The US has taken a leading role in the creation of the World Trade Organization. It is part of a growing network of international institutions through which America attempts to manage the global capitalist system.

- There have been several debt crises in recent years, and the US has taken the lead in organizing financial packages of assistance.

- Support has not been driven by altruism but as a means of maintaining global economic stability. The conditions on which aid is given often have a harsh impact on the poor of the receiving countries.

- America has become increasingly confident in its ability to play a hegemonic role in managing globalization, and this has led to charges that it acts in a unilateral and overbearing fashion.

A growing opposition

The effectiveness of American foreign economic policy in promoting an American conception of globalization has already produced a strong backlash. There have been many losers as well as winners from the economic dynamism unleashed by globalization, and many have argued that there are inherent properties in the globalization process that increase inequality (Hurrell and Woods 1995; Rodrik 1998). Globalization has allowed capital to take advantage of the fact that it has greater mobility than labour. Organized labour has been relegated to a reactive role, but there are signs that it is beginning to combine on a cross-national basis. There has also been a growth of other oppositional forces, whose focus is the environment, human rights, and similar social concerns. The emerging coalition of social movements, non-governmental organizations, and labour unions has shown its public face at recent meetings of the IMF, WTO, and G8. The most vivid demonstration occurred at the December 1999 meeting of the WTO in Seattle, at which assembled a coalition of opposing forces that matched the number of

official delegates. The violence attendant on the vociferous expression of opposition disrupted the meeting of the WTO and brought into clearer definition the oppositional movement.

American reaction was to recognize the substance of many of the criticisms and to pledge to try to incorporate some of them into a revised practice for the WTO. However, no ground was given on the value of trade liberalization. The American argument remains that there is no alternative to a market system, as a means both to economic growth and to increase global justice—or rather, that there is an alternative but that protectionism would be a short-sighted and ultimately counterproductive response to the difficulties of liberalization. The solution, as perceived by successive US administrations, is not to retreat from trade liberalization but to incorporate a wider range of nations within the fold. The richer democracies must take the lead in creating a framework, but it is an open architecture and it is only from the inside that less developed countries can progress.

There is little sign as yet of the opposition movement forcing the US to alter its policies. One possible exception is the Multilateral Agreement on Investment (MAI). This was an attempt to secure conditions for the accumulation of capital by creating binding international rules governing international investment. It would mean nation-states signing up to a conception of the relationship between state and capital that is a cornerstone of Western capitalism and would take the domination of the global economy by America, as the leading representative of this conception, to new heights. Perhaps it was fear of this that made opposition to the agreement so fierce. Criticized as a multinationals' charter and as a step too far in the global domination of capital, the MAI, like the WTO, became a rallying point for an emerging coalition of non-governmental forces brought into being by globalization. Although the shelving of the MAI was widely reported as a victory for the non-governmental opposition, in fact the outcome was determined by the struggle for power between nation-states.[9] The US overreached itself on this occasion and was forced to take a step back.

Key points

- American management of the global economy has produced a backlash of opposition. There have been many losers from globalization, and a coalition of labour unions, environmentalists, and other social movements has organized a series of high-profile protests on their behalf.

- America has not given ground, and continues to insist that a market economy is the only way to generate the wealth that will allow benefits to reach the poor.

- There are few signs of America changing its policies. When it has altered course this has been the result of opposition from other nation-states rather than from the protest movement.

Conclusion: from ordinary country to indispensable nation

The relative size of its economy and its domestic economic success in the first post-cold war decade has allowed America to define the terms on which globalization has taken place. The opportunity presented by the collapse of socialism has led the US to drive its free market ideology relentlessly; trade policy, regional policy, policy in international institutions, policies on aid and loans have all been marshalled to this goal. Beyond economics, policies towards China, Japan, Russia, and Latin America have all been given content by the larger goal of making the establishment of the market system across the globe irreversible. Within this framework the American goal is to maintain its own hegemony. Since the collapse of communism the US has achieved maximum influence in international economic affairs at minimum cost. It has regularly taken the lead in formulating policies, but has been able to insist that other countries pay a substantial part of the cost of carrying them out. This is a clear manifestation of hegemonic rent, which other countries pay to the US because it is driving policies that are in the interests of all in an integrated world economy.

The goal of governing the international economy, in addition to the benefits it brings to US economic interests, is also to provide an opportunity to promote American values. It is perhaps the fundamental premise of US foreign policy that capitalism and democracy are inextricably linked and that to promote the one is to further the cause of the other. The universalization of values associated with America, encapsulated by a version of democracy that enshrines human rights at its core, will ensure a benign peace. The purpose of promoting economic

---

[9] France in particular was wary of the influence the MAI would give to US-based multinationals.

integration is therefore to establish a chain of events that starts with the introduction of capitalism across the globe and proceeds via the establishment of democracy to a stable and secure peace that reflects American values and is in American interests. This is an extremely ambitious agenda. However much it is rationalized in terms of its universal benefits, it aims ultimately at nothing less than the universalization of the American model of economic, political, and social organization. Seen from the receiving end, the imperialist connotations are hard to avoid.

This begs the question of whether the US is capable of rising to the challenge. The most obvious danger is that of overstretch and involving itself beyond the limits of its resources. Even though advanced capitalist nations act increasingly in concert in the task of world economic management, there can be no doubt which country is first among equals. However, it is quite possible that American success stems not so much from the effectiveness of the American model as from its being the only candidate available to fill the vacuum in international power relations in the immediate aftermath of the cold war. If this is the case, then American dominance may not be sustainable. The Achilles heel of the American approach is likely to be the growth in inequality that its relatively free market approach has brought about. A more moderate social democratic approach to economic management has long prevailed in Europe over the aggressive free market philosophy that dominates in America, and the contest between the two visions has probably only just begun to be joined on the international level. When the global era has matured, the pursuit of the free market may yet come to be seen as an aberration. There is little talk these days of American decline, but only a decade ago it was the conventional wisdom. Have we, and the Americans themselves, been duped by its successes in the 1990s?

Some would argue that we have come full circle. In the post-cold war era US pre-eminence was characterized by economic power, but after 9/11 we entered a new era in which security issues, centred on a complex of international terrorism, weapons of mass destruction, and rogue states, have reclaimed their place at the apex of foreign policy. It is difficult to contest the view that 9/11 changed outlooks funda-

mentally but combating terror is about many things other than warfare. It is also about eliminating injustice and inequality, since these lie at the root of terror and have increased under US-sponsored globalization. It is the US that has insisted on the indivisibility of economics and politics by linking inextricably the free market with political liberty and democracy. Unless the future direction in which the US leads the global economy takes more account of inequality, the consequences will continue to threaten political stability and its own national interest.

The consequences may not manifest themselves in terrorism or in protest by the anti-globalization movement, but in the fact that inequality creates a lack of effective demand in the global market. The global market is relatively new and in an early stage of accumulation, but there is every reason to suppose that it will face this problem eventually, just as national markets of mature industrial economies did in the early part of the last century. American capitalism solved the problem by drawing workers into the economy as consumers, and in doing so it smoothed the rougher edges of capitalism and generated the engine of demand that had been drying up under a system in which workers were nothing more than a factor of production to be employed at the cheapest possible cost. If, after the cold war, we have embarked on the global stage of capitalism, it would follow that, in the early parts of this new stage, the system would exhibit renewed energy and dynamism. It would also proceed initially through a harsh regime in which economics runs ahead of politics and the new opportunities for profit are exploited at breakneck speed with little thought for the social consequences. Capital takes the driving seat at this point in the cycle, and this would certainly seem to be true of the last decade. But, as we have seen, a backlash has already emerged with a potency increased by an overlay of nationalism and cultural and religious militancy. It is not yet clear that the American response, governed as it understandably is by the events of 9/11, will be sufficiently broad. If, when hard choices have to be made, the US acts only to protect its own economic privilege, it will attract the flames of rebellion to itself. It will then be faced with capitulation, withdrawal, or repression, none of which is compatible with the goal of stable system maintenance. The US must reform the thrust of its international economic policy because a more just approach is required not only for its own continuing prosperity but for its leadership of international affairs.

QUESTIONS

1 What defines the American national interest after the collapse of communism?

2 What is the relationship between the long boom in the US domestic economy over recent years and American foreign economic policy?

3 Do the bilateral, regional, and global elements of US trade policy complement each other effectively?

4 How much control does the United States have over the policies of the International Monetary Fund?

5 Has the anti-globalization movement been successful in changing US foreign economic policy?

6 What role does foreign economic policy have to play in America's response to the events of 9/11?

7 For how long can America maintain its present domination of the international economy?

FURTHER READING

R. W. Cox and D. Skidmore-Hess (1999), *US Politics and the Global Economy: Corporate Power, Conservative Shift* (Boulder, Colo.: Rienner). Reveals some of the important connections between special interests and foreign economic policy.

J. E. Garten (1997), *The Big Ten: The Big Emerging Markets and How They Will Change Our Lives* (New York: Basic Books). The author was the architect of US trade policy and this book gives the rationale for his approach.

J. Goldstein (1994), *Ideas, Interests and American Trade Policy* (Ithaca, NY: Cornell University Press). Places trade policy in a broader intellectual context than usual.

P. Q. Hirst and G. Thompson (eds.) (1999), *Globalization in Question: The International Economy and the Possibilities of Governance* (Cambridge: Polity). Makes a persuasive case for the argument that the extent of globalization has been exaggerated.

P. Kennedy (1988), *The Rise and Fall of the Great Powers: Economic Change and Military Conflict from 1500 to 2000* (London: Unwin Hyman). This landmark book started the debate on American decline.

H. Nau (2002), *At Home Abroad: Identity and Power in American Foreign Policy* (Ithaca, NY: Cornell University Press). The latest perspective from an author famous for his anti-declinist view of America's role in the world.

W. Robinson (1996), *Promoting Polyarchy: Globalization, US Intervention and Hegemony* (Cambridge, Cambridge University Press). Clarifies the relation between economic policy and wider foreign policy.

J. A. Scholte (2000), *Globalization: A Critical Introduction* (Basingstoke: Macmillan). The literature on globalization is an essential background to this subject and this is an excellent introduction.

P. Trubowitz (1998), *Defining the National Interest: Conflict and Change in American Foreign Policy* (Chicago: University of Chicago Press). Brings up to date the debate on a fundamental concept.

WEB LINKS

Office of the United States Trade Representative

www.ustr.gov/ This site covers all the activities of the USTR, which is responsible for developing and coordinating US international trade and direct investment policy.

United States Department of the Treasury

www.ustreas.gov/ The international section of this site gives up-to-date information on US activity in the world economy.

White House Economic Statistics Briefing Room

www.whitehouse.gov/fsbr/international.html This site presents a range of facts and figures on the international position of the American economy.

United States Census Bureau

www.census.gov/foreign-trade/www/ This site has the most comprehensive foreign trade statistics available.

International Monetary Fund

www.imf.org/ This site is particularly useful for keeping up with current activities of the IMF, which is involved with many countries around the world at any one time.

World Trade Organization

www.wto.org/ This site gives details of current disputes and of the progress on the Doha agenda.

Organization for Economic Cooperation and Development

www.oecd.org/ The OECD is best known for its statistics relating to macroeconomics and trade. There is a wealth of information about the world economy available through this site.

Institute for International Economics

www.iie.com/ The IIE is a research institution devoted to the study of international economic policy. This site gives access to a wide range of studies.

16 Environmental policy

Elizabeth Bomberg

READER'S GUIDE

Environmental policy reflects wider themes of US democracy and politics. It illustrates the tension between states' rights and federal authority; it raises fundamental questions of justice and equity; and it typifies the crowded and fragmented nature of US policy-making. Perhaps above all it reflects Americans' paradoxical desire—noted in Chapter 11—for government action to protect the environment, while also protecting cherished (if contested) principles of individual liberty and limited government. This chapter begins by sketching the development of environmental policy and politics in the US. It then outlines the key characteristics of contemporary environmental politics as well as the varied actors which shape it. The third section explores in more detail the policy-making process and why it produces the outcomes it does. This section also examines prospects for change in a policy area marked by wider conflicts and a search for consensus in a divided democracy.

* The author would like to thank Neil Carter (University of York) and Larry O'Toole (University of Georgia) for their helpful comments.

Introduction: understanding US environmental policy and politics

The development of US environmental policy

Environmental policy today is amongst the most complex, politicized, and contested areas of national government policy. It was not always so. Before the 1970s the federal government had only a minor, indirect role in the formulation of environmental policy. Public concern over environmental degradation was limited, and interest groups engaged with something more than nature conservation were few. Certainly, political engagement with the environment is not new. It reaches back to the industrialization and urbanization of the nineteenth century, the nature writings of Thoreau and Leopold, and the conservation work of Scottish mountaineer John Muir. These personalities and their work reflect the long-standing American concern with the natural environment and how best to manage and protect it.

But the elevation of environmental concern to a prominent political issue began in the late 1960s. This politicization began with an expansion in the nature and number of environmental issues under debate: specific concerns about nature conservation spilled over into fear of pesticides in the food chain (Carson 1962), oil spills, acid rain, toxic waste, overpopulation and nuclear power. The concerns triggered wider political questions regarding who was responsible for these problems and who was best qualified to address them. The politicization also involved a dramatic shift in key actors: conservation or beautification groups gave way to broader, more radical social movements protesting not just environmental degradation but the wider paradigm of economic growth which had caused it. The original Earth Day in 1970 embodied this national expression of environmental awareness and protest. Public concern was heightened further by a series of well-publicized environmental disasters across the US: an oil spill off the coast of California in 1969, the discovery of a seeping waste dump in Love Canal, New York, in 1972, a nuclear accident at Three Mile Island, Pennsylvania, in 1979. Developments on the international level, such as the first UN conference on the environment in 1972, widened Americans' awareness of global environmental problems. Partly in response to these global events, partly to address domestic concerns, and partly to further their own institutional agendas, the US legislative and executive branches in the 1970s competed with each other to produce some of the nation's—if not the world's—most ambitious environmental policy and regulations. The National Environmental Policy Act (NEPA, 1969), the Clean Air Act of 1970, the Endangered Species Act (ESA, 1973), and the creation of the Environmental Protection Agency (EPA, 1970) established far-reaching and comprehensive regulations, institutions, and procedures for the control of pollution and conservation. These acts' provisions still profoundly affect US environmental policy today (see Table 16.1).

In 1980 Ronald Reagan was elected president and environmental policy became even more politicized. The Reagan administration and his Republican Party were unsympathetic to environmentalists' demands, and responsive to industry's complaints of regulatory burdens caused by environmental legislation. Using the cost of regulation as an issue to expand party support, the Republicans in Congress slashed the budget for environmental protection. But they were not successful in dampening public interest or federal engagement in environmental policy. Indeed, during Reagan's tenure, the number and membership of environmental groups grew significantly as citizens mobilized around the real or imagined threat to the environment posed by the Reagan administration.

During the 1990s the entire notion of a strong federal government administering and directing environmental policy was called into question as public concern over environmental issues waned and other social and economic priorities dominated. Yet even during this period federal action on environmental issues continued, spurred on by global agreements (such as the Rio Summit in 1992 or the Kyoto Conference in 1997) and increasingly active environmental groups at home. The result was that, in the space of three decades, environmental policy evolved from a modest local government responsibility into an ambitious and enormously complex system of national environmental programmes and regulation (Bryner 2000: 272).

Unique features of US environmental policy

Environmental policy poses unique challenges to any system of government. First, most pollution or environmental degradation is a by-product of legitimate activities of society such as growing food, providing goods and services or creating jobs (see Weale 1992). Governments thus have sought to regulate rather than halt these activities. But such regulation (say, restricting power plant emissions) heightens the perception that environmental protection clashes with other societal goals such as

Table 16.1 Landmark legislation and its implications

Legislation	Date	Key provisions	Implications
National Environmental Policy Act (NEPA)	1969	Required all federal agencies to prepare an Environmental Impact Statements (EIS) alerting citizens to a project and its possible environmental consequences.	First effort to integrate environmental concerns into other areas. Gave opponents of project chance to delay or even halt project if EIS not properly filed.
Clean Air Act	1970	Regulated discharges of several known pollutants, including automobile emissions; must be periodically re-authorized by Congress.	The Act's rigorous and open-ended provisions sparked ferocious debates about the proper balance between reducing risks to health and harming economic growth.
Water Pollution Control Act	1972	Restricted discharge of waste water into rivers and lakes; required companies to apply 'best available technology' to treat discharges.	'Best available technology' requirement resulted in cleaner water but was strongly opposed as expensive, unrealistic, and inefficient.
Endangered Species Act	1973	Required the US government to protect hundreds of endangered species regardless of the economic effect on the surrounding region.	Enormously controversial, especially when the fate of an endangered species (such as the Spotted Owl) appears to endanger the jobs and welfare of individuals or communities (say loggers in the Pacific Northwest).
Superfund	1980	Sought to restore lands spoiled by hazardous chemical and radioactive waste.	Ambitious and expensive, this Act also sparked endless rounds of litigation.

economic growth and prosperity. This tension has made regulation difficult and contested.

Secondly environmental goals (clean air, water, landscapes) are 'collective goods', which means they cannot be parcelled out only to those who pay for them. Individuals can enjoy the benefits of a public good (say, clean oceans) whether or not they have contributed to its production or maintenance. This dynamic creates a real temptation for individuals or firms to 'free ride' upon the efforts of others, hoping to secure the benefits without paying the costs. The third feature is the substantial technical element of contemporary environmental problems. Scientific expertise is needed to identify and frame a problem and determine possible solutions. Yet these scientific answers are never clearcut and seldom conclusive: Is there really a problem or risk here? How great? Who should decide? How clean is clean enough?

Fourthly, environmental problems are uniquely challenging because of their sheer scope. Pollution transcends state and national boundaries, and in some manifestations (such as global warming, see Box 16.1) is literally international in scope.

Environmental issues also cross established sectors of public policy into energy, industry, public health, agriculture, and transport. The entrenched structure of modern bureaucratic states makes it difficult to integrate environmental criteria into these established policy areas. Finally, in addition to crossing space, environmental issues cross time. The effects of many environmental problems are felt over the long term, affecting future generations whose interests are poorly represented in the policy-making process. Environmental policy thus raises unique issues of social and inter-generational justice (see Box 16.2).

In short, environmental policy is challenging for any system of government to manage. But let us add to these general features some elements particular to the American system of government. We will see that environmental policy is further distinguished by political tensions inherent in American politics and culture. One of these is the competing public expectations of what government should and can do. Another dynamic concerns the conflict between federal government and the individual states.

Box 16.1 Definitions

Command and control. The regulatory method whereby government sets uniform standards and stipulates the methods required to meet such standards. The term is especially attractive to critics of regulation because it implies a coercive, domineering government. In reality, most regulations are rarely applied in a coercive way, but the widespread use of the term represents an unmistakable rhetorical victory for critics of the regulatory approach (see Carter 2002: 287; Dryzek 1997).

Genetically modified organisms (GMOs). An organism whose genetic material has been modified by humans. Genetically modified crops are common in the US, especially soya. While GM foods can bring benefits such as reduced pesticide use and increased crop productivity, they also pose the risk of cross pollination (pesticide resistant genes could spread to weeds and pests) and a threat to biodiversity.

Global warming. A type of climate change caused, most scientists believe, by the accumulation of so-called greenhouse gases, mainly carbon dioxide (CO_2), in the earth's atmosphere. The US is the largest emitter of these gases, which result primarily from activities such as oil refining, power generation, and automobile emissions.

Policy network. Networks bring together actors engaged in a particular policy issue. These may be government actors from different branches as well as representatives from private firms, interest groups, and scientific experts. Each participant needs to bring with him or her some valued resource with which to bargain: information, ideas, finances, constitutional-legal power, or political legitimacy. Networks can be loose and open (as in air pollution control) or tight and exclusive (as, traditionally, in nuclear policy). According to network analysts, the bargaining and resource exchange among these actors determine the shape of policies.

Sustainable development. The idea that economic development needs to be balanced with social and environmental considerations. At the Rio Summit in 1992 it was adopted as a guiding principle for governments of all signatory nations; but the interpretation of the term varies dramatically and its implementation remains patchy.

Competing expectations

As earlier chapters in this volume have emphasized, American politics is infused with seemingly competing, if not contradictory, expectations of government's proper role in society. On one hand, and especially since the 1960s, the American public has demanded increasingly more goods and services from their government, and politicians have sought to deliver them. Americans have consistently favoured strong measures to protect the environment and have looked to federal government to develop and monitor these standards. The public's desire for a strong federal role is evident in opinion polls, election campaigns, and interest group mobilization (discussed below). At the same time, Americans treasure the constitutional notion of individual liberty and the limited government it implies. Advocates of reduced regulation have seized on this desire in their wider attempts to 'roll back' government regulations. For instance, the Republican's 1994 'Contract with America' advocated major cuts in the cost, scope, and reach of federal regulatory policy. Some of these elements were adopted, but others fiercely opposed and blocked by congressional Democrats. These debates were more than party clashes; they reflected broader disputes about the proper role of government, and the balance between the need for strong government action and the constitutional protection of individual liberties (see Box 16.3).

States' rights versus federal action

A second unique feature derives from US federalism and its attempt to balance local and national needs. Addressing the cross-border character of pollution clearly requires some sort of national policy and direction. Yet the area of environmental protection is marked by intense battles over states' rights and fears of federal encroachment. At first the division

Box 16.2 Environmental justice movement

The environmental justice movement refers to a mixed collection of small but numerous grassroots movements concerned with integrating environmental concerns with social equality and justice issues (Schlosberg 1999). Building on the spirit and tactics of civil rights protest, these groups rally against not just environmental degradation but the racial discrimination they feel is inherent within it. For environmental justice advocates, the effects of environmental degradation are part of a catalogue of miseries visited upon the poor, especially those from ethnic minorities. At its edges the movement makes charges of 'environmental racism'. Decisions, say, to site noxious industries, waste dumps, or industries in towns populated by racial minorities are based on calculations of race (see Cole and Foster 2001). These charges remain unsubstantiated, and a possible alternative explanation is class: environmental damaging industries are sited overwhelmingly in poor areas, whatever their ethnic make-up. But the movement offers a powerful reminder of the link between environmental issues and wider social concerns of justice and racial equality.

Box 16.3 Environmental protection and individual liberty: do property owners have the 'right to pollute'?

The 2000 confirmation hearings of the Bush nominee for interior secretary, Gale Norton, were lively. Opponents to her appointment unearthed several colourful quotes which they felt reflected Norton's unsuitability as warden of public lands. Amongst these was her earlier claim that property owners have the 'right to pollute'. The statement reflected property rights advocates' sentiment that any government attempt to regulate how individuals treat their own property represents a constitutional infringement on individual rights (see Rubin 2000). Opponents of Norton ridiculed the notion that polluters enjoy constitutional protection and rallied to block her nomination as interior secretary. The tussle reflected a wider debate about individual rights and responsibilities: when environmental protection clashes with individual rights, which should trump? The question can never be definitively answered because it rests ultimately on assessing the 'proper' balance between the rights of individual property owners and the majoritarian interests of the wider public. Such an assessment would ideally emerge from informed public debate, but no such debate emerged from the Norton nomination. In the throes of a very close nomination battle, Norton chose simply to disavow the statement. Her decision did nothing to settle constitutional debates, but it did help her secure the nomination by a comfortable margin.

of power seems straightforward enough: 'federal government's primary function is to establish policy, develop national standards, ensure that states enforce the laws . . . and provide some funding of compliance costs' (Bryner 2000: 274). State officials then use their discretion when adapting national efforts to match local circumstances. But in practice, as Chapters 5 and 12 stressed, the line between the federal or state domain is blurred and contested.

On one hand, few areas of policy place greater, more diverse, or more potentially intrusive demands on individual states. State governments are increasingly pressed to take on ever wider tasks, ranging from preserving wetlands to testing buildings for asbestos. These federal guidelines can be fantastically demanding, especially in areas such as water quality or toxic waste. States often complain that the federal government provides neither the technical support nor resources necessary to meet the

stringent demands set by the federal Environmental Protection Agency. At the same time, states object to what they see as the unwarranted intrusion into state jurisdiction. Moreover, federal regulation and standards can stifle sub-national innovation and autonomy (Scherberle 1997). In short, the line between state and federal jurisdiction is unclear precisely because both must work together: state and federal agencies must share rather than divide power in the formulation and implementation of environmental policy. The 'sharing imperative' does not come easily to either side, and the result is a constantly evolving relationship involving cooperation but also struggles between state and federal levels of government (see Box 16.4).

> ## Box 16.4 Federalism and the Wild West: the Sagebrush Rebellion and its legacy
>
> The federal government owns and manages massive tracts of land in the West. Historically it has allowed timber, mining, and ranching interests generous use of this land, much to the dismay of environmentalists. In the 1970s environmental groups successfully used litigation to block timber cutting and to create new wilderness areas. A counterattack quickly followed which became known as the Sagebrush Rebellion. Under the battle-cry of states' rights, powerful ranchers and mine owners in the West organized a series of legal and political battles to resist federal public land use policies and oppose federal ownership of these lands. The movements' legal efforts fizzled out by the early 1980s, but its legacy spawned several similar 'anti-federalist' resistance movements and challenges. In the 1990s, for instance, protests erupted after a Forest Service decision to halt construction on a road in a sensitive area of Nevada. The decision prompted the emergence of a 'shovel brigade' intent on building the road 'come hell or high water'.
>
> In all cases these movements have flown the banner of 'states rights' and anti-big government. And clearly, resentment of federal government or a perceived loss of state autonomy contributes to these protests. But at the heart of many of these demonstrations are not constitutional questions of federalism, but rather more mundane questions of which policy benefits whom. Should grazing and mining fees be raised? Should construction of a road be allowed to continue? Thus in environmental policy as in other areas, skirmishes over 'states' rights' often mask fundamental battles between preferred policies.

Key points

- The development of environmental politics and policy in the US has been rapid and contested.
- Environmental policy poses challenges to any state because of its cross-sectoral and complex character. In the US these general challenges are exacerbated by unique features of US politics, including the tension between individualism and government action, and between federal and state governments.

Main actors

Added to these unique features is the sheer diversity of actors and interests involved in US environmental policy. Of course, environmental policy across the globe is subject to a wide array of competing actors. But in the US these different actors and interests engage in a distinctly adversarial system of contestation that is greatly encouraged by the US system of fragmented government. The most important actors are examined below.

The presidency

Presidential leadership has played a major part in the initiation of environmental policy (Soden 1999).

Early in the twentieth century President Teddy Roosevelt set aside huge tracts of land for preservation as national parks (with plenty of opportunity for good hunting and fishing). Several decades later a less obviously 'environmental president', Richard Nixon, proclaimed the 1970s the 'environmental decade' as he signed the NEPA and created the EPA by executive order. The next Republican president, Ronald Reagan, left a profoundly different mark on environmental policy. Reagan was convinced that environmental regulations represented an unacceptable infringement on individual liberties and innovation. He set out to free business from this burden by slashing environmental budgets whenever possible and insisting that regulations be subjected to cost–benefit analysis (an order later carried out by George Bush Sr.).

Bill Clinton entered the presidency with an uneven environmental record from his previous tenure as Arkansas governor. But his administration's environmental credibility was greatly boosted by his vice-president, Al Gore, a long-time advocate of environmental issues and author of a leading book on the subject (Gore 1992). Clinton's most intense environmental activity, however, occurred during his last days in the White House when, in a frantic bid to leave a positive policy legacy, he issued a flurry of last-minute executive orders on the environment, including tougher diesel fuel emission standards and the designation of millions of acres of federal land as national monuments. When Al Gore lost the 2000 presidential election to George W. Bush the new White House team quickly signalled a change in tone and practice. Former oilman Dick Cheney became vice-president, and was chosen to chair a crucial task force charged with outlining US national energy policy. Key cabinet posts such as energy secretary (Abraham Spencer) and secretary of the interior (Gale Norton) were given to known critics of federal environmental legislation. Bush's early initiatives included proposals to further reduce regulation, open up the Alaskan wilderness to oil drilling, relax controls on arsenic levels in drinking water, and abrogate an international treaty on climate change. These moves quickly earned him a label as one of the most anti-environment presidents since the movement began.

But as John Hart and John Owen stressed in Chapters 9 and 10, presidents do not act alone in America's divided democracy. As in most policy matters, presidential impact depends on support in Congress, executive agencies, the media, and the public. For instance, Reagan's more radical revamping of laws and budget-cutting efforts were largely thwarted by divided government and a less enthusiastic public. Bush Sr.'s environmental policy leadership was marked by obvious conflict between the EPA and White House advisers over the pace and stringency of environmental regulations (Kraft 2000: 31). Clinton's brazen attempt to leave a positive environmental legacy was subsequently dampened as many of his executive orders were frozen or overturned. And Bush, too, has been thwarted in several of the proposals mentioned above. Presidents thus set the tone, but cannot determine the actual shape of environmental policy.

Bureaucratic agencies

A less visible actor is the bureaucracy. The number of agencies involved in environmental policy, like most policies, is staggering. At the federal level alone, responsibilities for environmental protection cross over several departments: Energy, Transport, Interior, but also, indirectly, Commerce, Agriculture, and Health. There is no Department for the Environment to coordinate and consolidate departmental duties, although one central agency, the EPA, is responsible for enforcing and administering policies. The EPA's regulatory task is thus daunting: it needs to enforce broad encompassing legislation such as NEPA or the Clean Air Acts and must also administer policies dealing with toxic waste and dangerous chemicals. Presidential appointment of its director has often reflected an administration's broad approach to environmental protection. For instance, Reagan's secretary of the interior, James Watt (who proposed wilderness areas be sold off at low prices), confirmed the worst fears of environmentalists. George W. Bush's appointment of Watt protégé Gale Norton originally elicited a similar outcry, though not enough to block her approval in the Senate (see Box 16.3).

The EPA is only one of several agencies involved in environmental protection. The major environmental Acts defining US policy (NEPA, ESA, and so on) are each enforced by a separate agency with its own priorities and modes of operation. Environmental rules and policies are thus often the result of turf wars between agencies over who 'owns' a particular issue and how it should be implemented or enforced. Nor do agencies simply follow the cues of their congressional or presidential masters. Many environmental laws are drafted in general terms, leaving to bureaucratic agencies wide discretion to draft actual rules and regulations. In short, the more general fragmentation and pathologies of US bureaucratic politics are in evidence amongst bureaucrats responsible for environmental protection.

Congress

Congress also plays a crucial role in the initiation and formulation of environmental policy. In the 1970s and 1980s it launched several environmental programmes, sometimes with the support of the president but often not. At first glance this leading role may seem odd given members' pursuit of particularistic interests and re-election. Case work and pork-barrelling—the supposed mainstays of congressional politics—are not easily amenable to environmental policy (except for limited specific projects such as designated research labs). But Bailey's study on Congress and air pollution (1998) suggests that environmental policy can flourish in Congress when it allows members to make a personal mark on policy or gain power and prestige within the legislature.

Of course, members can also block environmental policy or dilute its significance. The differential impact of Congress is partly explained by its internal decentralized power structure and fragmentation. Several different committees directly handle environmental issues, with several more— agriculture, transport, etc.—touching on them indirectly. In the House, for instance, aquatic pollution is covered by one committee; agricultural run-off (a main component of pollution) by another; irrigation and its environmental effects by yet another. The holistic treatment required by many environmental issues is not easily achieved in the decentralized Congress.

Finally, competition between Congress and the president defines environmental policy as it does other policy areas. Congressional and presidential attempts to adopt leadership roles are often at loggerheads. During the Reagan years, Congress blunted presidential attempts to cut environmental legislation and budgets. During Clinton's administration the Republican-led Congress in 1994 and 1996 played the opposite role, attempting to pass 'roll back' legislation in the face of presidential opposition. Under George W. Bush several battles were waged in the area of energy and environmental policy. In a typical struggle in 2001, Congress's own agency, the General Accounting Office, successfully demanded that VP Cheney hand over material related to the development of the Administration's energy policy (which Congress and many interest groups claimed was made in secret). In spring 2002, a Democrat-led Senate delivered a major defeat of presidential policy when it rejected Bush's plan for drilling in the Alaskan wilderness. Whatever the specific conflicts, the broader point is that environmental policy is often a forum for wider struggles of power between the two branches.

Courts

The courts' role in environmental policy is probably more pronounced in the US than in any other industrialized state. While not formally a policy-making body, the courts are called upon to ensure enforcement of laws and even to try agencies responsible for enforcing laws. Under provisions of the NEPA, environmental groups can use court battles to probe, delay, or halt construction projects or ensure agencies are enforcing agreed legislation. The Sierra Club and other environmental organizations have filed civil suits against the EPA for, among other things, its failure to implement regulation required by the Clean Air Act or NEPA. Some US environmental legislation positively encourages litigiousness. The 'Superfund' legislation covering toxic waste stipulated that those who polluted the land were responsible for paying for its clean-up. Indeed, one controversial clause suggested a single party was liable for paying for the clean-up even if the sources of waste were varied. The result was endless waves of litigation as large firms facing huge clean-up bills tried to recoup some of their costs by suing small businesses that had also contributed to the contamination (Nakamura 1993).

Parties

During the 1960s and 1970s partisan differences on environmental issues were muted. Both major parties, whether controlling Congress or the presidency, supported new environmental policies, albeit the Democrats with slightly more enthusiasm. By the 1980s, however, the partisan divide on environmental issues became more pronounced as Reagan's Republicans rode to power on a wave of anti-regulatory sentiment. The divide sharpened in the mid-1990s along similar lines. Controlling both Houses of Congress in 1994, the Republicans, with House leader Newt Gingrich in the lead, promised to roll back the state by removing a regulatory burden (especially on environmental issues) which, in their view, stifled prosperity and infringed economic and individual liberty. Even if their proposed actions were blunted by a less zealous public and presidency, the Republicans' actions did throw into sharp relief opposing partisan views, leading some analysts to argue in late 2001 that 'there are probably few other policy issues at present on which the difference between the two parties in Congress are so stark' (Dunlap et al. 2001: 30).

Yet the party in Congress is only one dimension of partisan activity, and outside the Beltway partisan differences are less pronounced. Both the Democrats and Republican parties remain broad churches; concealed within them are differences and nuances based on ideological and geographical cleavages. On environmental issues, for instance, moderate Republicans from the eastern seaboard are likely to share positions of moderate Democrats from the west. The point is illustrated by Vermont Senator James Jeffords's abandonment of the Republican Party in 2001, in part because of what he viewed as the executive's radically right views on the environment and other issues. Moreover, as broad parties, the Republicans and especially the Democrats, are able to soak up votes which, in other industrialized countries, might flow to a national Green party (see Box 16.5).

Box 16.5 Is America different?

(I): the case of the missing Green party

Virtually all Western industrialized countries have a national green party. In Western Europe many green parties are represented in parliament and even in national governments. In the US no national Green party existed until 2001, when the Association of State Green Parties in the US decided to file for status as a national party and name themselves the US Green Party (USGP). Despite the name change, the USGP is little more than a loose association of independent state parties. How can we explain America's lack of a stable national Green party?

Part of the explanation is found in the distinctive features of the US party system. Structural obstacles—a first-past-the-post electoral system; the expensive, often onerous procedures necessary to place minor candidates' name on ballots; the huge diverse population costly to reach and harder to mobilize—create a hostile environment for a fledging Green party just as they would for any small party (see Chapter 5). Add to this the all-embracing nature of the two major parties and the ideological moderation of a voting population which eschews radical parties. But other explanations are more specific to the environmental or green movement. In the US this movement is made up of very different strands. First, it includes a strong individualist and apolitical 'new age' contingent which focuses on the spiritual links between nature and the individual. For this movement, green politics is a personal

lifestyle choice, not a collective political goal to be pursued through party politics. Secondly, radical direct action groups such as Earth First! would shun conventional participation such as joining a party or voting. Finally, the many active professional interest groups provide a rich and often more effective outlet of expression for environmental goals.

The Greens' most notable political success was securing Ralph Nader as their presidential candidate in 1996 and 2000. But his candidacy could not overcome these many constraints. Nader attracted publicity for the Green party, and he fared especially well in north-west states (he garnered as high as 10 per cent of the presidential vote in Alaska). In addition, he siphoned off enough support from Democrat supporters to earn him the label of 'vote stealer' by the Gore camp. But in the end he polled less than 3 per cent of the national vote, well under the 5 per cent necessary to receive federal funding. Moreover, while Nader ran on the Green ticket, he himself declined to join the party, in part because of its strange mix of green and new age elements which sat uncomfortably with his broader leftist priorities. In sum, the green movement in the US is a loose and extraordinarily diverse (even by Green standards) collection of state parties and groups. Combined with the hostile conditions facing any third party in the US, it is not surprising that no coherent national Green party exists in America.

Environmental interest groups

Environmental sentiment which elsewhere might support a Green Party is in the US often channelled towards interest groups. The modern environmental movement broadly defined includes a vast array of different organizations, approaches, and goals. These include traditional conservation groups such as the Audubon Society; professional advocacy groups like the Sierra Club or the Natural Resources Defense Council, whose strength lies in a large membership and scientific and legal expertise; environmental justice advocates more concerned with the social and racial distribution and effects of environmental degradation (see Box 16.2); local grassroots protest groups; and more radical direct action groups such as Earth First! (see Gottlieb 1993: 6). Membership of one or more of these groups is high by comparative standards even if the incentives for joining may seem weak (see Box 16.6).

These groups can play an important role in shaping the outcome of elections, policy proposals, and public opinion. But they vary enormously in their ends and means. The Audubon Society is interested primarily in preserving a habitat for birds and wildlife, whereas Earth First!'s goal usually is to halt construction, full stop. Other groups are far more concerned with preserving spaces for hunting and fishing. Cooperation and coordination amongst these groups is therefore limited and almost exclusively focused on specific elections. Even here fragmentation is evident. In the 2000 presidential election, for example, environmental groups could unite in their opposition to the Bush candidacy but split over the question of whether to support Gore or Nader (Bomberg 2001).

Industry groups

Certain industry coalitions and conservative think tanks also have played a crucial role in shaping environmental debates. One of the best known is the Wise Use group, which favours few or no restrictions on the exploitation of resources. Making similar arguments are some influential conservative think tanks, such as the Heritage Foundation, which are usually set up as private, tax-exempt research and advocacy institutions and funded by foundations or corporations. These groups tend to downplay the severity (if not deny the existence) of environmental problems, advocate the use of the market to allocate

Box 16.6 Core academic debate

Environmental interest groups and collective action

In his classic study *The Logic of Collective Action* (1965), Mancur Olson argued that people are unlikely to join groups seeking 'collective goods' which cannot be restricted to its members. Crudely put: why should one spend time and money supporting an interest group when the benefits they obtain will come one's way regardless? The rational action is not to join but to 'free ride' on the efforts of others. According to this logic, environmental or other cause groups which can offer their members little in the way of personal welfare or material interests are harder to form and less likely to survive. Yet the explosion in the number and strength of environmental interest groups in the US (well over 10,000 exist) seems to defy this argument. The explanations are several.

It could be that Olson's logic is simply flawed and humans are capable of altruistic behaviour. Or it could be that the logic needs clarification in the context of environmental groups. Perhaps environmental protection is different from other collective goods. An ordinary citizen has little opportunity to influence national health or welfare policy, but anyone can organize a clean-up day. Or it may be that Olson is right about incentives but wrong about what environmental groups can offer. Maybe members of environmental groups *do* receive selective benefits such as organizational skills, the opportunity to meet new people, a sense of well-being, or the ability to contribute to shared goals important to them (see Moe 1980). In any case, the experience and development of US environmental groups have prompted other political scientists to challenge or qualify Olson's argument and refine our understanding of interest groups more generally (see Chapter 12).

scarce environmental resources, and favour the replacement of legislation with voluntary industry agreements (see Beder 2001).

Less obvious business interests also play an important role in shaping environmental regulation because of the cross-sectoral character of environmental issues. For example, American farmers are the most productive in the world, and to maintain that position use massive amounts of pesticides. Well represented in Congress, the agricultural lobby has been successful in limiting legislation designed to reduce the use of pesticides.

Scientific experts

Opposing interest groups exploit to their advantage the scientific uncertainty surrounding environmental issues. Scientific experts are employed by industry and environmental groups to add scientific legitimacy to their cause. An example is found in the area of global warming, which, in the view of a vast majority of scientists, is a serious ecological problem caused primarily by human activity. Yet some major oil companies, led by Exxon/Esso, are still able to find maverick scientists disputing the causes and very existence of global warming.

For their part, professional environmental groups such as Greenpeace and Friends of the Earth also now include scientists on their staff who can supply their own analysis and statistics concerning the type and extent of damage caused by various pollutants. Even if, as in the case of Greenpeace in the late 1990s, these groups sometimes exaggerate the scale of damage caused by industrial practices, the inclusion of scientists and trained experts on their staff suggests both the politicization of scientific expertise and its ambiguous role in environmental policy (Bomberg 1998: 133–4).

Public opinion

Public opinion sets the broad parameters of acceptable government action on the environment. Any radical slashing of government programmes or funding, as attempted during the Reagan administration or under the Contract with America, is not acceptable. Sweeping environmental legislation is embraced by the public, 'even at the risk of curbing economic growth' (Gallup Organization 2001). But support shrivels if such legislation adversely and directly affects consumers' wallets or choice (say in the form of petrol tax or road surcharge). Moreover, Americans' attachment to the car as a symbol of freedom and mobility is legendary; thus any restriction of automobile use is certain to meet fierce resistance. Beyond these broad guidelines, however, public opinion presents policy-makers with a fickle and contradictory guide to environmental issues. As in many policy areas the public is not informed or all that interested in the technical details or nuances of environmental policy.

A second problem is that public opinion is unpredictable. In recent debates surrounding the proper use of genetically modified organisms (GMOs) the American public's nonchalance is baffling to many Europeans. Yet Americans are intensely concerned with other particular risks—however small—to public health. For instance, reducing emissions of the many potential carcinogens released in relatively small amounts (as mandated in the Clean Air Act of 1970) is considerably more popular than measures to reduce the more obviously harmful CO_2 emissions from vehicles (Melnick 165: 161). Of course, the latter also appears costlier to individuals who might have to pay more for products or limit their private use of automobiles. Thus the public tends to support tough laws when costs are hidden (such as in the testing of water quality or protecting endangered species) but not if the personal costs are obvious.

This public attitude was on display in spring 2001, when President Bush came under fierce criticism for his proposal to raise allowed levels of arsenic in water. The threat to public health seemed direct and visible, and the public outcry intense (Bush later backed down). But his administration's Energy Plan developed that year, which advocated drilling in pristine wilderness areas and increased reliance on nuclear energy to meet undiminished public demands for fuel, received far less attention from the public. The wider point is that on these highly technical issues it is often difficult to include the public in political debate or anticipate and address their concerns.

Box 16.7 **Is America different?**

(II): the case of genetically modified organisms (GMOs)

To many Americans, Europeans seemed to be gripped by a near-hysterical anti-GMO fever. Efforts by bio-technology firms and politicians to assure the European public that GM foods are safe for humans and the environment have not succeeded. Europeans' opposition to GM foods continues to grow, fuelled by environmental group campaigning and resourceful entrepreneurs eager to claim that their product is 'GMO free'. Americans remain perplexed at the European reaction; their own view of GM foods is far more sanguine. How can we explain the transatlantic gulf?

To begin with, GM crops, especially soya, is big business and protects the livelihood of many American farmers. But the divergent attitudes are also linked to wider differences between the two populations' conceptions of

science and risk. In the wake of the BSE crisis in British beef, dioxin scares in Belgium, and tainted blood in France, Europeans are far less likely to trust science and scientists and their assessments of risk. The US has had no such major national food scare and scientists remain an object of trust, even if politicians do not. Moreover, most Americans believe that multinational corporations (such as the biotechnology firm Monsanto) need to be controlled but are not in themselves evil or unnecessarily greedy. Concerns over GMOs may increase in the US as the issue makes its way into international trade talks, and as transatlantic environmental NGOs sow their own seeds of doubt in the US media and public. But for now headlines of 'Frankenstein foods' are unlikely to capture the imagination of the average American.

Key points

- US environmental policy is populated by a considerably varied range of actors including government representatives and officials, interest groups, experts, and public opinion.

- Each set of actors holds starkly different notions of what environmental policy should be and how it should operate.

Environmental policy-making and policy

Policy-making dynamics

The varied actors introduced above interact in complex and unpredictable ways. The unpredictability arises from the sheer diversity of competing actors but also from an absence of a guiding principle or framework for identifying what should be the fundamental priorities or principles informing environmental policy. In both the industrialized and developing world, for instance, the broad principle of sustainable development guides the general policy of many individual countries as well as organizations like the European Union (see Lafferty and Meadowcroft 2000). In its most popular conception,

development is sustainable if it 'meets the needs of the present without compromising the ability of future generations to meet their own needs' (WCED 1987). The concept is terrifically flexible and open to interpretation (see Carter 2001). But at its core sustainable development requires that environmental protection and social development be integrated into more narrow conceptions of economic growth.

Following the 1992 UN Rio Summit, the Clinton administration set up the President's Commission on Sustainable Development, which issued several reports urging the public and private sector to reconcile social, economic, and environmental goals at all levels of government (Kraft 2000: 34).

But so far the US approach to sustainable development has been, in the words of Gary Bryner (2000), 'sorry—not our problem'. Without an overarching framework, US environmental regulation remains built on an ad hoc and complex statutory base made up of dozens of major and supplementary laws reached through bargaining and negotiation.

The absence of guiding principles is all the more noticeable because of the diverse and fragmented character of the US policy-making process. As the scope of environmental policy has expanded, so too have the number of actors and their competing claims. Any piece of environmental legislation is likely to be shaped, pushed, and pulled by a plethora of different committees, agencies, and actors described above. Policy output is thus the result of a long and often tortuous search for consensus in a fragmented system. Scholars have adopted different approaches to help analyse and capture this diversity. Classical pluralism and interest group theories suggest environmental policy emerges from the competition between different interest groups mobilizing resources to secure their goals (Bailey 1998: 17). So, pesticide measures are above all determined by skirmishes between agrichemical companies and farmers on one side and environmentalists on the other, with government agencies refereeing.

But government actors in Congress and in executive agencies are more than mere servants of interest groups. They pursue their own interests and agendas, which may pull policy in directions different from either interest group coalition. Bureaucratic actors, for instance, are interested in empowering agency control, Congress is interested in asserting congressional power. And, as described above, public opinion, the media, and experts can also influence the shape of policy. Thus a more revealing metaphor for understanding environmental policy-making is the idea of a policy network comprising actors from across the public and private sphere, each with a stake in a given environmental issue and willing to bargain with others to influence a given policy (Peterson 1995). Paul Sabatier (1999) has adapted this notion of networks (or coalitions) to help explain the development of clean air legislation.

Even the broad notion of networks does not capture fully the diverse character of US environmental policy-making. Legislation is also shaped by a core set of values and norms which define a country's 'policy style'. For instance, the highly individualistic American culture helps explain why government control of the means of production has not been employed as a method of pollution control (Bailey 1998: 16). The US regulatory style is also distinctively adversarial, formalistic, and legalistic. It relies heavily on formal rules, often enforced in the face of strong opposition from parties affected by them (Vogel 1986; Carter 2001: 290). This style encourages litigation rather than the development of consensual agreements between environmental groups and business, or between the EPA and businesses (Melnick 1999). A country's culture or regulatory style does not determine policy, but it does set the broad parameters within which policies tend to be framed.

Policy outputs

These dynamics have created uneven and often unpredictable policy outputs. The policy goals embodied in the early landmark legislation of the 1960s and 1970s were highly ambitious. Passage of these rigorous Acts clearly helped achieve lower levels of water, land, and—most dramatically—air pollution. But many provisions of these laws became politically explosive and were subsequently diluted. For instance, the 1973 Endangered Species Act requiring the government to protect hundreds of species (including majestic whales but also less popular flying earwigs) was later amended to allow exceptions in cases of overriding national or regional interests. Similarly, the Clean Air Act of 1970 was subsequently diluted with each further amendment. Nor did legislation introduced in the 1990s match the rigorous outputs of earlier decades. A modest energy tax introduced during the Clinton administration was compromised to a pulp and collapsed within a year (Bryner 2001: 142). And, the already weak conservation measures within Bush's energy plan were diluted further in Congress during 2001–2. On other environmental issues, however, environmentalists and their allies within Congress successfully forced the administration to retract some of its more drastic attempts to relax regulations in water quality or carcinogenic substances. The wider point is that environmental policy, especially in the absence of any overarching strategy, remains vulnerable to the vagaries of competing interests and political contests within Congress and between branches of government.

Policy change

Fragmentation and diversity are thus the enduring characteristics of environmental policy-making and outputs in the US. But environmental policies and policy-making also reflect the constantly changing and evolving nature of US politics. Change can be abrupt, especially in response to specific challenges or threats (see Box 16.8). But more often policy change is gradual, as policy-makers adapt incrementally to changes in domestic and international circumstance. In the US such change is evident in the development of new policy methods, and in the expansion of environmental policy concerns.

New tools

The primary means for achieving environmental protection thus far has been regulation: the establishment and enforcement of formal rules and targets. Under this method (which is often if inaccurately referred to as 'command and control') the government prescribes uniform standards, mandates the methods required to meet those standards, and assures compliance through monitoring and sanctions (Golub 1998). This method has brought dramatic environmental improvements but has come under attack in the last decades. One charge made is that traditional command and control methodology has been largely indifferent to costs. Early reduction in polluting emissions (for example, sulphur dioxide emissions from factories) were noticeable and often dramatic. But achieving the remaining marginal gains (such as squeezing out the last bit of sulphur emissions from factories) is far more costly. The 'squeeze' is especially true in the area of environmental health, where the US has spent more and more trying to eliminate smaller and smaller health risks (Melnick 1999: 161).

Secondly, these traditional techniques have not always proved the most efficient way to improve policy-making or environmental quality. The 'command' element has created an intensely adversarial and often litigious relationship between regulators and their subjects. The Superfund legislation, for example, has led to rounds of litigation which clog the system and reduce the likelihood of efficient policy-making. Thirdly, these regulations sometimes have simply not worked. Either they have not been implemented (see Kraft 2000) or they have not had

---

Box 16.8 11 September and its implications for US environmental policy

Like most areas of US politics, environmental policy was profoundly affected—at least in the short term—by the 11 September terrorist attacks. Of immediate notice was the rapid decline in the political salience of environmental issues. Concerns over clean air, endangered species, or environmental justice dropped below the political radar as threats of a more immediate nature preoccupied and consumed the American public. Similarly, criticism of Bush's environmental record and awkward handling of international negotiations was swept aside by the overwhelming public support for his performance as president.

A more lasting effect is a likely change in US energy policy. On one hand, the attacks increased the likelihood of more drilling and extraction of US oil reserves (including in pristine areas) as the US seeks to secure domestic sources of energy supply. Yet the attacks also raised the possibility of a more sober energy policy designed to reduce dependence on, and thus consumption of, oil reserves. Moreover, the attack made it far less likely that the administration's embrace of nuclear energy will continue, given fears of nuclear proliferation (including amongst terrorists) and the vulnerability of nuclear power stations as possible terrorist targets. It is still too early to know the more enduring effects of the attacks on environmental and energy policy. But radical change is not necessarily a given. Even an attack as momentous as that on 11 September must compete with entrenched routines of incremental environmental policy-making.

their desired effect. Many critics argue that these regulations have encouraged citizens and firms to avoid regulation rather than reduce the very activity the regulation was intended to curb. For example, traditional measures have done little to reduce energy consumption: today, per capita consumption of energy is higher in the US than anywhere else in the world and one quarter of the world's carbon dioxide emissions are created by this one country. Regulation does little to create incentives where they might matter most: in the wallet.

The methods of environmental policy have to a certain extent shifted in response to these shortcomings. The regulatory shift is not limited to environmental policy but is part of a broader and older agenda to 'reinvent government' by improving its efficiency and effectiveness (Osborne and Gaebler 1993). Most noticeable is the increasing adoption of economic tools (taxes, incentives, tradeable permits) and more collaboration amongst interested actors. The underlying principle behind economic tools is that companies (and consumers) will pollute less not because it is wrong or illegal to pollute, but because it is in their financial interest to pollute less.

These new methods also imply far more collaboration between government and business, and between federal authorities and the states. Instead of an adversarialism based on the threat of fines and court battles, the new approach suggests a much greater emphasis on government–business partnerships and voluntary or negotiated agreements. For example, under new agreements embraced by the Bush administration, the EPA would not set specific pollution limits but instead negotiate with industry over the reach and timing of practical environmental improvement.

But these measures are not without their critics. Most US environmental groups remain deeply suspicious of market-based approaches or voluntary compliance. They object on ethical grounds (such tools give firms the 'right to pollute') or are uneasy about market forces determining 'acceptable' levels of pollution. Above all, they fear that these new tools may allow major polluters to dodge responsibility and that collaboration will let more polluters 'off the hook'. More radical critics argue that market solutions perpetuate rather than address

the fundamental and capitalist root of environmental degradation: 'The basic paradigm remains unchanged: whenever big profits can be made the environment will be destroyed' (Beder 2001: 132).

Even if environmentalists' objections were assuaged (and some major groups have endorsed these new measures) these new tools pose an additional challenge to American political regulatory culture. Not only are current regulatory programmes deeply embedded; they are based on a far more contentious style of environmental policy-making. The consensual imperative these new tools imply (especially negotiated agreements) are foreign to US regulatory culture. Even industry, which stands to benefit from reduced regulation, may be uneasy about abandoning what is often a well-understood regulatory approach over which they exercise considerable influence (Bomberg 2001; Golub 1998: 7). The debate regarding new methods will continue. The most likely outcome is neither the total retention of traditional regulatory methods nor the full-scale adoption of new tools. For the immediate term, at least, the result will be some regulatory mix, a happy (or not) medium between government-enforced regulation and market-based tools.

New responsibilities

Policy change encompasses not just new tools but an ever-widening scope of issues and responsibilities. Environmental issues have become increasingly entangled with other domestic issues. Environmental policy has always spilled over into other policy areas such as agriculture or transport. But current environmental policy-makers now must address growing concerns over food safety and genetic engineering (see Box 16.7) and even questions of racial equality and civil rights.

The real increase in scope, however, is due to the 'internationalization' of environmental policy, that is, the extent to which US environmental policy is subject to wider global events, issues, and trends. Of course past environmental policy has also been affected by global problems and issues, but the impact of international agreements and events is increasingly apparent for several reasons. First, global environmental problems, especially climate change, no longer seem distant or 'foreign' to most US citizens. Among US citizens, recognition of global environmental problems now equals that of domestic problems of land or water pollution (Gallup Organization 2001). And international trade, once divorced from environmental concerns, now includes intense engagement by environmental interest groups and those opposing them. The 1993 North American Free Trade Agreement was only the first US trade agreement to include environmental provisions (Vogel 2000).

The growing link between domestic policy and international agreement means US foreign environmental policy actions have become increasingly important. Yet thus far, the US position in global environmental politics appears paradoxical. On one hand, the US is clearly an environmental leader in many respects. Its wilderness preservation policies have been used as a model elsewhere. Many of its environmental Acts are amongst the world's most comprehensive. Several key principles defining policy in other countries or globally (such as environmental assessment or emissions trading)

were codified in the US before being adopted by other nations.

Yet its global reputation is one of laggard, and with good reason. It has refused to sign or ratify several key international environmental treaties on matters such as biodiversity or toxic waste transport. It has stubbornly refused to push for environmental protection provisions in World Trade Organization agreements. And in climate change discussions the current Bush administration will be remembered for its clumsy refusal to support the Kyoto Protocol, despite the efforts of 178 other signatory countries (see Box 16.9).

Domestic politics shapes the US's international positions, but the opposite is also true: US domestic policy is increasingly susceptible to global events and issues. The need for foreign energy supplies in particular renders Americans and their consumption patterns acutely vulnerable to foreign events, governments and instability. Whichever way US environmental policy develops, it will be fundamentally shaped by international developments and obligations.

Box 16.9 America and the Kyoto Protocol

The 1997 Kyoto Protocol on climate change committed its signatories to reduce by 2012 their combined greenhouse gas emissions by at least 5 per cent of 1990 levels. The Clinton administration had signed the treaty, but when the time came to ratify in early 2001 the Bush administration publicly abandoned it. Bush contended the Kyoto limits would result in billions of dollars in industry losses, and therefore 'would not commit our nation to an unsound international treaty that will throw millions of our citizens out of work'.

Taken together with his refusal to sign other international treaties, Bush's Kyoto snub reinforced perceptions abroad that the new US administration had embarked upon a path of unilateralism. On closer examination, however, perhaps the Bush administration's Kyoto decision did not represent as dramatic a break with established US policy as it first appears. Rifts between US and European interpretations of the agreement, especially how agreed targets could be met, were already evident during Clinton's presidency. In particular, Europeans and other signatories insisted targets be achieved primarily through

cutting emissions at the source, whereas the US emphasized the use of emissions trading and other means. Moreover, under Clinton as under Bush, Senate ratification of the treaty was far from certain.

But style matters here, and Bush's outspoken disdain for the treaty, and his initial unwillingness to offer counterproposals, did far more to fuel distrust abroad than did the actual substance of US objections. Nor was the perception reversed when Bush unveiled his adminstration's own plan to combat global warming almost a year later. The plan announced in February 2002 reflected the strong influence of domestic interests. Relying on voluntary efforts and market forces to achieve cuts, it essentially preserved the status quo. It was praised by the National Association of Manufacturers and the National Mining Association for its 'bold leadership and flexible approach', but was met with predictable dismay from environmentalists and European signatories alike. Whatever the environmental merits or demerits of the plan, it suggests how the domestic and international dimensions of environmental politics have become increasingly intertwined.

Key points

- The environmental policy-making process is characterized by the lack of any overarching principle or goal (such as sustainable development) and the highly fragmented policy system in which policy is formulated.

- Change is also evident in US environmental policy-making. A shift away from traditional regulation and towards the use of financial tools and more collaborative methods is under way, but still hotly contested.

- Environmental policy has become increasingly intertwined with other domestic issues, but also with broader global issues of security, diplomacy, and trade.

Conclusion

The politics of the environment in the US is shaped by the unique challenges posed by environmental policy and, in particular, the devilish task of managing an issue that is fluid, encompassing, contentious, and very nearly unmanageable. American environmental policy is further distinguished by features distinctive to the US: competing if not contradictory expectations of government's role in the public sphere and competition between levels of government.

The main actors in environmental policy bring with them their own conceptions of the 'right' level of protection and how best to achieve it. While Congress, the president, and environmental interest groups are the most prominent players in environmental policy, less visible actors such as bureaucratic agencies, industry groups, scientific experts and the courts can each shape the form, content or strategy of environmental policy. Their influence varies across issue and across time, but all are potentially crucial to determining the success—or otherwise—of US environmental policy.

The policy-making process itself is defined by the competition, fragmentation, and divisiveness that characterize policy-making more generally. With no coherent overarching principle to guide general policy, the result is a set of enormously complex policies comprising ambitious domestic regulations, weaker supplementary legislation, weaker still international obligations and a very patchy record of implementation (Arentsen et al. 2000).

But change is also a constant in US environmental policy, and some leading analysts discern a shift towards a more enthusiastic embrace of sustainable development (Bryner 2001; Kraft 2000; Mazmanian and Kraft 2001). In addition to the more flexible tools and collaboration discussed above, many projects under way at the local and regional level suggest the eventual incorporation of sustainable development as a defining goal and organizing idea. An array of community or local projects—on transport, sustainable cities, or regional cooperation— embrace the fundamental requirement of sustainable development by explicitly integrating social, economic, and environmental goals (Mazmanian and Kraft 2001). US federalism in this context is an advantage rather than a hindrance to meaningful policy implementation. Whereas national adoption of sustainable development remains weak, experiments at the sub-national level are proving more successful and may eventually lead to adoption on a national scale (see Bryner 2000).

Yet such a shift has far to go, and it would be difficult to overestimate the challenge posed by sustainable development to national entrenched interests and procedures. Sustainable development requires that economic development endangers neither the present global environment nor future generations' ability to develop. The equity issues are unmistakable and intensely controversial, as seen in the development of, and response to, the environmental justice movement. The increase in collaboration and participation required by sustainable development is also far easier to achieve on the local than the national level. A reluctant Congress, in particular, has been slow to adopt any significant change in the dominant style or pattern of policy formulation. Finally, sustainable development requires a fundamental change in the attitude not just of policy-makers but also of private firms and public opinion more generally. The public's embrace of environmental protection and sustainability in the abstract is not (yet) accompanied by a willingness to change consumption patterns in any meaningful way.

In short, the enduring features of US environmental policy are not going to change radically or soon. Yet advocates of a more sustainable environmental policy can take heart: such change may be slow and incremental, but it is not impossible in a political system characterized by fragmentation and divisiveness, but also by innovation, resilience, and an ability to adapt.

QUESTIONS

1 How would you explain the apparent contradiction between the public's broad support for robust limits on pollutants, but its unwillingness to curb consumption to meet these targets?

2 Which actor dominates environmental policy-making?

3 Is the weakness of the US Green party due more to structural or ideological factors?

4 Would it be better to leave environmental policy to a group of experts insulated from public pressure or specific interests?

5 To what extent do domestic concerns shape US policy on global environmental issues?

FURTHER READING

Aldo Leopold's *Sand County Almanac* (1949) provides a classic collection of eloquent essays on American notions of land, nature, and the wilderness. For a passionate account of the environmental movement and its development see Gottleib (1993). For more detailed examinations of some of the other actors introduced here, see Bailey (1998) on Congress, and Soden (1999) on the presidency. Two experienced analysts, Vig and Kraft (1999), provide an authoritative collection of contemporary issues in US environmental policy, while Carter's (2001) wonderfully lucid introduction to environmental politics provides a useful account of US environmental politics from a comparative perspective. An excellent comparative examination of sustainable development is offered by Lafferty and Meadowcroft (2000) and a hopeful assessment of its potential in the US is suggested by Mazmanian and Kraft (1999). Finally, the US's international environmental role is explored in Harris (2001).

WEB LINKS

The official site of the Environmental Protection Agency provides (very!) detailed information on legislation and policies (**www.epa.gov**). The full range of environmental groups are represented on the web including the well-known Sierra Club (**www.sierraclub.org**), Greenpeace (**www.greenpeaceusa.org**), and the League of Conservation Voters (**www.lcv.org**), which tracks the voting records of members of Congress. More radical sites and views can be found through **www.gristmagazine.com**.

Think tanks and foundations opposing more robust environmental legislation include the Cato Institute (**www.cato.or**) and the Heritage Foundation (**www.heritage.org**). For in-depth analysis of specific issues, see the website of the Brookings Institution (**www.brookings.org**). Current developments and news are neatly indexed and available through Greenwire (**www.eenews.net**), but note that a subscription charge is levied for most full-length articles.

17 Social policy

Fiona Ross

READER'S GUIDE

This chapter describes and explains patterns of poverty and inequality in the United States and how social policy has responded to these challenges. It opens with a discussion of the relationship between the distribution of economic and social opportunity and the health of a democratic political system. Sharp divisions between rich and poor, blacks and whites, old and young, men and women may impede equality of opportunity and undermine America's pretensions to be a meritocracy. If inequities in the economic sphere affect the distribution of political resources in fundamental ways, political equality and political liberty can be diminished. The chapter examines trends in the distribution of inequality and poverty in the United States across time. Though the situation of some groups, such as the elderly, have consistently improved across time, children, minorities, and people living in female-headed households continue to suffer alarming rates of poverty. The chapter reviews and evaluates America's main anti-poverty programmes. It probes the politics of these policy choices, investigating why the United States is a welfare 'laggard' and why some programmes have fared better than others.

Introduction

Why does the United States of America, arguably the world's most economically and politically successful country, allow alarming rates of poverty to endure amidst spectacular levels of wealth? Why does such a rich nation not do more to alleviate the plight of its deprived and needy members? On a philosophical level, one might puzzle whether a country can justifiably claim to be the finest political system on earth when so many of its citizens are socially and politically marginalized by poverty.

The relationship between inequality and democracy is a matter of contention. Many advanced societies, America included, justify high levels of inequality in terms of a doctrine of meritocracy: differential rewards provide incentives for talented individuals to succeed and, so long as gain is based on merit, unequal rewards for unequal work is a just and appropriate system of economic distribution. Though political philosophers have long argued that an inequitable distribution of economic resources is likely to skew political power, high levels of inequality may only be problematic for democracy if political institutions deny the poor full inclusion in the political system. Many social conservatives argue that the Constitution, particularly the array of liberties protected by the Bill of Rights, ensure that the needy enjoy the same political rights and liberties as the affluent. Critics contend, however, that the accessibility of America's decentralized institutions to wealthy interests allows a tight relationship to flourish between economic and political power.

Empirical evidence leads social scientists to believe that high levels of poverty and inequality are problematic for democracy for a number of reasons. Inequality correlates closely with several indicators of social and political disintegration, suggesting that the broader wellbeing of the nation is affected by wide disparities in income between the rich and poor. Increased levels of social alienation, which have a dampening effect on political participation, are closely associated with a rise in economic inequality. Miringoff and Miringoff (1999: 108–9) cite evidence from the United Kingdom, a country that has experienced unusually fast rates of growth in inequality since the 1980s, to illustrate its impact on the physical health of a nation. Mortality and morbidity rates for children begin to decline at a significantly slower pace as income inequality rises. Life expectancy for the population at large also correlates positively with low levels of inequality.

In short, we have a number of social, political, and even physical reasons to be concerned about poverty and inequality in the United States. America tends to equate the strength of its economy with the vitality of its democracy. Yet economic expansion has not brought commensurate successes in the social realm. Social trends over the last three decades are far from an American success story.

Key points

- The relationship between inequality and democracy is contentious. Many liberal democracies, Britain included, justify wide disparities in the income levels of the rich and poor in terms of a doctrine of meritocracy.

Box 17.1 The 'social health' of America

A recent study by Miringoff and Miringoff (1999) entitled *The Social Health of the Nation: How America is Really Doing* argues that the concept of social health is ill defined and largely ignored by influential institutions in the United States, including the media and government departments and agencies. In contrast to economic indicators, on which key institutions report daily, critical social data on poverty, inequality, teenage pregnancy, housing, health, and education receive only intermittent and disjointed coverage. Miringoff and Miringoff (1999: 6) offer a nice summary of the contrast:

despite the significance of these trends, there is no *Social Report*, no Council of Social Advisors, no presidential press conference to convey these results and answer questions about them, no congressional committee to review and assess their consequences, no programs on the media to discuss their implications; in short there is no sustained attention to the social health of the nation.

As a result, America has been slow to predict and confront 'social recessions' and the nation has few tools with which to evaluate the significance of social data. The authors (p. 18) observe:

In both the medical sphere and the economic sphere, there are thresholds beyond which a critical point is reached: temperatures above or below a certain point, economic growth above or below a certain level. These lines, obviously arbitrary to some degree, are nevertheless instructive, in that they alert us to potential crises and conditions.... The child poverty rate has remained at or around 20 percent for more than a decade. When does this become significant?

- While political philosophers have long argued that high levels of inequality are problematic for democracy, political institutions, particularly the Constitution and the Bill of Rights, may ensure that the poor enjoy the same core rights and liberties as the affluent.
- Empirical evidence suggests that high levels of income inequality have political, social, and physical consequences, ranging from political alienation to slower improvements in child health.
- Social indicators receive comparatively little attention by influential institutions in America. The well-being of the nation and the health of American democracy are heavily defined in terms of the strength of the economy.

Patterns of inequality and poverty

Rates of inequality and poverty in America today are startling. Looking at social data at a single point in time, of course, does not tell us whether the poor can anticipate an improvement in their condition or whether we might expect their ranks to swell. Consequently, we need to understand social indicators at a given point in time and how they are moving across time. Is the *trend* line moving in a consistent direction, or is it stable across time, or is it fluctuating in response to cyclical conditions? Social data in America show all these things: poverty among the aged has shown marked and consistent improvement over time; though stabilizing since 1993, the gap between the rich and poor has widened significantly across time; poverty rates for people living in female-headed households have shown little change over the course of the past three decades.

Inequality levels

The United States has the highest level of inequality of any affluent democracy. America is currently home to three million millionaires and close to 40 per cent of the nation's wealth is in the hands of just 1 per cent of the population (Hutton 2002). The richest 20 per cent of Americans enjoy over 10 times the income share of the poorest 20 per cent (Miringoff and Miringoff 1999: 106). The US Census Bureau has been tracking levels of inequality since 1947. Its data is based on the Gini index (sometimes called a index of income concentration). The index ranges from 0.0 (complete equality of income) to 1.0 (complete inequality of income). It is based on gross pretax income and does not take account of non-cash government benefits such as Medicaid or Food Stamps. The most striking trend in inequality levels is the general decline in inequality between 1947 and 1968 and the reversal of this trend after this date, particularly after 1980. The rate of growth in inequality began to slow after 1993 and has remained statistically stable since (Jones and Weinberg 2000).

Explanations for rising levels of inequality in America are plentiful. Since the 1980s, the labour market has undergone a shift from manufacturing to technical services. Producer industries, with higher rates of unionization, created disproportionately well-paid jobs for unskilled and semi-skilled workers. These workers are increasingly pushed into poorly paid jobs in the tertiary sector (see Jones and Weinberg 2000: 10). Skilled workers, by contrast, have enjoyed significant wage gains, leading the distribution of wages to become more unequal. Changes *within* manufacturing also favour skilled workers. The Census Bureau notes the downward pressure on the low-skill wage due to globalization, immigration, and trade union membership. Policy choices are equally important, including a decline in the value of the minimum wage.

Change in the composition of households also affects inequality over time largely because married-couple units enjoy higher income levels. Rising rates of separation and divorce, single-parent families, out-of-wedlock births, and delayed first marriages reduce the number of traditional family structures. High-income men are increasingly likely to marry high-income women, thus contributing to the growth in income disparities (Jones and Weinberg 2000).

Poverty

The evidence regarding *trends* in poverty is mixed. After sharply rising during the 1980s and into the early 1990s (reaching a peak of 15.1 per cent in 1993), poverty rates have declined in recent years. The proportion of poor Americans fell from 12.7 per cent in 1998 and 11.8 per cent in 1999 to 11.3 per cent in 2000. Not since 1979 has the United States seen such 'low' poverty rates. The 2000 poverty rate came close to equalling the 1973 historic low of 11.1 per cent. Recent 'successes' can be largely attributed to continued economic recovery following the recession of the early 1990s. Poverty rates increase in the wake of recession and then slowly settle down. While these figures are positive, we need to be mindful of the fact that they capture trends at a time of economic growth. Record lows reported during periods of expansion are unlikely to be maintained or improved upon under less favourable conditions.

But poverty is not a problem that affects all sections of the population equally. Consequently, poverty rates need to be examined by race, age, and family composition.

Poverty by race

At the turn of the twenty-first century, 22.1 per cent of black Americans lived in poverty. This is the lowest poverty rate for black Americans on record. Still, this figure remains three times as high as the rate for white (non-Hispanic) Americans (7.5 per cent in 2000), and well over twice the rate for all white Americans (9.4 per cent). The Hispanic rate was just 1 per cent lower than that for black Americans (21.2 per cent in 2000).

Although the poverty rate for blacks has declined over time, the trend line has been unstable. Between 1959 and 1969 black poverty rates declined sharply (falling from 55.1 per cent in 1959 to 32.2 per cent in 1969). They have not done so since. During the 1970s, black poverty rates hovered around 30.3–33.5 per cent, rising again during the early-mid 1980s. After this point, they began to resemble the poverty rates of the 1970s. Only the thriving economy of the second half of the 1990s brought new gains over the poverty levels of the 1970s.

The story of poverty among America's Hispanic population is similar. The Census Bureau began data collection on Americans of Hispanic origin in 1972. After rising to 26.9 per cent in 1975 following the recession of the early 1970s, Hispanic poverty rates settled around the current rate and began to rise again sharply after 1980. Only since 1999 have Hispanic poverty rates begun to approximate the 1970s level. When viewed in historical perspective, the extent and persistence of poverty among America's Hispanic community is not cause for celebration.

Compared with black and Hispanic rates, poverty levels for white Americans have been lower and more stable across time. After declining from 18.1 to 9.5 per cent between 1959 and 1969, the poverty rate for white Americans underwent modest fluctuation during the 1970s (shifting between 9.9 and 8.4 per cent). After rising to over 12 per cent during the 1980s and 1990s, only since 1999 has the white poverty rate begun to approximate its 1970s level. The 2000 rate of 9.4 per cent (7.5 per cent for white non-Hispanics) is almost identical to the 1969 rate (9.5 per cent). Economic recessions affect racial groups in different ways. Whereas the poverty level for white non-Hispanic Americans increased to 9.9 per cent in 1993 (12.2 per cent for all whites), the rate for black Americans rose to 33.1 per cent (after a peak of 33.4 per cent in 1992) and the rate for Hispanic Americans to 30.6 per cent.

Poverty by age

We know from American research that childhood poverty is strongly associated with less schooling (2 years less), more criminal behaviour, various psychological pathologies and with lower earnings in adulthood (30 per cent less). Children from poor families are also much more likely to become poor parents later and thus, to reproduce the poverty syndrome across generations. (Esping-Andersen et al. 2000: 58)

Both old age and youth poverty rates decreased sharply up to the late 1960s. Old age poverty continued to improve well, whereas child poverty began to slowly increase during the 1970s, more dramatically into the 1980s, and rising again after the recession of the early 1990s. Despite recent improvements, child poverty in 2000 resembled the 1979 level, and rates remain significantly higher than during the pre-1970 period. The all-time low for child poverty (14.0 per cent) was recorded in 1969.

In 1974 the child poverty rate began to exceed that for elderly Americans. Two decades later, it was close to double the rate for the aged. Indeed, consistent reductions in old age poverty is one of America's greatest success stories. At the turn of the century, 10.2 per cent of aged Americans lived in poverty compared with 35.2 per cent in 1959. We should note, however, that the greatest drop in poverty among the elderly occurred during the 1960s and into the early-mid 1970s. While old age poverty has continued to decline, it has done so at a slower pace. Moreover, these rates look less impressive when viewed in comparative context. Poverty among the aged has improved across the OECD since the 1960s (see Esping Andersen et al. 2000: 177). A large number of countries currently boast rates below the 10 per cent level (Finland, France, Germany, Luxembourg, the Netherlands, and Switzerland) and in Austria and Canada fewer than 5 per cent of the elderly live in poverty. Among OECD nations, only Australia and the UK have higher rates of old age poverty than the United States (Esping-Andersen et al. 2000: 178).

Poverty rates among the elderly also differ significantly by race. While 8.3 per cent of white (non-Hispanic) Americans over 64 years of age were poor in 2000, 22.3 per cent of elderly black Americans lived in poverty. This figure represented a record low. A decade earlier, 33.8 per cent of black Americans over 64 years of age were poor. Hispanic elderly Americans recorded a poverty rate of 18.8 per cent in 2000. Again, this figure represented an all-time low. In 1990, 22.5 per cent of Hispanic Americans over the age of 64 lived in poverty.

Aggregate child poverty figures also mask important differences in the wellbeing of America's youth. In 2000, close to 31 per cent of black children (down from 46.6 per cent during the recession of the early 1990s), 28 per cent of Hispanic children (down from 41.5 per cent in 1995), and 9.4 per cent of white non-Hispanic children lived in poverty.

Part of the explanation for the stubbornness of America's child poverty problem is due to changes in family structure across time. Child poverty levels are also affected by economic changes that condition the job security and income levels of their guardians. By contrast, the welfare of elderly Americans does not fluctuate in response to recession. The persistence of child poverty is partially a function of policy choices, specifically tax and transfer decisions, on the part of the state. Most affluent countries report high rates of child poverty before the equalizing effects of taxation and spending. What differs in the United States is the limited effort on the part of the state to reduce child poverty. According to UNICEF, 'All other industrialized nations do more to lift their children out of poverty than the United States' (cited in Miringoff and Miringoff 2000: 84).

Poverty in female-headed households

People who live in a family headed by a female with no husband present are at high risk of poverty. While these Americans recorded their lowest poverty levels in 2000 (27.9 per cent), viewed in historical perspective, their situation has not shown marked improvement over time. After declining from a high of 49.4 per cent in 1959 to 39.8 per cent in 1966, poverty levels for occupants of female-headed households fluctuated between 35 and 40 per cent over the next three decades. Only in 1998 did their poverty rate fall below 35 per cent. What has changed across time are the number of Americans living in these families. In 1959 female-headed households constituted 10 per cent of all families. They now represent 17 per cent of American households (Dalaker 2001: 7).

There are marked racial differences in poverty rates among female-headed households. Poverty levels for black Americans residing in these families are close to double the rate for whites. In 2000, 22.1 per cent of people living in white female-headed households were poor (18.0 per cent of white non-Hispanics), compared with a rate of 38.7 per cent for blacks and 36.5 per cent for Hispanics. This was the first time the black and Hispanic rate had dropped below 40 per cent (approximating the

1966 rate for whites). While any fall in poverty is welcome, the permanency of these improvements is unclear.

Further social trends

Poverty and inequality levels are not the sole indicators that social scientists use to evaluate the well-being of a nation. Ask any European about social America and they will point to the absence of basic health care for millions of adults and children. By 2008, 55 million Americans will be without any form of health care coverage. Over 50 per cent of the uninsured are working 'low-income' Americans (those who survive on less than 200 per cent of the poverty line). Virtually all advanced democracies ensure that children enjoy access to a comprehensive range of health benefits. At the close of the twentieth century, 14.8 per cent of all children in America were uninsured. Disaggregated by race, 28.9 per cent of Hispanic children, 18.8 per cent of black children, and 13.9 per cent of white children lacked access to health care (Miringoff and Miringoff 1999). While new federal–state programmes are expanding child coverage, this is not the case for adults. There are also vast numbers of under-insured Americans. The consequences of these trends are well documented: people without health insurance are less likely to seek medical care at a timely stage, more likely to receive treatment through emergency room services and, unsurprisingly, suffer higher mortality rates.

A foreign visitor to any major American city is also likely to note the number of homeless people. Rates of homelessness are notoriously difficult to assess. Early estimates released by the Clinton administration put the figure somewhere between 4.95 and 9.32 million people, although later estimates suggested that the upper bracket could be as high as 12 million (Miringoff and Miringoff 1999: 141). Recent data indicate that somewhere between 700,000 and 2 million people are homeless each night, 7 per cent of whom are 'unaccompanied minors', 13 per cent are women, a staggering 36 per cent are families with children, and 44 per cent are men (**www.policyalmanac.org**). Half of the homeless population are thought to be black, 35 per cent are white, 12 per cent are Hispanic, 2 per cent are Native American, and 1 per cent are Asian. The Century Foundation reports that close to a third of the homeless have been without housing for at least two years (**www.policyalmanac.org**). These trends are integrally related to the poverty levels discussed above. They are also a direct function of the shortfall in low-income housing and the 'de-institutionalization' of people suffering mental health problems (Miringoff and Miringoff 1999: 141).

We noted at the outset of this chapter that social trends do not simply mirror economic indicators.

Box 17.2 **Definitions: defining poverty**

The US Census Bureau is the official source of poverty definitions and estimates in America. To determine how many people live in poverty, the Census Bureau adds pre-tax income to any cash benefits an individual or family receives from the state and compares this amount with their poverty threshold. Non-cash benefits, such as Medicaid, food stamps, or housing, are excluded from this calculation. Poverty thresholds are not adjusted for geographical differences in the cost of living, but they are indexed for inflation. In 1998 a family of four (comprising two adults and two children) with $16,530 to live on per annum was officially classified as impoverished. In 1999 this figure had risen to $17,029. In 2000 the poverty threshold was $17,463.

The Census Bureau also examines the severity of poverty using two measures. A ratio of income to poverty compares a family's income to its poverty threshold. By applying this measure we can tell how many people survive on less than 50 per cent of their poverty threshold and how many families are 'near poor' in the sense that their income level is under 125 per cent of their poverty threshold. In 2000, 4.4 per cent of people had a family income below 50 per cent of their poverty threshold (12.2 million) and 4.5 per cent of people were 'near poor' (12.3 million). An income deficit measure reveals the dollar shortfall in a family's income below its official poverty threshold. The income deficit for families in poverty averaged $6,820 in 2000 (see Dalaker 2001: 14).

America's claim to greatness looks rather less compelling when social data are considered. The trends described above are partially a function of the policy choices of the nation. The United States does not attempt to engineer equality of result among its citizens through extensive government programmes. It does not seek to ensure that all Americans enjoy a similar quality of life. The federal government, often in conjunction with the states, does provide numerous benefits and services that ease the lives of many Americans. Yet the omissions in programmatic coverage remain startling to many European observers.

Key points

- Rates of inequality in America are the highest in the industrialized world. After a sharp decline between 1947 and 1968, the Gini index has crept steadily upwards, especially after 1980. Though levels of inequality have been stable since 1993, income differences between rich and poor Americans remain dramatic in absolute terms.

- Poverty levels in America are among the highest in the industrialized world. Over 11 per cent of Americans were impoverished in 2000. Trends in the data reveal different poverty patterns across

age groups. The elderly, for example, have enjoyed significant reductions in poverty across time. Despite recent improvements, child poverty remains a stubborn problem. Current rates are significantly higher than those recorded during the pre-1970 period.

- Poverty levels also vary dramatically across racial groups. Black Americans continue to suffer three times the poverty rate of non-Hispanic whites. In 2000, 22.1 per cent of blacks were impoverished, the lowest rate ever recorded by the US Census Bureau. The poverty rate for Hispanics stood at 21.2 per cent in 2000. By contrast, only 7.5 per cent of white non-Hispanic Americans were poor.

- A growing number of Americans live in female-headed households. These people are at high risk of poverty and their situation has not shown marked improvement over time. Americans living in black and Hispanic female-headed households suffer double the poverty rate of non-Hispanic whites.

- Part of the explanation for these trends lies with the policy choices of the nation. Many affluent democracies have similar levels of child poverty *before* taxation and transfers are taken into account. What differs in America is the more limited effort on the part of the state to reduce child poverty.

Policy responses

If you are not wealthy, you had better have a good job or a responsible government. If you cannot draw subsistence or income from property . . . and are not blessed by the bounty of family, friends, neighbours or charitable institutions, you'd better have steady employment or a well developed welfare state. (Hicks 2000: 3)

Most of America's social programmes can trace their origins to two major bursts of policy activity during the twentieth century. President Roosevelt's New Deal, a far-reaching package of economic and social measures aimed at stemming the Depression and alleviating its worst consequences, went a long way towards bringing the state into the lives of

Americans. Before this time, social welfare was largely a matter for the institutions of civil society, most often the family, church, and charitable organizations. The next major burst of policy activity came three decades later as America entered a period of liberal progressive politics. President Lyndon Johnson's Great Society legislation led to the creation of two major health care programmes, Medicare and Medicaid, as well as a number of other initiatives, including public housing.

This section provides an overview of the major social programmes provided in part or whole by the federal government. Programmes fall broadly into three categories: insurance-based benefits, notably Social Security and Medicare; means-tested income maintenance cash benefits, such as 'welfare' (AFDC/TANF), Supplemental Security Income, and the Earned Income Tax Credit; and non-cash means-tested aid, such as food stamps, Medicaid, housing, and job training. Despite the range of benefits offered in part or full by the federal government, gaps in coverage, such as inadequate child health care, sick pay, and maternity leave, remain significant by European standards.

Insurance benefits

Social Security

Old Age, Survivors, and Disability Insurance (OASDI), typically abbreviated to Social Security, pays benefits to retired people, to the disabled (and their dependants), and to survivors of insured workers. Who qualifies from among this pool of potential eligibles and the amount they receive each month depends on their contribution record. Benefits are not means-tested. Rather, they are 'earned' in relation to contributions. Over 95 per cent of the workforce is insured under OASDI. Workers pay a 6.2 per cent payroll tax, as do their employers on wages up to $72,600, producing a total payroll contribution of 12.4 per cent. In total, close to 45 million Americans receive benefits, 62 per cent of whom are retired, 16 per cent the survivors of deceased workers, 10 per cent disabled under the age of 65, and 11 per cent the dependants of disabled or retired workers. Approximately 90 per cent of the elderly receive Social Security benefits. For almost two-thirds of beneficiaries (64 per cent) Social Security provides 50 per cent or more of their total income. For close to a third of recipients it provides 90 per cent of total income (www.ssa.gov). At the turn of the century, Social Security helped keep 40 per cent of recipients out of poverty. However, 8 per cent of beneficiaries remained impoverished, including 7 per cent of white and 21 per cent of black Social Security recipients (www.ssa.gov).

Despite its popularity, Social Security has come under increasing pressure for reform as a result of America's ageing population. The greying of America would be less important were it not for the fact that the pension system operates on a 'pay-as-you-go' basis, whereby current retirees are supported by the payroll taxes of current workers. At present, there are more than three workers to pay for the benefits of each retiree. By 2030, there will be just over two. At this point, 20 per cent of the population will be seniors and the fund will only be able to pay benefits at about 75 per cent of their full rate.

Medicare

Medicare provides health insurance for approximately 40 million people and has done much to improve the health and wellbeing of elderly, blind, and disabled Americans since its creation in 1965. It is a popular government programme, with 95 per cent of Americans saying that it is 'very important' or 'somewhat important' that Medicare survives (www.medicarewatch.org). While it is difficult to determine the unique contribution of a programme in isolation from other benefits and services, we know that close to 30 per cent of elderly Americans were impoverished in 1965—a figure that has now dropped by two-thirds (www.medicarewatch.org). Likewise, elderly Americans can now expect, on average, to live for three years longer than in 1965. A number of developments help account for this increase in life expectancy, but seniors' access to health care and hospital treatment is surely one explanation (www.medicarewatch.org).

Health coverage under Medicare is not comprehensive. The programme has two components. Part A provides in-patient hospital/hospice insurance and is funded by a 2.9 per cent payroll tax split between employers and employees. Part B, optional Supplementary Medical Insurance, pays 80 per cent of out-patient services and is financed by patient premiums and general revenues. While Medicare has been extended recently (the 1997 Balanced Budget Act added a number of annual cancer screenings, tests for osteoporosis and diabetes control to the programme), and prescription drug coverage is on the agenda, a number of services, including long-term nursing care, are not covered.

The demographic pressures that affect Social Security also apply to health care, though this huge entitlement is experiencing faster growth rates owing to new technologies and expensive prescription drugs. Recent predictions suggest that Part A will be insolvent by 2025. While more serious attempts to cut costs have been forthcoming over the last five years, the programme's popularity and political pressure from medical groups have reversed some big budget cuts and prevented major restructuring.

Income maintenance cash benefits

Welfare

For Americans, the term 'welfare' is synonymous with one programme: Aid to Dependent Children (ADC), later renamed Aid to Families with Dependent Children (AFDC) and, since the passage of the Personal Responsibility and Work Opportunity Reconciliation Act in 1996 (PRWORA), Temporary Assistance to Needy Families (TANF). Part of President Roosevelt's New Deal, ADC was initially a limited entitlement targeted at orphans and lone women with dependent children. The programme gradually expanded over the next decade and with some speed during the 1960s and 1970s. At its peak in 1994, it covered 14 million Americans. In 1996, President Clinton and the Republican-controlled Congress ended AFDC and replaced it with the block grant, TANF. This was the first time such a large-scale entitlement had been reduced to a block grant. The legislation created a fully-fledged system of 'workfare', departing radically from previous initiatives by imposing severe time limits upon the receipt of benefits.

Under TANF an individual can only receive welfare assistance for five years during their entire adult lifetime (counting from its enactment). Within two years of receiving welfare, claimants must work. At state discretion, this period can be reduced or abolished, forcing welfare recipients to work immediately—an option that close to 50 per cent of states have selected. Participation in community service is now mandatory after two months of receiving benefits. A family's benefit can be reduced pro rata for each day an individual does not work. At state discretion, the sanction may exceed the pro rata penalty to include the full denial of benefits.

Medicaid coverage can be terminated for adults (but not their children) who do not fully comply with work requirements. The new welfare system also stipulates that no person between the age of 18 and 50 (without children) can receive food stamps for more than three months in a three-year period. Children born on TANF can be excluded in the calculation of family benefits.

Supplemental Security Income (SSI)

In October 1972 SSI was created as a single federal income entitlement offering cash assistance to the poor aged, blind, and disabled. This means-tested benefit aimed to provide a minimum income guarantee for these 'deserving' categories of poor Americans and is funded out of general taxation. The programme was momentous in the sense that it 'federalized' what had been a highly varied system of state initiatives. Approximately 6.5 million people receive the benefit. The majority of recipients (approximately 55 per cent) are blind or disabled adults between the ages of 18 and 64. The elderly constitute close to a third of recipients, while blind or disabled children make up the rest of the programme's beneficiaries. In terms of numbers enrolled in the programme, SSI is relatively stable simply because its main source of expansion is through population growth.

Earned Income Tax Credit (EITC)

The Earned Income Tax Credit, first introduced in 1975, is perhaps America's most popular and successful cash benefit. It is targeted solely at working people and aims to lift families out of poverty by reducing their tax burden. In so doing, it attempts to 'make work pay' and ensure that employment is a feasible option for potential welfare recipients. Poor workers without children may claim the benefit but credit levels are severely restricted in such instances.

In total, close to 20 million people/families claim the EITC. It lifts approximately 5 million people out of poverty, around 50 per cent of whom are children. No other federal programme has reduced child poverty so effectively (www.policyalmanac.org). Owing to its success in alleviating poverty and encouraging work, sixteen states have introduced their own EITCs.

Box 17.3 **Core academic debate**
Has welfare reform worked?

The effects of welfare overhaul are a source of disagreement among both practitioners and academics. Within a year of the legislation's passage, supporters were celebrating plummeting welfare rolls while opponents predicted frightening rises in poverty and homelessness. The caseload has dropped by 50 per cent since the PRWORA was enacted, and close to 30 per cent of welfare recipients who remain on the rolls are working (Handler 2001: 1). Explanations for this dramatic fall vary. In May 1997 the Council of Economic Advisors claimed that over 40 per cent of the drop could be attributed to economic growth, state welfare experiments could claim credit for around 30 per cent of the fall, and measures to boost employment, such as the increase in the EITC, were responsible for the other 30 per cent (Katz 1997: 2603–10). Irrespective of government policy, the welfare caseload was expected to fall as the economy gained strength following the recession of the late 1980s and early 1990s. After reaching an all-time high in 1994, the number of people claiming welfare had been systematically declining *before* overhaul.

Most policy experts agree that the full impact of welfare overhaul on work and poverty will only be clear under less prosperous conditions. Welfare recipients are typically short on competitive skills and usually the first victims of economic swings (65 per cent of welfare recipients do not have a high-school education). The dramatic

early decline in the welfare rolls has already levelled off as those with the weakest skills and highest barriers to employment remain jobless. Estimates suggest that these people will be inadequately qualified for 90 per cent of all positions created over the next five years (Handler 2001: 35). Even the 10 per cent of vacancies that are suitable in terms of low skill requirements may be inaccessible for other reasons. Many of these people lack basic job skills, and a high proportion suffer from depression and drug-related problems. Recognizing this fact, the majority of states have decided to take advantage of federal provisions that permit them to exempt up to 20 per cent of their caseload from the PRWORA's work mandates/time limits, and six states are planning to use state funds to support welfare recipients with multiple employment barriers beyond the five-year limit (Handler 2001: 11).

It is also important to bear in mind that the welfare caseload is simply one indicator by which to evaluate the success of overhaul. We know that poverty levels have not declined at the same rate as the welfare rolls, in part because the low-wage labour market, where the vast majority of welfare recipients find jobs, has stagnated despite America's economic boom. As Handler (2001: 9) reminds us, leavers do not find a solid career and work their way up the employment ladder to affluence. They remain poor.

Non-cash benefits

Medicaid

Medicaid provides health care coverage to over 42 million poor Americans, approximately half of whom are children. The programme is a joint venture between the federal government and the states. The federal government sets a number of broad national mandates, leaving the states with considerable authority over eligibility, benefit levels, and payment criteria. Consequently, Medicaid provision varies across the country. On average, children can expect to receive Medicaid when their family income is less than 100–150 per cent of the federal poverty level.

As noted above, it is difficult to assess the precise impact of any given programme in isolation of other initiatives. A number of indicators lead policy analysts to believe that Medicaid has been a highly successful programme. Impoverished children who receive Medicaid enjoy better health than children from marginally better-off families who do not qualify for the benefit. The significant drop in infant mortality since Medicaid became available may be cited as proof of the programme's value (over 30 per cent of all births are now paid for by Medicaid). Moreover, had Medicaid not compensated for the decline in employer-financed health insurance since the mid-1990s, over 50 million Americans would lack access to health care.

The rising cost of Medicaid, particularly to the state governments, has led to a number of reform proposals, the most dramatic of which would transform the entitlement into a block grant. In 1995, GOP law-makers attempted to restructure Medicaid along with AFDC. President Clinton objected strenuously to the possibility of losing Medicaid as an entitlement and exercised his presidential veto power. It may only be a matter of time, however, before the states gain greater control over health insurance for the poor in the form of block grants.

State Children's Health Insurance Program (SCHIP)

The State Children's Health Insurance Program (SCHIP), a federal–state initiative to expand health care coverage for poor children, was launched in 1997 as part of the Balanced Budget Act. The programme is the most significant child health initiative since Medicaid was enacted in 1965. One of SCHIP's key aims is to ensure that children who are living in families that earn too much to qualify for Medicaid but too little to purchase private insurance through the marketplace have access to health care. Children who live in families with incomes up to 200 per cent of the federal poverty level may enrol in the programme. By 2000, SCHIP had insured 3.3 million children who previously lacked health care coverage. Despite the importance of SCHIP and Medicaid, 10 million children in America still lack access to medical care (**www.policyalmanac.org**).

Food stamps and nutrition

Hunger is a persistent problem in America. In 1999 the Department of Agriculture issued a report stating that approximately 3.5 per cent of households suffered from repeated hunger over the course of any given year. The anti-hunger advocacy group, Food Research and Action Centre (FRAC), reports that 4 million children under 12 years of age suffer hunger on any given day and close to 10 million others are 'at risk' of hunger (**www.policyalmanac.org**). The main initiative for addressing hunger in America is the food stamp programme (food stamps are

---

Box 17.4 **Categorical and block grants**

Social assistance programmes funded by categorical grants are often referred to as federal entitlements. They attempt to ensure a degree of uniformity in standards across America. Any American who meets eligibility criteria is entitled to the benefit regardless of the overall cost to the federal government. However, because the states usually make some funding contribution, in reality benefit levels can vary quite significantly across the country. Block grants, such as TANF, allow the states greater scope to devise their own programmes and set their own eligibility and payment criteria. Under these arrangements, the states can tailor their assistance programmes to local needs and serve as policy laboratories of the nation as a whole. They can also retrench programmes in the search for budgetary gains. In the case of Medicaid, governors have pressurized the federal government to turn the entitlement into a block grant partly because inflation throughout the health care industry is particularly

burdensome to the states. All but one state have an obligation to balance their budgets (and eighteen states are subject to fiscal restrictions). Consequently, Medicaid devours a rising proportion of state spending. Yet block grants come with risk. They are frequent targets in the federal budget cutting process. Local governments complain that block grants encourage the states to devolve costs and responsibilities to cities and counties where need and resources tend to be inversely related.

Critics of the block grant system also point to the negative effects of state competition on welfare provision. For example, TANF has been accused of encouraging a 'race to the bottom' in welfare provision. In order to prevent a 'welfare magnet' effect, whereby claimants cross state borders in search of higher benefits, the state governments have incentives to lower benefit levels and increase work requirements, especially in relation to neighbouring states. Added to this is the risk of business flight to low-tax states.

vouchers which recipients exchange for approved groceries at supermarkets—for example, alcohol and tobacco are excluded). Close to 18 million Americans qualified for food stamps in 2000. The federal government also funds a number of child nutrition programmes, such as the school lunch programme. Approximately 27 million children are fed at nursery and educational centres, costing almost $10 billion per annum (FY 2000). Other anti-hunger programmes include WIC (Women, Infants and Children), which assists approximately 7 million Americans in meeting basic food requirements.

Key points

- Social programmes fall broadly into three categories: insurance-based benefits (Social Security, Medicare), means-tested income maintenance cash benefits (AFDC/TANF, SSI, EITC), and non-cash means-tested aid (food stamps, Medicaid, housing).

- America's main social programmes can trace their origins to President Roosevelt's New Deal and President Johnson's Great Society. The most fundamental shift in the American safety net after these two bursts of social policy development has been the restructuring of AFDC from a federal entitlement to a block grant.

- The effects of welfare overhaul are a source of disagreement among practitioners and academics. While more Americans are working, it is clear that many ex-welfare recipients cannot find the type of stable employment that will lift them out of poverty. Only during less favourable economic conditions will we be able to assess the real impact of welfare reform with precision.

- Despite the range of anti-poverty initiatives provided in part or whole by the federal government, the gaps in guaranteed benefits render America 'exceptional' by European standards. Most apparent in this regard is the absence of adequate sick leave, maternity provision, and child health care.

The politics of social division

Given the empirical evidence pointing to the effectiveness of many anti-poverty initiatives, why does America not widen the reach of its social safety net? The answer to this question is complex, but what is clear is that it does not lie with the cost of developing and maintaining a far-reaching system of social protection. One explanation for the birth and expansion of welfare states emphasizes the level of economic development. If a nation's wealth constitutes the core explanation for welfare state development, we would expect America to provide its citizens with a comprehensive social safety net. A more compelling explanation than economics alone is that a combination of political institutions, ideas, and actors have coalesced in the Unites States in such a way that the momentum needed to create a fully-fledged welfare state never occurred.

Investigating the development of income security policy over the course of the last century, Alexander Hicks (2000) emphasizes the critical role played by the mobilization of workers via political parties and trade unions, and their representation in government and in the neo-corporatist bargaining networks. One key explanation for why the United States lacks the institutionally entrenched welfare state found in other affluent societies, therefore, is due to the fact that the working class failed to mobilize effectively behind a social democratic agenda. America never experienced the prolonged political pressure of a working-class movement that drove welfare state development in Europe. The New Deal and Great Society only serve to illustrate the isolated and crisis-driven nature of social expansion in the United States. Moreover, the broad welfare state consensus uniting parties of the center left and center right in Europe during much of the post-war period has been far less evident in the United States. Consequently, many of the New Deal and Great Society programmes have been subject to continuous political threat since their founding.

To the extent that welfare state development has been dependent on the success of social democratic politics, the lack of socialism as an attractive rallying cry for the working-class in the United States begs to be understood. Precisely why a working class movement, with socialism as its ideological *raison d'etre*, never became a mainstream political force in America has interested scholars for much of the past century.

The absence of working-class politics in the United States helps explain why America is a 'welfare laggard' in comparison to other affluent societies. How can we explain the variation in the fate of social programmes that America has instituted over the last century? Political support for social benefits depends to some degree upon whether they are insurance-based or income maintenance measures that have no link to contributions. Public support for income maintenance measures also differs depending on whether they provide cash or non-cash aid to the needy. Reflecting America's unease with the choices and behaviour of the poor, the most costly forms

---

Box 17.5 Is America different?
No socialism in the United States

By the outbreak of the First World War, twenty-seven cities across America had elected socialist officials, including several long-serving mayors. Eugene V. Debs, America's best-known socialist candidate, contested presidential elections in 1904, 1908, 1912, and 1920 (the Socialist Party was represented by A. L. Benson in 1916). Only eleven years after the founding of the Socialist Party in 1901, Debs won six per cent of the popular vote. Yet much of his success has been attributed to his personal charisma and the 'Americanized' version of the party doctrine (including a party preference for lower taxes). And, despite some success at the local level, few Socialist Party members were elected to Congress. Why did social-ist ideology have such little appeal in the United States at a time when other nations were organizing mass left-wing political movements?

This question has a long academic history, dating from the 1906 publication of Werner Sombart's *Why Is There No Socialism in the United States?* A recent treatise on the subject, *It Didn't Happen Here: Why Socialism Failed in the United States*, is offered by Lipset and Marks (2000). The authors suggest a number of cultural, structural, and institutional explanations. A basic suspicion of a centralized state and a deep-seated attachment to the value of property ownership do not sit comfortably with socialist ideology. The architectural impediments to the emergence of a powerful state, together with America's core belief in individualism and limited government, encourage radical thought to find expression in the form of liberalism rather than socialism. American institutions,

notably the two-party system and winner-takes-all electoral system, also present practical hurdles to the success of a third political force at the national level.

High levels of immigration, coupled with the ethnic heterogeneity of immigrants, likewise thwarted the development of a class-based political movement. The likelihood of forging a coherent movement from poor workers divided by culture, language, and religion was slim. Of some significance, the cultural and religious influences that immigrants brought with them to the United States were often inimical to class politics and socialist ideology, particularly Catholicism. Moreover, immigrants tended to develop their own social support networks in the form of fraternal and voluntary organiza-tions rather than seek protection through the state.

Class organizations also adopted mistaken strategies at decisive moments of their history. The decision of the American labour movement to oppose the state, rather than attempt to use its power to achieve its ends, proved to be a critical failing. Believing the state to be the handmaiden of corporate interests, the American labour movement resisted the creation of programmes that would expand the reach of government, including pensions, unemployment insurance, a minimum wage, and compulsory health insurance.

Added to these explanations must be governmental repression of socialists and communists in a number of high-profile episodes, the comparative prosperity of America, and the opportunity for social mobility.

of public assistance are 'in-kind' benefits, such as Medicaid. Indeed, the only popular form of cash assistance is the Earned Income Tax Credit.

Though most Americans are willing to help the needy, survey evidence indicates that they draw a sharp distinction between the deserving and undeserving poor. Americans disapproved of AFDC because, above all else, they believed welfare recipients should work irrespective of cost to the taxpayer. According to opinion polls, the same people who want government to spend more on the needy also believe that AFDC needed to be retrenched. Voters object to providing people with benefits in the absence of obligations. While most Americans agree that structural forces contribute to individual hardship, they rarely accept that market imbalances, unemployment, or inadequate education constitute insurmountable barriers to self-sufficiency. By extension, poverty is seen to derive in part from the behaviour and choices of the individual. Cope (1997: 204) makes note of this fact by pointing to the titles of state welfare reform initiatives, such as Colorado's 'Personal Responsibility Project', Missouri's 'Families Mutual Responsibility Plan', and Georgia's 'Personal Accountability and Responsibility Project'.

Although welfare overhaul was encouraged by appeals to the values of individualism and self-sufficiency, the racial politics of welfare reform were overt. The basic unpopularity of AFDC had much to do with the fact that it was overwhelming associated with black single mothers. As the programme's constituency changed over the years, so did its popularity. Handler (2001: 5) comments; 'Starting in the late 1950s and 1960s ... [its constituency changed] from largely white widows to divorced, deserted, and disproportionately never-married women as well as families of color. Welfare was now a "crisis".' Americans' misinformation regarding the entitlement contributed greatly to their dislike of the programme. Kuklinski et al. (2000) report extraordinarily high levels of public ignorance concerning welfare provision, culminating in a distinct anti-welfare bias. Up to two-thirds of respondents in their Illinois study were misinformed regarding the percentage of black people on welfare and 90 per cent provided incorrect answers when asked about the portion of the federal budget spent on welfare.

A fascinating study by Martin Gilens blames the media for perpetuating historical stereotypes of blacks as indolent. In so doing, even liberal-leaning outlets have conspired to 'racialize' welfare. Americans are not simply anti-welfare because they suffer from the misperception that it disproportionately helps blacks. Rather, the media feeds the public with images that welfare indulges slothful, undeserving blacks. The American public is neither anti-welfare on purely racial grounds nor because it is preoccupied with the values of individualism and self-sufficiency. Americans want to help the *deserving* poor, but they suffer from pervasive misinformation regarding welfare and this misinformation is racially distorted.

In contrast to welfare for the poor, Social Security and Medicare are victims of demography and the beneficiaries of politics. Of some importance, contentious proposals for restructuring Medicare won approval in the Senate in the latter stage of the second Clinton administration. Backed by the American Medical Association, these initiatives included an increase in the eligibility age from 65 to 67 years, a rise in 'Part B' premiums for doctors' visits for more affluent pensioners, and the introduction of a $5 per visit co-payment for home health care visits. Both the administration and the House rejected all three proposals and, in standard blame-avoidance fashion, a seventeen-member National Bipartisan Commission on the Future of Medicare was left to handle the programme's future. On Social Security, Clinton did manage to shift the debate somewhat during the second session of the 105th Congress but little was achieved in terms of policy change. President Bush's sixteen-member Social Security Commission reported on three main solutions at the end of 2001. The commission failed to recommend any particular action, and as all three options are likely to entail benefit cuts, sweeping reform is unlikely in the near future.

Key points

- According to Hicks (2000), welfare state development has historically depended upon the mobilization of workers via political parties and trade unions, and on their representation in

Box 17.6 Social justice, American style

In a book entitled *The New Politics of Welfare*, Bill Jordan explains how America's definition of social justice is integrally related to labour market obligations and the quest for economic efficiency. A just welfare state is one that emphasizes the 'work ethic' and requires all members of society to contribute to the economy in an active and productive way. Consequently, the American vision of social justice is one that renders its citizens subservient to the economic system. Participation in the economy is a moral issue. The doctrine, in Jordan's (1998: 3) words, rejects 'the continuing relevance of class and exploitation. . . . [and] emphasizes employability and equality of opportunity'. Handler (2000: 3) summarizes the American ethos well:

Failure of the 'able-bodied' to support oneself and family is considered a moral fault. Moral fault, in turn, is broader than failure to earn; it incorporates other forms of so-called deviant status and behaviour. Hence, it becomes easier to blame the victim rather than address structural issues.

Cope (1997: 190) emphasizes this point: 'The underlying message is that that the causes of poverty lie with the individual—not with economic shifts, exploitation, race or gender discrimination, disinvestment in education and social supports, or a lack of available jobs.'

Framed in such individualistic terms, welfare recipients must have their labour market responsibilities thrust upon them. Elaborate welfare systems are inherently misguided, and, far from ameliorating poverty, they are apt to induce social ills by discouraging individual responsibility. Social rights are limited to adequate education and access to training (Jordan 1998: 18). The deserving poor, that small group of people who suffer real need (as opposed to possessing slack work habits), are provided for through rigorous eligibility tests and tightly targeted benefits. The very concept of need, Jordan (1998: 99) argues, 'implies passivity, incompetence and dependence'. According to critics, this philosophy of social justice is heavily capital-friendly and provides for little de-commodification of labour. It is also insensitive to the politics of division which prevent the smooth application of meritocratic principles. Will Hutton (2002), a severe critic of the United States, argues that 'the inequality justified by this theory of social justice cannot be excused by more mobility and opportunity than in other societies, America's great conceit'. Recent investigations into levels of social mobility suggest that America does not compare favourably with Europe.

---

government and in the neo-corporatist bargaining networks. American workers never effectively organized behind a social democratic agenda in these ways.

- Socialist ideology was unable to provide an appealing rallying cry for American workers for a number of reasons. Recent research on the topic points to the importance of America's distinctive political culture, its institutions, high levels of immigration, mistaken strategies by the trade union movement, and state repression of left-wing politics.

- Most Americans want to help the needy. However, they draw a sharp distinction between the deserving and non-deserving poor. Welfare politics in America are founded on high levels of misinformation that is racially distorted. By contrast, Social Security and Medicare are victims of demography and the beneficiaries of politics.

- The American version of social justice emphasizes the 'work ethic'. Social rights are limited and heavily dependent on labour market obligations. Failure to work is a moral issue.

Conclusion

Levels of inequality in the United States are the worst in the advanced world. Poverty rates for many sections of American society are equally dismal in comparative context. In absolute terms, social data in America are alarming. Though trends in poverty levels for most groups have improved to varying degrees since the late 1990s, social scientists suspect that recent gains owe much to sustained economic expansion and are unlikely to be maintained under less prosperous conditions. Despite the importance of these trends, the 'social health' of America receives little sustained attention from influential political institutions.

The impact of inequality and poverty on the democratic health of a political system is a matter for debate. In the words of one prominent British commentator, 'The sumptuous and bleakness of the respective life styles of rich and poor represent a scale of difference in opportunity and wealth that is almost medieval—and a standing offence to the American expectation that everyone has the opportunity for life, liberty and happiness' (Hutton 2002: 22). Most Americans believe that the wealthy enjoy greater political opportunity than the poor. Recent scandals, such as the Enron affair, drive home the disproportionate power of corporate interests. Yet Americans' suspicion of a strong interventionist government, their basic faith in the efficiency of the market, their belief in the neutrality of the Constitution and the pluralism that it fosters help justify these inequities.

Whether the poor can be effectively helped through public policy is also a divisive topic in America. Liberals argue that reductions in poverty across time for groups such as the elderly indicate that policy can alleviate poverty and that the federal government can play a successful role in helping the needy. Poverty levels in America would be considerably higher, they argue, were it not for the effectiveness of government programmes. Though many liberals now shun the idea of a 'big' federal government, they are loath to see entitlements, such as Medicaid, transformed into block grants for fear of programmatic retrenchment.

Conservatives counter that the persistence of poverty since the days of the Great Society is evidence of policy failure. 'Compassionate Conservatism', embraced by President George W. Bush, advocates a policy agenda founded on the standard conservative principles of low taxes, reduced regulation, and smaller government combined with a social agenda that favours self-reliance over government redistribution and support. According to compassionate conservatives, 'throwing money' at the needy has encouraged a passivity and dependence among the poor, further isolating them from mainstream America. Wasteful government programmes have also had the effect of undermining civil society more generally. Ineffective state paternalism, therefore, needs to be replaced with a new reliance on individuals, families, faith-based groups, and local communities. In cases where state intervention is deemed to be absolutely necessary, the lower units of local government should be the first port of call.

Despite these political divisions, most Americans want to see the state help the deserving poor. In the case of health care, the views of the American public are quite clear-cut: they believe that all people should have access to decent medical services. With respect to work and welfare, however, the concept of 'deserving' becomes more restrictive. The deserving poor are vulnerable Americans who are either attempting to help themselves or are without the means to do so (such as children and the disabled). Hence, Americans support benefits, such as the EITC, which ease the lives of the *working* poor. By contrast, able-bodied Americans who do not actively participate in the economy are usually judged to be 'undeserving'. While recession, disadvantage, and discrimination may hurt their competitive position in the labour market, they are not an excuse for indolence. Consequently, welfare support should be accompanied by strict work-related obligations and time limits to ensure that assistance does not become a 'way of life'. The beliefs Americans hold about the poor, and particularly welfare recipients, of course, are not necessarily factually accurate. Survey evidence shows that they are based on high levels of misinformation that is racially skewed.

The politics of welfare are not simply a matter of public opinion. Social policy in America is affected by legal and financial relationships between the federal government and the states. In the case of welfare, the states lobbied heavily for the opportunity to run their own welfare programmes. Most were already operating under federal waivers at the time of overhaul. Likewise, the pressure for Medicaid reform is largely coming from the governors, most of whom are Republicans. Their desire to have the entitlement changed to a block grants is mainly driven by financial pressures. Yet block grants carry risk: they have been prime targets in the budget-cutting process across time and the states have frequently complained about unfunded mandates.

With the historic and current trend in social assistance granting considerable financial and policy authority to the state governments, the possibility of America developing a wider and more uniform social safety net is remote. While we might anticipate incremental expansion in particular areas, such as child health, overall the American safety net is likely to become more fragmented and uncertain. Indeed, geography is increasingly likely to determine the wellbeing of Americans who fall upon hard times.

QUESTIONS

1 To what extent are high levels of inequality and poverty compatible with democratic principles?

2 Is America's claim to be a meritocracy a convincing justification for high levels of poverty and inequality?

3 Evaluate the importance of racial differences in poverty levels in the United States.

4 How can we account for the different trends in old age and child poverty across time?

5 Discuss the significance of the rise in female-headed households in America.

6 Assess the social value of America's main anti-poverty initiatives. Which programmes, if any, would you like to see retrenched?

7 Do you agree with many Americans that welfare recipients should work for their benefits? Do you agree with imposing time limits upon the receipt of benefits?

8 Discuss the main explanations for the limited reach of America's safety net. What other factors might be important in thwarting the development of social programmes?

FURTHER READING

R. A. Cloward and F. F. Piven (eds.) (1993), *Regulating the Poor: The Functions of Public Welfare*, 2nd edn. (New York: Vintage Books).

G. Mink (1998), *Welfare's End* (Ithaca, NY: Cornell University Press).

D. Schmidtz and R. E. Goodin (1998), *Social Welfare and Individual Responsibility (For and Against)* (Cambridge: Cambridge University Press).

S. F. Schram (2000), *After Welfare: The Culture of Postindustrial Social Policy* (New York: New York University Press).

T. Skocpol (1995), *Social Policy in the United States: Future Possibilities in Historical Perspective* (Princeton, NJ: Princeton University Press).

WEB LINKS

www.ssa.gov official website of the Social Security Administration

www.hcfa.gov Health Care Finance Administration, Center for Medicare and Medicaid Services: detailed information on Medicare, Medicaid, and Schip

www.acf.dhhs.gov/news/welfare Department of Health and Human Services, Administration for Children and Families: detailed information on TANF, Medicaid, Child Poverty, state welfare, and social services

www.epn.org Electronic Policy Network: public policy news from a range of organizations

www.urban.org/welfare/overview.htm The Urban Institute: independent think tank conducting research into the effects of welfare overhaul

www.iwpr.org Institute for Women's Policy Research: investigates the impact of policy on women and their children

www.clasp.org Center for Law and Social Policy: researches the effects of law and policy on the poor

www.heritage.org Heritage Foundation: conservative think tank

www.cato.org Cato Institute: policy institute promoting limited government and free market values

www.policyalmanac.org Alamanac of policy issues

Part Four

Issues and controversies

American politics is about more than the institutions of government and the key public policies surveyed in the earlier parts of this book. Indeed, many students are especially interested in American politics because of the distinctive and ongoing controversies that distinguish it—either in nature or degree—from politics in other liberal democracies. In the final part of this book, the contributors tackle a series of such controversies, ones that have at once provoked intense divisions among Americans, attracted extensive scholarly commentary, and proved to be enduring features of contemporary American politics. As will become clear, these issues—from abortion to gay rights and multiculturalism—remain important subjects of conflict in America, not simply because millions of Americans disagree on matters of morals, rights, and public order (one of the more striking features of several of these controversies is how much consensus exists among the vast majority of Americans, even on questions such as abortion and gun control), but also because the design of America's governing institutions, the character of America's intermediary organizations, and the fragmented and complex nature of the policy process helps to perpetuate their salience.

Part Four

Issues and controversies

18 Abortion

Martin Durham

READER'S GUIDE

This chapter examines the long-running conflict over abortion in America. In particular, it explores the development of the abortion rights and anti-abortion movements, their relationship to the main political parties, and their efforts to secure greater or lesser access to legal abortion through the presidency, Congress, the Supreme Court, and state legislatures.

Introduction

In examining the politics of abortion in American politics, it would be wise to consider it in a number of ways. One is in terms of the structure of the American political system. American politics is premised on a separation of powers between the executive, the legislature, and the judiciary. All three have played important parts in the unfolding abortion conflict. The presidency has on a number of occasions played a crucial role in favouring one or other side. Congress has also been critical, both for the restrictive bills it has passed and for those it has rebuffed. Most importantly, the Supreme Court, both in decriminalizing abortion in 1973 and in returning on several occasions to exactly what restrictions might be acceptable, has been absolutely central to the conflict. Each of these institutions have impinged on each other, whether in the form of presidential vetoes of congressional legislation or in the form of the Senate's power to refuse presidential nominations to the Supreme Court, making abortion, as we shall see, an excellent case study of exactly how the American political system works.

But more can be learnt from a discussion of how the abortion conflict has unfolded. The importance of both rights and morality in political discourse in America is graphically illustrated first by the rise of a movement to gain access to abortion and then by the emergence of a movement to ban it once more. Indeed, one noticeable aspect of both movements is that both seek to argue in terms of rights, in an effort to maximize the possibility that it and not its adversary will finally settle the abortion debate in its favour.

Many other questions will make their presence felt in our discussion. In exploring the relationship between the executive, the legislature, and the judiciary at national level, we are in danger of ignoring one of the most important characteristics of the American political system, its federal nature. Many decisions are taken at state level, and this is particularly well demonstrated by the battles over exactly what restrictions can be legislated for in particular states. (In turn, the country's federal nature is likewise demonstrated by the role the Supreme Court has played in upholding such restrictions, or striking them down.) Another feature that is equally well illuminated by a study of abortion is the party system. America is a country in which many voters define themselves as Independents. Nonetheless, it remains a two-party system. This can lead to the situation where one holds the White House and another is dominant in Congress. It may well result in one party with a majority in one house of Congress and its opponent holding the majority in the other. The party system in America is not a firmly disciplined one, in which those who are elected on a party ticket consistently vote the party line. Instead, parties are broad coalitions based on areas of regional strength, and those who are elected as Democrats or Republicans are exposed to a variety of pressures. In the case of abortion, the quest for votes and the demands of activists have worked to put each party in particular (and diametrically opposed) positions.

One final point needs to be made. In examining abortion, we will learn much about the tensions that have divided American society in recent years. Frequently, abortion is taken to be emblematic of one of the most significant of these tensions, that between traditionalists and progressives. In important ways, this is true. As we will see, however, to characterize those who wish to reverse the liberalization of abortion as traditionalists may well obscure rather more about the role of the issue in American politics than it reveals.

Box 18.1 Definitions

Abortion: the deliberate termination of a pregnancy.

Anti-abortion movement: the constellation of organizations, set up in some cases before the *Roe* decision, in other cases after, in opposition to the legalization of abortion.

Abortion rights movement: the constellation of organizations, set up in some cases before the *Roe* decision, in other cases after, and created to bring about (or sustain) the liberalization of abortion law.

Christian Right: the constellation of organizations, set up in the mid-1970s and subsequently, committed to the mobilization of evangelicals in opposition to abortion, feminism, homosexuality, and other facets of what was seen as an increasingly non- or even anti-Christian society.

Pro-choice: the self-definition favoured by supporters of abortion rights through which they characterize their own stance as favouring 'a woman's right to choose' (and present their opponents as anti-choice).

Pro-family: the self-definition favoured by supporters of the Christian Right through which they characterize their own stance as defending the family (and present their opponents as anti-family).

Pro-life: the self-definition favoured by opponents of abortion through which they characterize their own stance as defending 'unborn human life' (and present their opponents as anti-life).

Abortion before *Roe*

In the development of the abortion issue in American politics, the key moment is the Supreme Court's 1973 decision, *Roe* v. *Wade*. It was that decision that marked a major gain for those who believed that abortion should be freely available, and a massive defeat for those who believed that it should remain illegal. Before discussing that decision, and the protracted conflict that has followed, we should first examine why abortion became illegal, and in order to do this we should turn our attention to the measures introduced by state legislatures in the mid-nineteenth century.

These measures ruled that, except when the woman would otherwise die, abortion was a crime. Abortion, it was held, was morally wrong and, to the degree that it continued to be widespread, would deprive the nation of the children it needed. This combination of moral and demographic argument was connected, in turn, with concerns over gender. If women refused to bear children, it was declared, then they were shirking their duties. The origin of these arguments can be traced to more than one source. In part, as we might expect, religion was crucial. However, given the dominating position then held by Protestantism, not only did the Catholic Church play a less important role in opposing abortion than it would do in the twentieth century, but part of the anti-abortion argument was entangled with fear of growing numbers of Catholic immigrants, and of the danger that abortion among native-born women posed to continued Protestant hegemony (Luker 1984: 15, 60; Mohr 1978: 87–90, 186–7; Petchesky 1984: 82–3).

The most important influence on how the issue was seen, however, was not religious but instead the increasingly important doctors' organization, the American Medical Association (AMA). Medical science, it declared, had established that the common assumption that abortion was permissible in the early stages of pregnancy was wrong. The embryo, it held, was alive from conception. Later writers have suggested that the key factor in the AMA's stance was concern not over the status of the foetus, but the status of its members. By successfully criminalizing most abortions, doctors drew a line between what could be seen as the unacceptable practice of medicine and the acceptable, and in doing so sought to ensure that only those viewed as medical professionals could decide the rare circumstances in which abortion might be permissable (Mohr 1978: 160–1; Luker 1984: 20–2, 27–35).

In the decades that followed, the circumstances in which an abortion might be held to be necessary were to prove sometimes contentious. Many doctors interpreted the legislation strictly. Others, however, interpreted risk to a woman's life more liberally. Faced with the danger that a doctor might be prosecuted, hospitals tended to establish abortion boards to review problematic cases. Many women, however, had to resort to illegal abortions, at times at the cost of their own lives. In 1959 a body concerned with legal reform, the American Law Institute, proposed allowing abortion on grounds both of the woman's health and foetal abnormality. The latter proposal was to become crucial in advancing the reformers' cause, in light of the furore that followed three years later over the effects of a drug that had been recommended for pregnant women, thalidomide. (Luker 1984: 54–7, 73–6; O'Connor 1996: 27).

Where in the nineteenth century the AMA had been crucial in the banning of abortion, in 1967 it declared itself in support of reform; and while in the previous century the fear of under-population had been important in securing the restriction of abortion, the belief that population was rising too fast now helped the abortion liberalization argument. The emergence in the mid-1960s of a women's liberation movement was also crucial, and increasingly the reformers' argument that abortion should be allowed on specified grounds was challenged by the more radical proposition that abortion was a woman's right. The forces supporting liberalization proved increasingly successful, with eighteen states deciding between 1966 and 1971 to change their abortion law. But in a number of states, demands for legal change were rebuffed, and in this the emergence of a counter-movement was crucial (O'Connor 1996: 30, 32; Staggenborg 1991: 18–21; Lader 1973: 178–80).

As with the forces on the other side, the anti-abortion movement involved a number of different elements. Crucially, however, it was connected with the Catholic Church, which had been central in the emergence of anti-abortion groups since the late 1960s and in 1971 the US Catholic Conference's Family Life Division set up a National Right to Life Committee (NRLC) to coordinate their activities. As we have seen, much of the conflict over abortion in the 1960s and early 1970s took place at state level. Ultimately, however, it would be at national level that the issue would be settled (*Front Lines Research* November 1994).

Key points

- Abortion was criminalized in nineteenth-century state legislation.

- While this was due in part to concerns over both women's role and the birth rate, the leading role in the criminalization of abortion was played by the medical profession.

- The emergence of an abortion rights movement a century later was also linked with concerns over women's role and the birth rate. The medical profession became increasingly sympathetic to reforming the abortion law.

- In the nineteenth century, religion played a part in the criminalization of abortion. In the twentieth century, when a movement emerged to oppose its decriminalization, religion was crucial.

Roe v. *Wade*

In 1970, a Texas federal district court decided in the case of *Roe* v. *Wade* that the state's restrictions on abortion were unconstitutional. It did not, however, issue an injunction against their enforcement, and both the state and the plaintiff sought to persuade the Supreme Court to review the case. Both supporters and opponents of abortion liberalization attempted to influence the Court's consideration of the case through what are known as *amicus curiae* briefs, by which individuals or groups seek to argue the grounds on which the justices should decide the issue. In January 1973 the Supreme Court pronounced on the issue, and by declaring its agreement with the earlier decision, made it impossible for nineteenth-century state abortion laws to continue to be enforced. Indeed, in a companion case, *Doe* v. *Bolton*, the Court also ruled that those reforming state laws which had been passed during the 1960s were also over-restrictive and unconstitutional (Craig and O'Brien 1993: 1–33; Faux 1988: 233–6, 280–1; Luker 1984: 126).

This did not mean that all restrictions were seen in this light. Instead, the Court set down, and would revisit later, where restrictions might be consti-

tutional. But, as both sides in the abortion conflict recognized, the decision in the two cases represented a far-ranging liberalization of the law.

In order to understand how the majority in the Court (the decision was reached by seven to two) came to its conclusion, we need to retrace our steps to an earlier decision in what had once been an equally controversial area, that of birth control. In 1965 the Court had ruled that for a state to make the provision of birth control to a married couple a crime was incompatible with what they described as the constitutional right to privacy. While not expressly presented in this way within the Constitution, this, it was held, was the implication of a number of the amendments which had been added to it. In a subsequent case, the Court extended the right of access to birth control to the unmarried. In 1973, the same right to privacy was extended to abortion (O'Connor 1996: 46; Craig and O'Brien 1993: 6–8, 26–7).

In reaching this decision, the Court declared that it was unnecessary to resolve when human life began. Instead, abortion should be seen differently depending at what stage in a woman's pregnancy it would take place. In the first three months, where abortion could be less dangerous to the woman than continued pregnancy, then the abortion decision was a matter in which state restrictions had no place. In the next trimester, in order to protect maternal health, the state could play a regulatory role, placing conditions in such areas as the qualifications of the abortionist and the facilities in which the operation could take place. Only in the final three months, when a foetus could potentially survive if born, could a state restrict those abortions not necessary on grounds of risk to the woman's health or life (Craig and O'Brien 1993: 28–30).

Key points

- The key moment in the development of the contemporary abortion conflict is the Supreme Court's 1973 *Roe* v. *Wade* decision.

- This held that nineteenth-century state legislation on the issue was unconstitutional.
- The Supreme Court held that only in the final stage of pregnancy could states restrict abortion on grounds other than protecting a woman's life or health.

Box 18.2 *Roe* and the liberalization of abortion

We, therefore, conclude that the right of personal privacy includes the abortion decision, but that this right is not unqualified and must be considered against important state interests in regulation . . . With respect to the State's important and legitimate interest in potential life, the 'compelling' point is at viability. This is so because the fetus then presumably has the capability of meaningful life outside the womb. (*Roe* v. *Wade*, 1973)

Abortion in the 1970s

In striking down both the 1854 Texas law and, in the companion *Doe* case, a 1968 Georgia measure, the Supreme Court fundamentally shifted the ground for the burgeoning abortion conflict. For abortion rights campaigners, who in the late 1960s had set up the National Association for the Repeal of Abortion Laws (NARAL), the Supreme Court had liberalized abortion law beyond the expectations of earlier reformers but had left the door open to earlier restrictions. Furthermore, that the decision nonetheless fell short of what the abortion rights movement would wish became clear following the Supreme Court's rulings first in a 1977 case, *Maher* v. *Roe* and then in 1980 in *Harris* v. *McRae*. There was, it concluded, no obligation on either states or the federal government to provide funding for women unable to afford abortions (Staggenborg 1991: 25; Craig and O'Brien 1993: 12, 91–4, 162–3).

For abortion opponents, it was the 1973 decision itself that was the problem. One response was to

reorganize the NRLC as a membership organization. Resting on often strong state organizations, much of its efforts were concentrated on establishing what restrictions could be secured in particular state legislatures and not subsequently struck down by the Supreme Court. But there was considerable activity too within Congress, with the vote that was eventually to lead to the *McRae* decision taking place in 1976. Named after its main sponsor in the House of Representatives, the Hyde Amendment initially only allowed the provision of Medicaid for abortions that were necessary because of the danger to the woman's life. Voted on every year, the Amendment was passed in a less restrictive form the following year, whereby abortion could also be funded in cases of rape or incest, before the original formulation was restored in 1981 (Paige 1983: 82–4; Craig and O'Brien 1993: 118–37, 162–3).

For both the abortion rights movement and anti-abortionists, members of Congress could prove amenable to restricting access to abortion. Presidents too took up the issue. Already, before the *Roe* decision, Nixon had directed military hospitals to follow state law on abortion, and it was subsequently suggested by a presidential aide that an anti-abortion stance could help win voters to the Republican Party. President Carter's declaration in the late 1970s that the federal government should not fund abortion suggested that where his predecessor sought to court anti-abortion support, Carter was unwilling to identify with the abortions rights argument. In 1980, however, the Democratic Party platform explicitly declared its support for the Supreme Court's ruling. Conversely, the Republican Party took an increasingly anti-abortion position. In 1976 its platform declared that while it favoured the continuance of debate on the issue, it supported a constitutional amendment to reverse the *Roe* judgment. In 1980 its support for an amendment was no longer accompanied by a call for further debate (O'Connor 1996: 44–5, 71–6; Craig and O'Brien 1996: 166).

Here, we need to think not only about why parties might take particular stances, but about how movements can frame issues. By framing, we mean the ways in which an issue can be represented in order to maximize potential support, and in this both the abortion rights and the anti-abortion movement have proved particularly adept. In identifying with how a movement had framed the abortion issue, a party could gain not only votes but more immediate support in the form of both donations and volunteers. For the Democrats, what had come to be described as a pro-choice stance might not only bring it support from abortion rights activists in election contests, but made it more attractive to those voters for whom feminist issues were highly salient. For the Republicans too, the abortion issue might prove advantageous in more than one way. While Catholic voters should not be seen as necessarily anti-abortion (or as treating the issue as the basis of a voting decision), to adopt what had come to be termed a pro-life stance was to bid for Catholic votes. But from the late 1970s, Republican opposition to abortion was also connected to another factor (Wilcox 1989: 1–19; Meyer and Staggenborg 1996: 640–1).

While at the time of the *Roe* decision the Catholic Church had been forcible in its opposition, Protestants had been less prominent. Some churches were among the early supporters of abortion law reform and those, usually evangelicals, who opposed the Supreme Court at the time were little noticed. The involvement of Billy Graham and others in the creation in 1975 of a specifically Protestant anti-abortion body, the Christian Action Council, marked a partial shift, but the most important development came later in the decade. In 1979 the creation of the Moral Majority marked the culmination of a gradual mobilization of a religious grouping that hitherto had played little role in politics. Its concerns particularly centred on what were described as pro-family issues, such as feminist rejection of traditional roles for women, the increasing acceptance of homosexuality, and, crucial for our purposes, the *Roe* decision. The creation of what became known as the Christian Right was not solely due to decisions taken within the evangelical community. Criticism of the moderate stance taken by leading Republicans in the mid-1970s had led to the inception of the New Right, a constellation of groupings which argued that the only way to remove liberal politicians from office was by taking up populist issues. One of these issues was abortion, and the defeat of a number of incumbents in the 1978 elections was widely attributed to the New Right's intervention. It is difficult both to clarify the impact of any single issue and to disentangle the role of the New Right as such from the specifically anti-abortion groups that also took part in the election contests. The subsequent creation of the Moral Majority and other Christian Right organizations represented a further complication for any analysis of the abortion issue's role in American politics. This would become particularly evident in the 1980 presidential election, and the events that followed it (Staggenborg 1991: 23; O'Connor 1996: 61; McKeegan 1992: 4–23; Jackson and Vinovskis 1983: 75–6).

Key points

- While they emerged before, the 1973 Supreme Court decision was crucial in the development of national movements to both defend abortion and to oppose it.

- Each movement has framed its stance in a way intended to maximize its appeal. Supporters of access to abortion describe themselves as pro-choice; opponents as pro-life.

- Much of the pro-life movement is Catholic. In the late 1970s, evangelicals organized a movement that opposed abortion as part of a broader agenda. Often described as the Christian Right, it characterizes itself as the pro-family movement.

Abortion and the Reagan administration

The election of Ronald Reagan brought to the White House a president who had denounced abortion during his election campaign but was centrally concerned with promoting an economic and foreign policy agenda. That he did not prioritize his opposition to abortion drew criticism from some within the anti-abortion movement. For most, however, what was crucial was that at last there appeared to be a real opportunity to seriously restrict or even ban abortion (McKeegan 1992: 31, 45–6, 59).

The new administration was active on a number of fronts. The first concerned government funding. This involved several aspects. One was the federal funding of organizations which either carried out abortions or might recommend them during counselling. Title X of the 1970 Public Health Service Act gave federal money to Planned Parenthood, a key provider of abortion. Efforts to end this proved unsuccessful, but in 1988 plans to ban abortion counselling or referral in federally funded clinics were announced. While Reagan was partly successful in this area, he was more successful in denying federal funds to providers of abortion overseas. Both the United Nations Fund for Population Activities (UNFPA) and the International Planned Parenthood Foundation (IPPF) received federal money, and anti-abortionists argued that it should be ended. In 1984, at an international population conference in Mexico City, the Reagan administration announced that it would not support family planning programmes in which abortion played a part, a policy that led to the defunding of the IPPF. (In a subsequent decision, the UNFPA was likewise deprived of funding; McKeegan 1992: 63–94, 113–21.)

Activity on abortion also took place in Congress. But if there were problems in what exactly a sympathetic president could achieve, there were even greater difficulties in winning over a somewhat less supportive group of federal legislators. In part, this was because anti-abortionists could not agree on what was wanted.

One possibility that had long been considered was an amendment to the Constitution. *Roe* had held that abortion was a constitutional right, but if the Constitution could be amended to declare that it was not, then the Supreme Court's decision would be overridden. But not only was there dispute as to what such an amendment should say, there were also practical problems in getting any amendment passed. To do so would involve first gaining a two-thirds majority in both Houses, and then achieving the support of three-quarters of the states. Some, indeed, argued that it would be more practical to attempt to deal with the issue through a conventional bill. A simple majority, it was argued, could prove within reach; passing an amendment was not (Craig and O'Brien 1993: 138).

Each of these disagreements was linked with divisions within the movement between what might be termed purists and pragmatists, divisions which we will return to later. In the event, none of the different approaches proved successful. Two did at least come to a vote. In 1982 both a constitutional amendment to return the abortion issue to state legislatures and a bill declaring that the foetus was a person were successfully filibustered. The following year, reintroduced in a modified form, the amendment was defeated in the Senate. President Reagan had intervened during the battle over the amendment, phoning senators in an attempt to persuade them to break the filibuster. The failure of these attempts to find a congressional resolution of the issue did not mean an end of anti-abortion hopes, however. What it did do was to give even more importance to another possible avenue, the nomination of new members of the Supreme Court (Craig and O'Brien 1993: 139–46).

Both the 1980 and 1984 Republican platforms

had explicitly called for the appointment of anti-abortion justices. During the Reagan years, three new justices were successfully nominated to the Supreme Court. Between the second and third, however, the White House attempted to secure the acceptance of a jurist seen by abortion rights supporters as particularly hostile to their cause, Robert Bork. The candidate elicited strong feelings from other groupings, notably African American civil rights organizations, and his defeat cannot be attributed to his stance on abortion alone. How we should understand the relationship between abortion and the administration is further complicated by a dispute of a different nature over the first nomination, that of Sandra Day O'Connor, where anti-abortionists unsuccessfully argued that the nominee had demonstrated a lack of sympathy for their stance. Nonetheless, Reagan's actions on this front should be seen as a serious effort to move the Supreme Court in an anti-abortion direction. (It is important here to note too a less publicized area, the successful nomination of nearly 400 federal judges, an area in which the White House's careful investigation of possible nominees' views potentially opened the way to more restrictive abortion decisions (O'Connor 1996: 88; Craig and O'Brien 1993: 63–4, 166–7, 173–8; McKeegan 1992: 129, 132–3, 137–40).

That, despite the hopes of 1980, Reagan failed to reverse *Roe* intensified divisions in the anti-abortion movement. We have already discussed the arguments over what should be put forward in Congress, in which the NRLC clashed with other more intransigent elements in the anti-abortion movement. Subsequently, a militant wing of the movement emerged, committed to ending abortion by direct action. Initially associated with groups such as the Pro-Life Action League, in the late 1980s the idea that access to clinics should be denied by organized blockades became the basis of a national effort by the newly formed Operation Rescue. As we will discuss, the adoption of a more militant strategy was ultimately to fail. But for mainstream anti-abortionists, the continued belief in more traditional methods was also to prove disappointing (Risen and Thomas 1998: 111–13, 258–88).

Key points

- The election of Ronald Reagan represented a significant opportunity for the pro-life movement.

- The administration was successful in some restriction of abortion.

- While it supported efforts to pass major restrictions through Congress, this proved unsuccessful.

- The administration appointed three justices to the Supreme Court in a bid to shift its stance on abortion.

- The administration was ultimately unsuccessful in seriously restricting abortion, and one of the most important developments of the period was a deepening divide between what could be described as a pragmatist and a purist strand of the pro-life movement.

From *Webster* to *Casey*

In 1983, in *City of Akron* v. *Akron Center for Reproductive Health*, Reagan's solicitor general submitted a brief to the Court calling for the reconsideration of the *Roe* decision. Three years later, in *Thornburgh* v. *American College of Obstetricians*, the solicitor general asked for it to be overturned. That the Supreme Court did not accede to such a call was a blow to the anti-abortion cause, if not to the credibility of the Reagan administration's claim to support it. It was not, however, until two later decisions, taken during the presidency of Reagan's successor, George Bush, that the issue of what would occur to the 1973 decision itself would emerge from the consideration of restrictions at state level (Craig and O'Brien 1993: 186–7).

The first case, *Webster* v. *Reproductive Health*

Services, concerned a number of restrictions which had been introduced in Missouri. States, it ruled by five to four, could refuse to allow abortions in public hospitals, and where in 1973 the majority of justices had declared themselves unable to decide where human life began, they now found no grounds to object to the statement in the preamble of the state's abortion law that life began at conception. It was a decision that was welcomed by the Christian Action Council, which declared: 'For 16 years, we've fought the effects of *Roe* v. *Wade*, and time and time again the Court has turned us down. Now, we finally have a ruling that goes our way.' Conversely, NARAL (which, following the *Roe* decision, had changed its name to the National Abortion Rights Action League) saw the decision as a major blow. The Court, it argued, had 'left a woman's right to privacy hanging by a thread and passed the scissors to the state legislature' (Craig and O'Brien 1993: 197–243; *Christianity Today*, 18 August 1989; O'Connor 1996: 30, 132).

Given the significance of both state legislators (who could pass legislation) and governors (who could veto it), both sides responded to the *Webster* ruling by attempting to influence election contests. This was a development which raised the profile of the issue for both incumbents and challengers. In a number of contests anti-abortion candidates were defeated, although in others they were successful. NARAL-supported candidates, however, proved so successful that increasingly the Republican Party began to distance itself from the hardline stance that had marked the Reagan years. It was not until 1992, in the case of *Planned Parenthood of Southeastern Pennsylvania* v. *Casey*, that it would become clear whether the anti-abortion or the abortion rights camp would find the

Supreme Court more sympathetic to its concerns (Craig and O'Brien 1993: 296–303; McKeegan 1992: 152–5; Staggenborg 1991: 139–41).

In its 1992 decision, the Supreme Court explicitly criticized the *Roe* majority's view that what states could do with regard to abortion differed depending on the duration of the pregnancy. A number of restrictions were upheld, and in accepting the constitutionality of a twenty-four-hour waiting period between a woman's consent to an abortion and the operation itself, the Court even reversed an earlier ruling in the 1983 *Akron* case. But it refused to reverse the *Roe* decision, arguing that to do so would lead to the spread of scepticism about the role of legal reasoning as against political pressure in the reaching of judicial decisions. Where abortion rights supporters continued to see *Roe* as in danger, now its opponents too saw the Supreme Court as refusing to support them (Craig and O'Brien 1993: 98–9, 321–62; O'Connor 1996: 144).

Key points

- In 1989, in *Webster* v. *Reproductive Health Services*, the Supreme Court decided in favour of a number of restrictions.

- Both the pro-life and pro-choice movements believed the *Roe* decision might soon be reversed.

- In the meantime, both movements sought to influence election contests, with the pro-choice side faring more successfully.

- In 1992, in *Planned Parenthood of Southeastern Pennsylvania* v. *Casey*, the Supreme Court supported a number of restrictions but declined to reverse its 1973 ruling.

Box 18.3 *Roe* in danger

We have not refrained from reconsideration of a prior construction of the Constitution that has proved 'unsound in principle and unworkable in practice' . . . We think the *Roe* trimester framework falls into that category . . . we do not see why the State's interest in protecting potential human life should come into existence only at the point of viability . . . (*Webster* v. *Reproductive Health Services*, 1989)

Box 18.4 *Roe* reaffirmed

The woman's right to terminate her pregnancy before viability is the most central principle of *Roe* v. *Wade*. It is a rule of law and a component of liberty we cannot renounce . . . (*Planned Parenthood of Southwestern Pennsylvania* v. *Casey*, 1992)

Abortion and the Clinton administration

While anti-abortionists had found it impossible to reverse *Roe*, every year on its anniversary they took part in a March for Life to protest the Supreme Court decision. During their presidencies, both Reagan and Bush had sent messages of support. The election of Bill Clinton, however, brought an abortion rights supporter into the White House and in January 1973, marchers were to receive not a supportive message but news of five executive orders signed by the new president. One concerned a long-standing facet of the abortion debate: whether or not abortions were permissible in overseas military hospitals. Two reversed decisions to forbid the use of foetal tissue for federally funded research and stop the import of the abortion pill, RU-486. The other two, however, reversed two of the key measures of the Reagan administration: the removal of federal funding from organizations carrying out abortions abroad, and the ban on such funding for clinics which provided abortion counselling (Craig and O'Brien 1993: 48, 170, 191–2; O'Connor 1996: 151).

If Clinton's executive orders represented a blow against the anti-abortion movement, so too did his later appointment of two Supreme Court justices. Indeed, the whole period of his administration was to prove highly unconducive, not least for the direct action wing of the movement, on which the Supreme Court ruled in three separate cases (Segers 1995: 232).

The first, *NOW* v. *Scheidler*, involved an attempt by the feminist National Organization for Women (NOW) to use the law against anti-abortion militants. NOW argued that Joseph Scheidler, the leader of the Pro-Life Action League, was trying to drive abortion providers out of business, and in its 1994 decision the Supreme Court ruled that such an effort did not have to be economically motivated to fall under legislation originally introduced to deal with activities by organized crime (O'Connor 1996: 159, 164–5, 167–8).

Militants were also constrained in other ways. At local level new measures forbade protesters to go within a specified distance of a clinic, while at national level Congress in 1994 passed the FACE (Freedom of

Access to Clinic Entrances) Act. The Court, in separate cases in 1994 and 1995, upheld both these provisions (O'Connor 1996: 164, 167; Risen and Thomas 1998: 361, 373–4; Segers 1995: 234–7).

This drawing to a close of the period of clinic blockades did not mark the end of militancy altogether. Already in the 1980s, a number of bombings took place against clinics. In the 1990s, as Operation Rescue and other direct action groupings went into decline, individuals not only bombed or set fire to clinics but also shot doctors. In March 1993 a doctor was killed in Pensacola, Florida; in August another was wounded in Wichita, Kansas; and in July 1994 a doctor and his driver were killed, once again in Pensacola. These actions, while denounced by mainstream anti-abortionists, received the support of a number of militants, and one of the assailants, Shelley Shannon, was found to possess copies of an anonymously authored Army of God manual which detailed how to attack clinics (McKeegan 1992: 111–12; Risen and Thomas 1998: 339–40, 351, 355–6, 362–4; Kelly 1995: 207).

If the Clinton years were marked both by the decline of such groups as Operation Rescue and by some sporadic anti-abortion violence, mainstream anti-abortionists also enjoyed little success. In 1994 the decision of a majority of Republican candidates to pledge that, if elected, they would seek the passing of a swathe of conservative legislation was followed by a landslide victory in the House of Representatives elections. The issues raised within the *Contract* had been deliberately chosen to maximize support, and it was on this basis that abortion was not included. This risked alienating the Christian Right, and partly in order to retain its support, the envisaged measures included the denial of increased payments to women who had additional children while on welfare and the removal of payments from young women who had had children outside marriage. This, however, opened up a fissure between a movement which had come into existence to oppose abortion and one which focused its concerns on the defence of the family. But it did not signify the destruction of the alliance between the Republican Party and anti-abortionists.

In part, this was because, despite the exclusion of abortion from the *Contract with America*, the majority of Republicans continued to vote for abortion restrictions when such measures came before the House. But it was also because a new development appeared to offer the possibility of making fresh progress in the battle against *Roe* (Balz and Brownstein 1996: 37–8, 55, 272–3, 281, 288–94; Jaenicke 1998: 1–9).

The anti-abortion movement's use of a variety of images of either the vulnerable foetus or an abortion in progress had from early on proved a potent weapon, and in the operation it described as partial-birth abortion, it found an issue in which the argument for a woman's right to choose could be presented as an advocacy of infanticide. While abortion rights supporters argued that the operation was rare and resorted to only in dire circumstances, anti-abortionists maintained that it was frequently used. A majority within Congress proved amenable to the arguments levelled at the operation, but President Clinton, declaring that without an exception for a woman's health, the banning of the operation was unacceptable, twice used his veto to block the measure from becoming law. In 2000, to the outrage of anti-abortionists, the Supreme Court ruled that a state law banning the operation was unconsti-tutional. Alighting on one particular form of abortion, anti-abortionists had declared that this could shift the ground on abortion as such. Despite their defeat by both Clinton and the Supreme Court, they continued to believe that it could do so (Condit 1990: 79–95; Alcoon 2000: 212–13; *American Prospect* 29 September–8 October 2001; *National Right to Life News* January 2001).

Key points

- The election of President Clinton offered a key opportunity to the pro-choice movement. The administration reversed a number of earlier restrictions and two justices were appointed to the Supreme Court.

- During the 1980s a militant wing of the pro-life movement had attempted to close clinics by direct action. Legal action in the 1990s made these tactics ineffective. During the 1980s some anti-abortionists engaged in bombings against clinics while in the 1990s two doctors were killed.

- Mainstream anti-abortionists continued to look for support from Republican members of Congress during the Clinton years.

Voters and parties

As we have seen, by the beginning of the 1980s the two main parties were identified with the two sides in the abortion debate. In the aftermath of the *Webster* decision, the party chairman sought to downplay its pro-life stance, arguing that the party should be seen as a 'big tent' open to different views on the issue. Party moderates had in 1989 established the National Republican Coalition for Choice, and in 1990 a former organizer for the New Right used more conservative arguments in an attempt to make a greater impact on the party through a new organization, Republicans for Choice. In subsequent conventions, pro-choice Republicans tried to change the party's stance on the issue or at least insert within the platform an acceptance of diversity. In 1996 the conservative candidate for the presidency, Bob Dole, identified himself with the latter effort. The strength of anti-abortion sentiment among Republican activists, however, particularly among the Christian Right sections of the party, made such a change impossible (Craig and O'Brien 1993: 300; McKeegan 1992: 173–4, 267–71; Melick 1996: 244–6; *Focus on the Family Bulletin* 23 September 1996; www.rcrc.org/0008nletter1.html).

The Democrats, for their part, experienced less problems with internal dissent. Following Carter's defeat, each of their presidential candidates ran on a pro-choice platform, and while a Democrats for Life grouping was active within the party, when the most prominent Democrat anti-abortionist, Pennsylvania governor Robert Casey, attempted to speak at the 1992 national convention, he was denied the opportunity to do so (www.democratsforlife.org; Kelly 1995: 211).

As with the Republican Party, this was in part a response to the pressure of party activists. For both parties, however, there was an important element of calculation as to what role the issue, and a particular stance on it, could play in elections.

We have already commented on the rival interpretations of the electoral contests that followed the *Webster* decision. There are disputes too as to the 1992 presidential election. The celebrated comment 'It's the economy, stupid!' has often been taken to capture the central factor in depriving George Bush of a second term in office. It has been argued, however, that for a crucial group of voters, it was support for abortion rights that decided how they would vote (O'Connor 1996: 148–50).

Both sides have continued to be active in election contests; in 2000, for instance, both NARAL and the NRLC were active in the contest between Bush and Gore. But, as we have seen, the abortion conflict does not only take place at national level, and it is to the state level that we now should turn (**www.naral.org/ mediaresources/publications/resident/chl.html**; *National Right to Life News* October 2000).

Key points

- Following the *Webster* decision, leading Republicans sought to distance themselves from the pro-life movement. Efforts to shift the party's stance on the issue, however, proved unsuccessful.

- While pro-choice Republicans were unsuccessful within their party, pro-life Democrats made even less impact.

Abortion and the states

In deciding whether a particular state legislature will prove favourable to a pro-life or pro-choice stance, a number of factors need to be taken into account. These include the strength of particular religious groupings within a state, the stance of the governor, and the number of women legislators. NARAL, while it has had some successes at state level, has been more effective at national level. A focus on state legislation, however, has proved well suited to an organization like the NRLC. This does not mean that it neglects lobbying at national level; indeed, it has been characterized as one of the more effective such organizations by an annual survey of members of Congress, congressional aides, and other Washington 'insiders'. But its creation in 1989 of a State Legislation Department has made it particularly well equipped to coordinate work in this area (*National Right to Life News* 9 March 1997, 15 March–December 1999; Byrnes 1995: 249–61; Hansen 1993: 226–9).

As we might expect, what measures can get through state legislatures has varied in a number of ways. We have already touched on the denial of public hospital facilities and the imposition of a waiting period and, more recently, measures against partial-birth abortion. A further area that has proved particularly attract- ive at state level has been the question of abortions under the age of majority, in which anti-abortionists have argued that this should involve parental consent or parental notification. The Supreme Court, however, has ruled that a minor could choose to seek a judge's consent rather than a parent's. The Court has also struck down a more contentious feature of some states' legislation: that a married woman should have her husband's consent before an abortion would be permissible (Craig and O'Brien 1993: 88–91).

In other areas anti-abortionists have met with greater success, notably in what is called informed consent, whereby a doctor must inform the woman of the dangers of abortion before she can give her written consent to the operation. But however successful anti-abortionists have proved at state level, and however willing the Supreme Court has proved to leave most of these restrictions in place, it remains the case that abortion is still legal. Whether that will remain the case will become clearer when we discuss developments since the Clinton administration. First, however, we need to pay more attention to what exactly is in dispute. As we have discussed, both in the 1860s and 1960s, a number of factors lay behind the demand for a change in the law. But how do we understand the development of the two antagonistic movements that have struggled around the issue since the 1973 Court decision? (Craig and O'Brien 1993: 329, 341).

Key points

- In achieving or averting restrictions at state level, a number of factors are crucial. These include the strength of particular religious groupings, the role of the governor, and the proportion of women state legislators.

- The pro-life movement has given considerable attention to the passing of such restrictions. The Supreme Court has accepted a number of these restrictions, but struck down others.

Movements and activists

We noted earlier the diverse roots of the abortion rights movement. While NARAL and NOW remained central (in the 1990s the former broadened its agenda to become the National Abortion and Reproductive Rights Action League), a key development since 1973 has been the organization of specifically religious groupings, notably the Religious Coalition for Reproductive Choice and Catholics for Free Choice. Religion has from its inception been a crucial factor for the anti-abortion movement, but for pro-choice activists too it can be important. But what has been most noticeable is the central role of the argument that the right to choose is central to women's rights (Segers 1995: 230; Staggenborg 1991: 59–60).

If the links between one movement and feminism are clear, does this mean that the counter-movement should be seen as anti-feminist? We have already noted the different priorities of the Christian Right and the pro-life movement. For the former, feminism is a threat to the family. But for those who have mobilized specifically to reverse *Roe*, the situation is more complex. Certainly there are points of contact between the overt traditionalism of the Christian Right and arguments made in the anti-

abortion movement. The American Life League, for instance, which describes itself as for life and the family, has published material against homosexuality, pornography, and sex education. But, where the Christian Right has argued that feminist attempts to add an equal rights amendment to the Constitution should be opposed because it would undermine the different sex roles of men and women, anti-abortionists have argued that they only oppose it because it could be used to advance abortion rights (*All About Issues*, May 1988, March–April, September–October 1992; Falwell 1980: 130; *National Right to Life News* 2 February 1997).

As Luker has shown, for many of the women who make up the base of the anti-abortion movement, feminist arguments for abortion are seen as denigrating the ways in which they have organized their lives. Tending to have more children than pro-choice women, and less likely to be employed, pro-life women believe that abortion is a rejection of women's role as a nurturer. But, as Staggenborg has noted, a 1980 survey of anti-abortion activists has shown that opposition to abortion is compatible with support for women's rights in other areas of their life. Indeed, in 1973, following a dispute within NOW, a specifically anti-abortion feminist grouping was set up. For Feminists for Life, abortion is not only an issue of human life but instead of liberating women, attempts to subordinate them to the needs of a male-defined society. Along with the appearance on the 1994 March for Life of a contingent from the Pro-life Alliance of Gays and Lesbians, the existence of a pro-life feminist grouping highlights the importance of distinguishing

---

Box 18.5 A pro-life argument

Medical and scientific evidence leaves no room for doubt that an individual is a unique human person at the point of conception and that a person's right to life should be respected by society and protected by law. (www.paprolife.org/wherewestand.htm)

between the Christian Right and the anti-abortion movement (Luker 1984: 160–3, 194–6; Staggenborg 1998: 77; Berr, Nurangor Hoebl and McNar 1995: 151–2, 154–60, 162–3; *Life Advocate* March 1994).

Key points

- While religion has played a key role in the pro-life movement, it also plays a role in the pro-choice movement.
- The pro-life movement is often taken to be opposed to women's rights. The Christian Right vehemently opposes feminism, and some sections of the pro-life movement share some of the Christian Right's concerns towards issues other than abortion.

Box 18.6 A pro-choice argument

We must cultivate respect for women as moral actors who make their childbearing decisions based on profound concerns about their own lives and the lives of their families . . . We must stress that abortion is a responsible choice for a woman who is both unwilling to continue a pregnancy and unprepared to care for a child. (**www.aclu.org/issues/ reproduct/rrujan98.html**)

- While pro-lifers and feminists are in conflict over the abortion issue, this should not be taken to mean that the former are necessarily opposed to women's rights in general.

Abortion after Clinton

The period following the *Webster* decision proved amenable to the abortion rights argument, and in 2000 the Democrat candidate, Al Gore, seemed well positioned to continue the run of pro-choice success in elections. The election of George W. Bush, however, was to see the return of a pro-life candidate to the White House.

Bush had already declared his opposition to abortion during his election campaign, and the 2001 March for Life received the news that the new president had restored a ban on the funding of organizations that provided abortions overseas. There have been other anti-abortion gains too. In 2000 John Ashcroft, who in the 1980s had sought to restrict abortion as attorney-general of Missouri, was successfully nominated to attorney-general in the Bush administration. The following year the president announced that 20 January would be National Sanctity of Human Life Day, and he then addressed the March for Life pledging his support for parental notification laws and his opposition to partial-birth abortion and public funding for abortion. Arguments continued over the funding of family planning organizations overseas, and in 2002 congressional pressure to provide funds to UNPFA was resisted by the White House (*Focus on the Family Citizen* March 2001; *New Yorker* 15 April 2002;

Washington Post 23 January, 16 May 2002; *National Right to Life News* February 2001).

Purists continued to be suspicious of the new administration, both because Ashcroft had declared during his confirmation hearings that *Roe* was the settled law of the land and because Bush's White House chief of staff had been reported as saying that while abortion was 'a high moral priority for the president', his policy priorities lay elsewhere. For mainstream anti-abortionists, however, Bush had not only been enthusiastically supported during the election but had continued to receive its support thereafter—just as for pro-choice activists, the return of a pro-lifer to the White House represented a grave danger. Their opponents, the Pennsylvania state organization of the NRLC noted in May 2001, were already mobilizing against what they described as an 'unprecedented assault on abortion rights'. NARAL had launched a four-year campaign to 'mobilize pro-choice Americans to block anti-choice Supreme Court appointments, restore pro-choice leadership in Congress, elect a pro-choice president and fight anti-choice initiatives at every level'. NOW had also launched a campaign which was seeking to lobby senators both in their home states and in the Senate itself. It was the Senate, both sides recognized, that would decide if any Bush nominees for the Supreme Court would be successful or not; and where NARAL and NOW feared *Roe* was in danger, the NRLC hoped it was (**www. rcrc.org/faxadres/jan01/01-01-19html** ; *Christianity Today* 11 June 2001; *National Right to Life News* July 2000, February 2002; **www.paprolife.org/ plunars 53101.html**).

Key points

- The election of George W. Bush offered the pro-life movement a significant opportunity.

- The administration has taken a number of anti-abortion initiatives.

- While the pro-choice movement has strongly opposed the Bush administration, pro-lifers are somewhat divided over the degree of support they are likely to receive from the president.

- The key issue is likely to be the appointment of Supreme Court justices.

Box 18.7 Is America different?

Abortion policy compared

The American anti-abortion movement is not the oldest in the world—the British was formed in the late 1960s and on the opposing side, Britain's Abortion Law Reform Association dates back to the mid-1930s. Nor is America the only country in which the abortion conflict is politically significant: Ireland has seen three national referenda on the subject. But in duration, intensity, and impact the American abortion conflict is particularly noteworthy, and why this should be raises questions as to how America is distinct.

As a country in which religious commitment is particularly high (see Chapter 22), America has produced a particularly powerful anti-abortion movement or, more precisely, movements. Linked primarily with Catholics, the pro-life movement, as it describes itself, has been joined by a second movement, the Christian Right or pro-family movement, which sees legal abortion as one of a number of attacks on the values of a Christian society. The Supreme Court's 1973 decision represented a significant achievement for those who argued that women had the right to choose abortion. For many Americans, however, such a right was incompatible with their view of society, and they turned to politics in order to try and reverse their defeat.

Such a decision would have been ineffective if the American political system had not had particular characteristics. In Britain, anti-abortionists have been forced to try to make a government grant sufficient parliamentary time to secure the passing of a restrictive bill. In the United States, conversely, power is not concentrated in the executive. Instead, it is dispersed, allowing the legislature, the executive, and the judiciary to check and balance each other. This should not be glamorized or frozen in time— at different points one or other has proved particularly powerful. But what it does mean is that for those who argue for the foetus's right to life, defeat in the judicial system does not mean that their only recourse is to the same court that has rebuffed them.

Instead—or often as well—they can attempt to find a more favourable response from the White House or Congress. Furthermore, as a federal system, the access points to political decision-making are not only at the national level but in the states. Movements can adjust their tactics according to their judgement of where they can best expend effort, and in doing so can also take advantage of the porous nature of America's party system, where pressure can be exerted both externally and internally on parties which are demonstrably willing to adopt movement priorities.

In thinking about what makes America different, it is important not just to consider one factor, but rather see how they affect each other. The USA and Canada are neighbours, and, as Meyer and Staggenborg note, both are federal states. Yet the abortion issue has developed very differently in the two polities. In part, they suggest, this is linked with the lesser significance of religion in Canada, in part with what until recently has been a lesser concern with rights, in part with the efforts of Canadian parties to keep the abortion issue out of national politics. It is not just the plurality of access points that we need to consider, but the party system and the values of the political culture that have also made America distinctive, and are crucial in understanding the importance of abortion (Meyer and Staggenborg 1998: 209–40).

Conclusion

As Richard Hodder-Williams noted in Chapter 8, the Supreme Court's 1973 decision did not settle the abortion issue. Instead, it nationalized it, encouraging the mobilization of pro-life and pro-choice movements and, over a longer period, also playing a central role in the coming into existence of a third movement, the Christian Right. Each has attempted to influence American politics through a number of access points. Before the *Roe* decision, anti-abortion and abortion rights campaigners had been active at state level and this continued to be the case after 1973. The Court had struck down not only nineteenth-century legislation, but also partial reforms gained in a number of states during the 1960s. Nonetheless, it did not rule out restriction altogether, and in the years that followed anti-abortionists have been particularly concerned to find what measures could succeed in state legislatures and not subsequently be struck down by the Supreme Court. But much of its energies, and those of its opponents, have been focused on the national level.

In part, this has involved lobbying members of Congress to vote in favour of or against legislation which will, for instance, provide funds for organizations providing abortions abroad or ban a particular form of abortion. This can take more than one form. Movements can affect politicians' decisions from both outside and inside their parties, and in the abortion conflict it has been particularly noticeable that the different movements have used both approaches. The Democrats have long been identified with the pro-choice argument; the Republicans with the pro-life. This is not a straightforward proposition in the latter case; the GOP has, on occasion, found that its commitment to an anti-abortion stance threatens its ability to win elections. But the emergence of the Christian Right in the late 1970s brought a large contingent of abortion opponents into Republican politics, and this makes the likelihood that in most circumstances it will take a pro-life stance all the stonger.

The pressure of abortion rights and anti-abortion movements on parties, and the pressure of activists within the parties, are both important in deciding presidential elections. Once in office, a president in modern American politics must consider the abortion issue. To take the most recent examples, both Bill Clinton and George W. Bush took up the question (in opposite ways) from the beginning of their administration. Under President Clinton, it was the pro-choice side which benefited; under his successor, it is the pro-life movement. The structure of the American political system, in which the separation of powers between the presidency and Congress (and the possibility that different parties can hold each) makes the future of the abortion issue an open question. Sections of the anti-abortion movement are extremely distrustful of politicians. How legal abortion can be reversed remains a matter of dispute among its opponents, and even if a president is successful in nominating Supreme Court justices, it may not be the case that the Court's future decisions will accord with a movement's agenda. Pro-choice activists, despite the attacks that abortion rights have experienced, have not lost what they achieved in the early 1970s, and even with an anti-abortion president, a movement that seeks the reversal of *Roe* can find as many obstacles as opportunities in the American political system.

QUESTIONS

1 Why was abortion severely restricted during the nineteenth century?

2 Why did a movement to liberalize abortion law emerge during the 1960s?

3 To what extent should the anti-abortion movement be seen as a specifically Catholic movement?

4 How useful is it to see the anti-abortion movement as necessarily linked to the American right?

5 How would you explain the successes and failures of the pro-life and pro-choice movements during the 1980s and 1990s?

6 Do you expect the Supreme Court's *Roe* decision to be still in place at the end of the George W. Bush administration? Why?

7 How would you account for the involvement of large numbers of women on both sides of the abortion conflict?

FURTHER READING

B. H. Craig and D. M. O'Brien (1993), *Abortion and American Politics* (Chatham, NJ: Chatham House). An excellent study of the politics of abortion which is particularly helpful in its discussion of legal decisions.

M. L. Goggin (ed.) (1993), *Understanding the New Politics of Abortion* (Newbury Park, Ca.: Sage). A wide-ranging collection of essays on the politics of abortion in the aftermath of the *Casey* decision. Particularly useful in its discussion of the state level.

K. Luker (1984), *Abortion and the Politics of Motherhood* (Berkeley: University of California Press). A path-breaking exploration of the contrasting lives and views of pro-life and pro-choice activists in California.

D. S. Meyer and S. Staggenborg (1996), 'Movements, countermovements, and the structure of political opportunity', *American Journal of Sociology*, 101(6): 1628–60. An illuminating use of the abortion conflict to examine how we might best understand the interaction between contending movements and government.

K. O'Connor (1996), *No Neutral Ground? Abortion Politics in an Age of Absolutes* (Boulder, Colo.: Westview Press). A comprehensive overview of the politics of abortion.

M. C. Segers and T. A. Byrnes (eds.) (1995), *Abortion Politics in American States* (Armonk, NY: M. E. Sharpe). A valuable collection of essays on the politics of abortion at state level.

S. Staggenborg (1991), *The Pro-Choice Movement. Organization and Activism in the Abortion Conflict* (New York: Oxford University Press). An exemplary discussion of the development of the pro-choice movement.

S. Staggenborg (1998), *Gender, Family and Social Movements* (Thousand Oaks, Ca.: Pine Forge Press), chap. 5. A thoughtful discussion of the relationship between the pro-choice and pro-life movements, gender, and the family.

WEB LINKS ~~Photocopy~~

Pro-choice sites

www.agi-usa.org Alan Guttmacher Institute

www.aclu.org/issues/reproduct/hmrr.html American Civil Liberties Union

www.crlp.org Center for Reproductive Law and Policy

www.feminist.org/rrights/intro.html Feminist Majority Foundation www.naral.org National Abortion and Reproductive Rights Action League

www.now.org/issues/abortion National Organization for Women

www.plannedparenthood.org Planned Parenthood Federation of America

www.rcrc.org Religious Coalition for Reproductive Choice

www.republicansforchoice.com Republicans for Choice

www.rpcc.org Republican Pro-Choice Coalition

Pro-Life Sites

www.all.org American Life League

www.unitedforlife.org Americans United for Life

www.armyofgod.com Army of God

www.cc.org Christian Coalition

www.democratsforlife.org Democrats for Life

www.feministsforlife.org Feminists for Life

www.nrlc.org National Right to Life Committee

www.paprolife.org Pennsylvania Prolife Federation

www.priestsforlife.org Priests for Life

www.prolifeaction.org Pro-Life Action League

www.rnclife.org Republican National Coalition for Life

19 Gun control

Robert Singh

READER'S GUIDE

America possesses the most heavily and legally armed private citizenry in the world. Although most Americans do not own guns, about one in six owns a handgun and approximately 250 million firearms are currently estimated to exist in the United States. Contrary to common non-American stereotypes, America does not lack gun laws—over 20,000 laws and regulations on all aspects of firearms production, distribution, and ownership exist—but most of these are state and local, rather than federal, laws, and their overall content is comparatively weak and highly permissive. For example, forty-two states now allow the carrying of guns concealed while only four states limit to one the number of firearms that can be legally purchased by an individual citizen each month. Most Americans support stronger gun control measures, especially at the federal level, but gun rights groups have been extremely successful since 1968 in minimizing federal government intrusion on the constitutional 'right to bear arms'. This is partly the result of a distinctive American 'gun culture' and the role of the Second Amendment to the US Constitution. The latter, especially, is widely—but inaccurately—perceived to prohibit strong gun control laws being enacted. But although both these factors are important, resistance to British-style gun bans is more directly due to the powerful political influence of sophisticated and well-organized gun rights groups such as the National Rifle Association (NRA). Operating in a candidate-centred and separated system of government where elected officials are typically risk-averse on controversial issues such as gun regulation, the NRA and its gun rights allies represent intimidating forces to most elected officials. The interest-group universe on firearms regulation is heavily skewed towards gun rights groups, which—as yet—is opposed only by a relatively poorly resourced gun control lobby and a mostly passive pro-control mass American public.

Introduction

America entered the twenty-first century doubly unique among contemporary liberal democracies: being governed by a Constitution designed in and for the eighteenth century and possessing the world's most heavily, and legally, armed civilian population. These two important and distinctive dimensions of America's divided democracy are closely linked. With the 'right to bear arms' popularly thought to be guaranteed by the Second Amendment to the US Constitution, many Americans regard widespread private legal access to guns as one of the key explanations of America's pronounced political stability and the historic preservation of constitutional rights and liberties in the republic. Informed by history and myth alike, American political development and comparative practice together confirm to many Americans that gun control is less about firearms than individual freedom—protections against not only criminals but also government. As Charlton Heston, president of the National Rifle Association (NRA), put it in 1999, the constitutional right of American citizens to own guns constitutes 'freedom's insurance policy'.

But to many both within and outside the United States, the high premium paid for that insurance policy is prohibitively costly. Americans seem, metaphorically and literally, to grip their firearms with an intensity and tenacity that defies all reason. After the horrific killings at Dunblane Primary School in Scotland by Thomas Hamilton on 13 March 1996, for example, successive British governments (Conservative and Labour) tightened already restrictive UK gun laws until a total ban on private possession of handguns was passed by Parliament in November 1997. By contrast, whilst America suffered over 30,000 deaths from gun violence each year during the 1990s—the equivalent of 2,000 Dunblanes annually—the most restrictive of a handful of firearms laws passed by the federal government during that decade comprised a five-day waiting period for prospective gun buyers and a ten-year ban on nineteen types of semi-automatic machine guns. Moreover, many state governments pushed during the 1990s not for tougher firearms regulations but instead for further 'privatization' and decontrol: laws allowing licensed individual citizens to carry guns concealed in public on their person and in their vehicles. The number of states with such 'right to carry' statutes increased from eight in 1985 to forty-two in 2002.

Such divergent international responses to the issue of the arming of private citizens perhaps suggests an American mindset on guns that is wholly exceptional. But only a minority of Americans own firearms (albeit a substantial minority) and a majority of the public consistently favours stronger gun controls, especially at the federal level. Yet America continues to lack restrictive gun regulations. In this chapter, the enduring reluctance of American governing institutions to enact strong gun laws is examined in a threefold context: first, the importance of firearms to American political culture; second, the constitutional protections afforded (and, importantly, not afforded) to private gun ownership; and, third, the asymmetrical influence on the firearms regulatory regime of gun rights organizations compared to gun control groups. Like the politics of abortion (examined in the previous chapter) and capital punishment (examined in the next), America's gun politics remains consistently controversial, divisive, and emotive not only because it addresses matters literally of life and death but also because it encompasses many of the central features of America's divided democracy more broadly: the US Constitution, individual liberty and civil rights, federalism, and the appropriate role of the state and government agencies in regulating individual conduct.

Firearms in America

Outside the United States, popular conceptions—animated in large part by American popular music, books, movies, and television—typically suggest that America possesses an excess of firearms, an absence of laws controlling them, and a citizenry that is either ignorant of, or intentionally blind to, the serious public health costs of gun violence and the desirability of more restrictive gun regulations. From John Wayne, Clint Eastwood, and Arnold Schwarzenegger to Ice Cube, *Natural Born Killers*, and Eminem, certain familiar popular American cultural icons depict this particular part of the western world as especially 'wild' about guns. But while the scale of guns in circulation in the United States is certainly distinctive in comparative terms, this popular picture is a partial and misleading stereotype in terms of both the complex regulatory regime on firearms and the nature of American public attitudes to gun ownership.

No reliable figures exist on the precise number of guns in circulation in America (partly as a result of popular resistance to registering guns with government officials and partly due to the relative ease of importing and selling them—even today, for example, travelling gun shows remain subject to minimal federal regulations). But most estimates suggest that almost as many firearms currently exist as people in the United States, and possibly more. Approximately 250 million guns have been estimated as existing in 2002. By any standards, then, America is distinctive in the extent to which firearms evidently make up a common part of the fabric of national life. Guns are a central and mainstream, not a peripheral and eccentric, aspect of modern America.

But if America is undoubtedly full of guns, it is not bereft of gun laws. Contrary to notions that America lacks laws regulating the production, import, export, distribution, sale, ownership, and use of firearms, in fact more than 20,000 such laws, regulations, and local ordinances existed by 2002–3. Where popular conceptions of America's lax regime do hold more purchase, however, is in regard to two crucial aspects concerning the substantive content of these many laws and regulations. First, the overwhelming bulk of firearm regulations exist at state and local, not national, level. During the entire twentieth century, the federal government enacted only eight laws regulating firearms nationwide, none of which approximates the restrictive provisions of most European states' firearms laws (see Box 19.1). Second, many of the laws that exist at both federal and state levels are comparatively weak in content. For example, of the fifty American states, only six—California, Connecticut, Hawaii, Maryland, Massachusetts, and New Jersey—had passed statewide bans on the private ownership of assault weapons by 2002. Similarly, as of 2002, twenty states administered neither a waiting period nor an instant check on prospective gun buyers to monitor them for possible prior criminal records (see Table 19.1). Only four American states prohibited the purchase of more than one gun per month by their citizens.

The central problem that analysts of America's gun politics therefore tend to address is not why America lacks gun laws—it does not—but why the thousands that do exist are so permissive in content. This is an especially pressing and vexing intellectual problem when two additional factors are taken into account: mass American attitudes on firearms and the public health costs of private legal gun ownership.

The American public's attitude to firearms is more complex and subtle than is typically imagined outside the United States. Again, contrary to Clint Eastwood-style depictions of a violence-prone citizenry ever ready to reach for the nearest .44 Magnum and have a nice day, most Americans do not own guns. By the end of the 1990s, official government statistics reported that slightly under half of all American households possessed a firearm (this included handguns, rifles, and assault weapons) while 'only' one in six Americans possessed a handgun. Moreover, since opinion surveys first began to ask Americans about their attitudes towards gun control in the late 1930s, consistent and decisive public majorities have expressed support for the passage of more restrictive gun laws, particularly at the federal level. Although, admittedly, some of

Box 19.1 Federal firearms legislation, 1934–2002

National Firearms Act (1934)

The violent gangster atmosphere of the Prohibition era and the attempted assassination of President-elect Franklin D. Roosevelt in 1933 facilitated the passage of this law. The measure imposed a punitive federal tax on the manufacture and distribution of gangster weapons (machine guns, sawn-off shotguns, and silencers) and required purchasers of those weapons to undergo FBI background checks and gain approval from local law enforcement officers.

Federal Firearms Act (1938)

The law prohibited the shipment of guns across state lines by manufacturers or dealers unless they possessed a federal licence, restricted the shipment of guns between states, and outlawed firearm sales to known criminals.

Gun Control Act (1968)

The assassinations of Martin Luther King, Jr. and Robert Kennedy in 1968, along with increasing levels of urban crime, inner-city riots, and violence, prompted passage of this federal law. The measure prohibited all traffic in firearms and ammunition between states and required serial numbers to be placed on all guns. It denied access to firearms to specifically defined groups (convicted felons, fugitives from justice, drug addicts, the mentally ill, and minors) and banned mail-order sales of firearms and ammunition. The importing of surplus military firearms and of guns and ammunition not certified by the secretary of the Treasury as legitimate souvenirs or for sporting purposes was banned. Interstate shipment of guns and ammunition to manufacturers, importers, and collectors who were properly licensed by the US government was also restricted. The measure also set the minimum age for firearm purchases at 21 for handguns and 18 for long guns.

Firearm Owners Protection ('McClure–Volkmer') Act (1986)

Often described as the 'zenith' of NRA influence on Capitol Hill, McClure–Volkmer overturned many pro-visions of the 1968 legislation, making inter-state sales easier. It also allowed gun owners to transport their fire-arms across state lines if unloaded and not readily accessible, and banned future sales and possession of machine guns by private citizens.

Gun Free School Zones Act (1990)

The measure made it a federal offence to carry a firearm within 1,000 feet of a school but was ruled unconstitutional by the Supreme Court in *US* v. *Lopez* (1995).

Brady Handgun Violence Prevention Act (1993)

Named after James Brady, who was shot during the assassination attempt on President Reagan in 1981, the law established a five-day waiting period (for states that did not already have one) in which background checks could be made on gun buyers. The background check provision was ruled unconstitutional by the Supreme Court in *Printz* v. *US* (1997), and the waiting-period provision lapsed in 1998.

The Violent Crime Control and Law Enforcement Act (1994)

Prohibited the manufacture, sale, and possession of nineteen types of semi-automatic weapons and copycat models, as well as some other semi-automatic guns. The measure outlawed magazines holding more than ten rounds of ammunition, banned juvenile possession of a handgun or handgun ammunition (with limited exceptions), and made it a crime to sell or give a hand-gun to anyone 18 years old or younger. It also barred firearms possession by someone subject to a restraining order because of threats of domestic violence. The Republican-controlled House of Representatives voted to repeal the law in 1996, but the initiative was not supported by the Senate.

The Domestic Violence Offender Gun Ban (1996)

This law prohibited anyone convicted of a misdemeanour or domestic violence offence from either buying or owning a gun.

Table 19.1 States with and without waiting periods

States with waiting periods (16)	States with instant checks (14)	States with no checks (20)
California	Colorado	Alabama
Connecticut	Delaware	Alaska
Hawaii	Florida	Arizona
Illinois	Georgia	Arkansas
Iowa	Idaho	Kansas
Maryland	Indiana	Kentucky
Massachusetts	Michigan	Louisiana
Minnesota	New Hampshire	Maine
Missouri	Oregon	Mississippi
Nebraska	Pennsylvania	Montana
New Jersey	South Carolina	Nevada
New York	Tennessee	New Mexico
North Carolina	Utah	North Dakota
Rhode Island	Virginia	Ohio
Washington		Oklahoma
Wisconsin		South Dakota
		Texas
		Vermont
		West Virginia
		Wyoming

these results vary according to the framing of the particular question (a common hazard with opinion surveys), most Americans have expressed support for stronger controls such as waiting periods, police permits, gun registration, and mandatory child-proof trigger locks.

One reason for such popular support—and a feature that suggests America is less distant from European experience than might be imagined—is the public health problems associated with firearms, not least the consequences of gun violence. In this regard, the empirical data depict a Hobbesian-style America where life is 'nasty, brutal and short'. More Americans have died since 1933 as a consequence of gun-related violence than were killed in all the wars (from the War of Independence and the Civil War through the First and Second World Wars to Korea, Vietnam, Iraq, and Afghanistan) that the US has fought combined. Since 1960, about three-quarters of a million Americans have died through gun violence. During the 1990s, approximately 38,000 Americans suffered gun-related deaths each year, almost evenly divided between suicides and homicides. In 1995, for example, 35,957 Americans died by gunfire: 18,503 in gun suicides, 15,835 in firearm homicides, 1,225 in unintentional

and accidental shootings, and 394 in gun deaths of unknown intent. These gun deaths were also disproportionately located among three demographic segments of the population: the young, men, and African Americans.

But if most or all Americans can agree that gun violence poses a serious public health problem, both its roots and resolution are the subject of acrimonious disagreement between progressives—who typically endorse stronger gun laws—and traditionalists, who invariably resist such measures as inappropriate, undesirable or unnecessary, and futile. As such, gun control both reflects and reinforces the broader 'culture wars' that contribute powerfully to the nation's divided democracy.

For progressives, the simple reason for America's high rates of gun violence is the widespread and poorly regulated private legal access to firearms. This is evident not only from comparative surveys but also from the data that has been collected on the nature of the perpetrators and victims of gun violence. For example, the ratio of non-gun homicides in America was three times higher than in England and Wales between 1985 and 1990 but fifty times higher in terms of gun homicides and 150 times higher in terms of handgun homicides.

Dizard et al. (1999: 13) argue: 'As terrible as our national rates of violence are, as tragic as the murders are, the facts make it hard to support the notion that we are in the midst of an epidemic of gun violence', and it is indisputably the case that—per capita—gun homicides in America were higher in the 1920s and 1930s than now, despite the far larger number of guns currently in private possession. Nonetheless, on most comparative measures, America's allowing millions of individual citizens legal access to guns seems clearly to account for the marked discrepancies in national gun murder and suicide rates.

Beyond this lie the sources of violent firearm usage. Although criminals frequently use firearms—whether obtained legally or illegally—the notion that gun violence is a product primarily of 'bad guys' misusing and abusing weapons that 'good guys' handle responsibly is unsustainable. Empirical studies suggest that most gun murders in America result not from violent encounters with strangers or criminals but from arguments among people who already know each other. Marvin Gaye's murder in 1982 (by his father during a family argument) is more the paradigm than John Lennon's in 1980 (by an obsessive stranger as Lennon was on his way home) on this view. The federal government's Uniform Crime Reports in 1991, for example, recorded that almost half of all murders that year (two-thirds of which were committed with firearms) were committed by an acquaintance or relative of the victim: partners, lovers, and friends. On this basis, stronger gun control laws and regulations may not eliminate gun violence completely, but they nonetheless represent rational steps towards its reduction.

But however much the progressive approach may appear obvious, compelling, and even unanswerable to many both within and outside America, many American traditionalists reject the gun control case wholesale, for four reasons.

First, many Americans simply deny that a clear or convincing distinction exists between the requirements of collective public safety (on the one hand) and the legal availability of guns for self-defence and recreational uses such as hunting and sport (on the other). On this view, guns are about *both* safety and pleasure, not an either/or choice.

According to the famous traditionalist slogans, 'guns don't kill people, people kill people', and hence 'if guns are outlawed, only outlaws will have guns'. Since the founding of the republic, private access to guns has been, and remains, a mainstay of American life, simultaneously ensuring public order, deterring (or punishing) criminals and government alike from intruding on individual rights and liberties, and facilitating the legitimate hunting and sporting uses of guns by responsible citizens.

Second, however tragic the thousands of gun deaths that occur each year in America undoubtedly are to most traditionalists as well as progressives, the proportion of such deaths is minuscule compared to those many millions of Americans who use guns responsibly—38,000 gun deaths annually compared to approximately 80 million gun owners and over 250 million guns in circulation during the 1990s, for example. More Americans die annually through road accidents than gun violence, and the overwhelming majority of gun owners—over 99 per cent—do *not* perpetrate murders, suicides, crimes, or have accidents with their firearms. Instead, they use them responsibly, whether for public safety or recreational purposes. The rights of a law-abiding majority (and the protections that flow from the exercise of those rights) should not therefore be trampled on because of the mistakes of a tragically and criminally irresponsible minority.

Third, something other than firearms appears to be at work in American homicide and suicide levels—whether this be a heritage of violence or a crisis of values and individual responsibility (or both). In 1990, for example, the official murder and non-negligent manslaughter rate was 9.3 per 100,000 persons, and firearms were used in two-thirds of these killings. But even if all guns were eliminated and those killers who used guns had substituted another weapon, America's murder rate would have remained at 3.1 per 100,000, higher than those of comparable industrialized democracies such as Canada, Sweden, and Japan. The overall suicide rate is also higher in several countries with stricter gun laws than it is in America, such as France. Moreover, if one removes entirely the gun homicides from the total US homicide figure, the latter remains at 31.3 per million citizens, a figure that is higher than every other comparable industrialized jurisdiction other than Northern Ireland.

Fourth, although official figures exist for the absolute number of gun violence victims, no reliable figures are available for the numbers of criminals deterred or defeated by the use—or threatened use—of guns. Almost by definition, a deterred criminal is not going to report this to the public authorities, and relatively few citizens who deter a criminal have an incentive to do so either. Moreover, guns have certain advantages that make them especially effective deterrents compared to other potential weapons such as knives, baseball bats, or fists: lightness, portability, allowing distance to use rather than requiring proximity, and ease of concealment. As such, the relatively weak in physical terms—such as women, the aged, or those with disabilities—can employ firearms for self-defence far more easily and effectively than they can other weapons against more powerful assailants.

In sum, by balancing the losses through gun violence against the purported benefits of gun ownership—from deterrence of criminals to protection against government—traditionalists and gun rights groups err on the side of responsible gun ownership and vigorous enforcement of the gun laws that currently exist. In their eyes, stronger gun control represents an undesirable, ineffective, and unnecessary step. But since most Americans support stronger gun laws, the reasons for the traditionalist case prevailing in public policy require analysis.

Key points

- No reliable figures exist on the total number of guns in America but these are generally estimated at over 250 million. Only a minority—albeit a substantial minority—of Americans own firearms, and about one in six Americans owns a handgun.

- Over 20,000 laws regulating firearms exist and most Americans support stronger gun laws. But the content of these laws is comparatively weak and permissive, and the federal government passed only eight gun laws during the twentieth century.

- Traditionalists and progressives differ strongly on the costs and benefits of both gun ownership and gun control.

America's 'gun culture'

One explanation of America's failure to embrace restrictive gun controls interprets this simply as an expression of a peculiar national affinity with firearms and the influential role—mythical and factual—that they have purportedly played in American historical development. The American historian Richard Hofstadter identified America as a 'gun culture', and that term appears especially valid and resonant today. Despite the pervasiveness of guns and violence in popular culture worldwide, no other nation shares the American predilection for such lethal weapons. Learning to handle a gun remains as much a rite of passage for boys in rural Alabama or Idaho as learning to drive or fish. Although only a minority own guns, when Justice Department figures record over 40 per cent of American households owning at least one firearm in 1996, their ubiquity seems clear. Moreover, as Table 19.2 shows, the popularity of decontrol measures among the individual states indicates that confidence in private use of guns is widespread. (Even the most convinced European opponent of gun control would be unlikely to endorse the carrying of concealed firearms as a reliable way to reduce crime and increase individual responsibility.) Love of firearms may be neither universal nor unrequited in the United States, but American passion for guns simultaneously reflects and reinforces the centrality of property rights and individual liberty to the nation's political culture and self-conception.

But whilst the comparative availability of guns

Table 19.2 Definitions: concealed-carry laws

By 2002, forty-two of the fifty states had enacted 'concealed-carry laws' (Vermont, in addition, had no law requiring either a permit or licence to carry firearms concealed, while the remaining seven states prohibited concealed carry entirely). Concealed-carry laws permit individual citizens to apply to the state for a licence to carry a weapon concealed (either on the person and/or in a vehicle). In 2002, twenty-eight states operated 'shall issue' laws, whereby every qualified applicant is automatically granted a licence; the responsibility falls on the state to explain why an applicant does not merit a licence. Fourteen states had enacted 'may issue' laws, in which the state need not automatically grant a licence and the responsibility rests on the applicant to explain why a licence is necessary (local police officers exercise the discretion to issue or deny concealed-carry permits to civilians in this case). Several states had also enacted laws to recognize the concealed-carry permits of other states' citizens when travelling through their territory.

'Shall issue' states (28)	'Shall issue' states (28)	'May issue' states (14 + DC)	'May issue' states (14 + DC)
Alaska	North Carolina	Alabama	Rhode Island
Arizona	North Dakota	California	
Arkansas	Oklahoma	Connecticut	
Colorado	Oregon	Delaware	
Florida	Pennsylvania	District of Columbia	
Idaho	South Carolina	Georgia	
Indiana	South Dakota	Hawaii	
Kentucky	Tennessee	Iowa	
Louisiana	Texas	Maryland	
Maine	Utah	Massachusetts	
Mississippi	Virginia	Michigan	
Montana	Washington	Minnesota	
Nevada	West Virginia	New Jersey	
New Hampshire	Wyoming	New York	

and the levels of gun violence in America are both remarkable, the gun culture explanation for resistance to stronger gun laws is not sufficient. First, as Mark Carl Rom noted when discussing the growth of the federal bureaucracy in Chapter 11, millions of Americans are content that—indeed, demand that—consumer products from cars to toys to airplanes be subject to more stringent government regulations than are firearms. For all their anti-government values, beliefs, and rhetoric, most Americans expect government to provide certain public goods through the regulation of private activities. Second, as recorded above, while millions of Americans possess some type of firearm, most Americans do not own handguns—the gun of choice in the overwhelming majority of gun crimes. Third, consistent and decisive public majorities have reaffirmed their endorsement of stronger firearm controls—including, in many surveys, majorities of gun owners themselves (which is unsurprising, since law-abiding gun owners should in theory have little to fear from regulations such as background checks).

Fourth, however much progressives may deride the message of George W. Bush and other gun rights supporters—that the gun violence seen in tragedies such as Columbine High School in Colorado on 20 April 1999 was a result more of the absence of the Ten Commandments in schools than of the legal presence of guns in almost half of all American households—much (arguably, most) of America knows little or nothing of gun violence, mass murders, or gangster crime.

Key points

- America is a 'gun culture' in the sense that millions of guns exist, and their use is often viewed as unremarkable and a rite of passage in many states.

- Such popularity cannot fully explain the lack of stronger gun laws, especially at federal level, since most Americans support tougher gun control.

The US Constitution and the right to bear arms

To gun rights groups such as the NRA, their strongest weapon in America's battles over gun regulation is not a firearm but a constitutional amendment. The Second Amendment to the US Constitution states: 'A well regulated militia, being necessary to the security of a free State, the right of the people to keep and bear arms, shall not be infringed.' Although even to some influential conservatives the amendment is poorly worded and now, some 212 years after its ratification, 'dangerously anachronistic' (Posner 1998: 223), to gun rights advocates the clarity of the Amendment is straightforward and supremely important—every American citizen enjoys an unfettered individual right to own a firearm (see Box 19.2).

Rather ironically, for all the popular attention and academic disagreement that the Second Amendment generates, it is arguably certain that other provisions of the US Constitution pose more formidable barriers to the enactment of stronger gun control. Not the least of these are the guarantees of state autonomy that the Constitution provides for in its federal provisions (elaborated in Chapter 4). For example, the background check provision of the Brady law was ruled unconstitutional by the Supreme Court in *Printz* v. *United States* (1997) on the basis of the Tenth Amendment: that the federal government did not have the authority to require local officials to execute federal policies (in this instance, to administer background checks on prospective gun buyers). Similarly, in *United States* v. *Lopez* (1995), the Court had struck down the federal Gun Free School Zones Act of 1990 that had prohibited possession of a firearm within 1,000 feet of a school. In this case, the majority held that since education was a state matter not subject to Congress's right to regulate under the Constitution's Commerce Clause—possession of a gun within the proscribed territory of a school was held neither to be, nor to affect, commerce—the Act was deemed unconstitutional (though carrying a firearm within a school is still a crime under the laws of most American states).

Since these were the first cases that the Supreme Court had faced since 1939 to rule on the constitutionality of federal firearms laws, the fact that the justices struck both down was less significant than the basis of the rulings. That is, the plaintiffs in both cases—supported by the NRA—chose not to rely on the Second Amendment but rather on the federalism provisions of the Constitution. Whether this was a pragmatic decision in the light of the Rehnquist court's approach to national–state relations, rather than a repudiation of the Second Amendment rationale, is debatable. Regardless, the importance of the Second Amendment should not be underestimated, not least since even gun control advocates unwittingly reinforce the perception of its salience by qualifying their pro-control position as not threatening the 'constitutional right' to own a gun. The apparent protection that the Amendment offers gun owners is thereby reinforced in the public mind by the proponents, as well as the opponents, of gun control.

Key points

- The Second Amendment is widely perceived—even by supporters of gun control—to limit or even prohibit strong gun laws, but its interpretation is open to argument.

- Constitutional guarantees are relative, not absolute, and the federalism provisions in the US Constitution arguably provide at least as powerful obstacles to strong national gun laws as the Second Amendment.

Box 19.2 **Constitutional influences**
Collective versus individual rights

Whether or not widespread legalized private access to guns is rational public policy, many contemporary disputes on firearms are rooted less in social policy than in law and, in particular, two markedly different interpretations of what the Second Amendment requires. The first interpretation—favoured by advocates of gun control—is the 'collective' or 'states' rights' approach. Collectivists focus on the preamble in the Second Amendment, 'A well regulated militia, being necessary to the security of a free State', which implies that the right to own firearms resides with the people collectively, through their support for militias. The Amendment gives states the right to establish militias, not a private citizen's right to own a gun. Moreover, these militias could be 'well regulated' by both state legislatures and Congress. Gun controls are therefore legitimate. This view has been dominant in federal courts and successive administrations for most of the twentieth century. In 1939, for example, the Supreme Court ruled that the government could make sawn-off shotguns illegal since there existed 'no reasonable relationship to the preservation or efficiency of a well-regulated militia'. Six former US attorney-generals—both Democratic and Republican—wrote in a letter to the *Washington Post* in 1992: 'For more than 200 years, the federal courts have unanimously determined that the Second Amendment concerns only the arming of the people in service to an organized state militia; it does not guarantee immediate access to guns for private purposes.'

Against that view, however, is an individualist interpretation supported by gun rights groups. This focuses on the clause, 'The right of the people to keep and bear arms shall not be infringed', which appears to guarantee an individual right to gun ownership. In 1791, 'the militia' and 'the people' were more or less regarded as the same thing. Even if elsewhere in the Constitution 'the people' means a collective entity, not individuals, it certainly does not mean 'the states'. Hence the universal right to 'bear arms' belongs to individual Americans. Moreover, when the Fourteenth Amendment was ratified after the Civil War, it stated that 'no state shall make or enforce any law which shall abridge the privileges or immunities of citizens'. This was adopted to make constitutional two other statute laws, the 1866 Civil Rights Act and a companion statute that stated that 'personal liberty . . . including the constitutional right to bear arms, shall be secured to and enjoyed by all citizens'.

Strong support for this individualist view came from the Bush administration in the spring of 2001, when US Attorney-General John Ashcroft stated that the Second Amendment 'unequivocally' conferred an individual right to gun ownership, and, in May 2002, when the Solicitor General Ted Olson filed two briefs to the Supreme Court that also held that the Constitution 'broadly protects the right of individuals . . . to possess and bear their own firearms'.

But even if this individualist interpretation is correct, as a substantial proportion of constitutional scholars believe, three points are noteworthy. First, if such an individual right does exist, then the NRA argument that any regulation will begin a slippery slope to confiscation of firearms is negated. For clearly, that slope must sooner or later run up against this core individual right. Second, no constitutional rights are absolute (whether to free speech or privacy), and all rights and liberties must be balanced against competing considerations, such as public order. Hence, a federal or state law that prohibited individual Americans from stockpiling 2,000 machine guns each month can still be upheld and need not be deemed to violate the basic individual right to gun ownership. Third, even if the Second Amendment limits what the federal government can do, it has not been 'incorporated' by the courts to apply to state and local governments, which in principle remain free to adopt whatever restrictive measures they wish on firearms.

The gun rights lobby

If neither the political culture nor the Second Amendment explanations can fully account for America's lax gun regulatory regime, we need to turn elsewhere—in particular, to the more 'practical' politics that feature the matrix of elected officials, political parties, organized interests, and governing institutions elaborated in Part Two of this book.

In this regard, gun politics in America since 1968 has been distinguished by two reliable features: first, crisis moments when, in the aftermath of notable gun violence incidents, a window of opportunity is created for the passage of new federal controls; and second, the rapid and decisive closing of that window by the longer-term dominance of gun rights groups, most notably the NRA. For example, despite the high annual rates of gun violence and horrific massacres such as Columbine in 1999, Republican control of Congress from 1995 to 2001 strongly assisted the NRA in frustrating any new restrictive federal firearms legislation (from regulating gun shows to mandating the installation by gun manufacturers of child-proof safety locks on guns). Gun rights groups' donations had generally been directed to both parties for most of the post-war period. But after 1994, these increasingly displayed a lopsided partisan character in favouring Republicans over Democrats—a function of the former's incumbency advantage in Congress, majority status in the House and Senate, and the national Republican Party's increasingly homogeneous conservative ideology and aggressively conservative congressional leadership.

Looming large over the politics of gun control, above all, is one supremely well-resourced and effective organization. The NRA is perhaps the model of an effective interest group. It gives organizational expression to the millions of Americans who believe passionately that their liberty, safety, and the very character of America are tied inextricably to the legal availability of guns. Although it is not the most extreme gun rights group (several others, not least the Gun Owners of America, compete for that title), the NRA provides an energizing and quasi-evangelical impetus to the gun lobby that few other interest groups match. With approximately four million fee-paying members and an annual income in excess of $100 million in 2002, the organization maintains a staff of over 300 employees, with in excess of sixty-five full-time lobbying staff. The pragmatic and ideological links to the arms industry honed by the NRA over decades effectively makes it the trade association for gun manufacturers. Moreover, the NRA's much-feared Institute for Legislative Action maintains a constant vigil on 'threats' to the right to bear arms, monitoring federal and state action on firearms and then prompting NRA members (by fax, direct mail, and email 'alerts') to contact legislators when new regulations are under consideration. The NRA's PAC (the Political Victory Fund) is also consistently one of the largest donors in American election campaigns. Faced by such passion, resources, and activism, elected officials who confront the constant election cycle mandated by the Constitution typically avoid antagonizing gun rights supporters.

That avoidance is encouraged still further by the asymmetry of the pro- and anti-gun lobbying forces. In particular, the groups that support new gun control laws tend to be considerably less well financed, and lacking in both a mass and an active membership, compared to gun rights groups. This is not to say that they lack support. The interest group coalition that supports gun control is a diverse one that includes many religious, educational, and social organizations such as the American Jewish Committee, the American Baptist Convention, the AFL-CIO, and Common Cause. But these are groups with aims far beyond gun control. Until 2001, the main dedicated (and, in effect, 'single issue') opponent of the NRA was Handgun Control Incorporated (HCI). Founded in 1974, HCI lacked resources until the murder of John Lennon in 1980 and the assassination attempt on President Reagan in 1981 helped boost its membership to over 400,000. But these numbers, and its budget of approximately seven million dollars, were both vastly inferior to the NRA's formidable resources.

Even in alliance with the National Coalition to Ban Handguns—renamed the Coalition to Stop Gun Violence in 1990—HCI remained relatively ineffective. For example, from 1968 to 1988 no proposals for tougher gun controls ever came to a floor vote in either house of Congress, while the Brady Bill that was eventually passed in 1993 had first been introduced to Congress some seven years earlier.

Nonetheless, developments towards the end of the 1990s suggested some shifts in the balance of influence in the political conflict over firearms. First, a series of gun massacres—several perpetrated by, and against, children—heightened national attention to America's lax gun laws. Second, and partly in response, pro-control forces saw one of the strongest mobilizations in their history. On 14 May 2000 (Mother's Day in America), for example, approximately 200,000 American women assembled in Washington, DC, to demand stronger gun control—the largest ever mass demonstration for gun control in American history. Third, trial lawyers and state and local public authorities began to litigate against gun manufacturers for the fatal consequences of gun violence, attempting to hold them responsible for the latter. Fourth, internet dotcom billionaire Andrew McKelvey established Americans for Gun Safety (AGS), a 'moderate' gun lobby that sought 'rational' gun laws while at the same time preserving the core right to bear arms. In 2001, AGS spent one-quarter of a million dollars in cinema adverts featuring Senator John McCain (R.AZ), the failed—but widely respected—2000 Republican Party presidential hopeful, endorsing the AGS's position on 'responsible' gun laws.

Such developments suggested that an American public notoriously passive in its support for stronger gun control might finally be galvanized into effective change. But in the aftermath of this gun control activism and litigation threats by trial lawyers and federal, state, and local authorities against gun manufacturers, both Republican-elected officials and gun rights groups mounted a fast, furious, and successful counter-mobilization. In 1999–2000, for example, the 106th Congress declined to act on proposals to impose a three-day waiting period so that police could run background checks on prospective buyers at otherwise unregulated gun shows.

Bills to ban the import of large-capacity ammunition clips and to mandate child-proof trigger locks also failed. By the summer of 2001, Florida—under Governor Jeb Bush—became the twenty-sixth state in only two years to pass legislation protecting gun manufacturers from lawsuits, one month after a unanimous New York Court of Appeals had ruled that victims of gun violence could not sue gun manufacturers. In the year following the Columbine massacre, the NRA's membership increased from 2.7 to 3.4 million and was estimated to have passed the 4 million mark for the first time in its history in 2000 (when Charlton Heston was re-elected as its president for an unprecedented third term). With George W. Bush's eventual victory in the presidential race, Moses appeared to have led his gun-toting followers to the promised land of a Republican White House and Congress that guaranteed no new federal firearms legislation (one NRA operative had, notoriously, even claimed during the 2000 race that the organization would be 'working out of an office in the White House' if Bush became president). A survey of Washington politicians, staff, and lobbyists in May 2001 for *Fortune* magazine saw the NRA supplant the American Association of Retired Persons as the most influential lobbying force on Capitol Hill (Sarasohn 2001).

Gun politics: the electoral connection(s)

The NRA and its gun rights allies are evidently powerful players, but what explains their influence? To this, attention must turn to the broader structures and dynamics of American government. In particular, the features explained in Part Two of this volume—weak parties, candidate-centred campaigns, and the imperative of localism—provide key explanations for the reluctance of American elected officials to resist the NRA.

Single issues rarely decide elections in America, and particularly not at presidential and congressional level. Nonetheless, precisely because America's elected officials are so 'vulnerable' (King 1997), each must calculate the most rational individual strategy to secure re-election. It is in this context that the threat posed by gun rights groups appears so potent. In an institutional environment where politicians enjoyed some collective cover from party (such as the UK), the incentives to challenge influential lobby groups would be greater. But in the fragmented, decentralized, and individualistic context of American government, most politicians (most of the time) instead pursue electoral strategies that are risk-averse and cautious. The choice that typically confronts most law-makers is to support gun control (and thereby antagonize a relatively small but particularly active element of the electorate that cares passionately about firearms) or oppose stronger gun control measures (and thereby, perhaps, lose a few votes from a larger public majority for whom firearms policy is one, and probably not a priority, of many issues informing their ballot decision). The optimal electoral choice, in this context, is not difficult to decipher.

Support for gun control measures in Congress is not uniform, however, and varies largely as a function of partisanship, rural versus urban constituencies, and region. That is, the more Republican, rural, and southern and western the congressional delegation, the greater the opposition to gun control; the more Democratic, urban and northeastern, the greater the support. Even here, however, Democrats in the South and West are heavily pressured to oppose new gun control measures, while Republicans in urban areas in the North and Midwest (especially those representing districts in cities such as New York) are heavily pressured to endorse gun control.

But increasingly gun control has contributed to, and in turn been affected by, the steady polarization of the main two political parties described in Chapters 5 and 6. Whereas in 1970 knowing a law-maker's partisan affiliation was a relatively

---

Box 19.3 **Is America different?**
Guns and American exceptionalism

America is clearly different to most other nations in allowing widespread and relatively lightly regulated private access to guns. But it is not alone in gun massacres or policy dilemmas. In the UK, for example, the number of handguns in circulation actually increased rather than declined after the 1997 handgun ban was passed. But America certainly remains distinctive in five important respects.

First, the American conflict over firearms is particularly highly charged and emotive. With gun rights groups describing government agents as 'jack-booted thugs' intent on confiscating weapons and gun control groups demanding that 'killing machines' be removed from America's streets, as Spitzer notes (1995: 97), 'rational policymaking recedes from view when political combatants spend most of their time screaming political obscenities at each other'. Second, the pro-gun rights lobby is broad, influential, and strategically and tactically adept, unlike the more narrow, parochial, and less sophisticated gun lobbies in most European nations. Third, whereas party politics powerfully assisted the passage of strongly restrictive firearms laws in the UK—the only diference between the Conservative, Labour, and Liberal

Democrat parties after Dunblane was whether to ban most or all handguns—gun control has instead gradually but inexorably polarized the main American political parties since 1968.

Moreover, with neither party capable of delivering a comprehensive and clear national programme of change in the context of a codified Constitution, federalism, and a separated system of government, and with divided party control of the White House and Congress the norm since 1968, prospects for reform at the federal level are modest. Fourth, single issues such as gun control and abortion rarely decide American presidential or congressional elections, limiting their salience to elected officials despite the preference of most Americans for stronger controls. Fifth and finally, the mass media is fragmented and localized, ensuring that national attention to gun violence is episodic rather than enduring. The fact that the *Washington Post* and *New York Times* reliably support gun control matters little in Alaska or Alabama. Taken together, the result is that in America 'the window of opportunity for gun control proponents had typically been brief' (Spitzer 1995: 126).

poor guide to their likely position on gun control, by 2002 it proved a generally reliable one. Republicans, with few but significant exceptions, reliably vote against new gun control measures. Democrats, with few but significant exceptions, reliably vote for them.

As Box 19.3 explains, this partisan context adds to the distinct constitutional and cultural factors that make the American conflict over guns comparatively unusual—and also enduring.

Key points

- Gun politics is dominated by the NRA and gun rights groups, who provide an energizing impetus to an active minority that opposes stronger gun control.

- In a candidate-centred environment with weak political parties, the incentives for most law-makers to support the passive pro-control majority over the active pro-gun minority are few.

Conclusion

Few progressive proponents of gun control entertain, much less advocate, the notion of a total ban on firearms in America. Much of the intensity and emotive character of the gun control conflict nonetheless arises from the sharply divided lenses through which guns and gun regulation are viewed. For traditionalists, firearms represent a central part of American culture, securing and protecting individual freedom and property rights and deterring government from infringing personal liberties, with gun ownership an individual citizenship right protected by the Second Amendment. But for progressives, twenty-first-century America is 'a congested, polluted society filled with traffic jams, shopping malls and anomic suburbs in which an eighteenth century right to bear arms is as out of place as silk knee-britches and tri-cornered hats' (Nelson 2001). On this view, the gun rights case rests on a combination of erroneous history, mistaken constitutional interpretation, and wilful ignorance of the public health costs of legalized private ownership of guns.

Gun control provides a clear example of an issue where public policy outcomes do not reflect majority preferences. The threefold combination of a powerful, vociferous, and skilled minority of gun owners represented by the NRA, a constitutional 'right' to firearms that is shrouded in historical and legal ambiguity, and a divided democracy that inhibits rather than encourages risk-taking by its elected officials together ensure that the desire of most Americans for stronger federal regulations

is regularly frustrated. Until and unless the mass American public prioritizes gun control at the ballot box as well as in the opinion survey, its prospects are modest if not minimal. Moreover, as the de facto privatization of security represented by concealed-carry laws shows, the public in many American states favours decontrol over new regulation.

But what is perhaps most striking, in comparative perspective, is not so much the polarization of the gun conflict in America's divided democracy as rather how much the gun rights and gun control lobbies in the United States share in common. Few of the latter demand outright prohibitions on firearms, as in Europe, even in the aftermath of mass murders committed by, and on, children. Most Americans realize that, aside from the practical political obstacles posed by gun rights enthusiasts, the Utopian character of a ban would be unenforceable. Even mild measures, such as the 1994 ban on assault weapons, were circumvented by manufacturers merely altering the shape or even the name of prohibited guns. But beyond this, many of the proposals that gun control groups make—from waiting periods to bans on large-capacity ammunition—would make relatively little difference to the grim statistics of gun homicides, suicides, and accidents. Ironically, the activism of gun control groups behind comparatively modest initiatives demonstrates precisely how central rather than peripheral firearm ownership remains to modern America.

QUESTIONS

1 What best explains the weak regulation of firearms in America?

2 Assess the arguments for and against repealing the Second Amendment to the US Constitution.

3 Should stronger federal gun control measures be enacted? What effect, if any, are they likely to have on gun violence, gun deaths, and gun crimes?

4 What makes the NRA such a powerful gun rights lobby and gun control groups so ineffective?

5 Evaluate the arguments for and against an armed citizenry in today's America.

FURTHER READING

M. Bellesiles (2000), *Arming America: The Origins of a National Gun Culture* (New York: Knopf). An important but controversial historical analysis arguing that the existence of a gun culture from the founding of the republic is a myth.

J. M. Bruce and C. Wilcox (eds.) (1998), *The Changing Politics of Gun Control* (Lanham, Md.: Rowman & Littlefield). An excellent collection on all key aspects of the recent federal and state-level politics of firearms.

T. Diaz (1999), *Making a Killing: The Business of Guns in America* (New York: New Press). A detailed analysis of the business forces driving the politics of gun rights groups.

J. E. Dizard, R. M. Muth, and S. P. Andrews, Jr. (eds.) (1999), *Guns in America: A Reader* (New York: New York University Press). A superb compendium of forty-three essays on all aspects of the gun debate, both pro- and anti-gun control.

S. Halbrook (1999), *That Every Man Be Armed* (Albuquerque: University of New Mexico Press). A strong pro-gun argument by one of the NRA's favoured lawyers that draws on a wide variety of authors, from ancient Greece to modern times, who support the notion of an armed citizenry.

D. A. Henigan, E. B. Nicholson, and D. Hemenway (1995), *Guns and the Constitution: The Myth of Second Amendment Protection for Firearms in America* (Northampton, Mass.: Aletheia Press). Three thoughtful essays by gun control advocates.

J. Leitzel (1998), 'Evasion and public policy: British and US firearm regulation', *Policy Studies* 19(2): 141–57. Comparison of the effects of regulation, and ease of avoiding them on both sides of the Atlantic.

J. Lott (1998), *More Guns, Less Crime* (Chicago: University of Chicago Press). A detailed, if controversial, case made for the effectiveness of concealed-carry laws in reducing crime.

J. L. Malcolm (1994), *To Keep and Bear Arms* (Cambridge, Mass.: Harvard University Press). A powerful historical analysis arguing that the Second Amendment was intended to confer an individual citizenship right of gun ownership.

R. Spitzer (1995), *The Politics of Gun Control*, 2nd edn. (Chatham, NJ: Chatham House). A readable overview of the key aspects of the politics surrounding gun control in America, sympathetic overall to the pro-control arguments.

WEB LINKS

Pro-gun rights organizations and resources

www.nra.org National Rifle Association

www.concealcarry.org Concealed Carry

www.guns-world.net Gun World

www.secondfreedom.net Second Amendment

www.keepandbeararms.com Keep and Bear Arms

www.sas-aim.org Second Amendment Sisters

www.gunowners.org Gun Owners of America

www.wagc.com Women Against Gun Control

www.pinkpistols.org/index2.htm Sexual Minorities' Self-Defence

www.gunownersca.com Gun Owners of California

www.grnc.org Grassroots North Carolina

www.kc3.com Kentucky Coalition to Carry Concealed

www.tennesseefirearms.com Tennessee Firearms Association

www.jpfo.org Jews for the Preservation of Firearm Ownership

www.ccops.org Concerned Citizens Opposed to Police States

Gun control organizations and resources

www.americansforgunsafety.com Americans for Gun Safety

www.bradycampaign.org Brady Center for the Study of Gun Violence

www.csgv.org Coalition to Stop Gun Violence

www.millionmommarch.org Million Mom March

www.house.gov/lofgren/dc/990427-crossfire.html Transcripts of CNN, 27 April 1999 *Crossfire* debate on gun control

20 Capital punishment

Robert Singh

READER'S GUIDE

America remains unusual among contemporary liberal democracies in both allowing for and implementing the death penalty for those convicted of carrying out certain crimes. The US Constitution allows—but does not require—individual states, the federal government, and the US military to impose capital punishment. Thirty-eight states currently allow for judicial executions, although the bulk of these occur in the South, with non-southern executions relatively rare events. But whether the current system meets the Constitution's guarantees of due process, equal protection, and adequate legal representation is highly questionable in the light of extensive evidence concerning the maladministration of the death penalty. Although public support for the death penalty is less strong than often imagined outside America, capital punishment remains a settled—albeit peripheral—part of the criminal justice system for two reasons. First, although the Supreme Court ruled the penalty unconstitutional in 1972, it reversed its position a mere four years later in the face of a widespread political backlash against abolition. Federal courts since 1976 have strongly endorsed the constitutionality of the death penalty and both expanded and refined the conditions under which it operates. Second, the vast majority of American elected officials—including many state judges and district attorneys—have embraced support for capital punishment to demonstrate their 'tough' credentials on questions of crime and 'law and order' more broadly. Although concerns across the political spectrum about the flaws in the system have recently prompted reforms at state and federal level and encouraged the federal judiciary to re-examine aspects of the capital punishment regime, these are better viewed as aimed at preserving rather than dismantling the death penalty.

Introduction

The election of George W. Bush as president in 2000 heightened international attention to America's capital punishment regime. During his six years as governor of Texas from 1995 to 2001, 152 convicted murderers were executed in the Lone Star state. In 1999, Bush notoriously parodied the pleas of a female death row inmate and 'born again' Christian, Karla Faye Tucker, to spare her life in an interview with *Talk* magazine. In 2000, Texas established an American record for the number of death row prisoners executed in a single calendar year (forty). The governor's apparently sincere insistence on the complete reliability of the Texas criminal justice system during the 2000 presidential election suggested to many Americans a conservatism that was more callous than compassionate—a view of the United States itself that is widely shared elsewhere in the world on the emotive issue of the death penalty.

Non-American bemusement and revulsion at America's support for capital punishment reflects not only deep disquiet at the principle of the state taking life but also the scale of America's judicial killings. In 2001, for example, sixty-six death row inmates—including federal inmate Timothy McVeigh, the Oklahoma City bomber—were executed in America, a slight drop from the eighty-five executed in 2000 and the record high of ninety-eight in 1999. As of 1 April 2002, 3,701 prisoners were awaiting execution across the United States in federal and state death rows. In contrast to Europe, where membership of the European Union now requires the abolition of capital punishment on the part of both current and prospective EU member states, all but twelve American states allow for the imposition and implementation of a death sentence for those convicted of perpetrating certain categories of crime. As the films *Dead Man Walking*, *Last Dance*, and *The Green Mile* suggested, America remains comparatively unusual among liberal democracies in not only allowing but also practicing judicial executions.

Like gun control, capital punishment eloquently illustrates the distinctiveness of America's divided democracy. Where liberal values trump those of majoritarianism in Europe on capital punishment in public policy outcomes (if not necessarily popular support), majority endorsement of the ultimate penalty remains a robust bulwark for the death penalty in most American states. Where the EU precludes a state from taking life through judicial executions, America's federal structure allows—but does not require—individual states, the federal government, and the United States military to impose the death penalty. Where even staunch conservatives in Europe have come to regard capital punishment as a barbaric, cruel, and savage practice unsuited for the twenty-first century, traditionalist support for the penalty far outweighs progressive opposition in most American states.

The politics of the death penalty is, however, more complex, subtle, and dynamic than many popular accounts of a primordial and macabre American enthusiasm for executions typically suggest. Despite the minimal evidence that capital punishment has any deterrent effect on prospective murderers and the substantial evidence of serious flaws in the administration of capital 'justice', the death penalty has been sustained as public policy in America through a combination of mass support for retribution, the association of capital punishment with the broader post-1960s fight against crime, and—ironically—federal judicial interventions that sought to abolish the penalty only to re-animate widespread political support for the punishment. Despite recent attempts by public authorities to reform the death penalty regime to eliminate its more egregious flaws, capital punishment remains an established—albeit peripheral—part of the criminal justice system and one of the more clear and conspicuous examples of America's 'exceptional' character.

The death penalty in America

American endorsement of capital punishment has been strong but uneven both over time and between the individual states. At the republic's founding the death penalty had been legal in the colonial states, and it remained so as the new nation was created in 1787. Although attempts at abolition succeeded in some states during the nineteenth century, most either retained or introduced laws allowing for the ultimate penalty. The traditionalist cast of most Americans' values, attitudes, and beliefs—deriving in large part from their strong religious and moral codes—powerfully supported the notion that some crimes existed for which life imprisonment was an insufficient punishment. And although the Supreme Court ruled the death penalty unconstitutional in 1972, it subsequently reversed its position in 1976 (see below). Capital punishment now remains as much a mainstay of 'law and order' in America as private legal access to firearms.

America's capital punishment regime, however, has altered substantially over time in three important respects. First, the types of crime that states decided should be open to punishment by judicial execution were gradually confined—until the 1990s—to those involving first-degree murder. Second, public executions were gradually eliminated, the last being held in Kentucky in 1936 (though pressures—from both supporters and opponents of capital punishment—to televise executions 'live' arose in states such as California and Texas during the 1990s). Third, the methods by which death row inmates were executed were steadily reduced. Currently, five methods are available across America—lethal injection, electrocution, poison gas, firing squad, and hanging—but individual states differ markedly as to which they use. Lethal injection has become easily the most popular method of dispatch since its introduction in Oklahoma in 1977. Only two states—Alabama and Nebraska—now require death row inmates to go to their doom in 'Old Sparky', the electric chair.

As prior chapters in this volume have stressed, federalism is a key contributor to America's divided democracy, providing for markedly different laws, regulations, and public policy outcomes according to where an individual citizen resides. Nowhere is this more graphic or fatal than in the case of capital punishment. For example, twelve states and the District of Columbia do not allow for capital sentences to be imposed for any crimes (nine of these are in New England and the northern Midwest). An individual who commits a murder in these states will not receive a death sentence but one who commits an identical crime in the remaining thirty-eight may do so. (In a curious reversal of the standard logic on rational criminal behaviour, the serial killer Ted Bundy deliberately sought murder victims in Florida during the 1980s precisely because he wished to receive a death sentence in that state rather than a sentence of life imprisonment in an abolitionist state.)

The result of the diversity that America's federal system allows is not merely a stark variance in the legality of capital punishment across the United States but also a highly uneven national pattern of death sentences, death rows (see Table 20.1), and actual executions among death penalty states. For example, of the 765 executions conducted between

Table 20.1 Death row prisoners by jurisdiction, 2002

California	606	Oregon	30
Texas	457	Virginia	28
Florida	383	US Government	25
Pennsylvania	247	Idaho	21
North Carolina	222	Delaware	20
Ohio	204	Maryland	16
Alabama	187	New Jersey	16
Illinois	175	Washington	14
Arizona	129	Utah	11
Georgia	124	Connecticut	7
Oklahoma	119	Nebraska	7
Tennessee	105	US Military	7
Louisiana	93	Montana	6
Nevada	88	New York	6
South Carolina	77	Colorado	5
Missouri	72	South Dakota	5
Mississippi	68	Kansas	4
Arkansas	41	New Mexico	4
Kentucky	41	Wyoming	2
Indiana	39	New Hampshire	0

Source: Legal Defense Fund, NAACP, 1 Apr. 2002.

the reinstatement of the death penalty as constitutionally permissible punishment in 1976 and 1 April 2002, almost all judicial killings took place in the South. Texas easily led the lethal league table with 262 executions, followed by Virginia (84), Missouri (56), Florida (51), and Oklahoma (50). By comparison, the lead executor among northern states was Delaware, with just 13. Similar variations also occur in specific years. Of the 85 executions that took place in 2000, for instance, almost 90 per cent of these occurred in the South. Of the 38 death penalty states, 24 carried out no executions that year and only three outside the South (Arizona, California and Missouri) conducted any. Texas, with 40, accounted for almost as many executions as the rest of the 49 states combined.

The reasons why the overwhelming majority of executions occur in southern states are several. First, the murder rate is much higher in the South than the North (in most years from 1976 to 1998, for example, the homicide rate in Texas, Louisiana, Arkansas, and Oklahoma alone was three to four times greater than in the New England region as a whole). This means simply that the opportunities for judges and juries to impose a capital sentence are greater in the South. Second, in a relatively impoverished and strongly traditionalist region, the access of defendants to good legal counsel is relatively limited compared to the North, where well-trained public defenders are frequently available for defendants in capital trials. Third, race historically played a key role in southern politics in general and criminal justice in particular. Although by the 1980s and 1990s black defendants were no more likely than white defendants to be executed in most states, the majority of southern prosecutors and district attorneys are white and evidence exists that—despite Supreme Court requirements of 'race-neutral' juries—both prosecuting and defending counsels seek to shape jury selection on racial grounds with an eye to the political leanings of blacks and whites (McFeely 2000).

Key points

- The death penalty regime has altered from colonial times, so that capital punishment is now applied almost always for crimes of murder. Lethal injection is the most common method of execution.

- Federalism ensures that states differ as to whether, how, and for what crimes states execute convicted criminals. Twelve states and the District of Columbia prohibit capital punishment, but it is legal in thirty-eight others and for the federal government and the US military.

- Even among the thirty-eight states that allow the death penalty, most do not execute death row inmates. Although some of the largest death rows exist in non-southern states, the overwhelming majority of executions occur in southern states for reasons of high crime rates, poor access to legal representation, and—to a diminished but still significant extent—racial bias.

Table 20.2 Death row USA, 1 April 2002

Death row inmates	Total no. (%)
Race	
White	1,678 (45.34%)
Black	1,593 (43.04%)
Latino/Latina	347 (9.38%)
Native American	41 (1.11%)
Asian American	41 (1.11%)
Unknown	1 (0.03%)
Gender	
Male	3,647 (98.54%)
Female	54 (1.46%)
Juveniles	
Male	83 (2.24%)
TOTAL	3,701

Source: Legal Defense Fund, NAACP.

The constitutionality of capital punishment

Although discussions of the death penalty frequently focus primarily on the (im)morality of the state taking individual life, this is less central to its longevity as public policy in America than the question of its constitutionality. Whatever the competing arguments about its morality and the reliability of its administration, the death penalty could not be implemented if federal courts held it to violate the US Constitution. Moreover, unlike gun control—where a specific constitutional amendment referenced the right to bear arms, albeit with a lack of textual clarity—the constitutionality of capital punishment is heavily contested because of the competing claims of distinct constitutional provisions that simultaneously allow deprivation of life but ban cruel and unusual punishments.

To most constitutional lawyers there seems little doubt that the Founding Fathers intended to allow for the death penalty in drawing up the US Constitution of 1787. Not only did certain provisions of the Constitution—such as the Fifth Amendment—expressly allow for the taking away of life, but others—such as the Eighth Amendment—were deliberately phrased in ambiguous ways that suggested even if certain forms of punishment could be banned (such as crucifixions or beheadings) the basic principle of government executions remained permissible if individual states and the federal government wished to legislate for these. For opponents of capital punishment, however, this is not an especially significant point. America has gradually abandoned a range of practices once regarded as normal—from bans on interracial marriage to the criminalization of homosexuality—but now deemed barbaric. For example, thirty states enacted sterilization laws (affecting the poor, African Americans, and convicted criminals) that resulted in the sterilization of over 60,000 Americans from 1907 to 1979. To abolitionists, capital punishment is equally uncivilized and deserving of a definitive ruling of its unconstitutionality.

But whilst mass sentiment concurs on the barbarity of eugenics, the American public broadly supports the death penalty. Although a plurality of Americans favoured abolition in the mid-1960s, a steep rise in crime rates from that period—combined with urban riots and growing public concern about social breakdown and a collapse of 'law and order'—helped shift opinion back to supporting capital punishment. That shift was rapidly accelerated by the popular backlash to the Court's abolitionist *Furman* v. *Georgia* decision in 1972. After the re-establishment of the death penalty's constitutionality in *Gregg* v. *Georgia* in 1976, support remained robust. Between 1977 and 1998, the proportion of those polled who supported the penalty fluctuated between 66 and 76 per cent, while those in opposition ranged from 19 to 28 per cent. Not only was public support higher than at any time since the first polls were taken in the 1930s but it was also strikingly consistent across regions and demographic groups. The most significant partial exception was African Americans, but people of all races—including a majority of blacks—favoured the penalty, whites by a four to one margin. Men, Republicans, and the rich supported it more than women, Democrats, and the poor, but only marginally more strongly.

But whilst relatively few Americans were abolitionist in principle, many nonetheless held reservations about the policy when offered alternatives. When polls during the late 1980s and 1990s asked whether murderers should be sentenced to death or life in prison without parole, slightly fewer than half favoured capital punishment. When the alternative was life imprisonment without parole combined with restitution to the victim's family, support dropped to just 30 per cent. An ABC poll in January 2000 also found that support had declined from 77 per cent in 1996 to 'only' 64 per cent.

Key points

- Whatever the competing moral and practical arguments about the death penalty, the constitutionality of capital punishment is

Box 20.1 Core academic debate
For and against capital punishment

The case for the death penalty

Most—though not all—social scientific examinations of the death penalty in America have concluded that capital punishment has no or minimal deterrent effect on crimes such as murder. But most Americans continue to value the death penalty despite this, for two main reasons. One is simply a desire for retribution, which stems in part from a reaction to a widespread loss of faith in the power of prisons and other institutions to rehabilitate criminals and partly from beliefs that crime rests on the free will of the criminal rather than social or biological forces beyond the criminal's control. As William Bradford Reynolds, an official in the Reagan Justice Department, wrote, 'Some crimes deserve death, and nothing else will quench our righteous anger, or vindicate our humanity, or inspire sufficiently profound respect or reverential fear of the law and the underlying moral order. Serving justice at times demands imposing the ultimate sanction' (Hickok 1991: 330). Secondly, with the end of public executions during the 1930s as a vehicle for the collective public condemnation of crime, support for capital punishment subsequently assumed a symbolic status—as a shorthand way of expressing concern about crime in general. For most Americans, some crimes exist for which life imprisonment is an inadequate punishment. Since relatively few of us within or outside America adhere to a complete prohibition on state killing—including times of war, in cases of crimes against humanity perpetrated by a Hitler or a Stalin or an Osama Bin Laden, or in particularly egregious crimes such as the bombing of the Alfred P. Murrah federal building in Oklahoma City in 1995—the key issue then becomes where the appropriate line is drawn (for example, only in cases of mass murder, in instances of individual homicides, or in non-homicidal crimes such as drugs smuggling or rape?).

The case against the death penalty

For many abolitionists, a sufficiently powerful motive force is simply the alleged immorality of the state taking individual life. But for others, beyond the vexed moral issue is a more 'practical' one of the equitable operation of any capital punishment system. In this regard, critics of the death penalty point to seven major flaws in its implementation in America currently:

1. No deterrent effect. Punishments should plausibly have a rational criminological and societal function. But only a minuscule proportion of those convicted of homicide receive the death sentence (about 0.1 per cent); of these, only a tiny proportion is executed. Beyond this, the twelve states that prohibit the death penalty experience crime rates no lower than those of the thirty-eight death penalty states.

2. Arbitrary sentencing and enforcement and class bias. Capital punishment is inflicted not on those who have committed the worst crimes but on those with the worst lawyers. Approximately 90 per cent of death row inmates cannot afford their own attorney, and stories abound of defendants who go on trial for their lives represented by lawyers who are inexperienced, unprepared, overburdened, and even drunk.

3. Racial bias and discrimination. Although black Americans make up only 11 per cent of the total American population, approximately 43 per cent of death row inmates in 2002 were black. Whites and blacks are murder victims in almost equal numbers, but approximately 80 per cent of prisoners executed since 1977 were convicted for the killing of a white person. Despite over 1,000 homicide victims in Kentucky being black, for example, every death sentence from 1977 to March 1996 was for the murder of a white victim. In 1998, of the 1,838 district attorneys and other officials who decide whether to seek a capital sentence in the thirty-eight death penalty states, only twenty-two were black and twenty-two were Latino.

4. Wrongful execution. According to the Death Penalty Information Center in Washington, DC, 100 death row inmates from twenty states were eventually released and cleared of capital charges from 1977 to 2002, out of some 6,000 who have been sentenced to death. Between 1987 and 1999, sixty-one condemned inmates were released. A few were beneficiaries of new evidence resulting from DNA testing, a technology unavailable when they were originally convicted. But most had been victims of dishonest prosecutors, law enforcement officials, or witnesses whose lies were only discovered several years later.

Box 20.1 **continued**

5. Alternative punishments. Providing that life imprisonment without parole is enforced, the prevention of a convicted criminal's reoffending is guaranteed while the possible problems associated with the death penalty are avoided.

6. Delays. The average wait between sentencing and execution grew from fifty-one months in 1977–83 to 134 months by 1995. Currently the average wait is approximately seven years—arguably a form of 'cruel and unusual punishment' in itself.

7. Excessive cost. Lawyers are more expensive than prison guards. A 1993 Duke University study found that the cost for each individual state execution in North Carolina—taking account of trials, appeals, and so on— amounted to $2.1 million, approximately twice as much as a sentence of twenty years to life in prison.

Perhaps unsurprisingly, the Geneva-based International Commission of Jurists concluded in a 1996 investigation of America's capital punishment system that it was 'arbitrary, and racially discriminatory, and prospects of a fair hearing for capital offenders cannot . . . be assured'.

Box 20.2 **Constitutional influences**
Cruel, unusual, and fair?

To most observers, the US Constitution allows for, but does not require, capital punishment. The Fifth and Fourteenth Amendments explicitly permit 'deprivation of life' as long as this occurs according to 'due process' of law. Whilst the Eighth Amendment prohibits 'cruel and unusual punishments', this was intended to ban barbaric punishments such as burning at the stake rather than to outlaw the principle of capital punishment as such. That is, the amendment was directed at the methods of implementation rather than the principle of judicial execution.

But this raises two important constitutional dilemmas. First, does the existing regime meet the requirements of due process, equal protection, and the Sixth Amendment's guarantee of adequate legal counsel? Second, who decides what counts as 'cruel and unusual' punishment? Does that term take its meaning from prevailing public sentiment—as the Supreme Court declared in *Trop* v. *Dulles* (1958)—if so, it merely restates majority opinion rather than protects minorities—or is there some timeless, independent content to the term beyond what temporary majorities may think? Both traditionalists and progressives face major problems on these questions. For traditionalists, the bulk of empirical evidence suggests that it is very difficult to argue that the administration of capital punishment does meet the procedural safeguards that

the Constitution mandates. For progressives, the death penalty represents the exemplar of the 'living constitution' notion, whereby practices once seen as unexceptional are now viewed as uncivilized. But if the meaning of cruel and unusual punishment is to be interpreted according to contemporary sentiment, it appears to guarantee only what the majority desires. That is, if its meaning is tied to the moral judgement of most Americans as to what counts as cruel and unusual, the clause is rhetorical and unnecessary, since it represents a restatement of the majority's will, not an independent curb on that majoritarianism.

Moreover, unlike the First Amendment, the Eighth contains an explicit limitation of the scope of its protections: it prohibits neither all punishments nor unreasonable, costly, useless, or discriminatory punishments, but only those held to be cruel and unusual. And most Americans clearly do not hold the death penalty to be cruel and unusual. Although the Court held in *Trop* that the Eight Amendment's meaning was not fixed immutably at its adoption in 1791 and instead 'must draw its meaning from the evolving standards of decency that mark the progress of a maturing society', the majority also ruled that 'the death penalty has been employed throughout our history, and, in a day when it is still widely accepted, it cannot be said to violate the constitutional concept of cruelty'.

strongly contested by constitutional scholars. Abolitionists claim the death penalty is by definition 'cruel and unusual' and hence prohibited by the Eighth Amendment. Others argue this clause applies only to the methods of execution, not the principle of capital punishment.

- Some pragmatists argue that the problem with capital punishment is that it fails to meet the procedural safeguards of the Fifth, Sixth, and Fourteenth Amendments. Others deny this, or argue that, even if this is the case, it does not outweigh the combined majoritarian, federalism, and Eighth Amendment defences of capital punishment.

- Majority public support for capital punishment since 1977 has been consistent and decisive but declines significantly when alternative punishments such as life imprisonment without parole are mentioned.

The politics of capital punishment

Since public support is strong but relatively shallow when alternatives are offered, what explains the failure of American abolitionists to persuade both the public and federal and state governing authorities to dispense with the death penalty? Beyond the predominantly traditionalist sentiments of most Americans on capital punishment, two main explanations account for why America's death penalty politics remain distinctive and resistant to abolitionism. First, American courts—and the federal courts, especially—have exerted a profound influence on the capital punishment regime, making the penalty a constitutional as well as a political matter for resolution. Second, traditionalist sentiments have proven tenaciously effective in encouraging public officials from presidents to district attorneys to oppose abolition for fear of looking 'soft' on broader issues of crime, social breakdown, and law and order.

The Supreme Court

Although Richard Hodder-Williams suggested in Chapter 8 that the term was broadly accurate, few death row inmates would be likely to concur with the description of the Supreme Court made by Founding Father Alexander Hamilton as the 'least dangerous branch' of the federal government. Ironically, the Court has proved a crucial actor in ensuring the maintenance and expansion of the capital punishment regime, in large part because its ill-conceived attempt to abolish the penalty in 1972 resulted in one of the most furious public responses to a judicial intervention on any issue witnessed in America since the Second World War.

In June 1972, the Supreme Court ruled by a five to four majority in *Furman* v. *Georgia* that the death penalty as then applied was unconstitutional because existing laws afforded judges and juries excessive discretion. Sentencing authorities did not know what factors to consider in deciding between a death or life sentence and arbitrary or discriminatory sentences were therefore inevitable. On identical facts, one jury might sentence a defendant to death while another might sentence a defendant to life imprisonment (or less). The ruling struck down the laws of the thirty-nine states that allowed capital punishment, required state courts to re-sentence over 600 prisoners then awaiting executions, and for the first time, imposed a de facto nationwide abolition of capital punishment across the United States.

As with the Court's ruling the following year in *Roe* v. *Wade* (1973), it was not only the nationwide effect of the decision but also its constitutional basis that provoked widespread disquiet among traditionalist Americans. Although five justices made up the majority that declared the death penalty to be 'cruel and unusual' punishment, they did not agree on the basis of their holding of unconstitutionality. Justices Brennan and Marshall ruled it so by definition, but the remaining three justices held the problem to be maladministration rather than morality. Justice Douglas identified racial and class discrimination as plaguing the system, while Justice Stewart saw arbitrariness as the problem, arguing: 'These death sentences are cruel and unusual in the same way that being struck by lightning is cruel and unusual.' Justice White, by contrast, concluded that the penalty was imposed so rarely by the states that it could not possibly serve a useful purpose. Whatever the flaws in the logic (each position was open to the challenge that it called for more, not fewer, executions, to remedy the defects and render capital punishment constitutional), Chief Justice Warren Burger—dissenting—predicted: 'There will never be another execution in this country.'

But Burger was decidedly premature. The legislative backlash in the states to *Furman* was broad, furious, and effective. States whose laws had been invalidated passed new statutes to repair the flaws identified in *Furman*. Fifteen introduced mandatory death sentences for particular crimes. Another twenty passed new statutes providing for various degrees of guidance for juries retaining discretion in sentencing capital punishment. By 1976, thirty-five states and the federal government had enacted new capital punishment statutes. Almost exactly four years after *Furman*, the Court declared in *Gregg* v. *Georgia* (1976) that the death penalty was not always unconstitutional, and approved new state laws that separated capital trials into two stages: one determining guilt or innocence and a second in which the life or death sentence was decided after consideration of aggravating and mitigating factors.

Much as the Court's intervention on abortion transformed the politics of the issue (see Chapter 18), both nationalizing and politicizing it as never before, so its rulings in *Furman* and *Gregg* turned capital punishment into a constitutional as well as a political issue. The Court rapidly constructed an intricate but extensive body of jurisprudence on the death penalty. One important result, in turn, was a shift in decision-making authority among the three branches of the federal and state governments, with concerns that had previously been determined mostly by elected federal and state legislators—or by governors during the clemency process—now

becoming constitutional questions to be decided ultimately by federal and state courts.

Among such questions, for example, were several that previously were matters for state legislatures to determine: should heinous crimes, such as rape, that nonetheless fell short of murder be subject to the death penalty? (no, *Coker* v. *Georgia*, 1977); was executing an accomplice to murder constitutional? (yes, *Tison* v. *Arizona*, 1987); if the defendant was 16 when he committed the crime, could he be executed? (yes, *Stanford* v. *Kennedy*, 1989); if the defendant was mentally retarded? (yes, *Penry* v. *Lynaugh*, 1989, but subsequently no, *Atkins* v. *Virginia*, 2002); and is a racially disproportionate death penalty system constitutional? (yes, *McClesky* v. *Kemp*, 1987). As Box 20.3 illustrates, in relatively few policy areas has the Court not only developed such a wide-ranging and detailed case law but also altered its views so rapidly on so broad a set of questions involving matters of literally life and death.

But the constant refinement of the capital punishment regime has not proved satisfactory even to members of the Court itself. Among more conservative justices, Antonin Scalia complained in 2002 of 'the fog of confusion that is our annually improvised Eighth Amendment "death is different" jurisprudence', while arguing that 'the choice for the judge who believes the death penalty to be immoral is resignation rather than simply ignoring duly enacted constitutional laws and sabotaging the death penalty'. By contrast, in June 1994 the retiring justice Harry Blackmun—one of the four dissenters in the landmark abolitionist *Furman* ruling—stated that the federal courts had evidently failed to develop adequate protections to ensure the fair and accurate application of the penalty: 'I feel morally and intellectually obligated simply to concede that the death penalty experiment has failed.' Such frustration is unsurprising, since the Supreme Court has in effect sought consistently since 1972 to reconcile two essentially irreconcilable goals: consistency across capital cases (which is best achieved by formal rules restricting jury discretion) and attention to the unique features of each death penalty case (which is best secured by allowing the jury unrestricted discretion in the light of all available aggravating and mitigating circumstances).

Box 20.3 Select Supreme Court rulings on capital punishment, 1972–2002

Furman v. *Georgia* (1972). 5–4. Ruled that the death penalty was unconstitutional under the 'cruel and unusual punishment' clause of the Eighth Amendment. Three justices found jury discretion produced a random pattern among those receiving the penalty that was cruel and unusual. Two justices found capital punishment a per se violation of the Constitution, as degrading to human dignity, arbitrarily severe, unnecessary, and offensive to contemporary values.

Gregg v. *Georgia* (1976). 7–2. Reaffirmed the constitutionality of capital punishment by upholding state laws that guided judges and juries when imposing death sentences.

Woodson v. *North Carolina* (1976). 5–4. Prohibited mandatory death penalty statutes as unconstitutional. Ruled that evolving standards of decency required that capital statutes treat the convicted as individuals.

Roberts v. *Louisiana* (1976). 5–4. Ruled unconstitutional a mandatory death sentence law for murderers of police officers in the line of duty because it did not allow for individualized sentencing.

Coker v. *Georgia* (1977). 7–2. Ruled that the Eighth Amendment's 'cruel and unusual punishment' clause prohibited punishments that are disproportionate to the crime. The death penalty for rape was therefore unconstitutional.

Booth v. *Maryland* (1987). 5–4. Prohibited 'victim impact statements' (where the emotional consequences of a crime on the family of the victim are elaborated) from

being introduced in the second—penalty—phase of capital murder trials.

McClesky v. *Kemp* (1987). 5–4. Upheld Georgia's death penalty law, despite a statistical study showing that Georgia defendants convicted of killing whites were eleven times as likely to be sentenced to death as were those who kill blacks, especially when the killer was black and the victim white.

Penry v. *Lynaugh* (1989). 5–4. Held that the Eighth Amendment does not preclude the execution of mentally retarded persons convicted of murder.

Stanford v. *Kennedy* (1989). 5–4. Ruled that the Eighth Amendment does not prohibit the execution of juvenile murderers as young as 16 (i.e. they were over 15 at the time of their crimes).

Payne v. *Tennessee* (1991). 6–3. Allowed the use of victim impact statements as evidence in sentencing trials.

Felker v. *Turpin* (1996). 9–0. Ruled as constitutional the Anti-Terrorism and Effective Death Penalty Act of 1996 that imposed strict limits on appeals and on federal courts' review of death sentences.

Atkins v. *Virginia* (2002). 6–3. Ruled that a series of laws enacted in eighteen of the thirty-eight death penalty states demonstrated that a national consensus had emerged against executing mentally retarded offenders, an unconstitutional 'cruel and unusual punishment'.

Ring v. *Arizona* (2002). 7–2. Held that a jury, not a judge, must decide whether a capital defendant receives the death penalty.

The elected branches

If the Supreme Court's interventions constitutionalized, nationalized, and politicized the issue of capital punishment, the elected branches of government at federal, state, and local level have strongly reinforced the death penalty's place as a settled element of American criminal justice policy.

In symbolic terms, much as abortion has become a litmus test for other issues of particular concern to American women (for those both pro-choice and pro-life), so the death penalty has become a proxy for broader questions of crime and 'law and order'.

America cannot be described as being 'soft' on crime. For example, with only 5 per cent of the world's population, America holds approximately 25 per cent of the global prison population. Despite having a higher proportion of its citizens behind bars than any other nation, support for capital punishment in particular signals an unequivocally 'tough' stance on crime, siding with law enforcement agencies; opposition signifies 'softness' on crime and criminals and insufficient concerns for the victims of crime. Consequently, much as few risk-averse politicians dare either to support strong gun regulations or to oppose the punitive paradigm on the 'drugs war'—

despite its chronic failure—so capital punishment consistently wins enthusiastic support rather than reluctant opposition from America's elected officials, especially during election years.

At federal level, for example, no American president of either main political party has opposed the death penalty. Indeed, since the Court's *Furman* ruling in 1972, Presidents Nixon, Reagan, George Bush, and George W. Bush all used the penalty to demonstrate their hardline credentials on law and order issues. For the Republicans, capital punishment offered a convenient issue on which to label Democrats as 'soft' on criminal justice. Most notoriously, George Bush relentlessly exploited the opposition of his Democratic Party opponent, Massachusetts governor Michael Dukakis, to the death penalty in 1988. Accusing him of having left the 'clear-cut path of common sense' and becoming 'lost in the thickets of liberal sociology', the notorious Willie Horton television advertisement—featuring the face of a convicted black rapist who had been temporarily released from prison in Massachusetts only subsequently to rape a white woman and murder her husband—helped strongly to increase the salience of the crime issue and derail Dukakis's campaign.

Such Republican successes were not lost on then Governor Bill Clinton, who returned to his home state of Arkansas in April 1992—interrupting his primary campaign for the Democratic Party's presidential nomination—to refuse to commute the sentence of Ricky Ray Rector, a mentally retarded black death row inmate. (Rector's comprehension of his imminent demise was so limited that on the night of his final meal he set his dessert aside to 'save it for later'.) Presidential campaign ads in 1992 stated that Clinton and Al Gore were 'a new generation of Democrats' who 'sent a strong signal to criminals, by supporting the death penalty'. Moreover, in the 2000 presidential election, none of the four leading contenders for the main parties' nominations (Gore, former Senator Bill Bradley, Governor Bush, and Senator John McCain) opposed the death penalty. Neither did the eventual vice-presidential candidates Dick Cheney and Joe Lieberman, and nor did erstwhile 'liberal' Senator Hillary Rodham Clinton (D.NY).

Alongside such presidential support stands a robust congressional endorsement of capital punishment. Particularly with the Republican takeover of Congress in 1994, pro-capital punishment forces enjoyed substantial successes in expanding and accelerating the death penalty process during the 1990s:

- *New capital crimes.* The 1994 crime bill—passed by the Democratic 103rd Congress (1993–4) and signed by President Clinton—created sixty new federal crimes for which the death penalty could be imposed and extended it to include certain drug offences.

- *Reducing delays between sentencing and execution.* The 1996 Anti-Terrorism and Effective Death Penalty Act extended recent Court decisions limiting death penalty appeals, imposing new restrictions on death row inmates' access to federal courts. Only one appeal in a federal court is now allowed, to be made within six months of sentencing. The average delay between sentencing and execution is expected to decline from an average of nine years during the 1980s to three by 2005.

- *Terminating funding for death row appeals.* The Republican 104th Congress (1995–6) ended federal funding to assist death row inmates' legal appeals. Congress also ended its financing of resource centres that helped indigent death row inmates find a lawyer. In 1995, the Republican Speaker of the House of Representatives, Newt Gingrich, advocated executing drug smugglers since mass executions ('27 or 30 or 35 people at one time') could provide an excellent deterrent.

When combined, these punitive measures meant that Congress and President Clinton (who signed the bills into law) effectively nationalized the death penalty in America. This is largely because the laws allow the federal prosecutor in a state to pre-empt jurisdiction from the state prosecutor in certain capital cases. If the federal prosecutor secures a conviction under federal statutes, whether or not the state law provides for a death penalty for the crime in question is immaterial to the imposition of a capital sentence.

This is not to suggest, however, that the quality of mercy among most state governments trumps that of justice any more than it does at the federal level. If anything, in most states the demands for retribution and 'effective' punishment ring especially loudly. Many politicians who campaign for statewide, state legislative, and judicial offices take their 'toughness' on crime to extraordinary lengths. For example, Al Checchi, an aspirant Democratic Party candidate for governor in California, launched his primary campaign in late 1997 by promising that he would extend the death penalty to include repeat child molesters and serial rapists. Pete Wilson, the incumbent Republican governor, had previously advocated the execution of children as young as 14. (Both intentionally misled the public, since the Supreme Court had already ruled such measures unconstitutional.)

During the 1980s and 1990s, state governors also became increasingly reluctant to commute capital sentences. Clemency—whereby governors (and, in the case of federal death row inmates, the president) can pardon a convicted criminal and transmute a capital sentence into one of life imprisonment—became in effect a political death sentence for governors, being granted in only about one case per year across the states. In the 1997 'off-year' elections, even the moderate Republican governor of New Jersey, Christine Todd Whitman, publicly demanded to know why none of the state's fourteen death row inmates had been executed under her watch. Her Democratic opponent in turn criticized her for waiting three years before taking action, claiming that he 'would take action on the death penalty from the first year' in office.

Locally, the district attorney of the county where the crime occurs decides whether a particular murder should be tried as a capital crime. Since, in most death penalty states, DAs (and many state judges) are themselves elected rather than appointed officials, both those who prosecute and those who adjudicate in capital trials may be vulnerable to electoral pressures. Such pressures inevitably shape the likelihood of disparate, discriminatory, and arbitrary rulings. For instance, Philadelphia County—an area with only 14 per cent of Pennsylvania's total state population—accounts for more than half of the state's total death sentences. Just one of seventy-nine counties in Texas accounts for almost one-third of the state's total death row prisoners: in

January 1998, 132 of 437 death row inmates were sentenced in Harris County, which achieved an execution rate higher than entire states such as Florida and Mississippi. The county's chief prosecutor, John Holmes, Jr. (the 'Texas Terminator') was elected four times as the Republican candidate for prosecutor and was unopposed in 1996. His view of the death penalty was clear: 'There's nothing worse than having a law and not enforcing it. That promotes disrespect for the law' (Langton 1999: 29).

None of this is to suggest that American opinion—either public, elite, or in the form of organized interests—is, or ever has been, uniformly pro the death penalty. Among those groups that have campaigned against capital punishment for decades are the Legal Defense and Education Fund, Inc. of the NAACP and the American Civil Liberties Union, in addition to a variety of state and federal politicians (such as President Clinton's attorney-general, Janet Reno). Although it had traditionally supported the penalty, the Roman Catholic Church—following the lead of Pope John Paul II—now opposes capital punishment, as do most Protestant denominations (Baptists, Episcopalians, Lutherans, Methodists, Presbyterians, and the United Church of Christ). Some figures—such as Sister Helen Prejean, the author of *Dead Man Walking*—have also achieved national attention for their abolitionist efforts.

Moreover, recent concerns about the high-profile releases of innocent prisoners from death row, news reports on flaws in the legal process, and adverse election-year attention to Texas in 2000 have combined to pressure public authorities strongly to reconsider the capital punishment regime. Even staunch conservative supporters of the death penalty, such as evangelical preacher Pat Robertson, talk show host and prominent Republican Oliver North, and columnist George Will expressed concerns during 2000–2 that the administration of the capital punishment system was 'broken'. In January 2000 George Ryan, the Republican governor of Illinois, declared a moratorium on all executions in his state, as did the Democratic governor of Maryland, Parris Glendenning, in April 2002. During the 107th Congress (2001–2), Senator Patrick Leahy (D.VT) also introduced a bill with bipartisan support—the Innocence Protection Act—to ensure access to DNA testing and better legal representation for defendants in capital trials.

But against this not only did the federal government expand the number of crimes eligible for death while reducing the opportunity for appeals, but also states that allowed but did not practise capital punishment resumed judicial killings. In 1999, for example, Ohio executed its first death row prisoner since the restoration of capital punishment in 1976, while Tennessee carried out its first execution in 2000. The terrorist attacks of 11 September 2001 did not result in a sharp upturn of support for the ultimate penalty. An ABC-NEWS.com poll of 7 May 2002 found that 65 per cent of Americans support the death penalty when no alternative is offered. When given the sentencing option of life without the possibility of parole, 'only' 46 per cent of Americans support the death penalty,

a proportion that was unchanged from April 2001 poll data. But the possibility of a capital sentence was readily entertained by the public for terrorists, and the examples of specific heinous crimes—from Timothy McVeigh's bombing of the federal building in Oklahoma to the destruction of the World Trade Center—lent strong support to the basic pro-capital punishment predisposition of most Americans.

Key points

- Most elected politicians at federal, state, and local level embrace capital punishment as a signal that they are 'tough' on crime and criminal justice issues, even though the death penalty is a minor and peripheral part of the criminal justice system.

Box 20.4 Is America different?

Europeans often use the death penalty as an example of how different—and, implicitly, how uncivilized—America remains in comparative terms. During the first years of the twenty-first century, the European Union, the Pope, the United Nations, Amnesty International, and other human rights organizations made strong objections to many American executions. The United States was even successfully sued by Germany in the International Court of Justice for executing two of its citizens in Arizona who were not informed of their rights under the Vienna Convention. Certainly, America is unusual in being the only industrialized liberal democracy other than Japan to allow and implement capital punishment. It also remains one the few nations—along with Iran, Iraq, Nigeria, Pakistan, and Yemen—that still execute juveniles. Moreover, the US was one of only ten nations (including China, Pakistan, Rwanda, and Sudan) to vote against the UN Human Rights Commission's April 1999 Resolution Supporting Worldwide Moratorium on Executions, which called for countries that had not abolished the death penalty to restrict its use—including not executing juveniles and limiting the number of capital offences.

But this picture requires some important qualifications First, many nations around the world do retain capital punishment. What is unusual is that most of these are the type of authoritarian regimes and 'rogue states' whose respect for democratic values and human rights is minimal. Second, as we saw above, public support for the death penalty in America declines significantly when alternative punishments are mentioned. Third, opinion surveys suggest that the mass public in many liberal democracies—including the UK, France, and Italy—favour the restoration of capital punishment, but are denied this by national political elites that are committed to abolitionism. In the light of a 1996 MORI poll that put popular British support for the death penalty at 76 per cent, Jonathan Freedland (1998: 31–2) persuasively commented:

Opponents of judicial killing have hardly won the argument among the British people. Instead our political system has simply failed to express the popular will . . . what is often a cause for self-congratulation—with progressive Britons imagining ours to be a more civilised society than the US—should perhaps be a trigger for self-doubt. American democracy ensures the public get their way, even if the result is not always pleasant. The British system cannot say the same.

- The federal government has expanded the number of capital crimes while reducing the quantity and quality of appeals that death row inmates can lodge, effectively nationalizing the death penalty in America.

- Although an important coalition of abolitionist interest groups exists and has secured some reforms of the capital punishment system, its influence is modest compared to that of traditionalist supporters of the death penalty.

Conclusion

No action by the state is more powerful than depriving its own citizens of their lives through judicial killings—however sanitised the prevalence of lethal injections may render such executions compared to the electric chair. It is therefore somewhat ironic that a citizenry generally suspicious of government in general and the federal government in particular evinces such a strong and abiding enthusiasm for judicial executions, the ultimate expression of 'big government'. That this should be the case in the face of a substantial body of empirical evidence on the flawed operation of the capital punishment system seems only more surprising given the extensive protections accorded to individual rights and liberties in the constitutions of the United States and the fifty individual states.

But the widespread concern for the victims of abusive law enforcement that existed in the 1950s and 1960s rapidly dissipated to concern for the victims of crime from the later 1960s as rising crime rates, urban riots, and a barely coded racial appeal to 'law and order' among elected politicians grew apace. The Supreme Court's abolitionist ruling in *Furman* appeared to many Americans not only to ride roughshod over traditional federal–state relations in an egregious act of 'judicial legislating' but also to do so on a highly dubious constitutional basis. Since the state legislative backlash against *Furman*, few American politicians have dared risk a direct attack on the principle, rather than the mechanics, of the death penalty. With federal courts

staffed by many Republican presidential appointees thanks to the Republican dominance of the White House (itself partly a function of voters endorsing the traditionalist appeals of Reagan and Bush), the 'least dangerous' unelected branch of the federal government has also reinforced the strongly pro-capital punishment inclinations of elected officials.

After a brief moment that stayed judicial executions from 1968 to 1976, capital punishment has once again emerged as an established—albeit peripheral—element of America's criminal justice system. In some states, death sentences and executions are now so common as to no longer be considered newsworthy. With 3,701 death row prisoners as of 1 April 2002, the death rate appears likely to increase over subsequent years (the annual number of death sentences currently exceeds the number of executions by a factor of three). The Supreme Court rulings in the summer of 2002 against the execution of mentally retarded inmates and requiring juries to determine capital sentences attracted considerable media attention and abolitionist celebrations. So, too, did Illinois governor George Ryan's decision on his last day in office in January 2003 to pardon all death row inmates in the state. But unless a decisive, unprecedented, and historically aberrant shift in mass American sentiment occurs—in the face of a growing range of capital crimes and reduced funding for a diminished number of appeals—the ranks of America's death rows and the macabre list of the judicially killed both seem destined to increase.

QUESTIONS

1 What best explains American support for capital punishment?

2 Critically assess the constitutional arguments for and against capital punishment.

3 Is capital punishment an issue that illustrates the excessive or insufficient power of unelected courts in America?

4 Why has opposition to capital punishment proven relatively ineffective in America since 1976?

5 'The strongest defence of capital punishment in America is that a federal system allows, but does not require, states to adopt whatever policies they so desire.' Discuss.

FURTHER READING

S. Banner (2002), *The Death Penalty: An American History* (Cambridge, Mass.: Harvard University Press). An elegant and comprehensive history of the penalty from the origins of the republic to the end of the twentieth century.

H. A. Bedau (ed.) (1997), *The Death Penalty in America: Current Controversies* (New York: Oxford University Press). An excellent collection of essays and information about capital punishment, with contributions covering all perspectives in the controversy.

D. R. Dow and M. Dow (eds.) (2002), *Machinery of Death: The Reality of America's Death Penalty Regime* (New York: Routledge). A set of powerful abolitionist essays by lawyers, wardens, and others active in the system.

M. Grossman (1998), *Encyclopedia of Capital Punishment* (Santa Barbara, Ca.: ABC-CLIO). A comprehensive A–Z of capital punishment in America and internationally.

H. H. Haines (1996), *Against Capital Punishment: The Anti-Death Penalty Movement in America, 1972–1994* (New York: Oxford University Press). A detailed analysis of the strategies and tactics of the abolitionist lobbies in America.

E. Hickok (ed.) (1991), *The Bill of Rights in America* (Charlottesville: University Press of Virginia), chs. 20–2. Constitutional arguments for and against capital punishment.

W. McFeeley (2000), *Proximity to Death* (New York: Norton). An account by an abolitionist historian of his involvement with several death penalty cases.

K. A. O'Shea (1999), *Women and the Death Penalty in the United States, 1900–1998* (Westport, Conn.: Praeger). A comprehensive analysis of the women who were executed in America during the twentieth century.

H. Prejean (1993), *Dead Man Walking* (New York: Random House). A detailed account of a Catholic nun's experiences in counselling inmates, and campaigning against the penalty, in Louisiana.

A. Sarat (ed.) (1999), *The Killing State: Capital Punishment in Law, Politics and Culture* (New York: Oxford University Press). A collection of essays on the law, politics, and cultural representations of capital punishment.

WEB LINKS

www.rightsforall-usa.org Amnesty International

www.aclu.org/executionwatch.html American Civil Liberties Union

www.deathpenaltyinfo.org/ Death Penalty Information Center

www.ncadp.org National Coalition Against the Death Penalty

www.TheJusticeProject.org The Justice Project

www.constitutionproject.org National Committee to Prevent Wrongful Execution

www.state.tx.us State of Texas

www.tdcj.state.tx.us/bpp/index.htm Texas Board of Pardons and Paroles

www.prodeathpenalty.com Pro-capital punishment site

www.murdervictims.com Victims' Rights

21 Gender

Vivien Hart

READER'S GUIDE

Is gender a factor in America's divided democracy? Women and men in America have equal rights to vote and hold office. Both sexes are members of political parties, advocacy organizations, and social movements. The constitutional promise of the equal protection of the laws extends to women and men. Government policies deeply affect the lives of both sexes. Nonetheless, the argument of this chapter is that gender remains a fault-line in America and a prime factor in women's involvement in politics. The concern of many women that government remains a predominantly male preserve challenges American values of democracy and equality. This chapter therefore first explores gender issues in voting, representation and office-holding. The lives of women and men differ in significant and unequal respects. The views of women and men differ on the public policies that are made by gendered political processes and affect those lives in many different ways. Three examples—constitutional equality, domestic violence, and peace and war—will show some of the complexities of making public policies that are gender-friendly and accepted as fair to all. Throughout the chapter we will find women active in their own cause, insistent on their full citizenship, and making a difference to American governance and public policy.

Introduction

A century and more ago, few Americans would have doubted that sex (biological differences between women and men) and gender (socially constructed expectations and norms of their different roles) divided women and men and excluded women from political and governmental activity. Most would have added that this was not just a fact, but a right and proper ordering of society. Governance was a part of the public sphere of life for which male attributes alone were suited, in which men participated, exercised power, and took all responsibility. The dominant construction of gender roles was a set of beliefs, ideals, and traditions by which white middle-class Americans lived and which they presented as the model for all. In this scheme, women's natural place was in the private sphere of home and family. Their responsibilities were for the domestic care and nurturing of husband and children, moral education, and social refinement. Those same female attributes of tenderness, sensitivity, and moral delicacy which equipped women for these tasks and gave them dignity and respect made them unsuited for the hurly-burly of the public sphere of politics and waged work, and made the public sphere unsuitable for their presence.

During the nineteenth century, a minority of women (and fewer men) began to question the assumption of gendered private and public spheres and the laws that enforced these. Women made their first bold public declaration in a meeting of barely 100 persons in the small town of Seneca Falls, in upstate New York, in 1848. The struggle for inclusion is still unfinished. Women started as outsiders. Men occupied the seats of power and would not willingly share their privilege. In addition, the structures of American government often worked against change. Women sought to inscribe their equality in the text of the Constitution, but constitutional amendments require super-majorities for passage. They brought lawsuits to win rights through constitutional interpretation by judges, a slow and technical route to social change. They pressed for new or revised legislation. But the division of functions in the American federal system meant that some of their campaigns must be aimed at the federal government, requiring national organization and a presence in Washington. Other concerns, such as the law of marriage and the family and many voting regulations, were the province of state legislatures. Then women could campaign closer to home but had to do so state by state. To form advocacy organizations required skill and money. Women had less experience, less income of their own, and less contact with moneyed benefactors.

Cultural as well as structural factors hindered women's progress. Any political action stepping outside their traditional place in society risked a backlash. Women were ridiculed, slandered, and arrested for speaking in public and marching in the streets. They were lectured on their place in life by judges who rejected their claims to vote or to practise law. Suffragists were jailed and force-fed when they chained themselves to the White House railings. Despite such obstacles, women have won many of the demands of 1848, for legal equality in marriage, access to education and the professions, the right to vote. We will see, however, how greatly gendered structural and cultural factors still influence American politics.

We will also see that the lines of division over gender in the American polity do not simply fall between women and men. Women are a majority, not a minority. If women agreed on every issue, they would carry the day! But differences among women work against any such unity. The cultural battles between traditionalists and progressives that feature in this book are central to the politics of gender. As we shall see, the definition of the family is intensely contested, with major effects for both sexes. Other factors also shape the politics of gender. Women are less well off than men, while class differences among women create different political priorities in employment or welfare policy. Class differences in the United States often overlap with racial and ethnic diversity. The poor woman is also more likely to be a woman of colour. Burdened with a history of double discrimination, by sex and by race, the African American woman's politics will often differ from those of her white counterpart and draw her into alliances with black men. Lesbian women feel marginal to politics dominated by heterosexual causes. They too have sometimes preferred to ally with gay men.

But nonetheless women do share a female identity. The deepest division among them concerns the nature of that shared identity and its political implications. In the next section, we join a debate that has run since the earliest days of women's political activism: about what women have in common. What women ask from politics differs depending on whether women determine they should be treated the same as and equally with men, or as fundamentally different from men with recognition and respect for that difference.

Box 21.1 Women and the Constitution

1848. Seneca Falls Declaration of Rights and Sentiments: women claim 'all the rights and privileges which belong to them as citizens of the United States.'

1868. Fourteenth Amendment: for the first time abandons the generic language of 'persons' and refers specifically to 'male citizens' only.

1870. Fifteenth Amendment: guarantees the vote regardless of 'race, color, and previous condition of servitude'; women fail to have sex added to this list.

1873. *Bradwell v. Illinois*: no right under the Fourteenth Amendment for women to practise law.

1875. *Minor v. Happersett*: right to vote is not one of the 'privileges and immunities of citizenship' guaranteed by the Fourteenth Amendment

1908. *Muller v. Oregon*: declares women's difference and weakness, permitting sex-specific labour laws.

1920. Nineteenth Amendment: gives women the vote.

1923. Equal Rights Amendment: first introduced to Congress.

1963. President's Commission on the Status of Women: says women should be directly granted the Fourteenth Amendment guarantee of 'equal protection of the laws'.

1967. *Loving v. Virginia*: strikes down state laws forbidding interracial marriage.

1971. *Reed v. Reed* and **1973** *Frontiero* versus *Richardson*: Supreme Court begins to give careful ('strict') scrutiny to laws discriminating between the sexes.

1972. Equal Rights Amendment: passes in both Houses of Congress, sent to the States for ratification.

1973. *Roe v. Wade*: conditionally legalizes abortion, citing a 'right to privacy' inferred from the First, Fourth, Fifth, Ninth and Fourteenth Amendments and the general ethos of the Bill of Rights. Many constitutional cases and attempts to amend the Constitution follow.

1976. *Craig v. Boren*: increases the degree of judicial scrutiny of laws making distinctions of gender. In contrast to *Muller v. Oregon*, laws that discriminate mostly presumed unconstitutional.

1981. *Rostker v. Goldberg*: upholds military draft for men but not for women.

1981. First woman Supreme Court justice, Sandra Day O'Connor, appointed by President Reagan.

1982. Equal Rights Amendment lapses, ratified by only thirty-five of the thirty-eight states needed.

1991. *UAW v. Johnson Controls*: employers cannot discriminate between the sexes on workplace hazards to fertility.

1993. Second woman Supreme Court Justice, Ruth Bader Ginsburg, appointed by President Clinton.

1995. Constitutional Equality Amendment: new campaign begun by the National Organization for Women.

2000. *US v. Morrison*: rejects right to freedom from gender-related violence.

Equality or difference?

Using the language of the Declaration of Independence, women's *Declaration of Sentiments* of 1848 proclaimed that 'We hold these truths to be self-evident: that all men and women are created equal.' Equality feminism, inspired by this simple statement, has been at the forefront of modern women's politics. Equality feminists minimize the political significance of the biological attributes of women. They argue that existing differences in the lives of women and men derive from cultural definitions of gender roles. The fact that women most often undertake the unpaid tasks of caring for children, partners, and friends is a reflection of internalized assumptions about their role and opportunities, not their choice. Pregnancy and childbirth apart, all else is shaped by a constructed package of beliefs about the nature and practice of gender—and what is constructed can also be reconstructed. Biased definitions can be rewritten, institutions can be changed, and social structures as well as citizenship can be made gender-neutral. The role of the state is to promote equality.

Equality feminists require public policy to enable women and men to work, to care, to live an individual life as a matter of choice. Radical feminism finds that pathetically inadequate. Agreeing only with the starting point, that biological sex differences are minimally significant, radicals view culturally created differences as evidence of men's power to construct and enforce an oppressive culture. Gendered roles leave women forever 'serving those who ruthlessly and effectively aggress against her' (Dworkin 1983: 17). Women who aspire to equality in this corrupted system are not addressing the problem: 'Facing the true nature of male power over women also means that one must destroy that power or accommodate to it' (Dworkin 1983: 236). Radical feminists are a minority in rejecting complicity with the oppressive male state, but the radical analysis of male power in religion and culture, sexuality, economy, and politics has influenced every school of feminist thought, including the third one we consider, difference feminism.

The feminism of difference starts from the opposite premise to these first two groups. Important aspects of women's lives are and always will be theirs alone, because of unchangeable characteristics that separate them from men. At their strongest, such theories rely on biological explanations. Female difference stems from woman's childbearing capacity, a physiological fact which may be extended into psychological definitions of maternal qualities of nurturing and caring. The state must support and value whatever difference is inherent in human nature, while ensuring that no disadvantage follows, and while equalizing every aspect of life where difference does not apply. At the extreme, radical believers in difference give absolute primacy to this maternal role and character. Those who believe motherhood to be the unchangeable essence of the female are known as essentialists. Few such would call themselves feminists, despite claiming a value and respect for women equal to that accorded for

other reasons to men. Difference feminists take a more complicated position. They seek to recognize both the biological essence and the cultural construction of gender roles, and to make this dual perspective a virtue. The state then has a special responsibility for the circumstances of pregnancy and motherhood. But many difference feminists also argue that, whether or not the caring character of women is their essential nature, women in fact do undertake the responsibilities of care—for children, families, partners, and society—often by choice. Governments must acknowledge and provide for this service to society.

In this chapter we see the practical implications of these views and the political agendas they generate. Consider just one example here, the institution of the family and its centrality to gender politics. States have banned interracial marriage in the past and few recognize same-sex relationships today. State regulation of reproductive rights has restricted women's control over their own bodies. Laws privilege motherhood. But minimal child care provision keeps some mothers at home, while welfare mothers must work outside the home. Employment and tax laws affect the household economy and the freedom of choice of its members. Equal pay and minimum wage legislation make work more attractive for women. But weak enforcement, confusion over how to address pregnancy costs and leave, the interrupted careers of mothers, 'glass ceilings' on women's promotion, all contribute to the abiding perception that women are 'secondary earners' in the family. The idea of paying wages for housework is treated as an outlandish proposition. The impact of each of these policies, direct or indirect, upon family roles and relationships, is contested by criteria of equality and difference. Hardly surprising then that a recent study of whether women's presence in politics had changed the agenda or outcomes concluded that it had indeed, and that the 'clearest and most consistent policy-related gender differences are evident in policies pertaining to women, children, and families' (Carroll 2002: xviii).

Access and representation

The politics of gender divides Americans along lines of sex but also divides women and men among themselves. Gendered political disputes are at the heart of American politics. Before we turn to explore three policy topics, we must look at the institutions within which decision-making takes place. Are these themselves gendered? Are women's voices and interests equally represented with men's? For if the forum of debate is biased, the outcomes may also be skewed and their legitimacy diminished in the eyes of citizens. Women are 52 per cent of the American population, and turn out to vote in greater numbers than men. Even given differences among women, these numbers suggest a potentially powerful public voice. While women have different views and allegiances, we will see that there is a broad tendency—the gender gap— for women as a group to vote somewhat differently from men. We will also see that, by contrast, relatively few women are elected to public offices. Why is this? And does this mean that, when gendered policies are up for discussion in federal and state legislatures, women's interests are not fully represented? Is it necessary to have women to represent women's interests?

Gender does make a difference in American elections. In 1920, the Nineteenth Amendment to the Constitution ensured women's legal right to vote. Suffragists were disappointed when far fewer women than men turned out to use their hard-won vote. But since 1974, while turnout in elections has plummeted, more women than men have voted. After 1965, when the Voting Rights Act addressed racism and exclusion, black women's voting rose faster than any other group in society (Baxter and Lansing 1983: 25, 70).

The American electorate is more female than male. In the 2000 presidential election, women constituted 52 per cent of the electorate. The result of that election was a virtual dead heat, with Republican George W. Bush and Democrat Al Gore both winning, in round figures, 48 per cent of the vote. But while the eventual winner, Bush, was the choice of 42 per cent of the women voting, Gore was supported by 54 per cent of women voting, a twelve-point gender gap in Gore's favour (figures almost exactly reversed for men, who voted 53 per cent Bush, 42 per cent Gore). Ninety-four per cent of black women voted for Gore, who also received strong support from women amongst the well-off (a fifteen-point gap from men), the unmarried (a fifteen-point gap), college graduates (an eighteen-point gap), and those independent-minded voters who identified themselves as neither Republican nor Democrat (a twelve-point gap) (Feminist Majority Foundation (FMF) 2001: 1, 3).

American voters participate in multiple elections at any one time. Separated powers and federalism allow that a voter may fail to elect one candidate of their choice while at the same time gaining other victories. A majority of women voters favoured the presidential loser in 2000, but the gender gap in Senate elections was decisive for their preferred candidate in nine Senate races. A fourteen-point gender gap helped elect Governor Jeanne Shaheen of New Hampshire, an eighteen-point gap Governor

Table 21.1 The gender gap in the 2000 presidential election (%)

Party identification	George W. Bush (Republican)	Al Gore (Democrat)
All women	43	54
All men	53	42
Republican women	90	9
Republican men	92	7
Independent women	39	51
Independent men	51	42
Democrat women	11	87
Democrat men	12	85

Source: Voter News Service poll, *New York Times*, 13 November 2000.

Ruth Minner in Delaware (FMF 2001: 8). The constitutional system, devised to ensure that no single faction can easily take over the whole system, enabled women to elect their preferred candidate to some key positions other than the presidency. Most of the candidates benefiting from the gender gap were Democrats and some were women. These facts suggest at least two important reasons why a gender gap might exist—the programmes of the parties and the sex of the candidates.

Women's party loyalties show a three-way split: 35 per cent identify as Republicans, 39 per cent Democrats, and 27 per cent Independents (FMF 2001: 3). In the 2000 presidential election party loyalists voted accordingly, giving Gore a head start among women. But of the Independents 51 per cent voted for Democrat Gore and only 42 per cent for Republican Bush. These non-partisan women greatly enlarged the overall gender gap in Gore's favour.

Partisanship explains part of women's distinctive political positioning. Non-aligned women lack party loyalty yet are more likely to support Democratic candidates. Why, since the 1930s, have proportionately more women than men voted for Democrats? Women's position in society, averaging lower incomes than men and bearing greater responsibility for children and for heath and welfare in general, predisposes them to the party associated with social policies—the Democrats. Women of colour see the Democrats as the party of civil rights. Women traditionally favour less military spending and more peaceful solutions—Democratic policies. The 2000 election revealed two further programmatic reasons why women voted for Gore: his support for abortion rights and for stronger gun control laws. Of all gender issues, abortion and reproductive freedom have generated the most bitter and unresolved struggle between pro-choice feminists and pro-life opponents, ever since the conditional legalization of abortion by the Supreme Court in *Roe* v. *Wade* (1973). In 2000, as usual, similar numbers of women and men supported the proposition that abortion should be legal in all or most cases (58 per cent of women, 55 per cent of men). But far more women voted in line with this belief. Of those with the strongest views, 77 per cent of women against 61 per cent of men voted for Gore. Far more women than men supported stronger

gun control laws (70 per cent of women, 50 per cent of men). Sixty-two per cent of this larger group of women voted for Gore (FMF 2001: 6).

In 2000, a disproportionate number of women candidates were among those winning seats with a marked gender gap. Although thirteen women and eighty-seven men constitute the new Senate, five women and four men, all Democrats, won the nine Senate races where the gender gap was decisive (FMF 2001: 8). The Democratic Party regularly fields more women candidates than do Republicans. In 2000, eighty Democrat and forty-two Republican women contested seats in the House of Representatives, with forty-two Democrat and eighteen Republican victories (**www.cawp.rutgers. edu/facts/elections/CandSummary2002.html**).

Did women prefer women candidates as well as Democratic policies, doubling their advantage? In the 1970s, poll evidence suggested that up to 13 per cent of the entire electorate simply would not vote for a qualified woman. By the 1990s that prejudice had dissipated. There may even be a slight preference among women voters for a woman candidate, from a belief that 'this country needs more women in high office' or that America might be 'a better place' if women governed (Cook et al. 1994: 126–7).

Behind such pragmatic arguments for women holding office lies a value-laden debate about the nature of representation. One view is that American democracy is itself undermined by so few women holding elected office. Representative democracy

Table 21.2 Percentage of elective offices held by women

Year	US Congress	Statewide elective	State legislatures
1979	3	11	10
1981	4	11	12
1983	4	11	13
1985	5	14	15
1987	5	14	16
1989	5	14	17
1991	6	18	18
1993	10	22	21
1995	10	26	21
1997	11	26	22
1999	12	28	23
2001	14	27	22

Source: Center for American Women and Politics, Eagleton Institute of Politics, Rutgers University.

must mean that those who govern will fairly represent the governed. For liberals, fair representation results from an electoral system that gives individuals the same access and weights their votes equally. Ideally, the electoral process aggregates individual views and transmits them to government. But government is not a mathematical process. In the legislature it transpires that some of those views are adequately spoken for, while minorities and the less powerful or articulate are outvoted or ignored. We have seen that American women do have distinctive views, but that policy-makers are mostly men. Both women and ethnic and racial minorities have argued that the liberal criterion of a fair and equal process is deficient: 'the franchise constitutes only the first step in achieving representation. If women and racially excluded voters ultimately got the vote, should they also achieve a minimal number of their own to speak for them?' The answer will be yes if it is true that 'only a woman finally will know what a woman's needs are' and can therefore speak for them (Maier and Klausen 2001: 6).

It has also been argued that women representatives don't just 'speak for' but also 'stand for' all women. In this view, fair representation involves 'some sort of physical or visible epitomization of the public': 'the quality of democracy as a whole—its value for men as well as women—is diminished if a significant group does not have its own members among the representatives' (Maier and Klausen 2001: 7). On this measure, of women representatives 'standing for' women, a simple count shows drastic underrepresentation. As to whether women representatives 'speak for' all women, some recent evidence suggests that indeed they do, consciously and with awareness of the diversity of women.

A pioneering survey found that women in state legislatures had different policy priorities from men, were more active on women's rights issues than men who shared their commitment, were more concerned to reshape the policy agenda and were more supportive of open and participatory government (CAWP 1988: 2–3). Women in Congress share these female priorities. Additionally, they feel that they represent women everywhere, not just the local voters who elected them. Congresswomen reported that, whatever their initial position, in office they learned that

women's concerns were neglected. Like other underrepresented groups, they found that the white male majority set the agenda from limited experience, 'given that so much that happens in this world is driven through a male perception' (Carroll 2000: 7). Senior Republican Marge Roukema spoke for most when she recalled being 'shocked to my toenails'. She had not 'wanted to be stereotyped as the woman legislator . . . but I learned very quickly that if the women like me were not going to attend to some of these family concerns, whether it was jobs or children or equity . . . , then they weren't going to be attended to.' Such 'commitment to representing women was widely shared by Congresswomen of different parties, ideologies, races and ethnicities, tenures in office, and institutional position' (Carroll 2000: 4).

Congresswomen's understanding of gender interests defied any simple distinction between equality and difference theories. The variety of examples they gave of 'the ties that bind' women together fall into 'four categories: care-giving, shared life experiences, discrimination, and work style' (Carroll 2000: 6). Care-giving and work style identified commonalities familiar from our discussion of difference theories: that women cared for families, were sensitive to others, and worked cooperatively. The same Congresswomen expressed strong equality positions when they spoke of shared life experiences and discrimination that left women disadvantaged across the board by comparison with men. They were also 'acutely aware of the differences that separate women and drive them apart', such as the demands of their districts, ideologies, or parties. Abortion was often the divisive factor. Conservative Republican representatives agreed with moderate Republican Connie Morella (R.MD) about some young women elected in a swing to the right in 1994:

I see a difference and I think it has basically to do with the abortion issue and the perception of the abortion issue as a divider because certainly women care about osteoporosis and women's health issues in general. They care about equity in the workplace. But the abortion issues have somehow clouded the thinking of some of the new women. They've seen this as a sort of barrier.   (Carroll 2000: 10)

Women are far short of numerical, 'standing for', representation in US institutions. Women representatives are conscious of the need to speak for all

---

Box 21.2 Congresswomen on women's shared identity

Women are the nurturing people in the nation. (Sue Kelly, R.NY)

I think we have an attunement, as a group, that men don't have . . . because of the role we have had all of our lives—the child-bearing role, the nurturing role—that we are more sensitive to social issues. (Carrie Meek, D.FL)

[Women] are more prone to try to find ways to work together, to bring people together. We do it with our kids, to get along with one another. (Sue Myrick, R.NC)

From just a physical standpoint, the way we have to dress, what happens to our bodies, having a period, having a baby, walking through life under those circumstances having to wear stockings every day, high heels at certain points—these

are things that just bring women together. (Susan Molinari, R.NY)

[Historically] without a voice or the opportunity to vote, their participation and their representation and their services are going to be different from men, and that puts us all in a similar category. (Karen English, D.AZ).

Every study that has been conducted in terms of women's achievement and gaining parity in every level of our lives—government, workplace, . . . access to health care—we find out that there is common ground for women to come together. We are facing, no matter our race, the same type of stigma, the same type of battles that every single woman faces in this nation. (Nydia Velazquez, D.NY)

Source: Carroll (2000).

---

women, even when they differ about their best interests. Perhaps what matters most for the female public, however, is neither the symbolism of a woman in office nor the concern of those women to speak with a gendered voice. It is whether the public policies that emerge from government are addressed to women's needs. In the next three sections we study three of many gendered areas of public policy where, in different ways, women have made a difference.

Key points

- Women are divided in their political loyalties, voting preferences, and policy preferences.
- The proportion of women in public office in America is far below the proportion of women in the American electorate.
- Female law-makers typically feel a responsibility to be particularly concerned with issues of disproportionate importance to women.

Public policy

The equality agenda

'You know we have the vote, the right to political equality, but we have not real equality yet,' said a suffragist in 1921. Since the *Declaration of Sentiments* of 1848, equality feminists have made their comprehensive goal of political, legal, economic, and social equality for women the most familiar aspect of gender politics. Winning the vote was doubly important for equality feminism. The right to vote advanced equality in itself. Also, it empowered women in the pursuit of other kinds of equality within the existing political system. The tactics have varied from the bold—amend the Constitution—to the

conventional—legislate step by step. Though none would say that America has yet achieved an equal society for women and men, equality feminists can be credited with changing the shape of public policy.

The attempt to add an Equal Rights Amendment (ERA) to the Constitution was the most ambitious campaign of equality feminists. What has been achieved both by and despite the ERA gives an insight into the structural and cultural factors that affect gender politics. In 1920, laws that made women unequal in marriage and as parents, at work, and in civic life, were mostly state laws. As suffragists had found, federalism could make life harder. Reforming state laws requires a campaign in one state after another, under different rules and addressing local preferences—precisely as the federal principle intends. Suffragists changed their strategy, and when the Nineteenth Amendment was ratified, states' resistance was wiped out at a stroke. An ERA had the same pragmatic attraction. The amendment was introduced in every session of Congress from 1923 to 1972 when it received the necessary two-thirds majority in both Houses. But while a constitutional amendment trumps the laws of separate states, ratification requires the consent of three-quarters of those states. After 1972, federalism's deference to state preferences assisted the defeat of the ERA. Thirty-eight states were needed to ratify. By the congressional deadline of 1982, only thirty-five had ratified and the ERA was lost.

Most opposing states were in the South, where fundamentalist religious groups, socially conservative life styles, and a presumption that less government was always better were strongest. These attitudes, as well as widespread vested male interests and business opposition, contributed to defeat. What put the ERA at the heart of the cultural divide between traditionalists and progressives in American politics, however, is that to many women the amendment seemed to cut deeper than a mere legal reform. This was a battle for the definition of gender roles themselves. A study of non-ratifying North Carolina found that the equality feminists' campaign, as they sought to reform the law, touched a much deeper nerve. For many women, gender 'was sacred': 'It was a given—a biologically, physically, spiritually defined thing ... an unambiguous, clear, definite division of humanity into two.' The ERA appeared to challenge this essentialist certainty: 'Ratification could become a referendum on all of these actions that challenged the concreteness and immutability of obligations identified with sex' (Mathews and De Hart 1990: 165–6). The amending process enables minorities, one-third plus one in Congress, one-quarter plus one of the states, to block change. When the ERA became understood as a choice between feminism's idea of constitutional equality and female essentialism's sense of threat to a whole-world view, a committed minority, geographically clustered within more than thirteen states, was able to veto change.

High stakes, as in the goal of a constitutional

Box 21.3 Constitutional Amendments: the Suffrage Amendment, Equal Rights Amendment, and Constitutional Equality Amendment

Nineteenth Amendment (ratified 1920)

The right of citizens of the United States to vote shall not be denied or abridged by the United States or by any state on account of sex.

Congress shall have power to enforce this article by appropriate legislation.

Equal Rights Amendment (unratified and lapsed 1982)

1. Equality of rights under the law shall not be denied or abridged by the United States or any state on account of sex.
2. The Congress shall have power to enforce, by appropriate legislation, the provisions of this article.
3. This amendment shall take effect two years after the date of ratification.

Constitutional Equality Amendment (proposed by NOW, 1995)

1. Women and men shall have equal rights throughout the US and every place and entity subject to its jurisdiction;

through this article, the subordination of women to men is abolished;

2. All persons shall have equal rights and privileges without discrimination on account of sex, race, sexual orientation, marital status, ethnicity, national origin, color or indigence;
3. This article prohibits pregnancy discrimination and guarantees the absolute right of a woman to make her own reproductive decisions including the termination of pregnancy;
4. This article prohibits discrimination based upon characteristics unique to or stereotypes about any class protected under this article. This article also prohibits discrimination through the use of any facially neutral criteria which have a disparate impact based on membership in ;a class protected under this article.
5. This article does not preclude any law, program or activity that would remedy the effects of discrimination and that is closely related to achieving such remedial purposes;
6. This article shall be interpreted under the highest standards of judicial review;
7. The United States and the several states shall guarantee the implementation and enforcement of this article.

amendment, attract strong opposition. Equality feminism's National Organization for Women (NOW) built its membership and reputation through leadership of the ERA campaign. Women's groups such as the Eagle Forum and Concerned Women for America, founded to oppose the ERA, have become permanent organizations that oppose NOW on reproductive freedom, gay rights, and almost every equality issue NOW adopts. Was the ERA a failure? The report card is mixed. The Constitution has great symbolic power in American politics and culture. Viewed in this light, inclusion in its text creates a different argument for an ERA. African American lawyer Patricia Williams once commented: 'Blacks and women are the objects of a constitutional omission.' Recognition of their rights 'is an affirmation; the affirmative action of hiring—or hearing—blacks is a recognition of individuality that includes blacks as a social presence, that is profoundly linked to the fate of blacks and whites and women and men' (Williams 1991: 121). The ERA promised women inclusion by name in the Constitution, and they still wait. But the ten-year ratification campaign educated supporters and opponents alike on the issues. It influenced the passage of legislation and judicial decisions in ways that advanced the equality agenda. America's federal structure was a problem, but its constitutional separation of powers meant that change could be sought in parallel through the constitutional text itself, state and federal legislation, and litigation. It failed ratification, yet many of the intended legal changes have been achieved without it.

Changes in federal law began before Congress passed the ERA. As feminism gathered momentum in the 1960s, Congress passed the Equal Pay Act (EPA) of 1963 and the Civil Rights Act of 1964 which banned discrimination at work on grounds of race or sex and created the Equal Employment Opportunities Commission. In 1972, legislation banned sex discrimination in education and sport. In the meantime court decisions gave women access to jury service and to pension, credit, and insurance equity. These victories on paper did not create instant equality in society. A decade after the EPA, NOW's ERA campaign distributed small green and white badges with the simple slogan '59 cents'. Fifty-nine cents to the dollar was the ratio of women's to men's pay in the 1970s. Challenged by such figures, specialist women's policy groups have multiplied, influencing political parties, legislatures, and government departments. Their watchfulness over the implementation of new laws helps ensure that women's rising levels of education, skill, and aspirations are supported by public policy. By 2001, women's pay average was (still) only 76 cents to the male dollar (US Bureau of Labor Statistics 2002: 1).

Some things the ERA could not have achieved. Equality feminism and American liberalism seek equality for every individual. Statistics and laws treating women as a group do not reveal or iron out differences between women, such as the poverty of many women of colour. In 2001, white women's average earnings were 15.5 per cent more than African American women, and 35.3 per cent higher than Hispanic women (US Bureau of Labor Statistics 2002: 1). Inequality between women and men, and among women, derives sometimes from direct discrimination, at other times from the way the labour market stereotypes many low-paid jobs as 'women's work', penalizes women who take time out for pregnancy, or endorses gendered beliefs that women will put their job second to their family responsibilities. Equality feminists have therefore had to address a much wider set of concerns than the EPA or ERA could solve. The EPA compared men and women doing similar work for the same employer, not the way in which women, especially women of colour, cluster in lower-paid jobs than men. The ERA contributed only indirectly, by raising awareness of inequality, to campaigns for comparable-worth legislation (the comparing and revaluing of whole job descriptions) or affirmative action (the positive effort to hire members of disadvantaged groups until a balanced workforce is achieved).

The most embedded gendered social institution is the family. The campaign for legal equality, whether for an ERA or at work, has inevitably bumped up against deep and value-laden divisions over the future of the family. All these equality measures are open to both radical and difference feminist criticism that they define equality as being equal with men—access to the same jobs, same pay, same promotion ladder. Meanwhile, social stereotypes still usually construct women as society's mothers and carers, so that equality at work is still accompanied

---

Box 21.4 Two women's organizations

National Organization for Women

Founded: 1966.

Current membership: More than 550,000, chapters in all fifty states and District of Columbia.

Funds: Membership dues, $35 annually.

Organization: Four elected national officers, a Board of Directors and Issues Committees; national office in Washington, DC.

Methods: Uses 'traditional and non-traditional means to push for social change . . . electoral and lobbying work and bring lawsuits . . . mass marches, rallies, pickets, non-violent civil disobedience and immediate, responsive "zap" actions.'

Original goal: End discrimination against women; implement 1964 equality legislation.

Long-term aims and current campaigns: Equal Rights Amendment, elect women, NOWPAC funds candidates. 'NOW's official priorities are winning economic equality and securing it with an amendment to the U.S. Constitution that will guarantee equal rights for women; championing abortion rights, reproductive freedom and other women's health issues; opposing racism and fighting bigotry against lesbians and gays; and ending violence against women.' In 2002 lobbying for stronger abortion access, Employment Non-Discrimination Act for gays, international women's rights, against George W. Bush's judicial nominations.

Website: www.now.org

Concerned Women for America

Founded: 1979.

Current membership: More than 500,000, chapters in almost all the fifty states.

Funds: 'Giving a donation of any dollar amount makes you a member of CWA.'

Organization: Beverly LaHaye, chairman since 1978. National office in Washington, DC with policy experts, and 'an activist network' receiving action alerts.

Methods: Local 'prayer/action chapters', education, lobbying, emphasis on media campaigns.

Original goal: Challenge NOW's claim to speak for the women of America; oppose the ERA.

Current mission statement: 'We help people focus on six core issues, which we have determined need Biblical principles most and where we can have the greatest impact. At its root, each of these issues is a battle over worldviews': Sanctity of Life, Definition of the Family, Education, Pornography, Religious Liberty, National Sovereignty. In 2002 lobbying for stronger anti-abortion counselling, against gay adoptions and Employment Non-Discrimination Act for gays, against international women's rights, for George W. Bush's judicial nominations.

Website: www.cwfa.org

---

by inequality in the work of the home. Acknowledging the shortcoming of an 'equality with men' strategy, the Family and Medical Leave Act of 1993 (FMLA) took a new tack. The FMLA requires employers to allow both women and men to fulfil the responsibilities of parenting and caring. The Act 'minimizes the potential for employment discrimination by ensuring generally that leave is available for eligible medical reasons (including maternity-related disability) and for compelling family reasons, on a gender-neutral basis'. The FMLA legislates on the basis that, childbearing apart, parenting and home-making are only culturally defined as women's work. But so far women have been more likely than men to take the unpaid leave, perpetuating the stereotype of their caring role or reflecting their lower, and more easily foregone, wages.

The equality agenda has advanced greatly since the 1960s. By 2000, few explicit sex distinctions survived in law. Why then, in 1995, did NOW propose a new 'Constitutional Equality Amendment' (CEA), longer and more explicit than the ERA? Legally neutral laws expose, but do not dissolve, all the cultural and structural factors that make women and men unequal. The CEA addresses men as well as women, and by banning 'discrimination based upon characteristics unique to or stereotypes about any class protected under this article' aims to bring the authority of the Constitution to work on entrenched beliefs about gender difference as well as equality. In the CEA, equality feminists continue to wrestle with the meaning of gender in politics, law, and the lives of women and men, and to find ways to push forward the slow process of social change.

Domestic violence

Women put violence within intimate relationships on the public agenda in the Seneca Falls Declaration of 1848. They complained that marriage made man the master of woman, 'the law giving him power to deprive her of her liberty, and to administer chastisement'. The largest nineteenth-century women's organization, the Women's Christian Temperance Union, campaigned against alcohol as a cause of wife-beating and family breakdown. As the states reformed their laws, husbands lost the right to 'chastise' their wives. But law enforcement agencies still preferred to keep out of domestic disputes. Intimate violence was rarely treated as criminal violence. Nineteenth-century campaigners might have been unsurprised to learn that only in 1992 did the Supreme Court admit the shocking incidence and nature of domestic violence as a factor in marital relationships and only in 1994 did the federal government legislate comprehensively on the issue. A women's campaign brought the issue from invisibility in the early 1970s to national recognition, in one of the clearest cases of women's activism bringing about change.

By the 1990s, even the stoutest defenders of family values and private relationships acknowledged the shadow that violence cast over the family ideal. Beverly LaHaye heads Concerned Women for America (CWA), dedicated 'to protect traditional values that support the Biblical design of the family' (**www.cwfa.org/library/family**). LaHaye travels the country warning that 'there is a concerted effort in our country to steal marriage and the family from our culture' and advocating family as the place where 'a man and a woman' will 'nurture each other and any children who may be born to the couple'. Criticizing unmarried partnerships, LaHaye cautions against a lifestyle that 'increases the risk of domestic violence for women' (LaHaye 1999: 2, 3). Her

implicit admission that violence occurs even within marriage betokens a consensus reached on the problem. The disagreement arises over what is to be done.

The CWA solution is that the family itself must be strengthened, especially through education about marriage but also using government programmes such as welfare to reward marriage and punish extramarital relationships. Preferring to inculcate moral values, LaHaye quotes that government 'can never, never substitute for strong families' (LaHaye 1999: 5). Equality feminists criticize the family as a hierarchy of male power and privilege where violence against women is a symptom. The family must be reformed in law to become an egalitarian partnership, and women protected by strong criminal law and enforcement. More radical feminists declare the family inherently oppressive, an instrument of male domination and female subordination that must be overthrown. This issue therefore challenges women, but not just on their theoretical positions. Proposing state intervention in intimate relationships is controversial and, for radical feminists, doubly problematic. Using one institution (the state) they mistrust as an agency of male power, to reform another (the family), equally an agency of male power, seems fruitless. Requesting the state to protect women appears to declare women helpless victims. Including lesbian violence betrays ideals of female relationships. In addition, this issue is perplexing for women of colour and ethnic minorities who hesitate to report incidents casting disadvantaged communities in a bad light or to challenge dominant ethnic ideals of male authority. The issue of gender-related violence illustrates all the questions of equality, difference, and power inherent in the politics of gender.

The public sphere ignored this problem for decades before the 1970s. Subsequently, with the knowledge that up to 90 per cent of gender-related violence is perpetrated upon women, this has been a public policy led by women. Radical critiques of the family were first to publicize wife-beating, as it was then known in the limited context of heterosexual marriage: 'Dependent on and subservient to men, women are always subject to this violence' (Dworkin 1983: 21). Radicals also acted first. Local groups set up shelters, women-run safe houses for 'battered women'. Shelters offered a temporary refuge, crisis hotlines, legal advice, and moral support. A 'commitment to women's self-determination, self-organization, and democratic participation' was to be both an organizing principle for themselves and an educational experience for the women they helped (Schneider 2000: 22). As more women spoke openly and shelters uncovered greater need than they could absorb, the media and social workers took notice and women mobilized to demand legislation and involvement by police and courts.

The leap from the scattered shelters of the 1970s to a bumper federal law, the Violence Against Women Act of 1994 (VAWA), challenged the women's movement. Despite their mistrust of male authority, shelters needed dollars to survive and state and city governments became major funders. As shelters

---

Box 21.5 Action on gender-related violence

1971. London, Chiswick Women's Aid establishes first shelter.

1972. First US shelters established in California and Minnesota.

1976. National Organization for Women Task Force on 'battering'.

1976. Nebraska becomes the first state to criminalize rape within marriage.

1978. US Commission on Civil Rights 'Consultation on Battered Women'.

1978. National Coalition Against Domestic Violence, national grass-roots organization, established.

1984. Family Violence Prevention and Services Act, first federal legislation.

1992. In *Planned Parenthood* v. *Casey*, the Supreme Court accepts evidence of violence and declares women cannot be required to have spousal consent to an abortion.

1994. Violence Against Women Act (VAWA) passed.

2000. In *US* v. *Morrison* the Supreme Court strikes down civil rights clause of VAWA.

2000. VAWA re-authorized by Congress.

---

multiplied and were accepted, radical feminists worried that they would be compromised by external funding and the formal organization and professionalism expected by government agencies. So great was the need that most found ways to work together. Meantime a National Coalition Against Domestic Violence formed (and still exists) and lobbying led to state law reform, litigation that advanced women's rights, and, eventually, federal legislation.

VAWA, fought for since the principle of federal support was established in 1984, made a series of important statements: that violence was a federal as well as a state problem; that law enforcement personnel required training in gender sensitivity and problems of cultural difference and rural isolation; and that funding must be given (and was) to activities from shelters to street safety to training programmes. The president spoke for and feminists hailed VAWA. Anti-feminists deplored the whole approach, which gave money to shelters and hotlines, 'feminist pork' according to Phyllis Schlafly of the Eagle Forum, but not to measures to restore traditional families. The most radical part of VAWA naturally attracted the greatest opposition. Subtitle C, 'Civil Rights for Women', created a new right: 'All persons within the United States shall have the right to be free from crimes of violence motivated by gender.' In addition, any 'party injured' could sue for damages in federal courts. This was a huge change of approach: 'For the first time, there is a law that explicitly links violence with equality.' Congress had agreed that gender-related violence impinged upon 'women's freedom to work, travel, live freely, and make choices about their own lives'. As Elizabeth Schneider concluded: 'It equates and connects the national with the individual, the public with the private' (Schneider 2000: 188). Opponents used federalism to defeat this breakthrough. In a case argued on one side by the Clinton administration and NOW lawyers and on the other by conservative public interest law firm the Center for Individual Rights, the Supreme Court decided that VAWA took national power too far: 'We accordingly reject the argument that Congress may regulate non-economic, violent criminal conduct . . . The Constitution requires a distinction between what is truly national and what is truly local.'

'Under our federal system', the judges concluded, the remedy for injured women must be provided by the states, not by Washington (*US* v. *Morrison*, 2000).

What has this thirty-year campaign, initiated and led by women, achieved? The family has lost its undeserved halo and a more realistic public accepts intervention. Much of VAWA remains in force, re-authorized in 2000 for five more years and providing vastly expanded programmes for supporting injured women, criminalizing attackers, and educating officials. More than 2,000 shelters and local service programmes exist. At the same time, funding remains inadequate, welfare laws push women into marriages, and the incidence of gender-related violence shows little decline. As we saw with the equality agenda, radicalism arouses opposition. The Supreme Court has blocked the civil rights remedy for gender-related violence. Since 2001, opponents have also won support from the Bush administration for programmes to encourage premarital sexual abstinence and the teaching of traditional family values. This issue is a fine example of how women can win change. It also exemplifies how cultural battles between traditionalists and progressives and structural battles over federalism resonate among women and provide strategic openings for their campaigns.

Peace and war

Is opposition to a 'man-making power of having war' the 'most feministic thing women can do'? Women who believe so join a history of peace action stretching from the Bowdoin Street Ladies' Peace Society of the 1820s to America's 'Greenham Common women', the Seneca Women's Peace Encampment of the 1980s. Jeannette Rankin, first woman elected to the House of Representatives, was the only member of Congress to vote against the entry of the United States into both world wars. Social reformer Jane Addams won the Nobel peace prize in 1931. Statistics repeatedly confirm that peace is not just the politics of a few exceptional women. Over twenty years,

the gender difference for force issues averaged 8 per-centage points . . . this almost completely reflects men selecting more violent options . . . . Gender difference in preferences

towards policies dealing with force and violence have consistently been moderately large. Sex differences in opinion toward other policies have been approximately half the size.   (Shapiro and Mahajan 1986: 49, 59)

Women have held out for peace even amidst rampant patriotic fervour. The Women's International League for Peace and Freedom (WILPF) was founded as America entered the First World War in 1917. Consistent with their principles, WILPF wrote to president and Congress on 12 September 2001 reminding them 'that for eighty six years, since our founding during World War I, [the League] has opposed war as a means of conflict resolution' (**www.wilpf.org/statements/letters_to_the_ government.htm**).

Difference feminists say that sex and gender attributes logically dispose women to support disarmament and peace: 'Women are the life-givers, the first care givers . . . Must mothers watch the slaughter of children in whom we have invested our lives?' asked the WILPF recently. From birthing to the social roles of women, 'in peace and war women are the ones whose work maintains community and life itself' (**www.wilpf.org/caring.html**). Equality feminists dislike the whiff of essentialism of slogans like 'Another Mother for Peace', but they too can explain a gendered approach to war and peace. Women's inequality makes them more dependent than men on programmes like welfare. Women are more likely to work in and take greater responsibility for their families' care in the (less well-paid) education and health sectors. Offered the classic political choice of spending limited resources on 'guns or butter', women find that the 'butter' of spending on social programmes urgently outweighs the financial and human costs of the 'guns' of war.

America's policy after the 11 September attacks, with unparalleled approval ratings for the 'war against terrorism', is a tough test for the peace-loving woman. Shortly after 11 September a typical poll found that 83 per cent of Americans 'continued to back military action against those responsible even if it leads to war'. Jennifer Pozner (2002) has looked behind the headlines that trumpeted unanimity. When citizens are offered something other than a stark alternative to fight or be victims, she finds, there is a gender difference. That 83 per cent contained 'pockets of hesitancy'. Women 'particularly,

Democratic women', are 'significantly less likely to support a long and costly war', as she quotes from the *New York Times*:

Men were also much more likely than women to support broadening the military action to encompass more targets. Forty-four per cent of women said they want a broad effort; 48 per cent said they wanted a limited strike or no military action at all. 'I'm against the bombing that is going to hurt innocent children and people,' said one respondent, 36-year-old Janice Cavolaski of Bel Air, Mn. 'I think that makes us as bad as them.'   (Pozner 2002: 20)

A widely-reported October poll was hailed as 'doing away' with the peace gender gap. It recorded a rise after 11 September from 24 to 47 per cent of women (compared to 51 per cent of men) supporting increased military spending, while equal numbers of women and men (64 per cent, with women's support up from 52 per cent) favoured the creation of a missile defence shield (Council on Foreign Relations 2001). Female pacifism had, it was said, been replaced by 'that instinctive maternal impulse to protect one's own' (*Christian Science Monitor*, 6 November 2001).

At the very least the figures suggest that women divide almost equally even on the war against terrorism, whereas men's support is, by a clear majority, for a strong military reaction. Given the gender biases in the nation's institutions that we noted earlier, has this difference been represented in policy-making? The Bush administration portrayed itself after 11 September as 'a bastion of women's empowerment' (Pozner 2002: 20) Boasting of women in senior White House positions, 'a Republican official told the *Washington Post* in early January [2002], George W. Bush "has not only erased any question about legitimacy, he has also erased the gender gap"'. With three 'Republican bigwigs', Condoleezza Rice, Karen Hughes, and Mary Matalin, the administration was giving Afghanistan a lesson in gender equity. Women were 'not only making the strategy; their gender is part of the strategy, a weapon to attack the Taliban's treatment of Afghan women' (quoted in Pozner 2002: 20). Does such empowerment—defined as women's presence in government—assure the representation of women's views?

Foreign policy issues following 11 September catapulted two women office-holders in particular into the public eye. Condoleezza Rice and Barbara Lee are African American women from similar origins, of similar ages, graduates, moving from a profession into public life. But there their lives diverge. Rice is National Security Advisor to President Bush, his closest White House influence and a hardliner on foreign policy. On 14 September 2001, Lee, a Democrat in the House of Representatives, cast the sole vote against a resolution authorizing the President 'to use all necessary and appropriate force' to prevent any future terrorist acts against the United States. There can be little doubt that the views of the 44 per cent of women supporting a broad military effort can reach the presidential ear with support from Rice, and were represented by over 500 members of Congress (including seventy-two women) who voted for open-ended presidential authority. One female representative publicly argued for restraint, in no way proportionate to the 48 per cent who said they wanted limited or no military action.

There is no simple gender difference over peace and war, restraint versus force, in world affairs. In this area of public policy, women as a group reveal what Jean Bethke Elshtain (1997: 305) has described as an abiding ambivalence. Women of all kinds advocate peace, while others give moral and practical support to war. Difference feminists deploy the language of motherhood. But while some mothers oppose militarism for endangering the lives they have nurtured, others take pride in mothering soldiers for the nation. Equality feminists divide over whether to oppose all wars or claim equality in the military. Foreign policy-making has been a stronghold of male elites, women's exclusion from public leadership and the military a survival of stereotypes of their proper sphere. Cynthia Enloe has showed us that women don't have to go to war to be implicated as active participants in 'friendly as well as hostile relations between governments' through their social roles 'as symbols' inspiring men to go into battle, 'as providers of emotional support' whether mothers, sisters and lovers or prostitutes, and 'as paid and unpaid workers' who necessarily sustain society, economy and the defence effort (Enloe 1989: 198).

Enloe invites us to analyse foreign and defence policy via a neglected question—where are the women? In the mainstream of American politics

Box 21.6 Condoleezza Rice, Barbara Lee

Condoleezza Rice

National security advisor to President George W. Bush, from January 2001, first woman in that position. Key role in formulating foreign policy, especially, since 11 September, for the 'war on terrorism'.

Born 1954, Birmingham, Alabama, in a segregated city where her parents nonetheless believed in education, religion, and opportunity for all. Entered the University of Denver at age 15, graduating at 19, continuing to an MA and PhD.

Rice has moved between academic positions and government appointments all her working life. Professor of political science at Stanford University in California since 1981, research on arms control, disarmament, and foreign policy, for six years as provost managed 1,400 faculty, 14,000 students, and a budget of $1.5 billion; worked on nuclear strategic planning for the joint chiefs of staff in 1986, as senior director of Soviet and East European affairs in the National Security Council of President George Bush Sr., in the election campaign of George W. Bush, and then as his senior White House advisor since January 2001.

Rice on foreign policy and the war against terrorism. 'When we were attacked on September 11th, it reinforced one of the rediscovered truths about today's world: robust military power matters in international politics and in security . . . Great powers matter because they can influence international stability for good or for ill due their size, influence and their will. Great powers never have, and never will, just mind their own business within their borders.' (April 2002, **www.whitehouse.gov**)

Barbara Lee

Democratic Congresswoman for the Ninth District of California since 1998. Attracted national and international attention in the wake of the 11 September attacks as the only Congressperson to vote against a key resolution authorizing the President to use military force when necessary.

Born in Texas, daughter of an army officer. The family moved to California in 1960. In 1973 graduated from Mills College, a women's college in Oakland, then gained an MA in social work at the University of California, Berkeley. Lee set up a community mental health centre while still a student. Later joined the staff of her Congressman, Democrat Ron Dellums, was active in city politics in Oakland; elected to the California State Assembly in 1990, state Senate in 1996 and Congress in 1998. Active in women's, environmental, and African American causes, for legislation for international programmes to fight AIDS, and for universal health care programmes.

Lee on foreign policy and the war against terrorism. 'On September 11, terrorists attacked the United States in an unprecedented and brutal manner, killing thousands of innocent people . . . Like everyone throughout our country, I am repulsed and angered by these attacks and believe all appropriate steps must be taken to bring the perpetrators to justice . . . Last week, filled with grief and sorrow for those killed and injured and with anger at those who had done this, I confronted the solemn responsibility of voting to authorize the nation to go to war . . . We must respond, but the character of that response will determine for us and for our children the world that they will inherit . . . A rush to launch precipitous military counterattacks runs too great a risk that more innocent men, women, and children will be killed. I could not vote for a resolution that I believe could lead to such an outcome.' (23 September 2001, **www.commondreams.org/views01/0923–04.htm**)

---

we have found that there is a consistent gender gap: more women than men favour less aggressive policies. Can politics at the margin hold the balance in a decision on foreign policy, as it can sometimes swing an election? In the war against terrorism, for the first time two women leaders present America with alternatives of war and peace. Has it made any difference that Rice and Lee have taken these roles?

Lee justified her vote in precisely the same language of racialized and gendered responsibility as the Congresswomen discussed earlier. Yet despite what we know about Congresswomen's sense of a gender community, gender identity was overwhelmed by patriotic national identity in the September crisis vote. Like Lee, other Congresswomen of colour have spoken for an international gender identity. 'I

Box 21.7 **Is America different?**
International gender differences

The answer is mixed. This selection of facts indicates the complexity of making comparisons.

Constitutions. The US Constitution requires 'the equal protection of the laws'. The UK does not have a written constitution but the Human Rights Act of 1998, embodying the European Convention on Human Rights, prohibits sex discrimination in the exercise of rights, and the European Union gives a fundamental right to 'equal pay for men and women'. Contrast the Canadian Charter of Rights and Freedoms which both guarantees that 'Every individual is equal under the law' and prohibits sex discrimination.

Voting. The gender gap, women above men:
US 2000 election: 12 per cent in favour of Democratic candidate
UK 1997 election: 1 per cent in favour of Conservatives, but a gender-generation gap of 35 per cent more women than men in favour of Labour in the under-30 age group

Representation. The percentage of women in parliaments in 2002 (lower house/US House of Representatives) is:
Sweden   42.7

European average	25.7
UK	18.4
USA	16.7
France	10.9

Leadership. Number of women as prime ministers or, in US, presidents or vice-presidents:
UK   1
US   0

Percentage of cabinet who are women:
Sweden	50
Blair cabinet 2002	30
European average	28
Bush cabinet 2002	22
Germany 1997	11

Equality organizations.
UK: Fawcett Society, founded 1866; 4000 members
US: National Organization for Women, founded 1966; more than 0.5 million members

Gender pay ratio. Average women's earnings as a percentage of average men's earnings:
UK   82
US   76

think that as American legislators, women in this body, we have a responsibility that goes beyond women in America ... We have a responsibility to protect women elsewhere', argued Latina Nydia Velazquez (D.NY). Her view was amplified by Rep. Carrie Meek, African American Democrat from Florida: 'I feel that a woman who is raped in Bosnia by the troops who were there, or a woman who is raped in Haiti ... [or] who has her genitalia mutilated in certain African societies, that I am partially responsible for that, for some amelioration of that' (Carroll 2000: 5–6). The issues of peace and war are a challenging test for understanding how democracy divides on lines of gender, and how this involves thinking about difference as well as equality, masculinity as well as femaleness, race and ethnicity as inseparable from gender identities.

How women's shared gender and race identities balance against national claims will challenge gender politics as international issues continue to dominate American politics.

Key points

- On issues as varied as reproductive rights, child care, domestic violence, and questions of war and peace, female representatives have had a major impact on the agenda of politics and policy outcomes.

- Despite these advances, many public policies remain 'gendered' and the advancement of the equality agenda for American women remains incomplete.

Conclusion

In the American polity, whose core values are individualism and equality, gender divides citizens into groups identified by their physical, social, and cultural attributes, and structures hierarchies of gendered inequalities, especially inequalities of power. The politics of gender run through every aspect of American politics: voting and office-holding, domestic and foreign policy-making. Women have been the primary actors in gender politics even without agreement on whether the ideal feminist world would achieve a gender-neutral equality, respect a form of gender difference, or restore male authority. Women of colour and lesbians have often chosen to work separately or in alliances of race or sexual orientation, but the story of feminist gender politics is also one of intersectionality—of women from many different backgrounds and with a multiplicity of interests sometimes uniting on common ground, at others making coalitions on behalf of sectional interests, or working independently. The story is also one of steady change over decades towards establishing women's voice and women's autonomy in the public sphere, and towards a still unattained but not unattainable state of gender justice in the roles, responsibilities, and rewards of American citizenship.

QUESTIONS

1　Compare and contrast the political consequences of demands for gender equality and gender difference.

2　What is the gender gap and what effect does it have?

3　Can only women represent women?

4　Why is the family so central to the politics of gender?

5　Was it worth campaigning for an Equal Rights Amendment?

6　What are the limitations of policies designed to equalize the circumstances of women and men?

7　Why have women been leaders on domestic violence policy?

8　Are women the peace-makers of America?

9　In the long run, would you expect the war against terrorism to bring out differences between women and men or bring them together?

FURTHER READING

There are now many books on gender politics. This selection expands on many of the questions raised in this chapter and on ethnic and racial politics and politics outside the mainstream. J. Squires, *Gender in Political Theory* (Cambridge: Polity Press, 2000), explains representation and other key political concepts. E. Freedman, *No Turning Back: The History of Feminism and the Future of Women* (New York: Ballantine Books, 2002), comes up to date and sets American feminism in global context. Two books concentrate on minority women: K. Anderson, *Changing Woman: A History of Racial Ethnic Women in Modern America* (Oxford: Oxford University Press, 1996) is an inclusive study, full of information on Hispanic, Asian, and Native American as well as black women; and see K. Springer (ed.), *Still Lifting, Still Climbing: African American Women's Contemporary Activism* (New York: New York University Press, 1999). S. J. Carroll (ed.), *The Impact of Women in Public Office* (Bloomington: Indiana University Press, 2001) covers national and state politics in electoral institutions, while C. J. Cohen, K. B. Jones, and J. C. Tronto (eds.), *Women Transforming Politics: An Alternative Reader* (New York: New York University Press, 1997) addresses radical and community politics as well as formal governance and has strong essays on minority women's politics. Alice Kessler-Harris, *In Pursuit of Equity: Women, Men and the Quest for Economic Citizenship* (Oxford: Oxford University Press, 2001) is the definitive account of the equality agenda. Finally, to make comparisons with the United Kingdom and Western Europe, use the short introduction by R. Henig and S. Henig, *Women and Political Power: Europe Since 1945* (London: Routledge, 2001).

WEB LINKS

www.cawp.rutgers.edu Center for American Women and Politics at the Eagleton Institute, Rutgers University: information on women running for office and holding office, and issues of representation, at all levels of US politics. Hosts a Latina politics section.

www.cwfa.org Concerned Women for America: claims to be 'the nation's largest public policy women's organization'. Research institute and reports, legislative campaigns, action alerts.

www.feminist.org Foundation for a Feminist Majority: advocacy group for women's representation and women's issues; information on current campaigns, background to issues, research reports, and extensive web links to other sites.

www.now.org National Organization for Women: feminist advocacy since 1966, especially for equality legislation, the Equal Rights Amendment, reproductive rights; policy papers, campaign notes, membership information.

www.usdoj/vaw Department of Justice Office for Violence Against Women: legislation, statistics, research reports, press releases.

www.wilpf.org Women's International League for Peace and Freedom: women's activism since 1917; lists current campaigns and links to many related websites.

22 Religion

Steve Bruce

READER'S GUIDE

This chapter reviews the change in the politics of religion from ethnic conflict to arguments about socio-moral issues. The example of the post-1978 'New Christian Right' shows how special interest groups can use the judicial, legislative, and electoral processes to press their agenda. The religious inspiration for the NCR creates a highly motivated core of activists which can achieve considerable success in local contests. However, such gains are routinely overturned when court cases are appealed upwards and when the same issues become the focus of contests in wider electorates. The structure of US politics creates unique opportunities for the NCR but finally prevents the re-establishment of a conservative Christian moral climate. This is not an accident, but stems from the fact that most Americans appreciate the importance of personal freedom and understand that the religious and social diversity of the United States requires a religiously neutral public arena.

Introduction

Unlike most western European countries, the United States is religious. While many other advanced industrial democracies have seen the church-going proportion of their citizens decline over the twentieth century to between 10 and 20 per cent, US church attendance is probably twice that. There are signs of decline in the last three decades. Detailed research shows a widening gap between what American say about their church-going and what they actually do (Hadaway et al. 1993; Marler and Hadaway 1997), but churches nonetheless remain powerful social institutions and religion provides a powerful source of public rhetoric.

A further difference from many European societies (especially those recently emerged from communist rule) is that the popularity of religion does not rest on one particular church (such as the Catholic Church in Poland or the Orthodox Church in Russia) enjoying a position of particular favour in the eyes of the state. The US Constitution is formally secular. Shortly after the 1789 Constitution was accepted, Congress decided to add explicit statements of individual rights to what was implied about the limited powers of the state in the main text. The first such amendment said: 'Congress shall make no law respecting an establishment of religion, or prohibiting the free exercise therof . . .' As we will see,

this still left much to argue about (Wilson 1990). Minimally it could be read as saying only that the USA could not have a state church. A more secular interpretation was put on it by Thomas Jefferson who, when he was president, said that the First Amendment erected 'a wall of separation between church and state' (Jelen 2000: 33). In the twentieth century that harder interpretation came to dominate the arguments. At the same time the 'free exercise' provision was given increasingly generous interpretation, so that the US now leads the world in its toleration of minority religions.

The formal secularity of the state had three roots. The first was painful experience: many of the

---

Box 22.1 **Constitutional influences**

The Supreme Court on church and state

'Congress shall make no law respecting an establishment of religion, or prohibiting the free exercise therof . . . '. Thus says the first amendment to the Constitution, passed in 1789 as part of a 'Bill of Rights'. The second or 'free exercise' clause has caused relatively little contentious precedent. Compared to most European countries, the USA has a strong record of religious toleration. Religion has not been allowed to trump secular social policy; for example, in *Reynolds* v. *US* (1879), the Supreme Court ruled that the free exercise clause did not justify Mormon polygamy. But the Court has often been more sympathetic to minority rights than has public opinion.

Far more contentious is the Supreme Court's interpretation of the 'establishment clause'. Contemporary disputes date from the 1940s. In *Everson* v. *Board of Education* (1947), the Court applied the clause to states as well as to the federal government and endorsed the Jeffersonian 'wall of separation' view of what it required. Justice Black wrote: 'The "establishment of religion" clause of the First Amendment means at least this: Neither a state nor the Federal government can set up a church. Neither can pass laws which aid one religion, aid all religions, or prefer one religion over another' (Jelen 2000: 12).

The separationist position was endorsed with two 1960s judgments: In *Engel* v. *Vitale* (1962), the Court ruled unconstitutional the New York state practise of starting

the school day with a non-denominational public prayer. The following year, in *Abington School District* v. *Schempp* (1963), the Court unanimously decided that a Pennsylvania law requiring ten verses of the Bible to be read at the start of the school day was unconstitutional.

In *Epperson* v. *Arkansas* (1968), the Court ruled that an Arkansas law prohibiting the teaching of Darwinian evolution was unconstitutional because the purpose of the law was to promote a particular religion. Creationists then tried the alternative of requiring that evolution be 'balanced' by their alternative but fared no better. In *Edwards* v. *Aguillard* (1987), the Court ruled that a Louisiana Balanced Treatment Act was unconstitutional: 'the purpose . . . was to restructure the science curriculum to conform with a particular religious viewpoint' (Supreme Court of the United States, 85–1513, 19 June 1987: 13).

The main standard for considering the establishment clause is Chief Justice Burger's judgment in *Lemon* v. *Kurtzman* (1971). A government policy would be invalid if it has the purpose or effect of advancing or inhibiting religion or involves 'an excessive entanglement' between government and religion. General state funding of church schools is thus prohibited because that would advance religion, but the state can provide chemistry textbooks to church schools because the state has a secular interest in promoting chemistry.

early American colonists had been persecuted for religious deviation in the European states they had left. The second was pragmatism. Although most of the colonies had established churches, they were not the same. Hence it would have been impossible to agree which should dominate the new nation. The third was the cultural influence of Enlightenment thought. Although most of the Founding Fathers were Christians, their faith was rather rational and liberal and they held that a modern and progressive society should not be constrained by the power of an established religion.

That, at the federal level, the USA was and is religiously diverse is not the same as saying that most Americans live in a religiously plural culture. Far from it. The patterns of settlement and later religious revival gave parts of America a very clear religious identity. In half of the counties of the US in 1950 more than half of those who belonged to a church belonged to the same one (Gaustad 1962: 159). That concentration was reinforced by most counties being bordered by others with the same dominant religion. Even in the major cities, diversity could be avoided. People tended to cluster by race, nationality, ethnicity, and religion. This dual pattern—strong sub-cultures within an overall structure designed to accommodate diversity—is central to understanding the continued public prominence of religion in two ways. First, in most societies there is a strong association between religious diversity and the decline of religion (Bruce 1999). Religion remains strongest where there is a consensual, supportive community. Then social institutions such as schools, colleges, and the mass media can socialize each new generation in the faith, and frequent interaction with the like-minded reinforces the shared culture. Put simply, it is easier to be a Mormon in Utah than in Berlin. But strong sub-cultures are also important in a second sense: they permit the dominant religious culture to enjoy public prominence. This creates an important source of tension. Members of what is, in context of the US as a whole, a minority live a lot of their lives in a social world in which they are a clear majority (Mormons in Utah or Baptist fundamentalists in southern Virginia), and hence can both misunderstand their relative importance and resent their lack of power nationally.

Table 22.1 Major faith groups in the USA, 1965

Some idea of the religious complexity of the USA is conveyed by the following data which describe claimed membership around the middle of the twentieth century. Note in particular the 'Number of Denominations' column in Table 22.2, which indicates the extent of division within what is already fragmented Protestantism.

Religious group	Membership	
	No. (000)	% of population
Protestant	69,088	35.6
Roman Catholic	46,240	23.8
Jewish	5,600	2.9
Eastern Churches	3,172	1.6
Others	582	0.4
TOTAL	124,682	64.3

Table 22.2 Protestant divisions in the USA, 1965

Protestant division	No. of denominations	Membership (000)
Baptist	29	23,812
Methodist	21	12,287
Lutheran	10	8,794
Presbyterian	9	4,420
Disciples/Churches of Christ	2	4,268
Mormons	5	1,963
Churches of God	10	530
Reformed	6	524
Adventist	4	402
Pentecostal	12	380
Brethren (German Baptists)	4	246
Mennonite	12	176
Spiritualist	3	176
Quakers	8	128
Evangelistic Associations	10	72
Moravian	2	67
Others	75	9,845

Source: Moberg (1972: 536–7).

Key points

- America is unusual among modern industrial democracies for popular participation in organized religion.

- The USA is a formally secular state which guarantees individual religious freedom.

- Religion in the USA is a mosaic: the religious diversity of the whole is made up of pockets of concentrated adherence.

Religion and politics before 1978

Religion was initially implicated in US politics through the medium of ethnic identity. From the inception of the Union until the 1950s there was considerable tension between Protestants and Catholics. The early settler white Anglo-Saxon Protestants (or WASPs) claimed for themselves virtues. They were loyal, hard-working, literate, democratic, independent, and diligent and they did not drink or gamble. In contrast, the Catholics who settled later were held to be poor, illiterate, vice-ridden, and in thrall to their priests. These respective vices and virtues were explained by religion. To the WASP 'nativists' Catholicism was a threat to the integrity of the USA (because Catholics owed their first loyalty to the Vatican) and to social progress (because Catholics lacked the admirable qualities of the WASPs). In the nineteenth century anti-Catholicism briefly became a major political force. The American party briefly held power in Massachusetts, and in 1856 its presidential candidate, Millard Filmore, won 21 per cent of the vote.

Forty years later the American Protective Association campaigned to prevent the entry of Catholics to the US and to curtail the rights of those already there (Lipset and Raab 1978: 79–82). The first revival of the Ku Klux Klan, in the 1920s, was as much an anti-Catholic as a racist movement: 'there was a general feeling that the election of every additional Catholic to public office would hasten the time when our government would be handed over to a foreign Pope' (Louks 1936: 106). But gradually anti-Catholicism faded as Catholics established themselves as a political power (and thus increased the costs of enduring religious conflict) and answered the disloyalty complaints by becoming fully immersed in US politics through the Democratic Party. Once the rise of the Soviet Union made WASPs worry more about Moscow than Rome, conservative Catholics and Protestants found themselves united in their fear of communism. That John F. Kennedy could win the presidency in 1960, when his co-religionist Al Smith failed in the 1920s, marked the end of anti-Catholicism.

However, anti-Catholicism had two enduring consequences for US politics. First, unlike their co-religionists in most European countries in the 1920s, US Catholics did not form Catholic parties; instead they worked through the Democratic Party and thus contributed to the demise of sectarianism. Second, outside New York and Chicago, the Catholic Church kept a low profile so that when, in the 1980s, socio-moral issues (on which Catholics had very clear value positions) again became highly charged, the campaigns were led by evangelical Protestants.

Although the most striking example of political mobilization of religious people since the 1970s has been of conservative Protestants supporting right-wing causes, we should not forget that religious values have also inspired liberal and progressive causes. Christians outside the slave-owning states of the South were at the forefront of the anti-slavery crusade. More generally, Christians were active in a wide range of social reform campaigns. We should also not forget that some causes which we now regard as reactionary interference with individual freedom (such as the prohibition of alcohol consumption) were once supported across the political spectrum as measures for the improvement of the working classes.

Nineteenth-century Christian interest in good works was not based on a modern ethic of human rights; it was paternalistic and philanthropic. It supposed that people who were harshly treated would not readily attend to the word of God; social amelioration was essential for spreading the gospel. It supposed that charity was good for the giver as well as the receiver (and hence was better than taxation). It also supposed that it was for the givers of charity and not the recipients to determine what was to their benefit. That way of thinking was threatened by the expansion of the franchise and the growth of trade unions. The poor and dispossessed started to act for themselves.

The end of philanthropy created a left-right rift within the Christian churches that coincided with a series of theological disputes. By the end of the nineteenth century, new thinking in science and in the arts and humanities was causing ordinary Christians to re-evaluate basic doctrines. Liberals were coming to see the Bible as a complex literary work that needed subtle reinterpretation to discover its message for the present age and to preserve it from refutation by new evidence about the age of the earth and the origins of species. Conservatives insisted that the Bible was the revealed word of God, true in every detail and mostly to be taken literally. Liberals were coming to a positive appreciation of the human potential that reached its fullest development in the optimistic 'Power of Positive Thinking' popularized by Presbyterian clergyman Norman Vincent Peale in the 1950s (George 1994). Conservatives continued to stress the basic sinfulness of people and their need for salvation. Liberals tended to suppose that the world was getting better. Many conservatives thought it was fairly bad and destined to get worse before the (not too distant) final Day of Judgement.

As they lost argument after argument in their churches, the conservatives, now dubbed 'fundamentalists', after an influential series of publications called *The Fundamentals of the Faith*, split off to form new sects, and from the 1920s devoted their energies to creating parallel institutions that would preserve the faith: schools, colleges, publishing houses, radio stations (and later television stations), revival crusade networks. This move from active involvement in public life and in social reform into pietistic retreat was hastened by the all-too-obvious evidence that conservative Christianity was losing influence. One obvious failure was the temperance cause. Instead of reducing drinking, the 1919 constitutional amendment to ban the manufacture, sale, and transport of intoxicating liquors created Al Capone and organized crime and in 1933 it was repealed. Another very public failure was the Scopes 'monkey trial'. In 1925 biology teacher John Scopes defied a Tennessee ban on the teaching of Darwin's theory of evolution. The prosecution in what became a national *cause célèbre* was led by William Jennings Bryan, the great Democrat populist, who rested his case on three claims. Darwinism was dangerous because to reduce the gap between animals and people would encourage the latter to behave like the former. Second, if there was a clash between science and the Bible, we should accept the Bible: 'It is better to trust in the Rock of Ages than to know the age of rocks' (Marsden 1980: 212). Third, the common sense of the ordinary American trumped the college learning of the scientists and liberal theologians. With a fundamentalist jury, three of whose members boasted that they had never read any book other than the Bible, the verdict was a foregone conclusion, but in the eyes of cosmopolitan America the evolutionists won the argument.

With the fundamentalists in retreat and concentrated in the parts of rural America that the elites easily overlooked, the mainstream churches assumed an easy command of liberal culture. Their ecumenical organization, the National Council of Churches, had the cornerstone for its prestigious office block in New York laid by President Eisenhower, and its slightly left-of-centre opinions were heard respectfully by US politicians. In the 1960s liberal clergymen became active first in various campaigns for black civil rights and desegregation and then in the anti-Vietnam War protests and the movements for gay and women's rights. Small numbers of fundamentalists were active in anti-communist organizations but the majority concentrated on soul-winning. Cosmopolitan journalists would write the occasional 'traveller's tale' about revival preachers sweating in tent crusades, but mainstream America largely forgot about the fundamentalists until the rise of the 'New Christian Right' in the late 1970s (Bruce 1988; Moen 1992; Wilcox 1992; Jelen 1991).

Key points

- In the nineteenth century religion inspired both anti-Catholic political movements and a range of progressive social reform campaigns.

- Between 1900 and 1930 conservative Protestants broke away from mainstream churches to form fundamentalist alternatives and created a distinctive sub-culture.

- Apart from some involvement in anti-communist campaigns, fundamentalists spent most of the twentieth century in retreat.

The rise of the New Christian Right (NCR)

Protest movements are stimulated by a conjunction of despair and hope: an intensification of what troubles people combining with some improvement in their circumstances that causes them to think action might be effective.

The positive roots of the NCR lie in the following. In the second half of the twentieth century there was a shift in economic power from the North (with its declining heavy industry) to the South. There was a shift of population. There was also a shift in political power. Since John F. Kennedy in 1960, every elected president has been from the South or the West. Lyndon B. Johnson was a Texan. Richard Nixon was from California. Jimmy Carter was from Georgia. Ronald Reagan was a Californian. Although a member of an old New England family, George Bush's political base was Texas. Bill Clinton was governor of Arkansas. George Bush Jr. was governor of Texas. Although it would be a mistake to say that the South had solved its race problem, the forced desegregation of the South had by the 1970s removed much of the stigma and made it clear that racial discrimination was not confined to the old Confederate states.

Within the sphere of religion, power had also shifted decisively to the conservative wing of Protestantism, which had been growing relative to the mainstream churches since the 1950s. The separatist institutions established by fundamentalists were bearing fruit. In particular, conservatives had made much better use of the new technologies of radio and television to create audience networks of committed supporters of their distinctive religion and social mores. They had also mastered the organizational virtuous circle. On air they solicited donations and offered free gifts to people who phoned in. From those contacts they built computerized mailing lists that could be used to solicit funds to buy more air-time to appeal for more funds and so on. Not all the radio and TV stars were fundamentalists. The Catholic bishop Fulton J. Sheen was popular in the 1950s, as was the liberal Peale, but big names were the fundamentalist Billy Graham and the Pentecostalist Oral Roberts

(who founded his own university in Tulsa, Oklahoma), and the main innovator was Marion G. 'Pat' Robertson. Robertson pioneered a new format by modelling his '700 Club' on the secular chat shows and news reviews. He also broke with the previous practice of buying air time on secular channels to create his own Christian Broadcasting Network. It is not easy to estimate the 'televangelism' audience, but Hadden and Swann (1981) suggest that in 1980 some twenty million people watched the top sixty-six syndicated religious TV programmes, and that the top ten shows attracted fifteen million viewers (just under 7 per cent of the population)—a considerable reach by any standards, and a powerful antidote to the sense of cultural inferiority that had plagued conservative Protestants since the 1920s.

The negative forces can be grouped under two headings. Fundamentalists were provoked into campaigning by cultural and social forces that reminded them of their marginality: black consciousness, feminism, gay rights, the anti-Vietnam War movement, the hippies, recreational drug use, mass media portrayals of sexuality, abortion, and the acceptability of divorce. All that would have been bad enough, but it came with a series of changes that threatened fundamentalist isolation. The federal state expanded and deepened its reach. Before 1960 there were twenty-seven federal regulatory agencies; by 1976 there were a further fifty (Janovitz 1978: 368). The federal courts imposed the will of the centre on the peripheries by, for example, ruling unconstitutional such locally accepted practices as beginning the school day with shared public prayers (see Box 22.1). Local media outlets were assimilated into national networks. Local newspapers were increasingly filled by syndicated national copy. Small family firms were bought up by large corporations. And, most importantly, increased affluence made it possible for fundamentalists to join the cultural mainstream (e.g. by owning televisions and going to the movies) at a time when that culture was becoming thoroughly abhorrent.

What brought the NCR to life was the stimulus of a

Box 22.2 What does the NCR want?

As well as being generally right-wing, the NCR wants:

- abortion banned;
- homosexuality made a crime;
- divorce made more difficult;
- women discouraged from working outside the home;
- public prayer in schools;
- sex education banned;
- tax relief for independent 'faith' schools;
- required teaching of creationism in schools.

group of professional right-wing lobbyists who saw in the fundamentalist milieu the potential for a new right-wing movement based, not on the traditional concerns of low taxes and an assertive foreign policy, but on cultural concerns. They persuaded televangelists such as Jerry Falwell to use their television audiences and church networks to mobilize conservative Protestants in support of a series of single-issue campaigns. In the late 1970s a number of organizations such as the Moral Majority and Religious Roundtable promoted voter registration drives, raised money, targeted liberal candidates, ran advertising campaigns in support of moral conservatives, lobbied legislators, ran slates of candidates for school board and council elections, organized boycotts of media outlets that offended their values, and in a variety of other ways sought to awaken a sleeping giant.

Key points

- The background to the rise of the NCR was a shift of economic and political power to the South, the relative decline of liberal churches, the increased permissiveness of mainstream culture, and increased imposition of the cosmopolitan centre on the peripheries.

- The crucial resource was the network of fundamentalist pastors and the networks of audiences for televangelism shows.

- The catalyst was the initiative of experienced conservative lobbyists who saw the potential for a right-wing socio-moral movement.

Evaluating the NCR

It is not easy to assess the impact of a diffuse movement that works on a variety of fronts, but I will summarize the impact of the NCR on the courts, on elections, on legislation, and on the general cultural climate.

The courts

There are two reasons why much of the work of the NCR has been conducted through the courts. First, many of its socio-moral concerns relate directly to the balance between the freedoms of the individual and the nature of the social order. Second, the courts play a vital role in interpreting the Constitution, and its specific references to the position of religion.

The NCR rejects the idea of minority rights. It wishes to impose on the entire culture what it claims to be the views of the 'moral majority' and sees minority (or in the case of women, majority) rights as a threat to its historical hegemony. Yet it is precisely when it has presented conservative Christians as a victimized minority that the NCR has had most success in the courts (Garvey 1993). For example, in 1995, in *Rosenberger* v. *University* of Virginia, the Supreme Court overturned a judgment that the university had been right to deny a Christian student group funding for an advocacy publication, when non-religious advocacy groups had been funded. In a five to four decision, the Court ruled that the Court of Appeal had been guilty of discrimination and that such funding did not violate the establishment clause of the Constitution. However, the oppressed minority appeal has worked only on very narrow ground. A Tennessee court agreed with fundamentalist parents that their rights were infringed when their children were required to read books explaining objectionable beliefs. On appeal, the verdict was overturned on the grounds that the lower court had not properly distinguished between knowing about beliefs and being compelled to embrace them. Parents could legitimately object to the latter but not to the former.

The argument that, if promoting religion is unconstitutional, then so is promoting 'secular humanism' has also failed. Funded by Pat Robertson, over 600 fundamentalists filed suit against the Alabama State Board of Education, charging that the board had violated their constitutional rights. Judge W. Brevard Hand found for the plaintiffs, but the unanimous verdict of the Appeal Court was that he was wrong to accept that all knowledge must be either Christian or secular humanist. The Appeal Court applied the narrower test of whether the textbooks at issue taught an identifiable philosophy of secular humanism, and concluded that they did not.

The courts also defeated another version of the parity argument when they ruled that the requirement to teach divine creation was unconstitutional. The Arkansas legislature had passed an 'equal time' bill that required that Darwinian evolution be matched with equal attention to the divine creation story of the Old Testament books Genesis 1–12. To establish that divine creation deserved such support, its promoters had to convince the court that a non-Christian would find the case as convincing as the secular alternatives. They failed miserably to even mount a consistent, let alone a persuasive case.

In summary, although the NCR was astute in presenting conservative Christians as a minority seeking only fair treatment, it actually gained very little by replacing the rhetoric of being a moral majority with that of being a persecuted minority.

The NCR has had very little success in using the courts to restore the primacy of its conservative socio-moral views. In one of the few decisions claimed as an NCR victory, the Supreme Court in 1986 held that the Due Process Clause (the basis for the general principle that the Bill of Rights applies not just to the federal state but also to state and local government) did not protect homosexual sodomy. However, in so doing the Court was explicitly returning the issue to the elected branches of government. There the tide has continued to run in a permissive direction despite the NCR. As of June 2001 the anti-sodomy laws of twenty-six states had been repealed (eight of them *since* NCR campaigning began in 1978). Those of a further nine states have been struck down by the courts, and in a further four, court cases are pending.

In the late 1980s the Supreme Court made three significant decisions on abortion, which, because it offends against conservative Catholic views, is probably the NCR's most popular issue. First, it expressed unhappiness about the time-limit rules laid down in the original *Roe* v. *Wade* decision of 1973; advances in medicine had altered the life chances for premature babies. Second, the Court allowed the government to restrict public funding for abortions. Third, it permitted states to require that minors notify their parents before having abortions. However, despite having a conservative majority, the Court has very pointedly declined to ban abortion, and has handed the issue back to the legislatures, where the fundamentalist record is at best mixed. While some states (e.g. Louisiana and Utah) enacted restrictive time laws, Maryland and Connecticut passed laws designed to preserve the right to abortion. Furthermore, the Court has protected the basic right to abortion where state laws have been too restrictive. Parental notification laws have only been permitted where there is a judicial 'bypass': a judge is able to waive the requirement if the minor is sufficiently mature or if telling a parent would not be in the girl's best interest. In 1997, by eight votes to one, the Court decided that a Louisiana attempt to weaken the judicial bypass was undue interference with a girl's abortion rights.

Finally, a major part of the NCR's agenda is concerned with the public presence of Christian symbols. The NCR wants public support for acts of religious worship and for the symbols of its distinctive religious culture. Despite the appointment by Reagan and his successor, George Bush Sr., of five conservative justices, the Supreme Court has followed the precedents of the earlier courts in refusing to permit government support for such acts and symbols. Equally noticeable is that the lower federal courts, heavily packed with conservatives by Reagan and Bush, have proved little more sympathetic.

Legislation

As we can see from the cases that find their way to the Supreme Court, NCR organizations have succeeded in promoting bills through legislatures in areas with strong conservative traditions, but they made very little headway in Congress. They found no shortage of politicians happy to make sympathetic noises, but few who would invest much political capital in promoting NCR causes. Ronald Reagan, for all his willingness to court fundamentalist voters, gave very little in return beyond such cheap gestures as declaring a 'Year of the Bible'. Even the 1994–6 Congress, with a Republican majority in both Houses, failed to deliver much. Despite its expensive lobbying, Christian Coalition had seven of the ten planks of its 'Contract with the American Family' wholly rejected. The partial successes concerned internet pornography. In announcing his retirement as director of Christian Coalition, Ralph Reed claimed four major achievements: welfare reform, the Communications Decency Act (a blanket anti-pornography measure), the Defence of Marriage Act (an anti-gay rights measure), and the Partial Birth Abortion Act. The first of these was not a specifically NCR issue, and within a year was unravelling. The second was voided by two federal courts. The Defence of Marriage Act has yet to face any serious tests, but is thought unlikely to prevent moves to recognise same-sex unions such as that being contemplated by Hawaii. The abortion Act was vetoed by President Clinton.

Elections

It is not easy to judge NCR impact on elections. Proponents of competing evaluations can readily list any number of contests from 1980 to 2000 to show that Christian Right support helped win or helped lose seats. On one side we have spokesmen for the American Coalition for Traditional Values saying that Roger Jepsen of Iowa lost his Senate seat in 1984 to a liberal Democrat because he turned his back on the religious groups which had supposedly helped him win in 1978 (McLaughlin 1984: 13). On the other side, we have reports that Virginia got its first black governor in 1990 because his white opponent was vocally anti-abortion until he discovered it was costing him the election (Brogan 1991). Abortion is also thought to have delivered the Western Massachusetts seat to a Democrat for the first time in its history: the Republican was against it. Liberal Republicans blame the defeat of George Bush Sr. in 1992 and Bob Dole in 1996 on the fundamentalist platform that NCR supporters foisted on the party. Movement conservatives argue that Bush and Dole lost because they showed insufficient commitment to that platform. But whichever explanation of defeat one prefers, the fact to be explained remains defeat and not victory. In 2000, the Republican standard was carried not by Gary Bauer or Pat Buchanan or any of the other NCR favourites but by George Bush Jr., who chose to present himself as a moderate 'compassionate conservative'.

It is possible to be impressed by figures that Christian Coalition used to describe itself (and were disputed even by some insiders). In 1997 it claimed 1.9 million members, 125,000 participating churches, and an annual revenue exceeding $27 million (Watson 1999). But it is easier to be impressed by how little the Coalition has achieved with all that money and support.

What the NCR has done best is to infiltrate the Republican Party (Moen 1992). Although Falwell and others initially promoted the movement as bipartisan, it was obviously more popular with Republicans than with Democrats, and during the 1980s many fundamentalists concentrated on taking over local branches of the party. But such entrism is of little value if the final product is rejected by the electorate as too extreme and too zealously focused on single issues. We might consider the case of the Virginia Republican Party in 1994. Virginia is a divided state. The majority of the state's population is found in the northern suburbs, which includes the fringes of Washington DC, where people are unusually affluent, socially liberal, and have low levels of church involvement. But the state also has large concentrations of conservative Baptists and Methodists and is home to Falwell's Liberty University and Pat Robertson's Regent University and broadcasting empire. In the 1980s Christian Right groups moved to infiltrate the Republican Party, something made relatively easy by the fact that party candidates are selected at a nominating convention which, like the Iowa caucuses, gives the advantage to any group able to mobilize committed supporters. In 1994 the convention nominated as its candidate for the Senate Oliver North, a former Marine Corps officer who had gained notoriety for his part in the Reagan administration's covert and illegal operation to supply arms to the right-wing Contra forces in Nicaragua. North had spent years cultivating the Christian Right and the gun lobby, and the support of those two groups of activists ensured him the nomination. Liberal Republican Senator John Warner was so horrified that he encouraged a more moderate Republican to run as an independent. On the Democrat side, the incumbent Chuck Robb was also challenged by an independent. The result was that Robb won an easy victory, made all the more remarkable by two things. First, over the country as a whole there was a major swing to the Republicans. Second, Ollie North spent approximately $20 million (about four times what Robb spent) and had the support of a vast army of conservative Christian volunteers.

Richard Nixon pointedly said that Republicans had to run to the right in the primary and then to the centre in the general election (Jelen 2000: 115). NCR activists in the party forgot the second part. Like the militant left's influence on the British Labour party in the early 1980s, the NCR's effect on the Republican Party in some areas was to shift it away from the middle ground that it needed to occupy if it was to win major elections. The Republican Party led by George Bush Jr. appreciated that, and although it is too early to be sure how a Bush administration will behave, its first round of appointments balanced a few NCR favourites such as John Ashcroft with liberal Republicans such as Colin Powell, whose disdain for 'movement' conservatism is well known.

None of this is intended to deny the obvious point that in small political units where conservatives are numerous, the NCR can achieve limited legislative and electoral success. However, as we move up from the city and county to the congressional district and the state to the federal government we move to units of greater cultural, social, and political diversity, and we see the potential for such pressure groups as the NCR steadily diminished.

A good example of 'small victory–large defeat' pattern can be found in the battle over creationism in Kansas. Members of the Kansas Board of Education have traditionally been elected on a very small turnout. In 1999 the board, dominated by fundamentalists, approved a science curriculum that made no mention of Darwin or evolution. There was a public outcry, led by the presidents of the state's major universities and supported by editorials in the Washington Post and the New York Times. On a much higher turnout, the fundamentalists were voted off the board the following year and evolution was put back on the curriculum.

General cultural climate

One may argue, as Falwell and others have frequently done, that the NCR re-established the respectability of conservative socio-moral positions and the right of fundamentalists to be taken seriously. It is certainly the case that the 1980s saw considerable publicity given to NCR activists and their views. However, while such exposure ensures a vigorous debate, it only guarantees to win that debate if it is the case that the previous liberal hegemony was achieved by stealth. But it was not. We can take examples from a variety of levels of the political system to make the point. When the televangelist Pat Robertson ran for the Republican nomination, the early impact of his highly committed supporters (which won him the Iowa caucuses) brought out liberal Republicans in such numbers that, despite spending unprecedented sums, he failed to win a single primary. In the

Kansas example, an initial fundamentalist victory was overturned once liberals appreciated that they could not take their hegemony for granted but had to become as active as the conservatives.

We take an even wider picture. The NCR has patently failed to force gays back into 'the closet'. There are now openly gay Congressmen and women. US TV channels air shows in which homosexuals are portrayed as normal people: the popular sitcoms *Ellen* and *Will and Grace* are good examples. The abortion rate has declined slightly. After rising from the 1972 level of 180 per 1,000 live births to 1985's 354, it fell back gently to 306 in 1997—a change resulting mainly from better contraceptive practice (US Centers for Disease Control and Prevention 2000). The divorce rate in 1940 among married women aged 15 and over was 8.8 per cent. It rose to a high of 22.6 per cent in 1981 and then fell back slightly to 20.5 per cent in 1994. The US Census Bureau now estimates that at least 40 per cent of marriages will end in divorce. One other central plank of the NCR approach to the family is its desire for a return to traditional gender roles. Here too there is no sign of the social trends going in the desired direction. Women made up 18 per cent of the US labour force in 1900, 30 per cent in 1950, and 46 per cent in 1997 (AFL-CIO 2001).

To conclude this very brief review, the NCR began with a great many advantages. It had ready access to the mass media through the products of televangelists such as Falwell and Robertson. It had the mailing lists of televangelism organizations to reach its potential supporters. It was led by some extremely skilled self-publicists. It was able to make use of the excellent existing networks of con-

servative Protestant pastors. Nonetheless, it failed to achieve significant progress on items which were specific to its agenda (as distinct from those ambitions such as increased defence spending which were shared with mainstream conservatives). It is always possible to argue that the NCR acted as a brake: that without it, America would have become more liberal and permissive. But unfortunately, claims for influence of this sort are untestable and have to remain in the realm of speculation. All we can do is look at the wish-list, look at what was achieved and compare the two. The conclusion must be that the NCR failed to end abortion, curtail divorce, prevent mothers working, outlaw homosexuality, balance the teaching of evolution with that of creation science, or restore the public primacy of conservative religion.

Key points

- The NCR has had some success in presenting conservative Christians as a legitimate minority, but has made little progress on its main goal of persuading the US state to accord priority to its distinctive socio-moral values.

- Initial NCR successes in the courts, in legislatures, and in elections have been reversed on appeal, in Congress, and in general elections.

- Twenty years of expensive NCR campaigns has failed to reverse the social changes that offend NCR values: public acceptance of homosexuality, divorce, abortion, women working outside the home.

The advantages and disadvantages of zealotry

Evangelicals bring a number of advantages to politics. They are highly motivated. They are used to giving large amounts of time, money, and energy to promoting the gospel. Once convinced that they could 'bring America back to God', they brought the same zealotry to politics and in venues where small

numbers of highly committed people could swing an outcome, they had some success. For example, in his run for the Republican nomination for president in 1988, Pat Robertson won the Iowa caucuses because there victory was determined by activists massing in a hall.

What is less often considered is that zealotry has a number of corresponding disadvantages. First, while the NCR leaders could work with conservative Catholics, Jews, and Muslims, many rank-and-file evangelicals could not sufficiently set aside their sectarian religion to create effective alliances. An Ohio chapter of the Moral Majority memorably preceded a meeting to discuss working with conservative Catholics with a lecture on the evils of Roman Catholicism (Wilcox 1987). Second, however much the zealots might have been willing to seek alliances, the groups they court have memories. The Catholic Church shares interests with the NCR (in the state funding for religious schools, for example, and on most socio-moral concerns), but Catholics can remember that fundamentalists used to be anti-Catholic. The black churches are conservative on moral issues but are only too well aware of the segregationist backgrounds of many older NCR supporters (such as Senators Helms and Thurmond) and are deeply suspicious of the economic liberalism of the NCR. Many Islamic groups would be at one with the NCR on gender roles, temperance, and personal sexual behaviour but are excluded by the Christian ethos of the movement and by its support for the state of Israel. As, so it happens, are most Jews, because fundamentalists are only interested in Israel for the part they expect it to play in hastening the Battle of Armageddon.

Finally, many non-NCR conservatives are alienated by the 'deep' message of the NCR. Skilled operators such as Falwell and Robertson try to confine their fundamentalist message to their core audience and speak more moderately to the wider public. But they often fail. For example, in the aftermath of the 11 September atrocities, Robertson on his *700 Club* show asked Falwell who was to blame. To frequent 'amens' from Robertson, Falwell replied:

[by] throwing God out successfully with the help of the federal court system, throwing God out of the public square, out of the schools. The abortionists have got to bear some burden for this because God will not be mocked. . . . the pagans and the abortionists and the feminists and the gays and lesbians . . . the ACLU [American Civil Liberties Union], People for the American Way, all of them who have tried to secularize America. I point the finger in their face and say 'you helped this happen'.   (Robertson 2001)

Non-fundamentalist conservatives are thus periodically reminded of just how narrow is the NCR's core vision.

Zealots are poor at compromise. Indeed, they define themselves against liberal Christians by noting that liberals accept a division of the social world into distinct spheres, each with their own values, while they, the fundamentalists, insist on ideological consistency. People driven by divine imperative are not good at trading losses in one area for gains in another.

Zealots become quickly disillusioned. They are brought to politics by apocalyptic imagery which creates expectations of success every bit as unrealistic as the bogeymen which stir them to action. Hence they are ill suited to the long haul. Religio-political mobilization thus tends to come in waves that are as short as they are intense.

Key points

- Zealots are good at politics in America because they are unusually committed to the cause; they are used to giving time, effort, and money; and they gain extra momentum from being inspired by shared beliefs and values and being highly disciplined.

- Zealots are bad at politics in America because their dogmatism makes them bad at forming alliances; they find it hard to compromise; and they have unrealistic expectations of the political process.

Structural advantages

There are two senses in which the NCR is a product of the open, diffuse, and federal nature of the USA. First, conservative Christianity remains stronger in the US than in any other modern industrial society because fundamentalists have been able to construct their own sub-societies to sustain their disticntive sub-culture. Second, in the following ways, the USA context allows interest groups easier entry into the political arena.

The weakness of parties

In most European countries, political parties are powerful institutions that dominate the political process. In the UK, the party chooses its candidates and determines its policy. Access to the mass media is free but allocated to parties, not individual candidates. Spending on elections is constrained and it is the parties, not the candidates, which pay. The party in power determines the legislative agenda and coerces its members to support it. The electorate recognizes the power of party by voting for party rather than for individuals.

As Robert Mason noted in Chapter 5, the major US parties are remarkably open. Candidates are selected locally and in diverse ways that allow small groups of activists to determine who shall represent the party. In many areas the candidate need not even be a member of the party. Where it is able to mobilize enough supporters, the NCR is able to impose its candidates on a reluctant Republican Party. With no effective cap on spending, elections can be extraordinarily expensive and candidates will often accumulate large debts (literal and metaphorical) to interest groups other than the party. In state legislatures and in both Houses of Congress, individual legislators are free to initiate legislation. It will not be passed unless it can command widespread support, but people can repay debts to interest groups by promoting pet issues. The weakness of party in turn means that how legislators vote on bills (no matter how frivolous) can be used against them at the next election. Hence the favoured NCR tactic of distributing the detailed voting records of liberals on rafts of bills that can (with varying degrees of plausibility) be construed as 'pro-family'. Party alignment is relevant in that there tend to be swings for and against that are based on perceptions of the effectiveness of the president, but candidates can run with or against their own parties.

Ironically, the reforms to election funding that followed the scandals of the Watergate era strengthened interest groups. Although they capped the amount of money that could be spent on behalf of a particular candidate, the rules did not constrain how much could be spent on promoting general issue positions (Sabato 1984). So rather than have individuals give money, say, to Senator Jesse Helms in North Carolina, NCR organizations could raise money to spend on advertising campaigns that promoted 'family values' in a way that made it very clear that anyone who shared those values should vote for Helms.

Many elections, little interest

Many public offices that in Europe would be filled by appointment are in the US filled by election. So, as Candice Nelson noted in Chapter 6, there are many more elections, most attract very low turnouts, and a small number of committed activists can have a major impact. And major elected offices are for shorter terms than is common in Europe: Congressmen and women have to face the electorate every two years. That candidates are judged more on personal record than the standing of their party gives a considerable advantage to the incumbent, who will insure that powerful interests are well served. But the need to be personally popular encourages gesture politics and timidity. An example of the consequence is the Arkansas state legislature's passing of the creation science bill. As it did not involve spending taxes, and opposition could be presented to the electorate as a vote against God, the majority acquiesced to the wishes of a handful of zealots.

Key points

- Socio-moral issues have become politicized in the US to a far greater extent than in any European democracy because the US has a higher proportion of conservative Christians.

- But much NCR success is explained by the open structure of US politics, in particular the weakness of the national political parties.

Structural constraints

The NCR has failed to 'bring America back to God'. So if the above description of 'opportunity structure' combines with the earlier points about the advantages of zealotry to explain the limited successes of the NCR, what features of the opportunity structure combine with the disadvantages of zealotry to explain why, overall, it has made little headway?

The NCR has formidable opponents. People for the American Way, for example, very effectively countered Pat Robertson's political ambitions by ensuring that what he said to his core religious audience was broadcast to the wider audience to which he was pitching as an entrepreneur whose business just happened to be religion. Liberal pressure groups can outspend the NCR. In the 2000 elections, nearly $250 million was spent on television advertising. Sixty per cent of that was spent by political parties; the rest came from special interest groups, and the ones that were not business-related were the trade union organization AFL-CIO, Planned Parenthood (which promotes contraception and is pro-abortion), the League of Conservation Voters, Americans for Job Security, and Emily's List, which raises money to promote women candidates (Associated Press 2001).

While single-issue organizations are well placed to mobilize support, single-issue election candidates tend to do badly because they are thought to be too narrow to be effective politicians. Even when the single issue in question is a popular one (e.g. limiting abortion), there are two obstacles to success-ful mobilization. The first is often overlooked when people use opinion poll data to show that this or that NCR agenda item is popular. Many people may indeed oppose abortion, but they might well accord that concern a low priority. The second obstacle is that the salience of some issue is not just a matter of how strongly people feel about it (relative to how strongly they may feel about other things). It is also a function of public agenda-setting. Turning a popular sentiment into political power depends on the importance of that issue at the time when political choices are made and the NCR is not free to set pub-lic agendas. That many people dislike abortion is of little use if abortion cannot be made the focus of an election. The relatively low priority that Americans accord socio-moral issues is demonstrated by Bill Clinton's career. Despite massive negative cam-paigning, he won two elections: the first because people thought he would be better than George Bush Sr. at managing the economy, the second because the economy was booming. Despite Clin-ton's sexual and financial scandals (and the con-siderable effort that NCR organizations put into reminding people of them), his approval ratings remained around 60 per cent. The 1998 elections marked the first time since 1934 that the party of the president made gains in the House in mid-term elec-tions (Jelen 2001: 105).

But perhaps the greatest obstacle to the NCR has been the general reluctance of Americans to support theocracy. With varying degrees of consciousness, most Americans seem to appreciate the practical benefits of liberalism and toleration. Some have a conscious commitment to the separation of church and state; others just have a vague sense that preachers should not be telling people what they cannot do. Survey after survey has shown that most Americans distinguish between morality and law. For example, a 1990 review of a series of polls showed that while three-quarters of Americans thought homosexuality immoral, a majority of those did not think that homosexual acts should be illegal (McKeever 1997: 37). A major survey sponsored by an organization in favour of greater religious influence on public life found that 58 per cent of the public thought it wrong for voters 'to seriously consider the religious affiliation of candidates'. When asked what they thought of faith-based charities receiving government funding for welfare programmes, 44 per cent were in favour but a quarter of the sample thought it only a good idea if such programmes stayed away from religious messages. Nearly a third thought it a bad idea for the state to fund religious organizations for any pur-pose. Most telling were the responses to questions about public prayer in schools. Only 12 per cent of evangelicals thought that such prayers should be specifically Christian and 53 per cent of evangelicals (the same as for the general public) thought that a moment of shared silence was the best solution to the problem (Pew Forum 2001).

Although the above point concerns social values, I have placed it in this section on structural constraints because the way in which this generally tolerant ethos is brought to bear on the NCR is through the centripetal nature of US politics and public administration. Although the federal structure of the USA allows far more autonomy for cities, counties, and states than is common in most European countries, the USA is in the end a single state and its political structure forces the most important matters to be decided at the highest level of generality. Any enthusiast may introduce a bill in the House of Representatives, but to have any chance of becoming law it must attract broad-based support. It must then pass the Senate, which, by giving two votes to every state irrespective of size, acts as a brake on regional and sectional interests. That senators are elected by the entire state rather than by a small congressional district means that they are much more likely to be moderates. Finally, bills have to be approved by the president, who answers to a national electorate, and they can only get past his veto with two-thirds support from Congress.

The court system is centripetal. The NCR had some successes in the lower courts but then saw the victories overturned as the cases were appealed upwards. Judges always interpret the law with one eye on what they think the people want or need. Federal judges answer to a large 'imagined community', and the justices of the Supreme Court, which has the final say on most matters that concern the religiously motivated, make their judgments in the light of what they take to be the interests of the US.

The same general point holds true for elections and party politics: in local elections with small constituencies (such as party selection meetings) the NCR could do well but then see its preferred candidate defeated in a full primary or the full election. And in the presidential elections, candidates such as Pat Buchanan and Pat Robertson have failed miserably.

What can easily be forgotten in using terms such as 'fundamentalist' to describe both Islamic Jihad in the Lebanon and Pat Robertson's Christian Coalition is that the vast majority of religious zealots in the USA accept the rule of law. They attempt to gain their goals by conventional electoral, legislative, and judicial action. They do not assert that the law of God trumps the laws of man and hence justifies serious criminal acts. For all the passion engendered by the abortion debate, only five or six people have been killed in the USA by anti-abortionists, and in all but one case the perpetrator has attempted to mitigate guilt by claiming to be mentally unstable. In not one case has any significant religious institution offered ideological legitimation for such acts.

In arguing for their values, US fundamentalists accept secular principles. They do not tell the courts that abortion should be banned because it offends God; they argue that it infringes the basic universal human right to life. They do not campaign for public prayers in schools by asserting that such is God's will. Instead they use the language of human rights. Unlike William Jennings Bryan, modern creationists do not say it is better to know the Rock of Ages than to know the age of rocks. Instead they argue that creation science fits the evidence every bit as well as the alternatives. They may privately oppose homosexuality and divorce because they are sinful, but in trying to promote their views they argue that they are socially dysfunctional. Whether fundamentalists present their case in terms of generally accepted secular norms because they are genuinely committed to a separation of church and state, of the public and the private, or because they reluctantly accept that there is no alternative, hardly matters. What matters is that the cultural diversity of the United States places a powerful constraint on the realization in the public sphere of any distinctive religious culture.

I will give one final example to illustrate the point. The case law built up by the Supreme Court over the second half of the twentieth century has established that state support for religiously inspired activities must be very narrowly constrained. At the same time, most American are sympathetic to religious institutions and recognize them as an important part of the fabric of civil society. Many NCR activists are now trying to capitalize on that public mood, while staying within the law, by promoting the idea that the government should be able to fund 'faith-based' social work and educational agencies. While in the abstract this is a popular direction, it seems highly unlikely that any successful legislation will survive the combination of judicial inspection and public prejudice. Very few people will object to public funding of the social-work initiatives of urban black pentecostal churches, but it is very difficult to see how any such initiative could exclude the Nation of Islam's alcohol rehabilitation work, Islamic education programmes, or the Church of Scientology's work with drug addicts and the mentally ill. Thus the problem of diversity is brought home. As a principle for the public administration of a religiously diverse country (half the citizens of which have no active religious commitment), permitting almost every-thing in private and almost nothing in public is attractively effective.

Key points

- NCR organizations face powerful opposition from well-organized liberal groups.

- Most Americans give relatively low priority to socio-moral issues in political choices and are

cautious about using the law to prevent immorality.

- The basically tolerant ethos is imposed on value-driven sub-cultures by the centripetal structure of the justice, legislative, and electoral systems.

- US fundamentalists are constrained by their own acceptance of rules of democracy, and NCR organizations increasingly concede the argument to their opponents by arguing for their agenda on secular, not religious, grounds.

Box 22.3 **Is America different?**
Religious differences

The USA is unusual in that levels of active participation in organized religion are twice as high as in European democracies such as the UK, France, and Germany. It differs from other countries with high degrees of religious participation in that, unlike Ireland or Poland, it does not have one dominant religion.

The constitutions of most modern democracies define a secular state and promise religious freedom, but the USA is unusual in the tolerant spirit in which the law is applied.

The size and the federal structure of the USA allow

sub-cultures an unusual degree of freedom to create and maintain their own sub-societies.

The structure of US politics (especially the weakness of the national parties) allows interest groups to engage directly in the political process in a way that is impossible in most European states.

The combination in the USA of a higher proportion of conservative Christians and an open political structure explains why there is nothing in any other modern democracies comparable to the New Christian Right.

Conclusion

In his excellent *Culture Wars*, James Hunter (1991) is careful to point out that behind the many specific arguments about school prayer, sex education, pornography in the arts, and the like there is a very general disagreement about the nature of authority. Though they may disagree on where it is located, conservatives share a common belief in the possibility of authoritative knowledge and guidance that transcends and constrains the individual. It may be a sacred text, a venerated tradition, or the official teachings of an organization, but there is some touchstone that allows one group of people to denounce another in what Islam

calls 'commanding what is good and forbidding what is bad'.

The problem for moral conservatives in the USA is that such certainty is being eroded. Despite being replenished by immigrants from more religiously traditional cultures, the proportion of the US population actively involved in religion is slowly declining. And within the church, synagogue, and mosque population there is a visible shift from conservative, authoritarian, and dogmatic faiths to increasingly individualistic and consumerist versions. Shibley (1996) documents this for new varieties of evangelicalism, which, as he points out, are 'world-affirming' rather than world-rejecting. They are no longer puritanical and oriented to obeying an authoritarian God. They are comfortable with prosperity and concentrate on offering therapeutic satisfaction: health, wealth, and happiness. Hunter (1987) noted among the young evangelicals he studied in the 1980s a creeping relativism. They were no longer as sure as their parents and grandparents that God requires the same things of all people. Even among conservative Christians, religion is becoming increasingly privatized. And even regular church-goers now select just which of their tradition's teaching they will accept. In brief, the assertive consumerism that Americans live out in other parts of their lives has now come to influence their religion.

QUESTIONS

1 The federal structure of US politics and public administration accommodates religious diversity, but does it also encourage conflict by letting religious sub-cultures misunderstand their relative importance in the country as a whole?

2 Why have socio-moral issues such as abortion, on which faith communities have strong views, not become as politicized in Europe as they have in the USA?

3 Does the fact that NCR organizations couch their agenda in secular terms show that they accept that theocracy is impossible?

4 Does the fate of the NCR show that US democracy is strong enough to resist zealots or does it show that the democratic process can be manipulated by special-interest groups?

FURTHER READING

S. Bruce (1988), *The Rise and Fall of the New Christian Right* (Oxford: Oxford University Press) and C. Wilcox (1992), *God's Warriors* (Baltimore: Johns Hopkins University Press) are good general introductions to the New Christian Right.

S. Bruce (2001), *Fundamentalism* (Cambridge: Polity Press) is a general survey of modern fundamentalism which pays particular attention to the differences between US and Islamic fundamentalism.

J. D. Hunter (1991), *Culture Wars: The Struggle to Define America* (New York: Basic Books) is an excellent account of the socio-moral disputes behind the NCR.

T. G. Jelen (2000), *To Serve God and Mammon: Church–State Relations in American Politics* (Boulder, Colo.: Westview) offers a clear account of the debates over the constitutional position of religion.

M. J. Rozell and C. Wilcox (eds.) (1996), *Second Coming: The New Christian Right in Virginia Politics* (Baltimore: Johns Hopkins University Press) offers a very detailed study of the role of the Christian right in Republican Party politics.

WEB LINKS

www.cc.org The Christian Coalition

www.falwell.com Reverend Jerry Falwell's site

www.au.org Americans United for Separation of Church and State

www.pfaw.org People for the American Way (a liberal group dedicated to opposing the Christian Right)

www.uscj.org United Synagogue of Conservative Judaism

www.nccbuscc.org United States Conference of Catholic Bishops

www.catholic.net Catholic Information Center

ecusa.anglican.org The Episcopal Church, USA

www.sbc.net/sbcsplash Southern Baptist Convention

23 Gay rights

Donald P. Haider-Markel

READER'S GUIDE

This chapter examines the emergence of civil rights and liberties issues of concern to lesbian and gay Americans. In particular it explores several key areas that help illustrate the debate and its evolution in America's divided democracy. Data from public opinion polls are used to show American attitudes toward same-sex relations, homosexuals, and policies that would ensure equality for lesbians and gays. The preferences of the public are then linked to national, state, and local public policies relating to gays and lesbians. Further, the evolution of the policy debate over homosexuality is explored in a multitude of government arenas, with particular focus on how opposing advocacy coalitions have tried to define this issue and how these definitions shape current and future policy-making activity in the United States.

Introduction

Attempts by lesbians and gays to achieve equality in American society clearly personify the divisions in American politics and culture over the role of government, and the balance of power between the national government and state and local governments, as well as conflicts in political traditions, such as traditionalism and progressivism.[1] Perhaps only abortion, gun control, and school prayer have evoked more cultural division and conflict than gay rights.

Following the success of other groups, gays and lesbians created a broad-based social movement to raise individual and societal consciousness regarding

[1] I use the terms 'gay' and 'lesbian' as well as 'gay' to simply refer to all homosexuals. However, when referring to the gay movement generally I am also including bisexuals, transgendered persons, and transsexuals. These additional individuals have been added under the rubric of the gay movement since about 1990, but much debate remains within the movement itself over the full inclusion of bisexuals, transgendered persons, and transsexuals and the representation of their interests.

sexual identity. This effort has included attempts to gain legal protections based on sexual orientation and gender identity, thereby making their personal lives a political issue. The gay and lesbian movement has evolved to become a regular player in local, state, and national politics. Among other activities, gay rights activists have worked to shape representations of gay people in the media and medical conceptions of homosexuality, to enact laws that protect individuals from discrimination on the bias of sexual orientation and allow same-sex couples to marry, to encourage companies and governments to offer insurance benefits for the same-sex partners of employees, and to pursue government action on diseases, such as HIV/AIDS, which have disproportionately affected gay men.

This chapter examines the American debate over gay civil rights and civil liberties by exploring several key areas that help illustrate the debate and its evolution in American politics. In particular I focus on (i) the central issues in the debate over homosexuality, (ii) the preferences and beliefs of the public and how they have changed over time, (iii) gay-related policy at the local, state, and national level, and (iv) how debate, issues, and government activity is likely to evolve in the future.

Issues in debate

Some observers argue that gays and lesbians are clearly an oppressed group. Similar to other minority groups, lesbians and gays face discrimination in various aspects of their lives, including harassment and violence based on their sexual orientation, as well as the specter of rejection by friends and family. In the workplace, research suggests that gay men earn less than their heterosexual counterparts and opinion polls consistently show the public has a strong dislike of homosexuals (Badgett 1995; Sherrill 1996; Yang 1999). And as a minority lesbians and gays often cannot protect themselves from a heterosexual majority, whether it is at the ballot box or the halls of a legislature. Further, unlike most other oppressed groups, lesbians and gays are not a clearly identifiable group, making it difficult for gays and lesbians to recognize one another and act collectively in the political arena to protect their civil rights and liberties.

Supporters of equal rights and protections for lesbians and gays argue that individuals and organizations should not discriminate against individuals because of sexual orientation. Such discrimination violates basic human rights, civil rights, and liberties as protected by the US Constitution and some statutory law. Further, some supporters suggest that it is morally wrong to discriminate or to commit violence on the basis of sexual orientation—that all people deserve to live free of harassment, discrimination, and violence, regardless of any characteristics they may hold (Vaid 1995).

Opponents of homosexual behaviour and government protection for homosexuals argue that homosexual behaviour is morally wrong (usually on the grounds of traditional religious beliefs) and question whether lesbians and gays have a legitimate claim to legal and other protections. They argue that homosexuality is not an innate characteristic like race or ethnicity, and therefore suggest that discrimination based on acquired or chosen orientations is legitimate. So rather than challenge the claim of civil rights as traditionally accepted in American society, opponents argue that civil rights protections can only be allocated on the basis of individual characteristics that cannot be changed or hidden. Indeed, public opinion polls suggest many believe that homosexual behaviour is chosen behaviour, suggesting that individuals can decide whether or not to be homosexual (Sherrill and Yang 2000). If gays choose their sexual orientation, it is less likely that they would be afforded legal protection based on that status. Thus, opponents often argue that lesbians and gays want 'special rights' rather than civil rights.

Nevertheless, medical and biological research examining the origins of sexual orientation has thus

---

Box 23.1 Political representation: openly lesbian Rep. Tammy Baldwin (D.WI)

Groups in society can use several strategies to ensure their interests are represented in government. One strategy is to elect public officials who are members of the group or who closely identify with the group. Since 1990 the number of openly gay and lesbian elected officials has increased dramatically. A vivid example of this change is Rep. Tammy Baldwin (D.WI), who made history in 1998 during an election season that some called 'the year of the lesbian'. Baldwin and three other lesbians ran for seats in the US House. Not only did Baldwin make history as the first lesbian elected to Congress, but she also became the first *non-incumbent* openly gay person elected to Congress. Rep. Baldwin had served two terms on the Dane County, Wisconsin, Board of Supervisors and was the first gay person elected to the Wisconsin legislature,

serving three terms in the state assembly before being elected to Congress. She was re-elected to Congress in 2000 and 2002. In a speech at the April 2000 gay march on Washington, DC, Baldwin offered hope for the future, suggesting that lesbians and gays should not doubt that Congress would pass significant hate crime legislation, and that states would ban sexual orientation discrimination and provide equal rights, including those granted through marriage. During her two terms Baldwin has focused on health care and education, with ties to civil rights issues. Organized opposition to her as a lesbian appears minimal, but it is clear that she had cleared a historic path that other lesbian and gay candidates are likely to follow.

---

far been inconclusive, even though evidence has accumulated suggesting a genetic predisposition to homosexuality (Tygart 2000). But even if a biological cause was discovered, opponents could still make an argument for discrimination on the basis of religious beliefs that firmly hold homosexual behaviour as immoral.

Still others suggest that local communities should decide these issues. As Chapter 4 detailed at length, American federalism allows for shared power between national, state, and local governments, and not all regions of the country share the same views on political issues. Individuals and groups should take advantage of this system and pursue local preferences on government involvement on issues such as homosexuality. State and local government involvement includes a range of issues from civil rights to adoption and fostering by homosexuals. If such issues are decided at the state and local level, it should be more likely that the greatest number of people will be satisfied with the outcome. However, some opponents of this view argue that racial and ethnic minorities would not enjoy their

civil rights and liberties in many parts of the country today if state and local governments had been allowed to be the sole arbitrators in this debate.

Key points

- Gays and lesbians and their supporters insist they have basic human rights that are violated in modern society.

- Significant evidence exists to suggest that gays and lesbians face discrimination, harassment, and violence because of their sexual orientation.

- Opponents argue that homosexuality is morally unacceptable and is a chosen behaviour not deserving of 'special' legal protection.

- The origins or causes of sexual orientation, heterosexual or homosexual, are currently unknown, though some research suggests genetic or biological origins. Beliefs about origins are important because they influence opinion towards gays.

Public opinion

In any democratic political system, elections play a key role in determining what the government does. However, in the interim between elections, policy-makers typically gauge citizen preferences through the use of public opinion surveys. Polls are also important to activists on both sides of a given issue. If activists can demonstrate that the public supports their position, elected officials and undecided citizens are more likely to be swayed by their arguments. But public opinion is fickle, and how questions are worded in public opinion polls can significantly alter how individuals respond to a given question.

Because the debate over homosexuality taps into core values concerning religion and morality, human rights, and the role of government in society, the public is often divided on many policy issues concerning gays and lesbians (Sherrill and Yang 2000). Opinions tend to vary significantly depend-ing on how a question is worded as well as how the issue is presented by the surveyor. However, broad trends in public opinion polls do suggest that public attitudes about sexual activities, relation-ships, marriage, and related issues have changed dramatically in America over the past thirty years. Attitudes about same-sex sexual relations, homo-sexuals, and the civil rights of lesbians and gays have become far more tolerant.

In their most simplistic form, opinions in the debate over homosexuality are shaped by attitudes individuals hold about sexual relations between persons of the same sex. If individuals believe that such relations are wrong, for moral or other reasons, these same individuals are less likely to have positive attitudes towards homosexuals as people, and are less likely to be supportive of policies that ensure equal treatment of gays and lesbians in society (Wilcox and Wolpert 2000). Furthermore, research demonstrates that individuals are more supportive of gay rights if they believe that homosexuality is not a choice, but instead can be attributed to a biological or genetic cause (Tygart 2000).

Since 1972 the General Social Survey has asked respondents to answer the following question: 'And what about sexual relations between two adults of the same sex, is it always wrong, almost always wrong, wrong only sometimes, or not wrong at all?' The responses to this question over time are shown in Fig. 23.1. Although strong majorities indicate that same-sex sexual relations are nearly always wrong throughout the time series, since 1991 the percentage of respondents indicating that these relations are sometimes not wrong or never wrong has nearly doubled. Opinion on same-sex relations has been incredibly stable since the 1960s, with a few minor changes, but most Americans clearly have little tolerance for activities that violate traditional religious values, even with recent surges in accept-ance. Thus, opinions on this question differ on the basis of adherence to traditional values. In particular, persons identifying with the Republican Party, the party most strongly associated with traditional values, are more likely to indicate that same-sex rela-tions are always wrong, compared to Democrats, who tend to espouse progressive values, 71 per cent to 56 per cent (Yang 1999).

Another way to explore American attitudes about homosexuality and homosexuals is to use what is traditionally referred to as a 'feeling thermometer'. The American National Election Study has used feeling thermometer questions to access feelings towards groups, such as homosexuals and environ-mentalists, for many years. Figure 23.2 shows the dis-tribution of feelings (average scores) toward gay men and lesbians on the feeling thermometer scale. Again, although feelings toward gays and lesbians have 'warmed' over time, the mean scores suggest that most Americans have unfavourable or cool feeling towards gays and lesbians. Indeed, across most of the periods in which the survey was conducted, gays and lesbians have average scores lower than any other group except illegal immigrants (Yang 1999). Respondent feelings toward homosexuals vary by individual charac-teristics, with those living in urban areas, those with higher levels of education, those with liberal and Democratic Party leanings, and women having warmer attitudes toward homosexuals (Haeberle

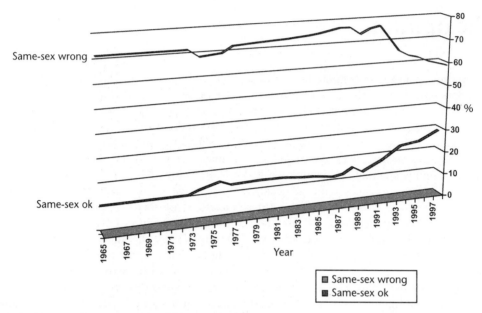

Fig. 23.1 Attitudes towards same-sex sexual relations, 1965–98

Notes: Data compiled by the author from Haider-Markel (1997) and General Social Survey (GSS) questions asked of adults in the US. The GSS question was: 'And what about sexual relations between two adults of the same sex, is it always wrong, almost always wrong, wrong only sometimes, or not wrong at all?' Responses were collapsed so that 'same-sex wrong' covers respondents indicating 'always wrong' and 'almost always wrong' and 'same-sex OK' covers respondents indicating 'wrong only sometimes' and 'not wrong at all'.

1999; Wilcox and Wolpert 2000). As such, these attitudes reflect long-standing divisions in American society between traditional and progressive values.

Attitudes about same-sex relations and towards homosexuals also influence attitudes about gay civil rights and civil liberties. Over the past thirty years both the General Social Survey and the Gallup Poll have asked American adults questions concerning their support for allowing books on homosexuality in public libraries, allowing homosexuals to teach, allowing homosexuals to speak in public, allowing homosexuals to serve in the military, and providing equal rights in terms of job opportunities. The responses to each survey question are displayed in Fig. 23.3 as the percentage of respondents indicating a response not supportive of gay civil rights and liberties.

The responses Fig. 23.2 reveal several interesting points. First, even in the 1970s a majority of Americans supported gay civil rights and liberties, although these were small majorities. Second, over time opposition to gay civil rights and liberties has dramatically decreased, even though most

Americans still do not have favourable attitudes about same-sex relations or homosexuals. Thus, Americans have some ability to separate their attitudes about the group from their attitudes (or tolerance) towards allowing the group basic civil rights and liberties. As with general attitudes about homosexuality, opinions on civil rights and liberties are shaped by conflicting traditional and progressive values. These values are reflected by partisanship, ideology, gender, education, and religious background. On average, Republicans, conservatives, men, the less educated, and those affiliated with orthodox, conservative, or evangelical religious denominations are less supportive of gay civil rights and liberties (Haeberle 1999; Wilcox and Wolpert 2000; Yang 1999).

Perhaps most interestingly, questions on gay civil rights mirror conflicting American attitudes over the proper scope and role of government in society. On the one hand they deplore centralized power, especially within government. On the other hand Americans have recognized legitimate roles for government in society, including national defence

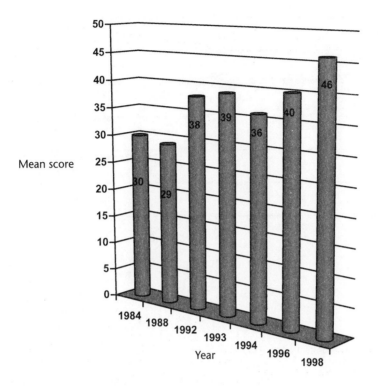

Fig. 23.2 Public feelings towards gay men and lesbians

Notes: Data are compiled by the author from Yang (1999) and the American National Election Study (ANES). Respondents were asked to state their feelings towards a group using a 0–100 scale, where a score of 50–100 indicates favourable or warm feelings and a score of 0–50 suggests an unfavourable or cold feeling, with the following question: 'How would you rate the following groups . . . gay men and lesbians, i.e. homosexuals?'

and the protection of civil rights and liberties. How-ever, more often than not Americans want to ensure protection from government rather than protection through government. As noted, most Americans believe that same-sex relations are wrong. Neverthe-less, they have increasingly supported the notion that government should not regulate these activities. When the Gallup Poll asked national adults in 1977 if 'homosexual relations between consenting adults should be legal or illegal', 43 per cent indicated illegal and 43 per cent said legal. The percentage of respondents indicating illegal peaked in the midst of the AIDS scare in 1988 at 57 per cent, but by 2001 the percentage of respondents saying it should be legal rose to a simple majority of 54 per cent (Newport 2001).

Furthermore, national surveys from a multitude of polling firms clearly show that large majorities of Americans favour equal rights for gays in housing, employment, public accommodations, and credit practices (Sherrill and Yang 2000). And a 2000 national poll by Princeton Survey Research reveals that Americans think gays and lesbians face more discrimination than any other group, including blacks, immigrants, and American Indians. How-ever, when asked if government should pass laws to ensure these rights are protected, majority support remains, but the margins drop between five and ten percentage points. For example, although most national polls show that about 80 per cent of Americans believe that gays should be treated equally or have equal rights in employment, a 2000 *Washington Post* poll suggests that 69 per cent also believe that homosexuality is not an issue the government should be involved in (Sherrill and Yang 2000). Americans clearly don't support dis-crimination against gays, but are more divided as to what role the government should play in ensuring

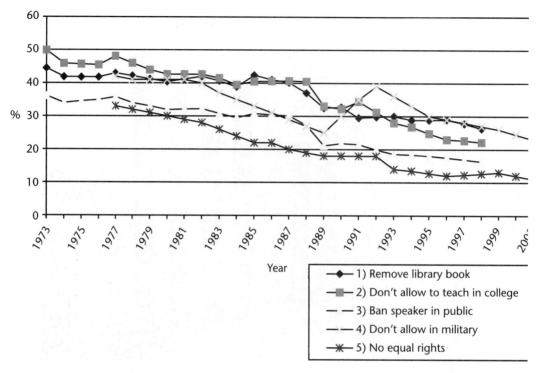

Fig. 23.3 Opposition towards homosexual civil rights and liberties, 1973–2001

Notes: Data compiled by the author from General Social Survey (GSS) (1–3) and Gallup Poll (4–5) questions asked of adults in the US. The responses to each survey question are displayed as the percentage of respondents indicating a response not supportive of gay civil rights and liberties. The questions: (1) 'If some people in your community suggested that a book he wrote in favor of homosexuality should be taken out of your public library, would you favor removing this book, or not?' (2) 'And what about a man who admits that he is a homosexual? Should such a person be allowed to teach in a college or university, or not?' (3) 'And what about a man who admits that he is a homosexual? Suppose this admitted homosexual wanted to make a speech in your community. Should he be allowed to speak, or not?' (4) 'Now I'd like to ask you about the hiring of homosexuals in specific occupations. Do you think homosexuals should or should not be hired for the following occupations: The armed forces?' (5) 'As you may know, there has been considerable discussion in the news regarding the rights of homosexual men and women. In general, do you think homosexuals should or should not have equal rights in terms of job opportunities?'

that discrimination does not occur or in addressing gay-related issues to any extent.

The variability in support for equal employment rights can also be seen when one examines support for homosexuals working in specific career fields. Starting in 1977 the Gallup Poll began asking adults in a national sample the following question: 'Do you think homosexuals should or should not be hired for each of the following occupations: salesperson, doctors, the armed forces, high school teachers, elementary school teachers, clergy?' The percentage of respondents indicating 'should not' in 1977 and 2001 are shown in Fig. 23.4. Even in 1977 most respondents suggested that gays should be allowed to be doctors, salespersons, members of the

military, and high school teachers. The strongest opposition was to allowing gays to be members of the clergy and elementary school teachers. By 2001, opposition to gays working in each of these career fields had dropped considerably, but sizeable minorities still opposed allowing gays to be members of the clergy and elementary school teachers (39 and 40 per cent respectively). The data indicate that even though Americans do not support discrimination against gays in principle, they are more supportive of discrimination when gays might hold positions that are associated with religious values or that largely involve working closely with young children.

Additionally, public opinion as it relates to homosexuality is argued to be important because it

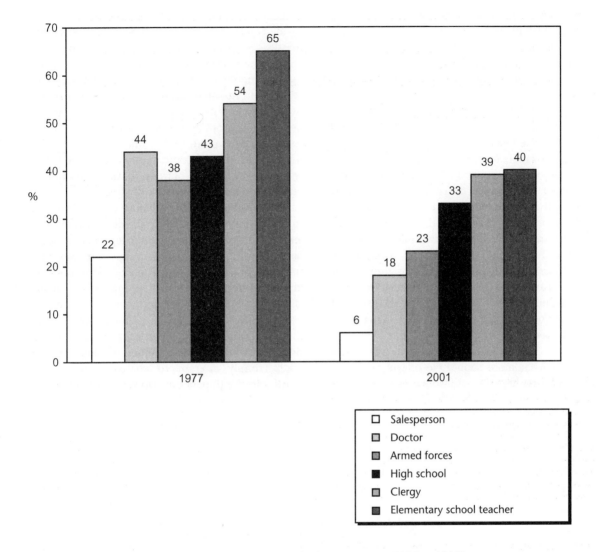

Fig. 23.4 Percentage opposition to gay employment rights by occupation, 1977 and 2001

Notes: Data compiled by the author from Gallup Poll (1977 and 2001) questions asked of adults in the US. Each occupation was listed following this question: 'Do you think homosexuals should or should not be hired for each of the following occupations?' Data values shown are the percentage of respondents indicating 'should not'.

shapes debate on the issue, and may influence the perceptions, opinions, and beliefs of elites, including interest group leaders and elected officials, who shape public policy. But can we assume first that elite opinions are similar to public opinion on these issues, and secondly that public opinion actually influences elite opinions and subsequent behaviour? We can briefly explore this issue by examining

published research. First, making use of unique data collected from surveys of state and local elected officials, Schroedel (1999) discovered that on average, state and local elected officials hold opinions on homosexuality similar to those of the public at large. However, those opinions are more strongly shaped by partisanship, ideology, gender, and religious affiliation than they are for the broader public. This finding suggests that some elites may be less tolerant and less compromising on issues involving homosexuality than the public at large. As such, state and local officials may find it difficult to resolve policy issues related to lesbians and gays.

A similar type of polarization on gay issues between traditional and progressive beliefs can be viewed in the behaviour of members of Congress. This polarization occurs over partisan (Republican and Democrat) lines and is more dramatic when compared to partisan differences on gay issues among the public. Lindamen and Haider-Markel (2002) compared the preferences of partisans in Congress to partisans in the mass public from 1970 to 1999. By averaging the gay-related voting records of Democrats and Republicans in Congress for each year, and averaging the responses of mass Democrats and Republicans to gay-related questions on the General Social Survey Lindamen and Haider-Markel (2002) were able to develop the data shown in Fig. 23.5. The data demonstrate that mass Democrats are somewhat more supportive of gay civil rights than are mass Republicans. More dramatically, con-

gressional Democrats and Republicans are highly divided on these issues, even though partisans in the masses show only small polarization. Further, both congressional Democrats and Republicans vote in a manner highly inconsistent with their partisan constituents in the mass public. Indeed, the researchers use statistical tests to show that there is no linkage between mass opinion and elite behaviour on gay issues (or vice versa). Such a finding is problematic for students of democratic theory, and suggests that winning the public opinion battle may not be enough for proponents of gay civil rights.

Finally, there are other equality issues of concern to gays and lesbians beyond discrimination in employment. Such issues include legal benefits similar to those provided by marriage, same-sex marriage, adoption rights, and equal access to housing, among others. As noted, opinions on policy issues related to gays are influenced by a variety of individual characteristics, including feelings towards homosexuality, partisanship, and education. Those who wish to influence public opinion might simply attempt to change these characteristics in the population. However, proponents of

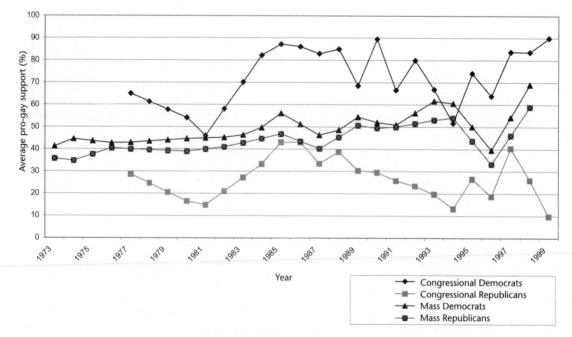

Fig. 23.5 Democratic and Republican pro-gay support: elite and mass opinion, 1973–99

Notes: Data compiled by the author based on Lindamen and Haider-Markel (2002).

gay rights argue that in order to educate the public about gays and lesbians, and subsequently change public opinion, gay individuals must publicly declare their homosexuality. This process, called 'coming out' or 'coming out of the closet', involves an individual telling friends, family, and co-workers his or her sexual orientation. Proponents believe that allowing more people to know gay people, and subsequently understand that gay people are largely like everyone else, will lead to a greater acceptance of homosexuality and support for gay civil rights. Multiple studies reveal this may be the case—the more gay people a person knows, the more supportive they are of homosexuality and gay civil rights and liberties. Figure 23.6 clearly demonstrates this phenomenon, with national survey data reproduced from Sherrill and Yang (2000).

As individuals know more gay people personally, they are more supportive of a series of gay-related policy issues, including same-sex marriage, which is most weakly supported by the general population. Thus, to shape both public and elite opinions on homosexuality, gay individuals must be public about their homosexuality, whether in the workplace, in a legislature, or at the dinner table. Almost by definition this process is precisely the notion of 'making the personal political' that American social movement activists have referred to since the 1960s. However, making one's personal life political, and thus threatening traditional family values and gender roles, is also what supporters of traditional values are so opposed to. These opposing and resolute positions shape the parameters of the policy debate in American political institutions, from city hall to the floor of the US Senate.

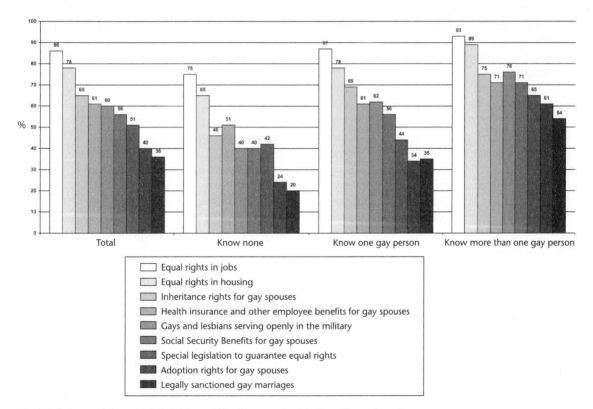

Fig. 23.6 Support for gay civil rights and liberties and familiarity with gay people

Notes: Data are compiled by the author based on survey results reported in Sherrill and Yang (2000). Survey was conducted of national adults in July 1998 by Princeton Survey Research Associates.

Key Points

- Although Americans still believe that sexual relations between persons of the same sex are generally wrong, tolerance of same-sex relations is increasing.

- Majorities of Americans believe that gays and lesbians should have equal rights, and support increases nearly every year.

- Although Americans oppose discrimination against gays in employment as a principle, survey data indicate that significant minorities approve of discrimination in certain professions, especially those that require contact with children.

- On average, political elites hold similar views to those of the public on homosexuality, but the views of elites are more strongly shaped by partisanship, which reflects the conflict between traditional and progressive values given the stances of the two main political parties.

- Opinions on gay civil rights and liberties are shaped by ideology, partisanship, religious affiliation, gender, and education level. Further, more familiarity with gay people leads to significant increases in support for gay civil rights and liberties.

Public policy

Although an understanding of public opinion on gay rights provides one with insight into the parameters of the political debate, an understanding of gay-related public policy helps to more fully illuminate the specific dynamics of gay politics in the United States. To start, gay-related policy has an intergovernmental dimension that cannot be ignored. Gay-related policies are debated in local, state, and national governments, and advocacy coalitions operating in this policy area are active in all of these venues. Indeed, a key strategy for advocacy coalitions and both sides of this issue is to pursue policies in the governmental venue they perceive to be most favourable to their views (Haider-Markel 2001). Furthermore, the traditional roles and authority of different levels of government in the US dictate the proper venue in which to raise an issue. For example, local and state governments have traditionally been responsible for regulating criminal behaviour. Therefore, laws that ban certain sexual acts have typically been adopted or reversed at the local or state level, with only cursory involvement by the federal government.

Second, a look at the policies affecting lesbians and gays will help us to understand the central issues involved in the debate, including the proper role of government and how public policy represents the government's codification of some values over others. Finally, our brief examination can demonstrate just how pervasive the debate over gay rights is in the US, and tell us something about what that debate will look like in coming years.

National level

Shortly after the modern gay movement began in 1969, many gay interest groups decided to focus their attention on the national government. This strategy was not surprising considering that it was the same strategy followed by other civil rights groups and because the tremendous growth in the federal government during the 1960s drew activists to Washington, DC. Gay rights groups have been successful in placing gay issues on the national political agenda, and have achieved some favourable policies through congressional action, executive orders, and bureaucratic rule-making (Campbell and Davidson 2000; Smith and Haider-Markel 2002). However, opponents of gay rights have also placed their issues on the national agenda and have been far more successful in the policy process.

Interestingly, gay issues reached the national political agenda based on arguments made by both

Box 23.2 Constitutional influences and issues

Proponents and opponents of gay civil rights and liberties often couch their arguments in terms of constitutional provisions. For example, proponents argue that all citizens are entitled to equal treatment under the Constitution and that Supreme Court decisions have made clear that the Constitution as a whole provides individuals with the right to privacy in their personal lives. Meanwhile, opponents argue that laws protecting gay civil rights are simultaneously unnecessary and unconstitutional. They argue that the Constitution already protects everyone's civil rights and liberties, so that no additional law-making is necessary. Further, they argue that specifically to protect homosexual behaviour in the law would violate the freedom of religion and separation of church and state clauses of the Constitution. To protect freedom of religion, they say, the government cannot regulate behaviour that is grounded in religious beliefs, such as rejecting homosexuality. And the separation of church and state clause would be violated if the government sanctioned homosexual behaviour by making it legal and protected when some religions state that homosexuality is a sin. Thus, by making homosexuality legal, the government is endorsing some religions over others.

Three of the most significant legal cases to address these issues came from US Supreme Court decisions in *Bowers* v. *Hardwick* (1986), *Romer* v. *Evans* (1996), and *Dale* v. *Boy Scouts of America* (2000). In *Bowers* v. *Hardwick* the Supreme Court rejected the right to privacy claims of a man convicted of illegal homosexual sex under Georgia's law banning homosexual sodomy. Deciding in *Dale* v. *Boy Scouts of America*, the Court ruled that the Boy Scouts of America could ban homosexuals from their organization in order to maintain the moral objectives of the organization. In these two cases, which have guided lower court decisions in a variety of gay-related issues, the Court upheld as constitutional discriminatory treatment of homosexuals and refused to accept the notion that privacy rights extend to homosexual behaviour. However, in *Romer* v. *Evans* the Court ruled that Amendment 2, a law passed by ballot initiative in Colorado that would have repealed existing gay civil rights laws and blocked the enactment of new laws, was unconstitutional because the law violated the equal protection rights of homosexuals. Specifically, the law would have unconstitutionally prevented homosexuals from using the political process to achieve policy goals. To some these three rulings are contradictory and leave unresolved the core constitutional issues related to gay civil rights and liberties.

opponents and proponents of gay rights. It began with concerns raised by the defence community over national security, and shifted to concerns raised by evangelical Christians over traditional values, lesbian and gay activists over equality and civil rights, and medical practitioners and civil libertarians, among others, over AIDS. Each of these groups defined homosexual issues differently. For example, during the 1950s members of the defence community tied the security threat posed by homosexual employees to the threat posed by communism (D'Emilio 1992: 68). Evangelicals framed their opposition to homosexuality in terms of declining moral standards and the rise of secular humanism (Vaid 1995). Starting in the 1960s, lesbian and gay activists argued that homosexuals were an oppressed group facing discrimination and the denial of their civil rights (Vaid 1995). In

the 1980s the AIDS epidemic brought new political actors into the debate over homosexuality, and these actors each brought medical and other perspectives into the debate.

In the 1950s members of Congress began the debate over homosexuality by linking homosexuality to communism. The Senate released a report on the security threat homosexuals posed to the federal government in December 1950 called *Employment of Homosexuals and Other Sex Perverts in Government*. This same issue was raised during the 1953 McCarthy hearings and appears to have led to President Eisenhower's Executive Order 10450 in 1953, which allowed federal employees to be dismissed for 'sexual perversion' (D'Emilio 1983). In 1954 Senator Wiley (R.WI) expanded the attack by sending a letter to the US postmaster demanding that a gay magazine be blocked from using the US mail because of its devotion to the 'advancement of sexual perversion' (Streitmatter 1995: 32). The postmaster complied until the Supreme Court overruled the decision in 1958 (Streitmatter 1995: 343).

The early lobbying efforts of a homosexual group, the Mattachine Society, so incensed Representative John Dowdy (D.TX) that he initiated hearings in 1963 on the issue and introduced a bill to revoke Mattachine's permit to raise funds. During congressional hearings, Mattachine representatives tried to frame homosexuality as a civil rights issue by discussing employment discrimination, but committee members used the hearing to speak against the immorality of homosexuality (D'Emilio 1983).

In the early 1970s gay activists increasingly attempted to present homosexuality in positive terms, by stressing discrimination and civil rights. These arguments convinced Representatives Bella Abzug (D.NY) and Edward Koch (D.NY) to introduce a bill to extend civil rights protections to gays and lesbians in 1974 (D'Emilio 1983). Presenting the issue as one of civil rights allowed gays to mobilize new actors, such as ethnic minorities and other traditional Democrats, for their cause. However, it was not until 1996 that a limited version of the 1974 bill reached a floor vote in either chamber (Campbell and Davidson 2000).

Starting in the late 1970s, religious conservatives around the country mobilized a backlash against gay civil rights. In Congress, Representative McDonald (D.GA) who was a chairman of the John Birch Society, a right-wing anti-communist group, introduced legislation to prevent a government legal agency from addressing cases that might promote gay rights and to block the District of Columbia from repealing its laws against homosexual sodomy.

The backlash against gay rights was assisted in the 1980s when religious conservatives argued that AIDS was a punishment from God for immoral behaviour. However, the AIDS epidemic brought renewed visibility to gay and lesbian issues, with Congress increasingly considering floor votes on AIDS and homosexuality. In fact, with the first congressional hearing on AIDS in 1982, AIDS became the focal point of most 1980s national activity regarding homosexuals. Gay lobbyists were successful securing funding for AIDS treatment and research by 1985,

but most 1980s AIDS legislation contained amendments prohibiting funds from being used to promote homosexuality (Vaid 1995). For example, in 1989 the Senate adopted, by voice vote, an amendment to AIDS funding legislation that prevented the distribution or production of materials for schoolchildren that would 'promote or encourage homosexuality, or use words stating that homosexuality is "normal", or "natural", or "healthy"' (Campbell and Davidson 2000).

During the 1990s gay lobbyists had more success in national policy, but as the decade progressed gay lobbyists also faced a number of demoralizing losses, including failing to remove the ban on gays in the military (see Box 23.3). Key victories included blocking an effort to overturn President Clinton's 1998 ban on sexual orientation discrimination for federal employees, pushing AIDS funding to record levels—exceeding $4 billion—, blocking Republican efforts to pass legislation prohibiting unmarried couples from jointly adopting children in the District of Columbia, and killing legislation that would have denied certain federal funds to localities with domestic partnership laws. Interestingly, this last piece of legislation was an attempt to block local governments from making their own choices on gay rights policy.

By 2001 the terms of the debate over gay rights at the national level had been cemented to reflect traditional and progressive values. Further, traditional values supporters had even reversed their arguments for local control on these issues, asserting that the national government should prevent local governments from supporting gay rights. In the debate over Washington, DC's domestic partner law, House Majority Whip Tom DeLay (R.TX) argued that opponents were not bigoted, but instead simply using their positions in the national government to uphold the tradition and sanctity of marriage. Rep. DeLay argued that allowing DC to go ahead with its domestic partners programme would 'radically undermine the special privileges and incentives of marriage by distributing them without requiring the unique commitment between a man and a woman' (Hsu 2001). Meanwhile openly gay Rep. Jim Kolbe (R.AZ) supported the local autonomy of DC, and argued: 'The fact is that traditional families have changed in our society. It is time to

---

Box 23.3 National policy highlights

Advocacy coalitions battling for and against gay rights have frequently turned to the national government to achieve their policy goals. Neither side always wins or always loses, but both sides can claim some victories. Highlights of these battles include:

- In 1998 President Clinton signed an executive order that prohibited civilian federal departments, agencies, and commissions from discriminating on the basis of sexual orientation.

- Between 1964 and 2001 Congress voted on nearly 300 bills and amendments addressing homosexuality and gay issues.

- In 1993 President Clinton established the first official liaison office for the gay community.

- In 1990 Congress passed the Hate Crime Statistics Act, which required the FBI to collect statistics on crimes motivated by sexual orientation bias.

- Conservatives have consistently attached language to

bills that prohibits positive discussions of homosexuality in everything from education programmes to agriculture training programmes.

- In 1990 President Bush signed the Americans with Disabilities Act, which protects persons with HIV/AIDS from discrimination.

- In 1993 conservatives were able to block President Clinton's attempt to allow gays to serve openly in the military.

- The Defense of Marriage Act became law in 1996. The law bans those in same-sex marriages from eligibility for federal benefits typically afforded to married couples.

- At the end of 2001 Congress passed a District of Columbia spending bill that allowed the city to spend funds for its domestic partner benefit programme for city employees. The programme had been banned from operating since 1992.

---

start bringing our country together. We should be uniting our country' (Hsu 2001).

Similar debate occurred over the amendment proposed by Senator Jessie Helms (R.NC) in 2001 to ban public schools from blocking Boy Scout troops from using public school space. Senator Helms argued that some schools were blocking access because the Boy Scouts refused to allow homosexuals in the organization. When reading his amendment into the *Congressional Record*, Senator Helms said:

For years, the Boy Scouts of America organization has been subjected to malicious assaults by some homosexuals and some liberal politicians simply because the Boy Scouts of America organization ... have steadfastly continued to uphold their moral and decent standards for scouting. . . . Mr. President, they never miss a beat, not one—those who demand that everybody else's principles must be laid aside in order to protect the rights of homosexual conduct, or they go on and on like Tennyson's Brook. These radical militants are up to the same old tactics when targeting an honorable and respectable organization, the Boy Scouts of America. . . . Only if they will accept homosexuals as their leaders and fellow scouts will these Boy Scouts be allowed to continue

their meetings on school property. But those very same meeting places at school remain open for more than 800 Gay–Straight Alliance clubs. These are homosexual school clubs that have been formed with the assistance of the Gay, Lesbian, and Straight Education Network, which is a radical group committed to promoting immoral lifestyles in the school systems of America. With groups such as these welcomed in our public schools, while the Boy Scouts are kicked out, schoolchildren need, it seems to me, to have the Boy Scouts stick around, and that is what I want to do with this legislation, if I can, and if the Senate will go along with it. . . . This arrogant discriminatory treatment of Boy Scouts of America must not be allowed to continue . . . (*Congressional Record*, US Senate, 14 May 2001)

Finally, research on congressional voting behaviour confirms the basic conflict between traditional and progressive values in national policy-making. Studies have shown that key predictors of legislators' votes on gay issues include partisan affiliation, personal ideology, religious affiliation, constituency preferences, and interest groups under certain circumstances. Legislators who are Republican, conservative, and affiliated with conservative religious denominations are more likely to vote against gay rights. Further, legislators whose constituents support gay rights and who receiving more campaign funds from gay groups than conservative religious interest groups are more likely to vote in favour of gay rights (Haider-Markel 1999).

State and local policy

Although most early local political efforts by gays were focused on police harassment, state and local governments now debate a multitude of gay-related issues, including anti-discrimination laws, hate crime laws covering sexual orientation, HIV/AIDS, homosexual sodomy, same-sex marriage, domestic partner benefits and official registries for domestic partners, adoption and foster care, and anti-gay harassment in schools. These issues are debated by legislatures, executives, school boards, bureaucrats in government agencies, and state courts. And although there clearly has been activity on gay issues at the national level, most of the policy-making activity has occurred at the state and local level (see Box 23.4 for highlights).

Indeed, state legislation concerning lesbian and gay issues began steadily increasing in the 1990s. In 1984 there were only six measures, five of which were anti-gay. By 1995 there were 129 gay-related bills or amendments in the states, seventy-eight pro-gay measures and fifty-one anti-gay measures. In 1996 the number rose to 274 pieces of gay-related legislation, 61 per cent of which were anti-gay. By 1997 almost every state considered at least one measure, and the amount of gay-related legislation reached 406, of which 52 per cent were anti-gay. The largest percentage of bills dealt with expanding hate crime laws and banning same-sex marriage. Democrats introduced 76 per cent of pro-gay measures and Republicans introduced 71 per cent of anti-gay measures (Jones 1997). By 1998 the number of gay-related bills dropped to 321, but for the first time a majority of measures were pro-gay rather than anti-gay. In 1999 there were at least 617 bills introduced, with the greatest number of bills addressing hate crime in reaction to the 1998 murder of a gay University of Wyoming student, Matthew Shepard.

Further, the pattern of politics on gay issues is

Box 23.4 **State and local public policy highlights**

The gay and lesbian civil rights movement has amassed a considerable list of public policy accomplishments at the state and local level. Although many of these successes can be attributed to key individuals and interest groups, successes in some states and localities but not in others also highlights the intergovernmental dimension of gay politics, as well as how traditional and progressive values and conflicts vary across the country. Highlights of the accomplishments include:

- Twelve states and the District of Columbia have passed laws to ban discrimination based on sexual orientation in public employment; another five states have similar laws through gubernatorial executive orders.

- More than 200 local governments ban at least one type of sexual orientation discrimination since 1972. Laws banning discrimination based on sexual orientation in private employment cover 38 per cent of the US population.

- Twenty-seven localities and three states ban discrimination based on gender identity.

- Court orders and legislation in eight states and eighty-three localities have provided some type of domestic partner benefits for public employees, such as health insurance.

- The state of California and forty-one localities have official registries to recognize domestic partners.

- In 2000 Vermont adopted the first civil unions law, providing legal recognition of same-sex partners and most of the legal benefits and obligations of marriage.

- Twenty-seven states have at least one type of law that records or punishes hate crimes motivated by bias towards perceived sexual orientation.

- Thirty-two states have nullified or repealed laws banning homosexual sex, typically called sodomy laws or laws banning 'crimes against nature'.

similar to the national debate, with key forces determining policy adoption or rejection including the preferences or tolerance of citizens, resources of gay interest groups, partisanship and party competition, conservative religious group mobilization, the preferences of political elites, and the presence of openly gay elected officials (Haider-Markel and Meier 1996; Button et al. 1997; Haider-Markel 2001). Haider-Markel (2001) illustrates the key role of religious conservatives and partisanship in policy-making on same-sex marriage bans in particular. He found that Republicans sponsored over 87 per cent

of the bills introduced and that conservative religious interest groups lobbied for 100 per cent of the bills. Additionally, in 81 per cent of the states there were public ties between same-sex marriage ban sponsors and conservative religious groups, and in at least 54 per cent of states conservative religious groups were directly involved in drafting the same-sex marriage bans. Religious conservatives have also clearly made use of the American federalist system by simultaneously pursing restrictions on same-sex marriage at the national, state, and even local level (Haider-Markel 2001).

The threat of direct democracy?

Even with dramatic changes in public opinion and public policy, gays and lesbians still tend to lose when their civil rights are decided in a majoritarian arena, such as ballot initiatives and referenda elections. Initiatives and referenda elections exist in twenty-four American states and hundreds of localities, and provide an additional policy-making venue for activists. The procedure allows citizens to place policy proposals directly on the ballot for a vote (initiative) once a requisite number of voter signatures have been collected, or to place a policy proposal on the ballot once it has been approved by a legislature (referendum).

Opponents of gay rights have made the most extensive use of direct democracy to achieve their political goal of protecting traditional values. Between 1972 and 2001 gay rights opponents have placed ninety-two anti-gay measures on state and local ballots (see Fig. 23.7). These measures have covered many topics, including bans on same-sex marriage, the repeal of existing and/or a ban on gay civil rights laws, the repeal of domestic partner benefits, and prohibiting 'positive' discussions of homosexuality in public schools. Of the ninety-two anti-gay measures, nearly 71 per cent have passed by popular vote. Although courts later overturned a number of these measures, and measures voted on since 1998 are more likely to fail, the election

results make it clear that the rights and liberties of lesbians and gays do not fare well when decided in a majoritarian venue.

Proponents of gay rights have used direct democracy to achieve policy goals far less frequently than opponents. Indeed, most gay activists have pursued their policy objectives in legislatures and courtrooms at the local and state level. However, between 1972 and 2001 gay activists put thirty-two pro-gay measures on local and state ballots, most of which would have banned discrimination based on sexual orientation. Nearly all of these efforts have failed, with 69 per cent being rejected by popular vote. This failure level is perhaps even more notable than the passage rate of anti-gay measures simply because courts have never overruled these popular vote decisions, and because gay activists have typically pursued direct democracy in states or localities where they believed they had popular support.

Key points

- Policy-making on gay-related issues occurs across all levels of government in the US, with activists on both sides trying to gain political advantage in more favourable venues.

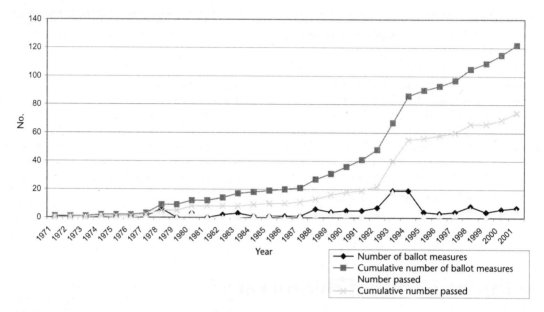

Fig. 23.7 State and local ballot initiatives addressing gay rights, 1972–2001

Notes: Data compiled by the author. Ballot measure counts include both pro-gay and anti-gay measures.

- At the national, state, and local level, the number and range of policy proposals has generally been on the increase since the 1980s.

- Gay activists do not fair well in majoritarian venues, such as the direct democracy process, where they lose two-thirds of the time.

- Gay-related policies are debated along partisan and ideological lines, with Republicans and religious conservatives typically opposing gay rights measures, and Democrats and liberals supporting these measures. However, interest groups and public preferences play a key role in determining government policy.

Conclusion

The political debate over homosexuality reveals several of the key elements of the American political system and its political culture—the nature of shared power among levels of government and the multiple access points this provides to the political process, the debate over the proper role of government, and the ongoing tensions between traditional beliefs and values and more progressive or liberal perspectives. Although only briefly outlined here, the politics of gay rights clearly illuminates many of these key issues.

The trends since 1990 further suggest that this debate is unlikely to disappear in the near future: groups and activists espousing traditional values continue to have a loud voice in American government, and gays and lesbians continue to expand their search for equality in every aspect of social and political life. Because the debate

Box 23.5 Is America different?
Rights and religion

The political debate over homosexuality and the rights of homosexuals is still relatively new in the US, and in most other countries of the world as well. And although the gay rights movement has made great strides in America since 1970, one must ask whether the politics of gay rights is different in America. On several points the answer seems to be yes. Even with the progress of the American gay rights movement, the US provides far fewer legal protections for homosexuals than many other industrialized nations. For example, approximately 48 per cent of the American population is protected from sexual orientation discrimination in public employment, but most European countries protect their entire population from discrimination in public as well as private employment, and in other areas, such as housing. Furthermore, the American political debate over homosexuality seems far more contentious than most other industrialized countries. Perhaps only Canada and Australia have as much pained public debate on the issue and have a formal organized opposition composed largely of conservative religious groups and political parties. And although Americans have increasingly grown more tolerant of homosexuals, the level of tolerance is still much lower than in most other industrialized nations. For example, the Netherlands provides civil marriage to homosexual couples, and Denmark and Norway adopted marriage-like institutions for same-sex couples in the 1990s.

So why is America different? Many explanations could be offered. However, there seem to be at least two key reasons. First, perhaps more than in some other countries, Americans tend to be nearly obsessed with concern over the rights of individuals and the proper role of government in protecting those rights. American political culture contains a significant strain of making the 'personal political'—that is, taking issues that have traditionally been isolated to the private sphere and making them public issues for debate, including the notion of a need for government action. And although most industrialized countries have experienced some development of what academics call post-materialist values, the development of these values in the US has led to decades of divisive debate (that some call a 'culture war') and government action at the national, state, and local level.

Second, compared to most other industrialized nations the US has significantly more religious activism in politics—from black church congregations marching for civil rights to evangelical Christians blocking abortion clinic entrances. This heavy reliance on religious values in political debate often means that issues will be discussed in moral terms. A moral discussion means that participation in the debate is easy for citizens—everyone has an opinion on morality—and that political actors will have a difficult time finding an acceptable compromise—morality is not something one can compromise on. Additionally, the design of the American system, which allows multitudes of political venues for citizen participation, means that any group who loses in one venue nearly always has another venue in which to raise the same issue, meaning that issues are rarely 'settled' as they are in countries with less accessible political institutions.

---

involves moral absolutes, compromise has been rare, and most policy change will likely be incremental. Similar to the issue of abortion, even seemingly definitive decisions made by governmental institutions will probably continue to be debated whenever one side perceives a political advantage.

However, increasing tolerance towards homosexuals and advances in medical science concerning the origins of sexual orientation make it likely that gays and lesbians will eventually achieve a significant level of equality in American society. Only on the issue of same-sex marriage does it seem likely that equality is many years away. And those who oppose gay rights may eventually be relegated to marginal debates on issues like affirmative action for gays. Regardless, the parameters of the debate are unlikely to change in the near future, with those defending traditional values believing that their core beliefs are under attack.

Box 23.6 Key concepts and definitions

AIDS (acquired immunodeficiency syndrome). A human biological disorder that severely inhibits the body's immune system. The syndrome is caused by the human immunodeficiency virus (HIV), which makes the body vulnerable to many diseases that a healthy immune system can typically cope with. The syndrome first began to be identified in the US in 1981 and has disproportionately affected the gay community, as well as racial and ethnic minorities, and intravenous drug-users.

Civil liberties. Constitutional protections protecting citizens from government.

Civil rights. Policies that protect individuals or groups from discrimination or arbitrary treatment by public or private organizations or persons.

Coming out. 'Coming out of the closet' involves an individual telling friends, family, and co-workers one's sexual orientation.

Federalism. A political system for organizing a country so that two or more levels of government have formal authority over the same citizens and land; multiple governments share power.

Gay. A male whose primary sexual and emotional attractions are toward other males. Also a general term for all persons whose primary or secondary sexual and emotional attractions are toward others of the same sex.

Gay rights. Policies that protect homosexuals from discrimination by public or private organizations or persons by ensuring equal treatment.

HIV. Human immunodeficiency virus that causes AIDS (see AIDS).

Homosexual. A person whose primary sexual and emotional attractions are toward persons of the same sex.

Lesbian. A female whose primary sexual and emotional attractions are toward other females.

Public opinion. The aggregation of the views of the mass populace, typically through random sample survey techniques.

Public policy. Any action (or inaction) by government to address a perceived public problem.

Transgender(ed). A general term describing persons who try to make their appearance and behaviour reflect those of a gender different from their own. The term can encompass transsexuals and transvestites, and transgendered persons can be heterosexual or homosexual.

Transsexual. Those persons who believe their sex at birth does not reflect their gender identity and who subsequently attempt to alter their physical appearance to reflect their 'correct' gender through the use of drugs as well as sexual reassignment surgery.

QUESTIONS

1 Are the politics of lesbian and gay civil rights unique in American society, or do they share characteristics with other societies, issues, or social movements?

2 How does American federalism, or the shared powers of different levels of government, influence lesbian and gay politics and public policy?

3 What accounts for the rise in public support for lesbian and gay civil rights?

4 Compare public policy related to gays in America and another country. How do they differ and what accounts for this difference?

5 Why do holders of traditional religious values take such offence at an individual's public declaration that he or she is gay?

6 Some conservatives argue that government should have nothing to do or say about private consensual sexual relations while others argue that the government should regulate certain kinds of sexual relations and activity. How can self-described conservatives hold such disparate viewpoints?

7 If one were to model the adoption of gay civil rights policy, what explanatory variables would need to be considered? Which could be ignored?

FURTHER READING

R. W. Bailey (1999), *Gay Politics, Urban Politics: Identity and Economics in an Urban Setting* (New York: Columbia University Press). An excellent examination of gay politics in urban areas, including elections, party politics, and interest group politics.

J. W. Button, B. A. Rienzo, and K. D. Wald (1997), *Private Lives, Public Conflicts: Battles Over Gay Rights in American Communities* (Washington, DC: CQ Press). The first of its kind, an empirically driven textbook of gay politics and policy at the local level.

M. Hertzog (1996), *The Lavender Vote: Lesbians, Gay Men, and Bisexuals in American Electoral Politics* (New York: New York University Press). A unique study that uses exit polls for national and state elections in 1990 and 1992 to analyse the voting profile of people who identify themselves as lesbians, gay men, or bisexual.

D. M. Rayside (1998), *On the Fringe: Gays and Lesbians in Politics* (Ithaca, NY: Cornell University Press). A detailed comparative analysis of gay and lesbian politics in the US, Canada, and England.

D. B. Riggle and B. L. Tadlock (eds.) (1999), *Gays and Lesbians in the Democratic Process* (New York: Columbia University Press). Examines gay politics in the arenas of public opinion and policy-making.

C. A. Rimmerman, K. D. Wald, and C. Wilcox (eds.) (2000), *The Politics of Gay Rights* (Chicago: University of Chicago Press). Examines gay politics, public opinion, and policy-making at all levels of government.

R. A. Smith and D. P. Haider-Markel (2002), *Gay and Lesbian Americans and Political Participation* (Denver: ABC-CLIO). Reference book examining gay political participation from voting behaviour to interest groups to symbolic representation in government.

WEB LINKS

National organizations

www.afa.net American Family Association

www.cc.org Christian Coalition

www.glad.org Gay & Lesbian Advocates & Defenders

www.victoryfund.org Gay and Lesbian Victory Fund

www.hrc.org Human Rights Campaign

www.lambdalegal.org/cgi-bin/pages Lambda Legal Defense and Education Fund

www.lcr.org/index.asp Log Cabin Republicans

www.ngltf.org National Gay and Lesbian Task Force

www.stonewalldemocrats.org/main.html National Stonewall Democrats

www.pflag.org Parents, Families and Friends of Lesbians and Gays

www.traditionalvalues.org Traditional Values Coalition

State organizations

www.calcape.org California Alliance for Pride and Equality

www.georgiaequality.org Georgia Equality Project

www.ifhr.org Equality Illinois

www.justiceinc.org Indiana: Justice, Inc.

www.kentuckyfairness.org Kentucky Fairness Alliance

www.freestatejustice.org Maryland: Free State Justice Campaign

www.tri.org Michigan: Triangle Foundation

www.prideagenda.org New York: Empire State Pride Agenda

www.equalitync.org Equality North Carolina

members.aol.com/RIAlliance Rhode Island Alliance for Lesbian and Gay Civil Rights

www.lgrl.org Lesbian Gay Rights Lobby of Texas

www.visi.net/vj Virginians for Justice

General information, media, and resources websites

www.advocate.com The Advocate

www.planetout.com/pno PlanetOut: NewsPlanet

www.gaysource.com/index.html The Source

www.qrd.org/qrd Queer Resources Directory

www.washblade.com The Washington Blade

24 Race and multiculturalism

Eric Kaufmann

READER'S GUIDE

In this chapter, we will consider how relations between America's ethnic groups have changed over time, and what this means in terms of elections, institutions, and public policy. Next, our focus will come to rest on multiculturalism—a major policy response to ethnic diversity which has proved extremely controversial. Furthermore, we will try to gauge the impact of these dynamics on American national identity. Finally, we will look at the traditionalist backlash against multiculturalism. The chapter is divided into two sections. The first treats pre-1960s developments. The second investigates issues and policies arising from that critical decade, and concludes with a look into the future of multiculturalism and ethnic relations in America.

Introduction

Few aspects of American politics remain untouched by ethnic—including race—relations. Part Four of this book has already considered a number of issues that pit traditionalists against liberal Americans in symbolic conflicts known as 'culture wars'. Gun control, abortion, religion, and the rights of women and gays all manifest this tendency. Moreover, these rifts have implications for American institutions. Often, traditionalists claim to espouse the 'will of the silent majority', and hence seek to legitimize themselves through populist democracy. On the other hand, liberals—including white progressives and their ethnic allies—have often been in the minority on cultural issues. In addition, they have tended to wield little power outside the nation's larger cities. Thus they have relied for legitimacy on the American Constitution, and have often sought entry points into the American polity that circumvent the majoritarian and territorial power centres of Congress. The judiciary, bureaucracy, print media, and political action committees thereby loom large in liberal (and ethnic minority) attempts to guard against what they perceive to be the 'tyranny' of the majority.

These fault-lines run sharply through American ethnic and race relations, as well as through the related attempt to weave these groups together into one nationality. This has its origin in the history of settlement in the United States. For example, white Protestants and African Americans (blacks) account for most of the rural and small-town population while 'newer' immigrants from Catholic Europe and Asia form a significant proportion of the metropolitan population of the north-east and west coasts. Continuing demographic change—natural increase, internal and external migration flows—forms the background against which we will confront the history of American ethnic (including race) relations. To begin with, the chapter examines the pre-1960s history of relations between the principal American racial categories and their component ethnic groups. The pre-1960s era was largely a period in which white Protestants of British, Irish, and Dutch descent dominated the institutions of American government. They defined the nation's identity and boundaries and populated the upper echelons of the educational, military, and corporate worlds. However, such dominance was not without challenge from a vociferous group of pluralist liberals and their urban allies from marginalized ethnic groups. They coalesced around institutions like the Democratic Party, the Catholic Church, and the AFL-CIO labour union. When the veil of white Protestant domination lifted in the 1960s, some, nursing bitter memories, moved to lay the foundations of what came to be known as multiculturalism.

The 1960s were indeed a revolutionary decade, but Vietnam and Watergate were only the most immediate outward manifestations of more deep-seated changes occurring beneath the surface of American life. In terms of ethnic relations, a number of important Supreme Court decisions combined with key pieces of Johnson-era legislation to launch the nation across new cultural frontiers (or the wilderness, as the opponents of these changes would have it!). Just as the clout of the newly liberated ethnic minorities reached its peak, however, cracks appeared within the ranks of the left. This split ethnic minorities along racial lines, leading many white ethnic minorities (or 'ethnics') to become increasingly conservative. One of the principal irritants for white ethnics was the emerging policy of multiculturalism, with its emphasis on race-driven policy. Accordingly, we look next at what 'multiculturalism', a slippery term even among academics, actually means. Here we find that it is popularly used to refer to at least two distinct phenomena: (a) the *demographic fact* of having many cultures living in the same territory and (b) the *public policy* of using proactive programmes to raise the status, wealth, and power of members of targeted minority cultures (usually based on gender or race).

In this chapter, we will focus on *ethnic* cultures, rather than those of gender, sexual orientation, or disability. This is because most of the fundamental conflicts surrounding multiculturalism are concerned with ethnic cultures. Furthermore, we are most interested in multiculturalism as *public policy*, though we will certainly address issues of demography. In policy terms, multiculturalism affects the three major social realms of culture, polity, and economy. Multiculturalism as *cultural* policy involves issues as diverse as the language and content of education; university admissions policies; the proclamations of leading politicians about national identity; immigration, census-taking, and naturalization practices; and legal/constitutional decisions about non-Western cultural rituals. Multiculturalism as *political* policy is implicated in debates about congressional redistricting; selection of party leaders, committee chairs, and candidates; minority representation on the courts, executives, and cabinets of the various levels of government; and minority access to (or, for opponents, 'capture' of) various parts of the federal bureaucracy. Finally, multiculturalism as *economic* policy (known as Affirmative Action) is extremely controversial, with the chief battles taking place over preferential hiring, federal and state contract compliance, and diversity training.

The reaction against multiculturalism from both traditionalists and classical or 'neo'-liberals has grown steadily since the 1980s, so we will change tack to trace their arguments and actions over the past quarter-century. We find that the 'backlash' against multiculturalism originates largely, but not entirely, from white America. Here we highlight the role played by grass-roots organizations like US

English and the Federation for American Immigration Reform. We also chart the opposition from sections of the influential (and largely Catholic or Jewish) East Coast intelligentsia. Finally, we note the stalemate between multiculturalists and their opponents, as reflected in the policies of the Clinton and Bush administrations. In conclusion, we take a look at the recent past and future of American ethnic relations, and what this says about the trajectory of American national identity for the twenty-first century.

Ethnic relations and politics before 1965

The American population at independence in 1776 was about 20 per cent black—most of whom were slaves. The rest of the population was largely white and relatively homogeneous: 60 per cent were English, 80 per cent British and 98 per cent Protestant. The small American population of just four million began to grow through large-scale immigration from the 1820s onward. This was the start of a human movement from Europe across the Atlantic that would total close to fifty million people. The inflow from the 1820s until the end of the Civil War in 1865 was almost entirely British, Irish, and German—the three largest European groups in the modern US.

Later, unlike Canada and Australia, immigration was more diverse—particularly in the period 1885–1925. This era saw a surge in immigration from Southern and Eastern Europe, which was primarily concentrated in the major cities. Immigration therefore led to a major divergence between the overwhelmingly WASP (white Anglo-Saxon Protestant) rural and small-town majority and the polyglot northern cities where Anglo-Protestants were a minority. These dynamics explain the ethnic politics of the 1885–1932 period, in which elite Protestant 'Progressives' and the rural Protestant masses joined together in a Republican coalition against the Democratic interests of the ethnically mixed cities and their southern allies.

The racial dimension of settlement

The original population of the United States was native Indian and Eskimo. However, the major push westward from the Northwest Ordinance of 1787 until Custer's Last Stand in 1876 completed the process by which the native population's influence was reduced to insignificance. Meanwhile, two other groups were annexed by the new United States of America in 1776: Hispanics, in the Spanish colonies of New Mexico and California, and French-speaking Acadians ('Cajuns') and Creoles in Louisiana. Of course, the most important non-immigrant group was the African-origin population, which made up 20 per cent of the total in 1776 and resided almost entirely in the rural South.

Ethnic politics, 1932–1964

The population pattern established from the 1840s, and especially after 1885, continued to explain white voting patterns into the late 1960s. In other words, the country's whites were divided into three groups: northern Protestants, who usually voted Republican; southerners—typically Democrats, and northern Catholics—also mostly Democrats; and blacks, who tended to back the Republicans, but began to defect to the Democrats due to FDR's support for public spending and fair employment practices. This alignment held relatively steady through Roosevelt's New Deal administration until the 1960s. It was also reflected in the Democratic Party leadership. For example, in 1960, the Democrat John F. Kennedy, the nation's first Catholic president, chose Lyndon Johnson, a southern Protestant, as his running mate. More importantly, Kennedy did not move to legislate for black civil rights in the South due to the power of the Democrats' large southern white contingent.

Key points

- For a century and a half after 1820, ethnic politics became highly significant. This often pits Catholic or Jewish immigrants in the north-eastern cities against rural Anglo-Protestants.

- Non-white ethnic groups were generally barred from playing a role in the political system until well into the twentieth century.

- In the first half of the twentieth century, African Americans tended to vote Republican for traditional reasons. Northern Protestants also supported the Republicans. White Catholics, Jews, and Southern Protestants backed the Democrats.

[handwritten annotation: Where to start – a stereotypical view of voting patterns before new deal]

Multiculturalism and national identity to 1965: *e pluribus unum?*

A nation's identity frequently involves a vision of how subgroups like ethnic minorities or different regions are connected to the nation as a whole. On American banknotes, for instance, one can find the Latin phrase *e pluribus unum*, 'from the many, one'. The American nation's identity was defined, for some two centuries, by northern white Protestants. This group generally saw the nation in two competing ways.

First, as a 'universal' civic nation which welcomed immigrants from every land and defined itself as a haven for those oppressed by political tyranny. This story has its origins in the flight of the Puritans from royalist tyranny in England in the 1620s. Second, as an ethnic nation which practised a more purified form of Protestantism, and was of more purely Anglo-Saxon ancestry than the Norman English in Britain. This second story later blended with a myth of the American as westward pioneer, which began to be immortalized in Cooper's *Leatherstocking Tales* in the 1820s. These views usually coexisted within the same individuals, leading to what the nineteenth-century writer Ralph Waldo Emerson called an attitude of 'double-consciousness'.

The origins of multiculturalism

By 1910, however, 'Liberal-Progressives' like John Dewey, Jane Addams, and Israel Zangwill had pioneered a new vision of a two-way melting pot which recognized the contributions of both natives and immigrants but sought to supersede both. Along with the old WASP assimilation and two-way melting pot came a third creed, Pluralism. Pluralism, the ancestor of multiculturalism, was first espoused in 1915 by an American Jew, Horace Kallen. Kallen believed that Dewey's project of a universal melting pot neglected the human instinct to bond with those of similar ancestry. In his words, 'men cannot change their grandfathers'. Kallen's ideas also appealed to romantic Anglo-Americans like Randolph Bourne, who popularized Kallen's ideas during 1916–17.

With time, Kallen's vision of America as a non-territorial federation of ethnic groups faded. In its place came a small 'p' pluralism which blended the ideas of Kallen and Dewey, becoming the mainstream ideology of American liberals until the 1960s. Symbolized in the thinking of Robert Park of the

University of Chicago, this theory agreed that ethnicity has value and that immigrants should not be forced to assimilate. However, the new pluralism rejected the idea that 'men cannot change their grandfathers': it felt that, so long as the immigrant was welcomed fully into the mainstream of American life, s/he would lose her/his ethnic attachments over three or four generations (Gleason 1992). The American ethnic historian John Higham refers to this approach as one of 'pluralistic assimilation', and stresses that it is fundamentally different from the multiculturalist theories of today.

Key points

- American national identity reflected the outlook of the dominant, northern WASP elite prior to the 1960s.

- American identity combined a civic focus on universal symbols like the flag and the Constitution with an ethnic focus on the story of westward Anglo-Protestant settlement.

- Immigrants were expected to assimilate to the WASP matrix of the English language and Protestant religion. This is known as Anglo-conformity.

- The Anglo-conformity model was challenged after 1905 by cosmopolitan liberals like John Dewey and Israel Zangwill—who coined the term 'melting pot'. They believed in a new American nation born of universal cross-fertilization.

- Multiculturalism has its origins in the Pluralist thought of Horace Kallen and Randolph Bourne during 1916–17. These writers wanted the United States to be a federation of ethnic groups.

Example of a change

The 1960s: a watershed decade

The decade of the 1960s proved extremely significant for all aspects of American cultural politics. The tumultuous changes in American gender, religious, and sexual relations form part of this story. Changes in ethnic relations constitute another dimension of this cultural-political earthquake. In terms of ethnic relations, three critical influences may be identified: the civil rights movement, immigration reform, and multiculturalism.

The civil rights movement

For years, black Americans and their white liberal allies had pressed the American government to live up to the promises of equality contained in the Fourteenth and Fifteenth Amendments of the Constitution. Nonetheless, this campaign came to little until the late 1940s. Even the federal government and military were segregated up to this time. However, a series of changes, notably fair employ-

ment practice laws, the landmark *Brown* v. *Board of Education* case, and African American public demonstrations helped to change this. This meant that states—especially in the South—would no longer be able to justify laws which enforced segregation along racial lines.

The public relations effect of the civil rights movement, broadcast on television and radio nationwide, helped to galvanize white public opinion behind the cause of racial equality. For instance, in a 1944 poll 52 per cent of whites endorsed the idea that 'white people should have the first chance at any kind of job'; by 1972, just 3 per cent did. Southern whites, however, formed a solid rump of opposition to civil rights in the 1960s. Furthermore, southern representatives were particularly effective due to their over-representation in Congress (especially as committee chairs). Recall that their influence formed part of the deal which allowed southern whites and northern Catholics to unite under the banner of the

Democrats. The power of the southern Democrats ('Dixiecrats') stayed the hand even of liberals like John F. Kennedy. Kennedy's assassination in 1963 shook up this crumbling alliance, and in 1964 the Democrat Lyndon Johnson passed the Civil Rights Act. This was followed by the Voting Rights Act of 1965. Together this legislation called for the enforcement of equal standards for African Americans in terms of voting, education, housing, public facilities, business, and other facets of public life.

Changing racial voting alignments

These symbolic steps, together with the increasing identification of liberal Democrats with the Civil Rights drive, helped to swing the black vote away from the Republican Party. In fact, between the 1950s and the 1970s the number of blacks who identified themselves as 'very liberal' in surveys rose from 25 per cent to over 60 per cent. The Democrats were also more willing than the free-enterprise Republicans to entertain new black social demands. These included greater social provision for deprived inner-city areas and support for the new affirmative action policies. This strategy proved so successful that in the past quarter century, roughly 85–90 per cent of African Americans have voted Democrat. Meanwhile, southern whites, feeling betrayed by Johnson, turned to the Republicans. The turning point was the 1964 election, in which Johnson defeated the right-wing Republican Barry Goldwater. Goldwater, seen as more sympathetic to southern values, lost badly in the election. However, the inroads he made among the southern white electorate marked the end of Democratic power in the once 'solid South'. Today, southern whites provide the Republicans' strongest group of supporters.

The 1960s also brought about shifts within other groups of voters. Younger, well-educated northern WASPs became more liberal, while northern white Catholics began to defect to the Republicans. This was partly caused by the influx of African Americans to the northern cities, where they competed for jobs and housing with the white Catholic working class. Furthermore, in the late 1960s and 1970s, Democratic policies unpopular among northern whites, like affirmative action and busing, hastened the change in political behaviour. Clearly, the northern Catholic/southern white backbone of the Democratic alignment of 1932–68 was starting to crack.

Key points

- The 1960s represents a watershed decade in American ethnic relations. Most of the key changes of the period originated in the 1940s and 1950s, but took off in the 1960s.

- The civil rights movement played a key part in this change. This mass movement united black ethnic leaders and white liberals in a battle to win political and civil rights for blacks in segregated southern states.

- The civil rights movement helped bring about an end to segregation in the South and to establish Fair Employment Practices commissions nationwide to enforce non-discrimination at federal and state levels.

- The success of the civil rights movement alienated many southern whites from the Democratic Party, but helped to win black support. After 1964, the Democrats lost their once predominant position in the South.

- When the civil rights movement moved to enforce integration in northern cities through affirmative action and busing, this alienated many traditional white Catholic Democrats, who began to switch to the Republicans.

Immigration reform

The second major 1960s policy change to affect American ethnic relations was a change in American immigration laws. By 1924 Asian immigration had been essentially stopped, while European immigration into the United States was based on a quota system designed to favour established groups like the British and Irish. In addition, immigration from Mexico, which began to increase during the Second World War, was controlled through mass deportations. Some of these, like Operation Wetback in the 1950s, led to the expulsion of over a million people. Yet attitudes were changing. Opinion polls showed that Americans were becoming more tolerant of increased immigration during 1945–65. After the Second World War, the ban on Asian immigration was lifted for foreign policy reasons—though the Asian quotas for China and Japan were restricted to several hundred people per year. More significant, therefore, were the tens of thousands of Hungarian and Cuban anti-communist refugees admitted outside their quotas in the late 1950s. Pressure from liberal Democrats like Harry Truman or John F. Kennedy helped to drive this change, but conservative northern Republicans and southern Democrats—many in key committee positions—allied to block changes that would have made American immigration policy 'colour-blind'.

The role of the Supreme Court

As in the case of civil rights, the Supreme Court played a key role in liberalizing policy. The conflict revolved around the disparity in population between districts. Thus congressional districts for state and federal legislatures remained relatively fixed, even as immigration and a domestic move to the cities changed the balance of population. In 1962, for example, Los Angeles County had 40 per cent of the population of the state but only one of the forty seats in the California Senate. At the federal level, one urban New York congressional district had a population of 800,000 while a rural one in the same state had just 91,000. This pattern gave great advantage to the white-Protestant dominated rural districts and helped a conservative coalition retain influence in a diversifying nation.

However, a series of Supreme Court cases during 1962 to 1964 altered this pattern. The newly liberal, activist Court ruled that congressional districts must contain roughly equal numbers of voters—with districts to be redrawn as the population changed its residence. The results were dramatic: the Democrats gained the electoral boost needed to see through their liberal policies in the 1960s. In addition, rural southern committee chairmen lost control to representatives from the more liberal urban north-east. The combination of reapportionment and the (related) rising influence of liberal Democrats from immigrant districts helped to usher in the Hart–Celler Act of 1965.[1] This law removed the old national origins quota system and replaced it with a colour-blind law that recognized only economic and humanitarian criteria.

The 'browning of America'

This change helped to unleash a wave of non-European immigration. For instance, just 25 per cent of immigrants in the 1950s were non-white. By the 1980s, however, 80 to 90 per cent of the inflow came from outside Europe. Together with a rising volume of illegal immigration from Mexico, and higher immigrant fertility rates, these movements transformed the composition of the American population. This demographic change has been nicknamed the 'browning of America'. Whereas the nation was 85 per cent non-Hispanic white in 1960, it remained just 69 per cent white in 2000. By 2050, whites will be a minority for the first time in the nation's history.

[1] For instance, the chairman of the House Judiciary Subcommittee on Immigration until 1963 was Francis Walter (R.PA), a defender of the National Origins scheme and co-sponsor of the restrictive McCarran–Walter Act of 1952. His replacement in 1964 by the reformist Michael Feighan (D.OH) smoothed the way for passage of Hart–Celler.

Immigration flows post-1965, as with the 1880–1925 stream, are highly concentrated by region. Immigrants today tend to move to metropolitan areas in the north-east, Florida, and California. In high-immigrant states, the rate of population change is dramatic. In California, for example, 85 per cent of the population was non-Hispanic white in 1960. Yet today, whites constitute a minority (47 per cent), and only a third of the under-5 population. Partly in response to the previous trends, native-born whites (and some blacks) have been moving out of high-immigration cities like New York and Los Angeles into more homogeneous interior ones like Denver, Las Vegas, and Atlanta. Many of these outmigrant whites, notably in the east, are Catholics and Jews who once voted Democratic. However, this has changed considerably. The recent influx of Hispanics and Asians has reinforced the trend of Catholic Republicanism which began in the 1950s. Indeed, New York Republicans like former Mayor Rudolph Giuliani and Governor George Pataki rely on the white Catholic vote.

The political loyalties of the new immigrants

The largest new immigrant category are Hispanics—now over 10 per cent of the national population (one in three in California)—and Asians. Yet one should be cautious before jumping to any firm conclusions about the allegiance of these voters. Racial categories like 'Hispanic' and 'Asian' have arguably less meaning than even the diverse 'white' label. In South Florida, to take a bellwether case, 'Hispanics' are divided into Cubans, Mexicans (or 'Chicanos'), and numerous Latin American groups like the Dominicans. Cubans tend to be middle-class and Republican. Mexicans and Dominicans tend to be working-class and vote Democratic. In California and Texas, the Hispanic population is mostly Mexican, working-class, and Democratic. Asians, on the other hand, are divided between the well-established, American-born Japanese, the well-to-do Chinese, Hindus, and (some) Arabs, and less well-off groups like the Filipinos and Vietnamese. Overall, Hispanics tend to vote Democratic (though less than blacks), Asians are slightly Democratic (though less than Hispanics), and whites are relatively Republican. Within these racial categories, though, it is important to bear in mind that differences of ethnic group, region, and class are very important.

Key points

- Like civil rights, immigration reform was a 1960s policy with great ramifications for American ethnic politics.

- The Supreme Court played a key role in immigration reform with its rulings that congressional districts must be reapportioned. This broke the power of a conservative coalition of Republicans and southern Democrats.

- The Hart–Celler Act of 1965 led to a dismantling of immigration policies which selected applicants on the basis of ethnicity. Together with wider global shifts, this has caused subsequent immigration to be overwhelmingly non-European.

- Immigration and differentials in ethnic birth-rates caused the white share of the American population to drop from 85 per cent in 1960 to 69 per cent in 2000. This share will fall below 50 per cent by 2050.

- The two main racial categories to gain from this 'browning of America' are Hispanics and Asians. However, both of these labels conceal significant ethnic diversity.

- Regional concentrations of Hispanics and Asians in California, New York, New Jersey, Texas, and Florida enhance their electoral power. Most Hispanics (apart from Cubans) vote Democratic, while Asian voters tend to float between the parties.

- Whites and some blacks have tended to leave high-immigration cities on the coasts for smaller interior cities in the West and South. Whites have also become more Republican in response to the new immigration.

Multiculturalism: the demographic reality of cultural diversity

Many ideas come to mind when Americans use the term 'multiculturalism'. This complexity finds an echo in Canada, Australia, and continental Europe. The first meaning of the word 'multiculturalism' refers to the *demographic fact* of many cultural groups occupying the same territory—in other words, cultural diversity. These groups need not be ethnic in nature, but could include cultures based on sexual orientation, gender, region, or lifestyle. On this definition, every inhabited space in the world is multicultural. However, it is true that certain spaces, like the five boroughs of New York or London, England (inside the M25), are more multicultural than others. Generally speaking, large migrant-attracting cities tend to be more multicultural than smaller centres. The great immigration waves of 1885–1925 and 1965–2000 can thereby be described as having increased the ethnic multiculturalism of the American nation. Likewise, the post-1960s differentiation of American society caused by sexual and gay liberation and the rise of popular subcultures has added another, trans-ethnic layer of multiculturalism.

Multiculturalism as public policy

In addition to describing the demographic fact of cultural diversity, multiculturalism is also used to describe a particular kind of public policy which is the subject of intense controversy.

Contemporary multiculturalism: cultural

We can distinguish three spheres of multicultural public policy: cultural, political, and economic. Multiculturalism policy often seeks to rectify cultural (or symbolic) inequities so as to improve the self-esteem of formerly stigmatized groups. Instruments of change can take the form of education policy; proclamations and speeches from leading politicians about national identity; immigration, census, and naturalization practices; and legal/constitutional

decisions about non-western cultural rituals. In terms of education policy, American legislators have attempted to rectify inequalities between black and white state schools by busing black pupils into white schools (and vice versa). In addition, the history and civics curricula have often been rewritten to portray deprived groups like African or Hispanic Americans in a more positive light and expand the amount of space devoted to their contributions to the nation. Frequently, this historical revision also involves a more negative and reduced treatment of established groups (i.e. Anglo-American), thereby generating majority-group animosity. Language is also an issue: in California, many Hispanic activists wish to see public schools teach their children a bilingual programme in both Spanish and English. Meanwhile, some African Americans have fought to replace standard English teaching with what they claim is the more authentic and expressive Black English Vernacular (BEV).

This process of revision began with Congress authorizing an ethnic heritage studies programme in 1972, but truly came into its own with the fully revised California and New York curricula of 1987. The early 1990s witnessed major battles in New York City over the introduction of a more radical curriculum which also sought to upgrade the contributions of gay and lesbian Americans. By the early 1990s, multiculturalism had made its mark on virtually every state in the Union. Proponents of multiculturalism claim that this effort has led to a more realistic portrait of the nation, while opponents counter that the new curriculum is as distorted in its way as the old. In actual fact, revision is very much a matter of degree. There clearly was a need to redress the short shrift given to, and poor portrayal of, Asians, native Americans, African Americans, and Hispanics in WASP-dominated school texts like David Muzzey's *American History*— read by half the nation's schoolchildren during 1911–61. On the other hand, some school districts in selected African American areas have endorsed a controversial Afrocentric curriculum. Though often moderate, in extreme cases Afrocentrism has advocated both anti-Semitism and falsehoods like the black origin of Egyptian and biblical civilizations. Other radical multiculturalists have dismissed European writers as 'dead white males' with little to say to non-whites and women.

In other spheres, multiculturalism finds expression in symbolic activities like official proclamations, when a president or governor might make mention of the nation's 'diversity' or rename a street after an important minority figure like Martin Luther King. Diversity has become a watchword even at induction ceremonies for new immigrants, and the census was reorganized in the 1980s to record the five main racial classifications of African, Hispanic, Asian, European, and Native American. Finally, there is disagreement over the degree to which American society shares common values which should condemn or prohibit certain cultural practices. Some of these involve less confrontational symbols, like the wearing of turbans by Sikh police officers or headscarves by Muslim schoolgirls. Others involve more serious issues: arranged marriage, the wearing of ceremonial weapons in public, female circumcision, animal sacrifice. Most multiculturalists would draw the line of tolerance at these practices— but some would not. Overall, multiculturalism policy stresses the significance of group rights for minorities owing to their deprived and marginal position within American society.

Contemporary multiculturalism: economic

While multiculturalism policy at the cultural level has led to heated debate in educational circles, economic multiculturalism—or affirmative action— has been an important battleground in many political campaigns. Affirmative action is a branch of multiculturalism policy that seeks to rectify economic inequalities based on race. It can take the form of preferential hiring and admissions policies, or government contract compliance. These are significant in the American context, because, while white ethnic groups perform at relatively similar levels, black and Hispanic Americans earn significantly less than whites. The situation for lower-echelon African American males is particularly difficult. On the one hand there has been a growth in

the black middle class, with the proportion of black households earning over $50,000 rising 46 per cent during 1970–90. University-educated black women even earn more than their white counterparts. On the other hand, black unemployment (already twice that of whites in 1960) is now closer to three times the white rate. Whereas blacks constituted a roughly representative share of the prison population in 1930 (20 per cent, as against 80 per cent for whites), they now account for half the prison population (as against just 40 per cent for whites). In fact, in many inner-city areas, a majority of young African Americans between 18 and 30 have had a criminal conviction. Together with a soaring rate of out-of-wedlock births, these trends point to a social crisis within the poorest third of the African American community.

How to rectify this situation? Since the early 1970s, one answer has been to guarantee blacks and other minorities a proportional share of desirable jobs, particularly in government. This is sometimes achieved through moral suasion rather than affirmative action, in the form of informal pressure to hire more minorities. At other times, however, public policy is brought to bear on the issue, and government departments and businesses are provided with minority hiring targets to meet. For example, a police department may be asked to increase the proportion of its staff that are non-white so that the department reflects the population composition of the region it polices. Universities may be ordered to admit minority students (even if underqualified in terms of grades) to meet diversity targets. And while private businesses cannot be forced to hire minorities, pressure may be brought to bear on private government contractors—those who wish to sell services to state or federal governments. This form of affirmative action is known as contract compliance, and affirmative action in this area is administered at the federal level by the Office of Federal Contract Compliance (OFCC). Sometimes, governments may also use minority set-asides which stipulate that a fixed proportion of contracts must be given to minority-owned businesses.

The rise of affirmative action is one of the more complex phenomena of our time. The term was first used in the 1930s in the context of taking affirmative action against racial discrimination, and its meaning remained unchanged until the mid-1960s. However, the civil rights coalition of white liberals and black leaders began to turn to a more proactive definition of affirmative action soon after the non-discrimination provisions of the Civil Rights and Voting Rights Acts were attained in 1965. They even garnered the support of prominent Democrats like Lyndon Johnson. As the 1960s progressed, the desperate state of poor northern blacks was expressed through a series of race riots in northern cities. In this atmosphere, the non-discrimination focus of federal agencies like the Equal Employment Opportunities Commission (EEOC) became committed to results-oriented policies. However, they were limited by the law and the non-discrimination remit of the Johnson administration. A plan by the city of Philadelphia to force construction contractors to hire a proportional share (30 per cent) of minorities was thus killed by the city controller, who feared that the plan violated federal contract law.

The true turning point occurred with the election of Republican Richard Nixon to the presidency in 1968. Though officially against multiculturalism, Nixon realized that if he revived the Philadelphia Plan, he could pit the white labour movement (which opposed quotas) against black affirmative action campaigners to split the Democrats. The result was a tactical manoeuvre that revived affirmative action and launched it at the federal level. After this 1969 legislative hurdle, progress was swift as the federal bureaucracy put the new law into effect. In 1970 the Department of Labor ordered all federal contractors to submit written affirmative action plans. A year later, the liberal Supreme Court Justice Warren endorsed lower court rulings stating that minority preferences did not violate the Civil Rights Act. Finally, in 1972, the EEOC's remit was broadened to include state governments and educational institutions.

The practice of affirmative action gradually became institutionalized as minority groups became established players within federal government departments concerned with affirmative action. Later, in the 1970s, the affirmative action agenda broadened to include women and non-black minorities. Some contend that affirmative action played a role in raising black average incomes, especially during 1965–75. Others argue that these increases would have occurred with or without the policy. Most agree, however, that the policy has helped well-educated blacks the most, but has had a limited effect on the fortunes of poor blacks. This does not mean that the policy failed, for it may well be the case that without it, the lot of both middle- and lower-class African Americans would be worse. However, all of this may be immaterial. Anti-affirmative action forces began to organize, and 1980 represented the high-water mark of success for affirmative action. From then on, as we will see, the policy either stalled or experienced setbacks.

Contemporary multiculturalism: political

A third pillar of multiculturalism policy is political multiculturalism. This refers to the drive to ensure minority representation in the institutions of government. Presidents, governors, and mayors; membership of cabinet, Congress, committees, the White House staff, and party executives; and representation on the Supreme and district courts are all areas of contestation. Most controversial is the attempt to increase minority representation through affirmative redistricting. Here the US is certainly more radical than other Western societies like Canada or Britain.

Much of the energy behind this policy was provided by the Supreme Court. Specifically, the *Thornburg* v. *Gingles* (1986) decision held that a minority group can claim a 'discriminatory effect' if 'its preferred candidates are usually defeated as a result of bloc voting by a white majority' (Canon et al. 1994: 24). In combination with 1982 amendments to the Voting Rights Act, these provisions provided for 'affirmative redistricting' to create districts whose make-up is as close to 65 per cent non-white as possible.

The new directives had an immediate impact in states where minority groups constitute a significant proportion of the population, but are too geographically dispersed to dominate a seat based on 'one person, one vote'. In many areas, black districts were mandated by the Justice Department. One district, known as 'I-85', connected two pockets of black voters at either end of a section of North Carolina interstate highway 85, running for a few hundred yards along either side of the road to avoid white majority areas in between. Though challenged by the Republicans, this district was deemed constitutional by the Supreme Court in 1992. Yet, as with affirmative action, the momentum behind this variant of multiculturalism has begun to encounter stiff resistance.

Key points

- There are two common meanings of the term 'multiculturalism'. One refers to the demographic fact of cultural diversity, the other to a particular public policy.

- The degree of demographic multiculturalism in the United States has increased dramatically due to immigration and post-1960s lifestyle differentiation. This is especially evident in the large coastal metropolitan areas.

- In terms of public policy, multiculturalism can take a cultural, economic, or political form. Cultural forms of multiculturalism include bilingual education, ethnic studies programmes, and a multicultural revision of history.

- Cultural forms of multiculturalism began in force in 1972, and gained ground with high school curriculum changes after 1987 which rapidly spread nationwide.

- Affirmative action developed quickly after 1970 due to the activism of some departments in the federal bureaucracy. The Supreme Court legitimated this with its key *Duke* v. *Griggs Power* (1971) ruling.

- Contract compliance, minority set-asides, and preferential hiring/admissions are the most common forms of this policy.

- Political varieties of multiculturalism policy try to ensure proportional minority representation in the institutions and leadership positions of government. One controversial form of this has been the policy of affirmative redistricting.

Multiculturalism in retreat, 1980–2001

The backlash against affirmative action

The 'bread and butter' realm of economics most frequently dominates American elections. Thus affirmative action (economic multiculturalism) was the first pillar of the policy to be exposed to the winds of majoritarian democracy. Public opinion polls from the 1970s to the 1990s were contradictory: they showed that a majority of both blacks and whites favoured programmes designed to help blacks succeed. On the other hand, a majority of both races also opposed the use of quotas. Furthermore, support for the idea of government assistance for blacks began to fall in the 1970s. Emboldened, opponents of affirmative action went on the offensive. The election of Ronald Reagan in 1980 marked the beginning of the majoritarian

comeback. Though the laws survived, Reagan's attorney-general, Edwin Meese, let enforcement of affirmative action lapse and curtailed the multicultural activism of the Department of Health, Welfare and Education. Black conservative and affirmative action opponent Clarence Thomas became head of the EEOC.

More importantly, the five Republican appointments to the Supreme Court of 1981–92 began to take their toll. Four of the five—Justices O' Connor, Scalia, Kennedy, and Thomas—oppose affirmative action. Together with Chief Justice Rehnquist, they formed an anti-affirmative action majority, and began to move against the policy. The landmark case in this regard is *City of Richmond* v. *Croson* (1989). Richmond, Virginia's plan for a 30 per cent minority set-aside was struck down because the Court determined that the city had provided insufficient evidence that discrimination persisted in the local construction industry. Citing a generalized 'systemic' discrimination in an industry was no longer considered adequate reason to use quotas. The Court further ruled that any policies of racial preference must be subject to 'strict scrutiny' by the Court. Few laws survive this high standard; thus the Court's decision heralded a cloudy future for affirmative action. The Republicans continued to chip away at affirmative action by successfully watering down the 1990 Civil Rights Act with a provision that discouraged the use of quotas. After 1992, President Clinton tried to hold the line on affirmative action by conceding to a 'mend it, don't end it' approach. Nevertheless, the direction of policy had been severely circumscribed by the Supreme Court.

The attack on the multicultural vision

Nathan Glazer, a long-standing foe of multiculturalism, recently suggested that, like it or not, 'we are all multiculturalists now'. Glazer was writing about the success of the multicultural curriculum and its seemingly irresistible energy in the New York City school system of the 1990s. However, the mainstream nature of his critiques also suggest that the arguments of those opposed to the policy had come of age. If one looks closely at the picture nationwide, it is evident that the juggernaut of multiculturalism has experienced important setbacks for almost two decades. In the the late 1980s and 1990s, for instance, cultural and political multiculturalism came under assault from several quarters. Intellectually, a chorus of anti-multiculturalist elite writers with liberal and/or Jewish backgrounds like Glazer, Allan Bloom, Arthur Schlesinger, and Seymour M. Lipset (to name just a few) began to inveigh against curriculum revision and racial preferences.

Political action at the grass-roots level also took off. Arguably the most important mass movement has been the campaign for Official English. Bilingual education had been given a strong push post-1970 by an increased foreign-born population and the determined action of the federal Department of Education. In reaction, during 1981–90, ten states in the South and Midwest adopted Official English by statute, a move that was engineered by conservative political elites.

Meanwhile, in 1983, a grass-roots organization, US English, sprang up to advance Official English measures in states with more liberal political elites. As a consequence, Official English measures were placed on the agenda of state legislatures outside the South and lower Midwest. During 1986–8 in Florida, Arizona, California, and Colorado, Official English laws were defeated in the state legislatures. However, all of these states have a popular initiative mechanism, which allows measures to be brought to a referendum as long as these are endorsed by the required number of signatories. Public opinion in these states favoured the idea of English Only, so the referendum process allowed the citizens of these states to force their legislatures to pass measures declaring English to be the state's official language. By the year 2001, twenty-six states adopted English as their official language and US English enrolled almost 1.2 million members.

Interestingly, many of the leading figures in the counterattack against multiculturalism are from ethnic minority backgrounds. US English president Mauro Mujica is a Hispanic immigrant from Chile and its founder, Senator Hayakawa, is of Japanese origin. Likewise, the head of the American Civil Rights Institute (ACRI), which opposes affirmative action in universities and the economy, Ward Connerly, is black. To some degree this is symbolic, allowing such organizations to maintain respectability. It is undoubtedly the case, though, that Official English is supported by a significant proportion of ethnic minorities. Proposition 63 (California's Official English bill)[2] vote, for example, showed 72 per cent of whites, 67 per cent of blacks, and 58 per cent of Asians in favour of the measure, though a majority of those identifying as 'liberal' were opposed. Similar trends appeared in Arizona.

Similarly, in 1997, California's bitterly contested Proposition 209 was passed with broad-based support (though strongest among whites and weakest among blacks). This measure compelled California to abandon racial preferences in hiring and university admission. The result in 1998–9 was that the proportion of Hispanic and black students in

---

[2] Proposition 63 has been followed by Proposition 227 (passed 2 June 1998), entitled 'English for the Children', which aims severely to curtail bilingual education.

the University of California system plummeted while white and Asian enrolments increased. Many California legislators, as well as the American Civil Liberties Union, the National Education Association, and other bodies fought to retain the state's affirmative action policies. More recently, a new pro-affirmative action movement, BAMN, has materialized to counteract the ACRI.

Despite their successes, US English and the ACRI have failed to attain similar victories at the federal level. Bob Dole, among others, came out strongly against multiculturalism and affirmative action in 1995. Though an Official English bill (Dole–Canady), backed by Newt Gingrich, passed 259–169 in the House, it later died in the Senate. A revamped 1998 bill was likewise defeated 238–182 in favour of a bipartisan amendment that would merely 'promote the teaching of English'.

Demographic multiculturalism under threat?

We have seen how multiculturalism policy is heavily contested, but is it the case that the demographic fact of multiculturalism has proceeded unopposed? To a degree, it is certainly true that no major section of the American political elite has elevated non-white immigration or the 'browning of America' into a high-ranking federal issue. This contrasts somewhat with the situation in Australia or in European countries like Norway, France, Switzerland, and Austria. Yet if one scratches beneath the surface to the popular level, it becomes evident that a reaction against changing demographics forms part of the backlash against multiculturalism. Opinion polls clearly demonstrate rising opposition to immigration since the late 1960s. A majority of Americans—between 60 and 80 per cent—now favour lower levels of immigration. African Americans (probably due to labour competition) are most in favour of reducing immigration, followed by whites, Asians, and Hispanics. The domestic migration patterns of white and black Americans—away from high-immigration areas—reflect this new mood.

The Federation for American Immigration Reform (FAIR), which has over 70,000 members, has provided a grass-roots focal point for immigration restriction since 1978. At the state level, a number of similar organizations also exist, and have scored important political successes. In California, for instance, grass-roots immigration restrictionist organizations won an important referendum victory when voters approved Proposition 187. This initiative, endorsed by Governor Pete Wilson and 59 per cent of state voters, sought to cut off public assistance to illegal immigrants, and was later declared unconstitutional by the state's district court. A majority of whites (64 per cent), African Americans (56 per cent), and Asians (57 per cent) backed the bill, but just one in three Hispanics voted in its favour. Even so, this demonstrates considerable cross-community support for this stringent measure.

At the federal level, immigration restriction has not proceeded very far, partly due to the Republicans' desire not to alienate Hispanic voters. This is especially important for the strategy of moderate Republicans like the Bush brothers. After 1996, their more liberal approach won out over the culturally conservative wing of the party represented by Bob Dole and Pat Buchanan. Recently, President George W. Bush has even made noises to Hispanic voters about reforming the Immigration and Naturalization Service so as to expedite the processing of Mexican Americans' naturalization claims. He has also pursued good relations with Mexico and given little succour to the immigration restrictionist lobby. With the Democrats unwilling to carry the issue forward either, an imminent reduction in the current immigration intake of one million per year looks unlikely.

Key points

- Many pillars of multiculturalism came under increasing attack after 1980. Affirmative action was the first aspect of this policy to encounter effective resistance from conservatives.

- The Reagan administration began to curtail the activities of federal bureaucrats on the affirmative action front after 1980, thus letting enforcement lapse. The Republicans also chose five new Supreme Court justices during 1980–92.

- The new Supreme Court began to rule against affirmative action in the landmark *Richmond* v.

Croson case in 1989. Racial preferences now had to satisfy the high standard of strict scrutiny by the Court, and could not use 'systemic' arguments.

- Cultural forms of multiculturalism also suffered a setback as half of American states adopted Official English laws from 1981 to 2001. In many states,

this occurred through popular initiatives spearheaded by groups like US English and ACRI.

- The backlash against multiculturalism appears to have reached a stalemate, with moderate Republicans and Democrats compromising on a mild, quota-free version of multiculturalism.

Conclusion

E Pluribus Unum. American national identity today continues the time-honoured struggle to forge unity out of a diversity of ethnic and other cultural groups. The struggle to integrate white and black, Catholic and Protestant, country and city, and capital and labour once defined the national conversation. Today, immigration and cultural fragmentation have added to the task. Hispanic and Asian 'new immigrants', more assertive African and Native American communities, as well as gays, women, and those with disabilities, are all pressing their claims for group rights. For some thinkers, this provides a golden opportunity to realize a new multicultural form of social organization. For others, growing diversity poses a threat to national unity that must be curtailed through an emphasis on assimilation to shared values. Some critics even advocate reducing immigration.

In this chapter we have traced the fractious history of relations between ethnic groups in America and the larger 'races' which encompass these. We saw that with the influx of Catholic Irish and Germans to the northern states, politics began to assume a more ethnic colouring. This intensified with the arrival of southern and eastern Europeans in large numbers around the turn of the last century. The pattern of a white Protestant countryside arrayed against the large, ethnically mixed cities of the north-east became important. Acts restricting the immigration of Chinese (1882), other 'Orientals' (1907), and southern/eastern Europeans (1924) highlighted the victory of the white Protestant forces.

Meanwhile, the political voice of black America began to be heard as millions of their number left

their agricultural quasi-serfdom in the Old South for the northern cities during 1925–65. Originally, these African Americans voted strongly Republican both for traditional reasons (Lincoln and his Republicans ended slavery) and because the Republicans tended to be more sympathetic than the Democrats to black civil rights. With the rise of the civil rights movement in the late 1940s and 1950s, however, it became clear that many leading white liberals were aligned with FDR's New Deal Democrats. The New Dealers were also more likely to pursue the public spending policies favoured by many blacks, thus a gradual shift in black voters' allegiances (toward the Democrats) took place.

The decade of the 1960s marks a watershed in the history of American ethnic relations. The civil rights movement hit its zenith during this decade, crowned by Martin Luther King's march on Washington of 1963 and the passage of the Civil Rights and Voting Rights Acts of 1964 and 1965. Following closely on from this emancipation was the rise to prominence of white ethnics. Kennedy became the first non-WASP president in 1960, and in 1965 the restrictive 'national origins' quota immigration laws were repealed. The multicultural movement, which called for a revision of the American story (as told in its classrooms and on its political podiums), gathered steam toward the end of the decade. So too did the 'affirmative action' crusade for racial and gender preferences in university admission, hiring, and government contract allocations. In addition, the Supreme Court began to play a more active, liberal role, with a series of landmark decisions which favoured desegregation

(1954), reapportionment (1962–4), and affirmative action (1971).

The political fallout from this critical, liberal decade was considerable. To begin with, the multiculturalism movement gained significantly. Multiculturalism has two principal thrusts. The first concerns the demographic fact of having many cultural groups living in the same territory. The second meaning of multiculturalism relates to public policy. Taking demographic multiculturalism first, the rapid rise in non-European immigration after the reforms of 1965—which has reduced the white population from 85 per cent to barely two-thirds of the total population in forty years—is highly significant. Whites are now a minority in California and will be a minority in the US by 2050. Hispanics have been the principal demographic gainers, and their regional concentration in California, Florida, Texas, New York, and New Jersey has rendered them an important political force. African Americans have drawn closer to the Democrats (80–90 per cent of this group have voted for the party since the 1970s), while many northern Catholics and southern whites defected to the Republicans post-1968. Hispanics, apart from the Cubans in Florida, tend to vote Democratic—though less decisively than blacks. Asians tend to split their votes between the two main parties.

Public policies of multiculturalism may act either in the economy (i.e. affirmative action on jobs, admissions, and housing), in politics (i.e. minority representation in Congress and in positions of influence), or in the culture (i.e. bilingual education or a multicultural curriculum). Multiculturalism as public policy surged ahead on all fronts from the late 1960s. In the economic sphere, affirmative action policies—spearheaded by an activist bureaucracy and legitimated by the courts—became institutionalized after 1970. Politically, the representation of blacks in Congress was accelerated in the 1980s by the use of affirmative redistricting and through pressures to include minorities in positions of influence. In cultural terms, the revision of school and university history, literature, and civics curricula proceeded apace, especially after 1987. This became especially controversial with the introduction of an Afrocentric curriculum in several New York school districts in the same year.

From 1980, however, the advance of multiculturalism policy began to be rolled back. Here, Republican control of the presidency from 1980 to 1992, in combination with its appointment of five Supreme Court justices, was vital. The enforcement of affirmative action was emasculated under Reagan, and in 1989 the Supreme Court raised the standards required to justify any racial preferences policy. Rumblings of discontent also began to resound from high-profile writers and academics, who took aim at what they perceived to be the illiberalism of multicultural education. The Official English movement gathered force as well, drawing the support of over a million Americans and driving through Official English statutes in over half the nation's states.

The battle over multiculturalism seems to have been fought to a stalemate as we enter the twenty-first century. Pluralistic assimilation, in a form Robert Park might recognize, appears to be the compromise for post-civil rights America. On the one hand, more radical demands of multiculturalism in terms of curriculum revision and affirmative action are unlikely to be realized. On the other, there is no returning to the 1950s. The national education curriculum will probably remain sensitive to its portrayal of minorities. Similarly, employers and state governors are aware of the need to increase minority participation in education, housing, and employment. This status quo highlights the balance between traditionalist and liberal forces that in many ways cuts across lines of race or ethnicity. This equilibrium is mirrored in the country's institutions: the Supreme Court and the Republican Party are relatively hostile to multiculturalism. The Democrats, sections of the federal bureaucracy, and some important political action committees favour it. Meanwhile, leaders of both parties have tended to moderate their demands.

Finally, the current situation reflects a post-1960s sea change in America's self-identity. Many now recognize that the US can no longer define itself as a white nation, but must embrace the stories and vantage points of once-marginalized groups. They understand that racial minorities are a significant and growing force in the political process. However, according to a recent multi-partisan workshop and report entitled *Becoming American/America Becoming*, the upsurge of diversity makes it all the more urgent to find points of unity and common understanding. The events surrounding 11 September seemed to provide some teeth to this abstract plea, rallying the nation behind polyglot New York and the American 'civilizing' mission. It remains to be seen whether this represents but a pause in the post-1960s fragmentation of the nation or whether it will restore a sense of unity not felt since the height of the cold war.

QUESTIONS

1 How have ethnic voting alignments changed over time, and why?

2 Why has immigration become an important issue?

3 What does multiculturalism refer to in the American context?

4 Provide some examples of struggles over cultural representation? How and why did these develop?

5 What is affirmative action? Do you support the policy?

6 Do the ends of attacking discrimination and inequality justify the means of racial preferences?

FURTHER READING

N. Glazer (1997), *We Are All Multiculturalists Now* (Cambridge, Mass.: Harvard University Press). A well-written, oft-quoted work which provides a useful history of the multicultural movement from a moderately 'anti' perspective.

D. T. Goldberg (1998), *Multiculturalism: A Critical Reader* (Oxford: Blackwell). A useful edited reader, whose writers advocate a more left-liberal approach than Glazer. See Part I in particular.

A. Hacker (1995), *Two Nations: Black and White, Separate, Hostile, Unequal* (New York: Ballantyne). Another landmark work which provides a detailed statistical picture of the socioeconomic differences between black and white America.

D. Jacobson (ed.) (1998), *The Immigration Reader: America in a Multidisciplinary Perspective* (Malden, Mass.: Blackwell). Provides a useful overview of the immigration debate. See especially chaps. 3–5 and 16–19.

D. King (2000), *Making Americans: Immigration, Race and the Origins of the Diverse Democracy* (Cambridge, Mass: Harvard University Press). Traces current debates over national identity and multiculturalism back to the battles against racism and immigration restriction which took place in the 1900–24 period.

J. F. Perea (ed.) (1997), *Immigrants Out: The New Nativism and the Anti-Immigrant Impulse in the United States* (New York: New York University Press). A useful collection of writings on the current immigration restriction and Official English movements.

A. M. Schlesinger, Jr. ([1991] 1993), *The Disuniting of America* (New York: Norton). A short, sharp, and insightful critique of the multiculturalism project by this famous Kennedy liberal and 'consensus' historian.

WEB LINKS

US Department of the Census, Population and Housing tables

www.census.gov/population/www/cen2000/tablist.html Provides information on the American population's ethnic and racial characteristics, by nation, state, and region.

US English

www.us-english.org Detailed site of the leading campaigner for making English the official language at federal and state level.

Federation for American Immigration Reform

www.fairus.org The principal organization of the drive to reduce American immigration levels. This comprehensive address also contains numerous links to historical, statistical, and opinion survey data.

American Civil Rights Institute

www.acri.org Important, California-based organization opposed to affirmative action, whether as racial or gender preferences. Headed by University of California regent Ward Connerly.

BAMN (Coalition to Defend Affirmative Action and Integration and to Fight for Equality by Any Means Necessary)

www.bamn.com A recent, impressive forum for those campaigning in favour of affirmative action, especially in California.

National Education Association (NEA), bilingualism issues

www.nea.org/issues/bilingual One of the forces behind multiculturalism in education, the NEA's site also provides some important discussion of the issues surrounding bilingual education.

Multicultural Pavilion

curry.edschool.virginia.edu/go/multicultural One of the leading pro-multiculturalism websites. Contains a wealth of information on American multiculturalism, notably in the sphere of education and culture.

American power before and after 11 September

Michael Cox

READER'S GUIDE

One of the more interesting consequences of the war against international terrorism is the discovery by many analysts of American power. However, if the experts had been more attentive they might have noticed that a power shift in favour of the United States is not just some recent phenomenon arising from US victory over the Taleban or the new Bush military build-up. Rather, it can and should be traced back to important trends going back to the early 1990s. What the war has done is to reveal the extent of the American renaissance in the post-cold war decade while consolidating America's position as hegemon. However, victory in war may not bring order in peace if the United States does not draw the correct lessons.

Introduction

On September 11, 2001, the post-Cold War security bubble finally burst. (Ashton B. Carter)[1]

11 September will go down as one of the more famous dates that have regularly punctuated the history of the modern world, a worthy rival in the minds of some to that other act of infamy when imperial Japan launched its own kind of surprise attack against the US Pacific fleet lying at anchor in Pearl Harbor. In fact, so famous (or infamous) has 11 September already become that it does not even have to be referred to in full, but simply by the shorthand use of two numbers—9/11. Certainly, no other event in the last decade has so dominated the headlines; and over time, no doubt,

[1] Quoted in 'The architecture of government in the face of terrorism', *International Security*, 26(3) (2001/2), p. 5.

the destruction of the Twin Towers and part of the Pentagon will inspire its own extensive academic literature. Indeed, it is already doing so, with the appearance of several books and the marketing of work (a good deal of which might have otherwise lay unread) devoted to dissecting the motives of the distinctly unappealing band of terrorists who instigated the massacre, the unfortunate country from which the attack was presumably planned, and the role of Islam in international politics. If nothing else, 11 September has proved to be a boon to the publishing world, making the previously intellectually unfashionable subject of international terrorism fashionable for the first time (and the dominant paradigm of the 1990s—globalization—distinctly unfashionable) while rendering the study of weapons and military budgets, large-scale wars, and soldiers academically exciting once again. As one conservative American recently observed, the tragedy visited upon the United States has had at least two beneficial effects upon intellectual discourse in the West: it has made us all more sensitive to real regions in real time and real space (regional studies are now back in vogue) and it has illuminated with stunning clarity the essential truth of realism: that we live in an international system where the conflict between the haves and have-nots, the ins and the outs, the settled and the dissatisfied powers, continues unabated.[2]

Not surprisingly, much ink has already been spilt trying to make historical sense of what happened on that bright, and most photographed, of autumn mornings. Out of the mass of words and the deluge of speculation, much of it best forgotten, a consensus of sorts appears to be emerging: simply put, that the world before 9/11 and the world after are very different places—almost different worlds altogether. A great and important corner has thus been turned, or so it has been suggested. Hence, in the same way that we talk of a post-war world (delineating the period after 1945) and a post-cold war era (the years following the collapse of the Berlin Wall), it is now reasonable to speak of a post-11 September world in which nothing will ever quite be the same again. However, it is not just the world which has changed; so too, according to the common wisdom, has the United States of America, and with it the contours of US foreign policy. As a well-known

scholar of American international affairs has forcefully argued, the terrorist attacks that 'destroyed the World Trade Center and damaged the Pentagon' were not just dramatic, but redefining moments that 'triggered the most rapid and dramatic change in the history of US foreign policy'. Nor should we assume that this will only last for a short space of time. As many now seem to believe, because of what occurred, the broad agenda of US foreign policy has changed for ever. The post-cold war era has finally come to an end: suddenly, tragically, and for good.[3]

Whether or not 11 September turns out to be as significant over the longer term for the United States as Pearl Harbor, the beginning of the cold war, or the collapse of the USSR remains to be seen. As one of the more cautious voices in the current debate has pointed out, we should beware of scholars bearing false analogies and dramatic tales of a new dawn.[4] What should not be in doubt, however, is the huge impact of recent events upon the ways in which many people now view the United States in general and American power in particular. 9/11 certainly proved something which many of us had always known: that like other countries around the world, the United States was deeply vulnerable. But it also pointed to something else too: that whatever its vulnerabilities the US had an enormous capacity to mobilize its vast assets when called upon to do so. In other words, it remained extraordinarily powerful. In fact, whereas before the war the overwhelming view was that the US was a confused and crippled giant led by an inexperienced president, today even the country's most rabid enemies appear to hold the last remaining superpower in some esteem. The political response that followed 11 September, the unexpected and speedy defeat of the Taleban, and the fact that this was achieved with minimal support from allies (the US did '98 per cent of the fighting, the British 2 per cent and the Japanese steamed "round Mauritius", opined one wit)—all this taken together has convinced even the most hardened of sceptics that America is not only a

[2] A. Garfinkle, 'September 11: before and after', *Foreign Policy Research Institute*, 9(8).

[3] S. M. Walt, 'Beyond Bin Laden: reshaping US foreign policy', *International Security*, 26(3) (2001/2), pp. 56–78.

[4] See C. Brown, 'The "Fall of the Towers" and international order', *International Relations*, 16(2) (2002).

country to be reckoned with now, but a power without peer or precedent. Moreover, there seems little likelihood of this changing in the foreseeable future. As one rather breathless report written by two very impressed British journalists suggested, America in 2002 was not so much a 'superpower as a behemoth on the planetary stage'.[5] Even that old theorist of US decline was forced to recant. Having spent a good deal of his intellectual energies in the late 1980s and 1990s defending the thesis that the United States was bound to go the way of other great powers—that is downwards—Paul Kennedy finally had to accept that this was one prediction of his that had turned out to be quite wrong. Indeed, the larger lesson to be drawn from what happened after 11 September, and one that was just as worrying to the Russians as it was to America's European allies, was that in nearly every single area there was 'only one player on the field' that now counted, and that was the United States. In a world of asymmetrical wars, Kennedy concluded, the most important asymmetry of all was not simply that which existed between the materially advanced West and its poorly endowed enemies, but the one between the US and the rest of the so-called major powers. The eagle, whose wings he thought had once been clipped, was now flying high.[6]

In this chapter I want to suggest that the 'new' American hegemony of which so many writers now speak in earnest is in fact not new at all, but rather the result of a combination of largely ignored trends which pre-dated 11 September. These trends were understood by some writers; indeed, a small but not insignificant literature had emerged by the beginning of the new century explaining why the next hundred years would be just as 'American' as the last one. But in the main these were lone voices in the intellectual wilderness. Popular pundits and academic international relations took little notice of such predictions. Fatally preoccupied as some of them appeared to be by the apparent incoherence of

US foreign policy in the 1990s, and fixated as many of them were with other developments in a complex post-cold war world, few serious writers detected the fact that a fundamental power shift was taking place in the world system. Not for the first time in history did the experts get things wrong. But they certainly got the 1990s wrong, and only woke up to the fact after 11 September when the United States, in an awesome display of power, willed an unlikely alliance into being, defeated an enemy, impelled others to change course, and began drawing upon its own resources that over time might not only revamp its economy but also leave it in an even more favourable international position than ever before.

To make sense of US foreign policy after 11 September, therefore, we first have to make sense of history, and in particular the international history of the 1990s. That done, we will then look at 9/11's impact on the United States. Here, one cannot but agree with the triumphalists: events since 11 September have left the US in a more dominant position than before. However, even at this moment in time, when the American candle is burning brightest, we should all be exercising some caution. The United States won a significant victory and, buoyed up by a public opinion that seems to hear no evil and see no evil, looks determined to press on and try and score others. But herein lies the danger. Hubris can easily lead to its own nemesis, and an America that is dizzy with success might find that the very scale of its achievements could easily sow the seeds of future problems. Winning one short war is one thing: achieving a durable and acceptable international order after the guns have fallen silent is something else altogether.

[5] P. Beaumont and E. Vulliamy, 'Focus—American power: armed to the teeth', *Observer* (London), 10 Feb. 2002.

[6] P. Kennedy, 'The eagle has landed', *Financial Times*, 2–3 Feb. 2002.

Before 11 September: the American renaissance

At the inception of the twenty-first century—not to mention the next millennium—books on 'The American Century' proliferate monthly, if not daily. We now have The American Century Dictionary, The American Century Thesaurus, and even The American Century Cookbook; perhaps the American century baseball cap or cologne is not far behind.   (Bruce Cumings)[7]

As we have suggested, the very success of the Bush administration following 11 September was built upon—indeed presupposed—a series of important changes in the position of the United States in the international system in the 1990s. Without these changes, which engendered an increasing sense of self-confidence about its global role, it is most unlikely that Washington could have acted in the way it did, with the self-confidence it did, and enjoyed the success it did in the weeks and months which followed the collapse of the Twin Towers. Which raises the central question: what were these changes that 'coincided' nicely to place the US 'at the pinnacle of the international system', and rendered earlier speculation about America's irreversible decline sounding like so much hot air?

As Steve Burman noted in Chapter 15, the story of the American renaissance begins where the related tales about the cold war and the Soviet Union unexpectedly ends. It was this quite remarkable turn of events, which together transformed the European landscape, altered the whole shape of the international system, led to a profound reconfiguration of the geography of the world system, and changed the ideological ways in which politics would now be conducted, which laid the foundation for US resurgence in the 1990s. Whether it would have happened anyway is a moot point. But the fact that 'actually existing socialism' went under, and did so with such apparent ease, opened up new vistas that would have been unthinkable a few years earlier.

There were a number of concrete ways in which the formal dissolution of Soviet power and communist influence around the world worked to America's long-term advantage. The first, quite simply, was by demonstrating in practice that planning and the conscious attempt to organize society other than through the mechanism of the market was bound to lead to disaster. A new civilization had been built in Soviet Russia which promised the earth; however, instead of creating abundance and freedom it had only produced deprivation and totalitarianism. Consequently it had been consigned—where Reagan said it would be consigned back in 1982—to the trash-heap of history, a timely reminder and warning to anybody else that this was the fate awaiting all those who tampered with the basic laws of economics. The implosion of official communism also made possible something which would have been impossible before: the creation of a truly 'open door' world economic system in which there were no longer any barriers standing in the way of the free movement of capital. Indeed, in one very critical sense, the collapse of the 'second' communist world with its inevitable knock-on effects into the 'third' only accelerated those pre-existing tendencies that were leading to that most important of modern economic phenomenon with which the United States in particular came to be identified: globalization. Finally, and from our point of view, most critically, the end of the USSR effectively removed the most serious source of organized state resistance to US power. At a stroke this changed the context of world politics and gave the United States a degree of strategic choice it had never had before. How it sought to exploit this novel situation became only too apparent in 1991 when it overwhelmed Iraqi forces with hardly a murmur emanating from Baghdad's traditional ally in Moscow. It was revealed yet again a few years later when the US gave the go-ahead for the NATO-led intervention in Kosovo. And it became clearer than the truth in Afghanistan when even the normally more nationalist leader Vladimir Putin signed up, almost without demur, to US war aims. In an earlier era where the international

---

[7] Quoted in his 'Still the American century' in M. Cox, K. Booth, and T. Dunne (eds.), The Interregnum: Controversies in World Politics, 1989–1999 (Cambridge: Cambridge University Press, 1999), p. 271.

environment had been less benign, such a move by a Russian leader would have been inconceivable. In a unipolar world it was not.

If the collapse of the communist 'other' laid the basis for American self-confidence in the 1990s—and made possible its final victory in Afghanistan in 2002—the long boom which began in 1993, and continued more or less without disturbance until the Bush presidency, gave it material meaning. Why and how this boom occurred remains the subject of much anguished speculation. Some would insist that the American economy was always fundamentally sound anyway. However, structure alone would not explain why the economy surged so dramatically after a period of relative inactivity in the early 1990s. It may well have been far more likely given America's 'natural' advantages. It may have also been made possible, as neo-conservatives insist, by Reagan's earlier package of radical economic measures. But there were other conjunctural factors at work, including the Clinton administration itself, whose laser-like focus on economic renewal, fiscal restraint, and the need to compete in a globalized economy played a critical part in generating much of the activity which followed. Certainly, without its intervention it is difficult to envisage what happened as Wall Street surged, unemployment fell, and profits (particularly in the new technologies) rose to new heights during a period of almost unprecedented expansion which lasted for a record 107 consecutive months. In the process, not only did the American share of world economic product rise from 25 to around 30 per cent (and US companies continue to dominate global markets), but Clinton himself even managed to eliminate the most obvious symptom of US economic weakness in the past—the budget deficit—the first president to do so since 1969. Symbolically this was of major importance, as Clinton well understood when announcing the good news in 1998. We have at last moved, he noted, from a 'red' period of deficits to a 'black' era of surpluses. This was not only good for America, he went on, but good for the world as a whole. It was also the most effective answer possible to those who had only a few years earlier been predicting further US decline. In the new American economy of the 1990s things that would have seemed inconceivable and improbable before now looked eminently easy. The

only way forward it seemed was up, and then up again.

This brings us then to the third source of American self-confidence at the turn of the new century: the collapse of the idea of the Pacific Century and with it the almost complete disintegration of the once widespread view that Japan represented a serious threat to US economic hegemony. Once held up as a rival form of capitalism that could not only compete with the United States but beat it hands down, by the end of the decade Japan looked less like the proverbial rising sun and more like a crippled giant. The transformation was truly extraordinary. In the early 1990s most experts, though not all, were still speculating in sometimes frenzied ways about the peculiarities of the Japanese 'way' and the menace this represented to America. A few years on, and such talk sounded like so much idle chatter. Certainly, by the turn of the century few serious analysts could see very much to be worried about, and none anticipated Japan displacing the US as the technological hegemon. This was clearly the view of an important report published in Japan itself in 1999.[8] It was also the opinion of an American study which had appeared a year earlier. As it showed, the US was still far ahead in all five of the most crucial sectors of the new information economy. In semi-conductors, American firms had even reclaimed both the technological edge and market share from Japanese companies, except in the low-end memory chip part of the market. Meanwhile, in microprocessors, US firms tightened their control of the global market, dominated the more lucrative software markets, and, in the latest surge in information technology prompted by the Internet and the World Wide Web, simply left Japan trailing in their wake. By the turn of the century the Japanese technological challenge had all but evaporated.

This in turn raises the question of Europe. Certainly if Japan presented a very different picture at the end of the 1990s from that at the beginning of the decade, the same could easily be said of the European Union as it coped in turn with the costs of German unification, the multi-layered process of transition in the East, EU enlargement, and further

---

[8] W. Horsley, 'Special report: the liberation of Japan', *Prospect*, Issue 63 (May 2001), pp. 52–6.

economic integration around its new currency, the euro. But in no way did any of these changes seriously impinge on the basics of power in the larger international system. Indeed, at the level of high politics, the 1990s tended to confirm US hegemony in the region rather than diminish it. The most obvious reason for this was Europe's disastrous showing in Bosnia. Having been left the problem to resolve by an American administration reluctant to get involved in the Balkans quagmire, US policy gradually moved from one of containment to engagement to full-scale involvement, as it became clear that the Europeans could not resolve the situation themselves. Determined to reach a Balkan settlement at all cost, it was the US which brokered the deal which finally led to some sort of peace. The fact that it was signed in Dayton, Ohio, and not Rome, Paris, or Brussels, tells its own particular story about the balance of power in the 'new' Europe. So too did the wider debates then taking place about the future of European security. The precise details of how the US moved from reasoned opposition to the idea of NATO enlargement in 1990 to ready acceptance of its necessity four to five years later is a story that has been told many times before. Suffice to say here that it was, in the end, an American decision, taken in Washington by US policy-makers, the significance of which was not lost on those like the French who had earlier argued strongly for a new set of security arrangements that might in the end provide a European answer to European problems. With NATO expansion it was clear that no such answer had been forthcoming, and that the United States would remain the critical factor in the new, or perhaps not so new, European security order.

Finally, any assessment of American power (which is of particular relevance to understanding the current situation) has to take account of that most important instrument of power: the military capabilities needed to deter enemies, control allies, preserve influence, and, if needs be, win wars. Here, the collapse of the USSR and the inability of other countries to justify military spending to sceptical publics, only emphasized the extent of US preponderance. A crude but accurate measure of this, was that in every year after 1992 the United States alone accounted for nearly 40 per cent of all the world's military expenditure; and while this repre-sented only 2.9 per cent of US GDP and 16 per cent of the US budget, this still meant that by the year 2000 America was spending just over $280 bn. on its 'defence', in real terms only 14 per cent less than that in an average year during the cold war itself. In comparison to its many dependent allies, and largely backward rivals, it was simply in a league of its own. Nor was this all. Half of all arms sales—close to $55 bn. in 1998—were American. It was the biggest manufacturer of conventional weapons. And its military R&D was seven times higher than that of France, its closest competitor. It was also one of the very few countries whose defence budget began to go up, rather than down, in the 1990s. Secretary of Defense William Cohen outlined the reasons why in 1997. After ten years of cuts, he explained, it was imperative to raise spending on the military. The cold war might have come to an end, but so too, he added, had the post-cold war era. We were now living in different and more difficult times, and the moment was ripe therefore for a new defence policy appropriate to the potentially long-lasting conditions of acute uncertainty. Moreover, without such a policy, he argued, the United States would be unable to provide the sort of leadership essential for global order. As an earlier and much-quoted defence review of 1992 had made clear, the US was not like other powers. It had wider international responsibilities, and these required a force structure capable of ensuring its continued dominance in the world—not just to deter likely enemies, but also to send an unambiguously clear message to more friendly regional players that the United States would not countenance any challenge to its hegemony. Much might have changed since the fall of the Berlin Wall and the end of the USSR, but one thing had not: the American urge to remain number one.

Key points

- The unmatched international influence of the United States pre-dated 11 September.

- The end of the cold war, relative decline of Japanese economic power, and uncertain development of the European Union contributed to the continued position of the US as the world's leading superpower.

11 September—and after

Some believe the first casualty of war is truth. But in this war, the first victory must be to tell the truth. And the truth is, this will be a war like none other our nation has faced. Indeed, it is easier to describe what lies ahead by talking about what it is not rather than what it is.   (Donald Rumsfeld)[9]

Thus after one of the more extraordinary decades of the post-war period, the United States presented a picture of itself to the world which would have been difficult to have envisaged ten years earlier, and unimaginable at the end of the problematic 1970s. Certainly, if opinion polls are anything to go by, Americans by the end of the 1990s appeared to feel more secure than at any point in the post-war period, in spite of the many obvious threats—including international terrorism—that were still facing the nation. Indeed, if we were to take the longer view and compare America's position within the international system in 1945—when it stood at the pinnacle of its power in an otherwise shattered world—and the one it held fifty-five years later, then a strong case could be made that by the turn of the century (and by the time George Bush took over in the White House) it was in a far more favourable situation. After all, in that crucial space of time two former enemies in the shape of Germany and Japan had been reformed and integrated into the wider international community, institutions had been consolidated that provided for a degree of inter-state harmony that would have once been regarded as Utopian, the other rival superpower had come and gone, the ideological alternative in the form of communism had finally been seen off, the challenge of national liberation had been contained, planning had collapsed as an economic option, the world economy had become more integrated and open, and everywhere it seemed people were increasingly being influenced by American ideas, American idioms, and American styles—even by the idea of America itself. The metamorphosis was truly breathtaking. The American 'empire' or what Halliday has aptly termed the 'unaccountable hegemon' was not only safe, at one level at least, it had never been so dominant.[10]

This then was the situation which confronted the United States as it entered 2002. Admittedly, the American economy was not performing as well as it had done before; a question mark also continued to hang over the legitimacy and competence of the newly elected president; and there were serious doubts being raised outside the US at least about its increasingly unilateralist behaviour abroad. Nevertheless, the world looked to be its oyster. Russia moreover was in decline, the once-miracle economy of Japan was in crisis, China was bothersome but marginal, Europe had few military assets worth talking about, and the United States possessed more weaponry than the rest of the major powers put together. Little wonder the Bush administration seemed so indifferent to the feelings of other countries: in its view, it had much to be indifferent about.

All this was brought into sharp focus by what happened on that tragic September day. For a country which had experienced a string of almost unbroken successes for the past ten years, the shock must have been very great indeed; the fact it was experienced in New York and Washington, and not thousands of miles away, must have made it all the more difficult to bear. Yet for the first time in history (or at least since the British burned the White House in 1812) the US homeland was subject to a direct attack, with the threat of more appalling acts of carnage to follow. Almost in an instant Americans were forced to confront the fact that no amount of power could bring them either the security they sought or the security they thought they had already acquired. Not only that: there were people out there who not only did not share their world-view but actually hated what the United States represented. Perhaps few in the Muslim world openly applauded what happened. Nonetheless, there were more than a few who appeared to take quiet satisfaction in seeing the hegemon hit where it hurt most, in those

[9] 27 Sept. 2001, 'America's new kind of war'. In **www. embassy.org.uk/terror172.html**
[10] See F. Halliday, *The World at 2000: Perils and Promises* (Basingstoke: Palgrave, 2001), pp. 90–109.

quintessential symbols of American power.[11] As one very moderate Muslim leader in Britain pointed out, though the attack was execrable it was understandable because the United States was just 'too domineering'. The banner brandished by a less moderate crowd in Pakistan made the point even more graphically. 'Down with the United States', it proclaimed. Why? Because it was 'unrighteous, seditious and arrogant'.

If 11 September produced its own particular form of political trauma, it also delivered what some at first feared might be a fatal blow to the American and world economic systems. For a few days at least, the situation seemed to totter on the edge. And even once things stabilized, they did not return to normal. Well over 600,000 job cuts were announced in the United States alone between 11 September and Christmas, more than for the whole five-year period between 1993 and 1997, and only 1,100 fewer than in all of 2000.[12] Particular sectors such as the airlines were especially hard-hit. 11 September also hit consumer confidence badly, with a massive reduction in individual spending as individuals and families retreated from the marketplace. Wall Street too suffered enormous losses as markets adjusted to what had happened. Nor was this all. Across the whole of the capitalist world the shock waves were keenly felt; and even as the dust began to settle, many continued to worry that in the new terrorist-threatened international economy, things could never be the same again. Indeed, some feared that globalization itself was now under threat as companies and countries adjusted to the increased costs of operating in a world where the very menace of terrorism was bound to impose increased costs on trade, capital, and information flows. Morgan Stanley in one assessment even estimated that US commercial insurance premiums alone would rise from $148 bn. in 2000 to $240 bn. in 2001, the equivalent of a new tax on the corporate sector. All in all, the economic outlook was hardly optimistic. Some in fact felt that 11 September marked not just a setback but a critical turning point in the more recent history of the global economy, with high growth and reasonable levels of prosperity situated on one side of the dividing line and deepening recession, possibly depression, standing on the other.

The costs of 9/11 to the United States therefore were enormous. Yet every crisis represents an opportunity as well as a challenge, and how the United States responded to this particular challenge was going to be crucial. Few doubted that the US would take military action. But hardly anybody could have anticipated the speed with which the regime in Afghanistan collapsed, and the extent to which the United States then found itself playing the role of regional arbiter in Central Asia within only a few weeks of having launched a war that many originally predicted would lead to disaster. Critics anticipated a military impasse: in reality, the war turned out to be a brilliant (and unexpected) success. The attack also provided the US with a larger rationale. Before 11 September the United States appeared to be floundering without purpose: following it, however, it was now playing a most active leadership role directing a loose but surprisingly obedient alliance of states in an ill-defined but very real war against something called international terrorism. And the results were not unimpressive. At least one source of global disturbance, in the shape of the Taleban regime, was destroyed; the US acquired new bases in countries within the former Soviet Union where before it had had hardly any influence at all; it secured at least one important source of oil; and it compelled a number of countries like Pakistan, Indonesia, and the Phillipines to deal with their own fundamentalists. Imperialism might be an inadequate and conspiratorial term by which to describe the process through which the United States increased its global influence post-11 September; but increase it, it undoubtedly did. Indeed, in much the same way that the international struggle against communism led (sometimes by design but more often than not through invitation) to an expansion of American influence after 1947, the war against the new global enemy known as terrorism helped extend American power after 11 September. Little wonder that certain analysts saw important parallels between the two.[13]

---

[11] See *Financial Times*, 12 Sept. 2001.

[12] M. Chung and P. Despaignes, 'Scant Christmas cheer for recession-hit US', *Financial Times*, 17 Dec. 2001.

[13] See A. Lieven, 'Fighting terrorism: lessons from the cold war', *Policy Brief* 7 (Oct. 2001), Carnegie Endowment for International Peace; and W. A. McDougall, 'Cold War II', *Orbis*, Dec. 2001.

The war did something else as well: it illustrated the extent to which the United States no longer seemed to require the active military support of its allies, except as bases or cheer leaders. Drawing what it felt was the central lesson from the war in Kosovo—that friends were politically necessary but militarily problematic—the United States decided from the outset to fight the war in Afghanistan on its own terms and largely with its own weapons. The result was one of the more impressive uses of US air power in modern times. This made life distinctly uncomfortable for its enemies on the ground. But it had important, and uncomfortable, consequences for its allies as well. US predominance was not just quantitative either. It was qualitative too. To take one example. Whereas only 6 per cent of the bombs dropped during the Gulf War were precision weapons, some 95 per cent of those dropped by the US in Afghanistan were in that category, a huge step forward in a relatively short space of time. Finally, the war was a great success for US intelligence. Sceptics made much of the fact that both the CIA and the FBI failed to anticipate the original attacks on New York and Washington; they said much less, not surprisingly, about the fact that the United States fought a very successful intelligence war on the ground—even, it seems, before the war began in earnest.

The Bush military build-up only confirmed the enormous power gap that already existed between the United States and the rest of the world. Significantly, Bush quite consciously linked his new expanded military budget both to the war against terrorism—even though most of the weapons he sought would make little difference to that particular struggle—and to what he seemed to suggest was the equally important war now being waged against economic recession. Rarely in recent American history had a peacetime US president been quite so explicit in making the connection; but he did, and in the process added another $36 bn. to the military budget of $328 bn. for 2002, and $48 bn. for 2003, a 15 per cent boost in all and the largest in two decades. This alone would make US spending on defence double that of all the European Union countries put together; and over five years would add another $120 bn. to a total defence outlay of some nearly $1700 bn. He also requested $38 bn. for homeland security programmes for 2003, double the level of spending for 2002 in a category of expenditure which did not even exist in 2001. As even Paul Kennedy was forced to admit, not only was the world's policeman likely to remain very well armed, but 'in military terms' it was now the only combatant left in the ring.

Finally, in terms of measuring America's response to the 11 September outrage we must take account of its impact upon the United States itself. Aside from the creation of a new cabinet post whose purpose was to deal with the problem of homeland defence, the Bush team acted decisively (some would say without due caution) in an attempt to reassure the American people that no such attacks would take place again in the future. This was by no means an easy job. Too little would achieve nothing, while too much might threaten civil liberties. In the end civil liberties appeared to take second place as Congress passed the 2001 USA Patriot Act on October 12. This gave the government significant new powers in dealing with the terrorist threat, which included amongst other things the power to tap phones, investigate bank accounts, and intercept e-mail traffic. This was then followed a month later by the quite incredible executive order signed by President Bush (without consulting Congress) making it legal to try alien terrorists in military tribunal courts with no criminal law or evidential rules of protection.

Of course, it would have been easier for civil libertarians to have opposed these moves if they had been widely opposed. But they were not. On the contrary, they proved to be massively popular in a nation which, having recovered from the initial trauma of 11 September, was now engaged in a spasm of nationalism whose most visible expressions were the mass flying (and mass sales) of the American flag and the almost perpetual singing of the US national anthem. Clearly, after the tragedy of 11 September Americans were seeking collective comfort and reassurance through such quite understandable rituals. The political consequences, however, were not without significance. For this almost unending wave of patriotism not only did much to bolster the Bush presidency, and Bush himself, but served to unite the country and generate a sense of shared identity. Moreover, in a hostile world where further action might be required to deal with the terrorist threat, this new sense of ideological cohesion was not to be underestimated. After all, if the US was to take action against either Iraq, Iran, or even North Korea—the three countries specifically mentioned by Bush in his 'evil axis' speech to Congress in February 2002—then it would need the backing of the American people. The Vietnam Syndrome so-called might not have been overcome completely as a result of 11 September. On the other hand, 11 September had done much— or so it appeared—to make Americans a good deal less reluctant to support US military action abroad.

Key points

- In addition to the devastating loss of life, 11 September caused major economic shocks to the US economy.

- The geopolitical implications of 9/11 nonetheless were, overall, beneficial to America's influence.

Power corrupts: absolute power corrupts absolutely

The war on terrorism is simply a euphemism for extending US control in the world, whether it is by projecting force through its carriers or building new military bases in Central Asia. (Paul Rogers)[14]

The impact of 11 September has thus been contradictory: there is no doubting that it did deliver a savage blow to American prestige, to the US economy, and to its international *amour propre*; however, such has been the strength of the American response that the longer-term result has been to enhance US credibility, to create a sense of international purpose where before there was none, and to unite the nation around some fairly powerful themes, while leaving the United States in an extraordinarily powerful position in Central Asia. It has also helped justify a massive military build-up that will leave the US in an even more dominant position than before. 11 September may also provide a set of economic answers to the problems posed by the American recession. Only time will tell.

Which brings us logically enough to the problem of the future. As has no doubt been repeated *ad nauseam* since the Taleban fell, it is critically important that the United States now draws the right set of lessons. At least two seem important: that the enemy state from which the aggression was originally planned was not especially secure or strong; and that the very nature of the attack legitimized some sort of response in the eyes of most people in that entity which has come to be known as the 'civilized world'. Nor was this support without justification. After all, what happened on that September morning was barbaric in the extreme. It was unprovoked. And it was launched by a band of zealots whose ideology was openly totalitarian. Moreover, in spite of Bin Laden's efforts, his group and their supporters in Afghanistan had little serious international support. Indeed, while many Muslims and Arabs might have had little liking for the United States, they had even less perhaps for the Taleban, who harboured a network of international terrorists whose activities gave Islam a bad name, and whose political rage was just as likely to be directed against other regimes in the Muslim world as it was against the West.

This litany of well-known facts draws us to our first, fairly self-evident conclusion: that attacking and destroying the regime in Afghanistan was (in spite of early pessimism to the contrary) a relatively easy task. Attempting to take the war against international terrorism forward against other countries which have no intention of attacking the United States and have far greater capabilities would be not only far more difficult but dangerous. Yet, if presidential rhetoric and recent revelations are to be believed, that is precisely what is now being considered in the highest circles around Washington. As

---

[14] Both quotes from the *Observer* (London), 10 Feb. 2002.

one recent report pointed out, it is becoming increasingly clear (though how clear remains open to speculation) 'that the US is not now engaged in a war against terrorism at all. Instead this is a war against regimes the US dislikes'—and Iraq is clearly the regime which the US dislikes most. How and when the 'war' against Saddam will be launched is not presently known. Nonetheless, regime change now seems to be the order of the day. Even the more 'moderate' Colin Powell has been reported as saying, that such a move 'would be in the best interests of the region, the best interests of the Iraqi people . . . we are looking at a variety of options that would bring that about'.[15]

Success in the war against Afghanistan is thus encouraging the United States to think 'creatively' about how to deal with other states and organizations it does not like. But it is also generating a series of perhaps equally important tensions between itself and its European allies. These had been simmering beneath the surface long before 9/11, to be momentarily checked by the horror of what subsequently happened in New York. However, the unresolved differences which existed before 11 September (on Kyoto and the ABM Treaty to name but two) have not gone away. The war moreover has only made matters worse—partly because of the way in which it was conducted by the US, and increasingly because of the American urge to carry it forward against other countries. However, there is something more fundamental, and this arises in large part because of the

sheer disparity of power between the US and its different NATO allies. NATO has always been an unequal partnership. But now the chasm between one of its constituent parts and the rest has grown exponentially, with potentially major implications for the future cohesion and even meaning of the alliance. The war in Afghanistan did not cause this to happen; what it did do, however, was reveal how great the gap has become and how much greater it is likely to become in the future. This will not undermine NATO—it is simply too important. Nonetheless, it could easily change its basic character. As the US ambassador to NATO, Nicholas Burns, warned, 'without dramatic action to close the capabilities gap, we face the real prospect of a future two-tiered alliance'—one part being what Lord Robertson has called the 'military pygmy' known as Europe and the other being the United States.

Key points

- The 9/11 attacks revealed the vulnerability of the United States but also, in the American response, demonstrated its singular power and resolution.

- Despite the interdependence that 9/11 suggested was an inescapable fact of the international system, the medium- and long-term response to this by the Bush administration remains unclear.

Conclusion

Any assessment of the future has to come to terms with another simple fact of international political life: the extent to which the United States itself is moving in an increasingly unilateralist direction.[16] This is not something new. Indeed, there has never not been a time when the US—because of its identity, geography, and Constitution—has reserved for itself the right to act when it likes, how it likes, and basically where it likes. This in some ways is the rare privilege enjoyed by all very powerful states. Even the Clinton administration was not immune to

the charms of unilateralism. As Madelaine Albright once put it, 'we will behave multilaterally when we can and unilaterally when we must'. The Bush team, however, has taken this whole approach onto a different, almost philosophical plane. This seems to be especially true of those around Donald Rumsfeld, whose world-view, it seems, is that power is what

---

[15] J. Borger and E. MacAskill, 'US targets Saddam', *Guardian*, 14 Feb. 2002.
[16] See P. Rogers, 'Right for America, right for the world', *World Today* 58(2), 2 Feb., pp. 13–15.

matters, that the United States has far more of this than any other country, and that to achieve results—as in Afghanistan—the United States should not be too sensitive about the political feelings of others when it decides it has to use its power. As one member of the Rumsfeld group recently admitted, the secretary of defense and his team are very firm 'believers in unilateral American military power'.[17] Nor is this outlook likely to have been dented by what happened in Afghanistan. But if this is the case, then the future direction of US foreign policy is likely to be very different from what we have come to expect from it in the past. When the war began there were those who hoped that this would curb the unilateralist inclinations of the Bush administration, and that it would emerge on the other side converted to the cause of coalitions and multilateralism. In reality, the war has had almost the opposite effect. This might not please important European leaders. It may upset America's allies. But to many in the United States, it now appears to be the only way to secure order in a world where its voice is now louder than ever and the fight against international terrorism has only just begun.

[17] Quoted in *Observer*, 10 Feb. 2002.

QUESTIONS

1 What was the main effect of 9/11 on American foreign policy?

2 To what extent, and how, did the terrorist strikes alter the existing foreign policy of the Bush administration?

3 Is American unilateralism either feasible or desirable in the post-9/11 world?

4 Is American influence in the international system more a function of its security or its economic power?

5 '9/11 brought the post-cold war era to a close, but did not establish a clear strategic vision for the post-9/11 world order.' Discuss.

FURTHER READING

K. Booth and T. Dunne (eds.) (2002), *Worlds in Collision: Terror and the Future of Global Order* (Basingstoke: Palgrave).

R. Gunaratna (2002), *Inside al Qaeda* (London: Hurst).

J. Hoge and G. Rose (eds.) (2001), *How Did This Happen? Terrorism and the New War* (New York: Council on Foreign Relations).

G. Kepel (2002), *Jihad: The Rise of Political Islam* (London: I. B. Tauris).

J. Nye (2002), *The Paradox of American Power* (Oxford: Oxford University Press).

M. Ruthven (2002), *A Fury for God: The Islamist Attack on America* (London: Granta).

S. Talbot and N. Chanda (2001), *The Age of Terror* (New Haven, Conn.: Perseus Press).

WEB LINKS

www.afpc.org/resources/mofas.htm Gives access to websites of most nations' foreign affairs ministries

www.infoctr.edu/fwl The Federal Web Locator: useful for federal agencies and organizations

www.foreignaffairs.org Foreign Affairs: magazine archives and links

usinfo.state.gov US Information Agency: broad coverage and links

www.state.gov/www/regions/internat.html Data on US foreign policy from arms control to environmental issues

www.unc.edu/depts/diplomat American Diplomacy: online journal of analysis

www.ceip.org Carnegie Endowment for International Peace

www.rand.org RAND

www.cia.gov Central Intelligence Agency

www.nato.int/structur/nids/nids.htm NATO Integrated Data Service: NATO and security issues

www.state.gov/index.html US Department of State

www.usip.org US Institute of Peace

www.imf.org IMF

www.ifo.usaid.gov US Agency for International Development

www.ustr.gov US Trade Representative

www.worldbank.org World Bank

counterterrorism.com Counterterrorism Page: documents events, strategies, tactics of terrorist groups, plus articles

www.defenselink.mil DefenseLINK: Pentagon

References

Aberach, J. D., and Rockman, B. A. (1976), 'Clashing beliefs within the executive branch: the Nixon administration bureaucracy', *American Political Science Review*, 70(2).

Abramowitz, A. I., and Segal, J. A. (1992), *Senate Elections*. Ann Arbor: University of Michigan Press.

Abramson, P., et al. (2002), *Change and Continuity in the 2000 Elections*. Washington, DC: CQ Press.

AFL-CIO (2001), 'Facts about working women', www.aflcio.org/women/wwfacts.htm

Albright, M. K. (1998), 'The testing of American foreign policy', Foreign Affairs, 77(2): 50–64.

Alcorn, R. (2000), *Prolife Answers to Prochoice Arguments*. Sisters, Ore.: Multnomah.

Aldrich, J. H., and Rohde, D. W. (1997–8), 'The Transition to Republican rule in the House: implications for theories of Congressional politics', *Political Science Quarterly*, 112(4): 541–67.

—— (2000), 'The consequences of party organization in the House: the role of the majority and minority parties in conditional party government', in Bond and Fleisher (2000: 31–72).

Amis, M. (2002). *The War Against Cliché: Essays and Reviews, 1971–2000*. London: Cape.

Anderson, B. (1983/1999), *Imagined Communities: Reflections on the Origin and Spread of Nationalism*, rev. edn. London: Verso.

Anderson, K. (1996), *Changing Woman: A History of Racial Ethnic Women in Modern America*. Oxford: Oxford University Press.

Anon. (1997), 'Reed resignation from CC reveals a split in the ranks', www.atheists.org/

Ansolabehere, S., Brady, D., and Fiorina, M. (1992), 'The vanishing marginals and electoral responsiveness', *British Journal of Political Science*, 22(1): 21–38.

Appleby, R. S., and Marty, M. (eds.) (1993), *Fundamentalisms and the State: Remaking Polities, Economies, and Militance*. Chicago: University of Chicago Press.

Arentsen, M., Bressers, H., and O'Toole, L. (2000), 'Institutional and policy responses to uncertainty in environmental policy: a comparison of Dutch and US styles', *Policy Studies Journal*, 28(3): 597–611.

Arquilla, J., and Ronfeldt, D. (eds.) (2001), *Networks and Netwars: The Future of Terrorism, Crime and Militancy*. Santa Monica, Calif.: Rand Corporation.

Associated Press (2001), 'Issue ad spending hit $250 million', *USA Today*, 2 Jan.

Bach, S., and Smith, S. S. (1988), *Managing Uncertainty in the House of Representatives: Adaptation and Innovation in Special Rules*. Washington, DC: Brookings Institution.

Badgett, M. V. Lee. (1995), 'The wage effects of sexual orientation discrimination', *Industrial and Labor Relations Review*, 48: 726–39.

Bailey, C. (1998), *Congress and Air Pollution: Environmental Policies in the USA*. Manchester: Manchester University Press.

Bailey, R. W. (1999), *Gay Politics, Urban Politics: Identity and Economics in an Urban Setting*. New York: Columbia University Press.

Baker, R. K. (2001), *House, and Senate*, 3rd edn. New York: Norton.

Balz, D., and Brownstein, R. (1996), *Storming the Gates: Protest Politics and the Republican Revival*. Boston: Little, Brown.

Banaszak, L. A. (1996), *Why Movements Succeed or Fail*. Princeton, NJ: Princeton University Press.

Banner, S. (2002), *The Death Penalty: An American History*. Cambridge, Mass.: Harvard University Press.

Barnett, L. (1988), 'The electability test', *Time*, 29 Feb.

Barry, J. M. (1989), *The Ambition and the Power: A True Story of Washington*. New York: Viking.

Baumer, D. C. (1992), 'Senate Democratic leadership in the 101st Congress', in Hertzke and Peters (1992).

Baxter, S., and Lansing, M. (1983), *Women and Politics: The Visible Majority*. Ann Arbor: University of Michigan Press.

Beaudry, A., and Schaeffer, B. (1986), *Winning State and Local Elections: The Guide to Organizing Your Campaign*. New York: Free Press.

Bedau, H. A. (ed.) (1997), *The Death Penalty in America: Current Controversies*. New York: Oxford University Press.

Beder, S. (2001), 'Neoliberal think tanks and freemarket environmentalism', *Environmental Politics*, 10(2): 128–33.

Beer, S. (1978), 'In search of a new public philosophy', in King (1990: 5–44).

—— (1993), *To Make a Nation: The Rediscovery of American Federalism*. Cambridge, Mass.: Harvard University Press.

Bellesiles, M. A. (2000), *Arming America: The Origins of a National Gun Culture*. New York: Knopf.

Bennett, A. (2000), *Popular Music and Youth Culture: Music, Identity and Place*. London: Routledge.

Bennett, L. W. (1998), 'The uncivic culture: communication, identity and the rise of lifestyle politics', *Political Science and Politics*, 31(4): 741–61.

—— and Entman, R. M. (2001), 'Mediated politics: an introduction', in L.W. Bennett and R. M. Entman (eds.), *Mediated Politics: Communication in the Future of Democracy*. Cambridge: Cambridge University Press.

—— and Manheim, J. B. (2001), 'The big spin: strategic communication and the transformation of pluralist democracy', introduction in L.W. Bennett and R. M. Entman (eds.), *Mediated Politics: Communication in the Future of Democracy*. Cambridge: Cambridge University Press.

Berman, L. (1979), *The Office of Management and Budget and the Presidency, 1921–1979*. Princeton, NJ: Princeton University Press.

Berry, J. (1999), *The New Liberalism: The Rising Power of Citizen Groups*. Washington, DC: Brookings Institution.

Bibby, J. F. (ed.) (1983), *Congress Off the Record: The Candid Analyses of Seven Members*. Washington, DC: American Enterprise Institute.

Biddlecombe, P. (2002), *The United Burger States of America*. London: Abacus.

Binder, L., et al. (1971), *Crises and Sequences in Political Development*. Princeton, NJ: Princeton University Press.

Binder, S. A., and Stephen, S. (1997), *Politics or Principle? Filibustering in the United States Senate*. Washington, DC: Brookings Institution.

Blum, J. G., and Gurevitch, M. (1996), 'Media change and social change: linkages and junctures', in J. Curran and M. Gurevitch (eds.), *Mass Media and Society*, 2nd edn. London: Arnold.

Bollen, K. A. (1979), 'Political democracy and the timing of development', *American Sociological Review* 44: 572–87.

Bomberg, E. (1998), *Green Parties and Politics in the European Union*. London: Routledge.

—— (2001), 'The US presidential election: implications for environmental policy', *Environmental Politics*, 10(2): 115–21.

Bond, J. R., and Fleisher, R. (eds.) (2000), *Polarized Politics: Congress and the President in a Partisan Era*. Washington, DC: CQ Press.

—— —— and Krutz, G. S. (1996), 'An overview of the empirical findings on presidential–Congressional relations', in J. A. Thurber (ed.), *Rivals for Power: Presidential–Congressional Relations*. Washington, DC: CQ Press.

Booth, K., and Dunne, T. (eds.) (2002), *Worlds in Collision: Terror and the Future of Global Order*. Basingstoke: Palgrave.

Brands, H. W. (1998), *What America Owes the World: The Struggle for the Soul of Foreign Policy*. Cambridge: Cambridge University Press.

Brinkley, D. (1997), 'Democratic enlargement: the Clinton doctrine', *Foreign Policy*, 106: 111–27.

Broder, D. S. (1972), *The Party's Over: The Failure of Politics in America*. New York: Harper & Row.

Brogan, P. (1991), 'Abortion issue returns to muddy the political and legal waters', *Glasgow Herald*, 27 July.

Bruce, J. M., and Wilcox, C. (eds.) (1998), *The Changing Politics of Gun Control*. Lanham, Md.: Rowman & Littlefield.

Bruce, S. (1988), *The Rise and Fall of the New Christian Right*:

Protestant Politics in America, 1978–1988. Oxford: Clarendon Press.

—— (1996), *Religion in the Modern World: From Cathedrals to Cults*. Oxford: Oxford University Press.

—— (2000), *Fundamentalism*. Cambridge: Polity Press.

Bryner, G. (2000), *Gaia's Wager: Environmental Movements and the Challenge of Sustainability*. New York: Rowman & Littlefield.

Burgoyne, R. (1997), *Film Nation: Hollywood Looks at US History*. Minneapolis: University of Minnesota Press.

Button, J. W., Rienzo, B. A., and Wald, K. D. (1997), *Private Lives, Public Conflicts: Battles Over Gay Rights in American Communities*. Washington, DC: CQ Press.

Campbell, A., et al. (1960), *The American Voter*. New York: Wiley.

Campbell, C. C., and Davidson, R. H. (2000), 'Gay and lesbian issues in the Congressional arena', in Rimmerman et al. (2000).

Campbell, J. E. (1993), *The Presidential Pulse of Congressional Elections*. Lexington: University Press of Kentucky.

Canon, D. T. (1990), *Actors, Athletes and Astronauts: Political Amateurs in the United States Congress*. Chicago: University of Chicago Press.

—— Schousen, M. M., and Sellers, P. (1994), 'A formula for uncertainty: creating a black majority district in North Carolina', in Kazee (1994).

Carroll, S. J. (2000), 'Representing women: Congresswomen's perception of their representational roles, www.cawp. rutgers.edu/pdf/congroles.pdf

—— (ed.) (2002), *The Impact of Women in Public Office*. Bloomington: Indiana University Press.

Carson, R. (1962), *Silent Spring*. Boston: Houghton Mifflin.

Carter, N. (2001), *The Politics of the Environment: Ideas, Activism, Policy*. Cambridge: Cambridge University Press.

Cashmore, E. (1994), *. . . and There Was Television*. London: Routledge.

Center for Political Studies, University of Michigan (1995–2000), The national election studies: electronic resources from the NES World Wide Web Site, www.umich.edu/~nes.

Center for the American Woman and Politics (1991), 'The impact of women in public office: findings at a glance', www.cawp.rutgers.edu/pdf/Findings.pdf

Chong, D. (1991), *Collective Action and the Civil Rights Movement*. Chicago: University of Chicago Press.

Church, T. C., and Nakamura, R. (1993), *Cleaning up the Mess: Implementation Strategies in Superfund*. Washington, DC: Brookings Institution.

Cloward, R. A., and Piven, F. F. (eds.) (1993), *Regulating the Poor: The Functions of Public Welfare*, 2nd edn. New York: Vintage.

Cohen, C. J., Jones, K. B., and Tronto, J. C. (eds.) (1997), *Women Transforming Politics: An Alternative Reader*. New York: New York University Press.

Cole, L., and Foster, S. (2001), *From the Ground Up: Environmental Racism and the Rise of the Environmental Justice Movement*. New York: New York University Press.

Coleman, J. J. (1996), *Party Decline in America: Policy, Politics, and the Fiscal State*. Princeton, NJ: Princeton University Press.

Collender, S. E., *Guide to the Federal Budget* (annual publication). Washington, DC: Urban Institute Press.

Collie, M. P. (1988), 'Universalism and the Parties in the US House of Representatives, 1921–80', *American Journal of Political Science*, 32: 865–83.

Collier, K. E. (1997), *Between the Branches: The White House Office of Legislative Affairs*. Pittsburgh: University of Pittsburgh Press.

Condit, C. M. (1990), *Decoding Abortion Rhetoric: Communicating Social Change*. Urbana: University of Illinois Press.

Cook, E. A., Thomas, S., and Wilcox, C. (1994), *The Year of the Woman: Myths and Realities*. Boulder, Colo.: Westview Press.

Cook, T. E. (2000), 'Senators and reporters revisited', in Loomis (2000: 164–93).

—— (2001), 'The future of institutional media', in L. W. Bennett and R. M. Entman (eds.), *Mediated Politics: Communication in the Future of Democracy*. Cambridge: Cambridge University Press.

Cope, M. (1997), 'Responsibilities, regulation, and retrenchment: the end of welfare?', in L. A. Staeheli, J. E. Kodras, and C. Flint (eds.), *State Devolution in America: Implications for a Diverse Society*. London: Sage, 181–205.

Corwin, E. S. (1957), *The President: Office and Powers*, 4th rev. edn. New York: New York University Press.

Council for Excellence in Government poll, conducted by the polling organizations of P. Hart (D) and R. Teeter (R), 21–8 May, 1 June, 1999. N=1,214 adults nationwide, accessed from **PollingReport.com**, 8 July 2002.

Council on Foreign Relations and Pew Research Center for the People and the Press (2001), 'America's new internationalist point of view', **http://people-press.org/reports/**

Cox, G. W., and McCubbins, M. D. (1993), *Legislative Leviathan: Party Government in the House*. Berkeley, Calif.: University of California Press.

Cox, M., Ikenberry, J. G., and Inoguchi, T. (eds.) (2000), *American Democracy Promotion: Impulses, Strategies, and Impacts*. Oxford: Oxford University Press.

Cox, R. W., and Skidmore-Hess, D. (1999), *US Politics and the Global Economy: Corporate Power, Conservative Shift*. Boulder, Colo.: Rienner.

Crabb, C. V., Sarieddine, L. E., and Antizzo, G. J. (2001), *Charting a New Diplomatic Course: Alternative Approaches to America's Post-Cold War Foreign Policy*. Baton Rouge: Louisiana State University Press.

Craig, B. H., and O'Brien, D. M. (1993), *Abortion and American Politics*. Chatham, NJ: Chatham House.

Cunningham, N. E., Jr. (1978), *Circular Letters of Congressmen to their Constituents 1789–1839*. Chapel Hill, NC: University of North Carolina Press.

Curran, J. (1996), 'Mass media and democracy revisited', in J. Curran and M. Gurevitch (eds.), *Mass Media and Society*, 2nd edn. London: Arnold.

Dahl, R. A. (1961), *Who Governs? Democracy and Power in an American City*. New Haven, Conn.: Yale University Press.

—— (1967), *Pluralist Democracy in the United States: Conflict and Consent*. Chicago: Rand McNally.

—— (1971), *Polyarchy; Participation and Opposition*. New Haven, Conn.: Yale University Press.

Dahlgren, P. (2001), 'The public sphere and the Net: structure, space and communication', in L. W. Bennett and R. M. Entman (eds.), *Mediated Politics: Communication in the Future of Democracy*. Cambridge: Cambridge University Press.

Dalaker, J. (2001), *Poverty in the United States: 2000*. Washington, DC: US Census Bureau: US Dept. of Commerce, Sept. 2001.

Dalton, R. (2002), *Citizen Politics: Public Opinion and Political Parties in Advanced Industrial Democracies*. New York: Chatham House/Seven Bridges.

Davidson, R. H. (1981), 'Subcommittee government: new channels for policymaking', in Mann and Ornstein (1982).

—— (1986), 'Committees as moving targets', *Legislative Studies Quarterly*, 11: 19–33.

—— Oleszek, W. J., and Kephart, T. (1988), 'One bill, many committees: multiple referrals in the House of Representatives', *Legislative Studies Quarterly*, 13: 3–28.

Davies, P. J. (1998), 'The media and US politics', in G. Peele, et al. (eds.), *Developments in American Politics 3*. Basingstoke: Macmillan.

Delli Carpini, M. X., and Williams, B. A. (2001), 'Let us infotain you: politics in the new media environment', in L. W. Bennett and R. M. Entman (eds.), *Mediated Politics: Communication in the Future of Democracy* Cambridge: Cambridge University Press.

D'Emilio, J. (1983), *Sexual Politics, Sexual Communities: The Making of a Homosexual Minority in the United States, 1940–1970*. Chicago: University of Chicago Press.

Derr, M. C., Naranjo-Huebl, L., and MacNair, R. (eds.) (1995), *Prolife Feminism Yesterday and Today*. New York: Sulzberg & Graham.

Derthick, M. (1999a), 'How many communities?', in Derthick (1999b).

—— (ed.) (1999b), *Dilemmas of Scale in America's Federal Democracy*. Cambridge: Cambridge University Press.

Diamond, M. (1992), 'The ends of federalism', in W. Schambra (ed.), *As Far as Republican Principles Will Admit: Essays*. Washington, DC: AEI Press.

Diaz, T. (1999), *Making a Killing: The Business of Guns in America*. New York: New Press.

Dinitto, D. M. (1999), *Social Welfare: Politics and Public Policy*. Boston: Allyn & Bacon.

Dizard, J. E., Muth, R. M., and Andrews, S. P., Jr. (eds.) (1999), *Guns in America: A Reader*. New York: New York University Press.

Dodd, L. C. (1986a), 'The cycles of legislative change', in Weisberg: 1986.

—— (1986b), 'A theory of Congressional cycles: solving the puzzle of change', in Wright, et al. (1986: 3–44).

—— and Oppenheimer, B. I. (eds.) (1993), *Congress Reconsidered*, 5th edn. Washington, DC: CQ Press.

—— —— (eds.) (1997a), *Congress Reconsidered*, 6th edn. Washington, DC: CQ Press.

—— —— (1997b), 'Revolution in the House: testing the limits of party government', in Dodd and Oppenheimer (1997a: 29–60).

—— —— (eds.) (2001), *Congress Reconsidered*, 7th edn. Washington, DC: CQ Press.

Donahue, J. D. (1997), *Disunited States*. New York: Basic Books.

Dougherty, K. L. (2001), *Collective Action under the Articles of Confederation*. Cambridge: Cambridge University Press.

Dow, D. R. and Dow, M. (eds.) (2002), *Machinery of Death: The Reality of America's Death Penalty Regime*. New York: Routledge.

Drake, F. D. and Nelson, L. R. (eds.) (1999), *States' Rights and American Federalism: A Documented History*. Westport, Conn.: Greenwood Press.

Dryzek, J. S. (1997), *The Politics of the Earth: Environmental Discourses*. Oxford: Oxford University Press.

Dudley, R., and Gitelson, A. R. (2002), *American Elections: The Rules Matter*. New York: Longman.

Dudziak, M. (2000), *Cold War, Civil Rights: Race and the Image of American Democracy*. Princeton, NJ: Princeton University Press.

Dumbrell, J. W. (1995), *The Making of US Foreign Policy*. Manchester: Manchester University Press.

—— (2002), 'Was there a Clinton doctrine? President Clinton's foreign policy reconsidered', *Diplomacy and Statecraft*, 13(2): 43–56.

Dunlap, R., Xiao, C., and McCright, A. (2001), 'Politics and environment in America: partisan and ideological cleavages in public support for environmentalism', *Environmental Politics*, 10(1): 23–48.

Duverger, M. (1954), *Political Parties: Their Organization and Activity in the Modern State*. London: Methuen.

Dworkin, A. (1983), *Right-Wing Women: The Politics of Domesticated Females*. London: Women's Press.

Easterlin, R. A., et al. (1982), *Immigration*. Cambridge, Mass.: Belknap Press.

Edelman, M. (1971), *The Politics of Symbolic Action: Mass Arousal and Quiescence*. Chicago: Markham.

Edwards, L. (2002), 'Slaying in black and white', in R. V. Wilcox and D. Lavery (eds.), *Fighting the Forces: What's at Stake in Buffy the Vampire Slayer*. Lanham, Md: Rowman & Littlefield.

Eggers, W. D., and O'Leary, J. (1995), *Revolution at the Roots: Making Our Government Smaller, Better, and Closer to Home*. New York: Free Press.

Elshtain, J. B. (1997), *Real Politics: At the Center of Everyday Life*. Baltimore: Johns Hopkins University Press.

Encyclopaedia of Associations site at: www.library.dialog.com/bluesheets/html/bl0114.html

Enloe, C. (1989), *Bananas, Beaches and Bases: Making Feminist Sense of International Politics*. London: Pandora.

Erikson, R. S., and Tedin, K. L. (1981), 'The 1928–1936 partisan realignment: the case for the conversion hypothesis', *American Political Science Review*, 75: 951–62.

—— MacKuen, M. B., and Stimson, J. A. (2002), *The Macro Polity*, 2nd edn. Cambridge: Cambridge University Press.

—— and Wright, G. C. (2001), 'Voters, candidates, and issues in Congressional Elections', in Dodd and Oppenheimer (2001).

Esping-Andersen, G., Gallie, D., and Myles, J. (2001), *A New Welfare Architecture for Europe? Report to the Belgian Presidency of the European Union*. Brussels.

Evans, C. L. (2001), 'Committees, leaders, and message politics', in Dodd and Oppenheimer (2001).

—— and Oleszek, W. J. (2000), 'The procedural context of Senate deliberation', in Loomis (2000).

Evans, P., Rueschemeyer, D., and Skocpol, T. (eds.) (1985), *Bringing the State Back In*. New York: Cambridge University Press.

Everard, J. (2000), *Virtual States: The Internet and the Boundaries of the Nation-State*. London: Routledge.

Falwell, J. (1980), *Listen, America!* New York: Bantam.

Faux, M. (1988), *Roe versus Wade: The Untold Story of the Landmark Supreme Court Decision that Made Abortion Legal*. New York: Macmillan.

Featherstone, M. (1995), *Undoing Culture: Globalisation, Postmodernity and Identity*. London: Sage.

Feminist Majority Foundation (2001), *How the Gender Gap Shaped Election 2000*. Preliminary Report, 24 Jan. 2001. www.feminist.org/research/ggap2000.pdf

Fenno, R. F. (1973), *Congressmen in Committees*. Boston: Little, Brown.

Fenno, R. F. (1975), 'If, as Ralph Nader says, Congress is "the broken branch", how come we love our Congressmen so much?', in Ornstein (1975).

—— (1978), *Home Style: House Members in Their Districts*. Boston: Little, Brown.

—— (1996), *Senators on the Campaign Trail: The Politics of Representation*. Norman: University of Oklahoma Press.

—— (2000), *Congress at the Grassroots: Representational Change in the South, 1970–1998*. Chapel Hill: University of North Carolina Press.

Ferejohn, J. A., and Weingast, B. (eds.) (1997), *The New Federalism: Can the States be Trusted?* Stanford, Calif.: Hoover Institution.

Ferguson, T. (1995), *Golden Rule: The Investment Theory of Party Competition and the Logic of Money-Driven Political Systems*. Chicago: University of Chicago Press.

Fields, B. J. (1990), 'Slavery, race and ideology in the United States of America', *New Left Review*, 181: 95–118.

Finlayson, A. (1999), 'Culture', in F. Ashe, et al., *Contemporary Political and Social Theory: An Introduction*. Buckingham: Open University Press.

Fiorina, M. P. (1981), *Retrospective Voting in American National Elections*. New Haven, Conn.: Yale University Press.

—— and Rhode, D. W. (1989), *Home Style and Washington Work: Studies of Congressional Politics*. Ann Arbor: University of Michigan Press.

Fisher, L. (1975), *Presidential Spending Power*. Princeton, NJ: Princeton University Press.

—— (1988), *Constitutional Dialogues: Interpretations as a Political Process*. Princeton, NJ: Princeton University Press.

Flanigan, W., and Zingale, N. (2002), *Political Behavior of the American Electorate*, 2nd edn. Washington, DC: Congressional Quarterly Press.

Foley, M., and Owens, J. E. (1996), *Congress and the Presidency: Institutional Politics in a Separated System*. Manchester: Manchester University Press.

Foote, J. S. (1994), 'The Speaker and the media', in Peters (1994: 135–56).

Fowler, L. L. (1993), *Candidates, Congress, and the American Democracy*. Ann Arbor: University of Michigan Press.

—— and McClure, R. D. (1989), *Political Ambition: Who Decides to Run for Congress*. New Haven, Conn.: Yale University Press.

Foyle, D. C. (1999), *Counting the Public In: Presidents, Public Opinion and Foreign Policy*. New York: Columbia University Press.

Francia, P., and Herrnson, P. (2002), 'Mobilizing the masses through local campaigns', *Public Interest*, 1(2): 4–6.

Frantzich, S. E. (1986), *Write Your Congressman: Constituent Communications and Representation*. New York: Praeger.

Freedman, E. (2000), *No Turning Back: The History of Feminism and the Future of Women*. New York: Ballantine.

Gaddie, R. K., and Bullock, C. (2000), *Elections to Open Seats in the US House: Where the Action is*. Lanham, Md: Rowman & Littlefield.

Gallup Organisation (2001), 'Poll topics and trends: environment', www.gallup.com/poll/topics/environment.asp

Gamson, W. A. (2001), 'Promoting political engagement', in L.W. Bennett and R. M. Entman (eds.), *Mediated Politics: Communication in the Future of Democracy*. Cambridge: Cambridge University Press.

Garten, J. E. (1997), *The Big Ten: The Big Emerging Markets and How They Will Change Our Lives*. New York: Basic Books.

Garvey, J. (1993), 'Fundamentalism and American law', in Appleby and Marty (1993: 28–48).

Gaustad, E. S. (1962), *Historical Atlas of Religion in America*. New York: Harper & Row.

Gellner, E. (1983), *Nations and Nationalism*. Oxford: Blackwell.

George, A. (1980), *Presidential Decisionmaking in Foreign Policy: The Effective Use of Information and Advice*. Boulder, Colo.: Westview Press.

George, C. V. R. (1993), *God's Salesman: Norman Vincent Peale and the Power of Positive Thinking*. New York: Oxford University Press.

Gerring, J. (1998), *Party Ideologies in America 1828–1996*. New York: Cambridge University Press.

Gerstle, G. (2001), *American Crucible: Race and Nation in the Twentieth Century*. Princeton, NJ: Princeton University Press.

Gilens, M. (1999), *Why Americans Hate Welfare: Race, Media, and the Politics of Antipoverty Policy*. Chicago: University of Chicago Press.

Gitlin, T. (1996), 'Television's anti-politics', *Dissent*, 43(1): 76–85.

Glazer, N. (1988), *The Limits of Social Policy*. Cambridge, Mass.: Harvard University Press.

—— (1997), *We Are All Multiculturalists Now*. Cambridge, Mass.: Harvard University Press.

Gleason, P. (1992), *Speaking of Diversity: Language and Ethnicity in Twentieth-Century America*. Baltimore: Johns Hopkins University Press.

Goggin, M. L. (ed.) (1993), *Understanding the New Politics of Abortion*. Newbury Park, Calif.: Sage.

Goldberg, D. T. (1994), *Multiculturalism: A Critical Reader*. Oxford: Blackwell.

Goldfield, M. (1997), *The Color of Politics: Race and the Mainsprings of American Politics*. New York: Free Press.

Goldstein, J. (1994), *Ideas, Interests and American Trade Policy*. Ithaca, NY: Cornell University Press.

Golub, J. (1998), 'New instruments for environmental policy in the EU: introduction and overview', in Golub (ed.), *New Instruments for Environmental Policy in the European Union*. London: Routledge.

Gore, A. (1992), *Earth in the Balance: Ecology and the Human Spirit*. Boston: Houghton Mifflin.

Gottlieb, R. (1993), *Forcing the Spring: The Transformation of the American Environmental Movement*. Washington, DC: Island Press.

Graebner, N. (ed.) (1984), *America as a World Power: A Realist Appraisal from Wilson to Reagan*. Wilmington, Del.: Scholarly Resources.

Graham, O. (ed.) (2000), *Environmental Politics and Policy, 1960–1990's*. Penn: Pennsylvania State University Press.

Greenwald, C. S. (1977), *Group Power: Lobbying and Public Policy*. New York: Praeger.

Greider, W. (1987), *Secrets of the Temple: How the Federal Reserve Runs the Country*. New York: Simon & Schuster.

—— W. (1992), *Who Will Tell the People? The Betrayal of American Democracy*. New York: Simon & Schuster.

Grossberg, L. (1992), *We Gotta Get Out of This Place: Popular Conservatism and Postmodern Culture*. London: Routledge.

Grossman, M. (1998), *Encyclopedia of Capital Punishment*. Santa Barbara, Calif.: ABC-CLIO.

Gunaratna, R. (2002), *Inside Al Qaeda*. London: Hurst.

Gyory, A. (1998), *Closing the Gate: Race, Politics, and the Chinese Exclusion Act*. Chapel Hill: University of North Carolina Press.

Hacker, A. (1995), *Two Nations: Black and White, Separate, Hostile, Unequal*. New York: Ballantine.

Hadaway, C. K., Marler, P. L., and Chaves, M. (1993), 'What the polls don't show: a closer look at US church attendance', *American Sociological Review*, 58: 741–52.

Hadden, J. K., and Swann, C. E. (1981), *Prime Time Preachers: The Rising Power of Televangelism*. Reading, Mass.: Addison-Wesley.

Haeberle, S. H. (1999), 'Gay and lesbian rights: emerging trends in public opinion and voting behavior', in Riggle and Tadlock (1999).

Haider-Markel, D. P. (1999), 'The institutional dynamics of morality politics: legislative voting behavior on lesbian and gay issues', *Policy Studies Journal*, 27(4): 735–49.

—— (2001), 'Policy diffusion as a geographical expansion of the scope of political conflict: same-sex marriage bans in the 1990s', *State Politics and Policy Quarterly*, 1(1): 5–26.

—— and Meier, K. J. (1996), 'The politics of gay and lesbian rights: expanding the scope of the conflict', *Journal of Politics* 58(2): 332–49.

Haines, H. H. (1996), *Against Capital Punishment: The Anti-Death Penalty Movement in America, 1972–1994*. New York: Oxford University Press.

Halbrook, S. (1984), *That Every Man be Armed: The Evolution of a Constitutional Right*. Albuquerque: University of New Mexico Press.

Hall, R. L., and Wayman, F. W. (1990), 'Buying time: money interests and the mobilisation of bias in Congressional committees', *American Political Science Review*, 84: 797–820.

Handler, J. (2000), ' "Ending welfare as we know it": the win/win spin or the stench of victory'. Typescript, UCLA School of Public Policy and Social Research.

—— (2001), 'Welfare reform: something old, something new'. Typescript, UCLA School of Public Policy and Social Research.

Haney Lopez, I. F. (1996), *White By Law: The Legal Construction of Race*. New York: New York University Press.

Hansen, J. M. (1985), 'The political economy of group membership', *American Political Science Review*, 79: 79–96.

—— (1991), *Gaining Access: Congress and the Farm Lobby, 1919–1981*. Chicago: University of Chicago Press.

Hansen, S. B. (1993), 'Differences in public policies toward abortion: electoral and policy context', in Goggin (1993: 222–48).

Harris, D. B. (1998), 'The rise of the public speakership', *Political Science Quarterly*, 113: 193–211.

Harris, P. (ed.) (2001), *The Environment, International Relations and US Foreign Policy*. Washington, DC: Georgetown University Press.

Hart, J. (1995), *The Presidential Branch: From Washington to Clinton*. Chatham, NJ: Chatham House.

Hartz, L. (1955), *The Liberal Tradition in America: An Interpretation of American Political Thought since the Revolution*. New York: Basic Books.

Heclo, H. (1978), 'Issue networks and the executive establishment', in A. King (ed.), *The New American Political System*. Washington, DC: American Enterprise Institute, 87–124.

Henig, R., and Henig, S. (2001), *Women and Political Power: Europe since 1945*. London: Routledge.

Henigan, D. A. E., Nicholson, B., and Hemenway, D. (1995), *Guns and the Constitution: The Myth of Second Amendment Protection for Firearms in America*. Northampton, Mass.: Aletheia Press.

Herbst, S. (1995), 'On electronic public space: talk shows in theoretical perspective', *Political Communication*, 12(3): 263–74.

Herman, E. S., and Chomsky, N. (1988), *Manufacturing Consent: The Political Economy of the Mass Media*. London: Verso.

Herrnson, P. (2000), *Congressional Elections: Campaigning at Home and in Washington*, 3rd edn. Washington, DC: CQ Press.

Hertzke, A., and Peters, R. M. (eds.) (1992), *The Atomistic Congress: An Interpretation of Congressional Change*. Armonk, NY: Sharpe.

Hertzog, M. (1996), *The lavender vote: lesbians, gay men, and bisexuals in American electoral politics*. New York: New York University Press.

Hess, S. (1991), *Live From Capitol Hill! Studies of Congress and the Media*. Washington, DC: Brookings Institution.

Hibbing, J. R., and Theiss-Morse, E. (1995), *Congress as Public Enemy: Public Attitudes Toward American Political Institutions*. Cambridge: Cambridge University Press.

—— —— (2002), *Stealth Democracy: Americans' Beliefs about How Government Should Work*. Cambridge: Cambridge University Press.

Hickok, E. (ed.) (1991), *The Bill of Rights: Original Meaning and Current Understanding*. Charlottesville: University Press of Virginia.

Hicks, A. (1999), *Social Democracy and Welfare Capitalism: A Century of Income Security Politics*. Ithaca, NY: Cornell University Press.

Higham, J. (1975), *Send These to Me: Jews and Other Immigrants in Urban America*. New York: Atheneum.

Hirst, P. Q., and Thompson, G. (eds.) (1999), *Globalisation in Question: The International Economy and the Possibilities of Governance*. Cambridge: Polity.

Hoge, J., and Rose, G. (eds.) (2001), *How Did This Happen? Terrorism and the New War*. New York: Council on Foreign Relations.

hooks, b. (1981), *Ain't I a Woman: Black Women and Feminism*. Boston: South End Press.

—— (1994), *Outlaw Culture: Resisting Representations*. London: Routledge.

Hrebenar, R. (1997), *Interest Group Politics in America*, 3rd edn. Armonk, NY: Sharpe.

Hsu, S. S. (2001), 'US House vote backs gay benefits; DC workers, partners would get coverage', *Washington Post*, 26 Sept.

Huber, E., and Stephens, J. D. (2001), *Development and Crisis of the Welfare State: Parties and Policies in Global Markets*. Chicago: University of Chicago Press.

Hunter, J. D. (1987), *Evangelicalism: The Coming Generation*. Chicago: University of Chicago Press.

—— (1991), *Culture Wars: The Struggle to Define America*. New York: Basic Books.

Huntington, S. (1991), *The Third Wave: Democratization in the Late Twentieth Century*. Norman: University of Oklahoma Press.

Hutton, W. (2002), 'Log cabin to White House? Not any more', *Observer*, 18 Apr.

Jackson, J. E., and Vinovskis, M. A. (1983), 'The "single-issue" issue', in Steiner (1983).

Jacobs, L., Lawrence, E. D., Shapiro, R. Y., and Smith, S. S. (1998), 'Congressional leadership of public opinion', *Political Science Quarterly*, 113: 21–41.

Jacobson, D. (ed.) (1998), *The Immigration Reader: America in a Multidisciplinary Perspective*. Malden, Mass.: Blackwell.

Jacobson, G. C. (1989), 'Strategic politicians and the dynamics of US House elections, 1946–1986', *American Political Science Review*, 83: 775–93.

—— (1990), *The Electoral Origins of Divided Government: Competition in US House Elections, 1946–1988*. Boulder, Colo.: Westview Press.

—— (2001a), *The Politics of Congressional Elections*, 5th edn. New York: Addison Wesley Longman.

—— (2001b), 'Congress: Elections and Stalemate', in Nelson (2001).

—— and Kernell, S. (1983), *Strategy and Choice in Congressional Elections*, 2nd edn. New Haven, Conn.: Yale University Press.

Jaenicke, D. W. (1998), 'Abortion and partisanship in the 104th US Congress', *Politics* 18(1): 1–9.

James, S. C. (2000), *Presidents, Parties and the State: A Party System Perspective on Democratic Regulatory Choice, 1884–1936*. New York: Cambridge University Press.

Jamieson, K., and Campbell, K. K. (1997), *The Interplay of Influence: News, Advertising, Politics and the Mass Media*, 4th edn. New York: Wadsworth.

—— and Waldman, P. (eds.) (2001), *Electing the President 2000: The Insider's View*. Philadelphia: University of Pennsylvania Press.

Janovitz, M. (1978), *The Last Half-Century: Societal Change and Politics in America*. Chicago: University of Chicago Press.

Jelen, T. G. (1991), *The Political Mobilization of Religious Beliefs*. New York, Praeger.

—— (2000), *To Serve God and Mammon: Church–State Relations in American Politics*. Boulder, Colo.: Westview Press.

Jentlesen, B. W. (2000), *American Foreign Policy: The Dynamics of Choice in the 21st Century*. New York: Norton.

Jewell, S. K. (1993), *From Mammy to Miss America and Beyond: Cultural Images and the Shaping of US Social Policy*. London: Routledge.

Johnson, C. (2000), *Blowback: The Costs and Consequences of American Empire*. New York: Metropolitan Books.

Jones, A. F., Jr., and Weinberg, D. H. (2000), *The Changing Shape of the Nation's Income Distribution, 1947–1998*. Washington, DC: US Census Bureau: US Dept. of Commerce, June 2000.

Jones, C. (1997), '"Laying the groundwork" pays off in the States', *Washington Blade*, 1 Aug.

Jones, C. O. (1982), 'Senate party leadership in public policy', in Kozak and Macartney (1982).

—— (1994), *The Presidency in a Separated System*. Washington, DC: Brookings Institution.

Jones, R. J. (2002), *Who Will Be in the White House: Predicting Presidential Elections*. New York: Longman.

Jordan, B. (1998), *The New Politics of Welfare: Social Justice in a Global Context*. London: Sage.

Jordan, G., and Weedon, C. (1995), *Cultural Politics: Class, Gender, Race and the Postmodern World*. Oxford: Blackwell.

Jordan, W. D. (1968), *White Over Black: American Attitudes Toward the Negro, 1550–1812*. Chapel Hill: University of North Carolina Press.

Kahan, M. (1999), *Media as Politics: Theory, Behavior and Change in America*. Upper Saddle, NJ: Prentice-Hall.

Kahn, K. F., and Kenney, P. J. (1999), *The Spectacle of US Senate Campaigns*. Princeton, NJ: Princeton University Press.

Katz, J. L. (1997), 'Longterm challenges temper cheers for welfare successes', *Congressional Quarterly Weekly Report*, 25 Oct: 2603–10.

Katz, M. (2001), *The Price of Citizenship: Redefining the American Welfare State*. New York: Metropolitan Books.

Kayden, X. (1989), *Manipulating Public Opinion: Essays on Democracy*. New York: Harcourt.

Kazee, T. A. (ed.) (1994), *Who Runs for Congress? Ambition, Context, and Candidate Emergence*. Washington, DC: Congressional Quarterly Inc.

Keith, B. E., et al. (1992), *The Myth of the Independent Voter*. Berkeley, Calif.: University of California Press.

Keller, R., and Melnick, R. (eds.) (1999), *Taking Stock: American Government in the Twentieth Century*. Cambridge: Cambridge University Press.

Kelley, R. D. G. (1994), *Race Rebels: Culture, Politics, and the Black Working Class*. New York: Free Press.

Kellner, D. (1995), *Media Culture: Cultural Studies, Identity and Politics Between the Modern and the Postmodern*. London: Routledge.

Kelly, J. R. (1995), 'Beyond compromise: *Casey*, common ground, and the pro-life movement' in Segers and Byrnes (1995: 205–24).

Kennedy, P. (1988), *The Rise and Fall of the Great Powers: Economic Change and Military Conflict from 1500 to 2000*. London: Unwin Hyman.

Kepel, G. (2002), *Jihad: The Rise of Political Islam*. London: I. B. Tauris.

Kernell, S. (1986), *Going Public: New Strategies of Presidential Leadership*. Washington, DC: CQ Press.

Kessler-Harris, A. (2001), *In Pursuit of Equity: Women, Men and the Quest for Economic Citizenship*. Oxford: Oxford University Press.

Key, V. O., Jr. (1942), *Politics, Parties, and Pressure Groups*. New York: Crowell.

—— (1955), 'A theory of critical elections', *Journal of Politics*, 17: 3–18.

—— (1959), 'Secular realignment and the party system', Journal of Politics, 21: 198–210.

Kiley, R. (1998), 'Introduction: globalisation and (post-) modernity and the Third World', in R. Kiley and P. Marfleet (eds.), *Globalisation and the Third World*. London: Routledge.

Kimball, D. C., and Patterson, S. C. (1997), 'Living up to expectations: public attitudes toward Congress', *Journal of Politics*, 59: 701–28.

King, A. (ed.) (1990), *The New American Political System*. Washington, DC: American Enterprise Institute.

King, D. (1995), *Separate and Unequal: Black Americans and the US Federal Government*. Oxford: Oxford University Press.

—— (2000), *Making Americans: Immigration, Race and the Origins of the Diverse Democracy*. Cambridge, Mass.: Harvard University Press.

King, D. C. (1997), *Turf Wars: How Congressional Committees Claim Jurisdiction*. Chicago: University of Chicago Press.

Kissinger, H. (2001), 'America at the apex: empire or leader?', *National Interest*, 64: 9–17.

Kleppner, P., et al. (1981), *The Evolution of American Electoral Systems*. Westport, Conn.: Greenwood Press.

Kornacki, J. J. (ed.) (1990), *Leading Congress: New Styles and Strategies*. Washington, DC: CQ Press.

Kozak, D. C., and Macartney, J. D. (eds.) (1982), *Congress and Public Policy: A Source Book of Documents and Readings*. Homewood, Ill.: Dorsey Press.

Krashinsky, M., and Milne, W. J. (1993), 'The effects of incumbency in US congressional elections, 1950–1988', *Legislative Studies Quarterly*, 18: 321–44.

Krasno, J. (1994), *Challengers, Competition and Re-election: Comparing Senate and House Elections*. New Haven, Conn.: Yale University Press.

Krehbiel, K. (1987), 'Why are committees powerful?', *American Political Science Review*, 81: 929–45.

—— (1998), *Pivotal Politics: A Theory of US Lawmaking*. Chicago: University of Chicago Press.

Kryder, D. (2000), *Divided Arsenal: Race and the American State during World War II*. New York: Cambridge University Press.

Kuklinski, J. H., Quirk, P. J., Jerit, J., Schwieder, D., and Rich, R. F. (2000), 'Misinformation and the currency of democratic citizenship', *Journal of Politics*, 62(3): 790–816.

Lader, L. (1973), *Abortion II: Making the Revolution*. Boston: Beacon Press.

Lafeber, W. (1994), *The American Age: US Foreign Policy at Home and Abroad since 1750*. New York: Norton.

Lafferty, W. M., and Meadowcroft, J. (2000), *Implementing Sustainable Development: Strategies and Initiatives in High Consumption Societies*. Oxford: Oxford University Press.

Lahaye, B. (1999), 'Protecting the traditional family', **www.cwfa.org/library/family/1999-09-24_hslda-fam.shtml**

Lang, K., and Lang, G. E. (2000), 'How Americans view the world: media images and public knowledge', in H. Tumber (ed.), *Media Power, Professionals and Politics*. London: Routledge.

Larson, S. G. (1992), *Creating Consent of the Governed: A Member of Congress and the Local Media*. Carbondale: Southern Illinois University Press.

Leitzel, J. (1998), 'Evasion and public policy: British and US firearm regulation', *Policy Studies*, 19(2): 141–57.

Lentini, P. (2002), 'Melbourne Punk: A "Banal" Politics of Difference?', in D. Crowdy, S. Homan and T. Mitchell (eds.), *Musical In-Between -Ness: The Proceedings of the 8th IASPM Australia–New Zealand Conference 2001*, (Sydney: University of Technology, Sydney Printing Services), 188–200.

Leopold, A. (1949), *A Sand County Almanac, and Sketches Here and There*. Oxford: Oxford University Press.

Lijphart, A. (1999), *Patterns of Democracy: Government Forms and Performance in Thirty-Six Countries*. New Haven, Conn.: Yale University Press.

Lindamen, K., and Haider-Markel, D. P. (2002), 'Issue evolution, political parties, and the culture wars', *Political Research Quarterly*, 55(1): 91–110.

Linz, J., and Stepan, A. (1996), *Problems of Democratic Transition and Consolidation: Southern Europe, South America, and Post-Communist Europe*. Baltimore: Johns Hopkins University Press.

Lippmann, W. (1955), *The Public Philosophy*. London: Hamish Hamilton.

Lipset, S. M. (1963), *The First New Nation: The United States in Historical and Comparative Perspective*. New York: Basic Books.

—— (1996), *American Exceptionalism: A Double-Edged Sword*. New York: Norton.

—— and Marks, G. (2000), *It Didn't Happen Here: Why Socialism Failed in the United States*. New York: Norton.

—— and Raab, E. (1978), *The Politics of Unreason: Right-Wing Extremism in America, 1790–1977*. Chicago: University of Chicago Press.

Loomis, B. A. (1979), 'The Congressional office as a small business: new members set up shop', *Publius*, 9(3): 35–55.

—— (1988), *The New American Politician: Ambition, Entrepreneurship, and the Changing Face of Political Life*. New York: Basic Books.

—— (ed.) (2000), *Esteemed Colleagues: Civility and Deliberation in the US Senate*. Washington, DC: Brookings Institution.

Lott, J. (1998), *More Guns, Less Crime: Understanding Crime and Gun-Control Laws*. Chicago: University of Chicago Press.

Louks, E. H. (1936), *The Ku Klux Klan in Pennsylvania: A Study in Nativism*. New York: Telegraph Press.

Lowi, T. (1979), *The End of Liberalism: The Second Republic of the United States*. New York: Norton.

Luker, K. (1984), *Abortion and the Politics of Motherhood*. Berkeley, Calif.: University of California Press.

McAdam, D. (1999), *Political Process and the Development of Black Insurgency 1930–1970*. Chicago: University of Chicago Press.

McDonald, F. (1994), *The American Presidency: An Intellectual History*. Lawrence: University Press of Kansas.

McElroy, J. H. (1999), *American Beliefs: What Keeps a Big Country and a Diverse People United*. Chicago: Dee.

McFeeley, W. (2000), *Proximity to Death*. New York: Norton.

McGrew, A. (ed.) (1984), *The United States in the Twentieth Century*. London: Hodder & Stoughton.

McKeegan, M. (1992), *Abortion Politics: Mutiny in the Ranks of the Right*. New York: Free Press.

McKeever, R. and Zvesper, J. (1999), *Politics USA*. London: Prentice-Hall.

McKeever, R. (1997), *The United States Supreme Court: A Political and Legal Analysis*. Manchester: Manchester University Press.

McLaughlin, J. (1984), 'The evangelical surge', *National Review*, 20: 13.

Madison, J., Hamilton, A., and Jay, J. (1961), *The Federalist Papers*. New York: New American Library.

Magleby, D., and Nelson, C. (1990), *The Money Chase: Congressional Campaign Finance Reform*. Washington, DC: Brookings Institution.

Maier, C. S. and Klausen, J. (eds.) (2001), *Has Liberalism Failed Women? Assuring Equal Representation in Europe and the United States*. Basingstoke: Palgrave.

Maisel, L. S. (ed.) (1998), *The Parties Respond: Change in American Parties and Campaigns*, 3rd edn. Boulder, Colo.: Westview Press.

Malcolm, J. L. (1994), *To Keep and Bear Arms: The Origins of an Anglo-American Right*. Cambridge, Mass.: Harvard University Press.

Mann, T. E. (1982), *Unsafe at Any Margin: Interpreting Congressional Elections*. Washington, DC: American Enterprise Institute.

—— and Ornstein, N. J. (eds.) (1982), *Congress, the Press and the Public*. Washington, DC: Brookings Institution and American Enterprise Institute.

Marler, P. L., and Hadaway, C. K. (1997), 'Testing the attendance gap in a conservative church', *Sociology of Religion*, 60: 174–86.

Marsden, G. (1980), *Fundamentalism and American Culture: The Shaping of Twentieth-Century Evangelicalism, 1870–1925*. New York: Oxford University Press.

Mathews, D. G., and De Hart, J. S. (1990), *Sex, Gender, and the Politics of ERA: A State and the Nation*. Oxford: Oxford University Press.

May, E. R. (1961), *Imperial Democracy: The Emergence of America as a Great Power*. New York: Harcourt, Brace & World.

Mayer, W. G. (1996), *The Divided Democrats: Ideological Unity, Party Reform, and Presidential Elections*. Boulder, Colo.: Westview Press.

—— (2000), *In Pursuit of the White House 2000: How We Choose Our Presidential Nominees*. New York: Chatham House.

Mayhew, D. R. (1974a), *Congress: The Electoral Connection*. New Haven, Conn.: Yale University Press.

—— (1974b), 'Congressional elections: the case of the vanishing marginals', *Polity*, 6: 295–317.

—— (2002), *Electoral Realignments: A Critique of an American Genre*. New Haven, Conn.: Yale University Press.

Mazmanian, D., and Kraft, M. (eds.) (1999), *Toward Sustainable Communities: Transition and Transformations in Environmental Policy*. Cambridge, Mass.: MIT Press.

Mead, W. R. (2001), *Special Providence: American Foreign Policy and How It Changed the World*. New York: Knopf.

Melich, T. (1996), *The Republican War against Women: An Insider's Report from behind the Lines*. New York: Bantam.

Meyer, D. S., and Staggenborg, S. (1996), 'Movements, countermovements, and the structure of political opportunity', *American Journal of Sociology*, 101(6): 1628–60.

—— —— (1998), 'Countermovement dynamics in federal systems: a comparison of abortion politics in Canada and the United States', *Research in Political Sociology*, 8: 209–40.

Mills, C. W. (1956), *The Power Elite*. New York: Oxford University Press.

Mink, G. (1998), *Welfare's End*. Ithaca, NY: Cornell University Press.

Miringoff, M., and Marque-Luisa, M. (1999), *The Social Health of the Nation: How America is Really Doing*. Oxford: Oxford University Press.

Miroff, B., Seidelman, R., and Swanstrom, T. (eds.) (2001), *Debating Democracy: A Reader in American Politics*. Boston: Houghton Mifflin.

Mitchell, T. (1996), *Popular Music and Local Identity: Rock, Pop and Rap in Europe and Oceania*. Leicester: Leicester University Press.

—— (ed.) (2001), *Global Noise: Rap and Hip Hop Outside the USA*. Middletown, Conn.: Wesleyan University Press.

Moberg, D. O. (1972), 'USA', in Mol (1972: 528–63).

Moe, T. M. (1980), *The Organization of Interests: Incentives and the Internal Dynamics of Political Interest Groups*. Chicago: University of Chicago Press.

Moen, M. C. (1992), *The Transformation of the Christian Right*. Tuscaloosa: University of Alabama Press.

Mohr, J. C. (1978), *Abortion in America: The Origins and Evolution of National Policy*. Oxford: Oxford University Press.

Mol, H. (ed.) (1972), *Western Religion: A Country by Country Sociological Inquiry*. The Hague: Mouton.

Moore, B., Jr. (1966), *Social Origins of Dictatorship and Democracy: Lord and Peasant in the Making of the Modern World*. London: Penguin.

Morris, A. D. (1984), *The Origins of the Civil Rights Movement: Black Communities Organizing for Change*. New York: Free Press.

Mule, R. (2001), *Political Parties, Games and Redistribution*. Cambridge: Cambridge University Press.

Muravchik, J. (1996), *The Imperative of American Leadership: A Challenge to Neo-Isolationism*. Washington, DC: American Enterprise Institute.

Mutz, D. C., and Martin, P. S. (2001), 'Facilitating communication across lines of difference: the role of the mass media', *American Political Science Review*, 95(1): 97–114.

Myrdal, G. (1944), *An American Dilemma: The Negro Problem and Modern Democracy*. New York: Harper & Row.

National Telecommunications and Information Administration (2002), *A Nation Online: How Americans are Expanding their Use of the Internet*. Washington, DC: Economics and Statistics Administration, US Dept. of Commerce.

Nau, H. (2002), *At Home Abroad: Identity and Power in American Foreign Policy*. Ithaca, NY: Cornell University Press.

Nelson, B. (2000), *Divided We Stand: American Workers and the Struggle for Black Equality*. Princeton, NJ: Princeton University Press.

Nelson, M. (ed.) (2001), *The Elections of 2000*. Washington, DC: CQ Press.

Nettl, J. P. (1968), 'The state as a conceptual variable', *World Politics*, 20.

Neuman, R. W. (2001), 'The impact of new media', in L. W. Bennett and R. M. Entman (eds.), *Mediated Politics: Communication in the Future of Democracy*. Cambridge: Cambridge University Press.

Neustadt, R. E. (1960), *Presidential Power: The Politics of Leadership*. New York: Wiley.

Newport, F. (2001), 'American attitudes toward homosexuality continue to become more tolerant', *Gallup News Service*, 4 June.

Nie, N., et al. (1979), *The Changing American Voter*. Cambridge, Mass.: Harvard University Press.

Niemi, R., and Weisberg, H. (eds.) (1993), *Classics in Voting Behaviour*. Washington, DC: CQ Press.

Noll, M. A. (ed.) (1990), *Religion and American Politics: From the Colonial Periods to the 1980s*. New York: Oxford University Press.

Nordlinger, E. A. (1995), *Isolationism Reconfigured: American Foreign Policy for a New Century*. Princeton, NJ: Princeton University Press.

Nye, J. S. (2002), *The Paradox of American Power: Why the World's Only Superpower Cannot Go It Alone*. Oxford: Oxford University Press.

O'Connor, K. (1996), *No Neutral Ground? Abortion Politics in an Age of Absolutes*. Boulder, Colo.: Westview Press.

O'Donnell, G., Schmitter, P. C., and Whitehead, L. (eds.) (1986), *Transitions from Authoritarian Rule: Prospects for Democracy*. Baltimore: Johns Hopkins University Press.

Olesek, W. J. (2000), *Congressional Procedures and the Policy Process*, 5th edn. Washington, DC: CQ Press.

Olson, M. (1965), *The Logic of Collective Action: Public Goods and the Theory of Groups*. Cambridge, Mass.: Harvard University Press.

Oppenheimer, B. I. (1997), 'Changing time constraints on Congress: historical perspectives on the use of cloture', in Dodd and Oppenheimer (1997a: 393–413).

—— (2000), 'Constituency size and the strategic behaviour of senators', in Loomis (2000: 151–4).

Ornstein, N. J. (ed.) (1975), *Congress in Change Evolution and Reform*. New York: Praeger.

—— and Fortier, J. (2002), 'Relations with Congress', *Political Science and Politics*, 35(1).

Orren, K., and Skowronek, S. (1998), 'Regimes and regime building in American government: a review of literature on the 1940s', *Political Science Quarterly*, 113: 689–702.

O'Shea, K. A. (1999), *Women and the Death Penalty in the United States, 1900–1998*. Westport, Conn.: Praeger.

Osborne, D., and Gaebler, T. (1993), *Reinventing Government: How The Entrepreneurial Spirit is Transforming the Public Sector*. New York: Plume.

Ostrom, E. (1990), *Governing the Commons: The Evolution of Institutions for Collective Action*. New York: Cambridge University Press.

Owens, J. E. (1997), 'The return of party government in the US House of Representatives, central leadership–committee relations in the 104th Congress', *British Journal of Political Science*, 27(2): 247–72.

—— (1999), 'From committee government to party government: changing opportunities for amendment sponsors in the US House of Representatives, 1945–98', *Journal of Legislative Studies*, 5(3/4): 75–103.

Page, B. I., and Shapiro, R. Y. (1992), *The Rational Public: Fifty Years of Trends in Americans, Policy Preferences*. Chicago: University of Chicago Press.

Paige, C. (1983), *The Right to Lifers: Who They Are, How They Operate, Where They Get Their Money*. New York: Summit Books.

Pakulski, J. (1991), *Social Movements: The Politics of Moral Protest*. Melbourne: Longman-Cheshire.

Palazzolo, D. J. (1992), *The Speaker and the Budget: Leadership in the Post-Reform House of Representatives*. Pittsburgh: University of Pittsburgh Press.

Parenti, M. (1986), *Inventing Reality: The Politics of the Mass Media*. New York: St. Martin's Press.

—— (1998), *America Besieged*. San Francisco: City Lights.

Patterson, O. (1999), 'Liberty against the democratic state', in Warren (1999).

Perea, J. F. (ed.) (1997), *Immigrants Out! The New Nativism and the Anti-Immigrant Impulse in the United States*. New York: New York University Press.

Petchesky, R. P. (1984), *Abortion and Women's Choice: The State, Sexuality, and Reproductive Freedom*. New York: Longman.

Peters, R. M. (1990), *The American Speakership: The Office in Historical Perspective*. Baltimore: Johns Hopkins University Press.

—— (ed.) (1994), *The Speaker: Leadership in the US House of Representatives*. Washington, DC: Congressional Quarterly Inc.

Peterson, J. (1995), 'Decision-making in the EU: towards a framework for analysis', *Journal of European Public Policy*, 2(1): 69–73.

Peterson, P. E. (ed.) (1994), *The President, the Congress and the Making of Foreign Policy*. Norman: Oklahoma University Press.

Pew Forum on Religion and Public Life (2001), 'It's wrong to base voting on religion, say most Americans', www.pewtrusts.com

Phillips, K. (1995), *Arrogant Capital: Washington, Wall Street, and the Frustration of American Politics*. Boston: Back Bay/ Little, Brown.

Polsby, N. W. (1983), *Consequences of Party Reform*. Oxford: Oxford University Press.

—— (1983), 'Some landmarks in modern presidential–Congressional relations', in A. King (ed.), *Both Ends of the Avenue*. Washington, DC: American Enterprise Institute.

—— and Wildavsky, A. (2000), *Presidential Elections: Strategies and Structures in American Politics*, 10th edn. Chatham, NJ: Chatham House.

Pomper, G. (ed.) (2001), *The Election of 2000: Reports and Interpretations*. New York: Chatham House.

Popkin, S. (1994), *The Reasoning Voter: Communication and Persuasion in Presidential Elections*, 2nd edn. Chicago: University of Chicago Press.

Posner, R. A. (2001), *Public Intellectuals: A Study of Decline*. Cambridge, Mass.: Harvard University Press.

Post, R., and Rogin, M. (eds.) (1998), *Race and Representation: Affirmative Action*. New York: Zone Books.

Pothier, J. T. (1984), 'The partisan bias in Senate elections', *American Politics Quarterly*, 12: 88–100.

Powlick, P. J. (1995), 'The sources of public opinion for American foreign policy officials', *International Studies Quarterly*, 39(3): 427–52.

Pozner, J. L. (2002), 'Missing in action: whatever happened to the gender gap?', *Women's Review of Books*, 19: 20–1.

Prejean, H. (1993), *Dead Man Walking: An Eyewitness Account of the Death Penalty in the United States*. New York: Random House.

Price, D. E. (1971), 'Professionals and "entrepreneurs": staff orientation and policy making on three Senate committees', *Journal of Politics*, 33: 316–36.

—— (2000), *The Congressional Experience*, 2nd edn. Boulder, Colo.: Westview Press.

Przeworski, A., et al. (1995), *Sustainable Democracy*. Cambridge: Cambridge University Press.

Putnam, R. (2000), *Bowling Alone: The Collapse and Revival of American Community*. New York: Simon & Schuster.

Rayside, D. M. (1998), *On the Fringe: Gays and Lesbians in Politics*. Ithaca, NY: Cornell University Press.

Rector, R., and Sanera, M. (eds.) (1987), *Steering the Elephant: How Washington Works*. New York: Universe Books.

Riesebrodt, M. (1993), *Pious Passion: The Emergence of Modern Fundamentalism in the United States and Iran*. Berkeley: University of California Press.

Riggle, D. B., and Tadlock, B. L. (eds.) (1999), *Gays and Lesbians in the Democratic Process: Public Policy, Public Opinion and Political Representation*. New York: Columbia University Press.

Rimmerman, C. A., Wald, K. D., and Wilcox, C. (eds.) (2000), *The Politics of Gay Rights*. Chicago: University of Chicago Press.

Risen, J., and Thomas, J. L. (1998), *Wrath of Angels: The American Abortion War*. New York: Basic Books.

Rivers, D., and Fiorina, M. (1989), 'Constituency service, reputation, and the incumbency advantage', in Fiorina and Rohde (1989).

Robertson, P. (2001), 'Transcript of *700 Club* interview with Jerry Falwell', 13 Sept. 2001. www.pfaw.org/issues/right/robertson_falwell.html

Rohde, D. W. (1979), 'Risk-bearing and progressive ambition: the case of the United States House of Representatives', *American Journal of Political Science*, 23: 1–26.

—— (1991), *Parties and Leaders in the Postreform House*. Chicago: University of Chicago Press.

Rose, T. (1994), *Black Noise: Rap Music and Black Culture in Contemporary America*. Hanover, NH: Wesleyan University Press/University Press of New England Press.

Rosenberg, J. (1999), 'For democracy, not hypocrisy: world war and race relations in the United States, 1914–1919', *International History Review*, 21: 592–625.

Rosenstone, S. J., and Hansen, J. M. (1993), *Mobilization, Participation, and Democracy in America*. New York: Macmillan.

Rozell, M. J., and Wilcox, C. (eds.) (1995), *God at the Grassroots: The Christian Right in the 1994 Elections*. Lanham, Md: Rowman & Littlefield.

—— —— (eds.) (1996), *Second Coming: The New Christian Right in Virginia Politics*. Baltimore: Johns Hopkins University Press.

Rubin, C. T. (ed.) (2000), *Conservation Reconsidered: Nature, Virtue and American Liberal Democracy*. Lanham, Md: Rowman & Littlefield.

Rueschemeyer, D., Stephens, E. H., and Stephens, J. D. (1992), *Capitalist Development and Democracy*. Oxford: Polity Press.

Rushkoff, D. (1994), *Media Virus: Hidden Agendas in Popular Culture*. Sydney: Random House Australia.

Ruthven, M. (2002), *A Fury for God: The Islamist Attack on America*. London: Granta.

Sabato, L. J. (1984), *PAC Power: Inside the World of Political Action Committees*. New York: Norton.

—— (2002), *Overtime! The Election 2000 Thriller*. New York: Longman.

Salisbury, R. (1984), 'Interest representation and the dominance of institutions', *American Political Science Review*, 78: 64–77.

Salisbury, R. H., and Shepsle, K. A. (1981), 'US Congressman as enterprise', *Legislative Studies Quarterly*, 6: 559–76.

Sarat, A. (ed.) (1999), *The Killing State: Capital Punishment in Law, Politics and Culture*. New York: Oxford University Press.

Sardar, Z. (1998), *Postmodernism and the Other: The New Imperialism of Western Culture*. London: Pluto Press.

Scheberle, D. (1997), *Federalism and Environmental Policy: Trust and the Politics of Implementation*. Washington, DC: Georgetown University Press.

Schlesinger, A. M., Jr. (1973), *The Imperial Presidency*. Boston: Houghton Mifflin.

—— (1991), *The Disuniting of America*. New York: Norton.

Schlosberg, D. (1999), *Environmental Justice and the New Pluralism: The Challenge of Difference for Environmentalism*. Oxford: Oxford University Press.

Schmidtz, D., and Goodin, R. E. (1998), *Social Welfare and Individual Responsibility (For and Against)*. Cambridge: Cambridge University Press.

Schneider, E. M. (2000), *Battered Women and Feminist Lawmaking*. New Haven, Conn.: Yale University Press.

Scholte, J. A. (2000), *Globalisation: A Critical Introduction*. Basingstoke: Macmillan.

Schram, S. F. (2000), *After Welfare: The Culture of Postindustrial Social Policy*. New York: New York University Press.

Schumaker, P., and Loomis, B. (eds.) (2002), *Choosing a President: The Electoral College and Beyond*. New York: Chatham House.

Scott, J. M. (ed.) (1998), *After the End: Making US Foreign Policy in the Post-Cold War World*. Durham, NC: Duke University Press.

Segers, M. C. (1995), 'The pro-choice movement post-Casey: preserving access', in Segers and Byrnes (1995: 225–45).

—— and Byrnes, T. A. (eds.) (1995), *Abortion Politics in American States*. Armonk, NY: Sharpe.

Shafer, B. E. (1983), *Quiet Revolution: The Struggle for the Democratic Party and the Shaping of Post-Reform Politics*. New York: Russell Sage Foundation.

—— (ed.) (1991), *The End of Realignment? Interpreting American Electoral Eras*. Madison: University of Wisconsin Press.

Shapiro, R. Y., and Mahajan, H. (1986), 'Gender differences in policy preferences: a summary of trends from the 1960s to the 1980s', *Public Opinion Quarterly*, 50: 42–61.

Shaw, R. (1999), *Reclaiming America: Nike, Clean Air, and the New National Activism*. Berkeley: University of California Press.

Sheingate, A. (2001), *The Rise of the Agricultural Welfare State: Institutions and Interest Group Power in the United States, France, and Japan*. Princeton, NJ: Princeton University Press.

Shepsle, K., and Weingast, B. (1987), 'The institutional foundations of committee power', *American Political Science Review*, 81: 85–104.

—— —— (1987) 'Reply to Krehbiel', *American Political Science Review*, 81: 929–45.

Sherrill, K. S. (1996), 'The political power of lesbians, gays, and bisexuals', *PS: Political Science and Politics*, 29: 469–73.

—— and Yang, A. (2000), 'From outlaws to in-laws: anti-gay attitudes thaw', *Public Perspective*, 11(1): 20–31.

Shibley, M. (1966), *Resurgent Evangelicalism in the United States: Mapping Cultural Change since 1970*. Columbia: University of South Carolina Press.

Shuker, R. (1994), *Understanding Popular Music*. London: Routledge.

Sinclair, B. (1983), *Majority Leadership in the US House*. Baltimore: Johns Hopkins University Press.

—— (1989), *The Transformation of the US Senate*. Baltimore: Johns Hopkins University Press.

—— (1990), 'Congressional leadership: a review essay and a research agenda', in Kornacki (1990).

—— (1992a), 'The emergence of strong leadership in the 1980s House of Representatives', *Journal of Politics*, 54: 657–84.

—— (1992b), 'The evolution of party leadership in the modern House', in Hertzke and Peters (1992: 259–92).

—— (1995), *Legislators, Leaders, and Lawmaking: The US House of Representatives in the Postreform Era*. Baltimore: Johns Hopkins University Press.

—— (2000a), 'Individualism, partisanship, and cooperation in the Senate,' in Loomis (2000: 59–77).

—— (2000b), *Unorthodox Lawmaking: New Legislative Processes in the US Congress*. Washington, DC: CQ Press.

Singh, R. (2002), 'Subverting American values? *The Simpsons, South Park* and the cartoon culture war', in Singh (ed.), *American Politics and Society Today*. Cambridge: Polity Press, 206–30.

Skocpol, T. (1992), *Protecting soldiers and mothers: the political origins of social policy in the United States*. Cambridge, Mass.: Harvard University Press.

—— (1995), *Social Policy in the United States: Future Possibilities in Historical Perspective*. Princeton, NJ: Princeton University Press.

Skowronek, S. (1982), *Building a New American State: The Expansion of National Administrative Capacities, 1877–1920*. Cambridge: Cambridge University Press.

Slater, D. (2001), 'Political discourse and the politics of need: discourses on the good life in cyberspace media', in L. W. Bennett and R. M. Entman (eds.), *Mediated Politics: Communication in the Future of Democracy*. Cambridge: Cambridge University Press.

—— and Taylor, P. J. (eds.) (1999), *The American Century: Consequences and Coercion in the Projection of American Power*. Oxford: Blackwell.

Smelser, N. J., and Alexander, J. C. (eds.) (1999), *Diversity and its Discontents: Cultural Conflict and Common Ground in Contemporary American Society*. Princeton, NJ: Princeton University Press.

Smith, A. (1991), *National Identity*. London: Penguin.

Smith, R. A., and Haider-Markel, D. P. (2002), *Gay and Lesbian Americans and Political Participation: A Reference Handbook*. Denver: ABC-CLIO.

Smith, R. M. (1993), 'Beyond Tocqueville, Myrdal and Hartz: the multiple traditions in America', *American Political Science Review*, 87: 549–66.

—— (1997), *Civic Ideals: Conflicting Visions of Citizenship in US History*. New Haven, Conn.: Yale University Press.

Smith, S. S. (1989), *Call To Order: Floor Politics in the House and Senate*. Washington, DC: Brookings Institution.

—— (1997), 'Forces of change in Senate party leadership and organization', in Dodd and Oppenheimer (1993).

—— and Deering, C. J. (1997), *Committees in Congress*, 3rd edn. Washington, DC: CQ Press.

—— and Flathman, M. (1989), 'Managing the Senate floor: complex unanimous consent agreements since the 1950s', *Legislative Studies Quarterly*, 14: 349–74.

—— and Gamm, G. (2000), 'The dynamics of party government in Congress', in Dodd and Oppenheimer (2000: 245–68).

Smith, T. (1994), *America's Mission: The United States and the Worldwide Struggle for Democracy in the Twentieth Century*. Cambridge: Cambridge University Press.

—— (2000), *Foreign Attachments: The Power of Ethnic Groups in the Making of American Foreign Policy*. Cambridge, Mass.: Harvard University Press.

Soden, D. L. (ed.) (1999), *The Environmental Presidency*. Albany, NY: State University of New York Press.

Sombart, W. (1976 [1905]), *Why is there no Socialism in the United States?* White Plains, NY: Sharpe.

Southern Poverty Law Center (2001), 'Reevaluating the Net', *Southern Poverty Law Center's Intelligence Report*, 102: 54–5.

Sparrow, B. H. (1996), *From the Outside In: World War II and the American State*. Princeton, NJ: Princeton University Press.

Spitzer, R. (1995), *The Politics of Gun Control*, 2nd edn. Chatham, NJ: Chatham House.

Springer, K. (ed.) (1999), *Still Lifting, Still Climbing: African American Women's Contemporary Activism*. New York: New York University Press.

Squires, J. (2000), *Gender in Political Theory*. Cambridge: Polity Press.

Staeheli, L. A., Kodras, J. E., and Flint, C. (eds.) (1997), *State Devolution in America: Implications for a Diverse Society*. London: Sage.

Staggenborg, S. (1991), *The Pro-Choice Movement: Organization and Activism in the Abortion Conflict*. New York: Oxford University Press.

—— (1998), *Gender, Family and Social Movements*. Thousand Oaks, Calif.: Pine Forge Press.

Stanley, H. W., and Niemi, R. (2000), *Vital Statistics on America Politics*. Washington, DC: CQ Press.

Stannard, D. E. (1992), *American Holocaust: Columbus and the Conquest of the New World*. New York: Oxford University Press.

Stears, M. (2001), 'Beyond the logic of liberalism', *Journal of Political Ideologies*, 6: 215–30.

Stein, H. (1988), *Presidential Economics: The Making of Economic Policy from Roosevelt to Reagan and Beyond*. Washington, DC: American Enterprise Institute.

Steiner, G. Y., et al. (eds.) (1983), *The Abortion Dispute and the American System*. Washington, DC: Brookings Institution.

Sterling, C. H. (2000), 'US telecommunications, industry ownership and the 1996 Telecommunications Act: watershed or unintended consequences?', in H. Tumber (ed.), *Media Power, Professionals and Politics*. London: Routledge.

Stevens, J. D. (1982), *Shaping the First Amendment: The Development of Free Expression*. London: Sage.

Stewart, J. G. (1975), 'Central party organs in Congress', in H. C. Mansfield (ed.), *Congress Against Itself*. New York: Praeger, 20–33.

Street, J. (2001), *Mass media, politics and democracy*. New York: Palgrave.

Streitmatter, R. (1995), *Unspeakable: The Rise of the Gay and Lesbian Press in America*. Boston: Faber & Faber.

Stubbing, R. A. (1986), *The Defense Game: An Insider Explores the Astonishing Realities of America's Defense Establishment*. New York: Harper & Row.

Sundquist, J. L. (1983), *Dynamics of the Party System: Alignment and Realignment of Political Parties in the United States*, rev. edn. Washington, DC: Brookings Institution.

Talbot, S., and Chanda, N. (2001), *The Age of Terror*. New Haven, Conn.: Perseus Press.

Tansey, S. (1995), *Politics: The Basics*. London: Routledge.

Tarrow, S. (1994), *Power in Movement: Social Movements, Collective Action, and Politics*. Cambridge: Cambridge University Press.

Therborn, G. (1977), 'The rule of capital and the rise of democracy', *New Left Review*, 103: 3–41.

Trattner, W. I. (1999), *From Poor Law to Welfare State: A History of Social Welfare in America*, 6th edn. New York: Free Press.

Trubowitz, P. (1998), *Defining the National Interest: Conflict and Change in American Foreign Policy*. Chicago: University of Chicago Press.

Tygart, C. E. (2000), 'Genetic causation attribution and public support of gay rights', *International Journal of Public Opinion Research*, 12(3): 259–75.

Underwood, D. (2001), 'Reporting and the push for market-oriented journalism', in L. W. Bennett and R. M. Entman (eds.), *Mediated Politics: Communication in the Future of Democracy*. Cambridge: Cambridge University Press.

US Bureau of Labor Statistics (2002), 'Highlights of women's earnings in 2001', www.bls.gov/cps/cpswom2001.pdf

US Census Bureau (2002), 'Voting and registration in the election of November 2000', www.census.gov/population/www/socdemo/voting.html

US Centers for Disease Control and Prevention (2000), *Abortion Surveillance: Preliminary Analysis—US, 1997*. Atlanta.

Vaid, U. (1995), *Virtual Equality: The Mainstreaming of Gay and Lesbian Liberation*. New York: Anchor Books.

Vig, N., and Kraft, M. (eds.) (1999), *Environmental Policy: New Directions for the Twenty-First Century*. Washington, DC: CQ Press.

Vogel, D. (1986), *National Styles of Regulation: Environmental Policy in Great Britain and the United States*. Ithaca, NY: Cornell University Press.

Walker, D. B. (1995), *The Rebirth of Federalism: Slouching Toward Washington*. Chatham, NJ: Chatham House.

Walker, J. L. (1983), 'Origins and maintenance of interest groups in America', *American Political Science Review*, 77: 390–406.

—— (1991), *Mobilizing Interest Groups in America: Patrons, Professions, and Social Movements*. Ann Arbor: University of Michigan Press.

Wallis, R. (1979), *Salvation and Protest: Studies of Social and Religious Movements*. London: Pinter.

Ware, A. (1985), *The Breakdown of Democratic Party Organization, 1940–1980*. Oxford: Clarendon, Press.

—— (1996), *Political parties and party systems*. Oxford: Oxford University Press.

Warren, M. E. (ed.) (1999), *Democracy and Trust*. Cambridge: Cambridge University Press.

Watson, J. (1999), *The Christian Coalition: Dreams of Restoration, Demands for Recognition*. London: Macmillan.

Wattenberg, M. (1998), *The Decline of American Political Parties 1952–1996*. Cambridge, Mass.: Harvard University Press.

Wayne, S. (2000), *The Road to the White House 2000: The Politics of Presidential Elections*. New York: Palgrave.

—— (2001), *Is This Any Way to Run a Democratic Election? Debating American Electoral Politics*. New York: Houghton Mifflin.

WCED (World Commission on Environment and Development) (1987), *Our Common Future (The Brundtland Report)*. Oxford: Oxford University Press.

Weale, A. (1992), *The New Politics of Pollution*. Manchester: Manchester University Press.

Weingast, B. R., and Marshall, W. (1988), 'The industrial organization of Congress, or, why legislatures, like firms, are not organized as markets', *Journal of Political Economy*, 96: 132.

Weir, M., and Skocpol, T. (1985), 'State structures and the possibilities for "Keynesian" responses to the Great Depression in Sweden, Britain and the United States', in Evans, et al. (1985).

Weisberg, H. F. (ed.) (1986), *Political Science: The Science of Politics*. New York: Agathon Press.

West, D., and Loomis, B. (1998), *The Sound of Money: How Political Interests Get What They Want*. New York: Norton.

White, D. W. (1996), *The American Century: the Rise and Decline of the United States as a World Power*. New Haven, Conn.: Yale University Press.

Whittington, K. E. (1999), *Constitutional Construction: Divided Powers and Constitutional Meaning*. Cambridge, Mass.: Harvard University Press.

Wilcox, C. (1987), 'America's radical right revisited', *Sociological Analysis*, 48: 46–57.

—— (1989), 'Political action committees and abortion: a longitudinal analysis', *Women and Politics*, 9(1): 1–19.

—— (1992), *God's Warriors: The Christian Right in Twentieth-Century America*. Baltimore: Johns Hopkins University Press.

—— and Wolpert, R. (2000), 'Gay rights in the public sphere: public opinion on gay and lesbian equality,' in Rimmerman, et al. (2000).

Wildavsky, A. (1969), 'Salvation by staff: reform of the presidential office', in Wildavsky (ed.), *The Presidency*. Boston: Little, Brown.

Williams, P. J. (1991), *The Alchemy of Race and Rights*. Cambridge, Mass.: Harvard University Press.

Wilson, J. F. (1990), 'Religion, government and power in the new American nation', in Noll (1990: 77–91).

Wilson, W. (1981 [1885]), *Congressional Government: A Study in American Politics*. Baltimore: Johns Hopkins Press.

Wolfinger, R. E., and Rosenstone, S. J. (1980), *Who Votes?* New Haven, Conn.: Yale University Press.

—— —— and McIntosh, R. A. (1981), 'Presidential and Congressional voters compared', *American Politics Quarterly*, 9.

Woodward, G. C. (1997), *Perspectives on American Political Media*. Needham Heights, Mass.: Allyn & Bacon.

Woolley, J. (1984), *Monetary Politics: The Federal Reserve and the Politics of Monetary Policy*. Cambridge: Cambridge University Press.

Wright, G. C., Riesel Bach, L. N., and Dodd, L. C. (eds.) (1986), *Congress and Policy Change*. New York: Agathon Press.

Wright, J. (1996), *Interest Groups and Congress: Lobbying, Contributions, and Influence*. Boston: Allyn & Bacon.

Wright, S. (2000), '"A love born of hate": autonomous rap in Italy', *Theory, Culture and Society*, 17(3): 117–35.

Yang, A. S. (1999), *From Wrongs to Rights: Public Opinion on Gay and Lesbian Americans Moves toward Equality, 1973–1999*. Washington, DC: National Gay and Lesbian Task Force.

Young, G., and Cooper, J. (1993), 'Multiple referral and the transformation of House decision making', in Dodd and Oppenheimer (1993: 211–35).

Zunz, O. (1998), *Why the American Century?* Chicago: University of Chicago Press.

Appendix

The Constitution of the United States of America

Preamble

We the People of the United States, in Order to form a more perfect Union, establish Justice, insure domestic Tranquillity, provide for the common defense, promote the general Welfare, and secure the Blessings of Liberty to ourselves and our Posterity, do ordain and establish this Constitution for the United States of America.

Article I

Section 1 All legislative Powers herein granted shall be vested in a Congress of the United States, which shall consist of a Senate and House of Representatives.

Section 2 The House of Representatives shall be composed of Members chosen every second Year by the People of the several States, and the Electors in each State shall have the Qualifications requisite for Electors of the most numerous Branch of the State Legislature.

No Person shall be a Representative who shall not have attained to the age of twenty five Years, and been seven Years a Citizen of the United States, and who shall not, when elected, be an Inhabitant of that State in which he shall be chosen.

Representatives and direct Taxes shall be apportioned among the several States which may be included within this Union, according to their respective Numbers, which shall be determined by adding to the whole Number of free Persons, including those bound to Service for a Term of Years, and excluding Indians not taxed, three fifths of all other Persons. The actual Enumeration shall be made within three Years after the first Meeting of the Congress of the United States, and within every subsequent Term of ten Years, in such Manner as they shall by Law direct. The Number of Representatives shall not exceed one for every thirty Thousand, but each State shall have at Least one Representative; and until such enumeration shall be made, the State of New Hampshire shall be entitled to chuse three, Massachusetts eight, Rhode-Island and Providence Plantations one, Connecticut five, New-York six, New Jersey four, Pennsylvania eight, Delaware one, Maryland six, Virginia ten, North Carolina five, South Carolina five, and Georgia three.

When vacancies happen in the Representation from any State, the Executive Authority thereof shall issue Writs of Election to fill such Vacancies.

The House of Representatives shall chuse their Speaker and other Officers; and shall have the sole Power of Impeachment.

Section 3 The Senate of the United States shall be composed of two Senators from each State, chosen by the Legislature thereof, for six Years; and each Senator shall have one Vote.

Immediately after they shall be assembled in Consequence of the first Election, they shall be divided as equally as may be into three Classes. The Seats of the Senators of the first Class shall be vacated at the Expiration of the second Year, of the second Class at the Expiration of the fourth Year, and of the third Class at the Expiration of the sixth Year, so that one third may be chosen every second Year; and if Vacancies happen by Resignation, or otherwise, during the Recess of the Legislature of any State, the Executive thereof may make temporary Appointments until the next Meeting of the Legislature, which shall then fill such Vacancies.

No Person shall be a Senator who shall not have attained to the Age of thirty Years, and been nine Years a Citizen of the United States, and who shall not, when elected, be an Inhabitant of that State for which he shall be chosen.

The Vice President of the United States shall be President of the Senate but shall have no Vote, unless they be equally divided.

The Senate shall chuse their other Officers, and also a President pro tempore, in the Absence of the Vice President, or when he shall exercise the Office of President of the United States.

The Senate shall have the sole Power to try all Impeachments. When sitting for that Purpose, they shall be on Oath or Affirmation. When the President of the United States is tried the Chief Justice shall preside: And no Person shall be convicted without the Concurrence of two thirds of the Members present.

Judgment in Cases of Impeachment shall not extend further than to removal from Office, and disqualification to hold and enjoy any Office of honor, Trust or Profit under the United States: but the Party convicted shall nevertheless be liable and subject to Indictment, Trial, Judgment and Punishment, according to Law.

Section 4 The Times, Places and Manner of holding Elections for Senators and Representatives, shall be prescribed in each State by the Legislature thereof; but the Congress may at any time by Law make or alter such Regulations, except as to the Places of chusing Senators.

The Congress shall assemble at least once in every Year, and such Meeting shall be on the first Monday in December, unless they shall by Law appoint a different Day.

Section 5 Each House shall be the Judge of the Elections, Returns and Qualifications of its own Members, and a Majority of each shall constitute a Quorum to do Business; but a smaller Number may adjourn from day to day, and may be authorized to compel the Attendance of absent Members, in such Manner, and under such Penalties as each House may provide.

Each House may determine the Rules of its Proceedings, punish its Members for disorderly Behavior, and, with the Concurrence of two thirds, expel a Member.

Each House shall keep a Journal of its Proceedings, and from time to time publish the same, excepting such Parts as may in their Judgment require Secrecy; and the Yeas and Nays of the Members of either House on any question shall, at the Desire of one fifth of those Present, be entered on the Journal.

Neither House, during the Session of Congress, shall, without the Consent of the other, adjourn for more than three days, nor to any other Place than that in which the two Houses shall be sitting.

Section 6 The Senators and Representatives shall receive a Compensation for their Services, to be ascertained by Law, and paid out of the Treasury of the United States. They shall in all Cases, except Treason, Felony and Breach of the Peace, be privileged from Arrest during their Attendance at the Session of their respective Houses, and in going to and returning from the same; and for any Speech or Debate in either House, they shall not be questioned in any other Place.

No Senator or Representative shall, during the Time for which he was elected, be appointed to any civil Office under the Authority of the United States, which shall have been created, or the Emoluments whereof shall have been encreased during such time; and no Person holding any Office under the United States, shall be a Member of either House during his Continuance in Office.

Section 7 All Bills for raising Revenue shall originate in the House of Representatives; but the Senate may propose or concur with amendments as on other Bills.

Every Bill which shall have passed the House of Representatives and the Senate, shall, before it become a law, be presented to the President of the United States: If he approve he shall sign it, but if not he shall return it, with his Objections to that House in which it shall have originated, who shall enter the Objections at large on their Journal, and

proceed to reconsider it. If after such Reconsideration two thirds of that House shall agree to pass the Bill, it shall be sent, together with the Objections, to the other House, by which it shall likewise be reconsidered, and if approved by two thirds of that House, it shall become a Law. But in all such Cases the Votes of both Houses shall be determined by Yeas and Nays, and the Names of the Persons voting for and against the Bill shall be entered on the Journal of each House respectively. If any Bill shall not be returned by the President within ten Days (Sundays excepted) after it shall have been presented to him, the Same shall be a Law, in like Manner as if he had signed it, unless the Congress by their Adjournment prevent its Return, in which Case it shall not be a Law.

Every Order, Resolution, or Vote to which the Concurrence of the Senate and House of Representatives may be necessary (except on a question of Adjournment) shall be presented to the President of the United States; and before the Same shall take Effect, shall be approved by him, or being disapproved by him, shall be repassed by two thirds of the Senate and House of Representatives, according to the Rules and Limitations prescribed in the Case of a Bill.

Section 8 The Congress shall have Power To lay and collect Taxes, Duties, Imposts and Excises, to pay the Debts and provide for the common Defence and general Welfare of the United States; but all Duties, Imposts and Excises shall be uniform throughout the United States;

To borrow Money on the credit of the United States;

To regulate Commerce with foreign Nations, and among the several States, and with the Indian Tribes;

To establish an uniform Rule of Naturalization, and uniform Laws on the subject of Bankruptcies throughout the United States;

To coin Money, regulate the Value thereof, and of foreign Coin, and fix the Standard of Weights and Measures;

To provide for the Punishment of counterfeiting the Securities and current Coin of the United States;

To establish Post Offices and post Roads;

To promote the Progress of Science and useful Arts, by securing for limited Times to Authors and Inventors the exclusive Right to their respective Writings and Discoveries;

To constitute Tribunals inferior to the supreme Court;

To define and punish Piracies and Felonies committed on the high Seas, and Offences against the Law of Nations;

To declare War, grant Letters of Marque and Reprisal, and make Rules concerning Captures on Land and Water;

To raise and support Armies, but no Appropriation of Money to that Use shall be for a longer Term than two Years;

To provide and maintain a Navy;

To make Rules for the Government and Regulation of the land and naval Forces;

To provide for calling forth the Militia to execute the Laws of the Union, suppress Insurrections and repeal Invasions;

To provide for organizing, arming, and disciplining, the Militia, and for governing such Part of them as may be employed in the Service of the United States, reserving to the States respectively, the Appointment of the Officers, and the Authority of training the Militia according to the discipline prescribed by Congress;

To exercise exclusive Legislation in all Cases whatsoever, over such District (not exceeding ten Miles square) as may, by Cession of Particular States, and the Acceptance of Congress, become the Seat of the Government of the United States, and to exercise like Authority over all Places purchased by the Consent of the Legislature of the State in which the Same shall be, for the Erection of Forts, Magazines, Arsenals, dock-Yards and other needful Buildings;—And

To make all Laws which shall be necessary and proper for carrying into Execution the foregoing Powers and all other Powers vested by this Constitution in the Government of the United States, or in any Department or Officer thereof.

Section 9 The Migration or Importation of such Persons as any of the States now existing shall think proper to admit, shall not be prohibited by the Congress prior to the Year one thousand eight hundred and eight, but a Tax or duty may be imposed on such Importation, not exceeding ten dollars for each Person.

The Privilege of the Writ of Habeas Corpus shall not be suspended, unless when in Cases or Rebellion or Invasion the public Safety may require it.

No Bill of Attainder or ex post facto Law shall be passed.

No Capitation, or other direct, Tax shall be laid, unless in Proportion to the Census of Enumeration herein before directed to be taken.

No Tax or Duty shall be laid on Articles exported from any State.

No Preference shall be given by any Regulation of Commerce or Revenue to the Ports of one State over those of another: nor shall Vessels bound to, or from, one State, be obliged to enter, clear or pay Duties in another.

No Money shall be drawn from the Treasury, but in Consequence of Appropriations made by Law; and a regular Statement and Account of the Receipts and Expenditures of all public Money shall be published from time to time.

No Title of Nobility shall be granted by the United States: And no Person holding any Office of Profit or Trust under them, shall, without the Consent of the Congress, accept of any present, Emolument, Office, or Title, of any kind whatever, from any King, Prince or foreign State.

Section 10 No State shall enter into any Treaty, Alliance, or Confederation; grant Letters of Marque and Reprisal; coin Money; emit Bills of Credit; make any Thing but gold and silver Coin a Tender in Payment of Debts; pass any Bill of Attainder, ex post facto Law, or Law impairing the Obligation of Contracts, or grant any Title of Nobility.

No State shall, without the Consent of the Congress, lay any Imposts or Duties on Imports or Exports, except what may be absolutely necessary for executing it's inspection Laws: and the net Produce of all Duties and Imposts, laid by any State on Imports or Exports, shall be for the Use of the Treasury of the United States; and all such Laws shall be subject to the Revision and Controul of the Congress.

No State shall, without the Consent of Congress, lay any Duty of Tonnage, keep Troops, or Ships of War in time of Peace, enter into any Agreement or Compact with another State, or with a foreign Power, or engage in War, unless actually invaded, or in such imminent Danger as will not admit of delay.

Article II

Section 1 The executive Power shall be vested in a President of the United States of America. He shall hold his Office during the Term of four Years, and, together with the Vice President, chosen for the same Term, be elected, as follows:

Each State shall appoint, in such Manner as the Legislature thereof may direct, a Number of Electors, equal to the whole Number of Senators and Representatives to which the State may be entitled in the Congress: but no Senator or Representative, or Person holding an Office of Trust or Profit under the United States, shall be appointed an Elector.

The Electors shall meet in their respective States, and vote by Ballot for two Persons, of whom one at least shall not be an Inhabitant of the same State with themselves. And they shall make a List of all the Persons voted for, and of the Number of Votes for each; which List they shall sign and certify, and transmit sealed to the Seat of the Government of the United States, directed to the President of the Senate. The President of the Senate shall, in the Presence of the Senate and House of Representatives, open all the Certificates, and the Votes shall then be counted. The Person having the greatest Number of Votes shall be the President, if such Number be a Majority of the whole Number of Electors appointed; and if there be more than one who have such Majority, and have an equal Number of Votes, then the House of Representatives shall immediately chuse by Ballot one of them for President; and if no Person have a Majority, then from the five highest on the List the said House shall in like Manner chuse the President. But in chusing the President, the Votes shall be taken by States, the Representatives from each State having one Vote; a quorum for this Purpose shall consist of a Member or Members from two thirds of the States, and a Majority of all the States shall be necessary to a Choice. In every Case, after the Choice of the President, the Person having the greatest Number of Votes of the Electors shall be the Vice President. But if there should remain two or more who have equal Votes, the Senate shall chuse from them by Ballot the Vice President.

The Congress may determine the Time of chusing the Electors, and the Day on which they shall give their Votes; which Day shall be the same throughout the United States.

No Person except a natural born Citizen, or a Citizen of the United States, at the time of the Adoption of this Constitution, shall be eligible to the Office of President; neither shall any person be eligible to that Office who shall not have attained to the Age of thirty five Years, and been fourteen Years a Resident within the United States.

In Case of the Removal of the President from Office, or of his Death, Resignation, or Inability to discharge the Powers and Duties of the said Office, the Same shall devolve on the Vice President, and the Congress may by Law provide for the Case of Removal, Death, Resignation or Inability, both of the President and Vice President, declaring what Officer shall then act as President, and such Officer shall act accordingly, until the Disability be removed, or a President shall be elected.

The President shall, at stated Times, receive for his Services, a Compensation, which shall neither be encreased nor diminished during the Period for which he shall have been elected, and he shall not receive within that Period any other Emolument from the United States, or any of them.

Before he enter on the Execution of his Office, he shall take the following Oath or Affirmation:—'I do solemnly swear (or affirm) that I will faithfully execute the Office of President of the United States, and will to the best of my Ability, preserve, protect and defend the Constitution of the United States.'

Section 2 The President shall be Commander in Chief of the Army and Navy of the United States, and of the Militia of the several States, when called into the actual Service of the United States; he may require the Opinion, in writing, of the principal Officer in each of the executive Departments, upon any Subject relating to the Duties of their respective Offices, and he shall have Power to Grant Reprieves and Pardons for Offences against the United States, except in Cases of Impeachment.

He shall have Power, by and with the Advice and Consent of the Senate, to make Treaties, provided two thirds of the Senators present concur; and he shall nominate, and by and with the Advice and Consent of the Senate, shall appoint Ambassadors, other public Ministers and Consuls, Judges of the supreme Court, and all other Officers of the United States, whose Appointments are not herein otherwise provided for, and which shall be established by Law: but the Congress may by Law vest the Appointment of such inferior Officers, as they think proper, in the President alone, in the Courts of Law, or in the Heads of Departments.

The President shall have Power to fill up all Vacancies that may happen during the Recess of the Senate, by granting Commissions which shall expire at the End of their next Session.

Section 3 He shall from time to time give to the Congress Information on the State of the Union, and recommend to their Consideration such Measures as he shall judge necessary and expedient; he may, on extraordinary Occasions, convene both Houses, or either of them, and in Case of Disagreement between them, with Respect to the Time of Adjournment, he may adjourn them to such Time as he shall think proper; he shall receive Ambassadors and other public Ministers; he shall take Care that the Laws be faithfully executed, and shall Commission all the Officers of the United States.

Section 4 The President, Vice President and all Civil Officers of the United States, shall be removed from Office on Impeachment for and Conviction of, Treason, Bribery, or other high Crimes and Misdemeanors.

Article III

Section 1 The judicial Power of the United States, shall be vested in one supreme Court, and in such inferior Courts as the Congress may from time to time ordain and establish. The Judges, both of the supreme and inferior Courts, shall hold their Offices during good Behaviour, and shall, at stated Times, receive for their Services, a Compensation, which shall not be diminished during their Continuance in Office.

Section 2 The judicial Power shall extend to all Cases, in Law and Equity, arising under this Constitution, the Laws of the United States, and Treaties made, or which shall be made, under their Authority;—to all Cases affecting Ambassadors, other public ministers and Consuls;—to all Cases of admiralty and maritime Jurisdiction;—to Controversies to which the United States shall be a Party;—to Controversies between two or more States;—between a State and Citizens of another State;—between Citizens of different States;—between Citizens of the same State claiming Lands under Grants of different States, and between a State, or the Citizens thereof, and foreign States, Citizens or Subjects.

In all Cases affecting Ambassadors, other public Ministers

and Consuls, and those in which a State shall be Party, the supreme Court shall have original Jurisdiction. In all the other Cases before mentioned, the supreme Court shall have appellate Jurisdiction, both as to Law and Fact, with such Exceptions, and under such Regulations as the Congress shall make.

The Trial of all Crimes, except in Cases of Impeachment, shall be by Jury; and such Trial shall be held in the State where the said Crimes shall have been committed; but when not committed within any State, the Trial shall be at such Place or Places as the Congress may by Law have directed.

Section 3 Treason against the United States, shall consist only in levying War against them, or in adhering to their Enemies, giving them Aid and Comfort. No Person shall be convicted of Treason unless on the Testimony of two Witnesses to the same overt Act, or on Confession in open Court.

The Congress shall have Power to declare the Punishment of Treason, but no Attainder of Treason shall work Corruption of Blood, or Forfeiture except during the Life of the Person attainted.

Article IV

Section 1 Full Faith and Credit shall be given in each State to the public Acts, Records, and judicial Proceedings of every other State. And the Congress may by general Laws prescribe the Manner in which such Acts, Records and Proceedings shall be proved, and the Effect thereof.

Section 2 The Citizens of each State shall be entitled to all Privileges and Immunities of Citizens in the several States.

A Person charged in any State with Treason, Felony, or other Crime, who shall flee from Justice, and be found in another State, shall on Demand of the executive Authority of the State from which he fled, be delivered up, to be removed to the State having Jurisdiction of the Crime.

No Person held to Service or Labor in one State, under the Laws thereof, escaping into another, shall, in Consequence of any Law or Regulation therein, be discharged from such Service or Labor, but shall be delivered up on Claim of the Party to whom such Service or Labor may be due.

Section 3 New States may be admitted by the Congress into this Union; but no new State shall be formed or erected within the Jurisdiction of any other State; nor any State be formed by the Junction of two or more States, or Parts of States, without the Consent of the Legislatures of the States concerned as well as of the Congress.

The Congress shall have Power to dispose of and make all needful Rules and Regulations respecting the Territory or other Property belonging to the United States; and nothing in this Constitution shall be so construed as to Prejudice any Claims of the United States, or of any particular State.

Section 4 The United States shall guarantee to every State in this Union a Republican Form of Government, and shall protect each of them against Invasion; and on Application of the Legislature, or of the Executive (when the Legislature cannot be convened) against domestic Violence.

Article V

The Congress, whenever two thirds of both Houses shall deem it necessary, shall propose Amendments to this Constitution, or, on the Application of the Legislatures of two thirds of the several States, shall call a Convention for proposing Amendments, which, in either Case, shall be valid to all Intents and Purposes, as Part of this Constitution, when ratified by the Legislatures of three fourths of the several States, or by Conventions in three fourths thereof, as the one or the other Mode of Ratification may be proposed by the Congress; Provided that no Amendment which may be made prior to the Year One thousand eight hundred and eight shall in any Manner affect the first and fourth Clauses in the Ninth Section of the first Article; and that no State, without its Consent, shall be deprived of its equal Suffrage in the Senate.

Article VI

All Debts contracted and Engagements entered into, before the Adoption of this Constitution, shall be as valid against the United States under this Constitution, as under the Confederation.

This Constitution, and the Laws of the United States which shall be made in Pursuance thereof; and all Treaties made, or which shall be made, under the Authority of the United States, shall be the supreme Law of the Land; and the Judges in every State shall be bound thereby, any Thing in the Constitution or Laws of any state to the Contrary notwithstanding.

The Senators and Representatives before mentioned, and the Members of the several State Legislatures, and all executive and judicial Officers, both of the United States and of the several States, shall be bound by Oath or Affirmation, to support this Constitution; but no religious Test shall ever be required as a Qualification to any Office or public Trust under the United States.

Article VII

The Ratification of the Conventions of nine States, shall be sufficient for the Establishment of this Constitution between the States so ratifying the same.

Amendments to the Constitution of the United States of America

Articles in addition to, and amendment of, the Constitution of the United States of America, proposed by Congress, and ratified by the several states, pursuant to the Fifth Article of the original Constitution.

Amendment I

Congress shall make no law respecting an establishment of religion, or prohibiting the free exercise thereof; or abridging the freedom of speech, or of the press; or the right of the people peaceably to assemble, and to petition the government for a redress of grievances.
(proposed 1789; ratified 1791)

Amendment II

A well regulated Militia, being necessary to the security of a free State, the right of the people to keep and bear Arms, shall not be infringed.
(proposed 1789; ratified 1791)

Amendment III

No Soldier shall, in time of peace be quartered in any house, without the consent of the Owner, nor in time of war, but in a manner to be prescribed by law.
(proposed 1789; ratified 1791)

Amendment IV

The right of the people to be secure in their persons, houses, papers, and effects, against unreasonable searches and seizures, shall not be violated, and no Warrants shall issue, but upon probable cause, supported by Oath or affirmation, and particularly describing the place to be searched, and the persons or things to be seized.
(proposed 1789; ratified 1791)

Amendment V

No person shall be held to answer for a capital, or otherwise infamous crime, unless on a presentment or indictment of a Grand Jury, except in cases arising in the land or naval forces, or in the Militia, when in actual service in time of War or public danger; nor shall any person be subject for the same offence to be twice put in jeopardy of life or limb; nor shall be compelled in any criminal case to be a witness against himself, nor be deprived of life, liberty, or property, without due process of law; nor shall private property be taken for public use, without just compensation.
(proposed 1789; ratified 1791)

Amendment VI

In all criminal prosecutions, the accused shall enjoy the right to a speedy and public trial, by an impartial jury of the State and district wherein the crime shall have been committed, which district shall have been previously ascertained by law, and to be informed of the nature and cause of the accusation; to be confronted with the witnesses against him; to have compulsory process for obtaining witnesses in his favor, and to have the Assistance of Counsel for his defense.
(proposed 1789; ratified 1791)

Amendment VII

In Suits at common law, where the value in controversy shall exceed twenty dollars, the right of trial by jury shall be preserved, and no fact tried by a jury, shall be otherwise re-examined in any Court of the United States, than according to the rules of the common law.
(proposed 1789; ratified 1791)

Amendment VIII

Excessive bail shall not be required, nor excessive fines imposed, nor cruel and unusual punishments inflicted.
(proposed 1789; ratified 1791)

Amendment IX

The enumeration in the Constitution, of certain rights, shall not be construed to deny or disparage others retained by the people.
(proposed 1789; ratified 1791)

Amendment X

The powers not delegated to the United States by the Constitution, nor prohibited by it to the States, are reserved to the States respectively, or to the people.
(proposed 1789; ratified 1791)

Amendment XI

The Judicial power of the United States shall not be construed to extend to any suit in law or equity, commenced or prosecuted against one of the United States by Citizens of another State, or by Citizens or Subjects of any Foreign State.
(proposed 1794; ratified 1795)

Amendment XII

The Electors shall meet in their respective states and vote by ballot for President and Vice-President, one of whom, at least, shall not be an inhabitant of the same state with

themselves; they shall name in their ballots the person voted for as President, and in distinct ballots the person voted for as Vice-President, and they shall make distinct lists of all persons voted for as President, and of all persons voted for as Vice-President, and of the number of votes for each, which lists they shall sign and certify, and transmit sealed to the seat of the government of the United States, directed to the President of the Senate;—The President of the Senate shall, in the presence of the Senate and House of Representatives, open all the certificates and the votes shall then be counted;—The person having the greatest Number of votes for President, shall be the President, if such number be a majority of the whole number of Electors appointed; and if no person have such majority, then from the persons having the highest numbers not exceeding three on the list of those voted for as President, the House of Representatives shall choose immediately, by ballot, the President. But in choosing the President, the votes shall be taken by states, the representation from each state having one vote; a quorum for this purpose shall consist of a member or members from two-thirds of the states, and a majority of all the states shall be necessary to a choice. And if the House of Representatives shall not choose a President whenever the right of choice shall devolve upon them, before the fourth day of March next following, then the Vice-President shall act as President, as in the case of the death or other constitutional disability of the President—The person having the greatest number of votes as Vice-President, shall be the Vice-President, if such number be a majority of the whole number of Electors appointed, and if no person have a majority, then from the two highest numbers on the list, the Senate shall choose the Vice-President; a quorum for the purpose shall consist of two-thirds of the whole number of Senators, and a majority of the whole number shall be necessary to a choice. But no person constitutionally ineligible to the office of President shall be eligible to that of Vice-President of the United States.
(proposed 1803; ratified 1804)

Amendment XIII

Section 1 Neither slavery nor involuntary servitude, except as a punishment for crime whereof the party shall have been duly convicted, shall exist within the United States, or any place subject to their jurisdiction.

Section 2 Congress shall have power to enforce this article by appropriate legislation.
(proposed 1865; ratified 1865)

Amendment XIV

Section 1 All persons born or naturalized in the United States and subject to the jurisdiction thereof, are citizens of the United States and of the State wherein they reside. No State shall make or enforce any law which shall abridge the privileges or immunities of citizens of the United States; nor shall any State deprive any person of life, liberty, or property, without due process of law; nor deny to any person within its jurisdiction the equal protection of the laws.

Section 2 Representatives shall be apportioned among the several States according to their respective numbers, counting the whole number of persons in each State, excluding Indians not taxed. But when the right to vote at any election for the choice of electors for President and Vice President of the United States, Representatives in Congress, the Executive and Judicial officers of a State, or the members of the Legislature thereof, is denied to any of the male inhabitants of such State, being twenty-one years of age, and citizens of the United States, or in any way abridged, except for participation in rebellion, or other crime, the basis of representation therein shall be reduced in the proportion which the number of such male citizens shall bear to the whole number of male citizens twenty-one years of age in such State.

Section 3 No person shall be a Senator or Representative in Congress, or elector of President and Vice President, or hold any office, civil or military, under the United States, or under any State, who, having previously taken an oath, as a member of Congress, or as an officer of the United States, or as a member of any State legislature, or as an executive or judicial officer of any State, to support the Constitution of the United States, shall have engaged in insurrection or rebellion against the same, or given aid or comfort to the enemies thereof. But Congress may by a vote of two-thirds of each House, remove such disability.

Section 4 The validity of the public debt of the United States, authorized by law, including debts incurred for payment of pensions and bounties for services in suppressing insurrection or rebellion, shall not be questioned. But neither the United States nor any State shall assume or pay any debt or obligation incurred in aid of insurrection or rebellion against the United States, or any claim for the loss or emancipation of any slave; but all such debts, obligations and claims shall be held illegal and void.

Section 5 The Congress shall have power to enforce, by appropriate legislation, the provisions of this article.
(proposed 1866; ratified 1868)

Amendment XV

Section 1 The right of citizens of the United States to vote shall not be denied or abridged by the United States or by any State on account of race, color, or previous condition of servitude.

Section 2 The Congress shall have power to enforce this article by appropriate legislation.
(proposed 1869; ratified 1870)

Amendment XVI

The Congress shall have power to lay and collect taxes on incomes, from whatever source derived, without apportionment among the several States, and without regard to any census or enumeration.
(proposed 1909; ratified 1913)

Amendment XVII

The Senate of the United States shall be composed of two Senators from each State, elected by the people thereof, for six years; and each Senator shall have one vote. The electors in each State shall have the qualifications requisite for electors of the most numerous branch of the State legislatures.

When vacancies happen in the representation of any State in the Senate, the executive authority of such State shall issue writs of election to fill such vacancies: Provided, That the legislature of any State may empower the executive thereof to make temporary appointments until the people fill the vacancies by election as the legislature may direct.

This amendment shall not be so construed as to affect the election or term of any Senator chosen before it becomes valid as part of the Constitution.
(proposed 1912; ratified 1913)

Amendment XVIII

Section 1 After one year from the ratification of this article the manufacture, sale, or transportation of intoxicating liquors within, the importation thereof into, or the exportation thereof from the United States and all territory subject to the jurisdiction thereof for beverage purposes is hereby prohibited.

Section 2 The Congress and the several States shall have concurrent power to enforce this article by appropriate legislation.

Section 3 This article shall be inoperative unless it shall have been ratified as an amendment to the Constitution by the legislatures of the several States, as provided in the Constitution, within seven years from the date of the submission hereof to the States by the Congress.
(proposed 1917; ratified 1919)

Amendment XIX

The right of citizens of the United States to vote shall not be denied or abridged by the United States or by any State on account of sex. Congress shall have power to enforce this article by appropriate legislation.
(proposed 1919; ratified 1920)

Amendment XX

Section 1 The terms of the President and Vice President shall end at noon on the 20th day of January, and the terms of Senators and Representatives at noon on the 3d day of January, of the years in which such terms would have ended if this article had not been ratified; and the terms of their successors shall then begin.

Section 2 The Congress shall assemble at least once in every year, and such meeting shall begin at noon on the 3rd day of January, unless they shall by law appoint a different day.

Section 3 If, at the time fixed for the beginning of the term of the President, the President elect shall have died, the Vice President elect shall become President. If a President shall not have been chosen before the time fixed for the beginning of his term, or if the President elect shall have failed to qualify, then the Vice President elect shall act as President until a President shall have qualified; and the Congress may by law provide for the case wherein neither a President elect nor a Vice President elect shall have qualified, declaring who shall then act as President, or the manner in which one who is to act shall be selected, and such person shall act accordingly until a President or Vice President shall have qualified.

Section 4 The Congress may by law provide for the case of the death of any of the persons from whom the House of Representatives may choose a President whenever the right of choice shall have devolved upon them, and for the case of the death of any of the persons from whom the Senate may choose a Vice President whenever the right of choice shall have devolved upon them.

Section 5 Sections 1 and 2 shall take effect on the 15th day of October following the ratification of this article.

Section 6 This article shall be inoperative unless it shall have been ratified as an amendment to the Constitution by the legislatures of three-fourths of the several States within seven years from the date of its submission.
(proposed 1932; ratified 1933)

Amendment XXI

Section 1 The eighteenth article of amendment to the Constitution of the United States is hereby repealed.

Section 2 The transportation or importation into any State, Territory, or possession of the United States for delivery or use therein of intoxicating liquors, in violation of the laws thereof, is hereby prohibited.

Section 3 This article shall be inoperative unless it shall have been ratified as an amendment to the Constitution by conventions in the several States, as provided in the Constitution, within seven years from the date of the submission hereof to the States by the Congress.
(proposed 1933; ratified 1933)

Amendment XXII

Section 1 No person shall be elected to the office of the President more than twice, and no person who has held the office of President, or acted as President, for more than two years of a term to which some other person was elected President shall be elected to the office of the President more than once. But this Article shall not apply to any person holding the office of President, when this Article was proposed by the Congress, and shall not prevent any person who may be holding the office of President, or acting as President, during the term within which this Article becomes operative from holding the office of President or acting as President during the remainder of such term.

Section 2 This article shall be inoperative unless it shall have been ratified as an amendment to the Constitution by the legislatures of three-fourths of the several States within seven years from the date of its submission to the States by the Congress.
(proposed 1947; ratified 1951)

Amendment XXIII

Section 1 The District constituting the seat of Government of the United States shall appoint in such manner as the Congress may direct: A number of electors of President and Vice President equal to the whole number of Senators and Representatives in Congress to which the District would be entitled if it were a State, but in no event more than the least populous State; they shall be in addition to those appointed by the States, but they shall be considered, for the purposes of the election of President and Vice President, to be electors appointed by a State; and they shall meet in the District and perform such duties as provided by the twelfth article of amendment.

Section 2 The Congress shall have power to enforce this article by appropriate legislation.
(proposed 1960; ratified 1961)

Amendment XXIV

Section 1 The right of citizens of the United States to vote in any primary or other election for President or Vice President, for electors for President or Vice President, or for Senator or Representative in Congress, shall not be denied or abridged by the United States or any State by reason of failure to pay any poll tax or other tax.

Section 2 The Congress shall have power to enforce this article by appropriate legislation.
(proposed 1962; ratified 1964)

Amendment XXV

Section 1 In case of the removal of the President from office or of his death or resignation, the Vice President shall become President.

Section 2 Whenever there is a vacancy in the office of the Vice President, the President shall nominate a Vice President who shall take office upon confirmation by a majority vote of both Houses of Congress.

Section 3 Whenever the President transmits to the President pro tempore of the Senate and the Speaker of the House of Representatives has written declaration that he is unable to discharge the powers and duties of his office, and until he transmits to them a written declaration to the contrary, such powers and duties shall be discharged by the Vice President as Acting President.

Section 4 Whenever the Vice President and a majority of either the principal officers of the executive departments or of such other body as Congress may by law provide, transmit to the President pro tempore of the Senate and the Speaker of the House of Representatives their written declaration that the President is unable to discharge the powers and duties of his office, the Vice President shall immediately assume the powers and duties of the office as Acting President.

Thereafter, when the President transmits to the President pro tempore of the Senate and the Speaker of the House of Representatives has written declaration that no inability exists, he shall resume the powers and duties of his office unless the Vice President and a majority of either the principal officers of the executive department or of such other body as Congress may by law provide, transmit within four days to the President pro tempore of the Senate and the Speaker of the House of Representatives their written declaration that the President is unable to discharge the powers and duties of his office. Thereupon Congress shall decide the issue, assembling within forty-eight hours for that purpose if not in session. If the Congress, within twenty-one days after receipt of the latter written

declaration, or, if Congress is not in session, within twenty-one days after Congress is required to assemble, determines by two-thirds vote of both Houses that the President is unable to discharge the powers and duties of his office, the Vice President shall continue to discharge the same as Acting President; otherwise, the President shall resume the powers and duties of his office.
(proposed 1965; ratified 1967)

Amendment XXVI

Section 1 The right of citizens of the United States, who are eighteen years of age or older, to vote shall not be denied or abridged by the United States or by any State on account of age.

Section 2 The Congress shall have power to enforce this article by appropriate legislation.
(proposed 1971; ratified 1971)

Amendment XXVII

No law varying the compensation for the services of the Senators and Representatives shall take effect, until an election of Representatives shall have intervened.
(proposed 1789; ratified 1992)

Index